☆ ☆
American Economic History
☆ ☆

HARPER'S HISTORICAL SERIES

Under the Editorship of
GUY STANTON FORD

HAROLD UNDERWOOD FAULKNER,

DWIGHT W. MORROW PROFESSOR OF HISTORY
SMITH COLLEGE

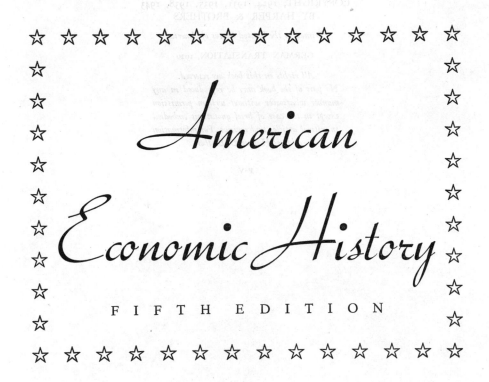

American

Economic History

FIFTH EDITION

NEW YORK   LONDON

HARPER & BROTHERS PUBLISHERS

To My Mother
HELEN UNDERWOOD FAULKNER

To My Mother

HELEN UNDERWOOD FAULKNER

Contents

the New Deal—Relief and security—Economic significance of the New
Deal

☆ ☆
Maps
☆ ☆

Graphs and Charts

☆　☆

Illustrations

xvii

Editor's Introduction

THE TRAILING clouds of glory that lay around our nation's youth have begun to fade away. With the war we reached middle age at a bound. We are now counting our resources, human and material, as we never did before. The results of the inventory are not wholly reassuring, and we are checking up our waning natural resources, our political institutions, our education, our social philosophy, to find where there is waste and lost motion. Mankind may not be at the crossroads, but it is dimly conscious that the road ahead is not the broad and happy highway of the past. It is more necessary than ever before that we should study our national history from every standpoint, and especially the economic. I think this book will be counted among the most useful of the aids yet provided for such study.

It may be well to point out that he who writes the economic history of any age or land undertakes a difficult task. If it be an economic history of the United States, as this volume is, the task is not less but rather more difficult. His subject is a country where nature has been bountiful and the exploitation of natural wealth has been less trammeled by old institutions and social customs than in Europe. Here the political individualism of a pioneer people has given freer play than ever before in human history to all the acquisitive impulses of men and groups of men. The faith of a youthful people that it lived in a land of inexhaustible resources and that nothing could happen to it that had happened to older lands where soil and forests became exhausted and the mineral wealth dissipated has opened the door for a material development unparalleled in the history of nations. How easy then for him who starts with the point of view implied in the title "economic history" to forget that the history of significant men and nations is, in its end results, but the charted field of a battle between their inherited ideas and unrealized ideals, on the one hand, and the material circumstances of their physical environment, on the other. I believe the author has written an account of our economic history free from the errors of one-sided materialism.

It is the achievement of this book that it is American history seen whole and sturdily, though from the given standpoint of its title. The reader has presented to him the picture of success and error in the discharge of an implied trusteeship. It is done dispassionately, without disproportion or vain glorification. Those who study it can draw their own conclusions and, if they master it, will find themselves in possession of the essential equipment necessary to a citizenship that will face in the next generation more complicated social and economic problems than it has in the past.

The student of economic history should be warned that he must face and master many facts. It is not a simple matter to grasp such data and wring their meaning from them. I believe that here, too, the author has given skillfully all the aid that any self-respecting student should require. He has gathered and integrated into an account that does not halt a remarkable and significant mass of tables, figures, and graphs. He has labored patiently that the student may read intelligently and be armed to test old conclusions or draw new ones. This is a difficult task for any author, but an essential one in an economic history. If an editor may not voice an opinion he can at least express his confidence that classroom use will prove that the author has achieved a large measure of success in writing a narrative that makes statistics an asset to teaching.

Neither teacher nor text writer is content to have a student think one book is the subject. A bibliography of material that will amplify, supplement, and enforce the text is essential. Such an aid to scholarship has been, as I can testify, one of the writer's chief concerns.

Guy Stanton Ford.

Preface to the Fifth Edition

☆ ☆

THE THIRD and fourth editions of this book were largely concerned with keeping it up to date. This is the first time since 1931 that the volume has been entirely reset. This has given the author a chance to rearrange or consolidate certain of the material, to make numerous deletions, particularly in the early part of the book, and to add new and pertinent information. It has made it possible for the publishers to design a new and more attractive format and for the author to improve the educational equipment by adding new maps and charts and to trace our economic development through forty pages of illustrations. Above all, this revision has afforded an opportunity to include and acknowledge the results of much significant research done in recent years by scholars in this field. So much fine work is being done in American economic history that any effort to integrate or interpret it has become increasingly difficult but at the same time an increasingly exacting and challenging task.

The author is very grateful that enough teachers have found this volume sufficiently useful to warrant another edition. Only through an understanding of our economic past can we plan wisely for the future; it is hoped that this and similar volumes may contribute in some slight way to the knowledge of our country so necessary in meeting the problems of the critical years ahead. The author is also grateful for the criticisms, suggestions, and help of many kinds he has received from scholars since the book was first published. Most textbooks which have gone through one or more revisions tend to become the cooperative result of many minds. For this aid, acknowledged in the preface of previous editions, the author again expresses his thanks.

HAROLD UNDERWOOD FAULKNER.

Northampton, Mass.
  December 1, 1942

☆ ☆
American Economic History
☆ ☆

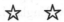

Physiographic Factors
and Natural Resources

PHYSIOGRAPHIC INFLUENCES

THE study of history, particularly economic history, must begin with a knowledge of the physical outline and resources of the unit under observation. Civilization has been defined as the process of conquering nature, but in that process nature has reacted quite as much on man as man on nature. "Thus," says Buckle, "we have man modifying nature, and nature modifying man; while out of this reciprocal modification all events must necessarily spring." [1]

Physical environment determines to a large extent where man shall live, what kind of work he shall do, what he may produce, and the routes over which he must travel and transport his products. Because of its influence upon his economic life, physical environment goes far to determine man's social and political point of view, his habits and desires, and even his physical frame. [2]

The history of the United States, written so largely in terms of the conquest of the continent, shows physiographic influence at every step. The contour of the coast fixed the place of the first settlements, the river valleys and mountain gaps pointed the routes westward, while the formation of the soil and the nature of its products determined the occupation of the settler after he had reached the new country.

GEOGRAPHIC DIVISIONS OF THE UNITED STATES

The North American continent forms a rough triangle approximately 3000 miles across at the north and tapering to a width of but a few miles at the Isthmus of Panama. Facing three oceans, it is influenced by each. The Pacific sends a stream of warm water against the western coast, which makes it habitable as far as Alaska, although, because of the Cordilleras, the

[1] Henry T. Buckle, *History of Civilization in England* (1862), I, 15.
[2] See Franz Boas, *Changes in Bodily Form of Descendants of Immigrants* (1912), compiled from *U. S. Immigration Commission Reports.*

effect is limited to the fringe of seacoast. The Gulf Stream of the Atlantic provides rainfall for the lower Mississippi and Gulf states, and its influence can be seen as far north as New England. The Arctic, where it touches America, cut off from the currents of both Atlantic and Pacific, is icebound and so makes unfit for habitation a large part of the northern half of the continent. A vast mountain range, the Cordilleras, traverses the western portion of the continent from Alaska to Panama. At its widest point, around the 40th parallel, this system has a breadth of about 1000 miles, with many of its peaks attaining a height of 14,000 feet. On the east the Appalachian system, bordering a fringe of seacoast and interspersed with fertile valleys, extends from Newfoundland to Alabama. It is nowhere as high as 7000 feet. Between these two mountain ranges lies an immense plain which, with the exception of a few patches of low mountains, stretches from the Gulf of Mexico to the Arctic. The drainage of this great plain is carried off by three main outlets: (1) the Mississippi and its tributaries, the Missouri, Ohio, Arkansas, and Red Rivers, emptying into the Gulf of Mexico; (2) the Great Lakes, draining into the St. Lawrence and the Atlantic; and (3) the MacKenzie, and the numerous streams running into Hudson Bay.

On this continent, roughly between the 25th and 49th parallels, lies the United States of America. In area it contains 3,026,789 square miles—over two-thirds the size of Europe. It has been divided geographically into six more or less distinct parts.

1. The eastern lowlands, or coastal plain, lying between the shore and the Appalachians. This region includes the eastern fringe of the states facing the Atlantic. Although the soil is not so fertile as that farther west, it is suitable for ordinary garden vegetables and for wheat, corn, and tobacco. It fortunately provided the first settlers with two indigenous plants—their chief cereal, corn, and their chief export, tobacco. As the agricultural center shifted westward, the future of the coastal plain became more and more wrapped up in manufacturing and commerce, the former made possible by the highly developed water power of the fall line, and the latter by the excellent harbors of the frequently indented coast. Two strings of cities mark the boundaries of the coastal plain; on the west the cities of the fall line—Montgomery, Augusta, Macon, Columbia, Raleigh, Richmond, Baltimore, Trenton, Hartford; on the east the seacoast cities—Savannah, Charleston, Norfolk, New York, Boston.

2. The Appalachian region, directly to the west, composed of parallel mountain ranges, including the Blue Ridge and the Alleghenies. The Appalachians extend from Newfoundland to Alabama, rising to heights of over 6000 feet in the White Mountains of New Hampshire and the Black Mountains of North Carolina. Between these mountain ranges, extending a

PHYSICAL MAP OF
THE UNITED STATES

Heights of land in feet

Over 10,000
6000 to 10,000
4000 to 6000
2000 to 4000
1000 to 2000
500 to 1000
Sea level to 500
Below sea level

Scale of Miles
0 100 200 300 400 500

CROSS SECTION OF THE UNITED STATES ALONG THE LINCOLN HIGHWAY

distance of 600 miles from New Jersey to Georgia, are to be found many fertile valleys. On both sides of the mountain systems, and especially to the west, are wide table-lands, merging gradually into the plains. In all, this section comprises some 300,000 square miles, only 12,000 of which are untillable, and contains in its fertile piedmonts and valleys, notably the Shenandoah, Cumberland, and Tennessee, some of the finest farming lands in America. The position of natural resources has given rise to a pronounced geographic localization of industries. Thus the nearness of the mountains to the coast in New England causes a rapid fall in the streams, and produces the water power which early made of New England a manufacturing center; the coal and iron deposits of Pennsylvania and the southern Appalachian states have given rise to the great iron and steel cities of Pittsburgh and Birmingham.

3. Lowlands of the Gulf states. This region includes Florida, southern Georgia, Alabama, Mississippi, Louisiana, and eastern Texas, where the rich black alluvial soil and the hot climate form an excellent combination for the staple crop, cotton, and for the vegetables and semi-tropical fruits which are becoming an increasingly important factor in the agriculture of this region.

4. The great plain of the Mississippi Valley. The Mississippi Valley consists of a relatively small delta section of alluvial soil, some twenty to thirty thousand square miles in area, and the great table-lands of the Appalachians and the Rockies. The wide fertile prairies and river valleys of this region make it the agricultural heart of the New World. It is here that immense crops of wheat and corn are raised; in the Mississippi delta, as in the Gulf states, cotton is king. The "Father of Waters" and its tributaries, the Ohio and the Missouri, furnish excellent natural transportation facilities which are augmented to the north by the Great Lakes and their connecting canals.

5. The Cordillera region. Although fertile valleys are to be found here and bits have been made artificially arable by irrigation, the greater part (at least nineteen-twentieths) is useless for agriculture. The great value of this region in the past has come chiefly from its mineral deposits of copper, iron, silver, and gold. As contrasted with the great Mississippi Valley which has the potential capacity to support an enormous population, the Cordillera region will probably always be sparsely populated, especially when its mineral resources are exhausted. Nevertheless, the increasing attention devoted to irrigation projects and dry farming is slowly laying the foundation for a permanent prosperity. Moreover, the vast projects at Boulder Dam, Grand Coulee, and elsewhere, designed not only to provide water for irrigation but also hydroelectric power, may well lay the foundation for light industries in the future.

6. A narrow region of low mountains on the extreme western coast. Of great fertility and extremely even and temperate climate this section has recently developed enormously the production of fruit. Although the Pacific coast is unfortunate in that it possesses but few natural harbors, the opening of the Panama Canal and the commercial importance of the Far East point to the increasing use of such facilities as are offered at the Golden Gate, Puget Sound, the Columbia River, and the artificial harbor at Los Angeles. Gold brought the first influx of English-speaking settlers to California, and the state still ranks first in the Union in the mining of gold; but its great present and future wealth depends upon other products, notably oil, fruit, and vegetables.

In the preceding paragraphs the emphasis has been placed upon *geographic* divisions. At the same time an effort has been made to point out their economic significance from the point of view of *human use*. For the economic historian the human-use region or division is much more valid for a proper understanding of the unit of land under study than the geographic.[3] Enough has been said, however, to make clear the close relationship between physiography and human use and to make possible their simultaneous discussion. In this connection it is suggested that one of the things that tends to make political history confusing is the fact that political boundaries are often quite artificial and have no relationship to economic boundaries. As Turner has emphasized, the United States is a federation of economic and cultural sections rather than a union of states.[4] It is through a study of these different economic sections, the interests of which are often in conflict, that we reach an understanding of the nation's economic and political history.

GEOGRAPHIC INFLUENCE UPON COLONIZATION

Although the American continent is accessible on its western side and the ancestors of the aborigines undoubtedly entered it from Asia, it was most fortunate that when the white man came to these shores he approached them from the east. Had the continent been turned around, its history would have been different, for the rugged Cordilleras would have presented to the pioneer a difficult if not impassable barrier. The accessability of continents is largely determined by the navigability of their rivers, and in this respect the American continent was most favored. After the forbidding Atlantic had once been crossed, the European found a land the ingress to which was simple. The St. Lawrence Valley connecting with the Great Lakes, the Hudson River opening through the Appalachians, and the Mississippi

[3] J. R. Smith and M. O. Phillips, *North America*, pp. 38–39.
[4] F. J. Turner, *Significance of Sections in American History* (1933).

with its innumerable tributaries penetrating the very heart of the continent pointed the way inland and made possible a more rapid settlement. Particularly was this true in the South where innumerable little rivers flowed into the sea, too small for the large freighters of today, but navigable for the tiny ships of the seventeenth century. To the north the Delaware, the Hudson, and the Connecticut Rivers cut the coastal plains as far as the Appalachians, and formed the natural highways for the early settlers.

Along these rivers settlements were planted, and down them were floated furs and tobacco, the two products that first linked the colonies with the markets of Europe. It is estimated that there are over 26,000 miles of navigable rivers in the United States, not counting the 2760 (meandered length, 4329) miles of shore line on the Great Lakes. Including indentations, the coast line on both oceans amounts to over 64,000 miles, with at least two-thirds of this directly accessible to Europe on the Atlantic and the Gulf of Mexico. With numerous rivers and an indented coast, good harbors were to be expected. The Atlantic and Gulf states show excellent examples of each harbor type: New York and Baltimore, of the drowned valley; Galveston, Provincetown, and many little harbors on the Carolina, Florida, and New Jersey coasts, of harbors formed from barrier reefs; New Orleans and Philadelphia, of river harbors. These and numerous other natural ports and river towns provided the points at which the raw materials for export could be gathered and the manufactured products of the mother country received and marketed.

CLIMATE AND RAINFALL

The territory now embraced in the United States was eminently fitted for those European races destined to settle and conquer the American continent. It lies between the lines of 40 and 70 degrees average annual temperature, representing a climate similar to that in the portions of Europe producing the most energetic and civilized races. Ellsworth Huntington and other students have found a close relationship between civilization and climate, and between physical and mental activity and climate.[5] A climate favorable to the rapid development of man must have a warm season long

[5] "Changes in the barometer," asserts Huntington, "seem to have little effect. Humidity, on the other hand, possesses a considerable degree of importance, but the most important element is clearly temperature. The people here considered [groups of factory operatives and college students] are physically most active when the temperature is from 60 to 65 degrees, that is, when the noon temperature rises to 70 degrees or even more. This is higher than many of us would expect. Mental activity reaches a maximum when the outside temperature averages about 38 degrees, that is, when there are mild frosts at night. Another highly important climatic condition is the change of temperature from one day to the next. People do not work well when the temperature remains constant. Great changes are also unfavorable. The ideal conditions are moderate changes, especially a cooling of the air at frequent intervals." Ellsworth Huntington, *Civilization and Climate* (1925), p. 8.

enough to grow plenty of food, and a cold season severe enough to make men work to lay up surplus food for the winter; it must in addition provide reasonably healthful surroundings. This combination the settlers found in most of the present United States.

Fundamental also in its effect upon the well-being of people is the amount of rainfall. Wheat, for example, man's most important food, can generally not be grown when the annual rainfall is less than 10 inches or more than 45. The average annual rainfall of the United States is 26.6 inches, varying from 5 inches in southern Utah to over 60 in the western valley of California and on the Gulf coast. The Pacific coast has a damp, insular climate which becomes drier toward the mountains, until in the great arid plateau moisture is almost lacking. The rainfall gradually increases, however, as we approach the Gulf of Mexico and the Atlantic. East of the Appalachians it averages from 30 to 50 inches a year. Since 20 inches is essential for agriculture and from 30 to 50 inches for ideal soil moisture, conditions for agricultural production are here most favorable. While the variations of both temperature and rainfall are greater than in Europe, the climate as a whole is essentially the same.[6]

In American economic history the subject of rainfall is of primary importance. The United States (except for some areas of the Pacific coast) is roughly divided into two parts: one east of the 100th meridian where rainfall averages more than 20 inches a year, and the other west of that line where rainfall averages less. East of this meridian agriculture is reasonably safe; there is rarely a drought lasting an entire season or covering any large area. West of it the average is less than sufficient. There are seasons when rainfall there is adequate for corn or wheat but these may be followed by seasons when droughts destroy crops, and winds whip up the dry pulverized soil, destroy the land, and drive the inhabitants out of the area. Lack of adequate rainfall on the Great Plains is the essential factor in the economic history of that region and is important in understanding our national policy in currency, banking, transportation, and other fields of economics.[7]

Adaptability of Europeans to American climate and conditions seems well established. Observations which have been made on groups of both Teutons and Celts who have been here for perhaps two hundred years and have kept their strain practically pure, point to the fact that the Europeans

[6] Interesting graphs showing the correlation between climate on the one hand, and wealth, occupations, income, intelligence, education, etc., on the other hand, are given in Jerome Davis and H. E. Barnes (eds.), *An Introduction to Sociology* (1931), II, 191–304.

[7] Interesting data on the importance of rainfall can be found in J. R. Smith and M. O. Phillips, *North America*, pp. 7–8, and Chap. XXIII. How rainfall delimits the corn belt is noted in O. E. Baker, *Economic Geography* (1925), p. 499; and in J. R. Smith and M. O Phillips, *op. cit.*, p. 366 n.

NORMAL

ANNUAL PRECIPITATION

| 0-5 | 5-10 | 10-20 | 20-40 | 40-50 | 50+ |
| IN | | | INCHES | | |

(From H. H. McCarty, *The Geographic Basis of American Economic Life*, Harper & Brothers.)

have not suffered physically from transplantation to America. They are no smaller in size, are as energetic, can withstand fatigue as well, and are as long lived as their kinsmen in Europe. Moreover, the energy and creative faculties of the immigrants were apparently challenged by the mighty task of subduing a continent, and the result was a sturdy and resourceful race. The transplantation of European civilization to America did, however, involve contact with unaccustomed diseases. To Europeans yellow fever was probably new, and, except in Spain and Italy, malaria was infrequent; these diseases, when encountered by colonists in America, created great havoc, both in the new settlements and when carried back to the Old World.[8] Fortunately these pestilences were largely confined to tropical and subtropical America, and they did not in the long run greatly delay the occupation of the present United States. Probably the greatest curse in the way of disease faced by the white settlers in this country was malaria, which appears to have been the most persistent frontier disease. Level lands and good rainfall on the Atlantic and Gulf coastal plains allowed stagnant water to gather and provided breeding spots for mosquitos; the disease often decimated early settlers and kept them out of certain sections.

It was the misfortune of the aborigines, on the other hand, that the settlers brought with them Old World maladies probably unknown here, which, as no immunity had been developed among the Indians, made rapid inroads on them when once started. Especially was this true of smallpox and measles. Tuberculosis probably occurred in sporadic cases among the Indians, but it did not assume the terrific death-dealing rôle it now possesses until after they had come in contact with civilization.

SOIL

Central North America is perhaps the choicest block of homeland in the world, containing as it does arable soil, minerals, and facilities for water transportation. Only 40 per cent of the land is arable, but the different types of soil and divergencies in climate make it possible to raise a variety of crops, and the area is so large that a severe food shortage has never been experienced. The significance of soil texture upon our history has never

---

[8] The origin of these diseases is still somewhat conjectural. "Yellow fever is generally believed to be a disease of American origin having its original habitat in the Antilles" (*Handbook of the Medical Sciences*, 3rd ed., 1917). Hookworm, that scourge of the South, was probably brought to America from Africa by slaves; present authorities do not believe the parasite to have been indigenous to the western hemisphere. Syphilis was long considered to have been a legacy to the Old from the New World, but the eminent German medical historian, Karl Sudhoff, concluded from his researches that sporadic cases had existed in Europe and Asia from remote antiquity. Syphilis did, however, appear in greatly increased and aggravated form in Europe during the fifteenth and sixteenth centuries, giving rise to the contemporary and subsequent belief that it came from America.

been fully appreciated by the general historian, but a close correlation be-tween qualities of the soil in a section and its prosperity is clearly dis-cernible to the student. Intensive studies of even small areas, such as Alabama, show a close relationship between soil fertility and the distribu-tion of crops, prosperity, races, and culture.[9] The Connecticut Valley, with its many colleges, its old publishing concerns, its famous newspapers, and its prosperous towns and villages, is also the most fertile strip of land in New England.

Economic history, in fact, might most logically commence with a study of the formation of soils and the varying resulting textures.[10] In North America particularly, such a study should include some reference to the glacial activity which occurred thousands of years before the white man came to America. Time and again glaciers a mile or more thick covered the northern part of the continent, affecting the future of mankind in both beneficent and detrimental ways. As the glaciers moved southward they leveled off ancient mountains, filled valleys with debris, scooped out the Great Lakes and thousands of others, turned the course of rivers, and scraped off the surface soil leaving bare rocks and pastures strewn with boulders in some places and in others leaving rich deposits to form the basis for future agriculture. Six times continental ice sheets advanced and retreated across the corn belt, mixing the subsoil with the surface soil and producing those rich limestone areas where agricultural productivity reaches its highest development. In other places they left swamps or sandy outwash plains in-dicating terminal moraines. The continental ice sheets at one time or an-other covered New England, the Lake states, most of North Dakota, and parts of Montana.[11] Certain regions of Wisconsin, Minnesota, Iowa, and Illinois were not covered by these glaciers, and a comparison of the civiliza-tion in the glaciated regions with that in the "driftless area" established a connection between geologic history and economic and cultural develop-ment which the student of history should carefully consider. Destroyer and creator, glacial action of bygone millenniums is still a potent factor in human lives.

INFLUENCE OF NATIVE PRODUCTS ON THE EARLIER SETTLERS

One of the great influences upon our history, next to topography, natural routes of travel, and climate, is the part played by the character and distribu-

[9] E. Huntington and F. E. Williams, *Business Geography,* Chap. V.

[10] An excellent introduction to the story of how the interaction of plants, wind, water, and weathered rocks produced various types of soil is given in C. E. Kellogg, *The Soils That Sup-port Us* (1941).

[11] For map, see *ibid.,* p. 28.

tion of the vegetable products. Presence or absence of forests, fertility and adaptability of the soil, and similar factors have determined both where the settler would erect his cabin and by what method he would support himself. The great variation in climate and soil has made it possible to raise in some part of our country practically every food product of importance, whether native or imported. In fact, the majority of plants of great economic value today have been of foreign origin.

The most pressing immediate need of the colonists was food. Even where the motive for colonization was the discovery of gold and silver, the practical question of keeping alive until the gold could be found intruded at once. Apparently it cost the Jamestown settlers years of suffering and the loss of many lives before they realized that the food supply should be their first concern. Lack of sufficient and proper nourishment was the greatest cause of the heavy mortality of the early years in Virginia, a fact that seems almost inexplicable when we consider the richness of the native food resources. The forests held an abundance of deer and other edible animals; the woods, bays, and marshes were plentifully supplied with every variety of wild fowl known to Englishmen; fish, both salt-water and fresh, were everywhere abundant. In the midst of such plenty the "starving time" in Virginia must be accounted for not by any scarcity of native food, but by the ignorance of the settlers as to how to gather and utilize the native products (for many of them were neither hunters, fishermen, nor farmers) and by their neglect of the cultivation of food crops—a neglect due to the hope of quick riches by other means.

Wood is vital to man's existence, especially in a primitive civilization where it provides shelter, fuel, means of conveyance on land and water, and even a considerable element of food. The early comers to the Atlantic seaboard found it thickly wooded; not an unmixed blessing, since land must be cleared of trees and underbrush before it can be made suitable for most agricultural uses. Far from unimportant was the forest as a source of food. The maple furnished sugar—in many cases the only sweetening except honey that was available. Beech, hazel, and hickory nuts, chestnuts, walnuts, and butternuts were found here. Most of the varieties of fruit trees have been imported, but the wild plum, cherry, persimmon, and mulberry were native to some part of the Atlantic seaboard.

Among the edible plants, either growing in a wild state or cultivated by the Indians when white settlers arrived, were maize, or Indian corn, pumpkins (or pompions, as they were called at first), squash, beans, rice, tomatoes, peanuts, Jerusalem artichoke, peppers, American aloe, sweet potatoes, watermelons, huckleberries, blackberries, strawberries, black raspberries, cranberries, gooseberries, and grapes. Vegetables and food-bearing plants of all kinds were imported, some of them entirely foreign and others European varieties of products native to America.[12]

To the Indian and early settler the animal life of the continent was of vast importance. Besides being a constant and oftentimes chief source of food supply, it furnished materials for clothing, shelter, and other necessities. Of the native animals, probably the most valuable to the aborigines were the deer east of the Mississippi and the buffalo which swarmed the great western plains, neither of which have any present economic significance. After the white settler appeared and the fur trade commenced, the smaller animals, such as the weasel, sable, badger, skunk, wolverine, mink, otter, and sea-otter, became important. There was a demand also for such fur-bearing rodents as the squirrel, hare, muskrat, and beaver. With the exception of the llama and the alpaca, which were used locally in South America as beasts of burden, and the dog, the American Indian never succeeded in domesticating any of the native fauna. Almost from the beginning, however, such common farm animals as horses, cattle, sheep, and swine were imported; the climate was found suitable for European livestock, and the vast grazing areas and easily grown food supported a rapid increase in numbers. Poultry of all kinds was introduced from Europe, and one variety of the innumerable wild fowl frequenting the American woods, the wild turkey, was taken to Europe, domesticated, and later brought back. The turkey was the one American contribution to domestic poultry, but the original native wild turkeys were in reality much larger than the barnyard product today, weighing as they did thirty or forty pounds. Such splendid birds sold for a shilling apiece, and so ruthless was their destruction that within a century after the settlement of America they had practically disappeared from the settled areas of the country.

The New World could furnish fish not only for the settlers but for all Europe. In his *New England Rarities* (1672) Josselyn enumerated over two hundred kinds of fish that were caught in New England's waters; Gosnold records that his ships in 1602 were "pestered with cod." Not only the ocean and bays, but the rivers, lakes, and brooks teemed with fish; often they were struck and killed with a stick and scooped up in frying pans. Besides their value as food and export, fish had worth to the early settler as fertilizer. As a consequence the fisheries were destined to assume a place of economic importance in the commercial life of New England.

GEOGRAPHIC INFLUENCE UPON OCCUPATIONS

In addition to the favorable elements for easy and rapid colonization produced by rivers, harbors, and a long indented coast line, there should be

[12] Lyman Carrier, *The Beginning of Agriculture in America*, p. 41.

noted especially the part played by the two greatest plants which America gave to the world—maize and tobacco. Maize yielded twice as much food per acre as the smaller grains, was less dependent upon seasons, could be cultivated without plowing and with the crudest implements, and grown with a minimum of labor. It provided a new and cheaper source of food, and the stalks furnished a more valuable forage than those of other grains. This plant largely helped to fix the early settlements in North America. Although the tobacco plant did not aid settlement in the same sense as did Indian corn, the fact that it soon furnished the basis of wealth to a large part of the country must be considered among the factors which contributed to the rapid transplanting of the European race.

In later years our history was influenced by the climatic adaptability of certain regions to certain products. Thus the southern states were found suitable for cotton culture, and that plant became, after the invention of the cotton gin, the great southern staple. It fastened slavery on the South, and in the train of slavery came many of the developments leading to the Civil War. The fertility and climate of the upper Mississippi Valley made it ideal for the cultivation of corn, and hastened settlement. Where mineral resources were at hand, economic life turned to them, so that in the Wyoming Valley of Pennsylvania, in the Rockies, and in the oil fields, whole communities have been built up around the extraction of minerals.

The harbors and rivers along the eastern coast not only fostered colonization but gave a turn to the occupation of the people. The barren soil of New England turned the settler's interest toward an easier means of livelihood than farming, and the nearby fishing made of the colonial and nineteenth-century New Englander a follower of the sea. New England became the center of colonial shipping and retained that position in later years during the heyday of the American merchant marine. With the passing of shipping as their leading industry, New Englanders turned to the abundant water power and found an outlet for their energies and a source of wealth in manufacturing. In the central Atlantic states, where fertile farm lands were combined with good harbors, rivers, and water power, the activities of the people were more diversified and spread over the major occupations.

One more section may be used to illustrate the effect of environment upon occupation. The first settlers in the Old Northwest (Ohio, Indiana, Illinois, Michigan, and Wisconsin) were chiefly farmers. The rest were rivermen, merchants, or others who took care of the needs of the farmers. Since much of the soil is fertile and particularly favorable to the growing of corn, large areas remain today an important part of our agricultural domain. The Old Northwest, however, had other wealth besides fertile soil. All the states in this region have soft coal. Oil, gas, and clay in Ohio, limestone in Indiana, and other valuable minerals are scattered through this section. With such wealth, it was not long before part of the people turned to mining and to the manufacture of products depending on minerals. Eastern Ohio and the region bordering on Lakes Erie, Huron, and Superior

(From H. U. Faulkner, Tyler Kepner, and Hall Bartlett, *The American Way of Life*, Harper & Brothers.)

have become one of the great manufacturing centers of the nation. At Youngstown and Cleveland, Ohio; at Gary, Indiana; at Chicago, Illinois, and in many other cities, great smelting plants turn iron into steel and other factories manufacture the steel into a thousand different commodities. In this region, with Detroit as the center, are produced almost all the American automobiles, and at Akron, Ohio, the rubber used in them is processed. The region is also important in processing agricultural products, particularly Chicago, the great meat-packing center of the world.

VARIETY OF PRESENT RESOURCES

Geographic influences are as powerful today as they have been in our past history. Furthermore, the present natural products of the country and the undeveloped resources will determine to a large extent our future in the political as well as the economic field. Let us examine briefly the natural products and resources of the United States.

In the variety of natural resources this country is rich beyond any European nation. Where most countries have two or three such assets, the United States leads the world in many. Her size and the variations of climate and physiographic factors endow her with a rich variety of natural products, animal, vegetable, and mineral. England, for example, has sufficient coal and iron for her needs, but her economic activities necessitate the importation of grains, meats, leather, cotton, certain minerals, including oil, and many other commodities essential to her industries and to the maintenance of life in her population. Italy and Norway have water power and food-stuffs, but must import iron and coal. France, although her resources and climate are varied, cannot supply her own needs in many essential products, such as petroleum, copper, and raw cotton.

The United States, on the other hand, with the exception of one or two minerals, such as chrome and tin (of relatively minor importance except in war time), rubber, and coffee, produces everything necessary for her own consumption and manufacture, and much to export. Food necessities of all kinds she has in abundance, enough to support a much larger population than her own, as was shown during the First World War and as could be increasingly demonstrated were more intensive methods of cultivation profitable. The United States exports food to many parts of the world, and although she imports various foods, such as coffee, tea, sugar, spices, and tropical fruits, nevertheless her imports are rather luxuries than absolute necessities. During the boom period of the late 'twenties we produced about 70 per cent of the world's oil, nearly 50 per cent of the copper, 38 per cent of the lead, 42 per cent of the zinc, 42 per cent of the coal, 46 per cent of the iron, 54 per cent of the cotton, and 62 per cent of the corn; we possessed 36 per cent of the developed horsepower of the world; yet the continental United States had only about 6 per cent of the world's population and land area.[13]

[13] *Commerce Yearbook, 1930,* Vol. II, Part II, "Comparative World Statistics." Percentages compiled from averages over several years, mostly 1925–1929. The United States leads all other countries in the world in the production of oats, barley, tobacco, and hogs, as well as in all the commodities mentioned above. These percentages, of course, vary with different years and differing economic conditions. During the depression years they dropped considerably. In 1936, for example, the United States produced about 61 per cent of the world's oil, 23 per cent of the copper, 24 per cent of the lead, 40 per cent of the coal, 34 per cent of the pig iron, 30 per cent of the zinc, 41 per cent of the cotton, and 51 per cent of the corn.

FOREST RESOURCES

At the present time the United States, with its 495,000,000 acres of forest, produces and uses one-half of the sawn lumber manufactured in the world. The forest belt of the American continent covers roughly the region east of a line drawn from the western shore of Hudson Bay south to Texas, a large area in the highest regions of the Rocky Mountains, and the Pacific forests in the Sierra Nevada and the coast ranges. For convenience in classifying the products, the timbered areas may be divided roughly as follows: (1) The Northeast.—The most important species in this section are the conifers, or soft woods, including white pine, spruce, and hemlock, although the various hard woods such as hickory, oak, and maple are found here also. (2) The South.—In the southern states four general types prevail, varying with the altitude: cypress and hard woods in the swamps and lower sections of the river valleys of the Atlantic and Gulf states; yellow pine in the rest of the coastal plain from Virginia to Texas; hard woods on the lower slopes of the Appalachians; and conifers higher up in the mountains. (3) The Great Lake region.—The southern part of this district contains considerable hard wood; in the northern section pine, tamarack, cedar, and hemlock predominate. (4) The Rocky Mountain division is chiefly noted for the western yellow and lodge-pole pines. (5) The Pacific coast.—This section produces soft woods; there is an abundance of Douglas fir, hemlock, pine, cedar, and redwood. The most important, the Douglas fir, attains its best development in the Puget Sound region, where it reaches a height of from two to three hundred feet.

Because of the enormous waste in clearing the land and the destruction of large areas by forest fires, the lumber industry has ceased to be important in most of these regions, and has been continually shifting. The northeastern states, which a half century ago produced more than one-half of all the lumber, now contribute less than one-tenth of the whole. Likewise, the pine forests of Michigan and Wisconsin, states which in the late 'eighties produced over two-thirds of the lumber, have rapidly declined. The Pacific States (including Nevada) are now the largest producers, with the southern states ranking second. Most of the lumber comes from Oregon, Washington, North Carolina, Alabama, and Mississippi. The chief hard woods are oak, red gum, and maple. The soft woods comprise over four-fifths of the total production, with yellow pine, Douglas fir, Western yellow pine, hemlock, and spruce, valued in the order named. It is estimated that originally the American forests covered 822,000,000 acres, with a stand of marketable saw timber of 5,200,000,000,000 square feet; this has now been reduced to 469,000,000 acres, with a stand of 2,215,000,000,000 square feet. "Stated in other fashion," says R. S. Kellogg, "nearly 60 per cent of the merchantable saw timber of the United States has been utilized or destroyed, and the bulk of it has gone in the past fifty years." [14] Conservative estimates suggest that we are consuming wood more than twice as rapidly as it is being replaced by natural growth, and it is obvious that unless strenuous and far-reaching methods are adopted to insure replacement the United States will be dependent upon imports for a large proportion of her supply. American production reached its maximum in 1909 when 44 billion board feet were produced; this had declined to less than 22 billion in 1938, and we are now importing large amounts from Canada.

The lumber supply of the future is dependent not alone upon replacement through scientific forestry but also upon the careful conservation of the remaining forests. Although three-fourths of the forest area is now given some kind of protection, the losses from fire are still great. The United States Forest Service reported that during the years 1920–1929 an average of 26,000,000 acres of forests were destroyed each year at an average annual loss of $37,000,000. Better protection has brought some decline in the 'thirties.[15] Preservation of wood also rests in part upon the adoption of less wasteful methods of cutting and marketing. Much less than half the wood taken from the forests reaches the retailer in marketable form.

AGRICULTURAL RESOURCES

Although the value of manufactured goods surpasses that of agricultural, agriculture continues to be the basic industry of the United States. Its products are the basis upon which many of our most important industries are built, and one-third of the labor force of the country is still employed in it. The leading crops in value in 1939 were corn, hay, cotton, wheat, oats, tobacco, potatoes, cottonseed, barley, and apples. Of vegetable foodstuffs, cereals are the most important, and of these maize, or Indian corn, takes first place. In 1920 the yield was over three billion bushels—in that year over 90 per cent of the world's crop—but this had declined to around two and one-half billion in the late 1930's. Corn is grown extensively in the cotton belt of the South, but three-fourths of our supply is raised in the so-called "corn belt" of the upper Mississippi Valley, which includes the states of Kansas, Nebraska, Illinois, Iowa, Ohio, Indiana, and Missouri. Here are to be found the ideal conditions for its growth—heavy rains alternating with much sunshine, and a soil which is drained easily and does not cake.

Wheat in the United States has only about half the acreage of corn and a valuation of only a third, but its position as one of the chief foods of man-

---

[14] R. S. Kellogg, *Pulpwood and Wood Pulp in America* (1923), p. 148.
[15] Nevertheless the statistics for 1939 show 212,681 fires which burned 30,449,000 acres at an estimated loss of $39,131,000.

kind makes it in some respects more important than corn. Introduced from the Old World by the earliest settlers, it has spread so widely that for some years prior to 1930 we led in its production.[16] In 1915, under the impetus of war needs, the production mounted to over a billion bushels, the largest yield in our history up to that time, but, like corn, the production has fallen off since then. Whereas about four-fifths of the corn produced is consumed on the farm and only about one-fifth offered for sale, almost all of the wheat is sold and converted into flour. Wheat is grown in forty states, but the leading states in 1939 were Kansas and North Dakota. Although these states lead in total production, the yield per acre in Washington is sometimes almost double.

The United States has led the world not only in the production of corn and wheat but also in that of oats and barley. The annual production of oats is around a billion bushels, about three-fourths of which comes from the North Central States. These states also produce about three-fifths of the barley and three-fourths of the rye.

Among the crops used for human foods which are grown in the United States should be mentioned rice and sugar, white and sweet potatoes. The center of American rice production is Louisiana, where it is grown mainly by irrigation, but a considerable amount is also produced in Texas, Arkansas, and California. Practically all of the cane sugar produced in the United States comes from Louisiana, but it furnishes only a fraction of the sugar used in this country, most of which is imported from Cuba, Puerto Rico, Hawaii, and the Philippines. The cultivation of sugar beets, however, has increased rapidly during the last few years.[17] Cultivation of white potatoes, the value of which in 1939 was over $250,000,000, is carried on in every state of the Union, but conditions are more favorable in the northern and northeastern sections. Sweet potatoes are grown extensively in the southern states.

In spite of the rapid substitution of motor power for animal power, the production of hay, curiously enough, was fifteen million tons greater in 1939 than in 1919. This may be explained by the fact that more hay is fed per animal unit, that a reduction in other farm crops usually results in greater hay production, and that more legume hay is being raised to improve the land by crop rotation.[18] In 1939 the value of the hay crop was second only to that of corn, with at least 15 per cent of the improved farm land given over to its production.

Ranking third in value among American crops, but the greatest of all crops in the South and still the greatest single item of export, is cotton. In

[16] Recent figures on production of wheat in Russia shows that country as the leader after 1930.
[17] The United States produces about one-tenth of the world's sugar beets, ranking third among the nations in this crop.
[18] *Yearbook of Agriculture, 1930*, pp. 308–310.

1939 the cotton yield was 11,817,000 bales, valued at over $536,744,000. This approximated nearly three-fifths of the world's crop, British India and Egypt ranking second and third, respectively. The cotton belt lies in a strip 1450 miles long and 500 miles wide, south of the 37th parallel and east of the 100th meridian, including all the southern states from North Carolina to Texas and California. About twenty-four million acres were given over to this staple in 1939. A superior type, known as Sea Island cotton, but representing in amount only about one per cent of the total product, is grown on the sea islands of South Carolina and the interior counties of Georgia and Florida. Before the First World War almost two-thirds of the cotton crop was exported, but now we are using nearly half of it at home.

Tobacco is grown east of the Mississippi in twenty-five or more states, mainly in the eastern coastal plain, the Appalachian region, and the Mississippi Valley plains. The total product in 1939 was over 1,800,000,000 pounds, and the chief centers of production were in North Carolina, Kentucky, and Virginia. Tobacco now ranks only sixth in value among the agricultural crops of the United States, although this country leads the world in its production and (including the crops of the insular possessions) furnishes about one-quarter of the world's crop. About three-fifths of the domestic growth is consumed here.

The great importance of the native animal life on this continent to the early settlers and pioneers has been mentioned. Possessing as it does the necessary requisites of temperate climate and immense pasturage areas, this country was destined to take its place as a leading source of animal products. It ranks first in the number of swine produced, second in cattle, and third in sheep. The best grazing lands for cattle are in the Great Plains, the Rocky Mountain table-lands, and their eastern slopes. The centers for milk production, however, are near the great cities, with New York leading in milk sold by farmers; Minnesota, Wisconsin, and Iowa are the leading states for dairy products. The swine country is, with the exception of Texas, identical with the region of the greatest corn production. While sheep are to be found in every state in the Union, the chief wool centers are Texas and the far-western states. The most important horse and mule markets are East St. Louis and Kansas City, both in the center of the horse-raising area. Mules are more numerous than horses in the southern states, because they can better endure the hot climate and hard usage. Owing to the fact that corn is the best cereal for fattening poultry, the center of the poultry industry is in the North Central States, from which comes over one-half of the billion-dollar annual yield of eggs and chickens.

Although the resources of the sea do not play as important a part in our economic life as they did in the colonial and early national period, they still provide a livelihood for some 130,000 wage earners, and foodstuffs valued at around $100,000,000 annually. The United States and Alaska together still lead the world in this industry. The western Atlantic from Newfoundland to the Chesapeake is one of the two most important fishing areas in the world. The shad, mackerel, cod, herring, halibut, bluefish, and oysters on the Atlantic coast supply in value about half of the annual haul

(From H. U. Faulkner, Tyler Kepner, and Hall Bartlett, *The American Way of Life,* Harper & Brothers.)

of the United States, including Alaska. The salmon fishing of Alaska and the Columbia River is the most important phase of this industry on the Pacific coast, the fisheries of which yield a catch worth annually $25,000,000. The Great Lakes supply herring, whitefish, trout, yellow perch, and many other varieties valued annually at about $6,000,000.

As in the case of lumber and certain other resources, the fishing industry has been characterized by tragic waste and disregard of the future. This is particularly true of the salmon fishing on the west coast where methods based upon momentary profits have reduced the haul and driven the fish farther and farther north.

MINERAL RESOURCES

In 1860 the value of the products of the mines and quarries (metallic and non-metallic) of the United States was placed at $90,000,000; in 1939 it had increased to $4,874,000,000. Of all the minerals, metallic or non-metallic, petroleum ranks first (1939) with a value of $1,265,000,000 or about one-quarter of the total valuation for all minerals. Although oil was produced originally to satisfy lighting needs, its field of usefulness has been widened until by distillation and other processes such commercial products as kerosene, benzine, gasoline, naphtha, heavy and lubricating oils, paraffin, and asphalt are manufactured. With the continued extension of the manufacture of gasoline motors and oil-burning engines, the value of petroleum in industry has constantly increased. Oil was first discovered in the Appalachian area, extending from New York to Tennessee, and originally most of the oil came from this region. It is found in many places, but the three chief fields today are (1) the mid-continent regions, including western Missouri, Kansas, and Oklahoma; (2) the California field, and (3) the gulf field, comprising the coastal plains of Texas and Louisiana. Although the United States produces about 60 per cent of the world's output, large amounts are imported from Venezuela, Colombia, and Mexico. The tremendous speed with which this country is consuming its oil resources has led certain geologists to sound frequent warnings and to predict that the peak of production will soon be reached.

Next to petroleum, coal is the most important of the minerals in point of value.[19] The anthracite deposits of the United States, located chiefly in Pennsylvania, are by far the most important in the world in both quality and quantity. The most important bituminous fields are in the Appalachian Mountains, extending from Alabama to Pennsylvania, but rich deposits are also to be found in many states of the Mississippi Valley and elsewhere. The aggregate coal areas of this country approximate 500,000 square miles, or about 13 per cent of its area.[20] The fact that these beds are well distributed is significant, for the expense of transportation of this essential commodity to industrial and commercial development is a big item in its ultimate cost. Also important is the fact that the richest deposits are within a few hours' haul of the great ports of New York and Philadelphia, and but a little farther from the manufacturing states of southern New England. If this had not been the case, the history of the northeastern United States after the Industrial Revolution might have been different. Moreover, the large deposits of coal in the Old Northwest have contributed greatly to make that area a great manufacturing center. On the other hand, it is extremely unfortunate that the production and use of this basic mineral are accompanied by so much waste,[21] and that the industry, especially since the ex-

[19] The anthracite production in 1939 was valued at $187,000,000 and bituminous at $732,-537,000. The value of coke, a derivative of coal, was $212,884,000.

[20] To these fuel resources the future historian will add the present peat swamps as yet almost wholly neglected; of these there are seven million acres in Minnesota alone. See E. K. Soper, *The Peat Deposits of Minnesota*, Bulletin 16, Minnesota Geological Survey (1919).

[21] It is estimated that only about 50 per cent of the bituminous coal is actually extracted from the mine, while another 10 per cent is lost in preparation and marketing. This says nothing of the waste in consumption. See *World Almanac, 1931*, p. 293.

pansion of mine capacity during the First World War, has been harassed by overproduction and by a chaotic labor market. A world-wide decrease in the demand for coal has been occasioned chiefly by the substitution of oil for coal, by the development of hydroelectric power, and by technical improvements in converting coal into steam and electric power.[22] The coal industry has been slow to adapt itself to all these changes; it is a classic example of unscientific production.

Next to coal and petroleum, the most valuable product of the mines is natural gas, the value of which was estimated in 1939 at close to $540,000,000. Little used before 1870 except for lighting purposes, and allowed to go to waste in large quantities, it has since come to be recognized as ideal for heat and power, and is now conserved as fully as conditions permit. Production has more than doubled since 1922, but here again some geologists predict exhaustion before many years. Only one-fifth is used for domestic light and heat; the remainder is used in industry. A notable development has been the invention of a process whereby gasoline may be extracted from the natural gas without injuring its utility for heating purposes. Over nine-tenths is so treated.

The most valuable, most widely distributed, and cheapest of the metals in the United States is iron. It is also the most important material used for machinery, tools, buildings, and other materials of industry which play so vast a part in an age of iron and steel. Iron is found in practically every state, but the great bulk of the ore produced comes from the Lake Superior district, including Minnesota, Michigan, and Wisconsin; the only other important source is the Birmingham region of Alabama and Tennessee. The Lake Superior region not only contributes almost nine-tenths of the iron ore but contains at least three-fourths of the available deposits. The ore is, moreover, of distinctly superior grade to that of the Appalachians and Rockies. The advantageous situation of Pittsburgh and Birmingham as regards both coal and iron gave them a start in the iron and steel industry, but the recent predominance of the Lake Superior ores has created a tendency for the manufacturing center of the iron and steel industry to shift slowly to such Lake shore points as Buffalo, Cleveland, Chicago, and Gary. The United States is particularly fortunate with regard to this metal, for her known iron resources appear to be nearly equal to those of all the rest of the world. On the other hand, certain alloys of iron of growing significance in our industrial life—manganese, nickel, vanadium, chrome, tungsten, and the like—are found here in small quantities or not at all.

From primitive times copper has been, next to iron, the metal most essential in the industries. This metal is so ductile and easily worked that the

[22]*Commerce Yearbook, 1930,* I, 11–12, 33, 266–268, 274.

ancients became exceedingly proficient in turning it to a variety of uses. Since the harnessing of electricity for man's use, and the invention of the telegraph and telephone, copper, because of its excellent properties as a conductor, has assumed a new importance. Its use is also widened by the fact that when combined with zinc it forms brass, and combined with tin it makes bronze. Improvements in extracting the metal, and the greater de-

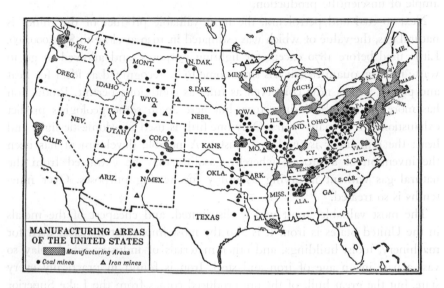

MANUFACTURING AREAS
OF THE UNITED STATES
▨ Manufacturing Areas
● Coal mines   △ Iron mines

mands for it, have made possible the increase of the world's annual output from 9000 tons in 1801 to almost 2,600,000 in 1937. Of this the United States contributes about one-third,[23] the three states of Arizona, Utah, and Montana producing almost three-fourths of the whole. The annual copper output of Arizona alone exceeds that of any foreign nation. The purest deposits are in the glacial districts of upper Michigan, but the greatest are in Arizona, which supplies over one-third of the American copper. The deposits in Montana, Nevada, and Utah have made possible the cities of Butte and Anaconda in Montana, Bingham in Utah, and the four Arizona towns of Bisbee, Morenci, Globe, and Jerome.

In the production of zinc, a comparatively new industry in this country (our first records of production are of 1873), the United States and Germany rank as the two largest sources of supply. The metal is used chiefly as an alloy of copper and tin, in paints, and also for galvanizing iron and steel to protect them from rust. Although twenty states mine zinc-bear-

[23] The United States is not only the leading producer of copper but also the leading refiner, importing as she does much copper ore from other nations for refining. Chile, exporting chiefly to the United States, is the second largest producer of copper ore.

ing ores, over two-fifths come from the region known as the Joplin, comprising southwestern Missouri, southeastern Kansas, and northeastern Oklahoma.[24]

Lead is another metal in whose production the United States leads, supplying over one-third of the world's total. Twenty-one states and Alaska produce it, but the output of most of them is small. Missouri, Idaho, and Utah yield three-fourths of the smelter production of lead, although Oklahoma, Kansas, Montana, and Colorado produce appreciable amounts. Advancing industrialization has increased the use of lead in its pure form and in its numerous alloys, and, like most metals, its production was greatly stimulated by the First and Second World Wars. One-third of the lead in times of peace goes into white lead for paint. Like other industrial minerals, the increase in its production has been spectacular, from 15,600 short tons in 1860 to 627,000 in 1939.

Of the remaining metals, aluminum has become the most important. Because of its firm texture and strength, but at the same time its lightness of weight and non-rusting quality, it is superior to other metals for certain purposes, particularly for cooking utensils and airplanes. Bauxite, the principal ore from which aluminum is derived, is mined chiefly in Arkansas, Georgia, Alabama, and Tennessee, although much of it in normal times is imported from British and Dutch Guiana. The bauxite is often shipped long distances to be processed into a whitish powder called alumina and this in turn is shipped to reduction plants located where electric power is cheap. The production of bauxite and its eventual reduction to aluminum have increased tremendously with the Second World War; this has been made possible by new hydroelectric power developments on the Tennessee and Columbia Rivers and elsewhere.

Of less significance in our industrial life, gold and silver, the so-called "precious metals," have played an important part in our economic and social history in promoting the migration of peoples and the founding of new commonwealths.[25] Before 1848 the gold mined in the territory of the United States was not large (a total of 1,187,170 fine ounces, 1792–1847). The discovery of deposits in California in 1848, however, quadrupled the world's supply by 1852, and the United States held first place until surpassed by South Africa in 1898. The production in California rapidly declined in the 'sixties, but the discovery of gold in the Comstock Lode in Nevada in 1859 helped to keep up the nation's supply. During the height of production from the Comstock Lode (1859–1869) the annual output averaged almost three million fine ounces; this average declined in the

---

[24] The production of zinc in 1939 was 491,058 short tons valued at $51,000,000.
[25] Below, Chaps. 10, 18.

'seventies and was not reached again until the gold discoveries in Alaska in the late 'nineties. During the first two decades of the present century the yearly production was between three and four million fine ounces, declining thereafter to only a little over two million in 1929. Artificial prices imposed by the New Deal legislation during the period of currency manipulation have sufficiently stimulated production to push it upwards to over five and one-half million fine ounces in 1939. The chief sources of gold in this country are now California, Alaska, South Dakota, Utah, and Colorado. About two-thirds of the metal is used for money or to maintain value for money; the rest is used for various commercial purposes.

Silver production had its great spurt in this country after the discovery of the Comstock Lode. Although the commercial needs for silver have, of course, increased, its decline as a monetary medium after the 'nineties caused its price to fall steadily. The production of silver was about 503,000 fine ounces for the decade 1850 to 1860; during the 1920's yearly production has ranged from 53,000,000 to 73,000,000. As in the case of gold, the government placed artificially high prices on silver and thus stimulated production in the late 'thirties.[26] Silver for all practical purposes is no longer a precious metal. If it were not for the fact that Senators from seven silver states sit in Congress to protect the price and future of this relatively unimportant mineral, the price would be less and its economic usefulness in industry much greater, to the benefit of the nation.

WATER RESOURCES

The importance of water in our economic history and in our present economic life can scarcely be overestimated. Water is valuable not only as the habitat of fish and certain fur-bearing animals, and as a cheap and convenient highway of commerce, but also as an inexhaustible supply of power which can be harnessed so as to fill an infinite variety of human needs. During the colonial period, rivers were the chief highways of inland commerce and continued so until the coming of railroads. In the early decades of the Industrial Revolution, water supplied the chief motive power for factories,[27] but during the 'eighties power derived from steam surpassed that from water, and by 1900 over three-fourths of the power used in manufacturing plants came from steam. This was due chiefly to the development of the coal resources which made it possible to locate factories at the most convenient points. The situation has changed greatly, however, during the last three decades. The rapid development of electricity and the inventions which have

---

[26] Production in 1939 was approximately 65,200,000 ounces valued at $44,000,000.
[27] Below, Chap. 13.

made possible the transportation of electric power over large areas have encouraged a return to water as the primary power. The project of "harnessing Niagara" was undertaken in the late 'nineties, and the success attained there has encouraged other stupendous projects, until today a network of giant power cables extends over the more thickly settled regions. Hydroelectric development has already gone far, notably in four sections: the North Atlantic, on the Merrimac, Connecticut, and Hudson Rivers; the St. Lawrence region, on the Niagara and other rivers, running into the Great lakes; on the Catawba and other rivers of the Carolina piedmont; and on the rivers of the north Pacific.

Nearly 25,000,000 horsepower, approximately one-half of the world's developed horsepower, was produced in this country by 1935, but the possibilities of water power are still in their infancy. The great new power projects which have come into operation at Boulder Dam on the Colorado, at Bonneville and Grand Coulee on the Columbia, and at various points on the Tennessee give some indication of the vast possibilities of electric power in this country. Probably less than half of the potential water power has yet been tapped. Nevertheless, steam has again been driven into a secondary position, and today two-thirds of the primary power used in manufacturing is derived from water.

IN CONCLUSION

To sum up, it may be said that the United States, with a few minor exceptions, furnishes every mineral necessary to a great manufacturing nation. In her fertile valleys and broad prairies she can produce foods, of both the temperate and the semi-tropical varieties, sufficient to support a population much larger than at present. She can supply enough leather, wool, and cotton for her own needs and a considerable amount for exporting. In addition to her sources of power from coal and petroleum, she has vast reserves of water power, the potentialities of which stagger the imagination. The United States comprises a world in itself. Not only is she the most wealthy and prosperous of the nations, displaying a higher standard of living than any other, but she is a country in which the real wages of work—food, fuel, shelter, and clothing—are higher and more abundant than elsewhere. Our resource area is at present second to none, and probably surpasses all others in the world. We have the bases for all the necessities and comforts of life for all our people. The possession of these apparently inexhaustible resources has helped to endow the American people with a hopeful and buoyant confidence, but at the same time has encouraged wasteful exploitation. Nature has done her part; it is the fault of man if this wealth has been wastefully used and inequitably distributed.

NOTE ON STATISTICS

In any work dealing with economics, wide use must be made of statistics, the nature of which should be better understood. "One of the prime objects of statistics," says W. I. King in his *Elements of Statistical Method* (p. 22), "is to give us a bird's-eye view of a large mass of facts, to simplify this extensive and complex array of isolated instances and reduce it to a form which will be comprehensive to the ordinary mind." To accomplish this, involved mathematics are used to develop economic formulas and scientific statistics, which then interpret the descriptive statistics compiled by the census and other agencies.

A word should be added as to the accuracy of statistical tables. Absolute accuracy in the material with which we are dealing is probably never possible, but since the aim is better comprehension of an entire field, relative and not absolute accuracy is the main desideratum. Statistics, as King says (*ibid.*, p. 64), are estimates rather than exact enumerations. It is impossible, for example, to obtain more than an approximate estimate of the number of bushels of wheat produced. Furthermore, statistics of varying kinds differ greatly in relative reliability. For instance, the number of deaths reported is relatively accurate, as the returns are required by law, but a tabulation of the causes of death may be far from correct. It should also be kept in mind that the use of round numbers sometimes gives a more accurate impression than the figures carried out, because when attention is directed to the digits the main point being demonstrated may be lost, especially in comparisons.

For a concise account of the manner in which facts for statistical study are collected, see *The Review of Economic Statistics,* Sept., 1920–Jan., 1921. Prefatory sections contain valuable material on methods employed and sources of information. For a clear and not too technical account of the nature of statistics, read Willford I. King, *Elements of Statistical Method* (1913), Parts I and II. Suggestive essays on the function of statistics in economics, history, political science, and sociology by E. R. A. Seligman, H. U. Faulkner, J. A. Fairlie, and W. F. Ogburn, respectively, can be found in W. F. Ogburn and Alexander Goldenweiser (eds.), *The Social Sciences and Their Interrelations* (1927). An excellent insight into the use and value of statistics may be gained from R. E. Chaddock, *Principles and Methods of Statistics* (1925), Chaps. I–III.

Most of the statistical information in this book is obtained from government sources. The government departments at Washington have statistical divisions that compile elaborate reports, and the Bureau of the Census now maintains a permanent staff that collects information. A large amount of data is conveniently reprinted in *The Statistical Abstract of the United States,* published by the Bureau of Foreign and Domestic Commerce of the Department of Commerce. *The Abstract of the Census of Manufacturers* and *The Abstract of the Census* are less bulky to use than the *Census* and condense the most valuable material of each census. *The Commerce Yearbook,* issued now in two volumes (I, *Domestic* and II, *Foreign*) and the *Yearbook of Agriculture* give valuable summaries of government statistics.

SELECTED READINGS

Harper's Atlas of American History, Introduction by D. R. Fox.
Semple, E. C., *American History and Its Geographic Conditions*, Chaps. I–III.
Hulbert, A. B., *Soil and Its Influence on the History of the United States*.
Kellogg, C. E., *The Soils That Support Us*, Chaps. I–III, IX, XVI, XVIII.
Huntingon, E., in Davis, Jerome, and Barnes, H. E. (eds.), *An Introduction to Sociology*, pp. 191–304.
Huntington, E., and Williams, F. E., *Business Geography*, Chap. V.
Smith, J. R., and Phillips, M. O., *North America*, Chap. I.
Chaddock, R. E., *Principles and Methods of Statistics*, Chaps. I–III.

2.

Economic Background
of Colonization

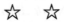

THE RISE OF MERCHANT CAPITALISM

THE discovery of America was brought about by a train of circumstances extending back through centuries of European history and culminating at the end of the fifteenth century. Intellectual, political, and, above all, economic factors contributed to make this a turning point in world history. The fifteenth century and the beginning of the sixteenth marked the height of the Renaissance, a period of inquiry and dissatisfaction with the old order. In political life the modern state was being erected on the ruins of feudalism; with the national state came a cessation of the private warfare of the Middle Ages, greater protection to travelers and merchants, and fewer tolls. More settled conditions encouraged the extension of trade and commerce, and the revived economic life led naturally to exploration and discovery. The latter was aided by the compass and astrolabe, by that time in general use, and by the improvement in the charts and maps; the news of scientific and commercial progress was disseminated by means of the printing press, invented about the middle of the fifteenth century.

Although the influences just mentioned all contributed to the great era of European expansion, particular emphasis should be placed upon the development of merchant capitalism, which transformed feudalism into a capitalist economy and gave a tremendous impetus to colonization and the development of overseas trade. Despite the condemnation of the church, money-lending continued throughout the late Middle Ages. Great private bankers, like the Medici of Florence and the Fuggers of Augsburg, accumulated surpluses as merchants and then turned to money-lending. By the end of the fifteenth century Flemish speculators were operating an exchange at Antwerp where commodities and the shares of joint-stock companies were bought and sold. These merchant princes and bankers helped to finance the struggle of kings against their feudal lords and contributed much to the eventual establishment of the great national states. Above all,

this capital accumulation contributed to the development of medieval industry and commerce which formed the immediate background for the discovery
of America.

As the chaos of feudal society gave way to national monarchical states,
a new impetus was given to the expansion of trade and the development
of merchant capitalism. Internally conditions became more stabilized, to
the benefit of trade and industry. In need of money to strengthen their position at home and their prestige abroad, the new monarchs encouraged industry within their realms and granted trading monopolies to groups of
adventurers willing to risk their fortunes in foreign commerce. The new
merchant and trading class was encouraged at the expense of the old nobility.
At the same time the Protestant Revolt weakened the prestige of the
Catholic church, which had frowned on interest-taking and excessive
profit-making and had emphasized the doctrine of the "just price" with
ultimate reward in the world to come. In many ways the foundations were
being laid for a great expansion.

Trade with the East

As for the immediate impetus to the discovery of America none was
more important than the desire on the part of Europeans to find a quicker
and cheaper route to the East. From the dawn of commerce Europe had
been dependent upon Asia for most of her luxuries and many of her necessities. The importance of spices in the Middle Ages is difficult to appreciate
today, when meat is kept fresh by cold storage or curing; but the monotonous
diet and coarse food of those times made spices and condiments so desirable
that they were frequently sent as gifts of honor from one sovereign to
another. Pepper from the Malabar coast of India was a staple import during
the Middle Ages and was used by all who could afford it. Cloves, cinnamon,
nutmegs from the Moluccas, and sugar from Arabia and Persia were more
expensive and less commonly used, but in great demand. Apothecaries obtained many of their drugs from Asia, among them rhubarb, balsam,
gums, aloes, cubebs, and camphor. The precious stones, which adorned the
persons of the upper classes in Europe, came almost exclusively from the
East.

Trade with the East, however, was not confined exclusively to such
luxuries as spices, drugs, and precious stones. An important class of wares
which served manufacturing industries, namely dyestuffs, found their source
there. Indigo was the chief staple of Bagdad, and Brazil-wood, producing a
red dye, came from India. Alum, considered indispensable for fixing colors
in dyeing and one of the most desirable products of the Levant trade, was
procured mainly in Asia Minor. Manufactured products, superior in work-

manship, material, and design to anything known in Europe, came also from the East: glass and cutlery from Damascus, Samarkand, and Bagdad; porcelain from China; a great variety of cottons and silks from India, China, Persia, and Asia Minor. Persian rugs, Cashmere shawls, taffeta silk, damask linen, and japanned ware all testify to the eastern nomenclature and origin of the most sought-after textiles, rugs, tapestries, and household luxuries.

In return for these products Europe could offer only woolen fabrics and such metals and minerals as arsenic, antimony, quicksilver, tin, copper, and lead. Although these products were much valued in the East, their weight and bulk made transportation on the long overland routes an arduous and unrewarded task. Gold and silver, on the other hand, were more easily transported and were consequently used freely to make up the balance. This movement of the precious metals from Europe to Asia was made possible by the fact that the monetary system of Europe in the Middle Ages was not highly developed. The continued movement of gold and silver to Asia, however, undoubtedly caused a scarcity of these metals in Europe, which was not relieved until the opening of mines in Mexico and Peru.

While trade with the Near and the Far East was a leading factor in the economic life of the Middle Ages, little was known by Europeans of Asia or the routes thereto. Trade had flourished in ancient times, but during the barbaric invasions of the fifth century and the succeeding conflicts this commerce had been largely broken up. A general awakening of economic life in the eleventh century set in motion with renewed vigor the intercourse with the East, a movement greatly aided by the Crusades (1095-1270). Not alone did the Crusades enlarge the vision and knowledge of Europeans by introducing them again to the learning and products of Asia, but they laid the foundations for the prosperity of the Italians in this trade. Towns at the extreme south of the Italian peninsula sprang into importance, as did Amalfi on the Bay of Naples, Genoa at the head of the Tyrrhenian Sea, and Venice at the head of the Adriatic.

MEDIEVAL TRADE ROUTES

The products of the East reached Europe over three main trade routes, of which the oldest and most important during the greater part of the Middle Ages was the central passage. Merchandise was gathered from India and the Far East and brought to Ormuz at the north of the Persian Gulf, and thence to Bossorah (Bozra) at the mouth of the Tigris, and up the valley to Bagdad. From Bagdad the routes spread like a fan either north to Tabriz, westward to Antioch, Damascus, or Jaffa, or west and then south to Alexandria. The southern route was chiefly a sea route leading from India across the Arabian Sea to the Red Sea. The cargoes in

TRADE ROUTES WITH THE EAST

Northern Route
Middle Route
Southern Route
All Water (Portuguese)

MANHATTAN DRAFTING CO INC. N.Y.

most cases were landed on the western coast and transferred to caravans, which carried them to the Nile, upon which they were floated down to Cairo. This route, although attended by difficulties of navigation, was the cheapest and quickest, and at the close of the Middle Ages the most important. The northern route, which was entirely overland, was in reality a system of routes leading from the inland provinces of China and India to the Caspian and up the Volga to central Russia and the Baltic, or to the Black Sea and thence to Europe.

The terminal points, then, of the eastern trade were such cities as Trebizond on the Black Sea, Constantinople on the Bosphorus, Acre, Beirut, Tripoli, Laodicaea, and Jaffa on the Syrian coast, and Alexandria at the mouth of the Nile. At these cities, and even in such inland points as Damascus, Aleppo, and Antioch, merchants from Spain, France, and Italy met the caravans and purchased what goods had escaped destruction from the elements and confiscation by pirates. The bulk of the Levant trade during the five hundred years from 1000 to 1500 rested in the hands of the Italians, and the three cities of Venice, Genoa, and Pisa struggled for supremacy in this trade, while Florence became a banking and manufacturing center. From the Italian cities the Oriental merchandise was distributed to northern and central Europe through two main channels. German merchants handled the overland reexport trade from Venice and Genoa. In the former city a building was set aside by the state for their use where they could bargain with the Venetians and be watched by the government. Through the St. Gothard Pass to Basel, Constance, Strassburg, and down the Rhine, or over the Brenner Pass to Munich, Nuremburg, or Frankfort were the usual routes. In addition to the overland passages through the Alps, a large amount of trade was carried on by sea with Lisbon, Bruges, and London. As far as northern Europe was concerned, it was in the Low Countries—at Antwerp, Bruges, Ghent, and other towns—that the lines of medieval commerce finally crossed. Here the goods of the Mediterranean and the Baltic were sent to be distributed later throughout England and France.

THE COMMERCIAL REVOLUTION

Our task so far has been, first, to point out the importance of the eastern trade[1] to the Europe of the Middle Ages; and, second, to show that the

---

[1] To show that the question of eastern trade routes is still a vital one it is necessary simply to call attention to the history of the Suez Canal and the attempt of Germany to cut in on this route by means of the Berlin-Bagdad Railway. The importance of this was never lost sight of during the First World War, as the campaigns in Palestine and the Euphrates Valley demonstrate. Two decades later Britain's life line was again threatened when Italy, anxious to dominate the Mediterranean, entered the Second World War to break British control of Gibraltar, Egypt, and the Suez Canal.

center of European medieval commerce lay in the Mediterranean basin. How this trade center shifted from the Mediterranean to the Atlantic, producing a Commercial Revolution, remains to be shown. The story involves the discovery both of new trade routes to the East and of the American continents.

Of the many factors operative in bringing this about, one stands pre-eminent—the eagerness of Europe for the products of Asia, coupled with the difficulty and expense of obtaining them over the existing trade routes. This made imperative the discovery of quicker and cheaper means of travel to the East. The old explanation that the capture of Constantinople by the Ottoman Turks in 1453 and the extension of their control over Syria and Egypt virtually closed the old trade routes and thus hastened the discovery of new routes is no longer accepted. The routes through Syria and Egypt did not, in fact, come under the control of the Ottoman Turks until a quarter century after Columbus discovered America. That the Turks raised the fees for foreign merchants and increased tariffs and tolls there can be no doubt, but the trade of Venice and other Italian cities continued to flourish throughout the sixteenth century. Moreover, investigations by Professor Lybyer have shown that there was no serious interference in eastern trade and no rise in the prices of eastern commodities in Europe after the Turkish conquests. He contends, on the other hand, that motives "related to religion, crusading, conquest, and adventure probably outweighed the seeking of spices in the minds of the great explorers and their royal supporters," and there is much to be said for this explanation.[2] If the Turkish interference is entirely discounted, there still remain the disadvantages of the old trade routes, which provided an important impetus for the burst of exploring activity in the fifteenth and sixteenth centuries.

Although such Italian travelers as Carpini and the three Polos had added much to the European knowledge of Asia, and the Italian cartographers led in the accuracy of their maps, it was left to the Portuguese to discover the new way to the East. Always a seafaring nation to whom the Atlantic coast of North Africa was not wholly unknown, they were spurred on by the enthusiasm of Prince Henry "the Navigator," a member of the Portuguese ruling family and a man in whom rare business ability was combined with the instinct of the explorer and the zeal of the missionary. One expedition after another was sent by him to explore the west coast of Africa. In 1434 Eannes rounded Cape Bojador, Cape Blanco was passed in 1441, and in 1445 Denis Diaz reached Cape Verde. It was not, however,

[2] A. H. Lybyer, "The influence of the Ottoman Turks upon the Routes of Oriental Trade," in the *Annual Report* for 1914 of the American Historical Association, I, 125–133.

until 1487 that Bartholomew Diaz discovered what he called the Cape of
Storms and what King John II of Portugal later christened the Cape of
Good Hope. Ten years later Vasco da Gama rounded the cape, pushed
up the east coast, and in 1498 reached India. Cabral, with a fleet, followed
in 1500.[3] The new sea route to India was complete and trade was rapidly
established. The strategic position of Portugal, combined with lowered
cost of transportation over the new route, threw the eastern trade into the
hands of the Portuguese, who took immediate advantage by laying the
foundations of an eastern empire which they ruled until the crowns of
Spain and Portugal were joined. With the opening of the new route to the
East the center of the world's trade shifted from the Mediterranean to the
Atlantic. Venice, it is true, continued a prosperous and important shipping
center for another century, but the loss of her eastern trade was a severe
blow. Merchants trading in eastern wares deserted the Rialto for the
bustling harbor of Lisbon, and the glory that had belonged to Venice now
passed to the Atlantic seaports.

THE DISCOVERY OF AMERICA

Portugal was not the only nation where men were dreaming of riches
through quicker routes to the Indies. Before da Gama had made his epochal
voyage to India, Ferdinand and Isabella of Spain, fresh from their conquests over the Moors, had paused in their building of a great Spanish
state to promise aid to the Italian navigator Columbus in his projected
westward voyage. Columbus, believing with all educated astronomers and
philosophers that the earth was round, thought that by sailing due west
he could reach the Indies. "I have always read that the world," said he,
"comprising the land and the water, is spherical, as is testified by the investigations of Ptolemy and others, who have proved it by the eclipses of
the moon and other observations made from east to west as well as by
the elevation of the pole from north to south." His thesis was of course
correct and not new; his mistake was in conceiving the world to be a smaller
sphere than it turned out to be. The greatness of Columbus lay not in the
originality of his conception, but in his courage in venturing the unknown
seas and in his pertinacity in pursuing his project. Sailing west in 1492
with his three little ships, he at length ran into what was probably one
of the Bahamas. He believed that he had discovered outlying islands of the
Indies, and returned in 1493, in 1498, and again in 1502, only to meet with
disappointment in his efforts to get through to India.

---

[3] Steering westward to avoid storms or calms, he was carried by the current to the coast of
Brazil, the point on the American continent nearest the Old World. If Columbus had not discovered America, another decade in all probability would have seen Europeans on American soil.

The efforts of Columbus were emulated by John Cabot, the Italian navigator in the service of Henry VII of England, who sailed due west in quest of Cipango, only to land on the barren shore of Labrador. Even after Balboa (1513) had discovered the great western ocean and Magellan's ship *Victoria* had circumnavigated the globe (1519–1522) in that greatest feat of navigation of all time,[4] explorers continued for a hundred years to seek for channels leading through or around America to Asia. This quest for a passage to the Indies led to the explorations of Verrazano (1524), Cartier (1534), Frobisher (1576–1578), Davis (1585–1587), and Hudson (1609). Although no natural opening through the American continents to Cathay was ever discovered, these voyages gave to Europeans their first knowledge of what is now the coast of the United States and of the two great rivers of the eastern coast, the St. Lawrence and the Hudson.

The Commercial Revolution, including as it did the discovery of America, had incalculable effects upon economic history. Only a few of the most important can be suggested here. The comparative cheapness of water transportation over the new routes to the Indies reduced the cost of Oriental goods and made possible their more general use. Long ocean voyages developed the construction of stronger and taller ships which could profitably carry to Europe the bulky commodities hitherto unknown, such as tea, coffee, Indian corn, and tobacco. All the influences tending to the development of merchant capitalism and economic imperialism were accentuated. The growth in business developed better methods of carrying on trade, new industries sprang into existence, manufacturing increased—all of which tended to break down the antiquated guild system. Even agriculture responded to the stimulus of new crops and the necessity of supporting a greater population which came with enlarged commercial activities. The slave trade was revived to provide the labor necessary to work the plantations of the New World. Not the least effect of the discovery of America was the plunder of Mexico and Peru. The flow of gold and silver from the mines of the New World put Europe definitely on a money economy and gave merchant capitalism a new lease on life. Trade with the Far East, which had been declining as Europe was gradually stripped of her precious metals, revived and flourished. The sudden flow of precious metals pushed prices upward. Since wages and rents lagged behind,[5] enormous

---

[4] Four centuries later (1924) the first circumnavigation of the globe by airplane was completed by United States Army fliers in 175 days. In 1931 Wiley Post and Harold Gatty girdled the globe in 8 days, 15 hours, and 51 minutes. Post, flying solo, cut the record in 1933 to 7 days, 18 hours, 49½ minutes.

[5] Adam Smith, writing in 1776, insisted that "the discovery of the abundant mines of America, seems to have been the sole cause of this diminution [between 1570 and 1640] in the value of silver in proportion to that of corn." *Wealth of Nations* (Cannan ed., London, 1904), I, 191.

profits were reaped by merchants, industrialists, and other enterpreneurs. This in turn stimulated commerce and industry and the results have permeated almost every phase of economic and social life.

Upon one class in Europe the Commercial Revolution had its greatest influence. While kings and nobles fought over colonial empires, the bourgeoisie or townsfolk, that new middle class just emerging, reaped the benefits. In every country the number of those dependent upon commerce and trade grew rapidly and the long process of the exaltation of the middle class at the expense of the landed aristocracy, the climax of which we see in our own day, was begun. In the arena of imperial politics the Commercial Revolution inaugurated a series of struggles for colonial possessions and commercial power during which maritime supremacy passed from Portugal to Spain and then, during the Dutch rebellion, to Holland. But England and France were both growing in national spirit and sea power and both made war upon the wealthy but diminutive republic until they had effectually crippled her. With Holland eliminated, England and France engaged in a series of seven great wars extending from 1689 to the overthrow of Napoleon, which left Great Britain supreme upon the sea and the foremost colonial power. All of these nations, however, while relinquishing their maritime supremacy, retained certain parts of their colonial empire in America.

MOTIVES FOR THE COLONIZATION OF AMERICA

As the idea was gradually brought home to Europeans that the new-found land was not the Indies but two mighty continents, not only did statesmen dream of new empires, and knights and merchants of new sources of riches, but the common man began to think of a new home across the seas where he might escape from the religious, political, and economic tyranny of the Old World. The motives for colonization were varied—religious, political, and economic being inextricably combined.

The age of the Reformation was one in which the religious motive was strong. Prince Henry sent his ships to find not only the Indies but also the fabled Christian kingdom of Prester John. "We come in search of Christians and spices," said Vasco da Gama. In the breasts of the early Spanish conquerors and explorers a consuming passion for gold was fused with a strong crusading spirit. "Gold is most excellent," said Columbus. "Gold is treasure, and he who possesses it does all he wishes to in this world, and succeeds in helping souls into paradise." [6] French Jesuit priests threaded the lakes and rivers in advance of the fur trader, baptizing as

---

[6] Fourth Voyage. Letter to Ferdinand and Isabella, written July 7, 1503. Original Narratives of Early American History Series, *The Northmen, Columbus, and Cabot*, p. 412.

they went. The religious impulse moved even the more prosaic English. Drake and Hawkins scoured the Spanish Main [7] to fight Catholics as well as collect booty. Later many felt with the Virginia Company managers that the first object of that plantation was "to preach and baptize into *Christian Religion,* and by propagation of the *Gospell,* to recover out of the arms of the Divell, a number of poore and miserable soules, wrapt up unto death, in almost invincible ignorance." [8] Sir George Peckham emphasized the benefits that would accrue to the natives brought by the white man "from falsehood to truth, from darkness to lyght, from the hieway of death to the path of life, from superstitious idolatry to sincere Christianity, from the devil to Christ, from hell to Heaven. And if in respect of all the commodities they can yield us (were they many more) that they should but receive this only benefit of Christianity, they were more fully recompenced." [9]

While the work of the priests in opening the routes for settlers should not be underestimated, even more important than the crusading spirit in promoting settlement was the desire for freedom from religious persecution at home. Separatists and Puritans founded New England to obtain religious liberty; but Puritan intolerance in turn drove Roger Williams and his followers to Rhode Island, banished Anne Hutchinson, and contributed somewhat to Hooker's settlement of Connecticut. Puritanism drove Cavaliers to Virginia and English Catholics to Maryland. French Protestants found refuge in the Carolinas; while Quakers, Mennonites, Moravians, and other sects found a home in Pennsylvania, New Jersey, and elsewhere.

Political motives also played their part. Each nation would secure for itself as much of the new land as possible. Settlements in the thirteen colonies were encouraged to check the northward advance of the Spanish and the southward and eastward pressure of the French. The four-cornered struggle for empire between Spain, France, England, and Holland during the sixteenth and seventeenth centuries contributed much in hastening the occupation of America. Divergence in political ideas, often derived from religious tenets, also sent many to the New World.

More important than the religious and political were the economic mo-

---

[7] The term Spanish Main properly means the coasts bordering on the Caribbean Sea, but is sometimes applied to the Caribbean itself.

[8] From "A True and Sincere declaration of the purposes and ends of the Plantation begun in Virginia . . . Set Forth by the authority of the Governors and Councillors established for that Plantation." Given by Alexander Brown, *Genesis of the United States* (1890), I, 339.

[9] Peckham, Sir George, *A True Reporte of the Late Discoveries . . . of the Newfound Lands,* a rare pamphlet published in 1583, reprinted in *Magazine of History with Notes and Queries,* Extra Number 68 in Vol. XVII, Extra Numbers (1920), p. 43. Sir George Peckham, a Roman Catholic, was a lifelong friend of Sir Humphrey Gilbert, and an associate in his colonizing ventures.

tives. It was the search for new routes to the Far East that led in the first place to the discovery of America, and during the next century it was the desire to find an opening through the continent that led to the explorations of Cartier, Frobisher, Davis, and others. When gold and silver were discovered in abundance by Cortez (1519) in Mexico, and by Pizarro (1531) in Peru, the dominating impulse of Spain was the exploitation of this source of income. The foundations of New Spain rested during the early years on the precious metals. Nor was the hope of quick riches through the discovery of gold and silver absent from the minds of the early English explorers whose appetites had been whetted by the good fortune of their Spanish rivals.

In time Europe came to realize that gold was not the only product of value which might be obtained from America. It is believed that even before the discovery of Columbus, fishing vessels from England and France had sailed out to the west until they found fish in plenty. Certainly in the fifteenth century the fishing fleets of many nations drew wealth from the Great Banks. The fur trade came soon to rival in value even that of gold. Sugar, tobacco, cocoa, and many other products, including timber and naval stores (tar, pitch, rosin, cordage, masts, etc.), demonstrated the value of the Americas to Europe as a source of raw materials. As a counterpart to the growth of manufactures in Europe came the appreciation of colonial settlements as a market for the finished products of the looms and workshops of the mother countries. In enumerating the benefits which England would derive from the establishment of colonies beyond the Atlantic, Sir George Peckham wrote that it would revive and promote especially the trades of "clothiers, wool men, carders, spinners, weavers, fullers, shearmen, dyers, drapers, cappers, hatters," and would repair "many decayed towns."[10] A pamphleteer, writing prior to 1606 on "Reasons for raising a fund for the Support of a Colony at Virginia," speaks of it as a place "fit for the vent of our wares."[11]

The economic motives so far mentioned involve to some extent state as well as private interest and participation. Other economic impulses concerned the individual more directly. The desire to escape the economic restrictions of the governmental guild regulations, the hope of bettering his fortunes upon a new soil where land might be acquired easily and the fruits of labor saved from a feudal lord, appealed to the poor but ambitious man. Younger sons of the nobility and impoverished gentlemen saw a chance in the New World to found a fortune or commence life anew.

There was also a feeling in the sixteenth and seventeenth centuries that

[10] *Ibid.*, p. 36.
[11] E. D. Neill, *Virginia Vetusta*, p. 30.

England was overpopulated, as, in fact, she was, and that the colonies would provide a natural outlet for the surplus population. Contemporary writers note the dangers of overpopulation and unemployment. The author of *Nova Britannia* speaks of "our land abounding with swarms of idle persons, which having no means of labor to relieve their misery, do likewise swarm in lewd and naughty practices, so that if we seek not some ways for their foreign employment, we must provide shortly more prisons and corrections for their bad conditions. It is no new thing but most profitable for our state, to rid our multitudes of such as lie at home pestering the land with pestilence and penury, and infecting one another with vice and villainy worse than the plague itself."[12] A statute of 1572 follows the precedent of half a century in complaining that England was "with rogues, vagabonds and sturdy beggars exceedingly pestered."[13] It is estimated that in Elizabeth's reign there were as many as ten thousand tramps, hundreds of whom were hanged every year, and many more inflicted with severe punishment. But in sipte of the stern measures taken against them, the unemployed—men, women, and children—continued to be a serious problem necessitating frequent legislation. Many factors contributed to make unemployment widespread over a long period—among them the disbanding of feudal retainers under Henry VII, the gradual break-up of the medieval manorial system, the dissolution of the monasteries and cessation of monastic charity, the inclosures of farm land into sheep pastures, and the close of the Elizabethan wars. Enormous numbers thus deprived of their customary occupations became highwaymen, beggars, or public charges. To men of this type America held out hope, and those in authority were in no wise loath to part with them.[14]

It is not easy in going through contemporary documents to determine with any accuracy the proportion of weight to be given to the various influences leading to American colonization. Individuals differed in their motives, and influences which carried weight in one period may have been of little importance in another. The numerous propaganda pamphlets written to encourage colonization attempted to include all arguments and to appeal to all men. In the end, however, it is safe to say that the underlying motive for interest in America on the part of the great majority—whether he be king, noble, or commoner—was the economic. On the part of the merchant adventurer it was profit, on that of the humble emigrant a chance to find in the New World opportunities for a better life.

[12] *Nova Britannia* (1609), reprinted in *American Colonial Tracts*, Vol. I, No. 6.
[13] 14 Eliz., Chap. 5. Extract given in George W. Prothero, *Select Statutes*, pp. 67–69.
[14] See Frederick W. Tickner, *Social and Industrial History of England* (1915), and Henry D. Traill (ed.), *Social England* (1910), III, index under "Beggars."

SELECTED READINGS

Cheyney, E. P., *European Background of American History,* Chaps. I–IV, VII, VIII.

Packard, L. B., *The Commercial Revolution.*

Nettels, Curtis, *The Roots of American Civilization,* Chaps. I–V.

Hacker, L. M., *The Triumph of American Capitalism,* Chaps. I–VII.

3

The Colonization
of America

COLONIAL SYSTEM OF SPAIN

Four nations—Spain, France, Holland, and England—strove to dominate the North American continent. Each nation had settlements in what is now the United States, and each nation in its efforts to reproduce on American soil a New Spain, a New France, a New Netherlands, or a New England, as the case might be, left here the imprint of its civilization. Although the statesmen of each of these four countries believed thoroughly in the regulation of the economic life of the colonies, nowhere was the idea carried to such extremes as in the treatment of the Spanish colonies by the home government. From 1503 until 1717 all commerce to and from the colonies had to pass through the city of Seville. At the American end the entry of goods during most of this period was limited to the two ports of Vera Cruz on the Mexican coast and Porto Bello on the Isthmus of Panama, the former receiving goods for Mexico and the latter for South America. By 1561 the development of piracy along the Spanish Main led the government to establish the system of yearly fleets which lasted nearly two centuries. Once a year two fleets would form under the protection of warships and sail to the West Indies, where they would separate, one proceeding to Vera Cruz and the other to Porto Bello. The arrival of the fleet at Porto Bello marked the period of the annual fair when the silver wedges from the Peruvian mines which "lay like heaps of stones in the street without any fear or suspicion of being lost" were exchanged for wines, figs, olives, cloth, iron, quicksilver, and luxuries from Spain. Besides gold and silver, which formed the chief item in the return voyage, cochineal, sugar, hides, and drugs were taken back.

This commerce was further restricted by the granting of monopolies on gunpowder, salt, tobacco, and quicksilver, by excises levied on goods sold, by export and import duties averaging perhaps 15 per cent, and by the king's royalty of one-fifth on the yield of the gold and silver mines. In the colonies the culture of olives, vineyards, tobacco, and hemp was forbidden, and intercolonial trade was restricted. The entire system was highly artificial and was seriously undermined by the wholesale smuggling after the English and Dutch had obtained a foothold in the West Indies and England had, through the Asiento (1713), secured the monopoly of the African slave trade with Spanish America.

A disproportionate emphasis may easily be placed on the part played by gold and silver in the economic life of Spanish America. Although they formed the chief items of export, the Spanish government was not indifferent to the establishment of agricultural colonies, nor were the colonists wholly occupied with extracting the precious metals. A great majority of the population lived by farming and ranching, the products of which, including hides, corn, the American aloe or agave, sugar, cocoa, vanilla, and cochineal, were more valuable than those of the mines. Around the two basic industries, mining and cattle ranching, was built up a prosperous and even wealthy civilization while the English and French to the north were still struggling to maintain a bare existence.

The economic unit of early Spanish America was the *encomienda,* a grant of land carrying with it the authority to command the services of a certain number of Indians. Begun by Columbus in the West Indies, it was later extended and applied almost universally on the continent. Under this system the Indians were forced to till the crops, tend the cattle, and work the mines for their Spanish overlords. While efforts were made to limit the duration of the *encomienda* system and detailed regulations were issued concerning the treatment of the Indians, forbidding their enslavement and advising their conversion to Christianity, it was to be expected that under such a system the natives would degenerate into serfs and often be subjected to the most cruel treatment. The conquest of a large territory with an inferior native population by a comparatively few adventurous soldiers bent on rapid accumulation of wealth made inevitable the transplanting of the only system of government known to these men—the feudal system of Europe.

Instead of exterminating or driving away the Indians as did the English settler, the Spaniard made serfs of the majority of them. In 1574, scarcely three generations after the conquest of Mexico, there were in the New World, according to Velasco (historian to the Council of the Indies), two hundred Spanish cities, towns, and mining settlements, containing 160,000 Spaniards, of whom about 4000 were *encomenderos* (lords of Indian serfs); the rest were settlers, miners, traders, and soldiers, controlling an approximate Indian population of 5,000,000 in eight or nine thousand villages. This was a half century before Plymouth was founded. Settling side by side, the Spaniard and Indian have eventually become so intermingled that a large proportion of the Spanish-American population are half-breeds.

Although the influence of Spanish civilization has been felt primarily in "Latin America," that influence has not been lacking in the region of the present United States. It was the Spanish who started the culture of citrus fruits in Florida and California, the manufacture of sugar in the West Indies, and cattle ranching and sheep raising in the Southwest; and their influence upon law and architecture can be traced. In all this the most important rôle was usually played by the missionaries who composed the cultural element of the Spanish vanguard. Spain was also responsible for the first permanent white settlements and the first explorations in the United States.

FRANCE IN AMERICA

Almost a century elapsed after the voyage of Verrazano before the first permanent French settlement was made at Quebec in 1608, but the genius of the French for exploration, and their talent for dominion, were notably demonstrated in the succeeding years. Dominated by patriotism, missionary zeal, and a desire to open up more territory to their traders, priests and explorers pushed their canoes up the St. Lawrence, along the Great Lakes, and down the Mississippi, until by the end of the century French posts extended from New Orleans at the mouth of the Mississippi to Fort Radisson near the western end of Lake Superior, and east to Nova Scotia.

The success of the French as colonizers did not measure up to their attainments as explorers and missionaries. The French as a whole cared little for colonization, while the persecuted Protestants, who might have furnished a valuable element for immigration, were forbidden to come. The most important cause of failure, however, was probably due to the source of economic wealth. The economic backbone of New France was the fur trade. To the Frenchman with initiative the harsh climate and stubborn soil of the St. Lawrence Valley made no appeal. The back country was rich in furs, and in the pursuit of these he penetrated ever farther into the interior. Adaptable in the extreme, he would often affect the manners and dress of the Indians, lead them on the warpath, live with them, and intermarry. This won to the French not only the bulk of the fur trade but the friendship of practically all of the Indian tribes, with the exception of the Iroquois. If wealth was to be gained in New France it must be through furs, and noble and peasant alike engaged in the business. At least a third of the population was occupied in gathering and transporting furs.

As the fur trade was the principal source of wealth, so it proved also to be the chief cause of weakness for the colony. So long as greater profits were to be made in peltries, it was difficult to interest settlers in agriculture, and the safest basis for a permanent colony was thus lacking. Instead of the 1,300,000 inhabitants which the English colonies boasted in 1754, nine-tenths of whom were engaged in agriculture, compactly settled along a fringe of seacoast and firmly established, the French had only about 80,000 scattered along the rivers and Great Lakes from the Mississippi to Nova Scotia. Beyond the barest necessities of subsistence, agriculture was neglected. There was some attention to fisheries, but practically no manufactures other than household in New France.

From 1600 to 1663 the efforts of the French to colonize and exploit the American mainland were in the hands of commercial companies, the most famous of which was known as the Hundred Associates. After that date the administration was taken over by the crown, and a government characterized by extreme absolutism and centralization was set up. To make complete the replica of the autocratic system of France in the New World, an order of nobility was created by Richelieu in the charter of the Hundred Associates. To induce members of the lesser nobility to remain in America, seigniories were granted them along the lake and river fronts. When the seigniories were inhabited at all the peasant settlers usually lived on a road perhaps a half mile back of the river or lake, with their fields sloping down to the water on one side and back into the forest on the other. These grants were usually four arpents (768 English linear feet) on the water front and ten arpents (1920 feet) deep. This long, narrow holding, peculiar to the French, had a twofold *raison d'être*. Comparative freedom from Indian raids made it unnecessary for the French to huddle in fortified villages, but their sociable nature inclined them toward living near one another.

With the seigniories went the rest of the paraphernalia of feudalism. The tenant was expected to pay rent to the seignior—trifling, to be sure, and generally in kind—to work for the lord a certain number of days a year, patronize his grist mill, present to him one fish out of every eleven caught, and render other feudal dues. Although remnants of this system outlasted the English conquest by half a century, the conditions in New France, in contrast to the situation in Spanish America, were not such as feudalism would thrive on. With plenty of vacant land and the fur trade to beckon them on, any attempt to impose a strict feudal system upon the inhabitants was doomed to failure, and the duties of the peasant to the seignior became more nominal than real. The lords themselves, hardly more prosperous than their tenants, were forced to till the fields with their own hands or take to the life of a fur trader. With the seigniorial system and despotic government went paternalism. Taught to depend not upon themselves but upon the home government, the settlers soon lost initiative in economic problems. With their trade shackled by petty restrictions and controlled by government monopoly, it is little wonder that private enterprise in industry was smothered and Canada never prospered under France.

During the century and a half of French colonization in America many trading posts and small settlements were planted in the territory of the present United States. Futile efforts in Florida (1562–1568) were followed after the settlement of Quebec by an extension of French power along the Great Lakes and in the Illinois Valley. The first French went to Louisiana in 1699, where they founded New Orleans in 1718. By 1775 there were several thousand French in the Illinois region and about 14,000 in Louisiana.

THE DUTCH IN AMERICA

The efforts of the Dutch to participate in the profits of the American trade led eventually to the settlement of the Hudson Valley and adjacent region. Henry Hudson in the interests of the Dutch East India Company had explored in 1609 the river which bears his name, and a trading post called New Amsterdam had been established in 1614 by some enterprising merchants of Amsterdam. In 1621 Dutch interests in America were taken over by the Dutch West India Company, a great private corporation founded by William Usselinex to which the States-General of Holland granted a monopoly of the trade not only of the American seaboard but also of the coast of Africa between the Tropic of Cancer and the Cape of Good Hope. This corporation, interested in trade in gold, slaves, and tropical products, equipping hundreds of privateers, supporting an army and a large navy with which it made war upon Spain and Portugal, found the fur trade of the Hudson Valley but a small item in its numerous enterprises; the valley consequently absorbed but a small part of the interest of the directors. This attitude is well expressed in the remonstrance of the company to the States-General against a peace with Spain, when they maintained that their object was not "trifling trade with the Indians nor the tardy cultivation of uninhabited regions," but "acts of hostility against the ships and property of the King of Spain and his subjects."[1]

In spite of the company's lack of interest in the Hudson Valley, much was done there in the way of trade and colonization. Fort Orange, upon the site of the present Albany, was built in 1622, a village on Manhattan Island was founded in 1623, and settlements were made later not only in the Hudson Valley, but in the Mohawk Valley, on Long Island, and along Delaware Bay. The West India Company, however, intent upon accumulating dividends, was not interested primarily in settling the country.

[1] J. R. Brodhead, *Collection of Documents,* I, 62.

The greatest profits were to be made in furs, and upon the promotion of the fur trade the chief energies of the company and its representatives were bent. Later shipbuilding was carried on to some extent, and eventually prosperous agricultural communities grew up.

The first farming in New Netherlands seems to have been done not by tenants but by servants working for the company which owned both the land and the stock upon it. After trading posts had been established the company became more interested in stimulating settlement, and a scheme of landed proprietors was introduced in 1629. Any member of the company who would bring over 50 persons at his own expense would receive a tract of land reaching sixteen miles along the river all on one bank, or half on one bank and half on the other, with no limit as to width; and under this impetus a number of wealthy Dutchmen, including the Amsterdam jeweler, Killian Van Rensselaer, carved out huge estates in the Hudson Valley. Upon these grantees, or patroons, were bestowed both proprietary rights and subordinate jurisdiction. The patroon could hold manorial courts, with the right reserved for the tenants to appeal to the company, could found townships and appoint officials for them. Upon their estates they had the monopoly of weaving and certain exclusive trading privileges. Here, too, as in New France and New Spain, an attempt was made to graft on the New World the feudal system of Europe. Under this system the most influential members of the company soon gained control of the choicest lands in the Hudson Valley. Here we have the origin of the large landed estates which existed in New York until well into the nineteenth century. Their influence can be seen in the economic history of New York State and was the cause of the "anti-rent wars" of the 'thirties and 'forties.

The Dutch, who had never accepted the feudal system in its entirety as had other Europeans, chafed under the unaccustomed rule of the company and manor barons. The patroon system was exceedingly unpopular from the start, and in 1640 the company attempted to modify it by reducing the extent of the patroonships and introducing a class of smaller proprietor who was to hold 200 acres tilled by five men brought over at his expense. Again in 1650 a further effort was made to increase the number of small farmers. A tract of land with implements and stock was granted to the settler, with the understanding that he pay a fixed rent and return the stock or an equivalent at the end of six years. In general the agricultural products and life were not unlike that found in New England, although the big plantations along the Hudson and Delaware Bay, where tobacco was a favorite crop, resembled those of Virginia.

The centralized despotism of the government of New Netherlands in the period before 1629 was modified after the introduction of the patroon system with its almost independent jurisdiction, but the principle of representative government was not recognized in New Netherlands until the closing years of Dutch occupation. At the same time the loss in efficiency and unity of control under a semi-feudal patroon system made the colony more susceptible to foreign conquest. Driven like a wedge between the English colonies in New England and the south, it was natural that Great Britain should cast covetous eyes upon the strategic territory of New Netherlands. In fact, English settlers were beginning to filter in from both east and south, many seeking that religious freedom which the Dutch were the first to recognize in America and which Englishmen had sought for in vain in all New England except Rhode Island. This influx of English, combined with the lack of interest on the part of the company at home, the corrupt and despotic government in the colony, and the growing sea power of Great Britain, led to its final conquest in 1664. When the English captured New Netherlands, it contained a population, according to the estimate of Stuyvesant, of about 10,000. Nineteen languages were spoken in New Amsterdam at that time, the city thus early partaking of the cosmopolitan tone which ever since has been a distinguishing feature.

EARLY ENGLISH COLONIZATION

England in the age of Elizabeth was ripe for exploration and colonization. The strong Tudor monarchy had destroyed the strength of the feudal nobility, broken the political and economic power of the church, and admitted to titled rank men whose minds were occupied with trade and commerce. With the growing strength of her national government and with a rapidly expanding economic life there developed an independent, self-reliant population eager for gain and commercial development, keen to challenge the maritime domination of Spain, and full of confidence in the destiny of England. While English sea captains like Sir John Hawkins and Sir Francis Drake roamed the Spanish Main to bait their enemy, capture his bullion, and sack his cities, more serious imperialists were dreaming of establishing plantations in the western wilderness. Men like William Hakluyt preserved the voyages of English sailors, wrote pamphlets to point out the social, economic, and political advantages of foreign possessions to England, and inflamed the minds of rich and poor with prospects of comfort and wealth to be gained by adventure abroad.

Just as private individuals had borne the burden of propagandizing for English expansion, so English colonization was accomplished by private initiative and with little or no aid from the British crown. The Tudors, Henry VII and Elizabeth, favored overseas expansion but did little more. The Stuarts, James I and Charles I, living in a period of rising prices, were always in need of funds and engaged in a continuous wrangle with their Parliaments over the question of taxes. They were, nevertheless, sincerely interested in colonization if it could be carried on without cost to them. The English kings held to the theory that title to and political jurisdiction of newly discovered or settled lands were vested with the sovereign. To preserve this title, but at the same time to encourage expansion, they were willing to grant to properly accredited persons (usually favorites of the crown) royal patents or charters to settle and exploit the new lands. This might serve to protect their rights and to increase the power and wealth of the nation and themselves, but at the same time it involved no direct cost to themselves or their government.

From the first patent granted to John Cabot in 1496 down to the Pennsylvania settlement in 1682, this was the general policy followed. Cabot, whose voyages (1497–1498) laid the foundation for England's claim to North America, was financed by Bristol and London merchants. To Cabot and his sons and heirs was given the right of a monopoly to whatever trade he might develop with the regions discovered except that the king was to receive a fifth of the profits. When Englishmen almost a century later (1578) again turned their attention to colonization, Elizabeth granted to that model knight, Sir Humphrey Gilbert, the exclusive right to "inhabit and possess at his choice all remote and heathen lands not in the possession of any Christian prince," but the crown was to receive "the fifth part of all the oare of golde or silver" that might be obtained. Gilbert made two voyages. His first expedition was scattered by a storm; his second in 1583 planted a small colony in Newfoundland which soon disappeared.

In the charter issued in 1584 Elizabeth passed on to Gilbert's half brother, Sir Walter Raleigh, the rights conferred in the early charter. Raleigh dispatched five expeditions to America and spent £40,000 of his personal fortune, but his efforts resulted in failure. His third expedition in 1587 actually planted a colony on Roanoke Island off the coast of Virginia. This colony vanished, however, because of failure in England to support the infant enterprise. His efforts, nevertheless, were not entirely lost. At least he proved that the initial stage of colonization was a task beyond the personal fortune of any single Englishman.

Raleigh's failure resulted in the next effort being made by a group of capitalists through the medium of a joint-stock company. These men, inflamed by the success of the East India Company, dreamed of establishing an outpost in America where traders and gold hunters might duplicate the success attained in India. The Virginia charter of 1606 created two companies, one consisting of "certain Knights, Gentlemen, Merchants, and other Adventurers, of our city of London and elsewhere"; and the other of "Sundry Knights, Gentlemen, Merchants, and other Adventurers, of our cities of Bristol and Exeter, and of our town of Plymouth." These two groups of stockholders, the big business men of their day, were known as the London and Plymouth companies. Upon them the king bestowed the coast of the present United States—to the first-named company the region between parallels 34 and 41, and to the second that between parallels 38 and 45, with the region between the 38th and 41st open to either on condition that neither settled within one hundred miles of the other. Attempts at colonization were immediately made by both companies, unsuccessfully by the Plymouth group on the Kennebec River in Maine, and permanently by the London Company, whose expedition planted a settlement in 1607 thirty miles up the James River.

The London and Plymouth Companies, it should be pointed out, were by no means the first groups to whom European monarchs granted monopolies of trade with privileges of colonization and government. At least seven, beginning with the Muscovy Company in 1554 and going down through the East India Company in 1600, had appeared in England alone. It was the practice of the monarchs of northwestern Europe, as we have noted, to dodge financial risk by granting monopolistic inducements to private companies.

The difficulties of the first Jamestown settlers were due in part to the inadequate financial strength of the original group of entrepreneurs and in part to the fact that the company's interest was in trade, of which there was little, and in gold, of which there was none. The first difficulty was overcome by a new charter in 1609 which (in addition to separating the London and Plymouth Companies) converted the Virginia enterprise into a joint-stock company. All were invited to purchase stock at a par value of £12 10s., the cost of transporting and equipping one settler, and all stockholders were entitled to dividends and a land grant. The capital thus raised was to be used to send settlers to America who were to work for the company for seven years. At the end of this period the improved land was to be divided among the stockholders, 100 acres for each share of stock. At the same time the rights of the company were specifically stated. They included complete control of the natural resources of the country, and the levying of export and import duties up to a certain amount. For twenty years the company was granted exemption from paying duty on goods imported in Virginia, and for all time it was to pay only 5 per cent upon goods brought into England. In return it was expected to colonize the country and to pay to the king one-fifth of all gold and silver acquired. Even these allurements did not produce enough capital, and in 1612 in a third charter the king authorized the company to raise further funds through lotteries. Eventually, the Virginia Company, as it was now called, sought to promote settlement by granting land to groups or individuals who would send over settlers or come at their own expense.

From the first arrival until the king revoked the charter in 1624, the colony was a true plantation. Most of the colonists were servants and employees of the stockholders who resided in England, and the fruits of their labor belonged to the company. In exchange for the products of the labor of the settlers, the company paid the cost of transportation to Virginia and was to supply them with food, clothing, medicines, furniture, tools, arms, and ammunition, all of which were kept in the common storehouses and allotted by the company's agent to the colonists. But the shiploads of lumber and other forest products gathered and sent to England paid only a small fraction of the expenses incurred by the London Company in its attempt to found the Virginia Plantation. It is important to remember that these commercial companies were more interested in dividends than in colonization, which, as in New Netherlands, was but a means to an end. For the stockholders in England, however, the Virginia Company represented only a heavy financial loss, but in world history its rôle was important, for it laid the foundations of the English world empire and the American nation.

The next permanent English settlement in the New World was that of the Separatists at Plymouth. Impelled by the hope that they might find in America an opportunity both for economic betterment and for the worship of God after the dictates of their own hearts, they negotiated with the Virginia Council for patents to settle in their land. A charter was eventually granted by the London Company, now under the control of Sir Edwin Sandys and the Puritan faction, giving the earnest little group the right to found a plantation and govern it by laws of their own in accordance with those of England. The London Company would not finance the settlement and the Separatists had to find assistance elsewhere. Eventually seventy London merchants subscribed £7000, a sum sufficient for the purpose. Under the terms of the "Articles of Agreement of Plymouth Plantation" each share was to be reckoned at £10. For "adventuring himself" each emigrant was counted as holding one share and was permitted to purchase as many more as he was able. For seven years all wealth produced by the colonists was to go into the common stock, and from this and supplies sent by the London merchants the colonists were furnished food, clothing, and other necessities. At the end of seven years "y° capitall & profits, viz. the houses, lands, goods and chatles, be equally divided betwixte y° adventurers, and planters; wch done, every man shall be free from other of them of any debt or detrimente concerning this adventure."[2] Those who came to the colony before the expiration of the seven years were to share proportionately, according to the time spent. Whereas the settlers in Virginia were merely servants of the company who were to receive at the end of the seven years nothing but their freedom, the Plymouth colonists were stockholders in a company for which they all worked and the profits of which they would all share. In addition, their efforts were to be directed by officials of their own choosing and not by representatives sent from England, as in the case of the Virginia Company. The whole plan was a far more generous arrangement than that under which the Virginia Plantation struggled during its first twelve years.

The merchants who had subscribed their money expected immediate and large returns, but the wringing of a mere subsistence from the stubborn soil demanded practically the entire time of the colonists. It is true that some wealth was secured by furs and fisheries, but never enough to return any profit to the stockholders. On their side, the London stockholders were not able to send over supplies in any degree sufficient for the needs of the suffering settlers. As in Virginia, a serious hindrance to success was the common store and the plan of cooperative industry. When famine threatened in the third year the system was abolished as far as agriculture was concerned, and land was allotted to each man for temporary use only. By 1627, the year in which the agreement with the London merchants ended, the colony was firmly established. Desiring to sever relations with the London merchants in a manner different from that prescribed originally, the colonists made arrangements whereby the interests of the London stockholders were bought out for £1800, to be paid in nine annual installments of £200 each. In return the merchants surrendered all claims upon the colony. The money was paid chiefly through profits in the fur trade.

Plymouth was eventually absorbed by the strong Massachusetts Bay Company, whose charter had been obtained in 1629 for commercial purposes, and whose stockholders were chiefly Puritan merchants. The pronounced High Church tendency of Charles I and his attempt at tyrannical government, which began in earnest in 1629 with the dissolution of Parliament and the imprisonment of men prominent in opposing his policies, gave to the activities of the company a different turn. To many of the leading Puritans, Massachusetts appeared as an ideal refuge from the hostile policies of the king. Since they belonged to the ruling classes at

[2] William Bradford, *History of Plymouth Plantation* (Commonwealth of Massachusetts edition), pp. 56–58.

home, they were unwilling to emigrate as the servants of a plantation company. Consequently they bought up the stock of the Massachusetts Company, pledged themselves to emigrate, and took over their charter with them. Thus we find Massachusetts Bay settled by the controlling members of the company itself and its form of government in the early years comparing rather strikingly to that of a modern corporation. The freemen, for example, may be compared to the stockholders, and the governor, deputy governor and eighteen assistants may be compared to the president, vice-president and board of directors. The place of meeting was not stipulated in the charter, which made it possible to transfer the whole corporation to America. The great migration of 1630–1640, which brought to America over twenty thousand settlers, including some of the best stock in England, has left a deep impress upon the whole political, social, and economic fabric of American life.

LATER ENGLISH COLONIZATION

Virginia and Plymouth were, as we have said, colonized by chartered commercial companies. They bore the brunt of settling a strange land far from the base of supplies. Subsequent English colonization was not attended with the hardships endured by the Pilgrim Fathers and the companions of the doughty Captain Smith. Later colonists could profit by the mistakes of their less fortunate predecessors, and it was now possible for private individuals to colonize with success. Later English settlements were founded not only by chartered companies but also by two other agencies— (1) migrating groups from existing colonies, and (2) wealthy proprietors. Examples of the first of these are Connecticut, Rhode Island, and parts of New Hampshire and Maine.

The little fishing settlements of Maine and New Hampshire were colonized in part by emigrants from England under the protection of Sir Fernando Gorges and Captain John Mason, who had received patents for this region, and in part by inhabitants of Massachusetts Bay, who by 1652 were successful in extending the government of the last-named colony over the new country. The colonies of Rhode Island and Connecticut were offshoots of Massachusetts Bay, the former settled by religious exiles, and the latter by pioneer farmers in search of more fertile land. Roger Williams established in 1636, on lands purchased from the Indians, a democratic commonwealth where for the first time in America religious toleration was put in practice. Windsor, Connecticut, was founded in 1635, and Hartford in the following year, by dissatisfied groups from Massachusetts. The settlers of neither Rhode Island nor Connecticut had a legal title to the land under

English law, being simply squatters on the king's domain; but both succeeded eventually in securing charters confirming their occupation.

Under the proprietary system the king granted a single individual (or a group, as in the Carolinas) estates in America which might be colonized and held by him practically as a feudal lord under the king with very extensive powers and rights, but in most cases with the restraining provision that he must make laws "by and with the consent of the freemen." Land was granted in this way to a number of men, of whom Gorges and Mason have been mentioned. The most important experiments, however, were those of William Penn in Pennsylvania and the Calverts in Maryland. New York for a time (1665–1685, with the exception of 1673–1674, when it was recaptured by the Dutch) was a proprietary colony of the Duke of York, who handed over New Jersey to his two friends Sir George Carteret and Sir John Berkeley. The last-named province, most of which came under the control of the Quakers until taken over as a crown colony in 1702, was settled chiefly by men attracted from the surrounding regions by the liberal land offers. The Carolinas were occupied either by Virginia frontiersmen pushing south or by immigrants direct from England. They were granted (1663) by Charles II to eight proprietors, the most active of whom was Anthony Ashley Cooper, later Earl of Shaftesbury. John Locke (his former tutor) worked out a highly elaborate model state with a feudal hierarchy, but it was not adaptable and was never put in actual operation. Proprietary rule in the Carolinas came to an end in 1729. Georgia, the last of the thirteen colonies, was founded in 1733, partly as a result of the desire of the British government to set up a buffer state against the Spanish in Florida, and partly through the philanthropic desire to help English debtors commence life anew. For these reasons a charter was given to a group of trustees in 1732, who were to be in control for twenty-one years. But few of the class for whom the colony was founded came, and the population grew slowly.

LAND TENURE IN THE COLONIES

The story of colonization raises for the first time (but by no means the last) the whole problem of land tenure. Despite Indian occupation, European monarchs assumed that the land belonged to them. In turn they granted it under certain conditions to joint-stock companies, to individual proprietors, to a group of proprietors as in the case of the Carolinas, or to a group of trustees as in Georgia. It was inevitable, as we have seen in New France, New Netherlands, and New Spain, that attempts would be made to transplant aspects of the feudal system to America. It was the existing land system in Europe and the only system the colonists knew. It was also inevitable that such a system in the long run was bound to fail in the new settlements. For one thing, the country was too vast; any system which would restrict the amount of land held was certain to be unsuccessful, for there was too much vacant land which could be obtained by mere occupation. The country was too sparsely settled to be controlled effectively and the authority of the proprietor or crown was too distant or too weak to enforce obedience. Moreover, the competition among proprietors for settlers was so great that it was impossible to impose onerous feudal dues. Furthermore, men who braved the dangers of frontier life demanded actual ownership. As a consequence, the quitrents of the proprietors were collected intermittently and with great difficulty, while laws restricting the amount of land which any single individual might own were generally evaded.

After attempts at cooperative agriculture failed in both Virginia and Massachusetts, they were followed by the parceling out of land. Eventually in Virginia, 100 acres were given in fee simple to each stockholder for each share owned upon the first division and another 100 acres per share when the grant was "seated." A shareholder also received as a "head right" 50 acres for every person he might transport. This privilege was later extended to all residents. After 1705 the crown granted 50 acres for five shillings on condition that a house be built and three acres of land cultivated within three years. Thousands of acres were granted for meritorious service or through favoritism. The Virginia law was so easily evaded that by 1700 the average plantation was 700 acres. In Massachusetts Bay every adventurer who emigrated or paid the passage of an emigrant was to receive 50 acres. The usual system in New England, however, was settlement under the group plan, in which a number of prospective settlers would secure from the General Court a grant of 36 square miles, upon which they would lay out the village, assign plots for homes and gardens, and later divide the arable and the pasture land. The land outside that owned in common was held ordinarily in fee simple.[3]

Penn and Baltimore, dominated as they were by altruistic motives, imposed small quitrents, but the competition for settlers in any case kept the quitrents low. This form of rent had originated in Europe as a money commutation of other services, and was looked upon as a boon. In America, small as it might be, it was considered an unjust relic of a hated system. Penn offered 500 acres to anyone who would transport and "seat" his family, and was willing to sell 5000-acre tracts for £100 and throw in 50

---

[3] For further comments on the New England system, see below, pp. 63, 99.

acres for each servant brought, but he reserved a quitrent of one shilling per 100 acres. In Maryland a settler was given 100 acres for himself, 100 more for his wife and for each servant, and 50 for each child. They were freehold grants subject to a rent of ten pounds of wheat per 50 acres. Anyone who would bring over five settlers was granted 1000 acres, subject to a quitrent of 20 shillings a year. For bringing over more men, larger grants were made which might be divided up and sublet under the manorial usage. A man with a musket and six months' provisions might receive 150 acres in New Jersey, with a like amount for each servant or slave, and 75 additional acres for each woman—conditions so liberal that many came in from the nearby colonies. In Carolina under the proprietors, the settler was granted 100 acres for himself, 100 acres each for his wife, child, or man servant, and 50 acres for each woman servant, with a quitrent of a half-penny an acre reserved. In Georgia the trustees allotted each man 50 acres and furnished tools, but forbade the ownership of more than 500 acres, and ordered the land entailed to the male heirs.

In spite of quitrents and other feudal regulations, the system of land disposal, as it actually developed, did not greatly hinder the normal expansion of the cultivated area. Nor did it prevent wide ownership of land among the population. It was, nevertheless, a source of much friction and discontent. The rent rolls of the crown and proprietors at the opening of the Revolution amounted to £37,500 annually, and about half of it was actually collected. The difficulties which arose over this and other phases of feudal tenure were a constant source of friction which contributed to the Revolution. Fortunately, primogeniture, entails, quitrents, and other appurtenances of the feudal system which prevailed in many of the colonies were mostly abolished during or shortly after the Revolution.

The most unfortunate aspect of the colonial land system was the fact that it developed to favor the building of large estates. It was by no means as democratic as might appear. Early arrivals obtained the best land; the rest had to take what they could get on the frontier. In New England, as we shall see, influential favorites of the legislature often secured the choicest land with little effort or expenditure. This was a great era of land speculation which favored the man close to the government, particularly if he had some capital with which to start. The ill effects of the land system were particularly accentuated in the South. Here it promoted social inequality and political corruption, and developed a landed aristocracy, at the same time hindering the westward advance of settlement. Land ownership might be widely distributed but it was so uneven in amount that a class society existed from the start.

SELECTED READINGS

Nettels, Curtis, *The Roots of American Civilization,* Chaps. VI, VIII.

Bourne, E. G., *Spain in America,* Chaps. XIV–XX.

Munro, W. B., *Crusaders of New France,* Chaps. VIII–XI.

Weeden, W. B., *Economic and Social History of New England,* Vol. I, Chaps. I–V.

Bruce, P. A., *Economic History of Virginia in the Seventeenth Century,* Vol. I, Chap. I.

Colonial Agriculture
and Labor

European Background

LIKE most aspects of American life, colonial agriculture was based on the knowledge and methods which the colonists brought from Europe, modified and influenced by American conditions. European agriculture of the seventeenth century was extremely primitive. The tools were few and crude. A plow, harrow, hoe, rake, spade, and sickle, with possibly a cart, represented the equipment of the most prosperous farmer. Little was known of stock breeding and this little could be rarely practiced for cattle and sheep were herded together in a common pasture. Since there was little food for animals during the winter, most of them were slaughtered in the fall. The lack of adequate care and of knowledge meant that cattle and sheep were smaller than they are today.

The use of land was likewise primitive. The more advanced farmers practiced a crude rotation of crops on a two- or three-field system. Under the latter one strip was planted with wheat, rye, or some other crop sown in the fall and harvested in the spring; a second strip was planted with oats, barley, peas, or some other crop planted in the spring and harvested in the summer or fall. The third field was allowed to lie idle in the hope that it would recover some measure of its fertility. What little fertilizing there was was accomplished by turning the livestock into the stubble after the crops were harvested.

Until the eighteenth century little progress had been made over the methods of ancient times. In that century, however, important agricultural advances occurred in England. Jethro Tull and Charles Townshend showed that clover and other crops would renew the soil more adequately than allowing it to lie idle. Turnips, it was found, provided winter forage for animals, allowing the farmer to keep his stock through the cold months and improve his breed. Another great farmer, Robert Bakewell, experimented successfully with methods of stock breeding and actually doubled the size of the breeds of sheep used in his experiments. American farmers of the eighteenth century came to know of these improvements but adopted them very slowly. There was little in the American environment to encourage their use. Rich virgin soil, with an inexhaustible supply to the west, was no incentive to scientific farming. The value of manure was hardly appreciated, crop rotation was rare, and "land butchery" was the usual practice. One observer said that the colonial farmer seemed to have but one object—the plowing up of fresh land: "The case is, they exhaust the old as fast as possible till it will bear nothing more, and then, not having manure to replenish it, nothing remains but to take up new land in the same manner." [1]

Considerable attention was given by farmers in the early years to experimenting with the environment. It was soon found that most of the common grains, vegetables, and fruits of northwestern Europe were suitable to American soil and climate, as were the various farm animals. But efforts to introduce subtropical fruits of the Mediterranean countries failed. The same was true of repeated attempts to raise silkworms and produce silk. These early efforts were doomed to failure not so much because the climate was unsuitable as because the scarcity and high cost of labor made production impracticable. Success in some cases came in later years when knowledge of plant breeding and scientific agriculture had made greater progress.

AGRICULTURAL ACHIEVEMENTS OF THE AMERICAN INDIAN

It is erroneous to picture the American Indian as a nomad, destitute of a permanent home and intent solely upon hunting and fighting. The Indian was the first American farmer, and agriculture played a large part in the economic life of the tribe. Cartier and Champlain saw fields of corn on the banks of the St. Lawrence, De Soto on the Mississippi, and Coronado in the Southwest. Henry Hudson observed a bark house filled with corn and beans stored by the Indians for winter use. The first settlers in the Ohio Valley found corn fields extending for miles along the river bank. General Wayne wrote in 1794 that he had never "before beheld such immense fields of corn in any part of America, from Canada to Florida." Regardless of where the warpath or hunting expedition might lead him, the warrior would return in the planting season and harvest time. Indications point to the fact that the villages built near these fields were often permanent, as in the case of the Pueblo Indians, or semi-permanent, as with the Iroquois of New York.

The extent to which the Indians practiced agriculture is difficult to determine with exactness. It varied, of course, with the different tribes and in

[1] *American Husbandry*, I, 144.

different parts of the country, ranging from tribes like the Apaches, who practiced it to a limited extent, to the southwestern Indians, who constructed reservoirs, irrigation system, and permanent cities, and hunted very little. The Atlantic coast Indians from Maine to Florida, with whom the English first came in contact, were farmers as well as hunters, and during the first years their corn helped keep the colonists alive. It is the testimony of explorers that the Indians in most parts of the United States relied upon corn and other cultivated products for their principal subsistence.

Indian agriculture in the main was built up around the cultivation of corn and tobacco. To prepare the ground, the Indian first girdled the trees or scotched the roots until they were dead. The dead trees and stumps, as well as brushwood, were then burned. With his stick or crude implement he then dug shallow holes three or four feet apart, into which he dropped a few grains of corn and beans. Between the hills he planted pumpkin and squash. It is believed that the coast Indians in some cases used fish to fertilize their fields. As the corn came up it was hilled, and as it ripened it was protected from the numerous wild birds by the children who watched from platforms erected in the middle of the field. After the harvest much of it was dried and stored away in pits or caves lined with bark or in corncribs, thus protecting it from rotting bacteria or fungi. Although far from efficient in their methods, the Indians produced at least a million bushels a year. Recent developments in agriculture have added little to the essential methods of raising corn practiced by the Indians. Like corn, tobacco was widely used by the Indians from the West Indies to Canada. It was cultivated in separate fields, but it also grew wild along the Atlantic coastal plain. Compared to the present product, the Indian tobacco was of an inferior grade. Nevertheless, Indian methods of cultivation were followed by the white man, as well as their methods of curing by the sun or open fire.

The third native American plant, destined in the years to come to be of world importance and to rank with wheat, corn, and rice as the world's greatest four foods, was the white potato. It is not possible to locate definitely its original habitat, but it is thought to be Peru or Chile. When introduced in England, this vegetable was called Virginia potatoes, but the careless nomenclature of those days (as evidenced by calling the great American bird the turkey) is no proof that Virginia was their original habitat. The potato was cultivated in various parts of Europe, but gained popularity first with the Irish, hence the colloquial name "Irish potatoes." Carried back to the New World, it found little favor in New England until the Irish settlers of New Hampshire encouraged its culture. Potatoes were, curiously enough, not considered edible by the early settlers, but were thought to contain some sort of poison and were carefully kept out of the reach of cattle and horses. Yet this despised tuber has been one of America's greatest gifts to the Old World and has kept countless thousands from starvation. Sweet potatoes, a native product in the South, were at once adopted by the English settlers and cooked in many ways. Though white potatoes were produced in very small amounts before the Revolution, large crops of sweet potatoes were characteristic of southern agriculture practically from the beginning. The sweet potato was a favorite food with the slaves as well as with the white settlers.

The tools of the Indians were of the crudest: the shoulder blade of an antler or deer, a flat stone (usually flint) chipped and tied by thongs to a stick, a clean shell, sometimes a mere stick, were their implements of agriculture. Most of the work was done by the old men, women, and children, but it was not uncommon for the younger men to go into the fields at planting or harvesting time. The work at such periods was often cooperative and accompanied by ceremonies and festivals.

The chief contribution of the Indian to the white man was in agriculture. Owing perhaps to the fact that his only domesticated animal was the dog, he had not advanced in civilization as far as the European, but he had made considerable progress. He understood the bringing of wild plants under control and the breeding of plants by seed selection. He had grasped the idea of fertilization and of working the soil. He practiced multiple cropping. He knew how to preserve foods—berries and fruits with syrup or honey, and fruit, vegetables, and meat by artificial or sun drying. The New England farm, cleared by tree girdling, with its rows of corn twined with bean vines, interspersed with squash and pumpkin and protected by scarecrows, was a counterpart of the Indian field. The Indian gave to the white man both his chief food and his principal export and taught him how to cultivate them.

NEW ENGLAND AGRICULTURE

Since the Pilgrims landed on the bleak New England shores in December, no foods of their own production could be expected until the next summer. Except for game, fish, and what corn they could purchase from the Indians, they had to rely on their rotting English supplies. It chanced that near them were cleared fields once cultivated by Indians who had been swept off in a great year of pestilence (1616–1617). The friendly Squanto showed the weakened Plymouth men the Indian method of cultivating corn, both "ye manner how to set it, and after, how to dress & tend it," [2] and thus contributed to save the colony.

[2] William Bradford, *History of Plymouth Plantation*, p. 121.

The great deficiency of the Indian as an agriculturist was his failure to domesticate animals. But the settlers immediately imported animals which multiplied rapidly. Cattle were brought in as early as 1624, and formed the basis of rapidly increasing herds and successful dairying. Hogs were raised in great numbers in New England, and a considerable export trade was developed in barreled pork. Horses of a very hardy variety were raised, particularly in Rhode Island, and exported in large numbers to the West Indies. Sheep were early introduced into Massachusetts and Rhode Island, where they were successfully developed and exported to the other northern colonies. Though these sheep were the old unimproved breeds, able to forage for themselves and to withstand hardships, conditions were at first hard for them, and special legislation was necessary to encourage sheep raising. Usually the sheep of the entire settlement grazed in common, under the care of a paid herder.

Besides corn, pumpkins, squash, and beans, the cultivation of which they learned from the Indians, the New Englanders raised peas, parsnips, turnips, and carrots from seeds which they brought with them. Wheat, introduced from England, was not immediately successful, but they had greater success with rye and buckwheat. Barley, oats, and other European grains were introduced generally and thrived, but other products experimented with were found unsuitable. Most of the nuts now growing in the woods were indigenous to America, and a valuable food for the pioneer. Many berries and fruits grew wild in New England—cranberries, huckleberries, blackberries, and raspberries; and cherry and plum trees. Apple trees were imported at once, and were especially successful in New England and the middle colonies. In his *Wonder-working Providence,* Johnson, writing of 1642, said that the settlers already had "apples, pears, and quince tarts instead of their former Pumpkin Pies."[3] Orchards were a part of every farm and the large apple crops caused them to be "reckoned as profitable as any other part of the plantation."

While the New England farmer of colonial times could with hard work obtain a living from the soil and might even become very prosperous, his methods were of the crudest and most primitive type. The great improvements in English agriculture which, as we have pointed out, led to the introduction of turnips, clover, and better grasses, to the more scientific rotation of crops, and to the abandonment of the three-field system, did not come until the eighteenth century and then interested Americans but little. What slight knowledge of improved agricultural methods the immigrant might have he was likely to discard when confronted with an abundance of virgin

[3] Edward Johnson, *Wonder-working Providence of Sion's Saviour in New England 1628–1651,* Original Narratives Series, p. 210.

soil. A harrow, a spade, a fork, all clumsily constructed of wood, were his chief farm tools. In the early days few could afford a plow; a town often paid a bounty to anyone who would buy one and keep it in repair. For twelve years after the landing of the Pilgrims there were no plows in Plymouth, and in the Massachusetts Bay Colony in 1637 there were only thirty-seven. One plow would do the work for a considerable territory. Such a thing as scientific farming was unknown, and even rotation of crops was rarely practiced. The land was used until its fertility was exhausted, and was then allowed to lie fallow or planted with natural grasses until it recuperated. Owing to the small size of the farms and the settlement in villages, "land butchery" was not practiced in New England to the extent that it was in the South, but methods were bad enough. Even to a contemporary observer tillage in New England was "weakly and insufficiently given: worse ploughing is nowhere to be seen, yet the farmers get tolerable crops; this is owing, particularly in the new settlements, to the looseness and fertility of old woodlands, which with very bad tillage, will yield excellent crops." [4]

Bad as their agricultural methods were, their treatment of livestock was worse. The same observer maintained that in all that concerned cattle the farmers in New England were "the most negligent ignorant set of men in the world. Nor do I know any country in which animals are worse treated. Horses are in general, even valuables ones, worked hard, and starved: they plough, cart, and ride them to death, at the same time that they give very little heed to their food; after the hardest day's work, all the nourishment they are like to have is to be turned into a wood, where the shoots and weeds form the chief of the pasture; unless it be after the hay is in, when they get a share of the after-grass." [5] During the early days when food was scarce, laws were passed forbidding the feeding of corn to animals.

With the exception of a few dollars' worth of salt and iron, many a New England farmer was practically self-sufficing. From his field he obtained grains, from his orchard fruits, and from his pasture land meat and dairy products. Flax from the field and wool from the sheep were spun and made into clothing by his wife and daughters. From honey and maple sap he obtained ingredients to sweeten his food; corn whisky and cider furnished him with strong drink. Every farmer had to be a Jack-of-all-trades, and his wife had to be just as able to turn her hand to anything. The New England farmer may have been self-sufficing, but it was not from desire. All who could raised a surplus, mainly for the West Indian market. The New England soil as a whole may not have been too good, but it was good

[4] *American Husbandry* (1775), I, 81.
[5] *Ibid.,* I, 80.

enough for intensive farming. It was not so much the soil as the greater
ease of making money in industry and commerce that turned New Englanders to other pursuits.

The early settlements in New England were made under agreements
whereby every shareholder or settler was entitled to a certain amount of land.
Further expansion usually occurred in the following manner. As vacant
land near the seacoast grew scarce, groups or congregations would obtain a grant from the General Court, to which they would move in a body
and found a town. The grants, commonly 36 square miles, were owned
by these proprietors and eventually divided among them. From the center
of the town where the meetinghouse stood, a wide street was laid out, and
along it house lots with perhaps six acres of garden land were assigned.
Eventually the rest of the land was distributed, each settler receiving a
share in the upland, meadow land, and marsh land, and rights in the commons. This system, in combination with the glacial soil, the rigorous climate,
and the land laws which allowed division among several heirs, was not
conducive to the development of great landed estates. The New England
farm continued to be a comparatively small affair; the New Englander lived
in a village and tilled the land with his own hands.

The New England villages, with their houses and gardens grouped compactly, with the village commons and the rights in the remaining land, is
reminiscent of the English manor. Much of the land was held in common, although cultivated separately, and the town meeting was the center
where plans were worked out and the cowherds, swineherds, and other
officers who cared for the village property were elected. The system described
was transitory. As the towns grew larger and the danger from Indians
lessened and as labor became diversified, the inhabitants were often glad to
sell their scattered strips, and the compact farm with its buildings and land
together appeared, resembling rural New England as we know it today.
The ease with which new land might be acquired, and an independent living assured, practically precluded a non-landholding labor class and necessitated much cooperation among the farmers. Houses were raised, fences
built, corn husked, and fields plowed by cooperative effort, and the gath-
erings were made the occasion of revelry as well as hard work.

Agriculture in the Middle Colonies

With the exception of the Hudson Valley, where the patroon system of
large landed proprietors was started by the Dutch and continued by the
English, the land system of the middle colonies resembled that of New
England in the sense that the holdings were generally small. There were
large plantations on the Chesapeake shore of Maryland, but even in this

colony the normal holding was small. The proprietors, Carteret, Berkeley, Penn, and the Calverts, anxious to encourage colonization, granted lands on the most favorable terms.

In these colonies the farmer found a climate closely approximating that of his native land and a soil much richer than in New England. In the fertile limestone deposits of the Mohawk, Hudson, Delaware, and Susquehanna River valleys, crops grew abundantly. Plenty of moisture and longer summers helped to make conditions ideal for farming. The soil of New Jersey was so rich, said Peter Kalm, the Swedish traveler, in 1749, that it made the settlers careless husbandmen. "They had nothing to do but cut down the wood, put it into heaps, and clear the dead leaves away. They could then immediately procede to ploughing, which in such loose ground is very easy; and having sown their corn, they get a most plentiful harvest. This easy method of getting a rich crop has spoiled the English and other European inhabitants, and induced them to adopt the same method of agriculture which the Indians make use of, that is, to sow uncultivated grounds, as long as they will produce a crop without manuring, but to turn them into pastures as soon as they can bear no more and to take in hand new spots of ground, covered since time immemorial with woods, which have been spared by the fire or the hatchet ever since the creation." [6] In the fertile soil the wheat and barley often grew so rank that it reached a height of six or seven feet, with little grain in the heads. An observer in the Mohawk Valley in 1665 wrote that he had seen fields in which wheat was raised for eleven years in succession on the same field, and farms which had not been manured for nine years. Although the same traveler mentions the irrigation of meadows in Pennsylvania, such care was rare, for the fertility of the virgin soil was not conducive to intensive farming. As in New England, rotation of crops was not practiced, but the land was allowed to lie fallow when it had worn out.

Although nine-tenths of the New Englanders were farmers, the inhabitants of the middle colonies were even more predominantly agricultural in their economic life. With the exception of furs and lumber, the exports of this section seem to have been almost entirely agricultural. Judging from the export statistics,[7] wheat must have been the chief export, the average acre yielding from twenty to thirty bushels, a larger crop than was common in England at that time. Corn was raised throughout these provinces, providing the bulk of food for cattle in the winter. Rye, barley, buckwheat, and oats were also generally grown, the latter with great success. Fruits suitable to a temperate climate grew in great abundance—apples in New

[6] Peter Kalm, *Travels into North America*, II, 193.
[7] See below, Chap. 5.

York, peaches and melons in the sandy soil of New Jersey and Delaware. "Peaches are of a fine flavor," says the author of *American Husbandry,* "and in such amazing plenty that whole stock of hogs on a farm eat as many as they will, but yet the quantity that rot under the trees is astonishing. . . . Watermelons are in such plenty that there is not a farmer or even a cottager without a piece of ground planted with them." [8] Large herds of cattle grazed on the coastal lowlands of Long Island, New Jersey, and elsewhere; hogs were abundant, running wild in the woods; and sheep were plentiful in Pennsylvania.

The agriculture of the middle colonies was somewhat influenced by the heterogeneous population. English, Dutch, Germans, Swedes, and other nationalities had their settlements, imported their particular strains of livestock, farmed with their own methods, and raised their favorite crops. Even with the unscientific and wasteful methods of the time, a rude abundance was easily obtained. For the European peasant it was a veritable land of promise.

Southern Agriculture

The first Jamestown settlers were careless farmers, being more intent upon gold hunting and exploration. The soil of Virginia was too rich and the climate too warm for English wheat. Disease and starvation carried off many of the first settlers; the remainder were kept alive only by the corn purchased from the Indians. Until 1612 the colony dragged out a precarious existence, but in that year John Rolfe began the cultivation of tobacco, a plant introduced into Europe a hundred years before and extensively grown in the West Indies. Conditions quickly improved as it was discovered that the Virginia soil was ideal for its growth. There was a great demand for the leaf in Europe and the gold hunters turned from their dreams of sudden riches to this slower but sounder basis of prosperity. Although Governor Dale frowned on the new occupation and in 1616 ordered that no man plant tobacco until he had put down two acres of his three-acre farm with corn, it was impossible to prevent the cultivation of tobacco to the detriment of grains and vegetables. In 1617 even the market place and streets of Jamestown were planted with it; the settlers found that the same amount of time and labor would yield per acre six times as much in tobacco as in grain, for it sold at times as high as twelve dollars a pound measured in present currency. By this time the Virginia Company, despairing of quicker riches, ordered its colonists to raise tobacco. The king (James I), out of his desire for revenue as well as dislike for the use of tobacco, "tending to a generall and new Corruption both of Men's Bodies

[8] *American Husbandry,* I, 139.

and Manners," levied a tax of one shilling a pound (about 20 per cent) in 1619, and in 1620 sought to limit the importation from Virginia and the Bermudas to 55,000 pounds. But no legislature either here or in England could stop the steady increase in production. The crop amounted to 20,000 pounds in 1616, to 60,000 in 1621, to 500,000 in 1627, to 23,750,000 in 1662, and to 130,000,000 in 1790. Virginia had discovered a staple crop and an economic basis of wealth.

Owing to the fact that the great staple crop was raised for exportation, it was necessary that the plantation be located on the river banks where the tiny ships of colonial days could sail up and load a cargo from each farmer's wharf. The land was accordingly rapidly taken up along the James, York, Rappahannock, and Potomac Rivers, then along the Chesapeake inlets, and then south into the Albermarle and Pamlico districts of North Carolina. When the land along the rivers were entirely occupied, the late comers were forced to set off a tier of farms immediately back of the river plantations and get the tobacco to their neighbors' wharves as best they might.

Tobacco, it was found, quickly exhausted the richest soil and necessitated the continual use of fresh land. Three years under the most favorable circumstances was the age of a tobacco field, after which it was turned over to other crops. White labor was scarce and costly, for each emigrant hoped to set up for himself, and gradually Negro labor was substituted. Supervision was essential for slave labor and it was believed that an overseer was too expensive unless he had twenty Negroes under him. This in turn encouraged large plantations. Therefore, the great plantations often had a thousand acres under actual tobacco cultivation besides land for other crops, a cattle range, and woodland. Many Virginia tobacco plantations were five thousand acres or over in size. These factors, combined with the ease with which the title to new land was acquired, are the chief causes for the large holdings in the South. Mere occupation and the payment of a small fee or quitrent were sufficient to establish ownership. "Head rights," or the granting of land to those who imported settlers, grants for meritorious service, and purely personal grants all contributed to the swelling of the large estates. The very ease, however, with which land could be acquired tended to make labor scarce and thus to a certain extent retarded the development of large estates. The typical southern holding, while much larger than the New England farm, was still moderate in size and the average southern white was a small farmer. Methods of agriculture, the emphasis upon the one staple, tobacco, and the geography of the country all tended to a system of settlement which prevented the growth of towns and promoted a distinctly rural life of scattered plantations in contrast to New England, where occupation usually began by founding a town.

Next in importance to the plantation system, which was undoubtedly the basic feature of southern agriculture, was the cattle range. Shifting arable land and large plantations made inclosures impracticable; the vast unoccupied regions could readily be utilized for cattle ranges. Cattle, horses, and swine roamed in droves, subsisting on roots and herbage, branded when possible, but wild and often hunted as wild beasts. Each settler had his "right in the woods," which gave him a share in the unbranded cattle. Although the technique of ranching in the West was derived from the Spaniard, the western cattle ranch, nevertheless, with its round-up and brandings, was a replica on a much larger scale and at a later date of cattle ranching during the early days in Virginia and the Carolinas. Plantations were often laid out with reference to cattle ranges, and the wild herds of livestock usually marked the fringe of civilization. The treatment of such livestock as was domesticated was even more unscientific than in the North. It was believed by many that housing and milking cows in the winter would kill them!

Passing south from Maryland and Virginia into the Carolinas, one found different conditions. Although cattle ranching was a feature in both North and South Carolina, in the first-named colony the farms were likely to be small and the products diversified, while the plantations of South Carolina were given over to the production of rice and indigo on a large scale. The farmers of North Carolina, most of whom were emigrants from Virginia—poor men, often former indentured servants or debtors—raised chiefly tobacco and corn on small farms.

Rice had been brought into Virginia by Sir William Berkeley in 1647, but its culture was soon abandoned. It was probably in 1693 that it was introduced from Madagascar and experimentation on its cultivation was begun by Governor Smith. Eventually it was found that the low and swampy coast lands of Carolina and the long hot summer produced an abundant crop. Work in the hot wet fields was impossible for white men, but with the importation of black labor, rice culture became profitable. By 1754 the planters exported annually from Charleston 104,680 barrels, and 125,000 by the opening of the Revolution.

The raising of indigo, the other great export crop of colonial South Carolina, was the result of experiments performed by Miss Eliza Lucas, the daughter of an English army officer, who was left in charge of the family plantation. A bounty had been granted in 1723 for the production of indigo, but no progress was made until her experiments demonstrated its practicability. A bounty of sixpence a pound was granted in 1748 by Parliament, and from then until it was eventually displaced by cotton immediately after the Revolution, the production of indigo was a constantly increasing source of wealth. In 1775 the quantity exported amounted to 1,150,662 pounds.

The fact that Virginia and the Carolinas were roughly in the same latitude as the Mediterranean naturally led to attempts to raise semi-tropical products there. The mulberry tree grew wild in Virginia, and a law was passed compelling each farmer to plant annually six mulberry trees for seven years. Even a premium of ten thousand pounds of tobacco to anyone who would produce fifty pounds of silk failed to make the industry profitable. Experiments in silk production were made in every colony and, encouraged by a parliamentary bounty (1769), continued down to the Revolution. Failure in the end came not from physical obstacles but rather from the prohibitive expense due to labor costs.

The cultivation of sugar cane was tried with little success until after 1751, when the Jesuits introduced the plant into Louisiana. Olives, lemons, pineapples, figs, ginger, almonds, and wine grapes were also planted unsuccessfully. Identity of latitude with Mediterranean countries did not carry with it identity of climate and soil, and few of the semi-tropical products would thrive. In many cases, as in silk production, the lack of cheap efficient labor prevented success. But Eliza Lucas, describing South Carolina in a letter, says they had "peaches, Nectarines and mellons of all sorts extremely fine and in profusion, and their Oranges exceed any I ever tasted in the West Indies or from Spain or Portugal."

CHARACTERISTICS OF COLONIAL AGRICULTURE

To lay down with exactness the characteristics of a period extending from 1607 to 1781 is difficult, owing to changing conditions in such an extended time. Certain general facts, however, can be stated. First of all, it is evident that colonial economy was predominantly agricultural. Even in New England, where commercial and industrial life was most developed, not more than one-tenth of the people were engaged in non-agricultural pursuits. In other colonies the proportion was far less. Although fish and naval stores were important export items, they were of far less value than the agricultural products shipped abroad. The economic life of the South came to rest upon large land grants, slave labor, and the export of such staples as tobacco and indigo. Nevertheless, it is important to remember that while the plantation system determined the economy of the South and the planters were the dominant influence in the government, they were at all times outnumbered by the smaller farmer. It has been maintained by a leading southern historian [9] that "nine-tenths of the South's landowners at any period in her history were small proprietors." The dependence of the prosperity of this

[9] W. E. Dodd, The South in the Building of the Nation, V, 74.

section on the success or failure of a single crop and upon the fluctuation of a foreign market led to repeated efforts on the part of colonial assemblies to stimulate a greater production of foodstuffs. In this movement the small farmer played a large part, so that by 1736 foodstuffs and flax were produced in sufficient quantity for both home needs and exportation, and by 1760 sufficient livestock for local consumption. In contrast to the South, northern agriculture was based upon limited land grants, free labor, and food crops designed chiefly for a home market.

If one is to understand colonial agriculture, or, for that matter, any phase of colonial economic life, he must always remember that he is dealing with a world dominated by a mercantilist philosophy. *Laissez faire* was utterly foreign to the minds of seventeenth- and eighteenth-century rulers. The products of America were to supplement, not to compete with, those of the home countries. Tariff regulations prevented the selling of certain agricultural commodities, particularly foodstuffs, to England. Other laws required that sugar, tobacco, cotton, wool, indigo, and other products be sent only to that country. This might give the colonists a monopoly of the English market, but it also to that extent limited the foreign market. At the same time both the English and colonial governments at one time or another encouraged by bounties the production of tobacco, flax, hemp, indigo, and other crops. It was an age in which innumerable laws restricted or encouraged, as the case might be, the normal development of colonial agriculture.

It is also easy, as we shall see in the next chapter, to emphasize the isolation and the self-sufficient aspect of the American farm. It is true that transportation facilities were poor and the typical small farmer had little ready money. At the same time there were always certain basic needs such as iron, salt, firearms, and ammunition common to all farmers, and innumerable other commodities which he greatly desired. There were taxes, mortgage payments, and other expenses. Even the small frontier farmer strove to raise a surplus which he could market, while the plantation owners of the South were primarily engaged in raising staple crops for export. That the small farmer was more self-sufficing than he was after the Industrial Revolution is obvious, but it is also clear that every effort was being made to escape that situation.

COLONIAL LABOR

In Europe during the seventeenth and eighteenth centuries there appeared to be an abundance of labor but a dearth of resources. In America the reverse was true. The Europeans who settled North America found a virgin continent still unexploited, with a wealth of raw materials awaiting the hand of man. Labor alone was scarce and from the earliest times the problem of obtaining a sufficient supply was most difficult. This is perhaps a partial explanation of the American philosophy of the glorification of work and of the Puritan hatred of idleness, as exemplified in many colonial laws. The supply of labor from the native population was practically negligible, for the Indian in the region of the present United States preferred to live his old life rather than to subordinate himself to the white man. The European, possessing enough initiative to pioneer in a new land, was not the type that would readily submit to the authority of others when the chance of becoming a free landowner was so easy and the inducement to strike out for oneself so alluring. The need for labor was greater in the South, where the staple crops were raised on large plantations, and less in the North, where the farmer and his family cultivated a small farm. There were consequently more servants of all types in the South, but in all sections the demand for them was keen.

In the North the scarcity of labor was partially met by cooperation. When an extraordinary situation arose, as at the time of a house raising or a ship launching, the neighbors were called upon and the project was accomplished by the associated efforts of the group. What laborers there were in the North were of two classes—free and non-free. Although there were always some of the former, their number was small, for a man with any capacity could with little difficulty become a landowner and attain a degree of independence.

The non-free laborers were of two classes—indentured [10] servants and slaves. The indentured servants were also of two classes—voluntary and involuntary. The voluntary indentured servant [11] was one whose servitude was based upon a free contract. Many a European, anxious to start a new life in America, gladly sold himself for a period of from three to seven years to shipmasters or emigration brokers in payment of his passage to America, his length of service depending on his ability to pay part of the passage money or his success in disposing of himself advantageously. A few Germans and others voluntarily indentured themselves in order to learn the language and obtain funds to start life more advantageously. The voluntary free servant was ordinarily entitled to two weeks to find a purchaser, but, as he was not allowed to leave the ship, this right was of little value.

The second class of indentured servants, those suffering involuntary servitude, were usually debtors, vagrants, or criminals deported by the

[10] The name indenture comes from the form of the contract, which was written in duplicate on a large sheet, the halves being separated by a wavy or jagged cut, called an indent.

[11] "Commonly call'd Kids," says Hugh Jones, *The Present State of Virginia* (1724), reprint by Sabin (1865), p. 53.

courts. The vagrancy laws since the days of Elizabeth had been extremely harsh in England. In addition, there were the various laws prohibiting the free movement of labor from one parish to another, because of fear that paupers might be thrown upon the parish for support. It was easy to fall into debt during hard times, and the penalty for debt was imprisonment. Over three hundred crimes in the seventeenth century were punishable in England by death. With the courts and prisons crowded with paupers, vagrants, debtors, and petty criminals, it seemed the most humanitarian as well as the most practical policy to ship them over to the colonies. In this way England was relieved of a burden and America supplied with much-needed labor. If these prisoners could pay their own passage money they were free to do as they pleased; otherwise (and this was true of almost all), they were sold for from seven to ten years. In spite of the scarcity of labor, "His Majesty's Seven Year Passengers," as they were called, were far from welcome, the colonists much preferring their room to their company,[12] but the protests of the colonies against being made a dumping ground for criminals were of little avail. The group of indentured servants was also recruited by the professional "spirits" or crimps who picked up thousands of children and adults and sold them to shipmasters engaged in the colonial trade. So extensive was this kidnaping in the latter half of the seventeenth century that Parliament passed legislation to curtail it, but the need for labor in the colonies was so great that Parliament showed little interest in enforcing the prohibition.

The rights of servants were to a certain extent protected. They were entitled to food, clothing, shelter, and medical attendance when sick, and they might own property. At the end of their service they were usually given an outfit and in some cases 50 acres of land. Although protected by law from unjust cruelty, the age was a hard one and the lot of the indentured servant, especially the involuntary, was exceedingly unenviable. On the one hand, the cost and need of labor were an incentive to considerate treatment, but on the other hand, the desire to obtain as much labor as possible in the number of years covered by the indenture was a spur to excessive driving. In many cases the lot of the slave was superior to that of the indentured servant, for the loss to the owner of an able-bodied slave was greater, and hence conducive to better treatment. Most of the servants in the North were recruited from indentured servants, as were those in the South during the seventeenth century, for slaves were at first unpopular and slavery grew slowly. In 1681 there were 6000 white servants in Virginia and but 2000 slaves. Thousands of "free-willers" came each year during the latter part of the seventeenth and early part of the eighteenth century, but the number

[12] *Ibid.*, p. 53.

gradually decreased until by the Revolution their immigration had practically ceased.

Of the white immigrants to the colonies during the colonial period, probably half came as indentured servants. It is estimated that in Pennsylvania, Maryland, and Virginia possibly three-fourths of the white population at the time of the Revolution were of this stock. Although most of the population growth during the colonial period came from natural increase rather than from immigration, it is evident that the indentured servants and their offspring formed a most important element in the early population of America.

While there seems to be little to justify the system of indentured servants, it did help to solve two problems. It enabled poor men to escape from Europe with a chance of starting life anew in a land of greater opportunities and it provided America with much-needed immigrants and laborers. For the average European laborer immigration on his own resources was impossible. Transportation to America cost from £6 to £10 and this amounted in money wages to three or four years' income for the pitifully underpaid English laborer. In terms of the wages obtainable in Europe, the indentured servant in America often sold his services at a reasonable price. Cruel as the system was, it was not without its defenders. George Alsop, himself an indentured servant, wrote home that "The servant of this Province [Maryland], which are stigmatiz'd for slaves by the clapper-mouth jaws of the vulgar in England, live more like Freemen than the most Mechanick apprentice in London, wanting for nothing that is convenient and necessary, and according to their several capacities, are extraordinarily well used and respected." [18] It should be remembered that the voluntary indentured servants in most cases represented men and women who had the courage and stamina to seek escape from an environment for which they were not responsible and which held out no hope. A good proportion who survived the ordeal in America achieved the better life which they sought and many rose to positions of importance in their communities.

COLONIAL SLAVERY

Today economic exploitation is often carried on by moving investment funds to the labor supplies, for that form of capital is concentrated in North America and Europe, whereas cheap labor is to be found in Asia, Africa, and South and Central America. Our forefathers, equipped with resources of land and raw materials, needed labor, and a partial solution was found in slavery. The reason why American farmers, chiefly plantation owners

[18] George Alsop, *A Character of the Province of Maryland*, p. 94.

in the South, turned from white indentured servants to slaves was the conviction that they were cheaper than any form of labor obtainable. An indentured servant cost on an average from £2 to £4 a year in capital investment; an able-bodied slave could be purchased for from £18 to £30. For this the slave owner received a lifetime of service, with the possibility of gain from increase in the slave's family.

During the fifteenth century Portuguese traders began to import into Europe Negroes from the "Slave Coast," the part of the west coast of Africa extending from Cape Verde on the north to Cape St. Martha on the south. From the time of the first Portuguese settlement in Africa in 1482 the traffic became regular, lasting for about four hundred years. The slaves were purchased from native brokers living in the coast towns, who obtained them from the tribes in the interior. The latter, well supplied with guns and ammunition, turned over their prisoners of war and the fruit of their raiding parties to be imprisoned in the slave pens along the coast until they could be shipped away.

The first Negro slaves were brought to America and sold at Jamestown in 1619 by a Dutch privateer; within a few years they were to be found in all of the colonies. Slaves were unpopular at first, notwithstanding the scarcity of labor; hence their number grew slowly and for half a century Negroes composed only a small fraction of the total population. The slave trade was a monopoly of the Royal African Company of England until 1698, when the traffic was thrown open; after this it expanded rapidly. Bancroft estimated the number of slaves in the American mainland colonies in 1714 at 59,000; in 1727 at 78,000, and in 1754 at 263,000. The first census (1790) showed over 697,000. At this time they formed two-fifths of the total southern population, varying from a small percentage of the total in Maryland and North Carolina to over twice the white population in South Carolina.

The slave trade to the English colonies was soon monopolized by British and American ships. The latter proved to be especially efficient. The usual procedure for the Yankee slaver was to load up with rum and other commodities in New England, sail for the Slave Coast and exchange his goods for Negroes, dispose of the latter in the West Indies or the mainland, and take on a cargo of sugar, molasses, and tobacco for the North. The voyage between Africa and the West Indies, known as the "Middle Passage," shows slavery in its gloomiest aspect and the slave dealers at their worst. Crowded in the smallest possible space and chained to the ships, the Negroes suffered untold agonies during the slow weeks of the Atlantic passage; if they fell sick, they were thrown overboard, lest they contaminate their fellows. But our ancestors were hardened to suffering and had few compunctions about slavery.[14]

A slave economy was adopted on the tobacco plantations of the South as the easiest way to fill the need for labor, and on the rice plantations of South Carolina as the only labor that could endure the climatic conditions on the hot, muggy rice fields. Slavery fulfilled an economic need, and as long as this continued it prospered. Toward the time of the Revolution, when the tobacco farms were wearing out, it fell into disfavor, only to be revived a few years later by the invention of the cotton gin.

SELECTED READINGS

Gray, L. C., *History of Agriculture in the Southern United States to 1860,* Chaps. I, XIV–XVI.

Sanford, A. H., *Story of Agriculture in the United States,* pp. 1–91.

Carrier, Lyman, *The Beginnings of American Agriculture,* Chaps. III–VII, IX, X–XXV.

Bidwell, P. W., and Falconer, J. I., *History of Agriculture in the Northern United States Before 1860,* Chaps. I–X.

Wertenbaker, T. J., *The First Americans,* Chap. III.

Phillips, U. B., *American Negro Slavery,* Chaps. I–VII.

Eggleston, Edward, *The Transit of Civilization,* pp. 293–307.

Bogart, E. L., and Thompson, C. M., *Readings in the Economic History of the United States,* pp. 28–40, 82–95.

[14] Peter Faneuil, one of the most honored and public-spirited citizens of Boston, was reputed (probably erroneously) to have made his fortune in the slave trade. Faneuil Hall, his gift to the city of Boston, was the scene of many patriotic meetings at the time of the Revolution and has been appropriately called the "Cradle of Liberty." These two facts led to the witty observation that the "Cradle of Liberty rocks on the bones of the Middle Passage."

5.

Colonial Commerce
and Industry

☆ ☆

Conditions of Colonial Commerce

THE American colonies from the beginning were destined to develop a large and thriving commerce. The whole theory of mercantilist economy envisaged the colonies as producers of commodities needed by the home country and in turn as purchasers of the latter's goods and services. This of necessity developed active commercial relations. Products of the forest and field were wanted in England and the colonists in a new country desired the manufactured goods of the more advanced nations. Even the tariff laws passed by the British government to prevent the importation of foodstuffs and other colonial commodities sometimes reacted to encourage commerce, for they forced the colonists, in need of money to purchase English manufactured goods, to find other markets for their products.

In the development of commerce the American colonists were particularly blessed by physiographic conditions. Excellent harbors dotted the coast of New England and the middle colonies. Coastal bays, indentations, and rivers in the middle and southern colonies made commerce easy. "The accessability of continents," it has been said, "is determined by the navigability of their rivers."[1] and this is especially true of a newly settled region. Numerous small rivers in the South allowed the tiny vessels of the period to sail directly to the private wharves of the planters. "None of the plantation houses, even the most remote," commented a Frenchman traveling in Virginia in 1686, "is more than 100 or 150 feet from a 'crik' and the people are thus enabled not only to pay their visits in their canoes, but to do all their freight carrying by the same means."[2]

Until the days of the railroad and automobile it was much easier to carry on commerce by water than by land. This was particularly true in a new country where roads were few and generally poor. It was not until the last third of the eighteenth century that regular stagecoach travel was

[1] E. C. Semple, *American History and Its Geographic Conditions*, p. 20.
[2] Durand, *A Frenchman in Virginia* (1923), p. 23.

established between a few of the larger centers. In 1771 the famous "flying machine" actually reduced the time between Philadelphia and New York to little more than a day and a half. As late as 1794 it took a week under the most favorable circumstances to travel by coach from Boston to New York.[3]

Under such conditions it was natural that most colonial commerce was carried on by water. Even so, the conditions were hard enough to give pause to a modern mariner. The boats were small and dependent on wind and weather, and the time consumed in crossing the Atlantic was exasperatingly long. The Pilgrims were at sea over two months between England and Cape Cod, and Peter Kalm more than a century later asserts that "it is common in winter time to be fourteen, nineteen or more weeks in coming from Gravesend to Philadelphia."[4] The weariness of such a voyage, the monotony of the diet, the discomfort in the cramped quarters, the misery in bad weather, the sickness from scurvy and contagious diseases which often accompanied a long passage, can easily be imagined. If the dangers on the high seas were safely passed, there were still the hazards of sand bars and reefs, many of which were not even charted in those early years; and the few lighthouses which existed before the Revolution were of but limited service.

Other factors also continuously harassed colonial commerce. Not the least of these was the lack of a convenient medium of exchange. As the balance of trade between England and the colonies was always against the latter, what little currency found its way to British North America was quickly drained away. Such currency as existed came chiefly through trade with the Spanish and French colonies or drifted in through the medium of privateering or even piracy. A contemporary writer asserts that money from the West Indies "seldom continues six months in the province before it is remitted to Europe." Barter was complicated by the fact that the amount of precious metals in the foreign coins varied, and also by the fact that although English coins were rarely seen, business was carried on in terms of pounds, shillings, and pence.

Conditions, of course, were not quite so bad as they might seem. International trade was conducted by drafts and bills of exchange; domestic trade, largely by barter of the stable commodities—beaver, skins, corn, wheat. "The term bills of students at Harvard College," says Dewey, "were for many years met by payment of produce, live stock, meats, and 'occasionally with various articles raked up from the family closets of student debtors.' One student, later president of the college, in 1649 settled his bill with 'an old cow,' and the accounts of the construction of the first college

[3] Edmund Quincy, *Life of Josiah Quincy*, pp. 47–48. Colonial travel is further developed in chap. 14.

[4] Peter Kalm, *Travels into North America*, I, 28.

building include the entry 'Received a goat 30s plantation of Watertown rate, which died.' "[5]

Efforts by the colonists to provide substitutes for metallic currency and barter were continuous. In Virginia and Maryland warehouse receipts for tobacco which had been deposited were successfully used. In 1690 Massachusetts issued bills of credit to pay the soldiers who took part in the expedition against Port Royal and Quebec, and this experiment in paper money was followed by all the colonies in the hope that such currency would fill a very evident need in commercial life. Acceptable at a premium over silver for the payment of taxes and generally specifying the date for payment, the early issues held up well, but as the issues became larger and the credit upon which they were based weaker, the result was disastrous. Depreciation followed excessive issue and the numerous emissions with their uncertain value hindered as much as they helped business. So-called "loan banks" in Massachusetts and Pennsylvania issued loan bills on real estate, personal security, and merchandise, but little is known of them. Disapprobation of these monetary issues by the colonies led to an act of Parliament in 1751 forbidding the further issuance of legal tender bills of credit in New England, a prohibition extended to the other colonies in 1764. Although bitterly resented, this legislation was far from being wholly effective. It is estimated that $22,000,000 in paper was still in circulation at the time of the Revolution.

Another source of more or less continuous annoyance to colonial commerce was the existence of piracy and, in time of war, privateering. Wars were frequent in the seventeenth and eighteenth centuries, particularly after the beginning of the "Second Hundred Years War" between England and France in 1689. In theory the difference between a pirate, a robber on the high seas, and a privateer, legally commissioned to war upon an enemy, was very wide. Actually, in practice it was sometimes exceedingly thin. The famous Captain Kidd started as a privateer and ended as a pirate. Despite the difficulties from pirates and privateers during the long years of warfare, their activities were not a complete loss to the colonists. Their booty and treasure had to be disposed of, and they were often smuggled into the colonies and sold cheap. Prominent merchants and even government officials connived at the practice. The Rhode Islanders were particularly active in it. One report in 1736 to the Board of Trade asserts: "These practices will never be put an end to till Rhode Island is reduced to the subjection of the British Empire; of which at present it is no more a part than the Bahama Islands were when they were invaded by the Bucanneers."[6] In any event the booty from this illicit traffic was large.

[5] D. R. Dewey, *Financial History of the United States*, p. 19.
[6] Quoted by M. W. Jernegan, *The American Colonies, 1492–1750*, p. 380.

Sober estimates suggest that New York alone for many years secured on an average of £100,000 in treasure annually in this way and that up to 1700 the greater supply of specie in the colonies was thus obtained.

THEORY OF COLONIAL TRADE

Reserving for a later chapter a more detailed discussion of British colonial policy, we need here merely outline its general purpose and effect. As we have already suggested, the theory behind the mercantilist policy was the subservience of the colonies to the political and economic welfare of the home country. This was the consistent and continuous policy followed for two centuries, clearly understood and repeatedly stated. The first Lord Sheffield once declared that "the only use and advantage of American colonies or West Indies islands is the monopoly of their consumption and the carriage of their produce." A member of the Board of Trade made this even clearer when he wrote in 1726: "Every act of a dependent provincial government ought therefore to terminate in the advantage of the mother state unto whom it owes its being and protection in all valuable privileges. Hence it follows that all advantageous projects or commercial gains in any colony which are truly prejudicial to and inconsistent with the interests of the mother state must be understood to be illegal and the practice of them unwarrantable, because they contradict the end for which the colony had a being and are incompatible with the terms on which the people claim both privileges and protection. . . . For such is the end of the colonies, and if this use cannot be made of them it will be much better for the state to do without them."

Could anything be clearer! After all, what was the use of an empire anyway? The only problem that remained was to determine how colonies in the long run could be made most valuable to the home country. Nor were those bodies of the British government which had supervision of colonial affairs (particularly the Lords of Trade and its successor, the Commissioners of Trade and Plantations) without definite ideas as to how this should be done. The commodities produced in the colonies and desired by England were encouraged by bounties and a monopoly of the home market. Those that came into competition with goods produced in England were kept out by high tariffs. Manufacturing in the colonies whose products competed with English products was discouraged or forbidden. Colonial efforts to ease the financial system by paper money— a system which forced the colonists to buy dear and sell cheap—were forbidden. Colonial laws to curtail the slave trade, a source of immense profit to British slave traders, were vetoed. Every possible attempt was made to center colonial trade in the home country where British capital might reap the profits of the carrying trade, of insurance, and of middlemen's commissions.

Although British mercantilism as a whole operated to the detriment of colonial economic interests and was probably the most potent influence in bringing on the American Revolution, it did not, curiously enough, discourage colonial commerce. For this there were three main reasons. First of all the colonies, being a new country where land and resources were plentiful and labor scarce, were normally producers of raw or semi-finished materials. They naturally fitted into the imperial system in which the colonies supplied the raw materials and the home country the manufactured products. In the second place, the colonies that produced commodities competing with those of Great Britain discovered other markets, particularly in the West Indies and southern Europe. Finally, when British laws came in conflict with colonial interests they were evaded. Despite the British Navy, already the most powerful on the sea, smuggling was rampant, and trade with nations forbidden by British law flourished.

ROUTES AND COMMODITIES OF COLONIAL TRADE

The chief markets for colonial products were England, the West Indies, and southern Europe. By an act of 1660 certain "enumerated" commodities raised on the British mainland colonies were required by law to be sent only to England—tobacco, cotton, wool, and indigo. To these were later added naval stores (tar, pitch, turpentine, hemp, masts, yards), rice, copper, iron, lumber, furs, pearl ashes, and other commodities. As the export staples of the southern colonies were largely tobacco, rice, and indigo, and to a lesser extent naval stores and furs, most of the export trade of these colonies was a direct trade with England. In return they imported dry-goods, hardware, furniture, and other types of manufactured goods.

In New England and the middle colonies the situation was quite different. These colonies had certain commodities—such as naval stores, lumber, furs, and metals—that were desired in the mother country, but their great staples—fish, grain, and other foodstuffs—were kept out of England by high tariffs. Their export trade with her was therefore relatively small and they were forced to find other outlets for their chief products. These outlets were primarily in the West Indies and to a lesser extent in southern Europe. To them New England sent mainly pickled and dried fish, pickled beef and pork, horses and livestock, and various kinds of building material. The exports to these regions from New York and Pennsylvania were chiefly flour and wheat. By the opening of the eighteenth century the West Indian islands had been turned largely into sugar and tobacco plantations unable to support themselves without the importation of cheap food for slaves and lumber for homes and for casks to transport sugar, molasses, and tobacco. In return the mainland colonies obtained molasses which they could turn into rum for the fishing fleet, the slave trade, or domestic use. They also obtained specie or various commodities which could be used to purchase manufactured commodities from England. Some idea of the variety and extent of colonial exports may be gained from the following rough estimates of exports in the decade preceding the Revolution furnished by a contemporary student:

AVERAGE ANNUAL EXPORTS FROM NEW ENGLAND, NEW YORK, AND PENNSYLVANIA, 1763–1766

NEW ENGLAND [7]

Codfish, dried, 10,000 tons, at £10	£100,000
Whale and cod oil, 8500 tons, at £15	127,500
Whalebone, 28 tons, at £300	8,400
Pickled mackerel and shads, 15,000 barrels, at 20s.	15,000
Masts, boards, staves, shingles, etc.	75,000
Ships, about 70 sail, at £700	49,000
Turpentine, tar, and pitch, 1500 barrels, at 8s.	600
Horses and livestock	37,000
Potash, 14,000 barrels, at 50s.	35,000
Pickled beef and pork, 19,000 barrels, at 30s.	28,000
Beeswax, and sundries	9,000
Total	£485,000

NEW YORK [8]

Flour and biscuit, 250,000 barrels, at 20s.	£250,000
Wheat, 70,000 qrs.	70,000
Beans, peas, oats, Indian corn, and other grains	40,000
Salt beef, pork, hams, bacon, and venison	18,000
Beeswax, 30,000 lbs., at 1s.	1,500
Tongues, butter, and cheese	8,000
Flax seed, 7,000 hhds., at 40s.	14,000
Horses and livestock	17,000
Product of cultivated lands	418,500
Timber planks, masts, boards, staves and shingles	25,000
Potash, 7000 hhds.	14,000
Ships built for sale, 20, at £700	14,000
Copper ore, and iron in bars and pigs	20,000
Total	£526,000

[7] *American Husbandry*, I, 59. [8] *Ibid.*, I, 124. Total incorrect as in source.

PENNSYLVANIA [9]

Biscuit flour, 350,000 barrels, at 20s.	£350,000
Wheat, 100,000 qrs., at 20s.	100,000
Beans, peas, oats, Indian corn, and other grains	12,000
Salt beef, pork, hams, bacon, and venison	45,000
Beeswax, 20,000 lbs., at 1s.	1,000
Tongues, butter, and cheese	10,000
Deer, and sundry other sorts of skins	50,000
Livestock and horses	20,000
Flax seed, 15,000 hhds., at 40s.	30,000
Timber planks, masts, boards, staves, and shingles	35,000
Ships built for sale, 25 at £700	17,500
Copper ore, and iron in pigs and bars	35,000
Total	£705,500

These figures also make clear the preponderant position of the fishing industry in New England and of agricultural products in the middle colonies.

The whole course of colonial commerce provides an interesting study in international trade and balance of payments, to say nothing of the ingenuity of the colonial merchant and sea captain in finding an outlet for the products of his region in the face of mercantilist restrictions. In addition to a certain amount of intercolonial commerce and the direct trade to and from England and to and from the West Indies, there developed various phases of the famous triangular trade. The imports of New England and the middle colonies from England were in some years eight times their exports. This trade was maintained in various ways. New England and the middle colonies exported their grain, meat, fish, and lumber to southern Europe, then carried wine, fruit, and other commodities to England where they were exchanged for manufactured products. Another triangular route was the carrying of the products of the New England and the middle colonies to the West Indies where they were exchanged for sugar, molasses, and other commodities; these were taken to England to be exchanged for manufactured goods that were brought back to the northern mainland colonies. As already pointed out, these manufactured goods from England were in part paid for by coin or bills of exchange on London obtained by the direct trade between the northern mainland colonies and the West Indies, a condition made possible partly by the fact that the exports from the West Indies to Great Britain were almost three times the imports.

No one ever made this clearer than Benjamin Franklin himself, testifying

[9] *Ibid.*, I, 181.

as the agent of Pennsylvania before a committee of the British House of Commons in 1766. After pointing out that Pennsylvania imported £500,000 worth of goods each year from Britain and exported to her but £40,000, he was asked, "How then do you pay the balance?"

"The balance," he replied, "is paid by our produce carried to the West Indies, and sold in our own islands, or to the French, Spaniards, Danes and Dutch; by the same carried to other colonies in North-America, as to New-England, Nova-Scotia, Newfoundland, Carolina and Georgia; by the same carried to different parts of Europe, as Spain, Portugal and Italy: In all which places we receive either money, bills of exchange, or commodities that suit for remittance to Britain; which together with all the profits on the industry of our merchants and mariners, arising in those circuitous voyages, and the freights made by their ships, center finally in Britain, to discharge the balance, and pay for British manufactures continually used in the province, or sold to foreigners by our traders."

Still another phase of the triangular commerce was the African slave trade which grew enormously during this period. The causes were: (1) the demand for cheap labor on the plantations of the islands and mainland, and for household servants in the northern colonies; and (2) the large profits which accrued from the trade to English interests and colonial shipowners. Not only were the shipping interests in New England concerned in the slave trade, but also the rum manufacturers who supplied the chief commodity used in the purchase of the Negroes. Until the Revolution almost all the Negroes were taken to the West Indies, and from there a certain portion were later brought to the mainland. From 25,000 to 30,000 slaves a year were transported to these islands, and perhaps 10,000 a year were taken from there to the continental colonies.

TRIANGULAR TRADE I

Considering the primitive conditions in America, such as lack of good transportation facilities and of liquid capital, and the other disadvantages, foreign commerce in the colonial period was extremely active and showed a high per capita value. Throughout the period there was a healthy increase that reached its apex in the decade of the 1760's. Although statistics are by no means dependable, a rough estimate for one of the later years enables the student to obtain a fairly clear picture of the amount and direction of this commerce. It will be noted, first of all, that northern com-

TRIANGULAR TRADE II

merce was more evenly distributed than that of the South. The colonies south of Pennsylvania carried on their commerce mainly with England. The North's discrepancy between imports from and exports to England is particularly evident. This unfavorable balance of trade with the mother country, however, was taken care of in the manner described by Franklin. For one thing, colonial merchants in the North usually owned their own

COLONIAL EXPORTS AND IMPORTS, 1769 [10]
(In pounds sterling)

Exports from	To				
	Great Britain	Southern Europe	West Indies	Africa	Total
North . . .	284,269	335,810	555,612	19,584	1,195,275
South . . .	1,247,245	216,923	192,292	690	1,657,150
Total . .	1,531,514	552,733	747,904	20,274	2,852,425

Imports to	From				
	Great Britain	Southern Europe	West Indies	Africa	Total
North . . .	504,614	54,909	594,421	877	1,154,821
South . . .	1,100,367	21,770	195,326	151,120	1,468,583
Total . .	1,604,981	76,679	789,747	151,997	2,623,404

[10] Figures from E. R. Johnson et al., *History of Domestic and Foreign Commerce of the United States*, I, 92, and F. A. Shannon, *America's Economic Growth*, p. 32. The North in this table includes all colonies north of Maryland.

ships, and profits from the carrying trade alone contributed much to even
the balance. Of all the commerce, that with southern Europe was most
important in maintaining an approximate balance, and this was true of both
North and South. Although the year 1769 showed a balance of trade in
favor of the South, this was generally not the case. Nevertheless, it was
deceptive, for the profits of the English middlemen and the shipowners more
than made up the difference and in the long run tended to throw the
plantation owners into a chronic state of indebtedness.

Conditions of Colonial Industry

The preeminence of agriculture in colonial economy has been stressed
again and again. Factory production as we know it today did not exist.
Even the "putting out" system—a method of production in which the
capitalist gathered the raw material, distributed it to individual workmen
in their homes, and later collected and sold the finished product—was rare.
Nevertheless a certain type of crude and somewhat primitive industry was
widespread. First of all, there was the typical household manufacturing.
On the average farm the housewife spun and wove the wool, flax, or cotton
for clothes, smoked and salted meat, dried and preserved fruit and vegetables. She made her own soap and candles and brewed her own beer.
Leather for shoes, gloves, and workclothes was produced and processed on
the farm. From his own wood lot the farmer procured timber for his
house and hard wood for his tools, furniture, and casks. The hard labor
involved in manufacturing all these necessities of living was not expended
by preference. The colonial farmer, like the farmer of today, would have
much preferred to exchange his surplus for manufactured goods. The
typical farm of the colonial period, however, was small, surpluses were
meager, and transportation was poor. The farm family manufactured its
own goods by necessity.

Another type of household industry existed, the products of which were
designed not for the home but for the outside market. During their spare
time in the winter months many farmers manufactured nails, shingles, barrel staves, or casks which found a ready market in the West Indian trade
or in the local fish and rum industry. In fact, by the end of the colonial
period this type of industry had often expanded into small local shops.
This form of industry—industry that was an adjunct of, or supplementary
to, agriculture and commerce—was typical of much colonial manufacturing.
The products included tools for farming, ships for the widespread commerce, naval stores and other ship supplies, and casks and containers for
tobacco, rum, molasses, and fish. Like industry on the farm, it was one of
necessity, stimulated at times by bounties, such as those on naval stores,

offered by the British government for commodities wanted in the home country.

Another type of manufacturing which may be described as village industries appeared as communities grew to a size that could support them. Most settlements of any size had a sawmill where the farmers could have their lumber prepared, a gristmill where their corn or wheat could be ground, and a fulling mill where cloth could be smoothed and dyed after it was woven. Such communities, if large enough, also supported a shoemaker, a tailor, a cabinetmaker, or other highly trained artisans who produced goods on order.

Delay in the development of colonial manufacturing for export and the general trade was not due to lack of resources. These existed or could be produced in abundance. It was not due to lack of capital. This could be obtained in England or from the surpluses of prosperous merchants, of whom there were many by the late colonial period. Nor was it due in the last analysis to lack of labor. The colonial population by 1776 was one-fourth that of England. Newly arrived immigrants, deprived of good land in the East, might have been induced to enter manufacturing; indentured servants and slaves were available. The lack of development was the result, among other factors, of the belief that greater profits were to be obtained in agriculture, commerce, and land speculation; but, above all, it resulted from the opposition of the British government. British mercantilism looked upon the colonies as a source of raw materials and a market for manufactured goods. Manufactured commodities that came into competition with British goods either in the colonies or in international trade were to be discouraged. At the same time every encouragement should be given to an economic system which would bind the colonies more closely to the needs of British mercantilism.

Even the most cursory survey of the actions of the Board of Trade and other groups in the British government or of their representatives in America during the century preceding the American Revolution bears out this contention. The policy can be seen in specific legislation to curtail the development of a colonial woolen or iron industry. Complaints of British manufacturers, for example, that the colonists were exporting woolens led to the Act in 1699 forbidding the shipment of wool, woolen yarn, or cloth produced in the colonies to any other plantation or country. In 1732 the exportation of hats was similarly prohibited. A law of 1750, while it permitted the entry of bar iron in England, prohibited in the colonies the erection of slitting or rolling mills, and plate, forge, or steel furnaces. Since it did not prohibit casting furnaces, the colonists could still make cannon, kettles, salt pans, and other utensils. This policy is also evident in the instructions to colonial governors to prevent the levying of duties on British goods brought to America or anything else that would in any way give preferential treatment to colonial manufactured products. It is apparent in the innumerable vetoes of colonial laws passed to encourage local manufacturing. It is clear in the veto of laws passed by southern legislatures to curtail the slave trade, for it was the business of the British government to perpetuate in the colonies the plantation system that was so profitable to the commercial and shipping interests of the home land. Far from being accidents of politics, say the Beards, such acts, instructions, and vetoes "were the matured fruits of a mercantile theory of state which regarded colonial trade as the property of the metropolis, to be monopolized by its citizens and made subservient in all things to their interests." [11]

INDUSTRIES OF THE FOREST

To the pioneer farmer the rich forest lands of America seemed only an obstruction to be cleared as quickly as possible in order to open up his farm. It was not long, however, before he discovered in the forests a valuable commodity for trade. Four industries were dependent upon the forest—lumbering, shipbuilding, the manufacture of naval supplies, and the making of potash. In addition, of course, there was the lucrative fur trade. Lumbering and shipbuilding were particularly active in the northern colonies where the rivers ran well up into the forests and sawmills could be run by water power at the fall line. There was a steady and profitable market in the West Indies and southern Europe, and many a farmer was able to attain prosperity by part-time work preparing wood for the market.

With an abundance of white pine, fur, and oak close to the water's edge and a ready supply of pitch pine for tar and turpentine, the colonists had at hand the raw products for shipbuilding. The cheapness of the raw materials overcame the high cost of labor, and the need for ships stimulated the industry from the start. As early as 1641 the General Court of Massachusetts declared the building of ships "a business of great importance for the common good" and provided for the appointment of inspectors "to survey the worke and workemen from time to time" with authority "to take view of every such ship, & all worke thereto belonging, & to see that it be performed and carried out according to the rules of their arte." [12]

Most of the shipbuilding in the colonies was centered in New England. The home demand for ships for the fisheries and the coasting trade must have exceeded the demand from abroad, but the prosperity of the industry was largely dependent upon the foreign market. Ships were constructed in

[11] C. and M. Beard, *Rise of American Civilization*, p. 193.
[12] *Records of the Colony of the Massachusetts Bay in New England*, I, 337.

New England at the close of the colonial period for $34 a ton, fully 20 to 50 per cent cheaper than the cost of construction in Europe. As early as 1676 New England builders were turning out thirty ships a year for the English market, and 300 or 400 commercial boats were built yearly by 1760. By this time one-third of the tonnage (398,000 tons) sailing under the British flag was American-built. Another factor, besides cheapness, which influenced the growth of colonial shipping was that the balance of payments with England continued to be unfavorable to the northern and middle colonies. On this account and also because of the scarcity of money in the colonies, English merchants from the sale of their cargoes would build ships and load them with lumber for Europe. By the 1770's the colonies were building around 25,000 tons a year.

In addition to the actual building of ships and exportation of lumber, the American colonies provided a valuable source for naval supplies, such as tar, pitch, rosin, and turpentine. These commodities, needed by the British navy and merchant marine, were imported chiefly from Sweden, Russia, and Poland. They were considered extremely important as colonial products in the days of mercantilism, the *summum bonum* of which was that a nation be self-sufficing. To encourage the manufacture of these commodities Parliament in 1705 placed a bounty of £4 per ton on tar and pitch imported from the colonies, £3 per ton on rosin and turpentine, and £6 a ton upon water-rotted hemp, all of which were later decreased. Colonial legislatures in some cases added to the bounties, but it was only in the Carolinas that the policy was successful in greatly stimulating the industry. About 82,000 barrels of tar, 9000 of pitch, and 17,000 of turpentine, altogether valued at £175,000, were exported in 1770.

The fur trade was an important forest industry and a valuable source of income for all the colonies in the early years and for some of them to the time of the Revolution. Although many types of furs were secured, the basic fur was beaver skins in the North and deer skins in the South. For these the white man traded guns, ammunition, rum, knives, axes, hoes, kettles, cloth, beads, trinkets, and other commodities greatly desired by the Indians. The sale of firearms and rum to the Indians was forbidden in most of the colonies, but the law was generally ignored. The Indians needed guns to obtain furs and a half-drunk Indian would part with his furs more easily than if he was sober; hence both commodities were considered essential to the trade.

Profits were ordinarily large, particularly in the early years. Later the Indians became wiser, but even then the white man's firewater tended to keep the trade on an unequal basis. Competition from French and Spanish traders, however, held the profits within some kind of limits. The English traders had the advantage over the French in that they were able to obtain commodities to trade with the Indians, particularly rum, at a much lower cost than the French, who had to import their brandy and other goods from France. Likewise the English traders traveled shorter distances than the *coureurs de bois*. These advantages were often thrown away for quick profits, particularly by the merchants of Albany, the center of the northern fur trade, by selling the cheaper English goods to the French traders. At all events the fur trade was large. The Champlain country of New York alone, when the traffic was at its height in the middle of the seventeenth century, exported 40,000 skins annually. By the end of the century traders in New York were tapping the furs of the Great Lakes, the traders of Pennsylvania had reached the Ohio, and those from Charleston, South Carolina, had penetrated a thousand miles into the interior.

The fur trade, however, has a much deeper significance in American history than its commercial and industrial phase. The fur trader pressing after the retreating game supply blazed the trail for the missionary and settler and pointed the way to the west. But though he opened the western routes and brought material prosperity, his unscrupulous treatment of the red men often resulted in Indian wars with their horrors and devastations. The most serious Indian troubles in the north arose from French influence, but the Indian wars of the Carolinas and Virginia were often attributable to disputes between Indians and fur traders.

The colonial rivalries of the seventeenth and eighteenth centuries went deeper than mere friction over the fur trade, though the latter was likely to be an immediate cause of irritation on this side of the water. New Netherlands was founded originally not as a colonization project but as a fur-trading post, and as such the Dutch East India Company was chiefly interested in it. The incessant slaughter of animals fast depleted the New England region, and by 1699 the annual export of New York had decreased to 15,000 skins. With the falling-off of the fur supply east of the Alleghenies, the English pushed westward, only to find the French firmly ensconced in the St. Lawrence Valley and already tapping the rich supplies of the Mississippi region. The decline of the fur trade east of the Alleghenies was coincident with the outbreak of King Philip's War (1675–1676).

The key to the situation rested in the friendship of the Iroquois, the most highly civilized and powerful of the Indians east of the Mississippi. Controlling as they did the Mohawk Valley, the gateway to the west, they were bound to play a leading rôle in the rivalries between the French and the English in the fight for the western fur trade. The unfortunate act of Champlain in 1609 in aiding Canadian Indians against the Iroquois, the subsequent mistakes of the French governors, and on the other hand the skillful diplomacy of Governor Dongan of New York (1684), won for the English the friendship of the Iroquois and the furs of the west and, in fact, determined as much as anything else which of the two nations should control the continent. The founding of the Hudson's Bay Company in 1670, headed by Prince Rupert, to which the English king gave a grant to trade in the regions draining into the Hudson Bay, was a direct stroke at the political and commercial interests of France and contributed, along with the friction on the southern border, to the succession of wars. Although we have no accurate records, it seems certain that the annual value of the furs exported from the British mainland colonies at the end of the colonial period was well over £200,000, a stake worth striving for. In fact, the French were ever ready to dispute with the English the control of the trade in the St. Lawrence, the Mohawk, and the Ohio Valleys, and with the Spanish the control of the southern Mississippi region; both Spanish and French competed with the settlers of the Carolinas.

INDUSTRIES OF THE SEA

Whether it was the chronic state of hunger under which Europe suffered during the Middle Ages or the desertion of the western coast of Europe by the food fish that drove the fishermen to push westward for their supply is uncertain. By 1300 they had reached Iceland, and at least a hundred years before there was an English settlement in New England, European fishermen were sailing regularly to the "Banks." By 1500 the deep-sea fisheries were in full operation and the Newfoundland waters were frequented by ships of England, France, Spain, and Portugal. To preserve the fish on the long trip home they had to be cured, and for this it was necessary to land and spread them out in the sun where the moisture could evaporate and the salt "strike in." The mystery which hangs over these early trips to the fishing banks, possibly because a great deal of the product was smuggled in on the return voyage, makes it impossible to determine at what date Europeans first began to land upon various parts of the coast to cure their fish. The Portuguese alone in 1550 had 400 fishing vessels in American waters; England in 1610 was said to have derived an income of ten million dollars from the sale of surplus fish. In consequence, European governments early in the seventeenth century awoke to the importance of possessing lands close to the fishing banks. This necessity provided one impetus to North American exploration, and resulted in disputes over lands close to the fishing grounds which have continued almost to the present day.

The New England settlers soon realized that wealth was to be found in the deep sea rather than upon the rocky soil. Said Captain John Smith,

"The maine Staple from hence to bee extracted for the present, to produce the rest, is fish; which however it may seeme a base commoditie: yet who will but truely take the pains and consider the sequell, I think will allow it well worth the labour." [13] An apparently exhaustless supply of cod and halibut was to be found off the Newfoundland banks, while closer to the coast mackerel, herring, bluefish, shad, and other varieties were plentiful. The demand for fish was widening in Europe, especially in Catholic countries. New England, close to the fishing grounds and with an abundance of shipbuilding materials at hand, was in a strategic position to profit, and after 1650 her prosperity was closely connected with fishing. Three hundred thousand cod, the great staple of the industry, were sent abroad in 1641, and by 1675 over 600 vessels and 4000 men were engaged in cod fishing. By the end of the colonial period the industry was worth £225,000 a year. As the market developed, New Englanders divided their fish in three classes. The largest and fattest, because they were the most difficult to cure thoroughly, were consumed locally. The second class, smaller and more easily cured, was exported to the Continent. The third class, sometimes tainted, damaged, or too small for the European or American market, was sold in the West Indies as food for slaves, usually in exchange for molasses. The latter, a by-product of sugar manufacture, was brought back and converted into rum. In addition to the manufacture of rum, which was a result of the fishing industry, the demand for salt was stimulated, and salt vats were erected at various points along the shore, where sea water could be evaporated. Fish, molasses, rum, and salt all contributed to make the cooperage industry one of the liveliest in the colonies.

Almost as important as fishing during the last hundred years of the colonial era was the whaling industry. Spermaceti, sperm oil, whalebone, and ambergris were in great demand. Whales were abundant off the New England coast and after 1700 New England seamen began to put off and harpoon the unwieldy monsters when they came up to breathe. When the whales were driven off the coast the whalers followed them to the arctic and antarctic regions. After 1732 an annual bounty of twenty shillings a ton (raised to forty shillings in 1747) was paid on vessels of 200 tons or upward engaged in whaling, and the consequent increasing values of the products spurred on the hunters. The most skillful whalers in the world came from New England and that province practically monopolized the business. Over 300 vessels and 4000 sailors were engaged in it at the outbreak of the Revolution, most of them hailing from Nantucket, New Bedford, Marblehead, and Provincetown. Upon the basis of spermaceti a candle-making business of some importance grew up.

[13] *Works,* Arber edition, p. 194.

INDUSTRIES OF THE HOME AND WORKSHOP

Mention has already been made of household industries, but it may be worth while again to emphasize the importance of this phase of colonial manufacturing. Few homes were without a spinning wheel and a hand loom and the larger part of the textiles used in the colonies were produced in the home. Most of this cloth was either wool or linen or a mixture of the two. Sheep were more commonly raised on farms in this period than in later years and flax was more widely grown. Hemp cloth or linen of varying degrees of fineness was the chief colonial textile; it served nearly all of the purposes for which cotton is used today. While the British government did what it could to discourage the production of woolen goods which came in competition with its own manufacturing, it was anxious to encourage the growth and use of hemp and flax. Several colonial assemblies offered bounties for the growing of these two commodities and others required that they be grown. Little cotton was grown in the mainland colonies until after the 1790's. Some was imported, but being a difficult fiber to work, it was generally mixed with linen or wool before spinning. Not only was spinning and weaving a universal household industry, but by the time of the Revolution the faint beginnings of the factory system could be seen in the grouping of several weaving machines under the same roof. Such shops could be found in certain of the larger towns such as Philadelphia and Lancaster.

It was impossible to produce iron utensils on most farms. The cost of importing them was so great, however, that iron works appeared in Massachusetts at Lynn and Taunton as early as the 1640's to exploit the bog iron common in those regions. In the eighteenth century the industry moved farther from the coast to use the rock ores in the uplands of New Jersey and Pennsylvania. Some copper was also mined in Connecticut, New York, and New Jersey.

The purpose of the iron mines was chiefly to supply the immediate needs of the colonists for wagon and sleigh tires, mill spindles, anvils, pots, kettles, forged plates, weights, bells, chains, anchors, guns, and cannon. In conjunction with these mines and smelting establishments usually were to be found some variety of casting works. Slitting mills furnished iron rods from which the farmers manufactured nails on winter evenings by means of a small furnace in the chimney corner. The colonial smelting furnaces generally were small and crude, producing from a dozen to twenty tons a week, but the principles upon which they worked were not unlike those employed in modern furnaces.

The development of iron foundries was not what the British wanted.

Pig iron might be produced in the colonies, but the colonials must not compete with the home manufacturers. By 1750 the casting of iron had reached such proportions that Parliament prohibited the erection of any slitting or rolling mill, plating, forge, or steel furnace, under a penalty of £200. Although iron manufacturing was restricted, the production of pig and bar iron was encouraged after 1757 by permitting their admission into the port of London free of duty. Exports which amounted to 1127 tons in 1728 grew under this stimulus to 7525 tons in 1771, valued at £20 a ton.

From the amount of furniture and other household utensils exhibited in antique shops as "colonial," one might gain the impression that most of our forefathers were engaged solely in this type of manufacturing. Most of the "antiques" date from the years after the Revolution. Nevertheless a large amount of household furnishings was manufactured either in the home or on order by local cabinetmakers. Some of it even entered the intercoastal trade. The loadings of New England vessels trading with the southern colonies and the West Indies show frequent items of furniture for export to these regions. Some glass was also manufactured. One experiment, that of the famous Baron Stiegel who set up a feudal state and glassworks at Mannheim, southwest of Lancaster, produced excellent glassware but otherwise proved unsuccessful.

An almost universal industry, household and otherwise, was the making of many kinds of liquor. It throve especially in the coast towns of New England, where the West Indian molasses was distilled into rum, particularly for the slave trade and the fishing expeditions. At one time twenty distilleries in Newport alone were engaged in the business. Not only rum but also beer, ale, and cider were exported to the West Indies. It must not be thought, however, that this liquor business was concerned entirely with exports; our forefathers were hard drinkers and a large proportion was consumed at home.

EXTENT OF COLONIAL INDUSTRY

It would be the merest guesswork to attempt even an approximate statement of the extent of colonial industry at various periods. Contemporary accounts are either inadequate, or exaggerated for the purpose of influencing prospective settlers or setting at rest the fears of the home government. The colonists' attempt at the time of the Stamp Act to free themselves from dependence upon British industry brought in 1766 and 1768 letters from the Lords of Trade to the colonial governors demanding an annual report on manufactures in their provinces. Though inadequate, these reports are a valuable source of information.[14] The general tenor of the replies was to

[14] A summary of these letters is given in Victor S. Clark, *History of Manufactures in the United States, 1670–1860*, pp. 207 ff.

depreciate the extent of colonial industry and to emphasize the dependence of the colonists upon Great Britain. While specific industries were mentioned, it was maintained that the wealthier classes bought imported goods and that the lure of the land turned the mechanic into a farmer, to the detriment of the development of manufacturing. Governor Bernard of Massachusetts went so far as to declare, "I do not think it necessary to send an annual account where I have nothing to inform of."

These reports, apparently aimed to reassure the British government that the colonists were in no position to become economically independent, belittled unduly the real condition of colonial manufacturing. A truer impression is given in a letter from Comptroller Weare to the president of the Board of Trade; he says: "Upon actual knowledge therefore of these northern Colonies, one is surprised to find out that, notwithstanding the indifference of their wool and the extravagant price of labour the planters throughout all New England, New York, the Jersies, Pennsylvania and Maryland (for south of that province no knowledge is here pretended) almost entirely clothe themselves in their own woolens, and that generally the people are sliding into the manufactures proper to the mother country, and this not through any spirit of industry or economy, but plainly for want of some returns to make to the shops."[15] An English writer stated in 1774 that "the inhabitants in the Colonies . . . do make many things, and export several manufactures, to the exclusion of English manufactures of the same kinds. The New England people import from the foreign and the British Islands very large quantities of cotton, which they spin and work up with linen yarn into a stuff, like that made in Manchester, wherewith they clothe themselves and their neighbours. Hats are manufactured in Carolina, Pennsylvania and in other Colonies. Soap and candles, and all kinds of wood-work, are made in the Northern Colonies and exported to the Southern. Coaches, chariots, chaises, and chairs, are also made in the Northern Colonies and sent down to the Southern. Coach harness, and many other kinds of leather manufactures, are likewise made in the Northern Colonies, and sent down to the Southern; and large quantities of shoes have lately been exported from thence to the West India Islands. Linens are made to a great amount in Pennsylvania and cordage and other hemp manufactures are carried on in many places with great success: and foundry ware, axes, and other iron tools and utensils are also become articles of commerce, with which the Southern Colonies are supplied from the Northern."[16]

When the colonist could afford it, he undoubtedly preferred to buy the finest grade of manufactures from abroad; but the essentials could be ob-

[15] Massachusetts Historical Society, *Collections,* 1st Series, I, 74.

[16] *Interest of the Merchants and Manufacturers of Great Britain in the Present Contest with the Colonies Stated and Considered* (London, 1774; reprinted in Boston), p. 12.

tained here, and the non-intercourse agreements prior to the Revolution demonstrated Franklin's contention that the colonist could supply himself with what was absolutely needed without recourse to Great Britain. To do so, however, at that time was abnormal, for colonial economy was primarily agricultural.

SELECTED READINGS

Hacker, L. M., *The Triumph of American Capitalism*, pp. 136–158.

Nettels, Curtis, *The Roots of American Civilization*, Chaps. IX, X.

Johnson, E. R., *et al.*, *History of Domestic and Foreign Commerce of the United States*, Chaps. I–XI.

Dewey, D. R., *Financial History of the United States*, Chap. I.

Tryon, R. M., *Household Manufacture in the United States, 1640–1860*, Chaps. I–VI.

Clark, V. S., *History of Manufactures in the United States, 1607–1860*, Chaps. I–IX.

Bogart, E. L., and Thompson, C. M., *Readings in the Economic History of the United States*, pp. 42–80, 96–105.

6

Frontier Expansion
Before the Revolution

Significance of the Westward Movement

CONFLICTING influences have contributed to the formation of American character and ideals. On the one hand, proximity to the ocean and intercourse with Europe retarded the development of a distinctly American civilization, while on the other the westward movement and frontier life continually worked to efface the European influence and to stimulate the growth of a new nation. The Appalachian barrier and the lack of transportation facilities, until the opening of the nineteenth century, kept the great majority of the people east of the mountains. As late as 1830 the center of population was still on the Atlantic coast. Nevertheless, even before this date, as afterward, one of the most important factors in the life and history of the people was the continued westward advance. The movement inland commenced almost immediately after the first settlements were made and lasted until about 1890, when the frontier lines moving west and east joined. "Up to our own day," says Professor Turner, "American history has been in a large degree the history of the colonization of the Great West. The existence of an area of free land, its continuous recession, and the advance of American settlement westward, explain American development."[1]

Leaving until a later time a more detailed discussion of the effects which the westward movement has had, we need here simply point out by way of introduction some of the most important tendencies resulting therefrom. The exigencies of pioneer life forced the settler, if he was to survive, to adapt himself to changed conditions; and although he carried with him the ideas and training of his youth, the influence of his European cultural background became progressively less. As settlers of various races were thrown together in a similar environment, there gradually evolved a composite type of American. The never-ending struggle against the forces of

---

[1] F. J. Turner, *The Frontier in American History*, p. 1.

nature, against hostile Indians and wild beasts, developed a self-reliant, keen, aggressive, individual type, characterized by antipathy to control and to any attempt to abridge his independence—what Burke called "a fierce spirit of liberty." The comparative equality of wealth in a new community, where each man stood upon his own feet, made it easy to forget the artificial customs of an old world and developed a distinctly democratic outlook. The West, as a result, has been the most democratic part of America, and our history has been full of the struggles between the democratic frontiersman and the more conservative Easterner. The elements which have gone to make up the life of the frontiersman have produced intellectually a type that is restless, energetic, and practical, and at the same time buoyant and optimistic.

For our political life the growth of the West with its different interests has meant the emergence of sectionalism and the demands of the Westerner for legislation promoting his own interests—internal improvements, free land, and an inflated currency. At the same time, however, his need for many things which only the national government could give him has been a most potent factor in the growth of nationalism. In the technique of government the drive of the West has been toward such democratic innovations as the direct election of United States Senators, woman suffrage, and the initiative, referendum, and recall. Economically, the growth of the West has brought virtual industrial independence for the nation, along with sectional specialization.

STAGES OF WESTWARD ADVANCE

Even during colonial times, rather clearly marked stages of westward advance were in evidence. The first was usually marked by the activities of the hunter, trader, or missionary. Traders and trappers like Daniel Boone and Jedediah Smith, and missionaries like Father Marquette and Marcus Whitman, are typical of the pathfinders who blazed the way. The trail of the hunter followed that of the wild animal and the Indian and eventually became a highway of civilization, and the trading posts erected at convenient points on the western trails grew into such cities as Albany, Pittsburgh, Chicago, and St. Louis. Following the trapper and the trader came the rancher, who occupied the land to exploit the grasses. Of all farm products, livestock was in those days the easiest moved, and from the "cow pens" of seventeenth-century Virginia and the Carolinas to the great modern ranches of the western prairies, the frontier ranchman has marked the farthest westward advance.

Close on the heels of the rancher came the farmer, the first wave dispersing in sparsely settled communities and wastefully exploiting the soil.

This preliminary farming stage was in turn succeeded by more or less intensive farming in denser settlements. Where conditions were favorable, the farming stage gave way to the final stage—city life with its manufacturing and commercial activities.

These stages through which most of our country has passed—the hunting, the ranching, the farming, the industrial—have all played their part in its development, and for almost three centuries this process has been repeated and the drama reenacted, coloring our history and determining our civilization. All these stages, of course, were not inevitable, nor did they always occur in the order named. Sometimes representatives of all the four groups landed pell-mell in a new region and contributed simultaneously to its development.[2] In general, however, the recurring stages so vividly portrayed by Professor Turner marked the outstanding epochs in our economic advance. "The Atlantic frontier was compounded of fisherman, fur trader, miner, cattle-raiser, and farmer. Excepting the fisherman, each type of industry was on the march toward the West, impelled by an irresistible attraction. Each passed in successive waves across the continent. Stand at Cumberland Gap and watch the procession of civilization, marching single file—the buffalo following the trail to the salt springs, the Indian, the fur trader and hunter, the cattle-raiser, the pioneer farmer—and the frontier has passed by. Stand at South Pass in the Rockies a century later and see the same procession with wider intervals between. The unequal rate of advance compels us to distinguish the frontier into the trader's frontier, the rancher's frontier, or the miner's frontier, and the farmer's frontier. When the mines and cow pens were still near the fall line, the traders' pack trains were tinkling across the Alleghenies, and the French on the Great Lakes were fortifying their posts, alarmed by the British trader's birch canoe. When the trappers scaled the Rockies, the farmer was still near the mouth of the Missouri."[3]

ROUTES OF WESTWARD MIGRATION

Navigable streams marked the first routes of westward migration. The hope of finding a passage through the newly discovered lands to the riches of Cathay led the earliest explorers to probe the innumerable rivers and estuaries with their tiny boats. Later the rivers and lakes offered to the fur trader the readiest access into the interior, and decades, even centuries, before the settler followed him he had clearly pointed out the routes of travel. Twelve years before the Dutch made their famous purchase of the island of Manhattan they had established a trading post at

[2] C. W. Alvord, in the *Mississippi Valley Historical Review*, VII, 403–407 (March, 1921).
[3] F. J. Turner, *The Frontier in American History*, p. 12.

Albany; by 1627 merchants of Jamestown were trading with Indians of the upper Potomac and Susquehanna. The French, who had stumbled upon the best route into the interior and had been forced by circumstances into the development of the fur trade, had discovered long before the opening of the eighteenth century the best routes between the basin of the Great Lakes and the Mississippi, and had used the key portages which the Indians made known to them.

There were four leading routes through the Appalachian barrier. The most northerly and the best, that by way of the Hudson and Mohawk to the Lakes, was closed to early settlers by the Iroquois. To the south was a second route leading from the headwaters of the Mohawk to the upper Allegheny. The third led across southern Pennsylvania to the Monongahela and thence to the Ohio, a line later followed by the Cumberland road. The fourth and most important to the pre-Revolutionary settlers was southward down the great Appalachian Valley and out through the Cumberland Gap or the Tennessee Valley. A possible route around the south of the Appalachians was closed by the Cherokees. While these routes were known to fur traders long before the Revolution, it was not until the latter part of the eighteenth century that settlers in any numbers followed them. Before that time the need of keeping in close touch with the European market had kept the white man near the rivers, and hostile French and Indians as well as the natural mountain barrier had all contributed to limit settlement east of the Appalachians.

THE FIRST FRONTIER

The first permanent English settlement, that of Jamestown in 1607, was largely a business venture, engineered by the Virginia Company. A few years only were necessary, however, to demonstrate the impracticability of the original plans, and it was not long before the land was broken up among individual owners, who, after about 1617, devoted themselves largely to raising the staple crop of tobacco. As the market for the crop was beyond the seas, it was necessary to remain close to the river. The early settlers took up land along the James, and from there spread north and south to other rivers, staking off their plantations on the bank and shipping their tobacco to Europe from their own wharves. As the land along the larger rivers was preempted, the region inland was tapped and the tobacco floated down in canoes and on rafts to the bigger streams. This tendency to remain near the rivers retarded the building of roads inland and the growth of urban life. Early Virginia was not unlike a federation of peninsulas.

The Virginian lowlands, cut into by many little rivers, were particularly adapted to a tobacco plantation economy. But tobacco raising under primitive conditions was wasteful and migration inland to fresh lands was rapid, a movement that was facilitated by the ease with which titles to new land could be obtained. New arrivals ascended the rivers to take up new lands as close to the water as possible. This type of westward advance left the frontiers open to Indian attack, and as the years went on the government made repeated efforts to control the frontier movement and to group the frontiersmen into towns at the first falls of the river in the vicinity of Richmond, Petersburg, and other places which might serve as outposts of defense against Indians. The frontier of Virginia also pushed south as well as west, and by 1700 the region of the Carolinas north of Albemarle Sound and east of the Chowan River had been occupied.

Whereas the westward migration of the Virginia colonists was more or less haphazard, in New England the colonial government attempted very definitely to superintend the founding of towns and the prescribing of their limits. Upon the request of a group of prospective settlers, the colonial governments of New England would grant a tract usually 36 miles square. "The settlement of a town normally began," says Professor Osgood, "with the laying out of a village plot and the assignment of home lots. This to an extent determined the location of highways, of the village common, and of some of the outlying fields. On or near the common the church was built, and in not a few cases the site that was chosen for the building went far toward determining the entire lay-out of the town. The idea of a home lot was a plot of ground for a dwelling house and outbuildings, for a dooryard and garden, and usually also an enclosure for feeding cattle and raising corn."[4] Common fields were usual, and provisions were ordinarily made in these pioneer towns for reserving lands for the support of a minister and schools. The attempt on the part of the government to control this frontier movement is seen in an order of the General Court in 1636, which directed that none go to the new plantations without the permission of a majority of the magistrates, an order which was probably evaded. On the other hand, the danger from French and Indian attack led the General Court in 1694, after enumerating certain "Frontier Towns," to forbid the inhabitants to desert these outposts on pain of imprisonment and confiscation of their land. The closeness of the New England frontier to the older settlements and the constant danger of enemy attack made the position and status of the frontier towns a matter of the most earnest concern.

With few exceptions, the expansion of Massachusetts Bay proceeded normally along the lines pointed out. In the case of the migrations from this colony to Rhode Island and Connecticut, migrants were squatters on the land, but eventually they obtained title and developed sufficient strength

[4] H. L. Osgood, *The American Colonies in the Seventeenth Century*, I, 438.

to push out frontier posts of their own by the New England township method. Settlement by townships by approved groups of men had many advantages, particularly in affording maximum protection against the Indians, but it also opened the way for controversies between the proprietors who received the grant and the non-proprietors who came in later and who might have no rights in the common or undivided lands. As the non-proprietors were often more numerous and gained control of the local government, the opportunities for friction were great.

The beginnings of Dutch settlement can be traced to trading posts on the Delaware River and at the mouth of upper reaches of the Hudson. Schenectady at the rapids of the Mohawk was begun in 1661, and in the succeeding years the intervening land along the two rivers was taken up under the patroon system and allotted to tenants by the patroons or the New Amsterdam officials. New Jersey was first settled by the Dutch, who emigrated from New York, and by the Swedes, who settled in 1638 on the Delaware. The Dutch conquered the Swedes in 1655 and were in turn (1664) brought under submission by the English, who turned the region over to two proprietors, Carteret and Berkeley. The latter sold his share in 1674 to two Quakers, and eight years later Carteret disposed of his to William Penn and eleven others. Consequently New Jersey was settled by Dutch from New York, Swedes, Quakers, and westward-moving emigrants from New England, all of whom were able to acquire land on advantageous terms. William Penn in 1681 was granted the territory west of the Delaware and between New York and Maryland; in the same year Philadelphia was settled. Penn founded the colony primarily as a home for oppressed Quakers, then opened it to the persecuted of all lands; and before the close of the century Quakers from England, Ireland, and Wales, Mennonites from the Rhine Valley, and a sprinkling of Scotch, Swedes, Irish, and French had established a thriving commonwealth.

Maryland to the south had been founded in 1634 by Lord Baltimore as a refuge for Catholics. The first settlement, St. Mary's, was begun about nine miles up the St. George, a tributary of the Potomac. Religious freedom brought immigrants of many sects, as did the liberal system of granting land. As the economic life of Maryland strongly resembled that of Virginia in its dependence on agriculture and its specialization upon a single staple, and as the geographic conditions were similar, her westward advance was like that of her southern neighbor. The Carolinas in 1700 boasted two patches of settlement, the northern around Albemarle Sound, in reality an extension of Virginia, and the southern extending from the Santee River south, with Charleston as its center. The southern colony, founded in 1670 under the patronage of eight proprietors, among whom

English Colonies in 1760
Settled areas
Disputed between England and France

THE ENGLISH CONTINENTAL COLONIES
IN 1760
SHOWING EXTENT OF SETTLEMENT
Scale of Miles
0   50   100   200   300

MANHATTAN DRAFTING CO. INC., N.Y.

were some of the most distinguished men in England, including Anthony
Ashley Cooper, later Earl of Shaftesbury, was commercially bound to
the West Indies, whence most of the inhabitants came. Settlement was
hindered at first by the attempt to impose an artificial system of government
—the Grand Model of John Locke—but after that plan had been discarded
the movement up the river was rapid. Excellent additions to the population
were furnished by the Scotch-Irish and by five hundred Huguenots who
left France after the revocation of the Edict of Nantes and took up 50,000
acres along the Santee.

It is evident even from this brief review of early settlement that by
1700 the American population had already taken on the heterogeneous character which has distinguished it to our own day. Most of the immigrants
during the seventeenth century came from England, but there was also a
sprinkling of people from other parts of the British Isles and from the
nations of western Europe. This trend, as we shall see, was to be even
more pronounced in the eighteenth century, when the great majority of
immigrants came from Ireland and Germany. As a matter of fact, migration
in the seventeenth century was not large; the population in all of the
English mainland colonies in 1700 was probably not more than 250,000.
Of this number, New England had about 80,000, Virginia 60,000, and
Maryland 30,000; the remainder was concentrated along the Hudson and
Delaware Rivers and in various areas in the Carolinas. Small as the population was, it was enough to occupy the coastal plains and to extend the area
of settlement to the fall line of the rivers. It was the eighteenth century
that was to widen the area to include the foothills of the Appalachian range.

INDIANS AND THE EARLY WESTWARD MOVEMENT

The insignificance of the Indian in the United States today in numbers
and power[5] makes it easy to underestimate his rôle in American history.
It should be remembered that the Indian, in a sense, prepared the way for
the European settler. Indian trails generally marked the routes inland taken
by the white men from the earliest days to the era of railroads. The clearings
made by the Indian for his crude farming were among the first occupied
by the newcomers, who not only used his land but adopted his methods
of agriculture. Furthermore, the Indians spurred on the white advance by
the temptations which they held out to the fur trader. The latter, returning
with tales of the rich western lands, continually whetted the desires of the

[5] F. E. Leupp, *The Indian and His Problem* (1910), p. 350, estimates the number of
Indians in 1492 in the continental United States area as between eight and nine hundred
thousand; the article "Indians" in the *New International Encyclopedia* quotes James Mooney,
United States government expert, as estimating the Indian population of the continent north of
Mexico at that time at 1,115,000. The 1940 census puts the Indian population at 333,969.

land-hungry settlers. On the other hand, however, every frontier had an Indian barrier to dispose of, and the problem of removing the red man, by purchase of land or forcible ejection through warfare, was a continual difficulty for almost three hundred years. The Indian held possession of strategic passes and gaps in the mountains, and was able to hold up immigration into the West. Again should be noted the effect of the Indian barrier upon the life and character of the people; frontier life meant danger from the Indians, which necessitated courage and self-reliance. Although the main burden of defense against the Indians rested upon the frontiersman, the latter naturally demanded aid from the more populous East. This provided a distinct trend toward nationalism. Indian dangers also developed more community life and less scattered settlement than would have occurred otherwise.

By the end of the seventeenth century the lands back to the fall line had been pretty well cleared of Indians, who were driven into the Piedmont region.[6] But this first foothold was not achieved without war and suffering. With the exception of Penn's colonies, where treatment of the Indians according to the Golden Rule kept the settlers relatively free from molestation, friction with the red men was frequent. The most serious of the seventeenth-century conflicts was with the Pequots in 1675, when all New England joined in one of the bloodiest Indian wars in our history. King Philip's War broke the power of the New England Indians, but their descendants, driven northward, continued in later years to aid the French in harassing the frontier settlements.

The tendency toward nationalism which the Indian danger fostered was seen most clearly in the colonial period. The need for mutual military defense had in 1643 brought Plymouth, Massachusetts Bay, Connecticut, and New Haven to form the New England Confederation, a real forerunner of the famous Albany Congress of 1754, in which an attempt was made to bring the colonies together for united action, chiefly with reference to Indian problems.

The Advance into the Piedmont

With the tidewater settlements fairly well secured, the colonists during the years from 1700 to the conclusion of the French and Indian War in 1763 pushed into the Piedmont region to take up the lands between the fall line and the Alleghenies. In New England this process was hastened when the old method of carefully guarded township grants to approved men was

---

[6] The term Piedmont, literally foothills, in American physiography designates that part of the Atlantic coastal plain lying between the low coastal plain proper and the Appalachian highlands. See Chap. 1.

replaced by the plan of locating towns in advance of settlement and then auctioning them to land speculators. Settlers pushing up the Housatonic Valley into the Berkshires founded Litchfield in 1720, Sheffield in 1725, Great Barrington in 1730, and Williamstown by the middle of the century. In 1735 four contiguous towns were laid out to connect the Housatonic and Connecticut River settlements. During these years most of the land between the Connecticut and the seacoast was also taken up, and by 1737 Connecticut had disposed of her unlocated lands. In New Hampshire settlement proceeded up the Merrimac and some distance up the Connecticut. The taking up of lands was also encouraged by the grants of Governor Wentworth of 120 towns west of the Connecticut in what was later Vermont. Although the New England expansion of this period was toward the north, it had all the essential characteristics of the westward movement.

A large and influential element in this frontier advance was furnished by immigrants from North Ireland, who with questionable accuracy have been commonly termed "Scotch-Irish," [7] a race well adapted to the rigors of pioneer life and *"par excellence* the Indian fighters." The Act of 1699 prohibiting the exportation of Irish wool from Ulster, the enforced payment of tithes to the Anglican Church, and the fact that between 1714 and 1718 many of the leases granted to the original settlers expired, all contributed in the early years of the eighteenth century to bring about a great migration of Scotch-Irish to America. So rapid was the influx into New England that the authorities shipped the newcomers to the frontier, where they settled in Worcester, founded Pelham, Warren, and Blandford, and, following the Connecticut Valley, settled in Windsor, Orange, and Caledonia Counties in Vermont, and Grafton County in New Hampshire.

Hemmed in by the Catskills to the west and with the Mohawk pass into the interior blocked by the Iroquois, New York during this period showed little expansive vitality. Notwithstanding the richness of the soil, the cultivation of the narrow ribbon of land along the two rivers proceeded slowly, largely because of the fact that the Dutch system of huge manorial grants was continued under British rule. With millions of acres of the choicest lands under the control of a handful of men who wanted to settle tenant farmers upon their lands, it was little wonder that the tide of immigration moved elsewhere. New York caught some of the first wave of the German-Swiss immigration, which, commencing in 1683, continued throughout the first half of the next century. This inflow, which came mostly from the Palatinate, Württemberg, Baden, and Switzerland, resulted from religious persecution,

---

[7] The non-Irish population who had settled in Ulster and other parts of North Ireland came from England as well as Scotland. Of those who came from Scotland, the great majority were Lowland Scots whose blood may have been more English than Scotch.

political discontent, and economic disorganization following the continental wars. Governor Hunter in 1710 tried to settle 3000 Germans on the Hudson near Saugerties to produce naval stores, but discontent with their lot led many of them to move on to the Mohawk Valley, where they settled in the country between Fort Hunter and Palatine Bridge. The Scotch-Irish moving on from New England mingled with the Dutch in the Mohawk region and entered the Cherry Valley in 1738.

Pennsylvania's reputation as a home for persecuted sects under Penn's magnanimous rule brought to her shores as permanent settlers, between 1700 and the Revolution, at least 100,000 Germans from the Palatinate and surrounding regions, the ancestors of the present "Pennsylvania Dutch"; 100,000 more were scattered along the frontiers of the other colonies from the head of the Mohawk to Georgia. The Pennsylvania frontier of this period was also the center of the great Scotch-Irish migration which brought to this country between 1730 and 1770 close to half a million. Probably one-third of Pennsylvania's population at the time of the Revolution was composed of Germans from the Rhineland, and another third of immigrants from northern Ireland. The cost of land in Pennsylvania in 1719 was ten pounds per hundred acres and two shillings quitrent; the price was raised in 1732 to fifteen pounds and a quitrent of a halfpenny an acre. But with the rapid influx of immigrants the management of the lands fell into confusion and a large proportion was occupied by squatters without title. James Logan, agent of the Penn family, disgustedly asserted that the Irish settled in "an audacious and disorderly manner," alleging that "it was against the laws of God and nature, that so much land should be idle while so many Christians wanted it to labor on and to raise their bread." [8] The Germans spread out in eastern Pennsylvania, and the Scotch-Irish, coming a little later, planted their outposts in the Cumberland, Juniata, and Susquehanna Valleys.

From Maryland to Georgia the story of the occupation of the Piedmont is much the same. As population increased and the rich lowlands were exhausted, more and more land was taken up until the fall line was reached. Then there moved up into the Piedmont a stream of new comers, mostly of the poorer classes, to claim lands under head rights, or settlers brought in by wealthy speculators to satisfy the requirements for obtaining their vast estates. Efforts were made by each of these colonies, for the purpose of protection, to lure men to the frontier by cheap or free lands and by exemption from taxation. For the same reason attempts were made to prevent the growth of large estates and to stimulate communal life. These efforts were only partially successful, for an aristocratic planter group occupied the Piedmont along with

[8] Quoted by H. J. Ford, *The Scotch-Irish in America*, pp. 271–272; also by C. A. Hanna, *The Scotch Irish*, p. 63.

a yeomanry of small farmers. By 1730 settlers from the coast had spread from thirty to fifty miles into the Virginia Piedmont, but in the Carolinas and Georgia the foothills had scarcely been touched.

After 1730 this westward movement from the coast was augmented by a steady stream of Germans and Scotch-Irish from the northeast. The Blue Ridge Mountains of Virginia and the pine barrens of the Carolinas abruptly checked the advance from the coast, but beyond these barriers lay rich lands in the great valleys of the Appalachians to which ready access could be had from the north. Impetus was given also by the fact that the best land in Pennsylvania was already taken up, whereas land in Maryland could be obtained at a cheaper price and in Virginia it was practically free. Accordingly, a steady stream of pioneers flowed through the Cumberland, Hagerstown, and Shenandoah Valleys into the great mountain trough, and finally out through the passes east into North Carolina or west some years later into Kentucky and Tennessee. By 1760 they had reached the uplands of Georgia. In the Piedmont were mingled the settlers of these two converging streams, the vanguard being usually the sturdy and venturesome Scotch-Irish.

Among the moving mass, as it passed along the Valley into the Piedmont, in the middle of the eighteenth century, were Daniel Boone, John Sevier, James Robertson, and the ancestors of John C. Calhoun, Abraham Lincoln, Jefferson Davis, Stonewall Jackson, James K. Polk, Sam Houston, and Davy Crockett, while the father of Andrew Jackson came to the Carolina Piedmont at the same time from the coast. Recalling that Thomas Jefferson's home was on the frontier, at the edge of the Blue Ridge, we perceive that these names represent the militant expansive movement in American life. They foretell the settlement across the Alleghenies in Kentucky and Tennessee; the Louisiana Purchase, and Lewis and Clark's transcontinental exploration; the conquest of the Gulf Plains in the War of 1812-15; the annexation of Texas; the acquisition of California and the Spanish Southwest. They represent, too, frontier democracy in its two aspects personified in Andrew Jackson and Abraham Lincoln. It was a democracy responsive to leadership, susceptible to waves of emotion, of a "high religious voltage"—quick and direct in action.[9]

Before the Revolution there had developed in the back country a society distinct from that in the tidewater regions. The men of the Piedmont were generally small farmers and trappers, destitute of wealth but well equipped with courage and initiative. Democratic and individualistic, they resented their political and economic subservience to the minority of the coastal plain. From the beginnings of the westward advance a distinct antagonism between the interior and the coast seems to have developed, and during this period it can be clearly seen in controversies between the plantation owners of Vir-

[9] F. J. Turner, The Frontier in American History, p. 105.

ginia and the small farmers of the Piedmont, between the backwoodsmen of Pennsylvania and the wealthy Quakers of the East, and between the frontiersmen of New England and the coast-town aristocracy. This antagonism was evident in the contests between the debtor class of the interior and the property-holding class of the coast, in the demands for a more democratic and representative government in which the frontier might be more justly represented, in the dissatisfaction over the defective administration of government and law under which the back country suffered, and finally in the different moral and intellectual outlook of the two regions.

Absentee landlordism was a curse of the early West. The hope of making fortunes in western land soon developed, and most of those who enjoyed means or influence speculated in land. "You may be pleased to know," said a Deerfield petition of 1678, "that the very principle & best of the land; the best for soile; the best for situation; as lying in yᵉ centre & midle of the town: & as to quantity, nere half, belongs unto eight or 9 proprietors each and every of which, are never like to come to a settlement amongst us, which we have formerly found grievous & doe Judge for the future will be found intollerable if not altered." [10] While the actual settlers cleared the land and bore the brunt of Indian wars, the proprietors profited financially in the security of the tidewater country. As the frontiersmen were the debtor class and as specie was difficult to obtain, they demanded paper money and the payment of taxes in kind—demands which were generally opposed by the older communities. The frontiersman was inclined to feel that his contribution to the defense of the colony exempted him altogether from the burden of taxation. Politically he felt that he was discriminated against by means of property qualifications and careful allotment of representation. The aristocracy of the tidewater and coast towns, although outnumbered, managed until the Revolution to keep control of the governments in their own hands. The counties of Chester, Bucks, and Philadelphia elected twenty-six delegates to the Pennsylvania legislature, and the five frontier counties only ten. Jefferson complained that 19,000 men below the falls legislated for more than 30,000 living elsewhere, as well as appointing their chief executive and judicial officers. The desire to escape from eastern control led to efforts to form such new states as Franklin and Vermont. Dissatisfaction over the administration of the government was keen. Officials were corrupt, and justice was expensive and slow, for the counties were large and it was sometimes necessary to travel long distances to court. Aid in time of war was uncertain. Finally, the intellectual outlook was different. In religious matters the frontiersman was likely to be a Dissenter or neglect the means of grace entirely. The social and economic con-

[10] George Sheldon, *History of Deerfield, Massachusetts* (2 vols, 1896), I, 189-190.

ditions under which he lived made him democratic and in most cases opposed to slavery. These differences in point of view accentuated the more pressing causes of antagonism.

This antagonism led to armed uprisings in at least two cases before the Revolution. When Governor Berkeley of Virginia failed to prosecute vigorously enough operations against the Indians, frontiersmen under Nathaniel Bacon took the matter in their own hands. Thereupon Berkeley (1676) declared Bacon and his followers rebels and attempted to arrest them. The backwoodsmen and small planters rose in rebellion behind Bacon, forced Berkeley to make concessions, gained control of the legislature, and inaugurated numerous democratic reforms. At the high tide of success Bacon died and the rebellion collapsed. Berkeley, with the backing of the tidewater aristocracy, was able to revoke the reform legislation and take such cruel revenge that Charles II declared, "That old fool has taken away more lives in that naked country than I did here for the murder of my father." Almost a century later (1769) rebellion broke out in South Carolina when the backwoodsmen, under the name of Regulators, demanded reforms and attempted to take the law into their own hands. Although they met the government party in arms on the Saluda, hostilities were averted when their demands were complied with. Two years later the Regulators of North Carolina and the militia of Governor Tryon clashed in the bloody battle of the Alamance. The frontiersmen were defeated, and the reins of government were held by the conservatives until the new constitution of 1776 recognized the rights of the interior. The failure on the Alamance was one influence that drove the first pioneers across the Alleghenies.

THE FRENCH BARRIER

Since 1604 the French had maintained permanent settlements in the New World, and during the seventeenth century had explored and laid claim to the region of the St. Lawrence, the Great Lakes, and the Mississippi. The English fur traders had disputed their possession of the Hudson Bay country, and the English colonists had sent a number of expeditions against Acadia. French ambitions in the Mohawk and Hudson had finally brought them into conflict with the British there. This region was so extensive that as yet there was little real trouble as long as the Stuarts, subservient to France, were on the British throne. When William of Orange, champion of the Protestant cause in Europe and bitter enemy of Louis XIV, became king in 1689, the aspect of affairs changed in America. In that year commenced a series of seven wars between France and England, known as the Second Hundred Years' War, which continued with brief intervals until 1815 and comprised sixty years of actual fighting. Rivalry for the commercial and colonial supremacy of the world was the underlying cause of these wars, the first four of which were fought in America as well as in Europe. In America, as far as the British mainland colonists were concerned, it was a battle for the control of the Ohio and Mississippi Valleys.

When this struggle reached its climax in the French and Indian War (1754-1763), the French were handicapped by lack of numbers, for the 80,000 inhabitants of New France were overwhelmingly outnumbered by the 1,300,000 English. Furthermore, they were not compact but scattered throughout a vast area. These disadvantages were partially compensated for by their centralized government, which functioned infinitely better in time of war than the disconnected colonial governments of the English, and by the fact that they already held the strategic points in the territories under dispute. However, the stronger economic strength of the English colonies, the superior sea power of Great Britain, the driving force of the elder Pitt, the great empire builder, and the persistence of the British soldiers, Amherst and Wolfe, proved in the end victorious and the great colonial empire of France passed largely to England. By the Treaty of Paris in 1763, France ceded to England all of Canada and the land east of the Mississippi; of her vast American empire she retained only the islands of St. Pierre and Miquelon off the coast of Newfoundland, to be used for drying fish, and the sugar islands of Martinique, Guadeloupe, and St. Lucia. From Spain England took Florida, but France ceded to Spain New Orleans and the country west of the Mississippi.

THE SPANISH BORDER

Spain remained a factor in the colonization of the present United States long after France had been eliminated, and the gradual advance northward of the Spanish frontier brought her into conflict with England, France, and the United States in turn. The first permanent white settlement in the limits of the present United States was made by the Spaniards at St. Augustine, Florida, in 1565, after they had destroyed a French colony fifty miles northward. With the cessation of French attempts to settle the Carolinas, no further impetus was given to the Spanish advance northward in Florida until the British settled Georgia in 1733. Hostilities commenced during King George's War, when Oglethorpe made an unsuccessful attempt to capture St. Augustine in 1740, and a return attack was made by the Spanish two years later. The Peace of Aix-la-Chapelle made no change in the Georgia-Florida frontier, but the Peace of Paris at the conclusion of the French and Indian War transferred Florida to England, in whose hands it remained until 1783, when it was returned to Spain.

In the meantime the Spanish frontier was gradually pushing northward from Mexico; the motive was the lure of fabled riches and the desire to win souls to Christianity, and missionaries, soldiers, and fur traders led the way. It was in 1598 that Juan de Oñate entered New Mexico with the definite intent to settle. Santa Fé, founded in 1609, became the capital of the new colony, whose limits were extended during the century as the Franciscans and Jesuits established new missions among the Indians. By 1680 there were more than 2500 Spaniards in the colony, and by the end of the century they had practically subjected the Indians. Eastern Texas, which had been temporarily occupied, 1690–1693, was reentered in 1716 by an expedition which founded San Antonio in that year. The expedition into Texas had been undertaken principally as a countermove against the French, who were making trading expeditions westward from Louisiana and establishing relations with the Indians of Texas and Arkansas. When war broke out in 1719 between France and Spain, the contest spread to the colonies, where it was waged along the whole border from Pensacola to the Platte River. The expedition of the Marquis of Aguayo (1720–1722), governor of Coahuila, into Texas clinched Spain's hold on the new province, although the territory in dispute between France and Spain continued to extend from the Trinity to the Mississippi. By 1700 Spanish ranches were to be seen in Arizona, but the Spanish advance into California did not occur until later. The Portola expedition founded San Diego in 1769, and the next year a post at Monterey was established. The year of the Declaration of Independence saw the beginnings of San Francisco; San José was founded in 1777 and Los Angeles in 1779. At the conclusion of the Revolution the land now encompassed by the United States was under the control of two nations, the infant American Republic and Spain, with Great Britain and Russia disputing the northern boundary line.

BRITISH WESTERN POLICY, 1763–1775

In the intercolonial wars just discussed, the Indians usually sided with the French, and the reason is fairly obvious. The French were chiefly interested in furs and provided a market where the Indian could dispose of the proceeds of the hunt; the English, on the other hand, wanted land, and their occupation of it meant an end to the furs. "Are you ignorant of the difference between the king of England and the king of France?" asked Duquesne of the Iroquois. "Go see the forts that our king has established and you will see that you can still hunt under their very walls. . . . The English, on the contrary, are no sooner in possession of a place than the game is driven away. The forest falls before them as they advance, and the soil is laid bare so that you can scarce find the wherewithal to erect a shelter for the night." [11] The

[11] Quoted by F. J. Turner, *The Frontier in American History*, p. 14.

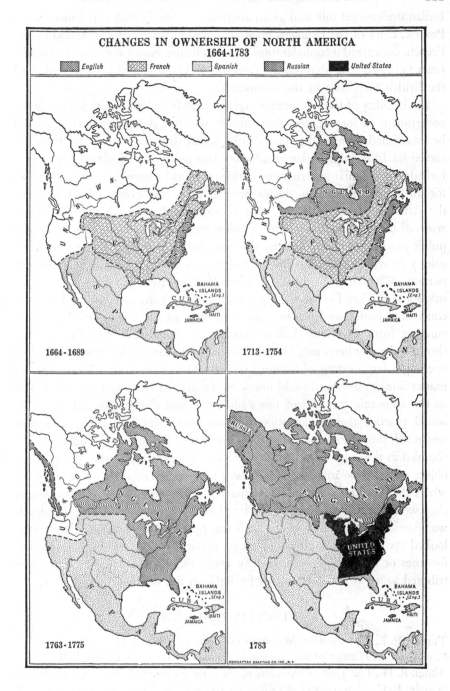

CHANGES IN OWNERSHIP OF NORTH AMERICA
1664-1783

Indian understood this, and as an aftermath to the French and Indian wars, Pontiac, chief of the Ottawas, greatest of Indian warriors and friend of the French, organized a confederation of tribes in the Northwest and during the years 1763 and 1764 attacked the frontiers of Virginia and Pennsylvania and the British forts west of the mountains.

The inability of the colonies properly to handle Indian affairs led the home government to formulate a policy under which a definite boundary should be established between the lands to be settled by white men and those reserved for Indians. In order to carry out this policy the Proclamation of 1763 forbade the colonial governors to grant warrants of survey or to pass patents for any lands beyond the heads or sources of the rivers which fall into the Atlantic Ocean from the west or northwest, all such territory being reserved for the use of the Indians unless purchased in the king's name at a public meeting of the Indians by the governor or commander-in-chief of the colony in which the land lay. In reality, a series of treaties, the most important of which were those signed at Fort Stanwix (1768) with the Iroquois and at Fort Lochabar (1770) with the southern Indians, established a continuous boundary line (in some cases west of the sources of the rivers) running from the Great Lakes west of the Appalachians to Florida and through the southern part of east and west Florida to the Mississippi, thus opening a large extent of territory to immediate settlement. This policy, no matter how well meant, could not long obviate the irreconcilable differences in the economic interests of the white man and the Indian. Although in actual practice the proclamation did not materially delay the movement westward, the attempt on the part of the British to control this advance was received in the colonies with dissatisfaction. Many believed that the primary object of the Proclamation of 1763 was to confine the colonists to territory where they could be kept in due subjection to the mother country and where they would be within reach of the trade and commerce of Great Britain. It was particularly resented, as we shall see, by wealthy land speculators, who looked upon western land as the easiest opportunity to recoup their waning fortunes or build new ones. In any event the Proclamation of 1763 contributed to the dissatisfaction that brought on the Revolution.

SELECTED READINGS

Turner, F. J., *The Frontier in American History*, Chaps. I–IV.
Paxson, F. L., *History of the American Frontier, 1763–1893*, Chaps. I, II.
Akagi, R. H., *The Town Proprietors of the New England Colonies*, Chaps. I–VII.
Semple, E. C., *American History and Its Geographic Conditions*, Chaps. IV–VI.
Mathews, L. K., *The Expansion of New England*, Chaps. I–V.

7

Economic Causes of
the Revolution

BRITISH MERCANTILISM APPLIED TO THE AMERICAN COLONIES

LIKE all revolutions, the revolt in America against British rule can be explained by no simple formula. It came from an interplay of many forces—economic, political, and social. Like most revolutions, however, that in America resolves itself in the final analysis mainly into a conflict between the economic interests of two groups. But it was more than a simple conflict between the economic interests of Britain and her mainland colonies; it was in many ways a revolt against a social and political system no longer applicable to conditions in America.

The economic conflict, as has already been suggested, rested upon a general theory of imperialism popular in the sixteenth, seventeenth, and eighteenth centuries and known as mercantilism.[1] It was a policy which aimed at building strong, wealthy, and independent national states, and its supporters believed that this could be achieved only by promoting economic independence and a favorable balance of trade. Specifically, they hoped to achieve this by (1) encouraging native shipping in order not to be dependent upon the ships of foreign countries to carry native products, and by providing an efficient navy with well-trained seamen in time of war; (2) protecting and aiding home agriculture so that the nation might produce for itself sufficient foodstuffs and raw materials for manufacture; (3) protecting and stimulating home industries in order to be self-sufficing industrially and to provide employment to citizens; (4) maintaining a favorable balance of trade in order to amass and keep in the home country as large an amount of metallic currency as possible. The nation which had the most gold and silver, it was believed, was the wealthiest.

The mercantile policy, it is obvious, was essentially concerned with the welfare of the mother country. If colonies were acquired, their purpose was to round out the economic life of the home country. It was their business to

[1] Above, pp. 78–79.

produce commodities not obtainable at home, chiefly raw materials, and to use manufactured goods produced in the mother country. Colonies were to offer opportunities for the development of a large merchant marine, profits to ship-owners engaged in the carrying trade, wealth to importers and exporters, and opportunities for the investment of capital. In brief, they were to sub-serve the interests of the mother country. If, in this process, the interests of the colonies were also served, well and good. If there was a conflict, it must be resolved to the benefit of the home country. Under no conditions, if it could be avoided, were colonies to be competitors.

Although the roots of British mercantilism were planted during the six-teenth century, it was not until the days of Cromwell and after that the great statutes were enacted upon which British mercantilism rested. By that time England had become a maritime power of importance and was beginning to build a colonial empire. The most famous of her Navigation Acts, passed in 1651, provided that: (1) no goods of the growth or manufacture of Asia, Africa, or America shall be imported into England or the dominions thereof, except in ships of which the proprietor, master, and a major part of the mariners are English; (2) no goods of the growth or manufacture of Europe shall be imported into England or the dominions thereof, except in English ships and in such foreign ships as do belong to that country where the goods are produced and manufactured; (3) no goods of foreign growth or manu-facture, that are to be brought into England, shall be brought from any other place than the place of growth and production, or from those ports where alone the goods can be shipped or whence they are usually shipped after transportation. The intent of this Act was to give to English or colonial shippers a monopoly of the carrying trade.

This Act was strengthened in 1660 by an "Act for the Encouraging and Increasing of Shipping and Navigation" (2 Charles II, Chap. 18), which provided that goods carried to and from England must be transported not only in British-manned ships but in British-built ships or ships built in the British colonies. The Act of 1660, besides providing for the protection of ship-ping and thus the development of the merchant marine, sought to regulate the trade of the colonies so as to add to the monopoly of navigation that of colonial commerce and markets. It was enacted that "no sugars, tobacco, cotton-wool, indigo, ginger, fustick, or other dyeing woods, of the growth, produce, or manufacture of any English plantations in America, Asia or Africa" should be shipped to any place whatsoever except England. This list was expanded in 1706 by the addition of the naval stores—tar, pitch, turpen-tine, hemp, masts, and yards; by rice in 1706–1730; by copper ore, beaver, and other furs, in 1722; by molasses in 1733; by whale fins, hides, iron, lumber, raw silk, and pearl ashes in 1764. The non-enumerated articles, chief of which were fish, grain, and rum, could be exported anywhere until 1766, but after that date exportation was confined to nations south of Cape Finisterre. The latter provision virtually excluded the colonies from direct export trade with any port of northern Europe except England.

Not only did England seek to control colonial exports, but by an Act of 1663 she sought to monopolize the handling of imports into the colonies. This Act prohibited by high duties the importation into the colonies of any European goods unless brought via the British Isles and in British (including colonial) -built and -manned ships, an Act which allowed duties and commissions to be collected in England before European goods reached America, and limited the profits of carrying such commodities to British or colonial merchantmen. Exceptions were made in the case of salt from Spain for the New England fisheries, wine from Madeira and the Azores, and provisions and horses from Ireland and Scotland. These laws were constantly evaded by colonial merchants who shipped such enumerated articles as sugar and tobacco directly to European ports without taking them first to England, under the pretense that the commodities were destined for another colony. In an effort to make this unprofitable, Parliament in 1673 enacted a law (reaffirmed and interpreted in 1696) levying a tax on enumerated articles shipped from one colony to another, equal in amount to the import taxes levied on the articles in England.

The British mercantilist policy was concerned not only with control of the carrying trade and the regulation of imports and exports, but also with control of the few manufacturing enterprises in the colonies. To prevent colonial manufacturing from coming into competition with the home industry, colonial governors were instructed "to discourage all manufactures and to give accurate accounts of any indications of the same." That representatives of the crown well understood the British attitude and were only too sympathetic with it may be seen in the words of Lord Cornbury, governor of New York, 1702–1708, who wrote to the Board of Trade:

I am well informed, that upon Long Island and in Connecticut, they are setting up a woollen Manufacture, and I myself have seen serge made upon Long Island that any man may wear. Now if they begin to make serge, they will in time make course cloth, and then fine; we have as good fullers earth and tobacco pipe clay in this Province, as any in the world; how farr this will be for the service of England, I submit to better judgements; but however I hope I may be pardoned, if I declare my opinion to be, that all these Colloneys, which are but twigs belonging to the main Tree (England,) ought to be kept intirely dependent upon and subservient to England, and that can never be if they are suffered to goe on in the notions they have, that as they are Englishmen, soe they may set up the same Manufactures here, as people may doe in England;

for the consequences will be that if once they see they can cloath themselves not only comfortably but handsomely too, without the help of England, they who are already not very found of submitting to Government, would soon think of putting in execution designs they had long harboured in their breasts. This will not seem strange when you consider what sort of people this Countrey is inhabited by. . . .[2]

In actual practice it was impossible for either British or colonial governments completely to control household industries or even those of the small shop. If Great Britain had been willing to import the fish and agricultural commodities of the northern colonies a greater importation of British manufactured goods could have been effected. Since she would not, a certain amount of colonial manufacturing was bound to develop.

There were two industries, however, that Britain guarded with a jealous eye—woolens and iron. England had already become a leading manufacturer of woolens and one-half of her exports to the colonies were woolen goods. So hostile were home manufacturers to competition that as early as 1699 a Woolen Act was passed providing that no woolen goods might be exported from the colonies or sent from one colony to another, and in the following year the duty on woolens imported into the colonies from England was removed. As a result of this legislation the manufacture of cloth for sale was checked and the hold of the English woolen merchants upon the American trade was prolonged for a century. The abundance of beaver gave the colonist a decided advantage in the manufacture of beaver hats. A petition in 1731 from a company of felt makers caused Parliament to institute an inquiry which disclosed that 10,000 hats a year were manufactured in New England and New York. Thereupon an Act containing the following provisions was passed: (1) that after 1732 no hat should be put on board a ship or cart for exportation to England, or for transportation from one colony to another; (2) that no one should make felt hats unless he had served an apprenticeship for seven years. No master should have more than two apprentices, and they could not serve for less than seven years, nor could they be Negroes. The penalty for violation was £500.

The iron industry, which had commenced in 1643 with John Winthrop's smelting furnace near Lynn, had grown by 1750 to healthy proportions. England was in need of iron, and conflicting interests until 1750 had prevented adverse legislation. To encourage the production of raw material but discourage the manufacture of iron products, a law was passed in 1750 providing (1) that bar iron might be imported duty free to the port of London, and pig iron to any port in England; and (2) that no mill or other engine for

[2] Letter to Secretary Hedges in 1705, in E. B. O'Callaghan (ed.), *Documents Relating to the Colonial History of New York*, IV, 115.

rolling or slitting iron, no plating forge to work with a tilt hammer, nor any furnace for making steel should be erected in the colonies. In 1757 it was provided that bar iron might be imported into any British port free of duty.

These restrictions upon manufacturing may not have seriously impeded American economic development, but the fact that England was so quick to protect the interests of her citizens at home as against those in the colonies did not go unnoticed. "A colonist cannot make a button, a horse shoe, nor a hobnail," complained a Boston newspaper in 1765, "but some sooty iron-monger or respectable buttonmaker of Britain shall bawl and squall that his honor's worship is most egregiously maltreated, injured, cheated, and robbed by the rascally American Republicans."[3] To the disgust of the colonists, these bawls and squalls were seriously considered by the British government.

Not the least among the economic conflicts between Britain and her colonies was the friction that arose over the currency policy. What metallic currency appeared in the colonies, whether English, Portuguese, or Spanish, was soon drained off to England because of the unequal balance of trade.[4] In their need to carry on the normal demands of trade, the colonists had resorted to the use of wampum, warehouse receipts, and other devices. In the end it was inevitable that various types of paper money should be tried. Massachusetts began it in 1690 when she issued paper money (without metallic backing) to pay her soldiers returning from the unsuccessful expedition against Quebec. It was the origin of paper money in America, and the money was kept near par by making it payable for taxes at 5 per cent advance over coin. Encouraged by the success of the first issue, she authorized a second in 1709. Connecticut, New Hampshire, Rhode Island, New York, and New Jersey followed before 1711, and other colonies later. Depreciation generally ensued, for this paper money was soon issued in excess of the domestic monetary demand at gold prices. In the meantime in 1704 the so-called "loan banks," designed to issue paper money on mortgages and real estate, were established in Massachusetts; but before these schemes could go far, Parliament intervened in 1741 and applied the Bubble Act of 1720, which put an end to these banks. In 1751 Parliament forbade the issue of bills of credit as legal tender in New England, and in 1764 extended the prohibition to the remaining colonies.[5]

---

[3] Boston *Gazette*, April 29, 1765. Quoted by C. and M. Beard, *Rise of American Civilization*, I, 195.

[4] Above, p. 76.

[5] These restrictive acts, says Dewey, "did not entirely suppress colonial paper money; under the exceptions prescribed, temporary treasury notes as well as notes of loan banks which had not been suppressed continued to circulate; so that in 1774 it was estimated that $12,000,000 were in current use." *Financial History of the United States* (8th ed., 1922), p. 30. Harlow (*American Historical Review*, Vol. XXXV, No. 1, Oct., 1929, p. 47) puts the figure probably more accurately at $22,000,000.

These Acts curtailing the right of the colonies to issue paper money were passed by the British Parliament mainly to safeguard the English creditor. Along with them went an Act of 1752 making the lands, tenements, and slaves of American debtors subject to levy in England for obligations of their owners. In America, interestingly enough, the problem of paper currency went far deeper than any protection of the English creditor. Here both the small debtor farmer and the plantation owner realized the opportunity afforded by an inflated currency to ease the situation in which they found themselves. These groups who were interested in paper currency, however, were usually opposed by the wealthier creditor merchants of the towns. British laws forbidding American paper money, in fact, came from petitions of wealthy colonists as well as British merchants.[6] In any event, British restrictions helped to alienate the great mass of small farmers and even the debtor plantation owners of the South. England's attitude on this matter did much to sow the seeds of discontent.

EFFECT OF THE "OLD COLONIAL SYSTEM"

In surveying the period from 1650 to 1763 to determine the actual effect of the mercantile system as applied to the British mainland colonies, it is evident that while the policy was essentially selfish and the interests of the colonists were sacrificed to those of the home country, its effects were by no means disastrous. On the whole, the American colonists enjoyed an economic prosperity and a political liberty unusual in the eighteenth century. British rule, as Adam Smith correctly stated, was "less illiberal and oppressive than that of any other European nation."

The explanation of this prosperity rests primarily on three facts. First of all, the interests of the colonists often ran parallel to those of the mother country. It was fundamentally sound for them to devote themselves to extractive industries. In the second place, although the bounties offered by England for various products in some cases produced artificial conditions, in others they aided a logical development and were a source of wealth for the colonists. Also beneficial in certain instances were the preferential tariff rates which gave the colonists a virtual monopoly of the British market. Typical of these were the substantial bounties offered on naval supplies and indigo, and the preferential treatment given in England to tobacco, lumber, iron, whale oil, and pot and pearl ashes. It should also be noted that the duty on commodities bound for the colonies via England was generally refunded so that in many cases the colonists could purchase these commodities cheaper than could the English.

[6] Curtis Nettels, *The Roots of American Civilization*, pp. 530–537.

The third reason, and perhaps the most important of all, why British mer-cantilism did not press more heavily, was the fact that the most harmful legis-lation was either evaded or not enforced. During the first half of the eighteenth century England followed the policy of Robert Walpole, who took for his motto *"Quieta non movere"* ("Let sleeping dogs lie"). It was during this period of "salutary neglect" that the West Indian trade reached such great proportions and that evasion of the Act of 1663 requiring European goods to be imported via England was so prevalent. Colonial merchants evaded the laws by loading tobacco or other enumerated articles without giving bond that they would be delivered in England, by loading or unload-ing at other than ports of entry, or by collusion with British customs officers. It was estimated that in 1700 one-half of the trade of Boston was in violation of the law. The evasion of the law continued actively until the 1760's, par-ticularly in the case of the Molasses Act of 1733. As we have seen, much of New England's prosperity was based upon the importation of specie and molasses from the West Indies and the manufacture from molasses of rum for the fur trade, the slave trade, and the fishing industry. This molasses the New Englanders could purchase from the French, Dutch, and Spanish islands more cheaply than from the British islands. At the behest of British plantation owners in the West Indies, Parliament in 1733 placed duties on goods imported from foreign plantations. This effort to protect British sugar planters to the detriment of New England trade fortunately remained a dead letter until 1763.[7]

In view of these facts, it appears that up to 1763 the colonists did not suffer severely from the "Old Colonial System" of England but on the contrary had grown rapidly in population and wealth. But it must still be remembered that the mercantile system embodied procedures that were likely to be detri-mental to colonial life. Disadvantages to the colonists were: (1) Monopoly of the carrying trade by English and colonial shippers removed foreign competition which may have had a tendency to make freight rates higher. (2) A middleman's profit had to be paid to the English merchant, since most of the colonial products had to pass through his warehouses. (3) The colonies were regarded as a source of cheap raw material for the English manufac-turer, and at the same time as a market for selling the finished product at

---

[7] David A. Wells, writing on the "American Merchant Marine" in Lalor's *Cyclopædia of Political Science* (I, 75), says of the colonial merchants, "Nine-tenths of their merchants were smugglers. One-quarter of all the signers of the Declaration of Independence were bred to commerce, to the command of ships and to contraband trade. Hancock, Trumbull (Brother Jonathan), and Hamilton were all known to be cognizant of contraband transactions and ap-proved of them. John Hancock was the prince of contraband traders, and, with John Adams as his counsel, was appointed for trial before the admiralty court in Boston, at the exact hour of the shedding of blood at Lexington, in a suit for $500,000 penalties alleged to have been incurred by him as a smuggler."

his own price. (4) The colonists' supply of gold and silver with which to pay for these manufactured goods was small and constantly being exported to England; yet one of their greatest sources of gold, the Spanish, Dutch, and French West Indies, was virtually closed to them. (5) Colonial efforts to ease the currency and credit situation were disallowed by the British government.

BRITISH POLICY AFTER 1763

Enough has been said to make clear the inherent clash between British capitalism and the expanding economic interests of American merchants, plantation owners, and farmers. While the colonies were young and the laws evaded, British mercantilism did not press too heavily. But in 1763 more than a century had passed since the first great Navigation Act of Cromwell. The colonies had grown in population and wealth and the disadvantages of the British colonial system were pressing more heavily upon them. To a certain extent colonial economic life had adjusted itself to these disadvantages, but further pressure was bound to cause trouble. It was the increasing of this pressure after 1763 which deepened the clash of interests and brought to a climax the forces leading to the Revolution.

Essentially there was no fundamental change in British policy after 1763 beyond strengthening and enforcing a policy already a century old—a policy based on protecting British interests and keeping the colonies in a subservient economic position. It is true that after the defeat of France in 1763 the great statesman, William Pitt, sought to weld more firmly the bonds which held the empire together. But these were essentially the old bonds by which the empire served the interests of British merchant capitalism. It was the protection of British sugar interests rather than dreams of a great empire that decided Pitt to take Canada instead of the French Islands of Guadelupe, Martinique, and St. Lucia at the end of the French and Indian War. It was, in fact, this clash between the sugar interests of the British West Indies and those of the northern colonies that brought the first measures leading directly to the Revolution.

The great commodity of colonial trade in the eighteenth century was sugar. By the 1760's British investments in Jamaica, Barbados, and other sugar islands amounted to the enormous sum of £60,000,000, six times the amount of British investments in the mainland colonies. Seventy "sugar lords" sat in the British Parliament to protect these interests. But absentee ownership, worn-out soil, inefficient management, and a high export tax at the island ports had put the British growers at a distinct disadvantage in comparison with those in the French islands. Colonial importers were buying their sugar and molasses at 25 to 40 per cent less from the French, and the British islands were supplying only one-eighth of the needs of the mainland colonists. Angered that this trade between the mainland colonies and the French islands continued even during the French and Indian War to the great advantage of the French, Pitt ordered the Navy in 1761 to stamp out smuggling in the foreign West Indian trade. In the same year colonial courts were ordered to issue writs of assistance (general search warrants) to aid in apprehending smugglers. That the colonists thus early understood the significance of this policy of tightening control is clear. James Otis thundered against the writs of assistance so eloquently that John Adams later called his speech the "opening gun of the Revolution."

With the end of that war, Grenville, the new Prime Minister, and Townshend, president of the Board of Trade, backed by George III, determined to end the policy of "salutary neglect." Believing that the American colonies should be brought under more direct supervision of the crown and that the colonists should help pay the war debts incurred in their defense, they decided (1) to enforce more strictly the laws of trade, and (2) to raise revenues in the colonies by means of the Molasses Act. It was this attempt to enforce the old commercial policy, along with the new imperialism, that was the greatest of all the causes of the Revolution. England's policy now became a real grievance and one which to the commercial interests seemed to spell ruin. Their opposition was immediate and strenuous.

The first measure under the new régime was the Sugar Act of 1764, designed to provide for the defense of the colonies. It cut in half the duties of the Molasses Act of 1733, in the hope that the removal of the prohibitive rates might induce merchants to be more honest and that some revenue might be raised. On the face of it this Act, which reduced the import duties on foreign molasses from sixpence to threepence a gallon, seemed more liberal than the Act of 1733, but the British government intended to enforce the new Act. British naval officers were to collect the customs duties, and cases arising from indictments for smuggling were to be tried by British admiralty courts. In addition, duties were laid on sugar, indigo, coffee, wines, silks, and calicoes, and at the same time the number of enumerated articles was increased. Economic depression was felt at once in New England and the middle colonies, and the reaction from it was apparent in the South.

The Sugar Act was supplemented in 1765 by the Stamp Act, which provided that stamps varying in cost from a halfpenny to £10 be affixed to licenses, contracts, deeds, wills, newspapers, pamphlets, almanacs, and other papers. The Stamp Act, following the Sugar Act so closely, created an excitement unparalleled in the colonies. When petitions and remonstrances failed, a boycott of English goods was inaugurated, merchants binding themselves to import no British goods until the Act was repealed. In England merchants and manufacturers were affected to such an extent that in 1766 the Stamp Act was repealed and the Sugar Act revised downward, although the concessions were accompanied by a Declaratory Act asserting the legal right of Parliament to legislate for the colonies "in all cases whatsoever."

Rejoicing followed the repeal of the Stamp Act, and opposition to the British government might have subsided had not the imperial authority in 1765 passed a Quartering Act, declaring that the colonists should provide for the light, lodging, and fuel of garrisons to be placed in specified districts. In 1767 Charles Townshend, who was now the leading spirit in the Cabinet, forced through Parliament the Townshend Acts, one of which imposed duties on glass, paper, painters' colors, red and white lead, and tea. Though not high, these tariffs fell on articles of general consumption and raised the cost of living. More dangerous than the duties were other features of the Townshend Acts which called for a reorganization of the customs service, with courts of admiralty established in the colonies to expedite cases of smuggling, and which provided that the money raised be used to pay the expenses of the civil government. The latter provision was particularly obnoxious because it would have removed from the colonists their chief weapon in their conflict with British officials. A special Act suspended the New York Assembly because it had refused to comply with a law of 1765 calling for the adequate quartering of soldiers. Irritating also was a part of one of the Acts that reaffirmed the legality of the writs of assistance.

Immediately following the passing of the Townshend Acts the colonists again resorted to their policy of non-intercourse. The boycott of 1768–1769 was more than a voluntary movement; it was backed and encouraged by political bodies, and it was much more thorough and universal than the non-importation movements following the Stamp Act. The value of English goods imported into New England and the middle colonies dropped from £1,363,000 in 1768 to £504,000 in 1769. While imports from England slightly increased in the southern colonies, the falling off for the whole country was over £500,000, sufficient to cause enough economic unrest in both England and America to bring about the partial repeal of the Townshend Acts in 1770.

As a matter of principle, in order to assert the power of the crown over the colonies, a tax of 3d. a pound on tea was retained, but a refund of 12d. a pound was allowed on tea exported from England to America, thus offering to America cheaper tea than could be purchased in England. Although the most tyrannical and objectionable aspects of the Townshend Acts, including the tax on tea, remained on the statute books, opposition to British policy collapsed rapidly after 1770. Non-importation broke down, trade was resumed, and prosperity returned. Imports, which had fallen to £1,604,000, jumped to £4,200,000 in 1771. Prosperous merchants, now making money in spite of import duties, turned their backs on radical political leaders and on the mobs they had so freely used against British policy, and sought to quiet agitation.

Trade Between Great Britain and the American Mainland
Colonies, 1745–1776 [8]

Any hope of ironing out the difficulties with the British government, however, was prevented by revolutionary agitators at home and by the stupid maintenance of her old colonial policy by Britain and her colonial agents. In Massachusetts Samuel Adams kept up a running fight with the governor in an effort to keep the revolutionary spirit alive. With others of similar mind, like Patrick Henry and Thomas Jefferson, he organized committees of correspondence throughout the colonies to exchange views and information. In the end it was the British government, unwittingly perhaps, that ended possibilities of reconciliation. The climax came in an effort to save the East India Company from bankruptcy. That famous company, which had long exploited the great riches of India with little interference, had fallen on evil days through extravagance or mismanagement. Its bankruptcy would drag with it a horde of British politicians and capitalists and must therefore be prevented. The company had 17,000,000 pounds of surplus tea stored in its

[8] E. R. Johnson, *et al., History of Domestic and Foreign Commerce of the United States,* I, 120.

warehouses. Among the measures adopted to save the company was one that gave it the right to sell directly to America and remitted the customary shilling-a-pound tax on all tea transshipped to the colonies. This would help the company find a market and at the same time provide the colonists with cheaper tea than they had ever enjoyed. Before the Tea Act of 1773 the colonists paid four profits—to the East India Company, the English middleman, the American middleman or importer, and the local shopkeeper. Allowing the company to import directly to the colonies eliminated two groups of middlemen as well as two profits. Furthermore, such an arrangement would inevitably give it a monopoly on the importation of tea to the colonies. If the company could be given a monopoly on tea, why not on other commodities that it transported from India? If a monopoly could be conferred upon the East India Company, a similar monopoly on other commodities might be granted to any company. Obviously, other principles besides that of taxation were involved. Instantly the most powerful class in the seaport towns was aroused. Merchants like Hancock, who had been importing and paying the duty on tea, now strenuously opposed the Tea Act, and their opposition, in conjunction with the activities of the radical politicians, led directly to the break with Great Britain.

When the tea arrived in American ports vigilance committees usually destroyed it or refused to allow it to be landed. In Boston a group of citizens disguised as Indians boarded the vessels and dumped the cargo of 342 chests of tea into the water. The "Boston Tea Party" was a direct challenge to British authority and Parliament responded by four disciplinary measures, known as the "Intolerable Acts." These Acts closed the port of Boston until the tea should be paid for, revised the Massachusetts charter so as to remove some of its liberal features, provided for the trial in England of colonial agents accused of violence in executing their duty, and revived the Quartering Act of 1765 for the purpose of stationing soldiers in Massachusetts. By another Act which had nothing to do with the Boston situation but was the result of long study over the problem of Canadian administration, the territory between the Ohio and the Great Lakes was annexed to the Province of Quebec. This last Act was not intended as a retaliatory measure, but it was resented as extinguishing the claims of Virginia, New York, Connecticut, and Massachusetts to these regions and placing them under an autocratic government in which the Roman Catholic Church was established by law.

With the passing of these Acts, events leading to the Revolution followed each other in quick succession. Immediately a third boycott was organized, encouraged by the different colonial assemblies and by the Continental Congress on December 1, 1774. The colonial merchants, made wiser by their serious losses in the former embargo period and unwilling to strengthen the hands of the non-merchant radicals, were loath to embark upon this system again, but public opinion carried all before it and the third boycott was more strictly enforced than either of the other two. English imports into the colonies dropped from £2,590,000 in 1774 to £201,000 in 1775. This shrinkage, enormous for the period just at the dawn of the Industrial Revolution, was a stunning blow to English factory towns and seaports, and Parliament was flooded with petitions. The king and his ministers would not yield, and in March, 1775, Massachusetts was declared to be in a state of rebellion; the fishermen of New England were forbidden the Grand Banks, and the trade of the New England colonies (extended in April to most of the other colonies) with other countries than Great Britain, Ireland, and the British West Indies was interdicted. Nine months later all intercourse with the colonies was prohibited.

From what has been said it is obvious that the economic causes of the Revolution emanating from the commercial policies of Great Britain were far from being "accidents of politics, conceived in the heat of controversy." They were, on the other hand, "the matured fruits of a mercantile theory of state which regarded colonial trade as the property of the metropolis, to be monopolized by its citizens and made subservient in all things to their interests," [9] and this policy had been consistently followed by Puritan and Cavalier, by Stuart and Hanoverian, by Whig and Tory. Fallacious in theory and disastrous in practice, mercantilism in Europe was in the saddle; and it was left to the mainland colonies of England in America to strike the first blow against it.

The Problem of Western Land

Among the major causes of friction between Britain and her mainland colonies was the changing policy after 1763 with respect to western land. Up to that time, as Professor Nettels makes clear, Britain had pursued a land policy which "reflected the purposes of British merchant capitalism." [10] The object was not to obtain revenue for the crown itself through land sales and quitrents; it was rather to promote settlement to provide markets for British goods and profits for British merchants. Small plots were granted to bona fide settlers and larger grants were made to speculators on condition that they settle a designated number of families on them. A rapid settlement of the frontier was also encouraged as a means of protection against the French and Spanish menace and for the promotion of the fur trade.

With the removal of the French menace in 1763 one necessity for pro-

[9] C. and M. Beard, *Rise of American Civilization*, I, 103.
[10] Curtis Nettels, *The Roots of American Civilization*, p. 602.

moting frontier settlement had ended. Uprisings of Indians under Pontiac in the same year which decimated the frontier of Virginia and Pennsylvania [11] also indicated a possible change in frontier policy. Various factors entered into any consideration of the British policy. With the great Canadian fur trade now in British hands it seemed wiser to many that further settlement of the West be discouraged or kept well under control lest the frontier destroy this lucrative business. British merchants also argued that further advance would extend beyond the mountains and be out of their reach. This advance would draw off settlers in the East and endanger the seaboard area where British capitalists had substantial investments. Moreover, if there was to be any development of the trans-Allegheny region it should be under the direct control of the British government so that British land speculators might have better access to the profits. A definite revival of interest in colonial land speculation was evident in England after 1763. Nor was the British government oblivious to the possibility of income from land sales and quitrents. These might provide funds for colonial administration which would both ease the burden of British taxpayers and at the same time free British colonial officials from dependence on colonial legislatures for financial grants.

In 1763 the British government issued the famous proclamation which forbade colonial governors to warrant surveys or grant patents "for any lands beyond the heads or sources of any of the rivers which fall into the Atlantic Ocean from the West or Northwest." Its immediate cause may have been to pacify the Indians, but all the considerations outlined above form part of its background. From the point of view of the colonists it was a new departure, but from that of the British colonial policy it represented the old subservience of American interests to those of British merchant capitalism.

Whatever the motives, the Proclamation of 1763 was bitterly resented in America. The resentment was strengthened when the crown in 1774 issued new regulations with regard to ungranted lands in certain of the old colonies and in the rest of the western lands. Quitrents on new grants were to be more than double the usual charge; there were to be no further free gifts of lands by the governors, and all tracts were to be sold at auction at not less than sixpence an acre. In America the Proclamation and the additional regulations cut across the interests of two groups—the bona fide frontier settler ever on the move to the West, and the large land speculator. With opportunities for investment by American merchant capitalists restricted by various kinds of British regulations, land speculation was the easiest way out. It was the natural and simplest way to make money quickly and few men of wealth were not actively engaged in it. While land specu-

[11] Above, p. 112.

lators in the colonies that had no western land were not averse to having the British rather than the colonial governments supervise speculation in this land, there was a feeling on the part of all that the new regulations

BRITISH COLONIES ON
EVE OF REVOLUTION

Scale of Miles
0   100   200   300   400

were a blow at American interests. Those who felt them most severely, perhaps, were the southern plantation owners. Many of them were finding it increasingly difficult to operate profitably under the restrictions of mercantilist regulations and many were sinking deeper into debt to British investors. The one way out was investment and speculation in western land. With this avenue of escape cut off, many were ripe for revolution. This helps to explain why great plantation owners in the South joined the patriot cause, whereas in the North a majority of the wealthy were Tories.

BACKGROUND OF THE REVOLUTION

Mercantilist regulations as they applied to shipping, commerce, manufacturing, and currency, together with the problem of western land, have been discussed in some detail. But they do not by any means give a complete picture of the economic and social causes leading to the Revolution. Historians of an earlier day made much of the battle over taxation and of the cry of "no taxation without representation." This, we know, has been overemphasized. In the literal political sense there had always been taxation without representation in English colonies from the beginning of colonization. Moreover, what new taxes were imposed after 1763 were quickly repealed (with the exception of a minor tax on tea) as soon as colonial opposition became strong.

There was, nevertheless, a psychological antipathy to taxation, both colonial and imperial, which must be recognized, and which undoubtedly played a part in the final break. No one has better summarized America's attitude toward taxation than Callender:

It was the fact that social conditions in the colonies were such as to render all taxation except for purely local purposes extremely unpopular. In the unorganized, dispersed society of the colonies it was impossible for men to recognize any connection between most of the governmental expenditures, which occasioned taxation, and their own interests and welfare. Taxes were a burden and did not seem to be justified by necessity, especially after the French had been expelled from the continent. That a great reluctance to pay taxes existed in all the colonies, there can be no doubt. It was one of the marked characteristics of the American people long after their separation from England. Down to the time of the Civil War it constituted one of the difficulties American statesmen always had to face. It was the principal rock upon which the confederation split, and Hamilton recognized it as the chief problem to be solved in the establishment of the new government. Until the Civil War it was strong enough to prevent the establishment of a respectable revenue system in either federal or state finance. It was this unwillingness to bear the burden of taxation that caused nine of the states to default in the payment of interest on their public debts in the early forties, and at least one of them to repudiate the debt altogether. It was fear of this also that caused so long a delay in levying adequate taxes to support the government during the Civil War. Here we have an explanation of that extravagant and, to us now, somewhat incomprehensible opposition to the slight burden of taxation which England proposed to levy upon the colonies.[12]

[12] G. S. Callender, *Selections from the Economic History of the United States, 1765–1860,* p. 123. Quoted by permission of the publishers, Ginn and Company.

Undoubtedly one potent cause in bringing about the separation was the period of depression or "hard times" which preceded the Revolution. This was in part a letdown from the artificial prosperity of the French and Indian War. It was also partly, but not entirely, the result of the commercial and financial legislation of the period 1763–1765 and the resulting economic dislocation. Other factors were at work to produce this economic depression, nor was it confined to the colonies. It was the period in England of both the Industrial and the Agricultural Revolutions, with the unrest and instability attendant upon these phenomena. With the introduction of the factory system and capitalism on a big scale came what was perhaps the first of the great cyclical fluctuations which in recent years have become so common.[13] The depression was accentuated by poor crops in England between 1765 and 1774.

The hard times in England were reflected in America; decreased buying power in England combined with the enforcement of the mercantile system was disastrous to the commercial classes of New England and the middle colonies, where commerce was the chief source of private fortunes. The revision and enforcement of the Molasses Act threatened ruin to the prosperity of merchants and shippers, and their misfortune reacted upon the southern colonies. The exports of New England in the ten years 1765–1775 reached the 1765 total only in 1768 and 1771. In the five years following 1765 her imports failed to reach that year's figure, although they were higher after 1770. Imports from England into New York reached the 1764 figure only once (1771) before the end of the Revolution. Exports from Virginia and Maryland did not reach the 1763 figure until 1775. The South as a whole did not feel this general economic recession as did the North, but the fluctuations in trade were indicative of increasing economic instability.

This depression, nevertheless, was felt not by the merchants alone; the farmers were also affected. The tobacco planters were discovering that a century and a half of wasteful methods had worn out their lands, and the poor crops in 1758 and later years brought a sharp decline in the amount of tobacco exported. The exportation of pig and bar iron reached its high point in colonial times in 1771 and decreased rapidly thereafter. Similar reductions in the production of other commodities could be traced, although some products, such as flax, that were covered by a substantial bounty showed decided prosperity. The business unrest and depression were accentuated both in England and in America by the three attempts to bring England to terms through non-intercourse. The Townshend duties on the necessities of life, the closing of the port of Boston, and the closing of the Grand Banks to New England fishermen were imperial mistakes

[13] See Chap. 29.

that hastened colonial rebellion. Hard times have always produced some kind of political unrest in our country; Bacon's rebellion represents an earlier instance in colonial history, and the pre-Revolutionary depression is another conspicuous example.

Although wealthy plantation owners in the South and many prominent merchants in the North supported rebellion, the American Revolution was not without its class and sectional struggles. Frontiersmen complained of injustice and the domination of colonial legislatures by the aristocrats of the older communities and believed that these were the men most loyal to England. The Revolution was in part a frontier uprising against eastern Tories. Both on the frontier and in the tidewater sections there was resentment on the part of the poor and the lower middle class against political disfranchisement, land laws such as primogeniture and entail which maintained an aristocratic class, a land system which favored wealthy speculators, and a social and economic system which everywhere pressed against them. Among the disfranchised and less favored there was a strong desire to diminish the power and prestige of the local aristocracies as well as the power of the British government. As one historian has aptly put it, "The Revolution was not merely a question of 'home rule'; it was also a question who should rule at home." [14]

One hundred and fifty years had passed since the first Englishmen had settled in America, a continent separated from the home land by 3000 miles of ocean and weeks of weary sailing. Under such conditions abiding loyalty after the first generation could hardly be expected if the strain became great. Perhaps one-fourth of the population emanated not from England, but from Holland, Germany, Sweden, Ulster, and South Ireland, many of the latter with an innate hostility toward Great Britain. Even in New England where the majority were of English descent, the bulk of the people, comments Ramsay, "knew little of the mother country, having only heard of her as a distant kingdom, the rulers of which had, in the preceding century, persecuted and banished their ancestors to the woods of America." [15] These factors, augmented by the aggressive and independent life of a new community, tended to develop self-reliance and to minimize the need of English protection, especially after the end of the French and Indian War. There was a gradual weakening of the ties and a growth of an independent social consciousness. The mere possibility, for instance, of the Church of England's extending its authority in the colonies aroused a storm of protest, and the efforts of Great Britain to circumscribe the power of the colonial governments were looked upon almost as an infringement of the rights of

[14] Carl Becker, in *American Historical Review*, Vol. XXIX, No. 2, p. 345.
[15] David Ramsay, *History of the American Revolution* (1811 ed.), I, 43–44.

a sovereign people. The settlers in America had up to the Revolution worked out their own destinies with little aid or interference from the outside. They were perfectly justified in feeling that they had a right to continue to do so, and they were in no mood to brook any change in status.

The most cursory examination of the factors in the controversy leading to the Revolution, as suggested in this chapter, leads one to discard quickly the old theory that the Revolution occurred because an English despot was seeking to regain his lost powers, as well as the other explanation that it was fought in protest to taxation without representation. Deep-seated causes of long standing were behind it, and it is easy to agree with Charles and Mary Beard, when they say: "Considered in the light of the English and provincial statutes spread over more than a hundred years, in the light of the authentic records which tell of the interminable clashes between province and metropolis, the concept of the American Revolution as a quarrel caused by a stubborn king and obsequious ministers shrinks into a trifling joke. Long before George III came to his throne, long before Grenville took direction of affairs, thousands of Americans had come into collision with British economic imperialism, and by the middle of the eighteenth century, far-seeing men, like Franklin, had discovered the essence of the conflict."[16] The development of a psychology which made independence desirable was a long process. "The Revolution," as John Adams asserted many years later, "was effected before the war commenced." It was "in the minds and hearts of the people."[17]

SELECTED READINGS

Beard, C. and M., *Rise of American Civilization*, Chap. V.

Nettels, Curtis, *The Roots of American Civilization*, Chaps. XXII–XXIV.

Hacker, Louis, *The Triumph of American Capitalism*, Chaps. XI–XII.

Van Tyne, C. H., *The Causes of the War of Independence*, Chaps, I, III, V, VII, X, XI.

Adams, J. T., *Revolutionary New England*, Chaps. VI–XVI.

Beer, G. L., *British Colonial Policy 1754–1765*, Introduction, and Chaps. I, XIII, XIV.

Johnson, E. R., *et al.*, *History of Domestic and Foreign Commerce of the United States*, Vol. I, Chap. III.

[16] C. and M. Beard, *Rise of American Civilization*, I, 201.
[17] *Works*, X, 292.

8

Economic Aspects of
the Revolution

CLASS AND SOCIAL DIVISIONS

IN spite of fundamental differences between the home government and the colonists, and long-continued friction, Americans were far from unanimous in demanding independence. The Tories, who supported the crown policy, were undoubtedly in the majority at the outbreak of hostilities but after 1776 they were probably in the minority. John Adams thought that at least one-third of the colonists remained loyal to Great Britain. Speaking generally, it may be said that the groups composing the Tories were: (1) the personal, political, or business followers, dependents, or friends of the royal governors; (2) the non-smuggling merchants of New England and the middle colonies whose interests were engrossed in the type of trade which could prosper without running counter to the English law; (3) many of the rich planters of the southern colonies; (4) the clergy attached to the Church of England and many of the rank and file of that denomination in the North; and (5) many of the most prosperous among the professional classes. In addition there was that great mass of the people, from natural conservatism or inertia opposed to change and habitually content with conditions as they are. The most cultivated, the most influential, and the wealthiest inhabitants of the coast towns from Boston to Charleston, Carolina, were likely to be loyalists.

Although the Whigs, or Patriots, were led by rich merchants like Hancock, able bankers like Morris, and aristocratic planters like Washington, the great strength of the rebellion came from the middle and poorer classes, "the plain people, as distinguished from the aristocracy."[1] So evident is this that some observers have seen in it "not so much a split between the colonies and the English government, as it was one aspect of a war between different divisions of the English people on both sides of the Atlantic," and "in reality but a battle in a great world-wide struggle between contend-

[1] J. F. Jameson, *The American Revolution Considered as a Social Movement*, p. 25.

ing social classes,"[2] in which capitalism has overthrown feudalism. The warm support of the Revolution by the great majority of the frontiersmen was to some extent a challenge by an agrarian and frontier people to both a waning feudalism and a rising capitalism, and the influence of the more radical western ideals was one of the most potent of the internal forces that brought the separation.[3] An intensely earnest minority, knowing its mind and active in its propaganda, took the lead and achieved independence. There was, as Ramsay says, "an animation in the friends of Congress which was generally wanting in the advocates for royal government."[4]

The most unfortunate page in the history of the Revolution was the civil war in which neighbor attacked neighbor. From thirty to fifty thousand Tories enlisted in the British Army and Navy, New York alone furnishing 15,000. Those to whom regular service did not appeal organized companies of militia under commissions from the crown which cooperated with the Indians in the cruel and useless warfare, of which the crowning examples were the Wyoming and Cherry Valley massacres. Loyalist privateering, of which New York was the center, somewhat balanced the depredations of the Patriots engaged in similar occupations. Governor Tryon's expedition in July, 1779, against the coast towns of Connecticut, which laid Fairfield and Norwalk in ashes, was the most serious Tory undertaking of the war. Wherever Patriots confronted Tories, there the fighting was fiercest.

The lot of the Tories not under the protection of the British Army was likely to be a hard one. Denounced and deprived of citizenship under the new state constitutions, they had no legal redress for their troubles. Laws forced them to pay for a cause they hated and at the same time denied them liberty to speak or write their opinions. Tarring and feathering, imprisonment, banishment and the appropriation of property, death—any of these might await the man whose loyalty to the Patriot cause was suspected. Whole communities of loyalists were driven into the back country to prevent their giving aid to the British Army on its approach. Eleven hundred Tory refugees sailed away with Howe's army to Halifax in March, 1776, and 3000 left with Clinton from Philadelphia in 1778. At least 35,000—some believe 100,000—eventually reached Canada and laid there the foundations of a new English commonwealth. The makers of British Canada were the Tories who left the thirteen colonies during the war.

To carry on a war efficiently with such a division of sentiment was im-

[2] A. M. Simons, *Social Forces in American History*, p. 70.

[3] The career and philosophy of Patrick Henry illustrate clearly the opposition of interests between the interior and the coast regions. See W. W. Henry, *Patrick Henry: Life, Correspondence and Speeches* (3 vols., 1891).

[4] David Ramsay, *History of South Carolina from Its First Settlement in 1670 to the Year 1808* (2 vols. in one, 1858), I, 147.

possible. Not only was there no unanimity as regards separation from England, but there was no unity among the colonies. Thirteen provinces jealous
of one another and with separate interests made impossible a close political
union or the formation of a body with sufficient powers to carry on a revolution. Only a common cause and a common enemy developed enough cooperation to keep an army in the field. The Continental Congress took
over the prosecution of the struggle, but it had little authority. It could
not impose taxes; it simply voted levies and asked the states to meet them.
Efforts to draw up a plan for a united government which would grant
legal power to a central body were blocked until 1781. The states on their
part either ignored the requests of Congress for money or handed over
what they saw fit. At the same time most of them insisted on maintaining their militia at home for their own defense. Though the success of the
war depended on the Continental Army, it was recruited and supported
under the aegis of a delegation of state representatives intrusted with insufficient authority to carry on the task.

ECONOMIC AND SOCIAL CHANGES

The American Revolution effected an economic as well as a political revolution. As the French Revolution of 1789 and the Russian Revolution of
1917 broke up the big landed estates and brought a radical change in the
agrarian economics of these two nations, so the years 1775-1781 in the thirteen colonies introduced changes in the land system as real if not as spectacular. Whatever institutions were not indigenous to the soil were bound
to disappear in the upheaval. For a century and a half Europeans had endeavored to transplant to America the feudal system of the Old World, and
vast estates were to be found in most of the colonies. As late as 1769 five-
sixths of the population of Westchester County, New York, lived on manor
lands. The exodus of the Tories not only removed the most conservative
class in the country, thereby throwing the local governments into the hands
of a new group, but made possible the breaking up of the large landholdings.
In November, 1777, Congress recommended that the states confiscate and
sell the loyalist property and invest the proceeds in Continental loan certificates. The idea found immediate favor. New Hampshire confiscated
twenty-eight estates, including that of Governor Wentworth. Massachusetts
confiscated the land of all who fought with England, including the Pepperell
estate containing thirty miles of coast land. In New York State the 50,000-
acre manor of Sir John Johnson, the Philipse manor of 300 square miles, the
Morris estate, and many other large holdings were broken up and sold,
usually in parcels of not over 500 acres. Everywhere crown and proprietary
properties were confiscated. The Penn estate taken over by Pennsylvania was

Hand-power Farming—Agricultural Tools in 1790.

Harvesting Wheat Before the Invention of the Reaper.

Stocking Frame—Spinning and Weaving (Eighteenth Century).

The Center of Colonial Industry.

From O. Turner, Pioneer History of the Holland Land Purchase of Western New York (1850)

Four Stages of the Frontier.

Pioneering by Train (Currier and Ives Conception).

Sod House on the Prairies—The First Home of Many Farmers on the
Great Plains.

Pawhuska, Oklahoma—A Typical Frontier Town of the Late 1880's.

Homesteaders Carrying Supplies From Railroad Station at Mandon,
North Dakota.

Wagon Train Setting Out from Helena, Montana, in the Late 1860's. (*Courtesy Northern Pacific Railroad.*)

Model of Whitney's Cotton Gin in the United States National Museum.

Eli Whitney, Inventor of the Cotton Gin and of Machinery to Make Interchangeable Parts. Yale University Library.

The Country Fair. Painting by J. A. Woodside.

Mechanized Farming in the Middle Nineteenth Century. (Currier and Ives.)

valued at nearly one million pounds sterling, and the State of New York received about 3,160,000 Spanish dollars for forfeited real estate. As in France during the Revolution, "country lawyers and newly rich merchants swarmed over the seats of the once proud aristocracy, so in the United States during and after the cataclysm a host of groundlings fresh from the plow and counting house surged over the domains of the Jessups, De Lanceys, and Morrises."[5]

Although the confiscation of crown and Tory estates did something to break up large landholdings, it by no means ended the great estates. Nor did it end the mania for land speculation so widespread in the years before the Revolution. Rather it seemed for the time being to increase it. States with western lands gave land bounties to soldiers, which in turn were bought and consolidated into large holdings. Sometimes small holdings were acquired by dummy purchasers for the same purpose. Virginia's practice of selling vacant lands as a means of paying state debts increased during the war and also stimulated speculation. Bending the state laws to their purpose, says Nettels, "promoters obtained great tracts in the West. They purchased at a discount the bounty warrants of soldiers unable or unwilling to migrate; they sent out servants to secure preemption rights; and they converted state certificates of indebtedness (which represented the values of depreciated currency) into claims upon the land. Estates as large as 140,000 acres came into being."[6] So much land, in fact, had been occupied beyond the Alleghenies that settlers pushing westward found it as difficult to obtain titles for reasonable amounts as earlier settlers had.

Along with the confiscation of land and its division into smaller parcels went a social revolution effected by a change to more democratic land tenure. Quitrents were the first to disappear. By 1786 every state but two had abolished entail, and within five more years primogeniture had gone, the new laws providing in some form or other for equality of inheritance. Jefferson's Act of 1776 probably released from half to three-quarters of the entire "seated" area of Virginia.[7] The significance of these laws in the development of a democratic society is, of course, obvious; one should also note the fact that this action was taken in many cases after the fighting had ceased. The war might be over, but the American Revolution, in a sense, had just begun.

---

[5] C. and M. Beard, *Rise of American Civilization*, I, 294. The Tories put their losses at $40,000,000, and the British government finally granted them $15,000,000.

[6] Curtis Nettels, *The Roots of American Civilization*, p. 684.

[7] Thomas Jefferson in a letter to John Adams, dated Monticello, Virginia, October 28, 1813, dwells with pride upon the fact that the laws of Virginia abolishing entails and primogeniture, "drawn by myself, laid the ax to the root of pseudo-aristocracy." Paul Leicester Ford (ed.), *Writings of Thomas Jefferson* (1898), IX, 427.

The Revolution had been ushered in with much condemnation of the autocratic methods of the British government. Consequently the new state constitutions reflected this feeling in the emphasis which they placed upon the so-called "natural rights of man"—life, liberty, and the pursuit of happiness; freedom of speech, of the press, and of worship; no taxation without the consent of the governed; jury trial; and so forth. In theory democracy had made great headway, but in practice it was otherwise. Most of the common devices by which an aggressive democracy could be checked were in use. The right to vote and hold office was limited to those who owned land or considerable taxable property; probably not one white man in five had even the franchise. Notwithstanding the illiberal provisions in the new constitutions, indications were not wanting that social readjustments were in progress. The Tory exodus decreased the power of the conservatives and strengthened the hands of such frontier radicals as Jefferson. The antislavery movement grew rapidly during the war, and by the end of the century a majority of the states had forbidden the importation of slaves, while all the New England states, with New York and Pennsylvania, had provided for abolition or gradual emancipation. The leavening force of the Revolution also played its part in religion. In 1770 there was an established church in most of the colonies, but during the war and in the years soon after, disestablishment took place, although religious tests of various kinds were still exacted from officers and legislators.

FRONTIER ADVANCE DURING THE REVOLUTION

The military events of the Revolution have overshadowed to a great extent the story of the frontier advance which won for us the "Old Northwest" and which went on simultaneously. Although the Proclamation of 1763 had forbidden settlement west of the Alleghenies, it was impossible to hold back the land-hungry settlers impatient to escape the restrictions of the conservative eastern counties. During the year of the Proclamation the first settlers pressed forward and established themselves on the upper Yadkin; six years later James Robertson and John Sevier led a band of Virginia frontiersmen to the Watauga Valley and planted settlements which by 1772 comprised thirteen stockaded forts. Disputes between Virginia and North Carolina over jurisdiction finally led to a meeting of representatives from the thirteen posts; they drew up the first written constitution adopted west of the mountains by American-born frontiersmen, and Watauga acted as an independent political community until incorporated as part of North Carolina in 1778.

The hunting trips of Daniel Boone and others had served to make known the wonders of the Kentucky country, and after 1769 settlers began to filter in, only to be driven out by the Indian attacks culminating in Lord Dunmore's War of 1774. After the Indian defeat of that year permanent occupation of central Kentucky began. In 1775 Judge Richard Henderson, a wealthy citizen of North Carolina who hoped to establish a proprietary colony from which profits might be derived through land sales and quitrents, founded the Transylvania Company, which purchased from the Cherokees the land between the Kentucky and Cumberland Rivers. Boone, as his agent, blazed the trail and erected a palisaded fort at Boonesboro, where Henderson soon arrived with the main body of colonists. Thus the business initiative of Henderson made practical the explorations of Boone and opened to the white man the fertile lands of Kentucky. After drawing up an exceedingly democratic constitution, the settlers petitioned Congress for admission as the fourteenth state, to be known as Transylvania. Virginia refused to recognize their independence, and the settlers submitted to her jurisdiction in 1776, the region (comprising the present boundaries of Kentucky) being attached as a frontier county. A further migration took place in 1779, when Robertson led an exodus of the most restless of the Watauga settlers into Tennessee and planted a colony at Nashboro at the bend of the Cumberland.

Still another effort was made by frontiersmen during this period to detach themselves from eastern control. The settlers about the headwaters of the Ohio, in what is now western Pennsylvania, West Virginia, and eastern Kentucky, a region claimed at that time by both Pennsylvania and Virginia, petitioned Congress unsuccessfully to be organized as the independent state of Westsylvania, declaring they never could be prosperous or contented while depending on a governing body four or five hundred miles distant. These attempts at state-making in Transylvania and Westsylvania illustrate only too clearly the lack of sympathy between the frontiersmen and their eastern neighbors, and the backwoodsmen's associations of Watauga, Boonesboro, and Nashboro exemplify the "social compact" in its simplest forms and are in marked contrast to the undemocratic features of the state constitutions being set up almost simultaneously.

The West in the Revolution

The frontier advance across the Alleghenies was the opening scene of the Revolutionary drama which records the winning of the lands between the mountains and the Mississippi for the infant republic. The British witnessed with uneasiness the few settlements beginning to dot the western slope, and from his headquarters at Detroit, Lieutenant-Governor Hamilton, known as the "Hair-Buyer," sent his Indian allies in raid after raid upon the hapless frontiersmen. George Rogers Clark, scarcely twenty-six years of age but a born leader with a commission from Patrick Henry of Virginia, raised a force in the spring of 1778 of some 250 men, descended the Ohio, and captured the old French posts, now held by the British, at Kaskaskia and Cahokia on the Mississippi, and Vincennes on the Wabash. Although Hamilton drove him out of Vincennes in December, Clark returned two months later after a 230-mile march across the "drowned lands," surprised and captured Hamilton and his garrison, and provided the basis of military occupation for the American possession of the Northwest at the close of the war.[8]

The winning of the Old Northwest helps to make clear the fact that the Revolution was to no small extent a frontier phenomenon. It was the men of the Piedmont region rather than those of the coast cities who were Whigs. After the first months there was scarcely a shot fired in New England. An appreciable part of the destinies of the Revolution lay in the hands of the frontiersmen: in Vermont under Ethan Allen, in New York under Gates and Herkimer, and in the Carolinas under Marion and Sumter, many of whom were not English but Scotch-Irish, German, and Welsh. As the situation came under the influence of the upland country the westward migration of the state capitals began and continued in the years following the war: in Virginia from Williamsburg to Richmond; in South Carolina from Charleston to Columbia; in North Carolina from Edenton to Raleigh; in Georgia from Savannah to Louisville, thence to Milledgeville and after the Civil War to Atlanta; in New Jersey from Burlington to Trenton; in New York from New York City to Albany; in Pennsylvania from Philadelphia to Lancaster and later to Harrisburg; and in New Hampshire from Portsmouth to Exeter. One of the demands of Shays's Rebellion was that the capital of Massachusetts be moved westward. The frontier, says Professor Turner, was the "vanguard of the Revolution and the advance guard of colonization."

EFFECT OF THE WAR ON AGRICULTURE

At the opening of the Revolution the population of the United States is estimated to have been in the neighborhood of 2,750,000. Of men between eighteen and sixty there were about 700,000, but at no time during the war was more than one-eighth of this number under arms in the colonial armies, and during most of the period probably no more than one-sixteenth. Con-

[8] Clark's exploit was probably not the deciding factor in the acquisition of the Northwest, although there is now definite reason to believe that it was fully known to American and therefore to British negotiators. See letter from Sargé to Franklin, edited by Lewis J. Carey, in the *Mississippi Valley Historical Review*, Vol. XXI, No. 3, pp. 375–378 (Dec., 1934). The matter was primarily a diplomatic problem in which Great Britain chose to favor the United States rather than France or Spain.

cerning the war there was widespread apathy, and the agricultural and industrial life of the people went on much as usual. After the first year New England, with the exception of the occupation of Newport and a few minor raids upon the coast, was free from the British. Agriculture was hardly affected. In New York, New Jersey, and Pennsylvania the depredations of both armies were to a great extent compensated for by the liberal prices the French and British paid the farmers in gold for supplies of all kinds; the farmers seemed only too willing to double their prices for the French and to sell their produce to Howe, while Washington's men shivered and starved at Valley Forge. That the colonies must have been plentifully supplied with profiteers and "sunshine patriots" we may gather from the words of John Adams: "The spirit of venality is the most dreadful and alarming enemy America has to oppose. . . . It will ruin America, if she is ever ruined. If God Almighty does not interfere by His grace to control this universal idolatry to the mammon of unrighteousness, we shall be given up to the chastisement of His judgements. I am ashamed of the age I live in." [9] "Such a dearth of public spirit and want of virtue," said Washington bitterly in 1775, "such stock-jobbing, and fertility in all the low arts to obtain advantage of one kind or another . . . I never saw before, and I pray God I may never be a witness to again. . . . Such a dirty mercenary spirit pervades the whole that I should not be at all surprised at any disaster that may happen." [10]

Blockade runners were always ready to carry the tobacco of the Virginia plantations to a waiting market in Europe. Comparatively speaking, the last twenty years of the century were the golden age for tobacco, for it was still the leading southern product, in 1791 surpassing flour as an export. The production of leaf tobacco rose from 101,800,000 pounds in 1774 to 130,000,000 in 1790, at which time over half of the southern population was either engaged in or dependent on its production. In the Carolinas the cultivation and export of rice went on, apparently with little interruption. In 1778 the first water mill adapted to cleaning and preparing rice for the market, and the model upon which subsequent improvements were based, was erected on the Santee River. While it is true that many phases of southern agriculture were not fundamentally affected by the war, at the same time it should not be forgotten that Patriot plantation owners suffered from the British raids and lost heavily by the confiscation of slaves. Likewise, the cessation of British bounties on indigo marked the beginning of the end of an important industry.

The interference in trade caused by non-importation agreements and the

[9] John Adams, *Familiar Letters*, p. 232.
[10] George Washington, *Writings* (Ford ed.), III, 246, 247.

first years of the war stimulated the production of wool throughout the colonies. The same was true of cotton in the South. The legislatures of Maryland, Virginia, and South Carolina urged upon their farmers the growing of cotton so effectively, apparently, that Hamilton, writing in 1775, said, "Several of the Southern colonies are so favorable to it that, with due cultivation, in a couple of years they would afford enough to clothe the whole continent." [11] American agriculture with its primitive wasteful methods was stimulated as a whole rather than injured by the war. Knowledge of European improvements was spread by the foreigners whom the war brought into the country. Quickened interest in agriculture was shown by the formation of several new societies for the promotion of agriculture. [12]

EFFECT OF THE WAR ON INDUSTRIAL LIFE

American manufactures were more directly affected by the war than American agriculture. The Revolution enfranchised American industry by doing away with all the annoying restrictions which the English Parliament under the influence of mercantilism had imposed when it sought to confine the colonies to the production of raw materials. During the boycotts preceding the outbreak of hostilities, the colonists refused to purchase English goods, and great efforts were made to stimulate the manufacture of such necessities as woolens and linens which had formerly been imported in large amounts. The spinning wheel came into renewed use. Large numbers of people pledged themselves not to eat lamb or mutton or to buy from butchers who sold it, that the wool might be saved for clothing; women of all classes turned to the production of cloth as a domestic business. The southern planters employed their poorer white neighbors at spinning or weaving or themselves built loom houses and trained their slaves to this work. Homespun was worn by the wealthiest. The necessity for wool cards led Connecticut to lend Nathaniel Niles, of Norwich £300 for four years to make wire for card teeth. Massachusetts in 1777 granted a bounty of £100 for the first 1000 pounds of "good merchantable card wire" produced in any water mill in her own territory from iron made in the American states. This activity in spinning and weaving during the early years of the war declined after the cargoes captured by the privateers began to be thrown on the market and importation was resumed.

The manufacture of munitions and necessaries of war was, of course, stimulated. The life in the colonies which made everyone a hunter had developed skilled locksmiths, and small gun factories sprang up at Sutton, Massachusetts; Waterbury, Connecticut; and North Providence. Connecticut

[11] H. C. Lodge (ed.), *Works of Alexander Hamilton* (1885), I, 153.
[12] Below, pp. 223-224.

in 1775 offered a bounty of 1s. 6d. for each gunlock manufactured, and 5s. for each complete stand of arms to the number of 3000. Congress in 1778 founded works in Springfield where cannon were cast—the predecessor of the present national armory established there in 1794. The casting and forging of guns and camp kettles was carried on in Pennsylvania and on the Hudson; new furnaces were built in many places in New England and the middle colonies. Rhode Island in 1777 provided for a bounty of £60 per gross ton for "steel of the best quality, or equal in goodness with good German steel," [13] made in the state during the next three years. In 1778 the legislature of Maine granted to the Reverend Daniel Little £450 to aid in erecting at Wells a building for the manufacture of steel. It is claimed that Jeremiah Wilkinson of Cumberland, Rhode Island, turned out in 1777 the first cold cut nail in the world. Massachusetts offered bounties on sulphur extracted from native ores, and Rhode Island for powder, but most of the powder used was imported. Attempts at mining and refining lead were made in Connecticut and at Cheswell, Virginia, but most of that used was obtained from abroad or from melting down lead roofs, window weights, and other commodities.

A very real shortage of many of the necessities was felt until 1777 in all parts of the country. When salt, molasses, and rum were cut off, attempts were made to supply the deficiency from sea water and cornstalks, but with indifferent results. The increase in newspapers during the war from thirty-seven to over one hundred brought an increase in paper mills. Small establishments were set up to manufacture various commodities formerly imported. Shipbuilding, an industry which had been stimulated by the Navigation Acts, was greatly restricted during the war. Limited as was the manufacturing, it is remarkable that so much was carried on. Labor, always scarce and expensive in the colonial period, became increasingly so during the war. Enlistments in the Army and on privateers, and the emigration of loyalists with their servants, decreased the supply. Wages of skilled and unskilled labor doubled from 1774 to 1784, giving an indication of the profits that were made in manufacturing, the rising cost of living, and the increased amount of money in circulation.

COMMERCE AND PRIVATEERING

The Revolution favored maritime commerce in two ways: first, in the opening of colonial ports to the world, and second, in stimulating privateering. The nonimportation agreements of the years preceding the war had exhausted the country of English goods; as a consequence, the merchants

---

[13] *Rhode Island Colony Records*, VIII, 240. Also see Victor S. Clark, *History of Manufactures in the United States*, I, 219–232.

of Spain, Holland, and France eagerly welcomed the new markets, discovering means of evading the British warships and privateersmen to such purpose that by 1777 there was little lack of foreign merchandise. Lists of imports during the war reveal items distinctly in the class of luxuries—such finer textiles as velvets, linens, silks, and broadcloths, as well as teas, coffees, spices, and wines. Later the ports were opened to English goods and considerable quantities were imported through New York. The articles were paid for mainly by exports of flour, tobacco, and rice, and by the money which found its way to the colonies through the medium of foreign loans and British quartermaster. These exported staples also had to run the gantlet of the British fleet and privateersmen. Although the British admirals reported the capture of 570 vessels between 1776 and 1779, exportation was sufficiently lucrative to continue with little abatement throughout the war. Twenty-four million pounds of tobacco alone were recorded in 1777–1778 by the British customs officials, about one-third of the ordinary consumption, received possibly under the pretense that it came from neutral ports, for the Dutch island of St. Eustatia and the French island of Martinique served as ports where cargoes could be transferred and neutralized.

Of almost equal magnitude with legitimate commerce were the operations carried on by privateers. It has been estimated that 2000 privateers were commissioned, of which the great majority came from Massachusetts.[14] Salem, which had been mainly a fishing town before the war, had 59 privateers carrying 4000 men in 1781, and probably 180 during the war. Nearly 200 commissions were issued by Rhode Island, where privateering became so popular that the Assembly found it necessary to check it and pass laws to limit the size of the crews. Newburyport sent out 22 vessels, and the Connecticut towns of New London, Hartford, and New Haven also engaged in the lucrative business, although more closely watched by the British fleet. Most of the operations were carried on from the smaller New England towns, for New York, Boston, Philadelphia, Newport, and Charleston were at one time or other under British control. With his usual routine voyage cut off, the American seaman found a natural outlet in privateering. Daring was necessary and the risk great, but the spice of adventure and the lure of profits drew the keenest and coolest. It was customary for the owners to split half and half with the crew, according to rank. Captured prizes were either taken to European ports, sold, and the money invested in merchandise to be brought home, or else, if the capture was effected off the American coast, brought in at once. More than 445 prizes were brought in by the

[14] "Six hundred and twenty-six letters of marque were issued to Massachusetts vessels by the Continental Congress, and some thousand more by the General Court." S. E. Morison, *Maritime History of Massachusetts*, p. 29.

Salem fleet. Elias Hasket Derby, the chief shipowner and the enterprising genius of this little town, died in 1799, worth about $1,000,000 realized from privateering profits, a stupendous fortune for those days. In the year 1776 alone, English West Indiamen to the number of 250 were captured, entailing a loss of £1,800,000, and insurance rates from the West Indies to England rose to 23 per cent. "Probably as many as ninety thousand Americans were, first and last," says Jameson, "engaged in these voyages, a number of men almost as great as served in the army, and greater than that of the army in any single year save one."[15] The constant heckling on the sea, and the continued losses incurred by the English merchants, undoubtedly increased the unpopularity of the war in England.

FINANCING THE REVOLUTION

The most difficult task which Congress had to handle was providing funds for carrying on the war. No power was given to it to levy taxes, and if such power had been given, it is doubtful whether legislation would have been practicable, owing to the colonists' hatred of any form of taxation and to the economic depression which would have made it extremely difficult to obtain money by taxation. The entire cost of the war measured in gold was only about $104,000,000, a sum which should have been easily raised. As a matter of fact, the generation which fought the war paid about half the cost, chiefly on account of the depreciation of the paper money which had been issued in lieu of taxes. Under the circumstances the resort to paper money seems quite natural. As England's control over currency had been one of the colonists' grievances, they expected that, with the restraining hand of the mother country withdrawn, recourse would be made immediately to fiat money.

The war had scarcely commenced when Congress (June 22, 1775) issued bills of credit for $2,000,000, to be redeemed for Spanish milled dollars by the states in proportion to population at a time and place not specified. From then until November 29, 1779, Congress authorized forty-two emissions of paper money to the amount of $191,552,380. To complicate the situation, the states began issuing competing paper currency; by 1783, eleven states had authorized paper to the amount of $246,366,941.[16] This was altogether more than the new nation had any need for, and as its value rested ultimately on the success of the struggle and the willingness of the states to redeem the paper, it was natural that depreciation should set in. In ringing proclamations Jay and others urged in the name of patriotism that all good

---

[15] J. F. Jameson, *The American Revolution Considered as a Social Movement*, p. 103.

[16] These computations were made by Professor Lewis J. Carey from tables in R. V. Harlow, "Aspects of Revolutionary France," *American Historical Review*, XXXV, 46–68 (Oct., 1929).

citizens accept it in trade. Patriots were exhorted and Tories forced to receive it. Buoyed up by the French and Spanish subsidies, the dollar held up fairly well until September, 1777, when it began to depreciate rapidly; in March, 1780, the Continental dollar sold for 2.45 cents, a value it held until the end of the war. In 1781 it took $100 in paper money to buy a pair of shoes, $40 to purchase a bushel of corn, $90 for a pound of tea, $1575 for a barrel of flour. "Not worth a continental" became the synonym of worthlessness. People with fixed incomes suffered, but it was the heyday for the speculator and the debtor. Chaotic as was the currency situation during the Revolution, its effect on economic life must not be overemphasized. The evils of fiat money in a primitive self-sufficing community are mitigated because relatively few people are forced to use it. Furthermore, the loss was distributed because the depreciation did not all come at once. The influx of European gold during the war, which brought in more metallic currency than the colonies had ever known, helped to ease the situation, even if the gold did not remain long in circulation. The issuing of paper money was probably the only means by which the war could be financed.

In addition to the issuing of paper currency, almost every other means was used to obtain funds. Certificates of indebtedness were issued by quartermasters in payment for supplies which they requisitioned. Domestic loans were floated first at 4 per cent and later at 6 per cent, but without great success. Equally discouraging was the result of the requisitions made upon the states; because of unwillingness to tax their own citizens and jealousy or distrust of their sister commonwealths, they failed to respond adequately to the demands of the Continental Congress. Lotteries were set up and prize money was taken from the sale of captures made by government privateers. Gifts were obtained from private individuals abroad, and loans and gifts from foreign governments. Including the expenses incurred by the states in maintaining their own militia, the cost of the Revolution in gold (in round numbers) has been estimated by Professor Seligman as follows:

Paper money	$41,000,000 (approx.)
Certificates of indebtedness	16,708,000
Loan-office certificates	11,585,000
Foreign loans	7,830,000
Taxes (requisitions upon the states) ..	5,795,000
Gifts from abroad	1,996,000
Miscellaneous receipts	856,000
State debts	18,272,000
	$104,042,000 [17]

[17] For a discussion of the payment of this debt, see below, pp. 159–160.

ECONOMIC REORGANIZATION AFTER THE WAR

As usually happens after a war, the American Revolution was followed by an economic reorganization that carried in its wake a period of uncertainty and hard times. During the conflict, labor and investment had been diverted from agriculture and legitimate trade to manufacturing and privateering. Men had gone into unwonted occupations which ceased when the war ended. Lowered prices resulting from the cessation of war demands, in combination with the importation of the cheaper manufactured goods of Europe, were fast ruining such infant manufacturing concerns as had sprung up during the war. The reabsorption of the disbanded army into economic life required time. So also did the replenishment of the stock of slave labor in the South, where thousands of Negroes had been taken off by the British and fleeing loyalists. South Carolina and Virginia had felt severely the ravages of war in the later years; New England had seen her fishing industry and the resulting West Indian trade ruined. Other states found business stagnant and conditions depressed.

Another factor which made the situation even more distressing was the British Navigation Acts. The American Revolution had been fought for freedom of commerce and in repudiation of the whole economic policy of Great Britain as it applied to the colonies. Instead, however, of remedying the situation, the War for Independence made matters worse. The only clause in the treaty of peace (1783) concerning commerce was a stipulation guaranteeing that the navigation of the Mississippi should be forever free to the United States. Jay at this time tried to secure some reciprocal trade provisions with Great Britain, but without result. Pitt in 1783 introduced a bill into the British Parliament providing for free trade between the United States and the British colonies, but instead of passing it Parliament enacted the British Navigation Act of 1783 which admitted only British-built and -manned ships to the ports of the West Indies and imposed heavy tonnage dues upon American ships in other British ports. This was amplified in 1786 by another Act designed to prevent the fraudulent registration of American vessels, and by still another in 1787 which prohibited the importation of American goods by way of foreign islands. The favorable features of the old Navigation Acts which had granted bounties and reserved the English markets in certain cases to colonial products were gone; the unfavorable alone were left. The British market was further curtailed by the depression there after 1783. Although the French treaty of 1778 had promised "perfect equality and reciprocity" in commercial relations, it was found impossible to make a commercial treaty upon this basis. Spain demanded as her price for reciprocal trading relations that the United States surrender for twenty-five years the right of navigating the Mississippi, a price which the New England merchants would have been glad to pay. France (1778) and Holland (1782) made treaties, but not on even terms; Portugal refused our advances. Only Sweden (1783) and Prussia (1785) made treaties guaranteeing reciprocal commercial privileges.

To make matters more galling, Americans needed European goods, especially the manufactured goods of England, which they were accustomed to from long usage. So necessary were they that in 1784 goods to the approximate value of £3,700,000 were imported and only £750,000 worth of goods sent in return; this meant paying the balance in specie or in other credits extended by foreigners to buyers in this country. John Adams was sent to England in 1785 and remained for three years in a futile effort to negotiate a commercial treaty; he argued unsuccessfully that "it is England's interest to cherish her trade with America, and if a hard policy is adopted America will trade elsewhere or build her own factories." There were not a few in Great Britain who realized the soundness of Adams' contention, but powerful mercantile interests prevented concessions. Under the leadership of Lord Sheffield[18] the British government took the position that the interests of the loyal colonies should be protected and that the American trade could be kept even if the old navigation laws were retained.

The weakness of Congress under the Articles of Confederation prevented retaliation by the central government. Power was repeatedly asked to regulate commerce, but it was refused by the states, upon whom rested the carrying out of such commercial treaties as Congress might negotiate. Eventually the states themselves attempted retaliatory measures, and during the years 1783-1788, New Hampshire, Massachusetts, Rhode Island, New York, Pennsylvania, Maryland, Virginia, North Carolina, South Carolina, and Georgia levied tonnage dues upon British vessels or discriminating tariffs upon British goods. Whatever effect these efforts might have had were neutralized by the fact that the duties were not uniform; they varied in the different states from no tariffs whatever to duties of 100 per cent. This simply drove British ships to the free or cheapest ports and their goods continued to flood the market. As Washington wrote to Lafayette in 1788, ". . . . it would be idle to think of making commercial regulations on our part. One state passes a prohibitory law respecting some article, another state opens wide the avenue for admission. One assembly makes a system, another assembly unmakes it."[19]

[18] His pamphlet, *Observations on the Commerce of the American States* (1784), was of great influence in this controversy.
[19] W. C. Ford (ed.), *Writings of George Washington*, IX, 254.

WEAKNESS OF THE CENTRAL GOVERNMENT AND DISSENSION AMONG THE STATES

It was the lack of a strong central government that tied the hands of Adams and Jay in their negotiations with foreign nations for reciprocal commercial treaties, and made it possible for certain states to nullify the retaliatory measures of the others against England. Under the Articles of Confederation (1781-1789) which created the so-called "League of Friendship," each state "retained its sovereignty, freedom, and independence," granting to Congress only such rights as could not be easily exercised by the individual states, such as the right to conduct foreign affairs, declare war, raise an army and navy, borrow money, emit bills of credit, etc. The right to levy taxes was not granted; Congress had merely the right to make "requisitions" which the states might or might not meet. A government without power to raise taxes was without power to provide for a standing army to enforce treaties, if they could be made. As a consequence, the government under the Articles of Confederation was one without power at home and without standing abroad. England openly violated the Treaty of 1783 by refusing to surrender the northwest trading posts; Spain trafficked with the western frontiersmen in an attempt to instigate a rebellion against the United States; and Barbary pirates levied blackmail on American merchant ships.

At home the union brought about by the Revolution seemed rapidly breaking up. Instead of one nation presenting a united front, there were again thirteen bickering states wrapped up in their old selfish provincialism, intent upon their own ambitions and problems. Pennsylvania attacked the Connecticut settlers in the Wyoming Valley as if they had been an intruding war party of Indians, and Connecticut and New York fought over the region of Vermont. These boundary-line disputes were only dramatic examples of the hostility which was ever present in commercial relations between the states. A classical example of these commercial wars occurred in 1787 when New York levied import duties and placed other hindrances in the way of New Jersey and Connecticut farm products, which had hitherto largely supplied the New York City market. New Jersey replied by levying a tax of $1800 a year upon a Sandy Hook lighthouse recently purchased by New York and essential to the safety of the harbor; and a mass meeting of business men in New London pledged themselves under penalty of $250 not to send goods to New York for a period of twelve months. Spectacular as these commercial wars sometimes were, their importance should not be exaggerated. Recent students have insisted that the process of commercial recovery was not greatly retarded by interstate jealousy and cutthroat commercial laws.[20] Discriminatory duties were exceptional after 1783, when it was usual to exempt the produce of American states from import duties and give preferential tonnage rates to American-owned vessels over foreign ships.

CHAOS IN THE CURRENCY

Even more disastrous to economic life than foreign trade restrictions, a weak central government, and interstate rivalries was the chaos in the currency. Congress and the several states during the war had issued $437,-919,321 in paper money, and in addition there had been much counterfeiting. The paper money of the states had depreciated in varying amounts, and the money issued by Congress, the Continental paper, had become practically valueless, simply a commodity in the hands of speculators. Since this money gradually passed from circulation as worthless, business again became dependent upon English, French, Spanish, and Portuguese coins. The innumerable varieties of money complicated barter. The appearance of foreign coins, however, did not wholly remedy the situation, for, as in earlier years, they were exported to pay for imports. With such a scarcity of currency and after two exceedingly trying years, it was to be expected that the old cry for paper money would again be renewed during the depression of 1785-1786, particularly by the farmer class, the debtors, and the poor generally. The business interests, realizing the effects of more paper money on trade, resisted the demand stubbornly. As their legislatures were again under the control of the large planters or wealthy merchants of the coast towns, Massachusetts, New Hampshire, Connecticut, Delaware, Maryland, and Virginia succeeded in escaping further paper money, but only after severe struggles. A mob crying out for paper and threatening the lives of the legislators surrounded the meetinghouse at Exeter, New Hampshire, and were dispersed by the militia. The farmers of central and western Massachusetts, strong for paper money and hot against the aristocrats of Boston who had gained control of the government through the conservative constitution in 1780, revolted under Daniel Shays, and were put down only after Governor Bowdoin had sent a good-sized army against them. The other seven states—Rhode Island, New York, Pennsylvania, New Jersey, North and South Carolina, and Georgia—yielded to the demand; but neither laws nor threats of bodily harm could in some cases make merchants take the money. The most exciting case in the judicial history of Rhode Island was fought on this question, when a certain John Weeden, a butcher, refused to accept scrip for meat. The judges held the statute unconstitutional and

[20] R. A. East, *Business Enterprise in the American Revolutionary Era,* pp. 249–250.

were summoned before the legislature and reproved, but their decision stood.

Important as was the question of paper money at this time from an economic point of view, its social significance was even greater. It served as a tangible issue around which social discontent could rally. The close of the Revolution found the old ruling aristocratic class weakened by the emigration of the Tories. The former middle class had pushed to the front and the small farmer was more of a factor. Dominated by more democratic ideals, this group opposed bitterly such projects as the promise of Congress to grant officers half pay for life and the founding of the Society of the Cincinnati. Their fear of an aristocratic class is seen in the abolition of primogeniture and entail, and the seizure of the rights of the proprietors in Pennsylvania and Maryland; their fear of a king, in the restrictions built around the executive in the new state constitutions.

But a counterrevolution had already set in. A new ruling class had possession of most of the state legislatures, a group whose economic interests were at variance with those of the small farmers. The latter, harassed by heavy debts, the scarcity of specie, and the depression of 1785-1786, were in no mood to see their welfare ignored by a new ruling class out of sympathy with the common man. Economic unrest and class antagonism reached their climax in Massachusetts in the rebellion of 1786, but the hard-pressed farmers who followed Daniel Shays only expressed more vigorously the feelings of thousands of small farmers in each of the states. Hundreds, disheartened, emigrated to the West, only to receive further evidence of the weakness of the central government. For there the Spaniards had closed the mouth of the Mississippi to their products, thus preventing their reaching a market. It was in this social structure and these conditions that the project of a new constitution and a stronger central government was launched.

How Critical Was the "Critical Period"?

From what has been said it is clear enough that the years between Yorktown and the adoption of the Constitution were difficult. Problems of readjustment after any war are serious. Whether these years were as "critical" as earlier historians have pictured them, however, is open to question.[21] Recent research has tended to emphasize the enlarging business activity during this period. First of all should be noted the rapid revival of commerce until it soon reached pre-war levels. It is true that under the Navigation Act of 1783 the British West Indies were closed to American ships,

[21] In 1888 the historian-philosopher, John Fiske, published a volume, *The Critical Period in American History, 1783–1789*, and many subsequent writers have followed his lead in emphasizing the darkness and chaos of these years.

but the demand for lumber and foodstuffs in these islands was so great that ways of evading the Act were quickly discovered. One method was to ship products to the French, Dutch, or Spanish islands whence they found their way to the British islands. The fact that half of the shipments to the West Indies from the United States went to Jamaica alone is ample proof of this. By the middle 1780's the navigation acts of the French, Spanish, and Dutch had been sufficiently relaxed to allow an active trade with their colonies. Moreover, trade with France and Holland developed to an amount above pre-war levels as these nations took certain "enumerated" products which during the colonial period could be shipped only to Great Britain. By 1787–1789 the trade with Holland had become more than 50 per cent as important as that with England, with a balance probably in favor of America. This revival of commerce brought in its wake, of course, a revival of the fishing and lumbering industries and a demand for foodstuffs, tobacco, and other agricultural commodities.

During the Revolution the slave trade passed into other hands and the three-cornered route became a thing of the past. The Yankee, however, soon found other opportunities for trade in the Baltic countries, the Near East, and the Far East. It was in 1785 that the *Empress of China* entered New York from Canton and in 1787 that the *Grand Turk* sailed into Salem from the same port; of forty-six foreign vessels entering Canton in 1789, eighteen were American. It was also during these years that the first New England mariners reached the northwest coast in search of furs; it was Captain Gray's famous voyage to Oregon and China (1787–1790) which opened the New England-Northwest-China trade, a lucrative traffic whereby the New Englander traded manufactured products to the northwest Indians for furs, and then sailed for China to trade the furs for Oriental goods.

Commerce was by no means the only field in which a vigorous spirit of business enterprise was evident. With British restrictions now lifted, the Bank of North America was established in 1781, the Bank of New York and the Massachusetts Bank of Boston in 1784. Throughout the country merchant capitalists, hitherto held in restraint by British mercantilism, were pooling their capital and organizing companies to exploit the West, to build turnpikes, bridges, and canals, and to promote manufacturing. The issuing of charters to American concerns was almost unknown in the colonial period, but between 1781 and 1785 state legislatures issued eleven and between 1786 and 1790 at least twenty-two more.

Americans were particularly loath to sacrifice such gains in manufacturing as they had made during the war. Many of these industries kept going. During this period the first cotton factory in the United States was built (1787) at Beverly, Massachusetts, and two years later Slater built his mill at Pawtucket. In 1788 a woolen factory was established at Hartford, with a capital of £1280, raised by subscription to shares at £10 each. Before the end of the period many of the large New England towns had commenced their manufacturing careers. At Philadelphia John Fitch and others who were experimenting with the steam vessel produced one that ran eighty miles a day. It was a period when society was alive not only to political changes but to the economic possibilities of the new nation.

It is true that the country suffered a depression in 1785 and 1786, but the letdown was due as much to overtrading and expansion as to any weakness of government. It did not last long and in the two years preceding the adoption of the Constitution, economic activity, as suggested by some of the dates in the preceding paragraphs, was again in full swing. Commenting on this activity, a leading authority on the period writes:

High rentals, building activity, and luxurious living actually impressed Franklin on his return to America in 1785. Stagecoach routes and facilities were steadily being increased in various regions. The paper industry continued to grow, and important companies were organized for iron and woolen manufacturers in 1786 and 1788. Above all, it is significant that capital was much sought after everywhere during the "critical" years. Interest rates were high in 1784. New York merchant-capitalists were even invited to New Jersey and Connecticut, being promised liberal treatment. . . . And if it be argued that all this merely emphasized a great lack of capital, rather than a general demand for it, it can be pointed out in reply that there was no difficulty in securing subscriptions of specie value for large amounts of bank stock in 1784 in Philadelphia, Boston and New York.[22]

THE STRUGGLE FOR THE CONSTITUTION

That the economic and social conditions of the 1780's presented many reasons for a stronger central government there can be no doubt. American economic expansion needed a more unified economic program, freedom of interstate commerce, a more stabilized currency, and other benefits which a strong central government could provide. Nevertheless, the student of American history must be on his guard not to overemphasize the effects of the weak government under the Articles of Confederation. "The defects of the old confederation," as Callender well says, "were then in no way responsible for the hard times. It had not produced them, nor could the best government in the world have removed them." [23] To no small extent it was the economic conditions that prevented government from functioning rather than poor government that caused the depression.

[22] R. A. East, *Business Enterprise in the American Revolutionary Era* (Columbia University Press), p. 242.

[23] G. S. Callender, *Selections from the Economic History of the United States*, p. 182.

Nevertheless, the movement for a constitution was supported most eagerly by those whose economic interests were most seriously affected by the weakness of the central government under the Articles of Confederation. It was also supported by many of the new ruling class who were frightened by the restlessness of the small farmers, particularly after Shays's Rebellion. Despite the economic expansion of the 1780's, investors in manufacturing and shipping desired a government strong enough to protect them against foreign discrimination. Capital was also being continually attacked by the debtor class, who were endeavoring to push stay laws and paper-money acts through the legislatures, and who sometimes in the local courts showed a disconcerting lack of interest in the rights of absentee capital. While ship-owners and manufacturers wanted protection from a strong central government, domestic merchants were anxious to demolish the barriers to inter-state traffic and longed for a stable and uniform currency. But among the most ardent advocates of the Constitution were naturally all those who held claims against the Confederacy. These included owners of Continental bonds, certificates of indebtedness, and paper money, who knew that a strong central government would be able not only to redeem its own securities but to tone up the state paper. Much of this paper, of course, was no longer in the hands of the original owners but had long since shifted into the possession of speculators. The foreign debt being excluded, it has been conservatively estimated that the increase in the value of Continental securities which resulted from the adoption of the Constitution and the sound financial policies of the new government was at least $40,000,000, which in value represented one-tenth of the total taxable value of the land in the thirteen colonies—obviously no mean stake to play for.[24] Another type of speculator anxious for a strong government was the investor in western land, a group that included a large number of the wealthy and prominent men of the time who undoubtedly agreed with a certain member of the Constitutional Convention who had "claims to a considerable Quantity of Western Country" and was "fully persuaded that the Value of those Lands must be increased by an efficient federal Government."[25]

Behind the movement for a new Constitution, then, were the commercial, financial, creditor, and speculating classes who were eager to safeguard and strengthen the rights of property. To be sure, these groups were in a minority, but they contained many men of ability, integrity, and broad vision who were powerful, active, and easily organized, for they were con-centrated in the towns and represented in each state. With such a group behind the movement, it was to be expected that the document would be

---

[24] C. A. Beard, *An Economic Interpretation of the Constitution of the United States*, pp. 34 ff.
[25] *Documentary History of the Constitution*, IV, 678.

DISTRIBUTION OF VOTES

IN RATIFICATION OF

THE CONSTITUTION

NEW ENGLAND
1787-1790

Based on Map

Prepared by O. G. Libby

Federal Majority

Anti-Federal Majority

Evenly Divided

BORMAY & CO., N.Y.

DISTRIBUTION OF VOTES
IN RATIFICATION OF
THE CONSTITUTION
———
MIDDLE AND SOUTHERN
STATES
1787-1788

Based on Map
Prepared by O. G. Libby

Federal Majority
Anti-Federal Majority
Evenly Divided

conservative in nature and the rights of private property and vested interests carefully safeguarded. The Constitutional Convention itself could hardly have been better picked to serve these interests. The left-wing radicals of the Revolution were notable for their absence, while more than half the delegates were either investors or speculators in public securities which would be benefited by the new Constitution. Much attention has been given by historians to the differences in the Convention and the great compromises which it wrought, but, as a matter of fact, its members were in pretty close agreement on essentials, and their facility in effecting compromises was due to their unity on the fundamentals.

Under the circumstances, opposition to ratification was bound to be extremely bitter, and it was long doubtful if the Constitution would be accepted. The opposition came mostly from the agricultural districts and debtor areas. "I believe it to be a fact," said Patrick Henry, "that the great body of yeomanry are in decided opposition to it." [26] Whether the people desired it or not it is impossible to know, for no more than one-fourth of the adult males voted in the election for delegates to ratifying conventions and probably not more than one-sixth of the adult males ratified it. As Professor Beard well says, "The Constitution was not created by 'the whole people,' as the jurists have said; neither was it created by 'the states,' as Southern nullifiers long contended; but it was the work of a consolidated group whose interests knew no state boundaries and were truly national in their scope." [27]

Although the Constitution was the work of a small minority, its adoption meant the elimination of many of the economic ills under which industry and commerce had struggled since the war. A reorganization of the government was essential and the immediate economic results were salutary. Its most important additions to the power of Congress were those relating to finance and commerce—it enabled the federal government to levy taxes, regulate trade, coin money, protect industry, direct the settlement of the West, and, as later events proved, to establish credit and redeem its securities. Under it freedom of trade was insured throughout the young republic. These prospective benefits were in the minds of the framers, and adequate powers were granted. [28]

Giving all due recognition to the many salutary economic effects brought about by a stronger central government, we should note at least three facts in respect to the Constitution. It was designed, in the first place, for a

[26] W. W. Henry, *Patrick Henry*, III, 578. Speech, June 24, 1788, in the Virginia Convention of June, 1788, convened to consider the question of the adoption of the United States Constitution.
[27] C. A. Beard, *An Economic Interpretation of the Constitution*, p. 325.
[28] Most of the economic clauses in the Constitution are in Article I, Sections 8, 9, and 10.

society distinctly agricultural and mercantile, and drawn up primarily by the leaders of these economic groups. Not only was this so, but it was the intent of the framers to protect these interests in case the structure of society might change in the future. In the second place, there was no intention on the part of the framers to set up an unmodified democracy. As a consequence, the readjustment of the Constitution a hundred years later to meet a great industrial development and more democratic conditions was fraught with difficulty, and further adjustments are subjects of current discussion. In the third place, the feeling was strongly expressed during the campaigns over ratification that the Constitution was a document more concerned with bolstering up the rights of private property, especially that invested in personalty, and not sufficiently interested in the generally accepted "Rights of Man." To make it more palatable and to secure its adoption, the first ten amendments, known as the Bill of Rights, were submitted by the first Congress and duly ratified. They guaranteed such fundamental rights as freedom of speech, press, and assembly, religious liberty, jury trial, and protection against unreasonable searches and excessive bails and punishments. The ninth and tenth amendments gave blanket protection against usurpations by the federal government of the rights of citizens and states. With the adoption of these amendments, it seemed that human rights as well as those of property had been covered by the Constitution. Unfortunately, these amendments have often not been so carefully guarded as have some other parts of this important document.

SELECTED READINGS

Beard, Charles and Mary, *Rise of American Civilization,* Vol. I, Chaps. V, VI.

Nettels, Curtis, *The Roots of American Civilization,* Chap. XXIV.

Jameson, J. F., *The American Revolution Considered as a Social Movement,* Chaps. I–III.

East, R. A., *Business Enterprise in the American Revolutionary Era,* Chaps. X–XII.

Hacker, L. M., *Triumph of American Capitalism,* Chaps. XIII–XIV.

Shultz, W. J., and Caine, M. R., *Financial Development of the United States,* Chaps. III–IV.

Clark, V. S., *History of Manufactures in the United States,* Vol. I, Chap. X.

Beard, C. A., *An Economic Interpretation of the Constitution of the United States,* Chaps. II, III, VI, X, XI.

Callender, G. S., *Selections from the Economic History of the United States, 1765–1860,* pp. 122–177.

Flügel, F., and Faulkner, H. U., *Readings in the Economic and Social History of the United States,* pp. 3–38.

☆ ☆

9

Finance and Tariff

☆ ☆

FISCAL POLICY OF THE NEW GOVERNMENT

IN spite of the widespread opposition to the adoption of the Constitution, the new government, when it commenced its labors in 1789, was comfortably controlled by the friends of that instrument. Eleven of the twenty-four Senators in the first Congress had helped to draft it, and a strong group of framers and ratifiers, led by James Madison, were in the House of Representatives. The first government was in no sense a coalition; only Thomas Jefferson in the Cabinet held lukewarm views toward the Constitution. Although certain concessions, as in the case of the first ten amendments, were made to the opponents, the early laws of the new republic were framed to meet the wishes of the conservative economic interests which had been responsible for the framing and adoption of the Constitution. They were essentially Federalist in policy.

Of the numerous problems which confronted the new government, none were more important than the financial. In fact, the chief items of legislation during the twelve years of the Washington and Adams administration had to do with financial matters. Since a major principle of the Federalist doctrine was a strong central government, one necessity was an ample income to establish and maintain such a structure. It was clear that the chief expenses would be the maintenance of an army and navy, the payment of principal and interest on the national debt, and the support of the so-called "civil list." Protection of the merchant marine, defense against the Indians, and preservation of the infant republic in the face of foreign aggression necessitated a military establishment. Debts must be paid if the credit of the new government was to be maintained. The general running expenses of the civil government must be met. As it turned out, about 50 per cent of the cost of government during the Federalist period went to the Army and Navy, about 30 per cent to the public debt, and the rest to the civil list and other expenses.

Washington offered the post of Secretary of the Treasury to Robert Morris, famous as the financier of the Revolution, but upon his refusal he appointed Alexander Hamilton. Under the latter's able leadership, a fiscal policy was inaugurated which established the new government on a firm financial basis. Duties on exports were forbidden by the Constitution, and it was natural to turn to tariffs on imports as the proper and easiest source for revenue. The Act of July 4, 1789, the first tariff act under the new government, was designed primarily for revenue, but it recognized the protective feature. There were eighty-one enumerated articles, upon over thirty of which specific duties were levied; the remainder called for ad valorem (appraised by value) rates varying from 7½ to 15 per cent. Upon all imported articles not enumerated a 5 per cent ad valorem duty was levied. Although the rates were exceedingly low, the average being not over 8½ per cent, some protection was given. The debates on the tariff brought out the conflicting interests of the various sections of the country. Duties were imposed to help the steel and paper mills of Pennsylvania, the brewers of New York and Philadelphia, the glass manufacturers of Maryland, the iron workers and rum distillers of New England. The by-products of the farmhouse were also aided by duties on nails, boots and shoes, and ready-made clothing. Luxuries, such as tea, coffee, sugar, and wines, were more heavily taxed. It was soon found, however, that the tariff of 1789 did not provide enough revenue, and increases were made in 1790, 1792, and 1794.

One of the last acts of the first Congress which adjourned on September 29, 1789, was to request Alexander Hamilton to make a report on the state of the finances. In compliance with this he submitted four reports: the first on January 14, 1790, which dealt with the public debt; the second, on December 13, 1790, which recommended an excise; the third, on the same date, recommending a national bank; the fourth, on December 5, 1791, was his famous report on manufactures advocating protection.

In his first report Hamilton showed that the total foreign debt to France, Spain, and Holland, with arrears of interest, amounted to $11,710,378; the domestic debt with arrears at 6 per cent amounting to approximately $40,414,086, and the existing state debts of about $25,000,000 totaled $77,124,-464. He proposed that the national government take over this debt of the states which had been incurred to aid the Revolution and that both state and national debt be refunded at par. This was necessary, he said, to place the credit of the government on a firm basis. There was but slight opposition to the principle of paying the foreign and federal domestic debt, but the proposal that the federal government assume the state debts aroused violent controversy. It was justly charged that the speculator was favored at the expense of the patriot, and certain states at the expense of others. Certain southern states, where the debts relative to the population were less than in the North, strongly opposed assumption of state debts, and many who had parted with their depreciated paper for a song bitterly resented the payment at par to speculators. The honest but suspicious Republican Senator from Pennsylvania, William Maclay, comments in his diary in January, 1790: "This day the 'budget,' as it is called, was opened in the House of Representatives. An extraordinary rise of certificates has been remarked for some time past. This could not be accounted for, neither in Philadelphia nor elsewhere. But the report from the Treasury explained all. . . ." The following day he writes: "I call not at a single house or go into any company but traces of speculation in certificates appear"; and a few days later: "Hawkins, of North Carolina, said as he came up he passed two expresses with very large sums of money on their way to North Carolina for purposes of speculation in certificates. Wadsworth has sent off two small vessels for the Southern States, on the errand of buying up certificates. I really fear the members of Congress are deeper in this business than any others." [1]

Hamilton finally prevailed against bitter opposition (August 4, 1790). His arguments were both economic and political. Refunding and assumption would establish the credit of the federal government, consolidate behind it the commercial and financial interests, and provide sound securities which might answer the purposes of money in business operations. "If all the public creditors," he urged, "receive their dues from one source, distributed by an equal hand, having the same interests, they will unite in support of the fiscal arrangements of the government." Washington's approval helped, as did the personal interests of many congressional holders of state and federal paper. Jefferson also cooperated by promoting a political deal by which the advocates of the measure, in return for southern votes, permitted the national capital to be located on the Potomac. Two years later he wrote disgustedly to Washington that he had been "duped" into this "by the Secretary of the Treasury, and made a tool for forwarding his schemes, not then sufficiently understood by me. . . ." It seems doubtful if the shrewd Virginian was as innocent as he claimed. His home state received one-sixth of the total assumption expenditure, a windfall which wiped out not only her entire Revolutionary debt but also most of her other debts. Whatever may have been the circumstances surrounding the passage of the bill, Hamilton's plan was sound in principle.

---

[1] E. S. Maclay (ed.), *Journal of William Maclay* (1890), pp. 177–179. In its details the bill was extremely complicated and not financially advantageous to the federal government. An interesting feature of the Funding Act of 1790 was the provision for cleaning up the Continental currency. In 1780 Congress had recommended to the states that the notes be taken up at forty to one, and $119,400,000 were received and canceled. Under the Funding Act of 1790 some $6,000,000 were taken in at the United States Treasury at the rate of one hundred to one in payment for government bonds. The rest were lost, destroyed, or never redeemed.

Hamilton's advice that an excise tax be levied was in like manner followed by Congress, but only after most strenuous opposition. It was his belief that an excise would both provide revenue for the national government and bring home to the most remote frontiersman who operated a still the power of that government. The tax accomplished its purpose, but it rested heavily and, it was felt, unjustly upon the frontiersmen, whose bulky products could be marketed only when reduced to the more concentrated form of whisky. The opposition of the Pennsylvania frontiersmen to the tax in the "Whisky Rebellion" of 1794 demonstrated both the hatred toward it and the strength of the new government in crushing disobedience. Under Jefferson the tax was modified and in 1802 repealed.

Hamilton's third recommendation was the establishment of a national bank. This was to be modeled after the Bank of England, a great institution privately owned but publicly controlled. In one respect Hamilton deviated from the English model by suggesting that the federal government own one-fifth of the stock. He urged the bank on the ground that (1) it would provide a much-needed paper currency, (2) it would furnish a safe place for keeping public funds, (3) it would benefit both the government and business by providing banking facilities for the carrying on of commercial transactions, and (4) it could act as a fiscal agency for the government in such transactions as the sale of bonds. There was a real need for such a bank, for at the time of the adoption of the Constitution there were only three banks in the United States—the Bank of North America in Philadelphia, the Bank of New York, and the Bank of Massachusetts in Boston. Furthermore, under the new Constitution the states were not allowed to issue money. That the proposed bank would have tremendous influence over the nation's currency and credit and the power virtually to dictate federal fiscal policies was obvious. This, however, was no drawback to the Federalist capitalists who at the moment controlled the national government and presumably would soon own the most of the bank.

To Jefferson and his followers, who advocated a strict construction of the Constitution,[2] the bank bill seemed highly dangerous. He saw in it the creation of a financial monopoly in the hands of seaboard capitalists which might operate unfairly and to the detriment of state banks. He argued that the bill was unconstitutional, and when he failed to prevent its passage, he organized a political party which drove the Federalists out of office in the campaign of 1800. Despite strong opposition the bank was chartered in 1791 for twenty years with a capital of $10,000,000, of which

[2] By "strict construction" is meant a limiting of the powers accorded to the national government by the Constitution to the exact letter of that document; by "loose construction," the broad interpretation of certain clauses of the Constitution and "the general welfare" phrase in Article I, Section 8, to include an extension to implied powers not specifically prohibited.

amount the government might subscribe $2,000,000 and private investors $8,000,000, one-fourth in specie and three-fourths in government bonds. The notes of the bank were to be limited to the amount of the capital stock and were to be receivable in taxes as long as they were redeemable at the bank in specie. Reports were to be made to the Secretary of the Treasury, who was authorized to inspect the affairs of the bank at any time. In spite of this strict government regulation, the bank was in reality chartered as a private corporation and as such met bitter opposition. The First United States Bank was nevertheless a salutary influence in the financial operations of the early republic, fulfilling amply the expectations of its advocates. Aided by the credit of the government, it was able to do business in a conservative fashion and acted as an efficient agent of the Treasury Department. By refusing to accept the notes of non-specie-paying banks it drove out fiat money and kept the paper at par.

The currency of the new bank was issued in terms of the dollar, the unit already adopted by the Congress of the Confederation. In 1792, after a report from Hamilton, Congress passed its first currency Act placing the valuation of the new American dollar at 24.75 grains of gold, the value of the Spanish milled dollar, and establishing the decimal system.[3] In the belief that a grain of gold was equal to 15 grains of silver, it was provided that a silver dollar should contain 24.75 times 15, or 371.25 grains of pure silver, the smaller coins to be of proportional weight. Free and unlimited coinage of both gold and silver was provided for in the Act, and both were made full legal tender. Although a mint was established in Philadelphia which in 1794 began the coinage of silver and in 1795 that of gold, little metal was brought in to be coined. This was due partly to the fact that the amount of precious metals mined in this country during those years was small, and partly to the fact that silver was slightly overvalued at the ratio of 15 to 1, thus discouraging the coinage of gold entirely, for under the working of Gresham's Law, cheap money drives out the better currency.[4] What gold was coined was speedily sent out of the country, and the nation was soon reduced to a silver standard. But the silver situation continued somewhat unsatisfactory because American silver dollars were exported to the West Indies where they were accepted in exchange for Spanish milled dollars of slightly greater value. The latter were brought

[3] The basic ideas for the American currency system were actually presented first by Jefferson in a report to Congress under the Articles of Confederation. Hamilton advised little that was new except to decrease slightly the amount of silver in the dollar.

[4] When two or more currencies of unequal value are in concurrent circulation, each being available for money payments, the poorer tends to drive the better out of circulation. The ratio 15–1 was accurate in 1792, but new discoveries of Mexican silver reduced the value of silver.

in, reduced to bullion, and presented to the mint for coinage. This was profitable to the importers of Spanish dollars but it provided no currency for the United States, and Jefferson stopped the practice in 1806 by closing the mint. From then until 1836 no silver dollars were coined. Until the coinage system was changed in 1834, paper money, coins of small denominations, and foreign coins supplied the need for currency.

The recommendations of Hamilton and the laws which followed were designed not only to end the financial chaos but to strengthen the federal government. Their implication was political as well as economic, and in the controversies over their adoption the group opposed to them speedily developed into the Republican party, destined before many years to assume under Jefferson the reins of government. As already suggested, these measures were especially heartening to the commercial and financial interests, but the settlers west of the Alleghenies also felt the benefits and strength of the new government. This was particularly true of the Treaty of 1795 with Spain, by which the "right of deposit" at New Orleans was obtained, a right which gave to the Westerners the privilege of landing their products and reshipping without the payment of duties.

It has long been the habit to attribute the success of the new federal government to the excellence of the Constitution and the soundness of the Hamiltonian economics, but this is only part of the story. The federal government was hardly organized before Europe was plunged into a war which brought new markets to American shippers, industrialists, and agrarians alike. The Constitution was launched on a wave of prosperity, and in the good times which followed the opposition to it rapidly disintegrated.

THE SECOND UNITED STATES BANK

Hamilton's idea of a banking system, modeled after that of Great Britain, in which a great bank under the joint control of private bankers and the government might regulate the currency and act as the fiscal agent of the government, was followed successfully in the First United States Bank of 1791. So useful was the bank that by the time its twenty-year charter expired many Republicans who had at first opposed it had been won to its support. Secretary of the Treasury Gallatin himself strongly advised its continuance. The House voted by a majority of one to renew the charter, but the Senate tied on the bill and Vice President George Clinton cast the deciding vote against it. The opposition of the West and of the state banks everywhere, along with the old Republican suspicion of the power and monopoly of the bank, ended its career.

With the restraining hand of a specie-paying national bank removed, numerous state banks sprang up, the number increasing from 88 to 246 in five years, and the money in circulation from 45 to 100 million. Their various notes circulated at a discount, sometimes as great as 50 per cent. The disorganized state of the currency was accentuated by the War of 1812, which the government financed with great difficulty. More than a year passed after war was declared before Congress summoned enough courage to increase the internal taxes, and the war was largely paid for by loans approximating $80,000,000 and treasury notes to the amount of $36,680,794. The latter usually bore interest and were receivable in all payments to the United States, but had no legal tender qualities. Owing to the opposition of New England, these loans were floated chiefly in the Middle Atlantic States, and with the exception of the first loan were sold at discounts running as high as 20 per cent.

The disastrous financial experience of the Treasury during the war and the chaotic condition of the currency led Secretary Dallas to urge the creation of a new United States bank. With the lessons of the war still fresh, the Republicans, who so long had denounced the earlier institution, now chartered the Second United States Bank in 1816 for twenty years; it provided that one-fifth of the $35,000,000 capital should be subscribed by the government and that five of the twenty-five directors should be appointed by the President. It was expected that the notes of the new bank, redeemable in specie on demand, would force the state banks to resume specie payment or drive their notes out of circulation. Although mismanaged during the first three years, after a reorganization in 1819 the bank efficiently handled the fiscal operations of the government and exercised a very salutary effect upon the currency. Nevertheless, the bank was strongly disliked in many parts of the country, particularly in the South and West. Its restraining influence upon the wildcat currency of the frontier banks aroused bitter opposition, as did the feeling on the part of the West that it was a dangerous monopoly in the hands of a few eastern bankers. Certain of the states attempted to tax branch banks out of existence, but Chief Justice Marshall in two famous decisions (McCulloch v. Maryland, 1819, and Osborn v. United States Bank, 1824) declared the acts unconstitutional, asserting that what the Constitution permitted the national government to set up no state might destroy.

The Second United States Bank, under the able direction of Langdon Cheves and Nicholas Biddle, rendered a real service to the nation. Unfortunately for its future, the question of its recharter aroused the latent hostility between the debtor and democratic West and the more conservative creditor East. Andrew Jackson, true son of the West, feared the bank as a dangerous monopoly prejudicial to the interests of the common man, and became convinced that Biddle and his associates were using the vast power of the bank to play politics. In his first message Jackson questioned both the constitutionality and expediency of the bank, but committees in both the House and the Senate reported favorably upon it. The supporters of Henry Clay (candidate of the National Republican party in 1832), scenting a political issue which they believed would carry them to victory in 1832, prevailed upon the bank to petition for the renewal of the charter four years before the existing charter expired, and Biddle, convinced that such a move would be successful, did so. Jackson vetoed the bill; the question of the bank was made an issue in the presidential election of 1832, and the victory of the Democrats spelled the doom of the bank. In an effort to frighten the nation into support of the bank, Biddle in 1833 ordered a contraction of loans and produced a credit stringency known as "Biddle's Panic." Instead of accomplishing the desired result, he merely convinced the people that Jackson was right and that the powers of the bank were dangerous to the nation. Jackson fought back by refusing to deposit government funds in the Second United States Bank. He had to remove two Secretaries of the Treasury before he could find one who would follow this policy, but in the end he dealt staggering blows to the bank before its charter expired in 1836.

BANKING AND CURRENCY, 1837–1862

The failure to recharter the Second United States Bank was a victory for the West, and it ended the attempt to control the currency by means of a central bank. Depositing government funds in selected institutions ("pet banks," as Jackson's political opponents called them) was far from satisfactory, however, encouraging as it did overexpansion of bank notes and laying the government open to the charge of favoritism. Arguing that it was not the business of the government to assume the management of domestic or private exchange or to engage in any kind of banking business, Van Buren proposed that the government establish an independent treasury to care for its own funds. By means of subtreasuries the government would collect its revenues in specie and make all disbursements in specie through its own officials. By this plan it was intended not only to divorce the government entirely from the business of banking, but also, by paying only specie, to promote the use of specie and thereby lessen the demand for bank notes. This independent treasury system was established after much opposition by the Democrats in 1840, discontinued by the Whigs in 1841, and then reestablished by the Democrats in 1846 (continuing until merged with the Federal Reserve System in 1913 and finally abolished in 1921 by an Act of 1920). In the meantime, the Whigs endeavored unsuccessfully to reestablish a central bank, and their failure ended until 1863 the circulation of paper money sanctioned by the federal government. The independent treasury system proved safe and efficient in handling the government funds, and also appeared to have had some success in restraining overexpansion of bank notes and in promoting the circulation of specie. Moreover, it prevented a financial crisis from tying up federal funds. One weakness was that it withdrew a portion of the nation's specie from circulation. As long as federal balances were small, no trouble might follow; but if the balances were large, the effect might be disastrous. The end of the Second United States Bank and the establishment of the independent treasury system did not, as we shall see, solve the fundamental question of control of credit. Whether this should be a function of government, of private bankers, or of a combination of both still remains a subject of controversy.

In spite of his frontier background, Jackson was a hard-money man, and in the furtherance of this policy legislation was enacted in the hope of restoring an American metallic currency. The Act of 1792, which established free and unlimited coinage of gold and silver at 15 to 1, overvalued silver, and under Gresham's Law gold disappeared. The silver dollar, it will be remembered, had been discontinued in 1806, leaving a miscellaneous collection of foreign coins as practically the only metallic currency. By an Act of 1834 (slightly amended in 1837) the ratio was changed from 15 to 1 to 15.98+ to 1, or approximately 16 to 1. At the same time, the weight of the gold dollar was reduced from 24.75 grains of pure gold to 23.22, while the weight of the silver dollar remained the same, that is 371.25 grains of pure silver. Under this new ratio, gold was overvalued and came into circulation again, while silver failed to appear. The overvaluation of gold was even more evident after the discoveries in California in 1848 reduced the price of that metal. It was only by debasing the fractional silver in 1853 that subsidiary silver was kept in circulation.

In addition to the metallic currency coined by the federal government, there was an increasing number of bank notes of various denominations issued by the state banks. The number of such banks increased from 307 in 1820 to 1601 in 1860, their capital from 102 million to 422 million, and their note circulation from about $16,600,000 to $207,000,000. As these banks were authorized by the states and in some cases their president and directors chosen by the legislature, the question of the constitutionality of their note issues was a pertinent one.[5] This question came before the courts in 1824 and was not definitely settled until 1837 when the Supreme Court made a distinction between bills issued on the credit of a state and those issued by an institution in which the state might be the sole stockholder;[6]

[5] Article 1, Section 10. "No State shall . . . coin money; emit bills of credit," etc.
[6] Briscoe v. The Commonwealth of Kentucky, 11 Peters 257.

the latter were held constitutional. In the earlier cases Marshall had attempted to restrict narrowly the note issues of banks, but the states'-rights court under Taney gave them wide leeway.

The issues of these banks obviously depended chiefly upon the safeguards provided by the states. In Massachusetts as early as 1809 a penalty of 2 per cent a month was placed upon banks which failed to redeem their notes on demand, and all banks incorporated after 1829 were restricted in their note circulation to one and one-fourth times the capital. The "Suffolk System," a method by which the city banks stood ready to redeem note issues and the country banks were required to establish redemption agencies in Boston, kept the New England bank notes at par. New York established a "safety fund" whereby each bank had to pay to the treasurer of the state an amount equal to one-half of one per cent of its capital stock until the payments should amount to 3 per cent, this fund to be used to redeem the notes of any bank which failed. These safety devices, however, were unusual. The legislatures were inexperienced and the pressure for easy money was great; the result was that the notes of hundreds of banks were in circulation, the value of which even an expert banker could hardly determine. Furthermore, counterfeiting was relatively easy. The difficulty of carrying on business under such handicaps can easily be imagined.

THE SPECIE CIRCULAR AND THE PANICS
OF 1837 AND 1857 [7]

With the downfall of the Second United States Bank came a rapid expansion in the number, capital, and note circulation of the state banks. An orgy of speculation followed which was aided by the distribution among the states in 1837 of the government surplus to the amount of about $28,000,000.[8] It was likewise spurred on by the mania for internal improvements and the inordinate speculation in western land. The income from the receipt of public lands jumped from $1,880,000 in 1830 to over $20,000,000 in 1836. Jackson, who was far from an expert on finance, clearly saw the essential unsoundness of the situation when he said in a message to Congress, "It was perceived that the receipts arising from the sales of the public lands were increasing to an unprecedented amount. In effect, however, these receipts amounted to nothing more than credits in bank. The banks lent out their notes to speculators. They were paid to the receivers [land agents] and immediately returned to the banks, to be lent out again and again, being mere

---

[7] For a general discussion of panics, see Chap. 29.

[8] The national debt was paid off in 1835, and during the next two years, for the only time in our history, the federal government was out of debt. The surplus which accumulated during this period was distributed to the states in the form of a loan, but it was understood at the time that it was to be an outright gift, and not a dollar has been recalled.

instruments to transfer to speculators the most valuable public lands and pay the Government by a credit on the books of the banks. . . . The spirit of expansion and speculation was not confined to the deposit banks, but pervaded the whole multitude of banks throughout the Union and was giving rise to new institutions to aggravate the evil." [9] The bubble of speculation was enlarged by the utterly reckless manner in which the states borrowed here and abroad for internal improvements and the prodigality with which they loaned their credit to unsound institutions.

The panic of 1837 was presaged by the crop failure of 1835. This prevented the farmers from meeting their obligations to the land speculators and merchants, and the latter could not pay their loans at the banks. The crop failure eventually produced a balance of trade against the United States, a withdrawal of foreign credits, and a need of specie to pay foreign creditors. In the midst of these accumulated difficulties Jackson hastened the crisis by issuing on July 11, 1836, his Specie Circular, an order which directed that future payments for public land had to be made in gold and silver. This served as a wet blanket to dampen the ardor of speculation in western land and shook the confidence in the circulating bank notes. The situation was further complicated by the failure of important mercantile houses in England toward the end of 1836, involving many English manufacturers and cutting down the demand for American cotton.

The panic which ensued was the worst that the nation had experienced up to that date. By the end of May, 1837, every bank in the country had suspended specie payment. The bank note circulation contracted from $149,-000,000 in 1837 to $58,000,000 in 1843, and the sale of public land fell off from $20,000,000 in 1836 to $1,000,000 in 1841. In that year Congress passed a special bankruptcy law under which 39,000 persons canceled $441,000,000 worth of debt. The depression continued to be severe for five or six years, holding back the expansion of both manufactures and agriculture.

Eventually recovery set in, and with the revival of business the country again experienced a period of remarkable growth. Spurred on by rising prices, due chiefly to the discovery of gold in California in 1848, railroad building was pushed on rapidly, new manufacturing establishments were set up, and the westward movement was accelerated. A temporary halt was called by the third great panic in our history, that of 1857. Overspeculation in the future of the country and overinvestment in railways upon which an adequate return was largely an expectation of the future, and in mineral resources, produced a setback, the causes of which closely resemble those of our other panics. As Schouler points out: "Premature railroads at the West

[9] Eighth Annual Message, December 5, 1836, in Richardson's *Messages and Papers of the Presidents* (1909 ed.), II, 1468.

had fostered premature cities, teeming with premature traffic for a premature population; and while canals and railroads had conspired to reduce the mileage rate of transportation, the dispersion of American farmers over a vastly wider area counterbalanced that advantage." [10] The failure of the Ohio Life Insurance and Trust Company in August, 1857, precipitated the panic, which was primarily financial and affected chiefly the financial centers and the speculative western railroad investments. Recovery was quick and the opening of the Civil War found the nation on the upgrade of a new cycle of prosperity.

TARIFF POLICY TO THE CIVIL WAR

Although the first American tariff was passed scarcely two months after the inauguration of Washington, until 1816 the various Acts had been primarily for revenue and had afforded only incidental protection. It is true that Alexander Hamilton in his *Report on Manufactures* had given classic expression to the arguments for protection, but a strong movement for a protective tariff waited upon the War of 1812 and its effects. The collapse of prices in land and agricultural products following the deflation of 1815–1818, and the fear that the dumping of European goods set free by the close of the war might snuff out the infant manufacturing, aroused an active interest in protection. In the years of ardent nationalism following the War of 1812, statesmen and economists, to say nothing of manufacturers, rang all the changes on the argument for protection of "infant industries." Still influenced by the war, all sections of the country united in supporting the tariff of 1816. The bill was introduced by William Lowndes of South Carolina, and John C. Calhoun, later a most uncompromising opponent of protection, led the fight for its enactment. It placed duties ranging from 7½ to 30 per cent ad valorem, giving special protection to cottons, woolens, iron, and other manufactured commodities stimulated by the recent war.

From 1816 until 1833 the movement for protection grew steadily. Men like the publicist, Mathew Carey, and the editor, Hezekiah Niles, formulated and popularized the arguments, and the popular political idol, Henry Clay, took the leadership in advocating it. To the "infant industries" argument Clay now added and emphasized the need for manufacturing to provide home markets for agricultural products and raw materials. In a famous speech in March, 1824, he pointed out the loss of European markets which the American farmer had suffered as a result of the close of the Napoleonic Wars, and asserted that only by developing industrial cities could the American farmer find a market for his surplus. In later speeches he tied up the movement for internal improvements with his plea for the tariff, showing that better trans-

[10] James Schouler, *History of the United States of America Under the Constitution,* V, 384.

portation facilities were necessary for the exchange of products between the farmer and industrialist. Such an economic development, he believed, would free American prosperity from dependence on European markets, and to his program he gave the name "American System."

While Clay was urgently advocating his "American System," diverse interests began to make themselves felt and to line up definitely the sections of the country on one side or the other. The center of the early movement for protection was in the middle and western states of that period—New York, New Jersey, Pennsylvania, Ohio, and Kentucky; they had felt keenly the disturbing effects of the war, and were anxious to develop a home market to dispose of their agricultural products. The South, on the other hand, was desirous of obtaining her manufactured articles cheaply and, with her chief market in Europe, naturally opposed protection. Manufacturing was being successfully carried on in the South, but it was relatively small in amount, and the great majority of the influential classes were convinced that her future lay in agriculture. New England at first was divided. The manufacturing interests, not yet powerful, were in favor of protection, whereas the shipping group and the merchants feared that a tariff would injure their business. As a consequence, she split her votes on the tariff until about 1830, when the manufacturers won control and lined her up on the side of protection. This change may be seen in the attitude of Daniel Webster, who opposed the tariff of 1816 but supported that of 1828. On the other hand, Calhoun, who had ardently backed the tariff of 1816, now led the opposition to the protective system.

In 1818 further protection was given to iron, and the duty of 25 per cent on cotton was extended until 1826. A general revision was undertaken after the election of 1824, at which time all the candidates had advocated protection. Not only was additional protection given to manufacturers of woolen goods, lead, glass, and iron, but 25 per cent was now granted to hemp manufacturers, and wool growers were specifically aided. This tariff received the support of the iron interests of Pennsylvania, the wool growers of Ohio and the Middle States, the hemp growers of Kentucky, and the manufacturers everywhere, but it incurred the disfavor of the northern shipper and the bitter hostility of the South, where much wool was used for Negro clothing.

The tariff of 1828 was the result of the agitation of the woolen interests for increased protection, aided and abetted by the Jacksonian politicians, who thought they saw a chance of promoting the interests of their candidate in the coming election. It was their intention to propose a bill so obnoxious that it could not pass, although the Jackson men of the North might vote for it and thus pose in the next election as the true friends of domestic industry.

By increasing the duties on raw wool, sailcloth, and molasses it was expected that New England would line up with the South to oppose the measure. John Randolph sarcastically observed that "the bill referred to manufactures of no sort or kind, except the manufacture of a President of the United States."

To the surprise of all, this bill was passed, but it was so unpopular that it was speedily dubbed the "Tariff of Abominations." It was on the statute books only four years, but during that time it aroused a storm of opposition, especially in the South. In 1832 a new bill removed many of the abominations and practically restored the tariff to the basis of 1824. Nevertheless, the bill was still essentially protective, and South Carolina in November, 1832, passed the famous Nullification Ordinance declaring the "tariff law of 1828 and the amendment of the same in 1832" to be null and void and not binding upon the people of South Carolina. President Jackson's uncompromising stand for national unity left South Carolina little hope of success, and in 1833 both sides agreed to a compromise tariff introduced by Henry Clay. The outcome was a victory for the nationalists under Jackson, but a lowering of the tariff in favor of the South. The Act of 1833 provided for a decrease of all duties exceeding 20 per cent in the tariff of 1832; this reduction was to be very gradual until 1842, when a sudden lowering was to create a uniform rate of 20 per cent on all articles. This 20 per cent level, however, remained in force only two months, from July until the passage of the more strongly protective tariff of 1842 in September.

The tendency of the tariff rates from 1832 to the Civil War was generally downward, although the principle of protection was never relinquished. The panic of 1837 so depleted the income of the national government that the protectionists were successful in restoring the duties in 1842 almost to a level with those of 1832. Passed by the Whigs, this Act was speedily repudiated when the Democrats came into power in 1845. The Walker tariff of 1846 classified imported commodities under schedules, A, B, C, D, etc. Luxuries were put into Class A and a tariff of 100 per cent was imposed; semi-luxuries into Class B with a 40 per cent tax; commercial products into the remaining classes, with duties varying from 30 down to 5 per cent. The Walker tariff changed the system from specific to ad valorem duties and introduced the warehousing system of storing goods until the duty was paid, an innovation permanently retained. The duties, while maintaining protection, were radically lowered by this tariff, and the tendency toward reduction was continued in 1857, when the free list was enlarged and the rates of the Walker tariff lowered by 5 per cent. The reductions of 1857 were the result of a treasury full to overflowing from the immense expansion of business from 1846 to

1857. From the latter date until 1861 the United States more closely approached a free-trade basis than at any time since 1815.[11]

It is extremely difficult, if not impossible, to determine the effects of the tariff system during the years preceding the Civil War. Undoubtedly the tariff legislation of the first seventy years of our history aided the growth of manufacturing and industry; it is equally true, however, that the emergence of the United States as an industrial nation was inevitable. The effect of the tariffs was chiefly artificial stimulation of a natural development. It is also undoubtedly true that the policy of protection was to a certain extent detrimental to the South, as southern political leaders contended. But it should be remembered that the South won in the tariff battle of the 1830's and that from then on until the Civil War the trend of tariff rates was downward. The tariff was but one of a number of causes which brought the economic decline of the seaboard South. Nevertheless, Southerners channeled much of their economic discontent into opposition of the tariff, and its psychological influence was important in bringing secession. Of one aspect of the tariff system, at least, the student of economic history can be certain. It was receipts from the tariff that mainly supported the federal government during this period. Except for one year (1836) such receipts were higher—usually from five to ten times—than all other sources of income put together.

SELECTED READINGS

Dewey, D. R., *Financial History of the United States,* Chaps. III–X.

Shultz, W. J., and Caine, M. R., *Financial Development of the United States,* Chaps. IV–XI.

Taussig, F. W., *Tariff History of the United States,* Part I.

Beard, Charles and Mary, *Rise of American Civilization,* Vol. I, Chap. XII.

McGrane, R. C., *The Panic of 1837,* Chaps. I–II.

Paxson, F. L., *History of the American Frontier,* Chaps XXVI XXVII.

Callender, G. S., *Selections from the Economic History of the United States, 1765–1860,* Chaps. X, XI.

Bogart, E. L., and Thompson, C. M., *Readings in the Economic History of the United States,* Chaps. X, XV.

Taussig, F. W., *Selected Readings in International Trade and Tariff Policies,* Part III, Chaps. XVII–XXI.

Flügel, F., and Faulkner, H. U., *Readings in the Economic and Social History of the United States,* Chaps. III and IX.

[11] Mention was made (p. 169) of Mathew Carey, Hezekiah Niles, and Henry Clay, prominent advocates of a protective tariff. A low tariff also had its exponents during this period, especially in the South, where Thomas Cooper of the University of South Carolina, T. R. Dew of William and Mary, and George Tucker of the University of Virginia, gave intellectual leadership to this group.

Westward Expansion from the
Revolution to the Civil War

THE WEST AT THE CLOSE OF THE REVOLUTION

ENGLAND and France fought over the lands between the Alleghenies and the Mississippi in the French and Indian War, but it was to the newly founded American Republic that this region was destined to go. The Treaty of 1783 recognized the boundaries of the United States as extending from the Atlantic Ocean and the St. Croix River on the east to the Mississippi on the west, and from the 45th parallel, the St. Lawrence River, the Great Lakes, and the Lake of the Woods on the north to the northern boundary of Florida on the south. The territory of the thirteen original colonies comprised 341,752 square miles, and the region beyond the mountains 488,248 square miles. How the country north of the Ohio was conquered in 1778–1779 by George Rogers Clark and his brave band of frontiersmen has already been told.[1] But fully as important as Clark's exploit was the actual occupation of the Southwest by the vanguard of settlers led by Boone, Robertson, and Sevier, whose hold on the Ohio and Cumberland Valleys was bitterly resented by the Indians.

The opening of the Revolution saw some six or seven thousand French scattered throughout the Mississippi Valley. Their settlements stretched from Biloxi on the Gulf of Mexico west to New Orleans, northward up the Mississippi to St. Louis and to Vincennes on the Wabash. For decades the French had experimented with plantation crops in the lower Mississippi Valley, had exploited the fur resources of the Missouri country, and had worked the lead mines in the present state of Missouri. Although the Spaniards in the years immediately after the Revolution held official title to Florida and to the vast region west of the Mississippi, Spanish settlements, except in the New Mexican region, were as yet few and thinly scattered.[2] Spanish Florida was little more than a string of huts and trading posts.

[1] Oliver Pollock, American agent at New Orleans, a little-known Revolutionary financier, helped make possible the success of Clark. See biographies by Bodley or James.
[2] Above, pp. 109–110.

Of settlers from the British colonies on the Atlantic seacoast, only two or three hundred by 1776 had broken through the mountain passes and settled along the Monongahela, on the upper Kanawha, and at Watauga on the upper Holston. The conclusion of peace, however, found 25,000 scattered along the head of the Cumberland, on the Kentucky River, on the Holston and French Broad, and in groups as far west as the Mississippi. Peace merely accentuated the movement of the population, which during the next half century swarmed into the region west of the mountains.

INTERNATIONAL BACKGROUND OF MISSISSIPPI VALLEY SETTLEMENT

The international aspect of the Mississippi Valley from 1783 to 1812 develops a tangled story of the three-cornered attempt on the part of Spain, France, and England to gain control of this region. Each of the three nations intrigued to stir up the Indians against the United States and to detach the settlers west of the Alleghenies from their allegiance to the new government. Although Great Britain had agreed in the Treaty of 1783 to relinquish the forts along the Great Lakes, she continued to hold them in the interest of the fur trade, the annual value of which was estimated at £100,000.[3] From these points of vantage she impressed upon the Indians the importance of not ceding land to the oncoming settlers, furnished them with arms and munitions, and encouraged them to oppose the westward advance. Her emissaries tried to induce Kentucky and Vermont to leave the Union. Wayne's victory over the Indians at Fallen Timber, followed by the Treaty of Greenville in 1795, opened most of Ohio to settlers, and nine subsequent treaties up to 1809 gave western Ohio and Indiana bit by bit to the white man. By Jay's Treaty with Great Britain in 1795 the British government promised to evacuate posts in the United States territory, but her active interference in the Middle West was not eliminated until the War of 1812.

The Spaniards, who had unsuccessfully attempted during the peace negotiations of 1781–1783 to prevent the thirteen colonies from obtaining the land west of the Alleghenies, now held Louisiana. From there they intrigued with the Creeks and Cherokees to bind them close to Spain and to use them as instruments to stem the advance into the Southwest. Their agents worked among the western leaders—men like George Rogers Clark (who offered his sword both to Spain and to France), Sevier, and Robertson—to foster movements for independence in order to erect buffer states between the thirteen colonies and the Mississippi. To the "Men of the Western Waters" free navigation of the Mississippi and the right of deposit at New Orleans was essential

[3] James M'Gill to Lt. Gov. Hamilton, Aug. 1, 1785. R. G. Thwaites (ed.), *Collections of the State Historical Society of Wisconsin*, XII, 72.

to their economic prosperity as the only outlet for their produce. Spain held the whip hand, and the indifference of the East made her overtures alluring. Discontent did not subside until Kentucky was admitted to the Union in 1792 and Tennessee in 1796, and until the Treaty of San Lorenzo, negotiated by Pinckney in 1795, had brought about the evacuation of the Spanish posts on the east bank of the Mississippi and the free use of that river with the right of deposit at New Orleans.

The career of France in the Mississippi Valley covered over a century. Her failure in the momentous struggle with England she did not consider as the concluding chapter. A few years later she joined with the American colonies in an effort to disrupt the British Empire, and at the peace negotiations strove strenuously both to limit the boundary of the American Republic to the land east of the Alleghenies and to obtain from Spain the return of Louisiana. After the Revolution, French diplomacy aimed to keep the colonies in America disunited, at the same time pushing French interests in the Mississippi. In Europe the effort to gain Louisiana from Spain was never dropped. This dream of resurrecting their lost empire in the New World for the triple purpose of checking England, of rendering the United States subservient, and of provisioning the French West Indies, was pursued under the Bourbons, the government of the Revolution, and the Consulate. Eventually Napoleon succeeded in acquiring Louisiana under the terms of the Treaty of San Ildefonso (1800), but held it only a short time. Realizing that it was hopeless to hold on to an overseas empire while England commanded the sea, that Louisiana was less valuable after the successful revolt in Santo Domingo, that he needed money to carry on the war with Great Britain, and that a successful war with that nation might enable him to recover the territory, Napoleon decided to sell the vast region between the Mississippi and the Rocky Mountains to the United States for a paltry $15,000,000. Jefferson understood the vital need of the Mississippi to the trans-Allegheny settlements and he was a man who could think in terms of a continent. A strict constructionist by principle, in this case he relinquished his constitutional scruples and in the face of much eastern opposition strongly urged the acquisition.

Notwithstanding the purchase of Louisiana, the fate of the Mississippi Valley was not fully determined until 1815, when the outcome at Waterloo laid to rest any further dreams of a French empire in America. In the meantime the War of 1812 had definitely eliminated England. The Second War for Independence was nominally fought over seamen's rights. In reality, however, it was a war of the West. Clay and the western "War Hawks" had pushed it in Congress. During the war Westerners, hungry for a greater empire, had unsuccessfully sought to annex Canada. With greater success the frontiersmen of the South had cleared the Creeks from southern and western Alabama and won the only notable land victory of the war at New Orleans. The war may have been a military stalemate but it ended British intrigues with the Indians in the Mississippi Valley. The results of the war were of interest chiefly to the West.

THE ORDINANCE OF 1787

Among the first problems which confronted Congress on the cessation of hostilities in 1781 was the disposition of the western territory. Under the vague but inclusive wordings of the original charters Georgia, South Carolina, North Carolina, and Virginia claimed that their boundaries extended west to the Mississippi. The Northwest was in dispute between Virginia, Connecticut, Massachusetts, and New York; six states—Maryland, Pennsylvania, Delaware, New Jersey, New Hampshire, and Rhode Island—had no claims on western land. Fear that the greater expansion of the states with western claims might impair their own relative importance, and jealousy because the fortunate states could use the western lands to pay off war debts, motivated these six states to repeated demands that the trans-Allegheny region be turned over to the national government. The fight was led by Maryland, who had demanded as early as 1779 "that a country unsettled at the commencement of this war, claimed by the British crown, and ceded to it by the Treaty of Paris, if wrested from the common enemy by the blood and treasure of the thirteen States, should be considered as common property, subject to be parcelled out by Congress into free, convenient, and independent governments, in such manner and at such times as the wisdom of the assembly shall hereafter direct." [4] Later she refused to ratify the Articles of Confederation until the states with claims promised to give them up. This they eventually did, though it was not until 1802 that Georgia, the last state, turned over her lands.

In 1784 Thomas Jefferson proposed a plan for dividing the Northwest Territory into a number of states with high-sounding classical names (Sylvania, Assenisipia, Metropotamia, Polypotamia, etc.), whose inhabitants were to enjoy most of the rights of the citizens of the older states and which were eventually to be admitted to the Union on equal terms as soon as their population warranted it. This plan was amplified in the more famous Ordinance of 1787, which provided (1) that not less than three nor more than five states were to be erected out of the territory, (2) that until the population numbered 5000 free male inhabitants the territory should be ruled by a governor

[4] Instructions of Maryland to her delegates, read in Congress May 21, 1779. Quoted by H. B. Adams, *Maryland's Influence upon Land Cessions to the United States* (1885), Johns Hopkins Studies, III.

and three judges appointed by Congress, who were to determine the local officers and make the laws, subject to veto by Congress; (3) that after the population reached 5000 the territories could have a two-house legislature, the lower appointed by the people and the upper a legislative council of five men selected by Congress from ten nominated by the lower house. The legislature could send a delegate to Congress with right to debate but not to vote. During this territorial stage the governor had power to veto; political rights were based on graduated ownership of land; a man owning 50 acres had the right to vote for a representative, but to be eligible for the lower house he must own 200 acres, for the upper house 500, and for the governorship, 1000 acres; (4) when any of the territories should have 60,000 inhabitants it might form a permanent constitution and state government and its delegates be admitted into Congress "on an equal footing with the original states in all respects whatever." This Ordinance laid down the principles of procedure which have since been generally followed in regard to new territory.[5]

Because the Northwest Ordinance of 1787 laid down the procedure upon which new states might organize, it has rightly received great emphasis from political historians. But it also had social and economic results of great importance. It established for the first time in history the principle that colonies were to be considered as an extension of the mother country and were to be put on an equal footing in every respect. The old mercantilist idea that they existed simply for the benefit of the mother country was abandoned. The Ordinance abolished slavery; guaranteed life, liberty, property, and religious freedom; and encouraged education. It did much to encourage millions to move westward.

EARLY LAND POLICY OF THE REPUBLIC

Even before the famous Ordinance of 1787 had been passed, the Congress of the Confederation was giving attention to the problem of land disposal

[5] "The so-called Ohio or Northwest Ordinance of July 13, 1787," said Eduard Fueter, the Swiss historian, "has been called one of the most important laws of the United States (from the point of world history it is perhaps the most important). . . . Thus the principle was abandoned that the welfare of the colonies ought to be subordinated to that of the mother country; rather was the principle established that colonies which are settled by a people are to be regarded as an extension of the mother country and are to be put on an equal footing in every respect." *World History*, p. 105, trans. by S. B. Fay (1922). Another famous provision of the Ordinance of 1787, which forever prohibited slavery in the entire region, reflected not only the anti-slavery attitude of the time but also the anxiety of the South to prevent possible competition in cotton, tobacco, and indigo. In respect to this prohibition, Professor Turner has said (and here he bears out the above quotation from Fueter): "While the importance of the article excluding slavery has often been pointed out, it is probable that the provisions for a federal colonial organization have been at least equally potential in our actual development. The full significance of this feature of the Ordinance is only appreciated when we consider its continuous influence upon the American territorial and State policy in the westward expansion to the Pacific, and the political preconceptions with which Americans approach the problems of government in the new insular possessions." *The Frontier in American History*, p. 132.

and laying the foundations of an American land policy. Despite a century and a half of experience, the problem was a difficult one. The Congress first of all had two objectives: it was anxious to promote settlement but at the same time to derive an income from the sale of public land. As most settlers were poor men with little or no capital, the two desires were hardly compatible. If the land was to be sold, should it be disposed of in large tracts or small ones? Sale in large tracts would play into the hands of wealthy land speculators; sale in small lots would benefit bona fide settlers who were generally poor. From the point of revenue, however, there were arguments against small sales. It might cost as much to survey the land as it was worth; buyers would purchase only the good land and leave the rest. It would tend to scatter the settlers rather than promote the compact settlements necessary for defense against the Indians. There was also the problem of settlement requirements. Should actual occupation of the land be required? Such a regulation would minimize speculation and favor the small buyer, but it might depress the value of the land. There were, of course, the important problems of price, of whether the land should be sold for cash or for credit (or both), and of where the land offices should be set up.

As all this involved the method by which a large part of the American continent was to be transferred from the government to private ownership, it was obviously a matter of primary significance. To the westward-moving settler the land policy of the government was of fundamental importance. Forced by necessity to tackle the problem, the Congress under the Articles of Confederation made a beginning in the Land Ordinance of 1785. This provided (1) for a rectangular land survey by the government, (2) for the setting aside of one thirty-sixth of the land for educational purposes, and (3) for the establishment of land offices for the sale of public lands at low prices. After a north and south line, known as the "prime meridian," had been established (the first one set up being the present boundary line between Ohio and Indiana), an east-west base line was established to intersect it at right angles. From the intersection of the prime meridian and the base line the surveyors ran out perpendicular lines at six-mile intervals. The crossing of these lines divided the land into squares containing 36 square miles. Each of these squares was to be a township and was subsequently to be subdivided into 36 squares each one mile square (640 acres), known as sections, Section 16 being reserved for the support of common schools. Most of the states admitted after 1842 reserved also Section 36 for school purposes, thus setting aside for education one-eighteenth of the land surveyed. An attempt was made to reserve Section 15 from each township for religious purposes, but it was voted down. In the history of American land policy the Ordinance of 1785 proved as fundamental as the Ordinance of 1787 did in the political life

of the new West. The method outlined in 1785 was generally followed during the next century.

It was in the methods of disposal rather than survey that policies changed.
Uncertain whether to follow the New England system of grants by townships
or the Virginia system of individual sales or grants, Congress in 1785 provided for both; half of the townships were to be sold entire and the other
half in sections of 640 acres. The land was to be sold at auction, with a minimum price of $1.00 an acre. An Act of 1796 raised the price to $2.00 an acre
but introduced a credit system that allowed a year for payment. As few
pioneers could command $1280, the demand arose immediately that the law
be changed to favor the settlers. As the political power of the West increased,
this demand was successful. In 1800 the minimum amount of land that could
be purchased was reduced to 320 acres and in 1804 to 160 acres. The time for
payment in the latter Act was extended to five years. New legislation in 1820
again reduced the amount to 80 acres and cut the price to $1.25 an acre. In-
ordinate speculation culminating in the panic of 1819, however, influenced
the Congress to abolish the credit system.

Perhaps the most important concession obtained by the West in the years
before the Civil War was the right of preemption, secured in 1841. For years
settlers had moved onto the public lands, cleared the forest, and laid out
farms without the formality of a purchase, only to find that they were illegal
intruders on government land; sometimes the land was sold over their heads
or they were driven off by federal troops. Settlers demanded the right to take
up the land that they wanted, whether it had been surveyed or not, and then
purchase it at the minimum price free from competitive bids. In actual practice they had sometimes succeeded in doing this before the law of 1841 made
it legal. Actual settlers would select their land and improve it and then
organize squatters' protective associations. These protective associations would
appear at the land auctions and make perfectly clear to any outsider that he
had better not bid on their land—that is, if he valued his personal safety. The
Preemption Act of 1841 was an important concession, but it was by no means
the ultimate goal of the western frontiersmen. But the next step, free land to
actual settlers, was not taken until the famous Homestead Act of 1862.

From this brief résumé of the more important land Acts, it is evident that
the land policy of the federal government became more liberal as time went
on. It is also clear that under them the West was settled, mainly by relatively
poor men. Nevertheless, the whole policy was by no means as just or as
democratic as might appear. One historian insists that "the liberalization of
the land laws, after 1820, must not be regarded as much more than a pious
gesture."[6] The chief weakness was the fact that in actual practice the laws

[6] Louis Hacker, *The Triumph of American Capitalism*, p. 209.

tended to favor the wealthy speculator rather than the poor settler. Three reasons (until the Homestead Act of 1862) were responsible: the government charged a price for the land beyond the capacity of the average settler, it set no limit on the amount that could be acquired, and it did not require actual settlement on, or improvement of, the land. Instead of promoting by such means a democratic society of small farmers, it threw the public domain into the hands of speculators. It is true that the government gave some land away —large grants to transportation companies, as in the case of the Illinois Central, and land bounties to veterans of Indian Wars and soldiers of the Mexican War. But the railroads sold their land to settlers or speculators and the veterans seldom actually settled on their land, preferring to sell their bounties at a small price to speculators. As the average settler did not have the money to purchase from the government for cash, he was forced to borrow from eastern capitalists at absurdly high rates or to buy from land speculators who had already bought the better land from the government. Even when he preempted the land he could not buy it except by borrowing. In many cases the pioneer worked himself out of debt; in others he improved the land, sold it to a newcomer at an advanced price, and then moved westward to take up a new farm which he might own free of mortgage. There were many sections where the land policy drove pioneer farmers into a state of tenancy rather than encouraged a democratic pattern of ownership.[7]

THE SETTLEMENT OF THE OLD SOUTHWEST

The first great trans-Allegheny migration, as we have seen, was south of the Ohio into Kentucky and Tennessee.[8] This went on steadily during the Revolution, the first census showing over 70,000 in Kentucky, and 35,000 in Tennessee. Repeated efforts by the pioneers of these two regions to free themselves from the parent states of Virginia and North Carolina were successful in 1792 and 1796, when the newly settled regions were respectively admitted to the Union as states. This migration had been undertaken chiefly by the yeomen farmers of the upcountry of the South who had originally found their way down the Great Valley from Pennsylvania, or by the small farmers who had been pushed out by the wealthier planters of the tidewater.

The Industrial Revolution, and especially the invention of the cotton gin in 1793, provided an apparently insatiable market for raw cotton and suddenly turned the eyes of the South to the development of a new staple. The tidewater lands of Virginia and the Carolinas seemed to be wearing out; this drove the southern planters to look westward for new and richer fields. The

[7] P. W. Gates, "Land Policy and Tenancy in the Prairie States," *Journal of Economic History*, I, 60–82 (May, 1941).

[8] Above, pp. 136–137.

demand for cotton was the chief determining factor in the second stage of the settlement of the Southwest, and as the importance of cotton increased, the planter pushed on behind the small farmer, who had first pioneered across the mountains.

By the side of the picture of the advance of the pioneer farmer [says Turner] bearing his household goods in his canvas-covered wagon to his new home across the Ohio, must therefore be placed the picture of the southern planter crossing through forests of western Georgia, Alabama, and Mississippi, or passing over the free state of Illinois to the Missouri Valley, in his family carriage, with servants, packs of hunting dogs, and a train of slaves, their nightly camp fires lighting up the wilderness where so recently the Indian hunter held possession.[9]

Or as Timothy Flint describes it:

The southern settlers who immigrate to Missouri and the country southwest of the Mississippi, by their show of wagons, flocks and numbers create observation, and are counted quite as numerous, as they are. Ten wagons are often seen in company. It is a fair allowance, that a hundred cattle, beside swine, horses and sheep, and six negroes accompany each. The train, with the tinkling of an hundred bells, and the negroes, wearing the delighted expression of a holiday suspension from labor in their countenances, forming one group; and the family slowly moving forward, forming another, as the whole is seen advancing along the plains, presents a pleasing and picturesque spectacle.

They make arrangements at night fall, to halt at a spring, where there is wood and water, and a green sward for encampment. The dogs raise their accustomed domestic baying. The teams are unharnessed, and the cattle and horses turned loose into the grass. The blacks are busy spreading the cheerful table in the wilderness, and preparing the supper, to which the appetite of fatigue gives zest. They talk over the incidents of the past day, and anticipate those of the morrow. If wolves and owls are heard in the distance, these desert sounds serve to render the contrast of their society and security more sensible. In this order they plunge deeper and deeper into the forest or prairie, until they have found the place of their rest.[10]

This was a new type of migration.

Just as the eighteenth-century frontier farmer had not been able to withstand the advance of the southern planter, so now the pioneer of the Southwest was in turn displaced. Unable to refuse the high prices which the planter offered him for his land, and outbidden in the competitive land sales, the small farmer had the option of adopting the slave plantation economy, of

[9] F. J. Turner, *Rise of the New West*, p. 92.
[10] Timothy Flint, *The History and Geography of the Mississippi Valley*, I, 191.

retreating to the less desirable soil of the mountains, or of again striking north or west for new lands. Hindered by poverty from adopting slavery, these pioneers left the rich black soil of the Southwest to the planters, retreating to the mountains to become the "poor whites" of the South, or pushing north of the Ohio or across the Mississippi to become again the founders of new states. With the decline of the yeoman farmer the Southwest fell under the control of the cotton aristocracy and cotton became in truth king. The invention of the cotton gin had increased production in South Carolina from 1,500,000 pounds in 1791 to 20,000,000 in 1801, and in Georgia from 500,000 pounds to 10,000,000. A similar increase was now to be seen in the new states. Tennessee, which raised 1,000,000 pounds in 1801, produced 45,000,000 in 1834. Louisiana, which raised pratically none in 1801, produced 62,000,000 pounds in 1834; the output of Mississippi and Alabama was even more. The ranking states in the production of cotton in 1820 were South Carolina and Georgia, but before 1834 Alabama and Mississippi pushed to the front. Cotton was clearly the staple of this region, and its importance is seen by the fact that after 1830 it furnished about one-half of the total value of the exports of the United States. It had the effect of confirming slavery as an apparently permanent institution. With the lessening of the Indian danger, settlement went on rapidly. Louisiana became a state in 1812, Mississippi in 1817, Alabama in 1819, and Missouri in 1821. Between 1812 and 1821 the population of Louisiana increased 41 per cent, Tennessee 61, Mississippi 81, and Alabama 142.

As the Old Southwest began to fill up it was inevitable that American expansion would clash with Spain. The Pinckney Treaty of 1795 had opened the navigation of the Mississippi to American ships, and obtained the right of deposit at the mouth and recognition of our ownership of the disputed land between the Yazoo and the 31st parallel. When Louisiana was purchased from France the territory governed by Spain included the land north of the Iberville and as far west as the Mississippi. Nevertheless, at various times attempts were made to incorporate West Florida with United States territory. By 1810 the advance to the Southwest had brought enough Americans into the region practically to control it. In that year they demanded from Spain a remodeling of the government, but shortly after declared their independence and applied for annexation to the United States. Orders were immediately issued by President Madison to take military possession of West Florida as far as the Pearl; thus by right of conquest alone was West Florida annexed. In 1819 Spain saw that it was useless to attempt to ward off further American aggression and agreed to give up East Florida, the United States assuming claims against Spain amounting to $5,000,000 and giving up all claims to Texas.

THE SETTLEMENT OF THE OLD NORTHWEST

The Land Ordinance of 1785 and the more famous Ordinance of 1787 prepared the way for opening to settlement the Old Northwest, the region north of the Ohio and east of the Mississippi. When this land was turned over to Congress, Connecticut, in order to foster religion and education and to reimburse those of her inhabitants whose homes had been burned by British raids during the Revolution, reserved a stretch of land 120 miles wide between the 41st parallel and Lake Erie which was known as "The Connecticut Western Reserve." In like manner, to redeem her military bounty certificates Virginia reserved 6000 square miles, known as the Virginia Military District, between the Scioto and the Little Miami, and Congress for the same reason reserved a block of land between the Scioto River and the Seven Ranges. The rest of the territory, with the exception of the lands sold to the Ohio and Scioto Companies and to Judge Symmes, was surveyed and sold by Congress to settlers under the existing laws.

Hardly had the Ordinance of 1787 been passed before the Ohio Company, composed chiefly of Massachusetts speculators under the leadership of the Reverend Manasseh Cutler, had purchased 2,000,000 acres of land north of the Ohio with depreciated soldiers' certificates, and in December of that year the Company's first settlers left Ipswich, Massachusetts, for the Muskingum River.[11] In the spring of 1788 they founded Marietta, where the Muskingum joins the Ohio and not far from the protecting guns of Fort Harmar. The Marietta settlers were followed in the same summer by a group from New Jersey under the leadership of Judge John Cleves Symmes, who settled Columbia and Cincinnati on part of the million acres between the Great Miami and the Little Miami which he and others had purchased. Some small French settlements at Detroit and in Illinois and Indiana already existed, but the pioneers of the Ohio Company and of the Symmes Purchase marked the first large entrance of Americans into the Northwest. The year 1790 saw the coming of Virginians into the Virginia Military District and the attempted settlement of groups of French, lured to America by the rosy promises of that most dubious of land speculative organizations, the Scioto Company, which was composed, according to Cutler, of "many of the principal characters of America." Connecticut, finding it difficult to induce individual buyers to take up land in the Western Reserve because of danger from Indians and the difficulty of access, finally sold most of the Reserve to the Connecticut Land Company, whose agent, General Moses Cleaveland, led a small party in 1796 to the site of the city now named for him.

[11] The history of the methods and negotiations by which the Ohio Company secured their land is an amazing story, which throws a flood of light upon the political morality of the period. See F. L. Paxson, *History of the American Frontier*, pp. 63 ff.

These settlers opened the way for the multitudes which began to pour into the Northwest in the thirty years following 1790. In the meantime western New York was being rapidly taken up. Mountains, tangled underbrush, and hostile Indians had dammed up the white man in the valleys of the Hudson and the lower Mohawk. It was not until after the Revolution that pioneers from Pennsylvania and New Jersey followed the Susquehanna and Tioga north to Seneca Lake and into the heart of the state, while from the east New Englanders, pushing across from Massachusetts and Vermont, laboriously ascended the Mohawk or struck directly west by land. A few log huts were to be found at Geneva, Bath, Naples, Aurora, Seneca Falls, Richmond, Palmyra, and Fort Stanwix, but the census of 1790 showed scarcely more than 1000 people in western New York. West of Seneca Lake the land had been sold by Robert Morris to the Holland Land Company; east of it the state had reserved 1,700,000 acres for military bounties. But the plots were soon broken up as the immigrants, chiefly from New England, took up the rich lands on the Tioga, Chenango, Genesee, and Mohawk, streams upon which were shortly to arise cities whose names harked back to classic Greece and Rome.

A combination of causes contributed to the amazingly rapid settlement of the Old Northwest. Immigration of home seekers from Europe, which had amounted to some four or five thousand a year, increased rapidly after the War of 1812, the number entering from 1815 to 1830 amounting to half a million. In the North the economic depression during the period of the Embargo and Non-intercourse Acts, the War of 1812 and immediately after, greatly stimulated the exodus to the West. In the South the planters deserted the worn-out tobacco lands of Virginia and North Carolina for the fresh alluvial soil of the Southwest, driving ahead of them the small pioneer farmer of the uplands, who moved on north into the Ohio Valley. Not only was immigration stimulated by economic causes, but the discontent, especially in New England, against the old religious and political oligarchy was potent in the movement. The gradually increasing liberality of the government in its western policy encouraged the taking up of new lands, and the extinction of the Indian titles between 1812 and 1830 opened up much new territory. The victories of William Henry Harrison in the Northwest and Andrew Jackson in the Southwest over the Indians marked the beginning of the rapid elimination of the red man from these regions.

After 1811, when the *New Orleans* was launched on the Ohio at Pittsburgh, the growth of the Northwest was aided by steam navigation. Before the advent of railroads the rivers formed the great avenues of travel and traffic, and upon them the immigrant or his products floated downstream in flatboats. By 1820 sixty steamboats plied on the western waters, and the succeeding years marked the golden age of the river boat. It took the old flatboat

months to make the journey downstream from Louisville to New Orleans, but the steamboat could cover the same distance in a few days. Besides these various economic influences speeding the westward movement there was, of course, the constant advertising which the West received during these years from the Louisiana Purchase, Pike's book on New Mexico, the Lewis and Clark exploration and the publication of their journal, the expeditions of Aaron Burr, the Indian victories of Harrison and Jackson—all of these kept the West vividly before the eyes of prospective settlers.

The influx into the Northwest was rapid from the start. The year that Marietta was founded (1788) saw 10,000 float down the river past this point; by 1803 the population of Ohio was sufficient for its admission as a state. While the prosperity of the East during the early Napoleonic Wars held back somewhat the exodus to the West, the movement was again stimulated by the embargo and the commercial difficulties preceding the war with Great Britain. An observer in Robbstown, Westmoreland County, Pennsylvania, a village on the highway to Pittsburgh, claimed that in one month toward the end of 1811, 236 wagons, with men, women, and children, and 600 merino sheep passed through to the West.

Old settlers in central New York declared they had never seen so many teams and sleighs loaded with women, children, and household goods traveling westward, bound for Ohio, which was then but another name for the West. One account describes the roads passing through Auburn as thronged all winter long "with flitting families from the Eastern states." Another from Newburg, in New York, declares that during one day in July six wagons with seventy persons, all from Massachusetts, entered and left the village for Ohio, and that scarcely a week passed without its citizens "witnessing more or less immigration of the same kind." [12]

"Old America seems to be breaking up and moving westward," wrote Morris Birkbeck, an English observer, in 1817, while journeying on the National Turnpike. "We are seldom out of sight, as we travel this grand track toward the Ohio, of family groups behind and before us." [13] The population of the Old Northwest (Ohio, Indiana, Illinois, Michigan, Wisconsin), which at the opening of the Revolution was composed of but a few thousand French, by 1810 numbered 272,324, by 1830 had increased to 1,470,018, and by 1860 amounted to 6,926,884. Indiana was admitted into the Union in 1816, Illinois in 1818, and Michigan in 1837. By 1830 Ohio had over one million people, more than Massachusetts and Connecticut combined. Indiana in the decade 1810 to 1820 grew from 24,000 to 147,000. That this increase in popula-

[12] J. B. McMaster, *History of the People of the United States*, IV, 383.
[13] *Notes on a Journey in America*, p. 31.

tion seriously drained the East is seen by the fact that Virginia and Massachusetts during the decade 1820 to 1830 remained almost stationary while the western states grew at a rate of 100 to 150 per cent. Chicago, a mere fur trading station in 1830, increased to over 100,000 by 1860; Cleveland, with only 6070 in 1840, numbered 43,000 in 1860. The chief cities of the West about 1830 were Cincinnati, or "Porkopolis," a meat-packing center in a rich farming district, with a population of 25,000; Pittsburgh, already an iron city with 12,000 people near the head of navigation of the most popular route (before 1825) to the West; [14] St. Louis with 6000, the point of exchange between the fur traders of the North and West and the steamboat trade of the Mississippi; and New Orleans, at the mouth, where the inland products were transferred to ocean boats.

The principal route over which influx traveled was the old road that Forbes had cut during the French and Indian War from Philadelphia to Pittsburgh by way of Lancaster and Carlisle.[15] Upon reaching Pittsburgh the immigrant transferred his effects to a flatboat and continued the journey down the Ohio and upon one of its tributaries to his chosen spot. Another important route was from Albany up the Mohawk to the Genesee turnpike, then to Lake Erie and Ohio. After the Erie Canal was completed in 1825 this route became more popular and contributed not only to the settlement of the Ohio Valley but to that of western New York. Another New York route was along the Catskill turnpike to the headwaters of the Allegheny. From Baltimore the traveler followed a turnpike to Cumberland, where began the National Road across the mountains to Wheeling on the Ohio, with branches leading to Pittsburgh. The wagon road from Virginia into central Kentucky was the chief southern route; from Kentucky and Tennessee many routes led to the Ohio in the region of Cincinnati or Louisville.

Although New Englanders founded Marietta and Cleveland, the majority of the population came from elsewhere. New England up to 1820 was still settling her own northern frontier and that of western New York. In Ohio the most numerous groups came from the central states of Pennsylvania and New Jersey, with Cincinnati as their commercial center. Next in importance were immigrants from Virginia, who outnumbered the New Englanders of the Western Reserve. Indiana and Illinois received in their northern counties some accessions from New England, but were mainly settled by the yeomen farmers of the upcountry of Virginia and North Carolina and by the restless pioneers of Kentucky and Tennessee who had been pushed out by the wealthier planters. From this stock came Abraham Lincoln. Many of these

[14] The real head of navigation was Old Fort Redstone above Pittsburgh, from which point many embarked.

[15] The present Lincoln Highway.

immigrants from the South were Scotch-Irish, the "Hoosier" element of Indiana coming chiefly from North Carolina. The native stock which settled the Mississippi Valley was preponderantly from the South. Nevertheless, the Northwest did not take on the tone of southern civilization. The poor whites of the South, with their Presbyterian and Quaker background, mingling with the pioneers from New England and the central states, developed communities of small farms rather than plantations, where slavery was forbidden and democracy was strong. The chief strain of direct immigration from Europe into the Old Northwest was German. Over half a million came between 1830 and 1850, and in the next decade another million took up lands in central Ohio around Cincinnati, in the Wisconsin counties along Lake Michigan, as well as in Indiana, Illinois, Michigan, and other states in the Mississippi Valley.

FRONTIER LIFE

The first task of the immigrant, whether he came by foot, horseback, crude wagon, or by river boat, was to decide upon a place to live. If he was a squatter his chief interest was to find some land distant from settlement where water was abundant and where a stream would furnish him a chance to reach a market for his produce and to purchase salt and the few necessities he might need during the year. If he intended to comply with the law, either he had purchased before going west, or else, providing he had been lucky enough to avoid the land speculators who swarmed the western towns, he filed a claim at the land office upon paying the price of the land. Arriving at the site he had chosen, usually with wood and water as prime elements in his choice, he built a rude log cabin, often with the help of neighbors. His next task was to clear away the underbrush and girdle the trees on enough land to plant the first year's corn. The fertility of the fresh soil would ordinarily yield fifty to sixty bushels per acre the first year, and further clearing normally produced seventy to a hundred the second year. The cattle, hogs, and horses could easily pick up enough food during most of the year, and with little attention his garden produced sufficient for the table. A rude plenty was thus provided, and by the third or fourth year the settler was in a position further to improve his house and to sell surplus products. If the site was good other settlers would soon appear, and in their wake might come a tanner or the builder of a sawmill, then possibly a professional innkeeper. The nucleus of a town having been formed, work was to be had for a blacksmith, carpenter, wheelwright, or saddler, and eventually one or more stores would grow up. This process of town development was noted in 1818 by Morris Birkbeck:

On any spot where a few settlers cluster together, attracted by ancient neighbourhood, or the goodness of the soil, or vicinity to a mill, or by whatever cause, some enterprising proprietor finds in his section what he deems a good scite for a town: he has it surveyed and laid out in lots, which he sells, or offers for sale by auction.

The new town then assumes the name of its founder:—a store-keeper builds a little framed store, and sends for a few cases of goods; and then a tavern starts up, which becomes the residence of a doctor and a lawyer, and the boarding-house of a store-keeper, as well as the resort of the weary traveller: soon follow a blacksmith and other handicraftsmen in useful succession: a schoolmaster who is also the minister of religion, becomes an important accession to this rising community. Thus the town proceeds, if it proceeds at all, with accumulating force, until it becomes the metropolis of the neighbourhood. Hundreds of these speculations may have failed, but hundreds prosper; and thus trade begins and thrives, as population grows around these lucky spots; imports and exports maintaining their just proportion. One year ago the neighbourhood of this very town of Princeton was clad in "buckskin," now the men appear at church in good blue cloth, and the women in fine calicoes and straw bonnets.

The town being fairly established, a cluster of inhabitants, small as it may be, acts as a stimulus on the cultivation of the neighbourhood: redundancy of supply is the consequence, and this demands a vent. Water mills, or in defect of water power, steam mills rise on the nearest navigable stream, and thus an effectual and constant market is secured for the increasing surplus of produce. Such are the elements of that accumulating mass of commerce, in exports, and consequent imports, which will render the Mississippi the greatest thoroughfare in the world.[16]

Later, as the resources of the community grew, there would come the demand for canals and better roads. The distance of the dwellings from one another made social intercourse highly valued, and husking bees, quilting parties, house "raisings," and even revival services contributed a boisterous but stimulating change from the day's drudgery.

Not all the settlers by any means remained upon the claims which they first selected. The large amount of unoccupied land and the ease with which it could be acquired developed a restless, moving people. Markets were usually at a distance and, prior to canals and railways, almost impossible to reach. In consequence, money was a scarce commodity of which the backwoodsman saw little in the course of his life. The quickest method of acquiring specie was to sell the partly cleared farm to a newcomer and "clear again for the tall timber." Some men repeated this process a half dozen times in the course of their lives—almost professional pioneers, who

[16] Morris Birkbeck, *Notes on a Journey in America*, pp. 103–105.

broke the way for more permanent home builders. As the population grew the latter were in turn followed by the capitalist.

The frontier stages have been well described in a much-quoted passage from J. M. Peck's *A New Guide for Emigrants to the West,* published in Boston in 1837.

Generally, in all the western settlements, three classes, like the waves of the ocean, have rolled one after the other. First comes the pioneer, who depends for the subsistence of his family chiefly upon the natural growth of vegetation, called the "range," and the proceeds of hunting. His implements of agriculture are rude, chiefly of his own make, and his efforts directed mainly to a crop of corn, and a "truck patch." The last is a rude garden for growing cabbage, beans, corn for roasting ears, cucumbers and potatoes; a log cabin, and, occasionally, a stable and corn-crib, and a field of a dozen acres, the timber girdled or "deadened" and fenced, are enough for his occupancy. It is quite immaterial whether he ever becomes the owner of the soil. He is the occupant for the time being, pays no rent, and feels as independent as the "lord of the manor." With a horse, cow, and one or two breeders of swine, he strikes into the woods with his family, and becomes the founder of a new county, or perhaps State. He builds his cabin, gathers around him a few other families of similar taste and habits, and occupies till the range is somewhat subdued, and hunting a little precarious; or, which is more frequently the case, till neighbors crowd around, roads, bridges, and fields annoy him, and he lacks elbow room. The preemption law enables him to dispose of his cabin and corn-field to the next class of emigrants, and, to employ his own figures, he "breaks for the high timber," "clears out for the New Purchase," or migrates to Arkansas or Texas, to work the same process over.

The next class of emigrants purchase the lands, add field to field, clear out the roads, throw rough bridges over the streams, put up hewn log houses, with glass windows, and brick or stone chimneys, occasionally plant orchards, build mills, school houses, court houses, &c., and exhibit the picture and forms of plain, frugal, civilized life.

Another wave rolls on. The men of capital and enterprise come. The "settler" is ready to sell out and take the advantage of the rise of property—push farther into the interior, and become, himself, a man of capital and enterprise in turn. The small village rises to a spacious town or city; substantial edifices of brick, extensive fields, orchards, gardens, colleges and churches are seen. Broadcloths, silks, leghorns, crapes, and all the refinements, luxuries, elegancies, frivolities and fashions, are in vogue. Thus wave after wave is rolling westward:—the real *el dorado* is still farther on.

A portion of the two first classes remain stationary amidst the general movement, improve their habits and condition, and rise in the scale of society.[17]

[17] Pp. 119–121.

While this picture by Peck was fairly accurate for those regions which were destined to a bright future, it was, of course, not universal. Many regions barely passed beyond the pioneering stage. In the Old Southwest particularly, there was in many sections a sharp differentiation from the steady advance described by Peck. The first or pioneering stage was the same; but in the second phase, instead of improved houses, better farms, and the accumulated evidences of thrift and plenty, there entered in the South the cotton planter who bought up the clearings of the pioneer, con- solidated the farms, and replaced the small white farmer with Negro slaves. The second phase thus often saw the country with a smaller popula- tion, certainly a smaller population of whites, than the first. After the steady cropping of the land without renewal and with inefficient labor came the third phase—that of general decline and gradual exodus. "In 1825," said a prominent citizen of Alabama in 1855, "Madison county cast about 3000 votes; now she cannot cast exceeding 2300. In traversing that country one will discover numerous farm houses, once the abode of industrious and intelligent freemen, now occupied by slaves, or tenantless, deserted, and dilapidated; he will observe fields, once fertile, now unfenced, abandoned, and covered with those evil harbingers—fox-tail and broom-sedge; he will see the moss growing on the mouldering walls of once thrifty villages; and will find 'one only master grasps the whole domain' that once furnished happy homes for a dozen white families. Indeed, a country in its infancy, where, fifty years ago, scarce a forest tree had been felled by the axe of the pioneer, is already exhibiting the signs of senility and decay, apparent in Virginia and the Carolinas; the freshness of its agricultural glory is gone; the vigor of its youth is extinct, and the spirit of desolation seems brooding over it." [18]

TRANS-MISSISSIPPI ADVANCE BEFORE 1860

When the United States purchased Louisiana in 1803 she divided the country into two parts—the Territory of Orleans, with New Orleans as its capital, extending to the present southern boundary of Arkansas, and the District of Louisiana, with St. Louis as its capital. In and around New Orleans there was scattered a heterogeneous population of French, Spanish, Americans, Negroes, and Indians; the upper Louisiana territory contained some ten thousand, of whom half were Americans. Thus by the opening of the century we find that white settlers from the East had crossed the Mississippi, lured by the lenient land laws of the Spaniards and the rich

[18] F. L. Olmstead, *A Journey in the Seaboard Slave States* (1856), p. 577.

fur trade. St. Louis had already become a market for furs and lead which were floated down the Missouri and the Mississippi.

The first real knowledge of the size and resources of the newly purchased land came from the famous expedition of Meriwether Lewis and Captain William Clark, the impetus for which was due to Jefferson. Starting from St. Louis in the spring of 1804 with a party of forty-five men, they ascended the Missouri 1600 miles to a point near the present Bismarck, North Dakota, where they spent the winter. Continuing up the river in the spring, they reached the Rockies and followed western streams until finally in November they floated down the Columbia to the Pacific, having covered over four thousand miles from the point of departure. On the return journey the little party broke into three detachments, uniting again near the confluence of the Yellowstone and Missouri, and reached their starting point two years and four months after their departure. Further explorations were carried on in 1805 and thereafter by Captain Zebulon Pike, who traced the Mississippi practically to its source and explored the Arkansas and Red Rivers, penetrating into the Rockies when he discovered the mountain which bears his name.

As the fertility and resources of the new purchase became better known, pioneers crossed the Mississippi and ascended the Missouri. Toward the south the cotton planters, ever hungry for fresh land, were crossing the river into Louisiana. Ahead of them were the cattle rangers, who from the first settlement of Jamestown had extended just west of the line of permanent settlement. The first Americans under Stephen F. Austin were welcomed by the Mexican authorities, but as American cattle rangers began to collide vigorously with the Spanish frontier cattlemen extending northward, and as numerous causes for friction—racial, political, and economic —developed, it was only a question of time before rebellion would take place. Not to be denied, American rangers and cattlemen rose against the Mexican Republic, won their independence in 1836 (recognized by the United States and many European countries, but not by Mexico), and petitioned for annexation to the United States. This was eventually consummated (1845) and led almost immediately to the Mexican War of 1846–1848, by which Mexico recognized the independence of Texas to the Rio Grande and was despoiled of the vast region which includes the present states of California and New Mexico, most of Arizona, Nevada, and Utah, and parts of Colorado and Wyoming. Eighteen million dollars was paid for it, and five years later $10,000,000 more for the Gadsden Purchase in order to push the boundary line south of the Gila River and in this manner insure the possibility of a southern transcontinental railway in United States territory. This was the conclusion of the long-cherished designs on Texas,

New Mexico, and California, which extended from the fantastic intrigues of
Burr to the actual conquest.

Oregon makes an interesting study in the westward advance, for its ac-

THE ADVANCE
OF THE
FRONTIER LINE

Technically, according to the census reports, the frontier is a region of
more than two and less than six people per square mile. Because of the
careful studies made by the census enumerators it is possible to reproduce
with relative accuracy the frontier line for each decade up to 1890. The above
map showing the frontier lines over thirty-year periods gives a picture of
population advance to the Civil War. It should be remembered, of course,
that by 1860 the discovery of gold in California and of silver in Nevada, and
the penetration of settlers into Utah, Oregon, and elsewhere in the Far West
had developed a frontier line far beyond that shown here.

quisition involved almost every influence which might stimulate settlement.
In 1788 Captains Gray and Kendrick visited the Northwest, laying the
foundations for a fur trade followed for many years by New England

merchants. On a second voyage in 1792 Captain Gray discovered the Columbia River, and claim to the Columbia Valley was further strengthened in the years 1804–1806 by the famous expedition of Lewis and Clark. In the meantime, the two English fur companies, the Hudson's Bay Company

OVERLAND TRAILS TO THE FAR WEST

Scale of Miles
0   100   200   300

The map above shows both the famous route taken by the Lewis and Clark expedition of 1804–1806 and the more common overland trails which developed to Oregon and California as settlers sought the fertile land of the Pacific coast and prospectors the gold and silver deposits of the mountains. A glance at the transportation maps on pages 491 and 505 will make clear that the same routes or variations of them were later followed by the great transcontinental railways.

and the Northwest Company, had commenced to penetrate the region, but their domination was soon disputed by John Jacob Astor and his American Fur Company which founded Astoria in 1811 as a basis of operations. During the War of 1812, Astor's interests were sold to the Northwest Company, and the latter was soon absorbed by the Hudson's Bay Company, which under the able leadership of Dr. John McLoughlin controlled Oregon for the next quarter century. Gradually a new wave of interest developed in

Oregon, this time among prospective settlers rather than fur traders. The great propagandist for the settlement of Oregon was Hall J. Kelley, a New England schoolmaster who published his *Geographical Sketches of Oregon* (1829),[19] organized a society to promote emigration to that region, and journeyed there himself in the early 'thirties. Business men of the type of Nathaniel J. Wyeth of Cambridge, Massachusetts, were again dreaming of commercial exploitation, and the Methodist Church in 1833 arranged to send missionaries to the Indians of the Northwest. The Far West was receiving a certain amount of literary exploitation from Washington Irving and others, and now letters from the missionaries began to spread the news of the fertile lands of the great Northwest. Only a handful of American settlers had trickled into Oregon in the 'thirties, but in the first years of the next decade migration commenced in earnest, and in 1846 an agreement was concluded with England, the only other nation now seriously claiming the land, whereby the boundary line of the 49th parallel was continued to the Pacific.

Profits from the fur trade and the lure of fertile lands were mainly responsible for the American occupation of Oregon, but it was the religious motive, so potent two centuries earlier in the settlement of America, that led to the founding of Utah. Persecuted and driven from one community to another, the Mormons, under their great leader, Brigham Young, left Nauvoo, Illinois, in 1846 for some retreat in the Far West. In the next year the advance guard reached the Salt Lake basin, and there the settlement was made. Sobriety, thrift, and skillful leadership, combined with an integration resulting from a unified religious purpose, quickly brought prosperity and plenty. Population was recruited by means of missionaries in the eastern states and in Europe, and the expenses of the immigrants were paid by a "Perpetual Emigration Fund." The efficiency of the migration and the rapidity with which a desert was turned into a thriving community mark the Mormon settlement as one of the most successful in American history.

Hardly had the Mormons established themselves in Utah and the great Southwest been acquired from Mexico before a remarkable impetus was given to the occupation of the west coast by the discovery of gold in 1848 on the mill race of John Sutter on the American River, about sixty miles from Sacramento. There was already a handful of American farmers in California, but now from the four corners of the earth prospective gold diggers flocked to the new land. By the end of 1848 at least 6000 had arrived, while in the next year probably 35,000 came by sea and 42,000 by

[19] A second edition (1831) of this pamphlet is reprinted in *Magazine of History with Notes and Queries,* Extra No. 67, Vol. XVII, and Kelley's *General Circular to all Persons of Good Character who wish to emigrate to the Oregon Territory* is reprinted as Extra 63, in Vol. XVI.

land; the population in 1850 was 92,597, more than that of the state of Delaware. The sea routes were either around the Horn or to the Isthmus of Panama, overland to the Pacific and up the coast. Engineers were sent out in 1849 to plan a railroad across the Isthmus; this was completed with great difficulty five years later, and did an enormous business until the first transcontinental line was completed in 1869. Overland there were two routes. The northern and shorter route, known as the Oregon Trail, led from St. Joseph or Independence near the Missouri along the Platte River to Fort Laramie. From Fort Laramie the trail led through the South Pass to Fort Bridger, where the traveler might turn south by way of the Mormon Trail and the "Hastings cut-off" to the Humboldt or proceed to Fort Hall and then bear south along the Snake River and Goose Creek to the American Desert. Proceeding along the Humboldt and the Truckee, he found himself at last in the heart of the gold region. The gold seeker traveling by way of the Southern, or Santa Fé, Trail, might strike southwest from Fort Leavenworth or Independence via Fort Dodge to Santa Fé or he might push due west from Fort Smith, Arkansas, along the Canadian or Red River to the Pecos, and thence to Santa Fé. At Santa Fé two routes could be followed: the northern, or "Spanish Trail," which connected with the "Mormon Trail," and the southern, known as Kearney's Route, which crossed the Colorado River near its mouth and led north to Monterey. Over these routes for the next twenty years "prairie schooners" by the thousands creaked their way, while multitudes endured every privation and suffering in quest of wealth. Those who escaped trouble with Indians and successfully braved the deserts still faced the risks of the cholera and typhoid prevalent in the unsanitary surroundings of the boom mining towns.

To the great majority of the " 'forty-niners" the lure of gold was but a snare and a delusion. True, a minority of the early gold seekers won wealth with pickax and cradle, but even in these early years the great profits went to the merchant, the hotel keeper, the transportation company, and the gambling house proprietor. After a few years the exportation of gold declined, but a more lasting prosperity was founded upon agriculture, industry, and other wealth-producing activities.

In 1850 it is no longer possible to draw a line south from the Canadian border to point out roughly the western frontier. In the two years after the discovery of gold thousands jumped across the prairies and laid the foundations of new commonwealths. Since 1848 there have been two frontiers in America, one moving westward and the other eastward. During the decade 1840 to 1850 Texas was annexed; the territories of Iowa, Wisconsin, and Florida were admitted as states, and the territories of Minnesota, Oregon, and New Mexico created. By 1860 California, Oregon, and Minnesota had

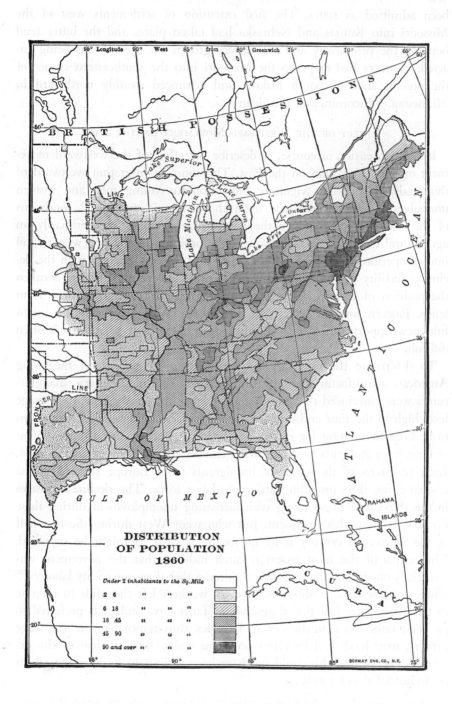

DISTRIBUTION
OF POPULATION
1860

Under 2 inhabitants to the Sq. Mile	
2 6 " " "	
6 18 " " "	
18 45 " " "	
45 90 " " "	
90 and over " " "	

BORMAY ENG. CO., N.Y.

been admitted as states. The first extension of settlements west of the Missouri into Kansas and Nebraska had taken place, and the bitter feud between the pro-slavery and anti-slavery groups for control was being enacted. Pioneers had crept up the Missouri into the southeastern corner of the present state of South Dakota and advanced steadily northward in Minnesota, Wisconsin, and Michigan.

EFFECT OF THE WESTWARD MOVEMENT ON THE EAST

It is much easier, of course, to describe the effect of the westward movement on the West than on the East. The constant migration westward of thousands of the most vigorous and ambitious young men and women undoubtedly had an influence upon the economic and social conditions of the seaboard states. Since the westward movement was primarily an agricultural expansion it soon brought the products of the rich western soil into competition with those of the East. This, in combination with the declining fertility of the seaboard states, tended, as we shall see, to weaken the position of eastern agriculture and depress the value of eastern farm lands. Eastern farmers were glad that in the West their children might find new opportunities, but the effect upon their own position was often difficult.

To determine the effect of the westward movement upon the rising American manufacturing industries is more difficult. Eastern manufacturers were convinced that the exodus of labor to the West kept the wage level high in the East and discouraged industrial development. There seems to be little foundation for this belief. There was always a large movement of farm boys and girls to the growing eastern cities as well as to the West. Each year tens of thousands of immigrants from Europe stopped in the eastern cities, thus providing an ample labor force. The decline of wages in the 1840's and 1850's along with increasing unemployment during these decades weakens this argument. Just who went West during the first half of the nineteenth century is by no means as clear as might be supposed. The results of the most recent research indicate that the movement was essentially one of farmers and their children rather than one of city laborers.[20] There are few data to show that factory workers left the mills to migrate to the West. The fact that thousands of farm boys and girls preferred to go West rather than to the eastern factories, thus removing *potential* wage earners, may have had its effect on wage scales. But in view of the declining wage scales, this could not have been serious in its long-run effects on industrial development.

[20] Carter Goodrich and Sol Davison, "The Wage Earner in the Westward Movement," *Political Science Quarterly*, L, 161–185 (June, 1935) and LI, 61–116 (March, 1936).

In any event, as the valleys of the Ohio and Mississippi filled up, eastern manufacturers found a market for their products. This promoted geographic division of labor and the interplay of commerce. As the years passed, the East became more and more a manufacturing section, the West a food-growing region, and the South a producer of cotton. During the first decades of the century the East shipped manufactured goods to the West, but the West sold most of its food products to the South, sending them via the river routes. The South in turn sold most of its produce to Europe, although some cotton was sent north. After the completion of the Erie and Pennsylvania canals, and especially after the opening of railroads, western products began to move east as well as south, and before the Civil War railroad iron had securely connected the region north of the Ohio with the economic interests of the Northeast.

Farmers, manufacturers, and merchants of the seaboard states might view with consternation the rapid development of the West, but not so the capitalist with a surplus with which to speculate in western land or in transportation facilities. This was probably the chief area of activity for American capital, particularly in the years which preceded the panics of 1819, 1837 and 1857. Writing of Illinois, Professor Gates sums up neatly the rôle of the speculator, but his description would apply to almost any region in the Middle West: "The rôle of the speculator has been one of profound importance in the history of Illinois. He preceded the settler, selected the choice locations, purchased them with land warrants or cash, surveyed and located them and then sought to turn immigration into his section. He was foremost in the advocacy of canals, railroads, plank roads and river improvements; to secure these his influence was exerted on the legislature, on county and city organizations and on Congress. As a factor in politics his influence cannot be overestimated."[21]

INFLUENCE OF THE WEST UPON EARLY AMERICAN POLITICS

Fear that the frontiersman with his radical ideas of democracy and strong tendency toward nationalism would upset the equilibrium of the nation and undermine the work of the founders was widespread in the East. Eastern fear of western democracy, in fact, has been a constant factor in American politics from the days of Bacon's Rebellion to the present time. Softening this fear was the widespread belief among statesmen, students of American conditions, and leaders of American thought that the West provided a "safety valve" against political and social discontent. As long as there was unoccupied land to which men might move when political, social, or economic conditions in the East became too hard, then

[21] P. W. Gates, *The Illinois Central Railroad and Its Colonization Work*, p. 119.

the nation would at least be saved from a revolutionary explosion. "Whenever social conditions tended to crystallize in the East," says Turner, "whenever capital tended to press upon labor or political restraints to impede the freedom of the mass, there was this gate of escape to the free conditions of the frontier." The West might be dangerous politically, but at the same time it was a safety valve.

Whether the West really acted in this way to any important extend is more than doubtful. The movement of dissatisfied eastern laborers, as has been suggested, was small. The cost of westward migration was too great for the poorer wage earner, so that the person in the East who suffered most from the economic system was practically prevented from escaping it. Moreover, population statistics appear to show that migration to the West was much greater during prosperity than in depression. Waves of economic discontent often appeared while there was an abundance of unoccupied land. This unrest seems to have been but little stronger since the disappearance of the frontier. Furthermore, social discontent seems frequently to have been more acute on the frontier than in eastern cities.

Whether the West acted as a safety valve or not, there can be no doubt as to its strong influence upon American politics. In state politics the aggressive frontiersmen demanded the rewriting of the state constitutions in the interest of democracy, as, for example, in New York in 1821 and Virginia in 1830. Gerrymandering and other devices were employed to ward off the growing power of the new communities, but without great success. The buoyant and intense spirit of the New West was not to be denied. In national politics the story was the same. The Federalists, representing the eastern aristocracy and what manufacturing and business interests there were at the time, lost control of the executive and legislative branches at the end of Adams' administration. With the accession of Jefferson, himself a Piedmont farmer, the influence of the western agriculturists was more in evidence, an influence which steadily increased as the representatives of one new state after another, elected by universal manhood suffrage, took their seats in Washington. During the period of the Republican presidents (Jefferson, Madison, Monroe, and John Quincy Adams) the spirit of the West was shown in the growth of strong national policies. The War of 1812 was a western war. The demands of the new communities led to the building of the National Road, notwithstanding the objections of the strict constructionists. The tariffs of 1816, 1824, and 1828 were passed only by the support of Kentucky and the Northwest, influenced chiefly by the arguments of Henry Clay, whose "American System" conceived of a manufacturing East as the logical market for the agricultural West. The famous decisions of the arch-Federalist, Chief Justice Marshall, while bitterly resented by the

Westerners, were generally in line with the nationalism so strong in the West. After 1820 there came a reaction from the nationalism of the previous years, which encompassed the South and West and swept Andrew Jackson into the Presidency in 1828. With his sincere belief in the ability and right of the masses to rule, Jackson, a true representative of the New West, bitterly fought privilege and vested wealth as he saw them in the Second United States Bank. Although strongly grounded in the idea of states' rights, his frontier training gave him a vision which made him stand firm against the nullification of South Carolina. Even the Whig party, in a sense a sort of resurrected Federalist party, which opposed him was led by a Westerner, Henry Clay.

SELECTED READINGS

Turner, F. J., *The Frontier in American History,* Chaps. IV–VII, XIII.
Bond, B. W., Jr., *The Civilization of the Old Northwest,* Chaps. I, II, X.
Webb, W. P., *The Great Plains,* Chap. V.
Mathews, L. K., *The Expansion of New England,* Chaps. VI–X.
Coman, K., *Economic Beginnings of the Far West,* Parts III and IV.
Goodwin, C., *The Trans-Mississippi West,* Chaps. IV–XIV.
Hacker, L. M., *The Triumph of American Capitalism,* Chaps. XV, XVI.
Semple, E. C., *American History and Its Geographic Conditions,* Chaps. X, XI.
Callender, G. S., *Selections from the Economic History of the United States, 1765–1860,* Chap. XII.
Flügel, F., and Faulkner, H. U., *Readings in the Economic and Social History of the United States,* Chaps. V, XI.

The Agricultural Era

Effect of the Westward Movement on American Agriculture

For almost three centuries the greatest single influence on American agriculture was the existence of an area of unoccupied land to which settlers were continually moving. This influence was particularly important in the century after the Revolution as the westward movement was stimulated by the increasing liberality of the federal land policy,[1] the growing tide of immigration, and the development of improved transportation facilities. That it was by no means easy to migrate to the West without at least a small backlog of capital is evident. Nevertheless, there were few men endowed with strength, ambition, and willingness to work who were unable to acquire land and make a new start in life. An ordinary laborer in the new country might save enough in a year to purchase his eighty acres, while a skilled mechanic or school teacher, both in great demand on the frontier, might purchase in less time. The proceeds from the sale of two horses or eight cattle would buy a quarter section. Under this policy and during the years 1783–1860 most of the land between the Alleghenies and the Mississippi was taken up, and the advance tide of migration swept into Texas, covered Missouri, and penetrated Kansas and Minnesota. The Mormons were carrying on agriculture around the Great Salt Lake and farms were rapidly developing on the Pacific slope.

Perhaps the greatest effect of this easily acquired land was to perpetuate the old-fashioned and criminally wasteful methods. The treatment of land in Virginia is thus described by Washington in a letter to Arthur Young:

The cultivation of tobacco has been almost the sole object with men of landed property, and consequently a regular course of crops have never been in view. The general custom has been, first to raise a crop of Indian corn (maize) which according to the mode of cultivation, is a good preparation for wheat; then a crop of wheat; after which the ground is respited (except from weeds, and every trash that can contribute to its foulness) for about eighteen months; and so on,

[1] Above, Chap. 10.

alternately, without any dressing, till the land is exhausted; when it is turned out, without being sown with grass seeds, or any method taken to restore it; and another piece is ruined in the same manner.[2]

The tobacco grower, when his land wore out, found it cheaper to take up new land than to care for the old, and tobacco culture advanced westward into Kentucky. The same was true a little later of cotton, this factor contributing to the rapid occupation of Alabama, Mississippi, and Texas. Northern agriculture was influenced in a similar way. Why, asked the farmer, must I cultivate intensively a small farm in Massachusetts or New Hampshire when an abundance of richer soil awaits the plow in western New York or the Ohio Valley?

After the pioneer had reached the new country the temptation was always present to skim the cream from the fresh land and then sell out and try his fortune farther on. As an observer in Missouri in 1849 commented, "Farming is here conducted on the regular skinning system . . . most of the farmers in this country *scratch* over a great deal of ground but *cultivate* none,"[3] a system which of course amazed the European traveler. Said Birkbeck in 1818, "The idea of exhausting the soil by cropping, so as to render manure necessary, has not yet entered into the estimates of the western cultivator. Manure has been often known to accumulate until the farmers have removed their yards and buildings out of the way of the nuisance. They have no notion of making a return to the land, and as yet there seems no bounds to its fertility."[4] Before the development of rapid water and steam transportation the pioneer farmer was handicapped by a lack of markets, which naturally lessened the incentive to improve his holdings. Enough could easily be raised to support his family without calling forth the latent possibilities of the new farm.

Even more harmful to agriculture than the case of acquiring fresh lands after the old had been ruined was the fever of land speculation that seized the American people and continued decade after decade during this period. Exaggerated, to be sure, but with elements of truth is the picture drawn by an Englishman:

Speculation in real estate has for many years been the ruling idea and occupation of the Western mind. Clerks, labourers, farmers, storekeepers, merely followed their callings for a living, while they were speculating for their fortunes. There are no statistics which show how many Yankees went out West to buy a piece of land and make a farm and home, and live and settle, and die there. I think that not more than one-half per cent of the migration from the East

[2] W. C. Ford (ed.), *The Writings of George Washington*, XI, 178 ff.

[3] *Cultivator*, New Series VI (1849), p. 302, quoted in P. W. Bidwell and J. I. Falconer, *History of Agriculture in the Northern United States, 1620–1860*, p. 272.

[4] Morris Birkbeck, *Letters from Illinois* (1818), p. 18.

started with that idea: and not even half of these carried out the idea. The German immigrants, indeed, were better entitled to be called settlers; but all classes and people of all kinds became agitated and unsettled, and had their acquisitiveness perpetually excited by land speculations in some shape or other— new railways, roads, proposed villages and towns, gold mines, water-powers, coal mines—some opportunity or other of getting rich all at once by a lucky hit. . . .

In the United States, vast numbers of the population became excited with dreams of sudden wealth, and the idea of a life of labour was scouted as the suitable destiny of mere timid, non-enterprising, weak people, or plodding Dutch or English, but altogether beneath the notice of Young America.

The people of the West became dealers in land, rather than its cultivators. Scorning cheap clocks, wooden nutmegs, and apple-parers, the Yankee, stepping from the almost ridiculous to the decidedly sublime, went out West, and traded in the progress of the country. Every one of any spirit, ambition, and intelligence (cash was not essential) frequented the National Land Exchange, a vast concern, extending from the Mississippi to the Pacific.

By convenient laws, land was made as easily transferable and convertible as any other species of property. It might and did pass through a dozen hands within sixty days, rising in price at each transfer; in the meantime producing buffaloes and Red Indians. Millions of acres were bought and sold without buyer or seller knowing where they were, or whether they were anywhere; the buyer only knowing that he hoped to sell his title to them at a handsome profit.[5]

Speculating on the progress of the country entered into the very soul of the pioneer and was part of his being.[6] In picking out a site for his claim the first consideration was its situation in respect to a possible rise in value. The typical frontiersman of these days was a man who laid out his claim, erected a rude cabin, and worked the land only until he could sell out at a profit. Upon the eastern farmer the effect of all this was demoralizing. He, too, imbibed the spirit of land speculation and many an eastern farm was put up for sale by the proprietor who was anxious to unload and try his fortune elsewhere. This trading on the progress of the country gave the American farmer a migratory tendency which was impossible under Old World conditions and unusual in a group which by its very occupation moved slowly. It broke down local attachments and discouraged intensive improvements; the farmer was building not for his descendants but for the first possible opportunity to sell. Eastern agriculture was further demoralized by western competition. After canals and railroads had provided an outlet for the bulky agricultural products of the West, the farmer of New England and the middle states found it difficult to compete successfully in the raising of grain and meat and was forced to reorganize his economy to that of truck

[5] D. W. Mitchell, *Ten Years in the United States* (1862), p. 325.
[6] See quotation from Peck, above, p. 192.

farming, fruit raising, dairying, or tobacco culture. Only the most favorably located or most fertile of the grain fields in the East could continue to compete with western grain. This reorganization took time and was attended with difficulties. Farming in the East was further handicapped by difficulty in obtaining sufficient labor. Higher wages and greater opportunities drained off to the nearby cities or the West the best of the farm hands, and tended to keep the labor cost higher in the East for both agricultural and industrial workers.

RISE OF COTTON

Undoubtedly the most striking feature in the agricultural history of the first half century of the Republic was the rise of cotton. During the colonial period little progress had been made in cotton culture. Lack of a market and the overshadowing importance of tobacco discouraged its growth, despite the efforts of colonial governments to the contrary. Some cotton was raised to be woven into cloth, but its use was confined to the poorer classes. Interruption of trade with Great Britain during the Revolution, which cut off the importation of foreign fabrics, turned the minds of Southerners to the production of cotton as a means of filling the need, and the legislatures of Maryland, Virginia, and South Carolina urged its possibilities upon their people. The chief difficulty with which the cotton grower had to contend was the separation of the seeds from the cotton fiber, a costly process even with slave labor.

The years 1790–1830 witnessed a veritable revolution in southern agriculture as far as the chief product was concerned. By the latter date cotton had become the principal southern crop and the largest single item of export from the country. This rapid development was occasioned, first of all, by the equally sudden opening of an available market. In England between 1767 and 1780 Hargreaves, Arkwright, and Crompton had constructed devices which were destined to eliminate hand spinning and substitute water power and later steam. In 1785 similar improvements in weaving were inaugurated by Cartwright; the result was an Industrial Revolution well under way in the early decades of the nineteenth century. Eventually the designs of these machines were smuggled into America [7] and factories established here. "In 1775, the cotton manufacture in England," says Adam Seybert, "was ranked 'amongst the humblest of the domestic arts'; the products of this branch were then almost entirely for home consumption; in 1797 it took the lead of all other manufactures in Great Britain, and in 1809, gave employment to 800,000 persons." [8] Rapid and cheap manufactures reduced prices and created demand. Any amount of cotton could now be manufactured; the problem was to obtain it. In the year 1786 almost by

[7] See Chap. 13.
[8] Adam Seybert, *Statistical Annals . . . of the United States* (1818), p. 92.

accident "sea-island" cotton was introduced from the Bahamas and was found to thrive along the seacoast. Because it had a longer fiber than the "short staple" variety, it was possible to separate the seeds by running the fiber between rollers turned in opposite directions. The demand for it abroad was immediate and its cultivation spread rapidly among the sea-coast farmers. The planters were the more ready to take up the cultivation of cotton because the tobacco lands were wearing out and the market for indigo and rice had been injured by the separation from Great Britain. The South badly needed a new crop at the same time that the factory owners of England were clamoring for the raw product.

The impetus for cotton culture was undoubtedly present. Only the difficulty of separating the seeds from the cotton held back expansion. Climatic conditions restricted the sea-island cotton to the coastal lowlands; the short-fibered upland cotton, upon which the greater part of the South had to depend, could be cleaned only with painful slowness at an average of about a pound a day per slave. The problem was solved in 1793 by Eli Whitney, a wide-awake Yankee and a mechanical genius, who had gone south to teach school immediately after graduating from Yale. In a letter to his father written in 1793 he tells the story of the invention of the cotton gin, one of the great episodes in American history:

I went from N. York with the family of the late Major General Greene to Georgia. I went immediately with the family to their Plantation about twelve miles from Savannah with an expectation of spending four or five days and then proceed into Carolina to take the school as I have mentioned in former letters. During this time I heard much said of the extreme difficulty of ginning Cotton, that is, separating it from its seeds. There were a number of very respectable Gentlemen at Mrs. Greene's who all agreed that if a machine could be invented which would clean the cotton with expedition, it would be a great thing both to the Country and to the inventor. I involuntarily happened to be thinking on the subject and struck out a plan of a Machine in my mind, which I communicated to Miller (who is agent to the Executors of Genl. Greene and resides in the family, a man of respectability and property) he was pleased with the Plan and said if I would pursue it and try an experiment to see if it would answer, he would be at the whole expense, I should lose nothing but my time, and if I succeeded we would share the profits. Previous to this I found I was like to be disappointed in my school, that is, instead of a hundred, I found I could get only fifty Guineas a year. I however held the refusal of the school until I tried some experiments. In about ten Days I made a little model, for which I was offered, if I would give up all right and title to it, a Hundred Guineas. I concluded to relinquish my school and turn my attention to perfecting the Machine. I made one before I came away which required the labor of one man to turn it and with which one man will clean ten times as much cotton as he can in any other way before known and also cleanse it much better than in the usual mode.

This machine may be turned by water or with a horse, with the greatest ease, and one man and a horse will do more than fifty men with the old machines. It makes the labor fifty times less, without throwing any class of People out of business.[9]

The contraption in its first crude form consisted of a cylinder equipped with teeth projecting through strips of metal which drew in the cotton fiber leaving the seeds behind, and a second roller, equipped with brushes to free the teeth from the lint, that revolved in the opposite direction. Operated by hand, the machine would clean fifty pounds a day; with water power, a thousand. Whitney's idea was to set up his engines throughout the South and gin the cotton for the planters at so much a pound. But the demand was so great that his machines were stolen and his patents infringed. South Carolina paid him and his partner, Miller, $50,000 for the unrestricted use of his machines and North Carolina paid $12,000, most of which was spent in lawsuits to protect the patent.

EFFECTS OF THE COTTON GIN

The effects of the invention of the cotton gin were immediate and far-reaching. Cotton became the greatest commercial crop of the South and the largest single export of the United States. With the exception of 1808, the year of the Embargo Act, and 1812-1814, the war years, the growth of cotton culture was rapid and steady. The production in 1790 was 4000 bales of 500 pounds; after the invention of the gin, it jumped to 73,222 in 1800. Each decade following saw roughly a doubling of production: 177,-824 bales in 1810; 334,728 bales in 1820; 732,218 bales in 1830; 1,347,640 bales in 1840; 2,136,003 bales in 1850; 3,841,416 bales in 1860.[10]

[9] "Correspondence of Eli Whitney," *American Historical Review*, III, 99–101.

[10] AVERAGE ANNUAL PRODUCTION AND EXPORTS OF AMERICAN COTTON FOR FIVE-YEAR PERIODS, 1791–1865, AND AVERAGE ANNUAL PRICES FOR MIDDLING UPLANDS COTTON IN NEW YORK AND LIVERPOOL

Years	Average Annual Production in the United States in Pounds	Average Annual Exports from the United States in Pounds	Percentage of Crops Exported	Average New York Prices for Middling Uplands — Cents	Average Liverpool Prices for Middling Uplands — Pence
1791–1795	5,200,000	1,738,700	33.43	31.7	No data
1796–1800	18,200,000	8,993,200	49.41	36.3	No data
1801–1805	59,600,000	33,603,800	56.38	25.0	15.4
1806–1810	80,400,000	52,507,400	65.38	18.9	18.4
1811–1815	80,000,000	42,269,400	52.83	14.8	20.5
1816–1820	141,200,000	91,144,800	67.38	26.2	16.7
1821–1825	209,000,000	152,420,200	72.93	16.2	9.2
1826–1830	307,244,400	254,548,200	82.84	10.9	6.5
1831–1835	398,521,600	329,077,600	82.57	11.9	8.0
1836–1840	617,306,200	513,315,800	83.15	13.0	6.7
1841–1845	822,953,800	691,517,200	84.03	7.7	4.7
1846–1850	979,690,400	729,524,000	74.46	8.7	5.2
1851–1855	1,204,422,800	990,368,600	76.51	9.6	5.4
1856–1860	1,749,496,500	1,383,711,200	79.51	11.5	6.7
1861–1865	No data	No data	No data	58.9	19.1

Source: *The South in the Building of the Nation*, V, 211.

Cotton, which in 1810 constituted about 22 per cent of the value of the total export, reached over 57 per cent in 1860. In value the exports of cotton increased during the same years from $66,758,000 to $333,576,000. Its importance in the export trade explains the source of southern wealth, the South's attitude on the tariff, her overconfidence at the beginning of the war, and her eventual failure.

The invention of the cotton gin and the rise of cotton culture were important in the opening up of the Southwest. Beginning in Georgia and South Carolina, cotton growing after 1800 spread into North Carolina and southeastern Virginia and across the mountains into Tennessee. After men realized that the rich alluvial soil of Alabama and Mississippi was better suited to cotton than the uplands, prospective growers entered in a steady stream, pushing before them Indians, Spaniards, and cattle ranchers. Crossing the Mississippi, they drove the cattlemen into Texas, contributed in bringing about the Mexican War and its resulting annexations, and by 1860 had preempted the coastal regions of Texas. The exhausting methods of early cotton culture, as with tobacco, wore out the soil and impelled the planter to search for further virgin land. As late as 1820 over half the cotton grown in the country was raised in Georgia and South Carolina. By 1850 Alabama had taken first place, with Georgia second, Mississippi third, and South Carolina fourth. In 1860 Mississippi (1,195,699 bales), Alabama (997,-978 bales), and Louisiana (722,218 bales) raised over half the total product, and the yield from Texas (405,100 bales) now surpassed that of South Carolina (353,413 bales). The most pronounced periods of expansion in the Southwest were in the flush years preceding the crisis of 1837 when land speculation there reached its highest point, and in the period immediately following the annexation of Texas. With the shifting of the center of cotton culture went a shift in the centers of trade, of wealth, and of political power. The importance of Charleston and Savannah declined, while Memphis, Mobile, and New Orleans rose as commercial centers. In the decade 1850–1860 New Orleans handled about half the cotton crop. By that time the center of the cotton kingdom had shifted to the Southwest.

The effects of the invention of the cotton gin permeated the whole social as well as the economic life of the South by fastening upon it the system of slavery. Slavery as an institution was decidedly under fire in the years immediately following the Revolution. Intelligent planters were beginning to question the economic soundness of the entire slave system as it operated in the South at that time. Wrote Washington in 1794: "Were it not that I am principled against selling negroes as you would cattle in the market I would not in 12 months be possessed of a single one as a slave. I shall be happily mistaken if they are not found to be very troublesome species of property ere many years have passed over our heads." [11] Men like Washington and Jefferson freed their slaves and with other prominent Southerners urged the abolition of the whole iniquitous system. In the North the movement to end slavery was making rapid progress.

The trend toward abolition was halted by the invention of the cotton gin. Cotton was a crop preeminently adaptable to slave labor. Almost the entire Negro family could work in the cotton fields during the greater part of the year. A single overseer could supervise a large number of slaves, and cotton culture as a whole was suitable to the crude and wasteful methods of ignorant slave labor in a country where large stretches of fresh land could be taken up as the old wore out. Although the number of slaves increased from approximately 698,000 in 1790 to almost 4,000,000 in 1860, the increase was not rapid enough to meet the demand, and as larger regions were brought under cultivation the demand for slaves grew. Before the cotton gin was invented a good Negro brought $300, but twenty years later the price had doubled. The average value was around $800 in 1830, $1200 in 1850, and from $1400 to $2000 in 1860. Abolition sentiment died away not only in the South but also in certain of the border states, where it had been strongest. The movement of cotton production to the West and South left a surplus of slaves in the border states, particularly Virginia, and their disposal became an active business. At the same time the law prohibiting the slave trade was openly evaded along the whole coast. Fearful of the increasing criticism of the system, the slave owners, ably represented in Congress, met attacks boldly and worked unceasingly to extend the slave area.

In the North the effects of the rise of cotton were also felt. The infant textile industries of New England were stimulated; and north of the Ohio the farmers found a market for their pork, corn, flour, and whisky. This stimulated agriculture and brought prosperity to the Middle West, but it also favored the rapid extension of slavery and the development of the plantation system in the Southwest. [12]

OTHER ASPECTS OF SOUTHERN AGRICULTURE

By far the greatest southern product during the colonial period was tobacco. The last decade of the century saw it at the height of its importance, when over half the population of the tobacco states was engaged in or dependent on its cultivation. It headed the list of exports in 1791, when more than $4,590,000 worth was shipped abroad. Still the leading export in 1800, it declined rapidly in importance, owing to the disastrous effects of the

[11] Quoted in W. A. Mazyck, *George Washington and the Negro* (1932).
[12] P. W. Bidwell and J. I. Falconer, *History of Agriculture in the Northern United States, 1620–1860*, Chap. XIII.

Embargo Acts and the War of 1812, the competition of Cuba, Colombia, and Sumatra, high import taxes imposed on it by foreign countries, the gradual exhaustion of the land, and the rise of cotton. The effect of the shifting of land and slaves from tobacco to cotton was distinctly noticeable; the industry remained practically stationary until 1840, when exports again equaled the amount shipped in 1790. The substitution of flue curing for the old-fashioned charcoal fire, and the introduction of a new yellow-leaf species so improved the product as to give the industry a new life; the population increase widened the home market. Between 1850 and 1860 the production more than doubled, so that at the opening of the war the South continued to be the greatest producer of tobacco in the world. About half the crop raised at this time was exported to England and Germany.

Virginia continued to be the leading tobacco state, but the center of tobacco culture moved steadily west. By 1859 the yield of Kentucky, Ohio, Tennessee, and Missouri was greater than that of the tidewater states—Virginia, Maryland, and North Carolina. Virginia and Kentucky together furnished more than half the tobacco grown in the United States. Louisville and St. Louis were the western centers of the tobacco business.

Sugar cane was brought by the Jesuits from Santo Domingo to Louisiana in 1751, but sugar was not successfully refined until toward the end of the century, when Etienne de Bore made a spectacular success of growing and refining sugar on his plantation near New Orleans. His experiments were followed by a rapid increase in the production of sugar. The average annual production from 1820 to 1830 was 52,000 hogsheads; this increased to an average of 280,000 hogsheads in the decade 1850 to 1860. Although most of the southern states raised some sugar, it was only in Louisiana that the cultivation assumed large proportions; in 1844 in that state there were 762 sugar estates cultivated by 51,000 slaves and capitalized at $60,000,000. By the time of the Civil War at least 180,000 slaves were engaged in sugar production. Most of the sugar consumed in the Mississippi Valley was refined at New Orleans, St. Louis, or Cincinnati. Unlike most southern crops, sugar expanded under the protection of a high tariff, which it needed to compete with West Indian sugar. Its production was also more highly mechanized than that of other southern crops.

Rice, which had been a leading colonial crop along the seacoast of South Carolina and Georgia, continued to be successfully grown, the production more than tripling from 1820 to 1850. The high watermark was reached in 1850, after which a decline set in. Until that year South Carolina raised more than half the crop, with Georgia producing most of the rest. The rice grower as a class was undoubtedly the most scientific and intelligent farmer in the pre-war South. Forced by necessity to use the same soil continually, his attention was early turned to the use of fertilizer and the reclamation of swampy land. The fact that only the moist soil was suitable for rice resulted in plantations of diversified products quite different from the cotton and tobacco plantations. The rice grower was encouraged in his efforts by a steady market and the acknowledged fact that the Carolina product was the best in the world. His chief problem was to meet the acute competition for slave labor produced by the rapidly developing cotton and sugar plantations in the southwestern states.

Another crop of considerable importance in certain sections of the South was hemp. The beginnings of this industry were almost simultaneous with the settlement of Kentucky. Hemp became as important here in the early years as tobacco had been in early Virginia. It was used principally for bagging and rope for cotton bales and for cloth for Negroes, but the market extended to the North and East. From Kentucky hemp growing spread into Tennessee, Arkansas, and Missouri, where it was an important factor in winning the latter state to slavery. Henry Clay, the champion of the "American System," was, it should be noted, the representative of the Kentucky hemp growers. Kentucky in 1850 produced 17,787 tons of hemp, Missouri 16,028, and Tennessee 595.

Although the economic life of the South was dominated by the commercial crops already described, other crops were raised, chiefly for home consumption. In addition to the usual garden vegetables, cereals were produced in 1859 as follows: Indian corn, 433,067,000 bushels; wheat, 49,-158,000 bushels; oats, 32,163,000 bushels; rye, 4,070,000; and barley and buckwheat in small amounts. The southern soil was more adaptable to corn than the other cereals, and it served as the chief food for the slaves. The crop, however, was barely half that raised in the five states north of the Ohio, and was not adequate for southern needs. These crops nevertheless, occupied the attention of a majority of the small farmers, who surpassed the plantation owners in number. In the animal industry the South, particularly Kentucky, was famous for the excellent speed horses bred there. Kentucky was also noted for breeding short-horn cattle and Hampshire hogs. Virginia's preeminence in sheep raising during these years can be traced back to Washington's interest and the subsequent efforts of agricultural societies. That the activity of the South in livestock was not confined to fancy breeding is evidenced by the estimated value of all livestock, which the census of 1860 placed at $381,778,601.

Agricultural Advance into the Region of the Old Northwest

More significant in the history of American agriculture than even the rise of cotton was the opening to agriculture of the region between the

Ohio River and the Great Lakes, westward into the prairies of Iowa and Kansas. The lands of western New York and northern Ohio, probably at one time covered by water, are endowed with a fine rich soil, free of boulders and easy to cultivate, and blessed with a climate tempered by the expanses of water. Nearly 100,000 square miles of water surface furnish the finest inland navigation in the world, facilities augmented by a natural outlet through the Mohawk Valley to the eastern coast. Tributaries of the Ohio and the Missouri permit the produce of the North Central States to be carried by way of the Mississippi to the markets of Europe and the southern states. Natural highways were supplemented in the early decades by the Erie Canal, the Pennsylvania Canal, and the Cumberland Road, and after 1840 by the railroads which were easily built in this region.

The first settler, pressing into the wooded stretches bordering the Ohio and its tributaries, found the soil richer perhaps, but the problems much the same as on his New England or Kentucky farm. It was a case of clearing the forest and duplicating the old crops. It was also a process of duplicating old methods of pioneering and farming. The first year was devoted to erecting a crude log cabin and clearing enough land to plant a garden patch and two or three acres of corn. Subsistence came largely at first from hunting and fishing or from livestock that the pioneer may have brought with him. In subsequent years the farmer enlarged his cornfields, expanded to other crops, and improved his house and added other buildings.

As the land was taken up and the advance pushed into Indiana and Illinois, Minnesota and Iowa, the pioneer found himself in a different type of country with new problems to be faced. Here was to be found prairie land without forest, which made building expensive and firewood scarce. Frequent absence of water was a deterrent. The tough prairie soil was extremely hard to break with the early wooden plows, and at first there was a mistaken idea that it was not fertile. Occupation of the prairies was also held up by the lack of transportation facilities which made it impossible to market the surplus profitably. When the real richness of the soil was realized, especially after the invention of the steel plow and other farm machinery, and after artificial transportation facilities had been developed, the land was quickly put under cultivation and occupation was the more rapid because the land needed little preparation for sowing. Practically no clearing was necessary; the soil was simply broken with a plow or ax, and a crop of corn planted. The first crop usually broke up the sod sufficiently to let it rot, and in the second year a crop of wheat was possible.

The development of the Lake region and prairies depended largely upon markets and transportation. The Industrial Revolution was turning western

Europe into an urban manufacturing civilization and was beginning to make itself felt in America in an increased demand for foodstuffs. This was particularly true after the repeal of the Corn Laws in 1846, which opened Great Britain to American foodstuffs. An important market also developed in the South, the planters here believed it more profitable to purchase food and turn the entire labor energy of the slaves to raising the staple crop. As a consequence, the North Central States developed into a great food-producing region, whence the products moved eastward by canal and railroad and south by steamboat and rail in two continuous streams. Western New York and northern Ohio became interested in fruit growing and dairying, while the rest of the Middle West produced meat and cereals.

What little exportation of foodstuffs there had been from this region prior to 1825 had been in the form of beef, pork, and mutton on the hoof. Before the era of canals and railroads and the development of the packing industry, the farmers of the western counties of Pennsylvania, Maryland, Virginia, and Ohio annually took great droves of cattle and hogs along the highways leading to Philadelphia and Baltimore. "During the summer and autumn, along these lines of travel, so many drovers passed that an observer, a mile or more away, could know of the passing of stock, for far up in the air he could see long moving lines of rising dust." [13] Livestock raising has always been a leading frontier occupation, for every frontier has provided animal food at low cost. In the Middle West, where hog growing was destined to become a great industry, conditions were especially favorable. Hogs at first could find maintenance on the mast [14] and herbage of the forests on the fringe of civilization; later on, corn, their principal food, was found especially adaptable to the soil and soon became the leading crop. About 1818, meat packing as an industry came into existence west of the Alleghenies. The development of markets, of transportation, and of banking facilities, and the growth of a sufficient population to provide a steady supply of animals had progressed far enough by this time to build up a considerable meat-packing industry in Cincinnati. In the early years meat was preserved by salting and smoking and, as this process did not require large capital, packing establishments sprang up in many of the larger towns. Nevertheless, Cincinnati retained the leading position until 1860, although the center moved continually westward. As Chicago grew in size, its superior transportation facilities, combined with its nearness to the new pork states, enabled it to take the lead. Upon the meat industry

[13] I. F. King, "The Coming and Going of Ohio Droving," Ohio State Archæological and Historical Society Quarterly, XVII, 249 (1908).

[14] Fruit of the oak and the beech or other forest trees.

and the manufacture of such by-products as leather goods, fertilizers, glue, candles, soap, lard, salt, and barrels, the early prosperity of both Cincinnati and Chicago rested. This industry is still basic in these centers.

The chief stimulus for cereal production in the early years came from the need for food for animals and ingredients for the manufacture of whisky. Corn was too bulky to transport, but it could be fed to animals, which in turn could be driven perhaps hundreds of miles to the market. Corn and rye could be reduced to the less bulky and more concentrated form of spirituous liquors. It was this fact that made whisky a characteristic pioneer product, and explains the opposition of the frontier farmer of Pennsylvania to Hamilton's excise tax. Corn during this entire period remained by far the chief agricultural product, although little found its way out except in the form of whisky or meat.

After the opening of the Erie Canal and the growth of railroads it was possible to ship cereals east as well as south, and there was a great impetus to other lines of cereal production. Wheat was consigned either to millers at Cincinnati, Louisville, and St. Louis to be prepared for local and southern consumption, or to the east via Buffalo and Pittsburgh. Some eventually reached Europe via New York or New Orleans. The Middle Atlantic States in 1850 still produced more wheat than the North Central, but in the next decade western production increased 125 per cent to 15.5 for the Middle Atlantic. As the western wheat grew in importance, the milling center shifted from the coast streams to Rochester on the Erie Canal, then to Chicago and St. Louis, and eventually to the great mills of the northwest.[15]

BEYOND THE MISSISSIPPI

The extension of agriculture beyond the Mississippi into Missouri, Minnesota, Iowa, Kansas, and Nebraska was a continuation of the frontier experience of the states north of the Ohio, with essentially the same products

[15] Farm statistics for the regions now occupied by the states of Ohio, Indiana, Michigan, Illinois, Missouri, Minnesota, Iowa, Nebraska, Wisconsin, and Kansas. (Area, 384,510,080 acres.)

	1840	1850	1860	1870
Population......................	3,352,000	5,404,000	9,092,000	12,967,000
Cash value of farms, including machinery and livestock..........	....	$914,637,000	$2,523,256,000	$5,132,815,000
Corn, bu......................	105,853,000	222,209,000	406,146,000	439,112,000
Wheat, bu.....................	27,518,000	43,842,000	95,004,000	194,764,000
Oats, bu......................	30,335,000	42,329,000	62,951,000	159,690,000
Rye, bu.......................	1,141,000	840,000	4,105,000	6,473,000
Barley, bu....................	472,000	832,000	4,909,000	10,608,000
Buckwheat, bu................	886,000	1,602,000	4,105,000	6,473,000
Hay, tons.....................	1,594,000	3,336,000	7,059,000	12,440,000
Butter and cheese from dairies, pounds......................	20,880,000	105,110,000	181,308,000	228,367,000
Cheese from factories...........	....	....	....	23,904,000
Value of animals slaughtered	....	$25,419,000	$62,722,801	$208,586,441

and civilization. Farther south in Louisiana and Arkansas, the fringe of settlements was pushed beyond the Mississippi long before the region east had been occupied, and tobacco, cotton, sugar, and cereals were grown. American advance into Spanish territory began in 1821, when Moses Austin, a native of Connecticut, obtained a grant from the Spanish government upon which to plant a colony of settlers from the United States, and in the same year his son, Stephen, established the first Anglo-American settlement in the Brazos and Trinity Valleys. Probably 30,000 Americans followed Austin's band in the next fifteen years, taking up land mainly along the rivers between San Antonio and Nacogdoches and the coast; most of them were Southerners who either brought their slaves and raised cotton or engaged in ranching.

The reason for their migration was the opportunity to obtain better land at less cost than was possible in the United States where the best land in the South was already preempted and the minimum price of what remained was $1.25 an acre. This immigration took place during the revolutionary epoch when Mexico was winning her independence from Spain. Welcomed at first by both Spaniards and Mexicans, the new settlers soon provided cause for friction. Attempts by the Mexican government to prevent further immigration, to abolish slavery, and to eliminate home rule were but a few of the causes which led inevitably to insurrection. The land-hungry Americans revolted, won their independence from Mexico in 1836, and were annexed to the United States in 1845.[16] By 1860 Texas had a population of 604,000 living on 42,891 farms and raising 405,100 bales of cotton, in addition to her extensive ranching industry.

It should also be remembered that American farmers by 1860 were laying the foundations for a great agricultural empire on the Pacific coast. The population of California had increased from 92,000 in 1850 to 380,000 in 1860, providing a growing demand for the products of local agriculture. At the same time placer mining was giving out, and many of the Forty-niners, who had been farmers before their migration to California, began to see great agricultural opportunities in the new state. Already the Pacific region was occupied with large-scale ranching—both cattle and sheep—and was raising substantial crops of barley, wheat, and other cereals.

EFFECT OF THE INDUSTRIAL REVOLUTION AND WESTERN AGRICULTURE UPON THE EAST

In rural New England during the first half of the century changes were enacted which brought about a veritable agricultural revolution. As in colonial days, farm life at the opening of the century was characterized by

[16] Above, Chap. 10.

self-sufficiency. With few markets for his produce, the farmer was unable to buy from without; what he needed in the way of food, clothing, and tools was raised or manufactured mainly on the farm. After 1810 this condition began to change gradually as the Industrial Revolution slowly transformed New England into a manufacturing center.

The urban population, which in 1860 amounted to about one-third of the total population of southern New England, provided a market for agricultural products. Farming, which had been uniform, began to give way to specialization: intensive farming of root crops in the regions adjacent to the cities, wool growing in the hilly country, and the fattening of beef cattle in the Connecticut Valley. New markets created new interest in farming, which was augmented by agricultural societies and by the use of improved machinery after 1830, particularly the iron plow.

No sooner had the New England farmer accustomed himself to the new conditions than a second readjustment was forced upon him by the growth of railroads. Cheap transportation made it impossible for him to compete with western wool, beef, and pork; in consequence, although corn continued to be the agricultural backbone of New England, the production of beef and pork declined. Attention was turned to dairying and truck gardening, and on the rich bottom lands of the Connecticut in the three decades after 1840 there developed a spectacular extension of tobacco culture as the increasing use of cigars provided a market for the superior wrappers grown there. This agricultural upheaval brought striking changes to rural life. The self-sufficient domestic system broke down before the factory system. Markets for agricultural products brought ready money to the rural districts, new comforts to the farmer, and a higher standard of living. Women released from household industries sought work in the factories. At the same time many men, discouraged by the uncertainties of this period of readjustment, followed the lure of new opportunities in the cities or of richer lands in the West. The whole situation was further complicated by a readjustment of land values usually, but not always, detrimental to the farmer.

What was happening in New England was taking place to a lesser extent in the middle states. The richer farm land in this region enabled it to compete for a longer period with the products of the West and it remained an important agricultural section throughout these years. Nevertheless, developing industry in the Hudson and Delaware Valleys and in growing seaport towns furnished an increasing local market for foodstuffs and brought an agricultural readjustment to meet the demand. The seaboard South, on the other hand, had little to compensate her for the competition of western cotton and other products. No important industrial development created large cities, and cotton found its outlet in New Orleans and other Gulf cities. Like New England the seaboard South was dotted with deserted farms, but unlike New England it was unable to adjust itself or turn its energy into new channels. Southern leaders like John Taylor of Caroline and Edmund Ruffin urged diversification of crops and conservation of soil by scientific agriculture, but their call fell on deaf ears. With his capital tied up in land, his soil wearing out, and labor draining off to the Southwest, the eastern plantation owner seemed able to do little. It is this situation which explains in part the discontent leading to secession.

Technical Advances in Agriculture

The period from 1830 to the Civil War witnessed the beginnings of revolutionary changes in American agriculture. Fresh agricultural labor as well as enlarged markets was provided by the rapidly increasing population resulting from (1) natural growth in a civilization conducive to large families, (2) immigration which amounted during these years to over 4,500,000, and (3) the growth of the factory system with its increase of the urban population. The rapid building of railroads after 1850 stimulated the farmer by bringing both the products and the markets of the world to his door. The discovery of gold in California and an increased demand for foodstuffs due to the repeal of the English Corn Laws in 1846 both helped to raise prices. Scientific agriculture made rapid strides, but especially to be noted was the invention and adoption by the American farmer of labor-saving machinery. This development was slow in the quarter century after the Revolution, but gathered speed in the years from 1810 to 1840, and thereafter proceeded with lightning-like rapidity.

In a nation where land was plentiful but labor scarce, it was to be expected that the first great advances would come in labor-saving rather than in land-saving devices. "In Europe," said Jefferson, "the object is to make the most of their land, labor being abundant: here it is to make the most of our labor, land being abundant." American farming implements were designed to increase the yield per man rather than the yield per acre; in the latter we have not kept up with more thickly populated countries. For years after 1800 a farmer's equipment consisted usually of a crude wooden plow, harrows, hoes, shovels, forks, and rakes, poorly constructed and often homemade. The first great improvement was the metal plow, which came into general use after 1825. Colonial plows had been covered with strips of iron, and as early as 1790 Charles Newbold of New Jersey was working on the idea of a cast-iron plow, which he finally patented in 1797. He spent his entire fortune of $30,000 to introduce his invention, but the farmers would have none of it, many claiming that the iron poisoned the soil and made the weeds grow. The conception of an improved plow was not lost sight of, men like Jefferson and Webster making studies of types and materials. Eventually Newbold's plow—one solid piece of cast iron—was improved on by Jethro Wood of New York, who in 1819 patented a plow, the different parts of which interlocked and could be replaced if broken. Manufacturers and inventors infringed his patents, but the farmer profited. Eventually mold-boards were designed, more adaptable to breaking the matted grasses of the prairies, the sticky soil of which also necessitated a smoother surface. This was provided by the steel mold-board first made in 1833 by John Lane of Chicago, and a few years later by John Deere. The life work of James Oliver of South Bend, Indiana, resulted in 1869 in the chilled-steel plow, which eliminated blowholes and made the metal less brittle. After the 'thirties the metal plow was adopted rapidly by the farmer. In Massachusetts alone in 1845 there were 73 plow-manufacturing concerns with an output of 61,334 plows and other implements. In 1855 the number of establishments had decreased to 22, but the yield had increased to 152,688 plows valued at over $700,000. Two factories in Pittsburgh in the 'thirties were turning out plows at the rate of 34,000 a year. Quantity production brought lower prices.

Simultaneously with the improvement in plows came the invention of the mowing and reaping machines to keep pace with the increased production which the new plows made possible. The grain cradle had come into use about 1800 and had considerably facilitated both the cutting and the gathering of the grain, but harvesting was still a painfully slow process. Many men experimented during the following years on the problem of a reaper, and many minds contributed to the eventual machine. A patent for a mowing machine had been granted to William Manning of New Jersey in 1831, but the two men who succeeded in building a practical reaper were Obed Hussey and Cyrus McCormick, whose patents were dated, respectively, 1833 and 1834. Hussey's machines, which could mow fifteen acres a day, were good enough to demonstrate the possibilities of a reaper and he had little competition for almost a decade. His poverty and mistakes in policy, however, prevented large-scale production and in the end other manufacturers were to reap greater fame and fortune. The greatest success was experienced by Cyrus McCormick, of Scotch-Irish ancestry, who had emigrated from Pennsylvania into the Shenandoah Valley and who inherited from his father a mechanical genius and an interest in farm machinery. Turning his attention to the development of a practical reaping machine, he continued, after securing his first patent, to manufacture reapers in his workshop on the Virginia farm and to perfect further improvements. Believing his machines would be more practical on the level land of the West, he moved in 1845 to Brockport, New York, on the Erie Canal, and three years later to Chicago, where by 1860 he was turning out 4000 machines a year.

The principle of these early mowers and reapers was the same—a number of blades or "wipers" swept the grain against the cutting surface, after which it was pushed on to a receiving table and automatically shoved off when enough had been gathered to make a sheaf. Laborers following the machine tied the sheaves. These early machines, clumsy as they were, showed their superiority over hand labor and improvements came rapidly. By 1855 nearly 10,000 were in use. At the International Exposition at Paris in that year an American reaper cut an acre of oats in twenty-one minutes, one-third of the time consumed by the foreign makes. In 1857 the United States Agricultural Society held a national trial at the New York State Fair at Syracuse, where forty mowers and reapers were entered. The results demonstrated that the most serious disadvantages, such as side draft, clogging, and inability to begin in standing grain, had been practically eliminated. Moreover, new features such as the header, invented by George Esterly of Wisconsin, were being added to increase the usefulness of the machines. In the succeeding years the reapers were widely introduced, a fact which explains the great crops in spite of the labor shortage during the Civil War.

A necessary further improvement was furnished when a satisfactory thresher was added to the mechanical devices upon which the farmer could depend. With the old-fashioned hand flail progress was painfully slow; from eight to sixteen bushels a day was the average production per man. Experiments went on in both Europe and America in an attempt to devise flails which could be attached to cylinders and driven by horse or steam power, but it was not until 1850 that the separator was attached to the thresher and the whole process of threshing and winnowing was carried on in the same machine. At the Paris Exposition the American machine entered by Hiram and John Pitt won first prize, threshing 740 liters in an hour as against 410 liters by an English machine, its nearest competitor.

The invention and improvement of other farming implements accompanied the greater inventions. The horse hay-rake, which did the work of from eight to ten men, came into use about 1820, and the curing of hay was aided years later by the invention of the tedder. In the decade of the 'forties seed drills for sowing wheat were introduced, and between 1840 and 1860 came the corn planter and various types of cultivators which by the latter date had been widely adopted.

Wide-awake farmers of the time were not unaware that a revolution in agricultural methods was under way. As early as 1839 Judge Jesse Buel, a prominent agitator for scientific farming, wrote:

The disparity between the old and new implements of culture is great, not only in the time employed, but in the manner in which they do their work, and in the power required to perform it. The old plow required a four-cattle team, and two hands, to manage it, and the work ordinarily was but half executed. The improved plow is generally propelled by two cattle, requires but one man to manage it, and, when properly governed, performs thorough work. Harrows and other implements have undergone a like movement. Besides, new implements, which greatly economize the labor of tillage, are coming into use, as the roller, cultivator, drill-barrow, etc., so that a farm may now be worked with half the expense of labor that it was wont to be worked forty years ago, and may be better worked withal.[17]

This remarkable development which Judge Buel described in 1839 was but the beginning. A much more important period of agricultural transformation came in the next two decades, the years which witnessed the introduction of seed drills, corn planters, cultivators, and many other types of machinery, particularly the mower and the reaper. Said the Census of 1860: "By the improved plow, labor equivalent to that of one horse in three is saved. By means of drills two bushels of seed will go as far as three bushels scattered broadcast, while the yield is increased six to eight bushels per acre; the plants come up in rows and may be tended by horse-hoes. . . . The reaping machine is a saving of more than one-third the labor when it cuts and rakes. . . . The threshing machine is a saving of two-thirds on the old hand flail mode. . . . The saving in the labor of handling hay in the field and barn by means of horserakes and horsehayforks is equal to one-half."

SCIENTIFIC FARMING

In England the work of Arthur Young, Jethro Tull, Viscount Townshend, Robert Bakewell, and others in the eighteenth century had demonstrated to Englishmen what might be done in the way of scientific farming. Little interest was shown in agricultural improvements in the colonies, and it was not until after the Revolution that many wealthy American farmers became interested in better methods. The lead was taken by planters like Washington and Jefferson, who were farmers on a large scale and intensely interested in agricultural experiments. Washington, who has been described as "not only the greatest man, but the greatest agriculturist of the period," turned from tobacco raising to an intensive cultivation of other

[17] *The Farmers' Companion* (ed. of 1839), p. 123, quoted by P. W. Bidwell and J. I. Falconer, *History of Agriculture in the Northern United States,* p. 281.

products. He was the founder of the mule-raising industry in the country, the fine Kentucky breed of later years descending directly from the best asses of France and Spain sent him as presents by Lafayette and the king of Spain. His experiments in sheep raising, continued by George Washington Parke Custis, did much to better the breed of sheep in the South. A few of the excellent merino sheep had been smuggled out of Spain, but it was not until the Napoleonic Wars that it was possible to obtain them in large numbers. Jefferson and Robert Livingston were especially interested in the introduction and wide distribution of merinos, a mania for which swept the country in the years 1810–1816. A "strange and incomprehensible infatuation," commented Birkbeck. "There is not a district, scarcely a spot that I have travelled over, where a flock of fine wooled sheep could be kept with any prospect of advantage, provided there were even a market for the carcase. Yet by the ragged remains of the merino family, which may be recognized in many places, I perceive that the attempt has been very general."[18] The importation of merinos and other breeds nevertheless greatly improved the stock. A similar improvement also took place in the quality and size of cattle. English shorthorn or Durham cattle were imported into Kentucky in 1817, and in succeeding years great numbers were bought by farmers who desired to better their stock. Henry Clay in 1817 imported the first Herefords, but this breed did not develop rapidly until it was found adaptable to the Texas ranges in the 'seventies. Other standard breeds were imported and farmers came to take more interest in bettering their herds.

Until 1840 the usual mode of travel was by horseback, and this fact undoubtedly explains the early improvement of breeds of horses. The thoroughbred stallion, Messenger, progenitor of the Standard-bred horse so closely connected with the agricultural history of Kentucky, was brought into New Jersey from England in 1788. The American saddle horse, also largely bred in Kentucky, is descended from the thoroughbred stallion, Denmark, brought into Kentucky in 1839. The Morgan horses of New England were also excellent types. The best kind of American horse as developed by the Kentucky breeders was a saddle horse with easy motion and a rapid walk.

Knowledge of these superior breeds, of the new inventions, and of the improved methods of tillage was disseminated by five means: (1) agricultural societies, (2) agricultural fairs, (3) farm periodicals and literature, (4) agricultural schools, and (5) government aid. The beginnings of all of these are to be found in this period. The Philadelphia Society for Promoting Agriculture was founded in 1785 and included in its membership

[18] Morris Birkbeck, *Notes on a Journey in America*, pp. 87, 88.

Washington and Franklin. Similar societies were founded in five other states before 1800.[19] The first half of the century saw other organizations springing up all over the country, whose purpose was to spread information, lend mutual aid, and stimulate improved methods by holding fairs and offering prizes—pioneers in the great task of agricultural education.

A distinguishing feature of American agricultural life is the county fair. The first agricultural fair was held in Washington in 1804, but the idea took root chiefly through the influence of Elkanah Watson, who in 1807 exhibited two merino sheep in the public square of Pittsfield, Massachusetts, and who three years later persuaded some of his neighbors to join him in an exhibition of livestock on the village green. From this exhibition came the Berkshire Agricultural Society, the first permanent fair association in America. Watson pushed his idea in other states and similar societies were rapidly founded. The first state aid for agricultural fairs was granted by New York in 1819, when $20,000 was appropriated for two years. The United States Patent Office in 1858 printed a list of over 900 agricultural societies, most of which were state or county organizations that existed for the purpose of holding fairs. The interchange of ideas, the new information obtained, and the rivalry promoted by these fairs made them of great importance, especially during this period, in demonstrating the worth of the new machinery.

Agricultural journalism sprang up along with the associations and fairs. Its real beginning dates from 1819, when John S. Skinner founded *The American Farmer* at Baltimore, a weekly paper which enjoyed continuous publication until 1833—a venture quickly imitated in other parts of the country. Of these papers, perhaps the best in the East was *The Cultivator* (1834–1853), founded in Albany by Jesse Buel, and in the West, *The Prairie Farmer,* founded in 1840.

Agricultural education in America undoubtedly had its start with special instruction in the existing schools, perhaps the first being the establishment in 1792 of a professorship of natural history, chemistry, and agriculture at Columbia University. The first institution devoted principally to the teaching of agriculture was the Gardiner Lyceum, established in 1822 at Gardiner, Maine, which for the next ten years maintained its distinctive agricultural character. Other seminaries were founded with the same purpose in view, but agricultural education had to wait on state aid before it became a real factor. The state constitution of Michigan, adopted in 1850, provided for

---

[19] The Philadelphia Society for Promoting Arts, "mainly for improving agriculture," had been founded twenty years before, as well as a similar society in Pennsylvania, but little is known of their activities. The New Jersey Society for Promoting Agriculture, Commerce and Arts was established as early as 1781. See Carl Raymond Woodward, *The Development of Agriculture in New Jersey, 1640–1880* (1927), pp. 51–52.

a college of agriculture. In accordance with this provision the legislature appropriated $40,000 for buildings, instruction, and maintenance, and in 1857 a state college of agriculture was opened, the first institution of its kind in America. Two years later Maryland and Pennsylvania followed the example of Michigan in establishing state-supported institutions. The great growth of agricultural education, however, followed the passing of the Morrill Act in 1862.

National aid to agriculture began in 1839, when Congress appropriated $1000 to be expended by the Commissioner of Patents for the collection of statistics and investigations for the promotion of agriculture. After 1842, with the exception of one year, gradually increasing appropriations were made for this purpose. Annual agricultural reports were printed after 1854. Agricultural matters were handled by the Patent Department until 1862, when a separate bureau of agriculture was set up. These modest beginnings of federal and state interest in the problems of the farmer hardly presaged the immense government activity along this line in recent years.

AGRICULTURAL TRENDS, 1783–1860

In this brief review of American agriculture during the period from 1783 to the outbreak of the Civil War three great developments stand out. First of all there was the great expansion of the farming area which was to cover the larger part of the Mississippi Valley and turn America into the greatest agricultural region in the world. In the second place there was a rapid development of agricultural specialization in which specialized commercial agriculture in well-defined areas was taking the place of the self-sufficient farm. Finally there was the real beginning in America of scientific agriculture and the mechanization of farm methods.

In many ways these years were the brightest in American agricultural history. This was an era of confident expansion in which the future seemed secure. Widening markets in Europe kept pace with expanding farm areas in this country. Factories abroad and at home absorbed the cotton crop and industrial centers purchased foodstuffs. Except for panic periods prices were generally higher and farmers were able in turn to buy the products of forge and factory. In the South slaves, the chief property of the plantation owner, rose in value, and in the Old Northwest the rapid settlement combined with good prices pushed up the value of lands. In such a situation it was natural that the talent of the nation should turn to scientific improvements, to the invention of farm machinery, and to agricultural education. Agriculture was the nation's primary interest. Transportation facilities were developed and industry was organized to serve its needs. The period, in truth, was America's agricultural era.

SELECTED READINGS

Bidwell, P. S., and Falconer, J. I., *History of Agriculture in the Northern United States, 1620–1860*, Chaps. XI–XXV.

Gray, L. C., *History of Agriculture in the Southern United States to 1860*, Chaps. XXVII, XXXIX.

Hutchinson, W. T., *Cyrus Hall McCormick*, Chaps. III, IV, VII, VIII.

Sanford, A. H., *The Story of Agriculture in the United States*, pp. 92–199.

Bidwell, P. W., "The Agricultural Revolution in New England," in the *American Historical Review*, Vol. XXVI, No. 4 (1921).

Hammond, M. B., *The Cotton Industry*, Chaps. I–III.

Flügel, F., and Faulkner, H. U., *Readings in the Economic and Social History of the United States*, pp. 153–187.

The American Merchant Marine
and the Development of
Foreign Commerce

COLONIAL SHIPPING AND THE REVOLUTION

SOME attention has been given to the history of shipbuilding and the merchant marine during the colonial period and the Revolution. We have seen how the colonist, dependent upon the ocean for communication with the home land and with other colonies, began to build ships almost immediately upon his arrival. The best of material was at hand and the market was steady. Meager agricultural possibilities and proximity to the fishing banks literally drove the New Englander to the sea, and having discovered a road to wealth, he pursued it aggressively.

The fisheries and the West Indian trade absorbed most of the ships built, although Europeans, after the Yankee ships had demonstrated their superiority, bought heavily. Shipbuilding was a favored and protected industry from the start. At the opening of the Revolution at least one-third of the tonnage under the English flag was American-built; Massachusetts was said to own one seagoing vessel for every one hundred inhabitants. So anxious was England to increase her power on the sea that Parliament forbore from passing legislation directly antagonistic to the building of ships; lax enforcement and easy evasion of the Navigation Acts up to 1763 permitted extensive commerce and normally developed a shipbuilding industry.

The immediate effect of the Revolution upon American merchant shipping was disastrous. The fishing industry off the New England coast was for the time being effectually limited and the British Navy broke up the intercourse with the West Indies, Spain, and Portugal. As the war progressed, however, merchantmen discovered ways of evading the enemy, and shipping interests found in privateering an outlet for their energies and compensation for their losses. While the slow heavy ships were driven from the sea, the lighter and more easily managed were mounted with guns and directed against English commerce. Between four and five hundred privateers were in commission in 1781; their crews numbered almost as many men as were serving in the Continental Army. Silas Deane in 1777 wrote Robert Morris that as American privateers and cruisers "sailed quite around Ireland and took or destroyed seventeen or eighteen sail of vessels, they most effectually alarmed England, prevented the great fair at Chester, occasioned insurance to rise, and even deterred the English merchants from shipping goods in English vessels at any rate, so that in a few weeks forty sail of French ships were loading in the Thames on freight, an instance never before known."[1] He adds that "even the packet boats from Dover to Calais were for some time insured." A witness before a special parliamentary inquiry in 1778 stated that the losses suffered by British merchants from American privateers "could not be less than two million two hundred thousand pounds." Privateering served the purpose not alone of harassing the enemy but of keeping alive the maritime spirit and holding capital to the shipping industry. In consequence, the close of the war found the American merchant marine in a fairly prosperous condition.

PERIOD OF UNCERTAINTY, 1781–1789

The years between the Revolution and the adoption of the Constitution were years of uncertainty for the American shipping interests. The West Indian trade, so important to the colonists, was hit hard by British Orders in Council issued at the conclusion of the Revolution. Americans might sell lumber, rice, naval stores, tobacco, and live animals to the British West Indies, but not packed meat and fish. Even more disastrous was the decree which forbade entrance of American ships to the island ports. Although these orders were so evaded that by 1787 the West India trade was in a measure restored, the fact that as many as 15,000 slaves in the West Indies are said to have died from starvation between 1780 and 1787 shows only too clearly that trade in the bulky articles of foodstuff was greatly restricted. British shipowners were forbidden the privilege of purchasing vessels built in America, and the list of American products which could lawfully be imported into England was restricted chiefly to naval supplies. Our ambassadors failed in their attempts at relief through treaties, and retaliatory measures were unproductive because of interstate jealousies. Many shipowners were ruined, and shipbuilders and seamen were destitute of work. No group of interests saw more clearly the need for the encouragement and

[1] The Deane Papers, II, 108, New York Historical Society Publications. Letter, dated "Paris, 23rd. August, 1777," to Robert Morris, who was a member of the Secret Committee of Congress. This entire letter, pp. 106–111, is well worth reading for its account of the activities of "American ships of war, private as well as public."

protection of a strong central government and no group more ardently demanded it.[2]

Perhaps the greatest influence in restoring maritime prosperity was the opening of new sources of commerce. In February, 1784, the *Empress of China* sailed from New York to Canton, returning in May of the following year with a cargo of tea and silk, and in 1785 Elias Hasket Derby of Salem sent his *Grand Turk* to the Far East. Yankee merchants had found a new trade route and a new market, and within five years they had broken the long monopoly of the East India Company and were trading regularly with Asia. They had yet to discover, however, a readily salable commodity for the Chinese trade. Late in 1787 Captains John Kendrick in the *Columbia* and Robert Gray in the *Lady Washington* set out from Boston to engage in the fur trade on the northwest coast, and Gray with a load of peltries continued to Canton where he exchanged them for tea.[3] This first adventure proved unsuccessful financially, but it "solved the riddle of the China trade," [4] and for years thereafter New England traders exchanged clothing, hardware, and various knicknacks for sea otter and other furs which found ҁ ready market at Canton.

GROWTH AND PROSPERITY, 1789–1807

Commerce with the Far East ushered in the golden age of American shipping, but it was not the Canton market alone which lured the venturesome and aggressive sea captains in the decades after 1790. Merchantmen from Salem and other coast towns carried the American flag into every port where Yankee ingenuity could secure access or trading ability secure profits. Sensitive in the extreme as merchant shipping is to outside influences, the favorable reaction occasioned by the adoption of the Constitution, by tonnage taxes imposed on foreign vessels, by the establishment of public credit, and by increased demand for American products resulting from the European wars, was nevertheless astonishing. The tonnage registered for foreign trade jumped from 123,893 in 1789 to 981,017 in 1810. The imports carried in American bottoms—the most important method of determining the real prosperity of a merchant marine—increased during the same period from 17.5 per cent to 93 per cent, and exports in American bottoms from 30 to 90 per cent.

Shipping interests had been among the most ardent in supporting the new Constitution, and the first Congress hastened to their protection. The first Act passed by the first Congress (with the exception of a formal

---

[2] Above, p. 153.

[3] It was on the second voyage of the *Columbia* in 1792 that Gray sailed into the river which bears the name of his ship and laid the foundation for American claims to this region.

[4] S. E. Morison, *The Maritime History of Massachusetts*, p. 51.

statute with reference to the taking of oaths) was the Act of July 4, 1789, which, although designed for the "encouragement and protection of manufacturers" and for obtaining revenue, gave real aid to shipping by allowing a discount of 10 per cent in the tariff duties on imports brought to this country in ships built and owned by American citizens. In order to encourage the newly developed trade with the Far East, this same Act allowed a reduction in the duty on tea imported direct from the East; this made the tariff paid by the American ship less than half that of the foreign vessel, and at the same time dealt a blow to the East India Company by placing high duties on tea bought in Europe, even if imported in American ships. The next Act of the same Congress, that of July 20, 1789, imposed a duty of six cents a ton on American-built ships owned by Americans upon entering our ports, but charged thirty cents a ton on American-built ships owned by foreigners, and fifty cents a ton on foreign-built and -owned ships. It was provided at the same time that American ships in the coastwise trade should pay tonnage duty only once a year, while foreign ships must pay it at every entry. This Act presaged the early absorption of the coastwise trade by American ships.

An Act of 1790 on the government and regulation of seamen provided a code of law in advance of the time. It stipulated that a written contract must be entered into between master and seamen specifying the voyage and rate of wages; without this no master could have full control of his men. He was also required to pay them the highest current wages, with the ship itself as a guaranty. Masters were liable to severe penalties for abandoning American sailors in a foreign country, and seamen who signed articles and deserted their ship might forfeit their wages and be brought back under compulsion. With but few changes, this was the basis of the law covering seamen until the salutary modifications of the La Follette Act of 1915. The development of a strong merchant marine was also aided by the creation in 1798 of an American Navy, which repeatedly gave a good account of itself in the succeeding years.

Much of the remarkable growth in shipping was absorbed in the first years of this period in the Far Eastern trade, but when the energies of the European nations were taken up with the Napoleonic Wars, American merchantmen were to be found wherever business was to be obtained. "The unfolding of the great West," says Marvin, "had scarcely begun. Kentucky was not admitted to the Union until 1792; Tennessee, until 1796. Not only did most of the American people live within reach of the ocean, but the ocean everywhere seemed to be the nearest, the most natural, and the most inviting field of adventure. It was true of many more American towns than tide-encircled Boston that 'Each street leads down to the sea.' Down these streets went most of the young men who had dreams in their heads and iron in their blood, and they always found ships waiting."[5] It was the day when "the streets of London, the quays of Lisbon, and the Hong of Canton were more familiar sights to the merchants of the coast than were the somber forests and stump-studded clearings of Western America."[6] "At the end of 1793," says Ugo Rabbeno, "the tonnage of the United States exceeded that of every other nation except England; their foreign trade ranked in point of value next to that of England, and, proportionally to the population, the United States were the first commercial nation of the world."[7] Between 1795 and 1801 the average annual net earnings of the American merchant marine were believed to exceed $32,000,000.

The two decades after 1789 were not, however, years of peaceful and uninterrupted development. During practically the entire period we were in difficulties with our chief rivals, England and France, and between 1801 and 1805 our tiny Navy engaged in war with Tripolitan pirates in defense of our merchant marine. In 1792 war broke out between France and Austria, a war which was eventually to involve all Europe and to continue, with but two short interruptions, until 1815. The superiority of the British Navy was soon apparent and it was not long until the merchantmen of France and her allies had entirely disappeared from the sea. The result was to throw the carrying trade of France into the hands of American merchantmen flying the flag of the only neutral nation of importance on the ocean. While all Europe was engaged in a life-and-death struggle, Yankee merchants and shipowners reaped handsome profits from transporting the products of the French, Dutch, and Spanish colonies. Intent upon weakening her foe as well as hindering this new rival, England began to enforce the so-called "Rule of War of 1756," by which she maintained that a neutral might not enjoy in time of war a carrying trade prohibited in time of peace. This would have prevented American merchantmen from trading with the French West Indies, as the latter had been theoretically closed before the war. Provisions were considered contraband of war, and the warships and privateersmen of both England and France were ordered to capture any vessels so laden. As the chief exports of the United States were provisions, the effect, if the orders were enforced, would be disastrous.

Especially irritating was the claim made by Great Britain that British sailors found on American ships might be taken and forced to serve on British men-of-war. In the later years of the war, as seamen became scarcer, she became more and more unscrupulous in her use of this alleged right;

[5] W. L. Marvin, *The American Merchant Marine*, p. 43.
[6] C. and M. Beard, *Rise of American Civilization*, I, 400.
[7] Ugo Rabbeno, *The American Colonial Policy*, p. 141.

the State Department believed that in 1806 and 1807 as many as 6000 American seamen were serving under compulsion in the British Navy. As to the number of impressed seamen who were American-born it is impossible to know, for English sailors were deserting by the thousands. "Every English vessel," says Henry Adams, "which entered a Virginia port was at once abandoned by her crew, who hastened to enter the public or private ships of the United States. The captain of any British frigate which might happen to run into the harbor of New York, if he went ashore, was likely to meet on his return to the wharf some of his boat's crew strolling about the town, every man supplied with papers of American citizenship." [8] As England at this time did not recognize the alienation of nationality, she resented this on legal as well as practical grounds.

Although the chief trouble was with England, the first actual fighting occurred with France. Rightly or wrongly, she felt that under the Treaty of 1778 we were in duty bound to aid her in the war with Great Britain; she therefore resented Washington's proclamation of neutrality (1793), and she maintained that in the Jay Treaty (1794, ratified in 1796) and in several other ways we had violated our treaty agreements with her. Her resentment led to repeated violations of our neutrality and insults to our government; the "XYZ affair" created a great stir in this country. While war was never officially declared, France in 1796 stated informally that the alliance with the United States was at an end, and Congress on July 7, 1798, voted to abrogate all treaties with her. Organization of a Navy Department (1798) and other preparations for war were pushed forward, and Congress suspended commercial intercourse with France and her dependencies. Between 1798 and 1800 naval engagements between the two nations were fought in the West Indies and 84 French ships, mostly privateers, were captured. A treaty in 1800, which for the time being settled the chief points in controversy, closed this episode.

Notwithstanding interference from British warships, French privateersmen, and Tripolitan pirates, the years up to 1807 were prosperous for American shipping and agriculture. Registered tonnage in foreign trade had mounted from 123,893 tons in 1789 to 810,163 in 1807; exports, from $20,754,000 in 1792 to $108,343,150 in 1807; and imports, from $29,200,000 in 1792 to $138,500,000 in 1807. The proportion of this trade (import and export) carried in American ships jumped from 23.6 per cent in 1789 to 92 per cent in 1807. Only in two subsequent years (1825 and 1826) was this mark surpassed. The shipbuilding industry was especially prosperous, taking care not only of this remarkable growth in local tonnage, but actually, between 1789 and 1812, selling over 200,000 tons to foreigners. The rapid in-

---

[8] Henry Adams, *History of the United States of America*, II, 334–335.

crease in exports was made up chiefly of provisions, a market for which had been created by the war. Europe, too busy fighting to raise sufficient foodstuffs, called increasingly upon America to furnish grain and meat, as well as such raw materials as cotton, wool, and leather. While the prices of foodstuffs and raw materials soared, farmers reaped a golden harvest, shared by the shippers who transported the products and the merchants who during these prosperous years were able to dispose of increasing amounts of imported goods. Sailors' wages rose from eight to thirty dollars a month and foreigners became naturalized in order to partake of the huge profits of American shipowners. The whole situation was remarkably similar to the early years of the First World War, 1914–1917, when the United States as the great neutral profited from supplying foodstuffs and other products to the warring nations.

This period, one of prosperity not only for merchant shipping but for the country at large, was halted in 1807. The year 1805 witnessed the two great battles of Austerlitz and Trafalgar, the former leaving Napoleon master of the Continent, and the latter leaving Great Britain mistress of the sea. By this time both nations had come to the conclusion that only through economic boycotts could eventual victory be gained. Already in 1804 English Orders in Council had declared French ports from Ostend to the Seine under blockade; these orders were extended in May, 1806, to include the coast from Elbe to Brest. From Berlin Napoleon, recently victorious over Prussia, issued his answer in the form of a decree declaring the British Islands under blockade. A year later, in November, 1807, England issued a second Order in Council declaring that no neutral vessel should trade with the ports of France or her allies without touching and paying duties at a British port. Napoleon, now thoroughly convinced that the ruin of England could be brought about only by the strict enforcement of the "Continental System," retaliated with the Milan Decree of 1807, declaring that any vessel sailing to or from Great Britain or her colonies was liable to seizure, as was any ship that submitted to the Orders in Council of 1807 and paid duties to England. It is true that these were to a certain extent merely paper blockades, impossible of enforcement on the part of France with her Navy driven from the seas, and inadequately enforced by England; but they resulted in the capture of about 1600 American ships and $60,000,000 worth of property. These orders and decrees, if enforced, meant the virtual prohibition of neutral trade, and hence the elimination of American ships from the European trade.

This utter disregard of neutral rights and the heavy losses inflicted upon American shipping, accompanied as they were by such virtual acts of war as the firing upon the American frigate *Chesapeake* by the British man-of-war *Leopard,* finally aroused Jefferson to action. Anxious to preserve peace, he believed that Europe could be brought to terms by an embargo. At his advice Congress in December, 1807, passed an Embargo Act which prohibited American ships from sailing to foreign ports and permitted coasting trade only under condition that the owner give bonds double the value of the cargo that it would be relanded in the United States. This applied even to the smallest fishing smack. The navy and revenue cutters were put at the disposal of the executive by later Acts. Instead, however, of starving Great Britain into submission, the Act bade fair to ruin our own shipping. American exports dropped from $108,343,150 in 1807 to $22,430,960 in 1808; imports, from $138,500,000 to $56,990,000. New York, said a British traveler at that time, "was full of shipping, but they were dismantled and laid up. Their decks were cleared, their hatches fastened down, and scarcely a sailor was to be found on board. Not a box, bale, cask, barrel, or package, was to be seen upon the wharves. Many of the counting houses were shut up or advertised to be let; and the few solitary merchants, clerks, porters, and laborers that were to be seen, were walking about with their hands in their pockets. . . . The coffee-houses were almost empty; . . . The streets near the waterside were almost deserted; the grass had begun to grow upon the wharves. . . ." [9] The testimony of this traveler may not have been unprejudiced, but McMaster estimates that 55,000 sailors and 100,000 mechanics and laborers were thrown out of work and that during the period of the Embargo Act ships lost $12,500,000 in net earnings. The customs revenues sank from $16,000,000 to a few thousand. Thirteen hundred men in New York City alone were thrown into prison as debtors whom the embargo had ruined.

The losses sustained by the shipping interests as a result of the Embargo Act were colossal, especially in New England, where one hundred Massachusetts towns adopted resolutions against it. Smuggling was rampant, and from certain New England ports "loaded vessels literally fought their way to the sea," for New Englanders found that they could carry on a prosperous commerce notwithstanding the many adverse factors. In spite of widespread opposition, Jefferson's theory of an economic boycott was a sound one, and there is evidence pointing to the fact that, if it had been continued long enough, it might have accomplished the desired result. [10]

[9] John Lambert, *Travels Through Canada and the United States of North America in the Years 1806, 1807 and 1808* (1810), II, 65.
[10] W. P. Trent in his excellent sketch of Jefferson in *Southern Statesmen of the Old Régime* (1897), p. 80, comments as follows on Jefferson's efforts to avoid war: "In short, what chiefly affects me when I study the whole matter is the pathos of it,—a philosopher and a friend of peace struggling with a despot of superhuman genius and a Tory cabinet of superhuman insolence and stolidity."

Even so, subsequent non-intercourse or embargo measures did bring success. Britain repealed her Orders in Council in 1812, unaware that this country had declared war a few days earlier.[11]

The pressure of the shipping interests, however, was so strong that in March, 1809, the Embargo Act was repealed, and for it was substituted the Non-intercourse Act, which prohibited trade only with Great Britain and France and their possessions. This Act was repealed in 1810, and new legislation, called the Macon Bill, was enacted; this provided that as soon as either England or France withdrew her decrees against our shipping, the Non-intercourse Act would be revived against the other country. Napoleon immediately announced (August 5, 1810) that the Berlin and Milan Decrees were repealed, and Madison issued a proclamation reviving the Non-intercourse Act against England if she did not repeal the Orders in Council before February 2, 1811. She ignored the proclamation and Napoleon, in spite of his announced repeal of the two decrees, continued, as before, to seize and rob American ships wherever he could lay hands on them. Nevertheless, the years 1809 and 1810 showed increases in both imports and exports and the registered tonnage in foreign trade reached 981,019 tons in 1810, a mark not equaled again until 1847. In spite of all the setbacks and discouragements, it had been a period of remarkable growth and prosperity, the worst blow being the Embargo Act imposed by our own government.

THE WAR OF 1812

The year 1811 found the United States fast drifting into a war with England. Although France and England had both apparently vied with each other in heaping insults upon our government and bringing losses upon our shipping, it was the latter nation that was in a position to enforce her attitude and to cause the most trouble. In order to give merchantmen a chance to reach a safe harbor, Congress imposed a third embargo in the spring of 1812 and on June 18 declared war. The causes, as reviewed by Madison in his message of June 1, were violations of our flag on the high seas, confiscation of our ships, illegal impressment of seamen, blockade of our ports, the obnoxious Orders in Council, and the inciting of Indians against our borders. All but one of them had to do with violations of the rights of American merchantmen; yet it was the young "War Hawks" of the South and West, led by Henry Clay, who urged the war in Congress, and the representatives of western farmers and plantation owners whose votes made it possible. Agriculture, like shipping, had suffered from interference with commerce, for the produce of the farms and plantations comprised a large

[11] This is told in full in W. W. Jennings, *The American Embargo* (1921), and L. M. Sears, *Jefferson and the Embargo* (1927).

part of our exports. It was the decline of the prices of agricultural commodities that was the all-important underlying cause and for this farmers and planters rightly held Great Britain responsible. But it was also the Indian menace and the desire to annex Florida and Canada that fed the flames of the war spirit rising along the whole frontier. "Agrarian cupidity," cried John Randolph, "not maritime right urges the war. Ever since the report of the Committee on Foreign Relations came into the House, we have heard but one word—like the whip-poor-will, but one eternal monotonous tone—Canada! Canada! Canada!" [12]

On the other hand, New England, which had been most disastrously affected by the British Acts, bitterly opposed the war, many believing that it "originated in hatred to *New England* and to commerce; in subservience to the mandate of the Tyrant of *France.*" [13] Federalist statesmen believed that new agrarian empires arising in the West as a result of the war would further jeopardize the waning influence of the seaboard states. Not only did New England in certain instances refuse to fight or lend money to carry on the war, but she actually rendered aid to the British and made preliminary movements toward secession. In England the result of the embargoes had been to raise the cost of food. With war in sight the Orders in Council were withdrawn five days after war had been declared in the United States. Modern cables might have prevented the conflict.

The War of 1812 was primarily a war on the sea. With the exception of the battle of New Orleans which was fought after peace had been signed, the conflicts on land were of minor importance and were usually unsuccessful to American arms. Before the declaration of war both Clay and Calhoun had talked glibly of the ease with which the militia would capture Canada, but all attempts to invade that region met with utter failure. On the other hand, the American Navy of but twenty-three vessels of all classes gave an excellent account of itself, capturing 254 naval and merchant ships of the enemy before being destroyed or shut up in American harbors. By the end of the war the British Navy, numbering at that time about one thousand ships, had effectually blockaded the American coast and captured some 1400 merchant vessels and fishing boats. Exports dropped from $61,316,832 in 1811 to $6,927,441 in 1814; imports during the same period from $53,400,000 to $12,965,000. The most effective work on the American side was done by the privateersmen, who took 1300 prizes valued at $39,000,000. The self-reliant American seaman, realizing that he was fighting his own battle, was at his best aboard a privateer. That his work bore fruit may be gleamed from the words of a

---

[12] *Annals of Congress,* 12th Cong., I, 533.
[13] Declaration of a Barnstable County Peace Convention, quoted by S. E. Morison, *The Maritime History of Massachusetts,* p. 198.

resolution of Glasgow merchants passed at a meeting in September, 1814, which said:

That the number of privateers with which our channels have been infested, the audacity with which they have approached our coasts, and the success with which their enterprise has been attended, have proved injurious to our commerce, humbling to our pride, and discreditable to the directors of the naval power of the British nation, whose flag, till of late, waved over every sea and triumphed over every rival. That there is reason to believe that in the short space of less than twenty-four months, above eight hundred vessels have been captured by that power whose maritime strength we have hitherto impolitically held in contempt. That at a time when we are at peace with all the world, when the maintenance of our marine costs so large a sum to the country, when the mercantile and shipping interests pay a tax for protection under the form of convoy duty, and when, in the plenitude of our power, we have declared the whole American coast under blockade, it is equally distressing and mortifying that our ships cannot with safety traverse our own channels, that insurance cannot be effected but at an excessive premium, and that a horde of American cruisers should be allowed, unresisted and unmolested, to take, burn, or sink our own vessels in our own inlets, and almost in sight of our own harbors.[14]

By the spring of 1813 flour was selling in England at $58 a barrel, beef at $38, pork at $36, and lumber at $72 a thousand. Peace, which was signed on December 24, 1814, made no mention of the causes of the war—impressments, right of search, or blockades—but with the removal of the causes and the record our seamen had made in asserting their rights, it seemed likely that the latter would not soon again be called into question. What immediate gains there were came to the West, where the Indian power in the Northwest and Southwest was effectually broken and the way prepared for the annexation of Florida and a rapid extension of the frontier.

The natural reaction after the war was immediately felt. The conclusion of peace released shipping and the registered tonnage for foreign trade went up from 674,600 in 1814 to 854,300 in 1815. Exports increased from $6,927,400 in 1814 to $93,281,100 in 1818; imports from $12,965,000 in 1814 to $147,103,000 in 1816. This sudden prosperity was not entirely healthy. The flood of imports glutted the market and forced manufacturing concerns which had been established during the war to suspend operations. This, combined with the disturbed and unsettled financial condition, brought in 1818 a sharp decrease in tonnage registered in foreign trade, and in 1819 a marked decrease in both exports and imports.

The years immediately following the war marked the beginning of legislation to establish commerce on the principle of reciprocity. The Act of

[14] Quoted by W. L. Marvin, *The American Merchant Marine*, p. 129.

March 3, 1815, provided that all discriminating duties imposed by former laws on the tonnage of foreign vessels or the goods imported therein would be repealed in the case of any foreign nation that abolished its discriminating and countervailing duties against us. On the other hand, an Act was passed in 1817, in imitation of the European navigation laws, forbidding the importation of goods from any foreign port except in American vessels or vessels of the country from which the goods came, and at the same time closing the coasting trade to foreign vessels, but providing for repeal in the case of nations that removed such restrictions upon our vessels. An Act of 1828 provided for reciprocity with foreign nations in the indirect carrying trade. The result of these three Acts was a long series of reciprocal treaties with foreign nations, commencing with the treaty of July 3, 1815, with Great Britain, which abolished differential duties with respect to direct trade between the two countries. This was followed by a treaty with France in 1822 and Prussia in 1828, guaranteeing reciprocal liberty in commerce, and in the succeeding years with most of the countries of Europe and Central and South America. It was not until 1830 that England opened the West Indian ports to the United States commerce, and the restrictions of the Act of 1817 against her were removed.

REVIVAL OF MARITIME PROSPERITY

The years 1820 to 1830 witnessed a second period of remarkable growth and prosperity. Although the amount of tonnage registered in foreign trade did not equal that of 1815–1817 or the figures of the next two decades, the proportion of American carriage in the foreign trade reached 92.5 per cent in 1826, a larger percentage than has been attained before or since. J. R. Soley maintains that "in every respect we may say that this period represents the most flourishing condition of shipping in American history." [15] Not only were we carrying practically all of our own goods, but the reputation of Yankee shipbuilders for turning out models which in speed, strength, and durability surpassed any vessels to be found brought about the sale between 1815 and 1840 of 540,000 tons of shipping to foreigners. A fully equipped 500-ton sailing vessel cost $37,500 in America and $43,000 in England. Generations of New England shipbuilding had produced the most skilled artisans in the world, and northern Europe had lost many of her shipwrights, drawn here by higher wages. To man these ships there were the aggressive and intelligent Yankee sailors who appeared equally at home on the cod banks, in the whaling ships, or on the rigging of a transatlantic packet. Notwithstanding higher wages, it cost less to run an American vessel, for a smaller

[15] In N. S. Shaler, *The United States of America,* article, "The Maritime Industries of America," I, 539.

crew was carried. Of the world's total whaling fleet in 1842, it was estimated that 652 out of 882 sail were American vessels.

It was during this decade that the development of the packet ship occurred. The first line of sail packets, the Black Ball Line, had been founded in 1816

PERCENTAGE OF EXPORTS AND IMPORTS IN AMERICAN VESSELS [16]

Each symbol represents 10 per cent of all exports and imports   PICTOGRAPH CORPORATION
(From H. U. Faulkner and Tyler Kepner, *America, Its History and People*, Harper & Brothers.)

The proportion of a nation's commerce carried by its own merchant marine is a good index of the prosperity of that merchant marine. The golden era of our shipping was before the Civil War, after which came a rapid decline. Shortage occasioned by the World War brought a new revival.

between New York and Liverpool. A second line to Liverpool began operation in 1822, and in 1823 a third line to Hull. These packets, larger and better than the ordinary merchant ships, specialized in high-grade freight and passenger traffic. They made their trips regularly, sometimes in eighteen or twenty days, and were especially designed for transatlantic work. They were the predecessors of the present steam lines and their service was so excellent that they remained in operation long after the steamship became dominant.

With all this prosperity it should be remembered that tonnage in foreign trade was less in 1830 than in 1820, and that with the increasing population there was a relative falling off in per capita tonnage from 12.54 cubic feet in

[16] Statistics from J. R. Soley in N. S. Shaler, *The United States of America;* from *Statistical Abstract, 1921,* p. 426, and *ibid., 1930,* p. 460.

1807 and 13.43 in 1810, to 4.25 in 1839 and 8.63 in 1855, the date marking the highest point of the clipper-ship era. Most of the elements which contributed to the later rapid decline were already making themselves felt.

OVERPRODUCTION AND DECLINE

In the history of ocean navigation the decades from 1830 to 1860 marked the most important advance that the world had yet seen. Far-sighted shipbuilders turned from wooden to iron ships and equipped them with steam power rather than sails. These years were also significant in the history of the American merchant marine. Although registered tonnage in foreign trade increased rapidly,[17] the percentage of our trade carried in American bottoms fell. The American merchant marine was definitely on the decline.

Robert Fulton had demonstrated the practicability of steam as a motive force for propelling ships in his memorable voyage up the Hudson in 1807, and steam craft were on the Mississippi as early as 1812.[18] Notwithstanding the fact that the *Savannah,* a 300-ton vessel built in New York and equipped with steam as well as sails, had made a twenty-seven-day trip across the Atlantic in 1819, eighty hours of which she traveled under steam, it was generally considered that steamboats were adaptable only for river and coast navigation. The utilization of coal in the production of steam and the invention of the screw propeller, both of which occurred in the 'thirties, hastened an inevitable development.

Englishmen had been experimenting with steam packets on short services to Rotterdam, Hamburg, and Gibraltar for a number of years before the *Sirius* and the *Great Western* in 1838 made the trip to New York by steam only in seventeen and a half and thirteen and a half days, respectively. These records proved that wooden side-wheeled steamers could make the trip in a shorter time than the fastest sailing packet. The British government was farsighted enough to realize that the motive power of the immediate future was steam, and in 1839 it heavily subsidized the Cunard Company, which began its career in 1840 with four side-wheeled wooden ships. This policy of subsidization, which has been continued to the present time by Great Britain, aided materially not only in giving her maritime interests a start in the new type of ships but in helping them win and hold supremacy on the ocean. The Peninsular Company, afterwards the Peninsular and Oriental, was established in 1837, and the Pacific Steam Navigation Company in 1840; both were subsidized.

Almost as revolutionary as the gradual substitution of steam for sailing vessels was the very gradual substitution of iron and later steel ships for those of wood. With an abundance of coal and iron close to the sea, with skilled mechanics and cheap labor, and with a metallurgical industry de-

[17] See graph, p. 528.   [18] See Chap. 14.

veloped far in advance of ours, Great Britain forged ahead from the start. Already by 1853 one-fourth of the total tonnage built there were steamships, and more than one-fourth were made of iron. In the same year 22 per cent of our tonnage was constructed for steamships, but scarcely any iron ships were built here. The Yankee shipbuilder, overconfident in the recognized superiority of his inimitable clipper ship, was blind to the fact that the future of the sea was for the nation which could build the cheapest and best iron steamships. The clipper was fast but uneconomical. Built of wood, it could not be expanded indefinitely. Moreover, steamships in the long run were to prove safer and even faster than the beautiful clipper ship.

The thirty years from 1830 to 1860 were characterized by extremely rapid production in shipbuilding. The 538,136 tons registered in foreign trade in 1831 had increased to 1,047,454 in 1847 and to 2,496,894 in 1862, a figure that represented the culmination of our shipbuilding tonnage until surpassed in World War I. From 1848 to 1858 shipbuilding was maintained at an average of 400,000 tons a year. This construction was caused, in the first place, by the development after 1845 of the above-mentioned justly famous American clipper ship, the fastest sailing ship afloat, an extraordinary product of decades of shipbuilding and the intense rivalry between steam and canvas. Designed for speed, the clipper was built on sharp lines and carried a maximum of canvas. She was intended primarily for long voyages, and was used especially for the California and Far Eastern trade. Given a fair breeze, she could outdistance a steamship. It was not uncommon for a clipper to sail over 300 miles a day; the *Flying Cloud* on a 90-day run to San Francisco made 374 miles on one day. The *Comet,* on an 80-day voyage from San Francisco to New York, averaged 210 miles a day. Records of 86 days from Singapore to New York, 84 from Canton to New York, and 96 from Manila to Salem were made between 1851 and 1853. It appeared that the American shipbuilder, before he relinquished his supremacy, was intent upon demonstrating the heights of efficiency and speed to which a sailing ship could attain.[19]

In the second place, there was an increased demand for shipping. This was occasioned chiefly by the discovery in 1848 of gold in California. The overland routes were slow and perilous, and the demand for passage and shipments to the Golden Gate swamped accommodations. The Yankee packet could make the trip around the Horn in about three months, thus giving a prolonged lease of life to the building of sailing ships. The wars between

[19] It is believed that the lines of the clipper ship were originally derived from a type of Chinese coasting vessels known as the "Singapore fast boat," a half-block model of which (now in the Clark Collection at the Massachusetts Institute of Technology) was brought from China by Captain R. H. Waterman. The first clipper in this country, the *Rainbow,* was designed by John W. Griffiths and built in New York. The greatest of the clipper ships, including the *Flying Cloud,* were built in Massachusetts by Donald McKay, a Nova Scotian trained in the shipyards of Isaac Webb in New York.

Great Britain and China in 1840–1842 and 1856–1860 threw a part of the China trade into American hands. The revolutionary outbreaks of 1848 interrupted European trade, with a resulting benefit to Americans; and the Crimean War, for which many European boats were engaged in transporting troops and supplies, gave new openings to American ships. In addition, the natural increase in commerce due to the growth in population, wealth, and production necessitated increased shipping. In no commodity was the increase in production so great as in cotton; production increased from 4000 bales of 500 pounds in 1790 to 3,841,416 bales in 1860. Our exports increased from $19,012,000 in 1791 to $333,576,000 in 1860, and of this last the exports of cotton were valued at $191,806,500. Imports increased during this same period from $29,200,000 to $353,616,000. Increasing immigration also contributed to the demand for shipping facilities.

Notwithstanding these demands, there was a decidedly unhealthy element in this remarkable activity in shipbuilding. In the first place the demand from Europe resulting from the Crimean War was abnormal; between 1854 and 1859 the European nations were buying 50,000 tons of shipping as against 10,000 tons in normal years. Furthermore, the increase in the building of sailing ships unfortunately came at a time when their days were numbered, for between 1850 and 1860 the share of ocean freight carried by steamers increased from 14 to 28 per cent. When the abnormal demand for sailing ships abated, as it did in 1858, it meant that shipyards built and equipped to produce wooden ships and shipwrights trained for a type no longer in demand would be idle, and that foreign shipyards already engaged in building iron steamships would be in a decidedly superior position. The panic of 1857 precipitated the crash. In 1858 the shipbuilding output, which had been maintained for the preceding ten years at an average of 400,000 tons a year, dropped to 244,000 and in 1859 to 156,000. At the same time the combined imports and exports carried in American bottoms were steadily declining, only 65.2 per cent being carried in 1861 as against 92.5 per cent in 1826.

The decline of the American merchant marine was by no means due solely to British subsidies and the technological superiority of iron steamships. Many other factors were involved. In the first place the importance of certain of the old trade routes declined. The great revival of the carrying trade after the Revolution was to no small extent the result of the opening of the China trade and of the Napoleonic Wars. The wars were over by 1815. The China trade declined with the disappearance of the sea otter, with the substitution in America of European porcelain for Chinese pottery, and with the change in the styles of men's clothes which no longer demanded large quantities of silk. Only tea remained as an important article of Far Eastern commerce and its importance was waning as Brazilian coffee replaced tea as the national drink.

Even the West Indian trade which had been the backbone of colonial commerce fell off. Nor did the Treaty of 1830, which opened the British West Indian ports to American ships, revive it. As opportunities lessened, profits became smaller and more uncertain. Great fortunes had been made in the Far Eastern trade in the early years of the century and profits were fair a half century later in the California trade, but as a whole commerce and shipping no longer offered outstanding opportunities.

As chances for profit declined in shipping, capital found new and more profitable fields for investment. Manufacturing, which grew rapidly after the War of 1812, absorbed some of it; and considerable amounts were drawn into such internal improvements as canals and railways. Between 1820 and 1838 the states contracted debts of over $110,000,000 for building roads, canals, and railroads; from 1830 to 1860 over 30,000 miles of railroad were built, most of the capital coming from private investors. The minds of the venturous and ambitious turned from the sea to the unexploited West, and capital turned from shipbuilding and the carrying trade to the development of natural resources.

The elements contributing to the decline of the merchant marine were already apparent before the Civil War, and the result would undoubtedly have been the same if that conflict had not occurred. The war, however, accentuated a tendency already existing and dealt a blow from which the merchant marine failed to recover until artificially revived during the First World War. In 1861 registered American tonnage in foreign trade amounted to 2,496,894 tons and in 1865 to 1,518,350, and the percentage of imports and exports carried in American ships dropped in the same years from 66.2 to 27.7. The decrease of some 900,000 tons in these years was due chiefly to two causes. The first was the loss sustained from Confederate cruisers such as the *Alabama*, built and fitted out in England contrary to the laws of warfare. The second and more important was the sale during the four years 1862–1865 of 751,595 tons of shipping abroad, occasioned by lack of confidence, the decline in profits caused by continual Confederate captures and high insurance rates, and the decline in the export business resulting from the cessation of cotton shipments abroad.

Whaling and Fishing

The whaling industry was definitely retarded during the Revolution and the continental wars, 1775–1815, but revived after Napoleon's final defeat. The recorded tonnage had increased from practically nothing in 1814 to 35,-000 tons in 1820, and then steadily, during the golden age of the industry, to 157,000 in 1841 and 198,000 in 1858. After that year the decline set in. Before 1791 whaling had been confined to the Atlantic, but gradually cruises were extended into other oceans; after 1835 the industry was largely confined to the Pacific. Almost the entire whaling fleet hailed from New York and New England. Sag Harbor, New York, boasted 63 vessels in 1846, though the great center was New Bedford, Massachusetts, and the smaller towns close by; their fleet numbered over 200 vessels in 1857 and employed over 10,000 seamen. Nantucket ranked second and New London third as whaling ports during this period, the former relinquishing her colonial supremacy because of the shallow harbor which prevented the entrance of the large vessels. Many of the coast towns engaged in the traffic on a smaller scale and derived rich profits. Boston and New York were the chief exporting centers; the chief foreign markets for sperm oil were the West Indies, South America, and northern Europe; and for whalebone France, England, and the Baltic region. The larger part of the oil product was absorbed in the domestic market. During the height of its prosperity the products of the whaling industry surpassed in value those of all the rest of the fishing industry combined. In New England whaling ranked next to textiles and boots and shoes. The average annual production from 1835 to 1860 was 118,000 barrels of sperm oil, 216,000 barrels of whale oil, and 2,324,000 pounds of whalebone, with an average annual value of about $8,000,000. After 1850 the decline was rapid, owing partly to the growing scarcity of whales, but chiefly to the increased use of mineral oils and gas as illuminants.

The cod-fishing industry suffered the same early setbacks as whaling experienced during the two wars of independence, but eventually recovered after the passage of a series of laws that remitted most of the duty on the imported salt which was used. The registered tonnage engaged in cod fishing increased from 25,000 in 1790 to 136,700 in 1860. In that year close to 2500 vessels with crews numbering 18,000 were fishing for cod, the annual value of which was about $3,000,000. After 1818 an increasing number of vessels went out after mackerel, the maximum tonnage before 1860 reaching 73,800 in 1849. During this period also, commercial fishing for herring, halibut, and oysters began. Maine and Massachusetts monopolized the cod fishing, the catch being about evenly divided between them. The two chief centers were Portland and Castine, Maine, and Gloucester and Marblehead, Massachusetts. The latter state sent out the major part of the mackerel fleet. Despite the expanding fishing fleets and large catches, the fishing industry never attained the relative economic importance that it held throughout the colonial period.

COMMODITIES AND PAYMENTS

Foreign commerce quickly reestablished itself in the decade after the Revolution and by 1790 its value amounted to more than three times that of the 1760's. As a result of the increased European demand for foodstuffs and raw materials during the Napoleonic Wars, its value had again more than trebled by 1800. Interrupted by the embargo, the War of 1812, the post-war readjustment, and other factors, foreign trade declined from the high figures of 1807 and did not reach them again until 1835. Since then the trend has been generally upward.

IMPORTS AND EXPORTS BY DECADES [20]

Year	Total Exports	Total Imports
1790.	$20,200,000	$23,000,000
1800.	70,972,000	91,253,000
1810.	66,758,000	85,400,000
1820.	69,692,000	74,450,000
1830.	71,671,000	62,721,000
1840.	123,609,000	98,259,000
1850.	144,376,000	172,510,000
1860.	333,576,000	353,616,000

During this entire period, about 50 per cent of the imports comprised manufactured goods ready for consumption. Textiles, metals, and earthen goods were imported from England and the Continent; wines from southern Europe; molasses, sugar, rum, and coffee from the West Indies; specie and bullion from Mexico; hides, indigo, and coffee from South America; and tea, silks, china, and spices from the Orient. England supplied the greater part of the imports, but as the years went on trade with continental Europe, especially France, increased, while the West Indian trade declined. In return for imports, as the accompanying table shows, we sent out raw materials for use in manufacturing, and foodstuffs.

EXPORTED MERCHANDISE BY GROUPS, PERCENTAGES OF TOTALS [21]

Year	Crude Materials	Manufactures for Further Use in Manufacturing	Manufactures Ready for Consumption	Foodstuffs in Crude Condition — Food Animals	Foodstuffs Wholly or Partially Manufactured
1820	60.46	9.42	5.66	4.79	19.51
1830	62.34	7.04	9.34	4.65	16.32
1840	67.61	4.34	9.47	4.09	14.27
1850	62.26	4.49	12.72	5.59	14.84
1860	68.31	3.99	11.33	3.85	12.21

[20] Compiled from *Statistical Abstract, 1921*, Table 482, p. 836.
[21] Compiled from *ibid., 1921*, Table 482, pp. 848–849.

In the South, tobacco and rice gave way to cotton, which, after the invention of the gin, became our largest single export. By 1860 it comprised 60 per cent of our exports. Along with rice, tobacco, and sugar, approximately three-fourths of our exports came from the South. From the northern and middle states wheat, flour, corn, hides, wool, naval stores, and furs found their way to foreign markets. England, continental Europe, the West Indies, and the Orient were the principal markets. Great Britain during this period absorbed from 30 to 50 per cent of our exports, chiefly cotton for her mills, and foodstuffs after the abrogation of the Corn Laws in 1846. The trade with South and Central America was relatively small, Brazil being the chief purchaser. Business was carried on mainly through New York, Philadelphia, Baltimore, Boston, and New Orleans, although Salem, Newburyport, Plymouth, and many other seaport towns were important trade centers, particularly in the earlier decades. Preeminence in foreign trade depended in the end on communication with the interior, and the building of the Erie Canal made New York's position secure as the leading commercial city on the Atlantic seaboard. The activities of Philadelphia, Baltimore, Boston, and other seaport towns in pushing canals and railroads were based on the hope that western products might be shipped to Europe through them. During the years from 1790 to 1860 our imports from Europe were larger than our exports. In the balance of international settlements the huge debits in this country were offset in the main by the freight profits earned by the merchant marine, by the commissions of merchants in the reexport trade, by investments of European capital in the United States, and by the movement of specie and bullion. Until 1849 this specie movement was made up in the main of gold and silver coin and bullion from Latin America and the Orient trade; the United States tended to use the quantities she received in excess of domestic monetary requirements as an invisible export item to Europe. After 1849 this country became the greatest gold-producing country in the world, and consequently an important part of the balance of international payments consisted of this commodity. Even so, the balance of trade for the entire period was against this country. Estimates put foreign holdings in federal, state, railroad, and other securities at over $222,000,000 in 1853 and $1,465,500,000 in 1869.

No account of either commerce or the merchant marine would be complete without some mention of the coastwise traffic. Legislation in 1789 [22] favored the American merchant marine to an extent that virtually excluded foreign vessels from participation. The coastwise trade to the South was concerned with distributing northern or European goods among the southern coastal towns. The northward movement consisted mainly in loading western

[22] Above, p. 230.

foodstuffs at New Orleans, or cotton, sugar, tobacco, and other products at New Orleans, Mobile, Charleston, and elsewhere, and bringing them to the northern cities for use or export. The most important aspect of this trade was the so-called "cotton triangle." Vessels carried cotton directly from a southern port to Europe; returned to New York with freight or immigrants, and sailed southward on the coastwise run with freight or ballast. An alternative route used only two sides of the triangle. Coastwise vessels picked up southern cotton and brought it to New York, whence most of it was shipped to Europe. European goods in return were first brought to New York and then distributed throughout the South. After the discovery of gold the intercoastal trade grew in importance as hundreds of vessels each year plied between California and the eastern seaboard. That the coastwise trade was of extreme significance may be seen from one estimate which put the value of commodities thus transported in 1852 at $2,600,000,000 as against $374,425,000 for foreign commerce. The value of the commodities carried in the coastal traffic was more than double that carried on either canals or railroads.[23]

SELECTED READINGS

Johnson, E. R., *et al., History of Domestic and Foreign Commerce of the United States,* Vol. I, Chaps. XII–XIV and XIX (by T. W. Van Metre).

Marvin, W. L., *The American Merchant Marine,* Chaps. IV–XIV.

Soley, J. R., in N. S. Shaler's *The United States of America,* Vol. I, pp. 518–624.

Morison, S. E., *The Maritime History of Massachusetts, 1783–1860,* Chaps. III ff.

Albion, R. G., *The Rise of New York Port,* Chap. VI.

Pratt, J. W., *The Expansionists of 1812,* Introduction, and Chaps. I, II.

Flügel, F., and Faulkner, H. U., *Readings in the Economic and Social History of the United States,* pp. 194–206, 208–219, 680–682.

[23] E. R. Johnson, *et al., History of Domestic and Foreign Commerce of the United States,* I, 344.

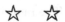

13

The Rise of
the Factory System

☆ ☆

T HE years 1790 to 1860 marked a period in which the United States passed
from a condition of economic independence upon Europe to one in which
the ordinary wants of manufactured goods could be supplied at home. The
period also saw the gradual rise of the factory system when the foundations
were laid for the Industrial Revolution. These years can be divided into
three periods.[1] The first, 1790–1815, was characterized by economic dependence on Europe for the finer type of manufactured goods. But also during
this period international disturbances brought succeeding crises in our economic life, interferences with international trade, and the birth of the factory
system. In the second period, 1815–1840, small factory production grew
gradually and manufacturing made an aggressive entrance into political
controversies. During these years manufacturing was largely dependent upon
water transportation for the distribution of its products.

The third period, 1840–1860, profited from the discovery that the use of
coal was practical for iron smelting and steam power. It was marked by the
rise of railroads which greatly facilitated transportation and by the introduction of many new improvements in machinery which quickened and diversified manufacturing enterprises. These were the years when manufacturing
grew rapidly and the little mills began to take on some of the characteristics
of the modern factory. In other words, they ceased to be adjuncts of merchant
capitalism and became definite integrated units where skilled managers
supervised the machine production of standardized products by labor that
had been removed from the home or small shop. Factory owners were no
longer merely merchants or commission men; they became actual manufacturers with factory production as their chief interest. In these years America
began definitely to feel the effects of the Industrial Revolution.

In the whole period from 1790 to 1860, agriculture still continued to occupy
the chief energies of the people. Moreover, until 1850 at least, the bulk of

[1] These divisions follow in general those of Victor S. Clark in his *History of Manufactures
in the United States, 1607–1860*, Chap. XI.

general manufacturing was still carried on in the home or small shop. During most of the period, shipping and the industries dependent upon it absorbed a disproportionately large share of capital and labor. Milling and meat packing, industries closely allied to agriculture, rose first, followed by textiles and then by the metal industries. Unoccupied public land across which the frontier advanced was a determining factor in the history of manufactures, as it was in agriculture, especially as it affected the labor market.

ECONOMIC DEPENDENCE ON EUROPE

The Revolution, as we have seen, brought political independence but by no means economic independence. Products of the colonial period which had been exported to Europe still found a market there and we continued to import European manufactured commodities. Manufactures which had grown up during the Revolution were smothered by the cheaper British goods thrown onto the American market on the resumption of peace. Moreover, certain industries which had thrived in the old "three-cornered traffic" were largely destroyed by the prohibition of trade in English provisions in the West Indies. There was every indication that America would again sink into a subservient position, producing the raw materials which Europe needed and taking the latter's goods in return. Competition with England in the production and sale of manufactured goods seemed out of the question.

It was not only the difficulty of competing with Europe that held back the development of manufactures; internal factors were of equal importance. After two hundred years of settlement there still remained an apparently exhaustless supply of unoccupied land; the lure of an independent life with profits to be secured both from agriculture and from rising land values attracted the average man more than existence as an industrial laborer. Agriculture was still the primary industry, the one from which the greatest returns were to be obtained. Unoccupied western land was the main cause of the scarcity and consequently high cost of labor, the chief deterrent to the growth of manufacturing. Marketing the agricultural products seemed the most important problem to be solved, and what liquid capital remained from agriculture and commerce was drawn into schemes for turnpikes, canals, railroads, and river and ocean vessels. In particular the infant manufacturing industry had to compete for capital with the shipping industry during the golden era of the merchant marine. Net earnings of the latter between 1795 and 1801 were estimated at $32,000,000 a year, three-fourths the total value of agricultural exports during the same years; the tonnage built in American dockyards increased from 202,000 in 1789 to 1,425,000 in 1810. Nor were American carriers content with transporting their own produce; they scoured the seas in search of business. In some years during the first decade of the century the foreign goods transported exceeded domestic products in value. Between 1791 and 1800, 35 per cent of the goods received were reexported, largely in American ships. This competition for capital, of course, kept interest rates high, making it difficult for manufacturers to borrow money for operating expenses or expansion. It was the age of merchant capitalism in which the credit and transportation facilities were geared to the needs of the merchant rather than of the manufacturer.

Rising manufacturing had to contend—except during the periods of the First and Second Banks of the United States—with inadequate banking facilities and a currency situation that was fantastic.[2] Furthermore, after about 1830 it had to operate under a federal government that was dominated by southern plantation owners little interested in the development of manufacturing. This group opposed a protective tariff, a strong central banking system, a transcontinental railroad built in the North, free land for homesteaders, a government immigration plan. With the Supreme Court under their domination, legal decisions gave little encouragement to the type of free capitalist enterprise necessary for the rapid development of the factory system.

In the face of these contending factors, it is a source of wonder that any progress whatever was made. Yet it was during the years most discouraging to industrial life that the birth of the factory system took place and American manufactures established themselves. The chief contributing causes were (1) the partial shutting off of European imports during the Revolution (1775–1783), the Embargo and Non-intercourse Acts, and the War of 1812–1814; (2) the existence of an abundance of raw materials, especially cotton, iron, and fuel, and of water power; (3) the immigration of skilled and unskilled European laborers in continually increasing numbers, in many cases persons unused to agriculture and willing to engage in industry; (4) government aid through protective tariffs; (5) the versatility and genius of a resourceful people; and (6) the gradual appearance of small amounts of accumulated capital. To make possible the use of these small accumulations the states began to charter corporations.

Certain other factors also must be considered as part of the background for the growth of manufacturing. There were savings in freight rates which tended to overcome the higher cost of labor in this country. There was the discovery of gold in California which made it possible for the United States to enjoy an unfavorable commodity balance in international trade and thus purchase abroad iron, machinery, and other products needed to develop manufacturing. Underlying all of these factors, however, was the phenom-

[2] Above, pp. 164 ff.

enon of a rapidly expanding domestic market that was being made ever more available by the continued improvement in transportation facilities.

Although the small amount of surplus capital in the country was largely drawn into other fields, sufficient was attracted to manufacturing to give the latter a start. Considerable amounts came from commercial firms who withdrew their capital from commerce during the uncertain years preceding and following the War of 1812. Similarly shipowners and sea captains during the same period turned from the carrying trade to cotton manufacturing. With the decline of the East Indian trade, capital in Salem and Providence shifted to manufacturing as did that in New Bedford with the passing of the whaling industry. Merchants with surpluses, especially those who wished to assure themselves of a supply of the finished product, invested actively in manufacturing. In a sense, many of these merchants were already manufacturers. As had been done in England in the years before the Industrial Revolution, they had gathered the raw materials, distributed them to the farm house and small shop to be turned into manufactured goods, and then collected them for sale in the markets. But undoubtedly the largest number of establishments originated from small shops and water mills whose owners reinvested their accumulations until their enterprises assumed respectable proportions. The profits from manufacturing were normally large, affording both new capital for extension and a stimulus to outsiders to invest. From the inaccurate and inadequate census estimates it is probable that the capital invested in manufacturing was about $50,000,000 in 1820 and $1,000,000,000 in 1860.

EUROPEAN BACKGROUND—THE INDUSTRIAL REVOLUTION IN ENGLAND

The Industrial Revolution in America was preceded and made possible by a similar transition in England. For thousands of years economic processes had been carried on in essentially the same manner. Thread was spun and cloth woven by hand; this was true of other manufactured articles. These handicraft operations were usually carried on either in the home as a by-industry to farming or in a little shop attached to the house where the master craftsman, surrounded by his journeymen and apprentices, laboriously turned out his products. During the eighteenth century and the first quarter of the nineteenth, various inventions were made which were destined to revolutionize the world, changing the everyday life of mankind more profoundly than had anything in any previous age. England, the first of the European nations to free herself from the shackles of guild regulations, possessed of a thriving commerce and accumulated capital, free from the internal devastation of the European wars, and rich in coal and iron, was the logical starting point for this great advance.

The Industrial Revolution, the result of the work of thousands of experimenters, began in the textile industry. In 1733 John Kay invented the "fly-shuttle," a device by which a weaver, instead of reaching across to throw the shuttle back and forth, could jerk a string to accomplish the same purpose. This simple contrivance allowed the weaver to work on a much wider piece of cloth and with greater rapidity. The speeding up of weaving brought increased demand for thread; but it was not until 1770 that James Hargreaves, a Lancashire weaver, patented an improvement on the old-fashioned spinning wheel whereby eight spindles connected by a band to a horizontal wheel, and turned by a crank, could spin eight threads at a time. While Hargreaves was still working on his "spinning jenny," Richard Arkwright, a barber of Preston, patented a machine in 1769 which drew the carded cotton through a series of rollers, each set revolving at a greater velocity than the preceding set, and turned out cotton thread strong enough to be used as warp. His original patent called for a machine worked by horses, but in 1771 water power was used and his "water frame" made the manufacture of cotton goods a commercial possibility and himself a wealthy man. A further improvement in spinning was made in 1779 by Samuel Crompton, who combined Hargreaves' "jenny" and Arkwright's "water frame" in a machine called a "mule," which turned out a better thread at quicker speed and enabled England to compete with India in the finer textiles. Since the spinners were now far ahead of the weavers, it was quite logical that the next advance should be in weaving. The invention, strange to say, was the result of the labors of a Kentish clergyman, Edmund Cartwright, who knew absolutely nothing of machinery when he first set to work on the problem. By 1785 he had constructed a power loom for weaving, propelled first by horses and then by steam. The demand for cotton was now so great that increasing numbers of southern planters were turning from raising tobacco to cotton, a transition made possible by Eli Whitney's cotton gin. These inventions in cotton machinery were but the beginning of the revolution in textiles. Other inventors followed with machinery for other fabrics.

Simultaneously with the improvements in textile machinery came the practical steam engine. The properties of steam had been known to the ancient Egyptians, and interesting experiments had been made toward the end of the seventeenth century by Dennis Papin, a Frenchman, and by Thomas Savery. Thomas Newcomen patented an engine in 1705 to pump water out of the mines; it was capable of doing the work of fifty men but was slow and expensive to operate. In 1763 James Watt, a Scottish engineer, was given a model of one of Newcomen's engines to repair. In 1769 he patented an improved engine which effected a great saving in fuel and time by drawing off the steam into a separate condenser, thus keeping the cylinder continually warm and making it possible by automatic controls to use the same steam in forcing the cylinder both ways. In company with Mathew Boulton, a wealthy manufacturer, Watt began the commercial manufacture of steam engines. To a man of his genius it was not difficult to apply the backward and forward motion of the piston to the turning of wheels or the driving of a steam hammer. Industry was now to a great extent emancipated from water power and factories sprang up in the large cities. These engines not only facilitated the mining of coal and iron, but they provided a greater market for both materials.

The improvements in manufacturing which brought increased production were followed by striking advances in the methods of distribution. The years of the Industrial Revolution saw great progress in road building under the direction of such men as Telford and McAdam. James Brindley constructed the Bridgewater Canal, opened in 1761, for the purpose of carrying coal from Worsley to Manchester. The success of this canal led in the next decade to a wave of canal building, similar to that in the United States after 1825, which connected most of the principal rivers and centers in England. Machinists since the 1780's had realized the possibilities of connecting the piston of the steam engine to a wheel revolving in water, but it was not until 1803 that William Symmington demonstrated the practicability of the steamboat on the Clyde and 1807 that Robert Fulton demonstrated this for Americans. In that year a Watt engine drove the *Clermont* from New York to Albany, a distance of 150 miles, in 32 hours. In 1833 the *Royal William,* the first ship to cross the Atlantic by steam alone, made the distance from Pictou, Nova Scotia, to London in 20 days. What Fulton accomplished for water traffic the Englishman, George Stephenson, building on the work of Trevithick and others, did for land transportation. In 1829 Stephenson's engine, "The Rocket," in a trial test between Liverpool and Manchester attained a speed of twenty-nine miles an hour, demonstrating beyond doubt the feasibility of steam railroads.

With the substitution of power-driven machinery for hand labor and the utilization of steam in factories and for transportation purposes, the Industrial Revolution was well-nigh accomplished. Its results are the civilization in which we live. The introduction of machinery produced an immense increase in production, with a corresponding increase in wealth and a general transformation of business methods to take care of this increase. It enhanced enormously the wealth, power, and numbers of the rising middle class. At the same time it brought into being what was virtually a new class, that of the industrial wage earner. Most of the added wealth produced by the Industrial Revolution was absorbed by the middle class; the industrial wage earners, separated from the land and concentrated in the slums of the new cities which sprang up around the factories, were reduced to extremes of poverty and degradation. The sharp distinction in wealth and opportunity in the new era was soon felt in politics. The middle class, leaning on the *laissez-faire* philosophy of their own economists, Adam Smith, Ricardo, and others, demanded and won a commanding position in the government. To the industrial worker the displacement of the landed aristocracy by the middle class brought no advantage. Stirred to wrath by legislation which discriminated against their interests, workmen followed the example of their industrial masters and agitated for political rights. This agitation, commencing with the Chartist Movement (1838–1848) and continuing to the present day, has resulted in political democracy and in a long list of Acts promoting social betterment. Machinery has cheapened the process of printing, a factor which, combined with the growth of the urban population, has quickened intellectual life and been a spur to progressive thought. Upon international relations the Industrial Revolution has had an immense influence. The search for raw products, the scramble for new markets and for a place to invest some of the surplus wealth created by machines have become acute. The result is a new imperialism bringing in its wake militarism and the conquest of economically backward peoples.

Beginnings of the American Factory System

In America industry went through somewhat the same evolution as in England, but much more rapidly. Self-sufficing manufacture for household needs had developed there into the handicraft or domestic stage where the work might be done at home, but the products were sold elsewhere by retail or wholesale. In the later years of this stage work was sometimes done in the home but it was on a commission basis, the merchant capitalist distributing the raw materials to be worked up. In the United States household manufacture for family needs was general everywhere at the end of the eighteenth century, except, perhaps, in some plantation districts, and this type of manufacture continued in the frontier regions long after it had disappeared from the seacoast. Household manufacture for the general market was also carried on at this time, the craftsman sometimes working on the raw material supplied by the merchant capitalist. The manufacturing artisan who had confined his energy to custom work was extending his operations to a general market, and some mills and furnaces were operating on a scale that approached factory production. At the same time itinerant artisans wandered from house to house making shoes and doing other skilled work beyond the ability of the family. In other words, all these stages of industry—the household, the domestic, and their various modifications—were contemporary in America on the eve of the Industrial Revolution. Although the United States passed from "mother-and-daughter power to water-and-steam power" in a short period of some seventy years, almost all phases of the household and domestic stages were to be found here. Rapid as was the transition, it would have come even more quickly had not the poverty and remoteness of frontier life, which existed in so many sections, held it back.

The Industrial Revolution took place first in England. This advantage, which was fast making her the workshop of the world, she was loath to lose, and attempts were made to keep the secrets of the new machinery from spreading. The emigration of trained operatives was prohibited by an Act of 1765. In 1774 an Act, which remained in force until 1845, was passed prohibiting the exportation of textile machinery, plans or models; it was supplemented in 1781 to prohibit the exportation of any utensils used in textile manufacturing. A statute of 1772 prohibited citizens engaged in printing calico, linens, or muslins or in manufacturing textile machinery from emigrating; another of 1785 prohibited the emigration of workmen employed in steel and iron manufacture and the carrying out of tools; and another Act of 1789 prohibited the emigration of coal miners.

These measures, however, did not materially delay the introduction of machinery into this country, after interest had once been aroused in manufacturing. The years from the close of the Revolution to 1800 were a period of experimentation. Factories in which the jenny was used were established in 1787 at Philadelphia, at Beverly, Massachusetts, and in succeeding years at other places in New England and New York—undoubtedly the first cotton mills in America. Of these only the mill at Beverly survived; it produced bed ticking until 1807, when it was ruined by the embargo. The first successful Arkwright mill was built in 1789 by Samuel Slater, an English emigrant who had served an apprenticeship in one of Arkwright's factories at Belper and had been induced to come to America by bounties offered here for the improved machinery. Through the influence of Moses Brown, a Quaker merchant of Providence, Slater came to Rhode Island, and in 1790 his mill, erected at Pawtucket, spun the first machine-made cotton warp in America. The beginnings of the American factory system can truly be traced to Slater and his Pawtucket mill. "The first attempt systematically to develop an extensive water-power for general manufacturing purposes," says Clark,[3] "was probably the conception of Alexander Hamilton," whose initiative resulted in the incorporation in 1791 of a company in New Jersey for the manufacture of textiles on the falls of the Passaic. The company itself was short-lived but it founded Paterson, which eventually became an important textile city.

The first spinning machines set up were run either by hand or by horsepower. Later, especially in New England, water power was used extensively, and for a while almost exclusively, for both spinning and weaving. Steam was probably first used in America for pumping mines in New Jersey and Rhode Island during the last decades of the eighteenth century; it is believed

[3] Victor S. Clark, *History of Manufactures in the United States*, I, 404.

that it was first applied to mill machinery in a sawmill in New York in 1803. In the years following, either the imported low-pressure engines of the Boulton-Watt type or the high-pressure engines of Evans were introduced in sections where water power was not to be obtained. By 1812 several of Evans' engines were in use west of the Alleghenies, and by 1817 steam engines were being manufactured not only on the coast but at Pittsburgh, Louisville, and Cincinnati. The Census of 1830 showed that 57 of the 161 plants in Pennsylvania used steam, although the factories listed in New York, New Jersey, and all the New England States with the exception of Massachusetts used water power. Of 169 plants in that state, 39 used steam. Where coal was available it gradually came into use as the fuel for steam engines, but until toward the middle of the century most engines were stoked with wood. Generally speaking, however, water power was mainly used in early manufacturing and accessibility to it determined the location of industry.

When manufacturing by machinery was once firmly established, American inventors enthusiastically took up the ideas of European engineers, adapted them to conditions here, and contributed new improvements. Labor scarcity did much to stimulate inventions, but ignorance as to what had been done in England led to duplication. Of American contributions, perhaps the most famous was that of Eli Whitney, who not only invented the cotton gin but as early as 1807 applied the principle of standardization of parts and interchangeable mechanism in the manufacture of firearms. Another notable advance was the Goulding condenser, which greatly simplified and quickened the carding of wool. The first successful power loom for weaving in America was constructed by a Boston merchant, Francis Cabot Lowell, who on a trip to England in 1810–1812 had made a careful study of textile machinery. With the aid of a mechanical genius, Paul Moody, Lowell designed and constructed a new set of spinning machinery and a power loom which were set up at Waltham in 1814. Here, for the first time in the world, it is believed, all the processes of spinning and weaving were brought together in the same factory. In concentrating all the processes in one factory the "Waltham system" took a long step toward modern factory production. In the succeeding years many American inventors, of whom perhaps Samuel Batchelder and William Mason are the best known, perfected machines for knitting and lace making and for manufacturing linen and cotton in figured designs.

Not only in textiles were American machinists making progress. Oliver Evans of Philadelphia invented a high-pressure steam engine which was used successfully. Rumsay, Fitch, and Fulton made notable experiments in the application of steam to water transportation, and John Stevens of Hoboken directed his attention to a railroad engine. Geissenhainer in 1830 successfully smelted iron ore with anthracite coal, and in 1851 William Kelly of Kentucky independently discovered the principle of the Bessemer method of decarbonizing molten metal by forcing air through it. Elias Howe in 1846 invented the sewing machine, a machine equally suitable to the home and the factory and one that not only proved an immense boon to women but revolutionized the clothing and shoe industry. The work of Morse in introducing the magnetic telegraph effected a similar revolution in methods of communication. These men and hundreds of other inventors must be given the chief credit for the establishing of American manufacturing. The Patent Office, which reported an average of 77 inventions annually from 1790 to 1811, recorded 544 patents in 1830. In the decade 1840–1850, it issued 6480 patents, and in the next decade 28,000.

While due credit is given to the work of the inventors, recognition should also be accorded that remarkably large and brilliant group of entrepreneurs and capitalists who built upon the labors of the technicians, men who planted little factories in out-of-the-way places which became the foundation for important industries and thriving cities. Among the many who quickly come to mind are Nathan Appleton and Abbott Lawrence, who were leaders of the group responsible for the manufacturing development of Lowell and Lawrence; Edmund Dwight, who played a similar rôle in Chicopee and Holyoke, and William Gregg of Graniteville, South Carolina. One of the ablest of them was Patrick Tracy Jackson (1780–1847), whose activities exemplify the entrepreneur at his best. Apprenticed to a Newburyport merchant at the age of fifteen, he became a sea captain in his early twenties, retired from the sea at 28 to engage in the exporting and importing business, and with the curtailment of his shipping interests by the War of 1812 found an outlet for his energy in the manufacture of cotton. Joining his brother-in-law, Francis C. Lowell, he aided in the establishment of the famous Waltham factory and managed it in its early years. When the local power resources were exhausted Jackson and his associates moved to the Merrimac and erected mills around which grew the city of Lowell, the "Manchester of America." Finding transportation facilities from his new mills to Boston inadequate, Jackson turned a ready ear to the reports of steam railroads and was chiefly responsible for the first one in New England. Sailor, merchant, manufacturer, railroad builder—his life epitomizes the economic history of New England during the first half of the nineteenth century.[4]

The development of the Industrial Revolution, of course, followed no

---

[4] The number of these business men of great ability during this period is amazing. Besides Appleton, Lawrence, Lowell, Dwight, and Jackson, the student is referred to the sketches of Nathan P. Ames, Benjamin Talbot Babbitt, Richard Borden, Charles Goodyear, Ward Cheney, Jonas Chickering, Alvah Crocker, Samuel Downer, Arthur M. Eastman, Charles Tillinghast James, and scores of others included in the *Dictionary of American Biography*. A study of the lists of directors of New England banks, insurance companies, and railroads, as given by Vera Shlakman, *Economic History of a Factory Town*, Appendix A, shows the small and closely knit group of financial and industrial entrepreneurs who promoted the economic development of New England during the first half of the nineteenth century.

fixed rule. Some factories were merely the extension of tiny mills already in existence; some were the work of inventors or technicians who also had capital, as in the case of Lowell; others were established by business men who had little or no technical knowledge but could obtain capital. Some were personally managed by the owner or his friends, while many, particularly in the large centers of New England, were controlled by absentee owners and conducted by resident managers. Each type of industry had to develop its particular technique of production and distribution. In at least one industry the expanding market produced by the Industrial Revolution was met by the expansion of old methods rather than by new machinery; the shoe industry did not introduce new machinery until after 1860, but in the meantime the little handshop increased in size until a more minute division of labor became necessary. In the shoe centers of New England there appeared the main "factory" where the cutting, packing, and shipping were done, and many little shops or even private homes about the town where specialized operations, such as binding, stitching, soling, and lasting, were carried on—the whole an excellent example of a primitive industry expanding to meet changed conditions without new machinery. Not until power was applied to shoe machinery did the industry become a factory industry in reality.

THE TEXTILE INDUSTRY

Following Slater's success at Pawtucket, spinning mills sprang up at various points, but most of them had been closed by 1800. During the next decade, however, new impetus was given to cotton spinning, particularly by the Embargo Act. The first Census of Manufacturing in 1810 recorded 269 cotton mills. The movement started by the embargo was further encouraged by the War of 1812. The mills around Providence alone, at that time the center of cotton spinning, increased from 41 to 169 during the three war years. New England emigrants carried manufacturing into the Hudson and Mohawk Valleys and into the central lake region of New York, and mills sprang up in the South and west of the Alleghenies. Before the Census of 1820 was taken, cylinder machines run by water power had been introduced for printing cloth, and Lowell had erected on the Charles his power loom for weaving.

The return of peace and the flooding of American markets by the pent-up English goods was disastrous to the infant industries. Comparatively few survived. Nevertheless, the tariff of 1816, new labor-saving devices, and a world-wide business revival enabled new mills to rise on the ruins of the old. Although the Census of 1820 showed 250,000 spindles in operation (a 213 per cent increase since 1810), using 10,000,000 pounds of cotton (176 per cent increase), the production in 1820 was undoubtedly less than half that in 1815. After 1820, despite the crises of 1837 and 1857, textile manufacturing continued to increase rapidly. Between 1820 and 1831, the number of spindles more than quadrupled and the factory looms increased tenfold. Cotton manufacturing increased 150 per cent between 1840 and 1860. At the same time the price of cotton yarn and cloth was reduced to less than a fourth of its cost prior to the introduction of machinery. Sixty-nine per cent of the cotton manufacturing in 1860 was concentrated in New England. The growth of the industry after 1840 as obtained from the census reports follows:

COTTON MANUFACTURING [5]

	1840	1850	1860
Mills	1,369	1,074	1,091
Spindles	2,284,631	. . . .	5,235,727
Cotton consumed (bales) . . .	237,000	641,240	1,056,726
	(500 lbs.)	(425 lbs.)	(400 lbs.)
Capital invested	$51,102,359	$76,032,578	$98,585,269
Value of product	$46,350,453	$65,501,687	$115,681,774
Workers (average)	72,119	94,956	122,028

Although the Census of 1860 showed 1909 establishments manufacturing woolen goods (including mixed goods), with an invested capital of $35,520,-527, consuming close to 90,000,000 pounds of wool, employing on an average 48,900 operators, and producing $68,865,963 worth of cloth, we were still dependent on England for considerable quantities of both raw wool and manufactured goods. The manufacture of woolens developed more slowly than that of cotton, notwithstanding the fact that woolen cloth was used from the time of the early settlements and the adaptability of large parts of the country to sheep raising was thoroughly demonstrated. This was due to several causes. English statesmen, acting under the policies of mercantilism, in 1699 forbade the exportation of wool or woolen cloth from the American colonies, and by other Acts sought to discourage in every possible way the manufacture of woolens so that the American market could be retained by England. Great Britain excelled in the colonial period, as she still does, in the manufacture of woolens, and it was difficult to compete even after the assistance rendered by the high tariffs following the War of 1812. Moreover, woolen machinery was introduced into this country at a later date than cotton machinery. Furthermore, a far larger number of farms produced wool than cotton and this tended to prolong the household production of woolen cloth.

[5] Eighth Census (1862). Manufactures, III, xix.

Nevertheless, the manufacture of woolen cloth slowly passed from the home to the factory. Colonial sheep produced wool suitable only for coarser cloths; but after 1790 improved breeds were gradually introduced from Spain, Ireland, and England, and these, bred with the existing stock, bettered the product and made possible the manufacture of excellent woolens from domestic sheep. Simultaneously with the growing of improved wool came the gradual shift from household to factory manufacture. Little weaving had been done outside the home before the Revolution, and household weaving had undoubtedly increased during the troubles with the mother country. In 1788 a mill which produced 5000 yards of cloth a year was founded in Hartford, and another mill at Stockbridge, Massachusetts. Just as Samuel Slater had evaded the British law and brought to America knowledge of the cotton machinery, so two brothers, John and Arthur Scholfield of Yorkshire, emigrated in 1792 and aided in establishing factories in Massachusetts in 1793, and later in Connecticut, where the most improved woolen machinery was set up. The Census of 1810 reported 24 factories and 1682 fulling mills. Steam was first used in woolen manufacturing at Middletown, Connecticut, in 1811. The average annual factory production in these years was probably not over 10,000 yards, an exceedingly small amount in comparison with that still woven at home. The War of 1812 gave woolen manufacturing its first real foothold, the new factories turning out military equipment, cloths for the Negroes, and even fine woolens. The fact that about this time knee breeches were no longer worn also brought a wider demand for woolen goods. It was estimated at the conclusion of peace that $12,000,000 had been invested in woolen mills, the product of which was valued at $19,000,000. Connecticut, the leading state, had 25 factories employing 1200 operatives. Manufacturing establishments had also been founded west of the mountains at Louisville and Cincinnati.

The conclusion of the war and the subsequent heavy importation of accumulated European goods ruined many of these mills and was a potent influence in bringing about the tariff of 1816, in which a 25 per cent ad valorem rate was imposed on most woolen goods. The incomplete returns of the Census of 1820 showed that over 100 factories with 700 looms had survived the post-war depression. This depression had in like manner affected the farmers, thus lengthening the life of household manufacturing; as late as 1830, even in the leading textile states of New England, more woolen cloth was woven at home than in the factories. There was some improvement in the decade of the 'twenties, but as a whole it was a precarious period for the industry. After 1830 normal prosperity returned and woolen manufacturing firmly established itself, securing control in certain lines of the domestic market. It is not until the decade of the 'forties that it can truly be said that the factory-made product had the upper hand and that the domestic industry was in a decline. Although the production of worsteds remained small and the manufacture of broadcloths declined, the industry as a whole showed healthy progress during the next twenty years, with an increasing output of cassimeres, satinets, flannels, blankets, felts, and carpets. The statistics for these years follow:[6]

Year	Woolen Factories	Capital Invested	Value of Product	Employees
1840	1420	$15,765,124	$20,696,999	21,342
1850	1817	26,071,542	43,542,288	34,895
1860	1909	35,520,527	68,865,963	48,900

Before the introduction of the factory system flax held first place in homespun products. With the introduction of spinning and weaving machinery for cotton and wool, the latter fabrics became cheaper and displaced flax. Factories for the manufacture of cordage, sailcloth, and the finer grades of flax goods existed, but their numbers were few, their life was precarious, and their output, though of good quality, was not large. The duty on imported flax in 1828 practically killed the industry. In the late 'forties it slowly revived, the Census of 1860 showing the total value of linens, apart from homespuns, to be $700,000.

Hemp was used extensively in the manufacture of bagging and bale cloth. The center was in the Ohio Valley, especially in Kentucky, where the manufacture of bale cloth was one of the earliest industries. Later Missouri became a competitor. The Census of 1860 reported the output of bagging at 9,540,000 yards, of which Kentucky produced 5,750,000 and Missouri 3,680,000.

Unsuccessful efforts had been made at various points in the Connecticut and Willimantic Valleys to manufacture silk in the early decades of the century, but lack of cheap labor and indifferent success in the cultivating of mulberry trees held back the development of the industry until about 1840. In 1838 the Cheney brothers started their famous factory at South Manchester, Connecticut, and shortly thereafter John Ryle took over the tiny factory that Christopher Colt had started at Paterson, New Jersey. In the next twenty years these and other plants manufactured thread from the raw silk imported from the Orient, and commenced to weave broad silks, but with little success. Silk manufacturing was still in its infancy in 1860, when the census reported 42 silk mills in the Northeast turning out thread

[6] Eighth Census, *Preliminary Report,* p. 66.

but only one factory making woven goods. The total value of silk products is given as $6,589,171, with the centers of the industry in Connecticut and New Jersey.

METALS

The development of modern industry is closely bound up with the story of iron, a substance which now enters into the construction of machinery, buildings, ships, and the innumerable needs of an "iron age." In the seventeenth and eighteenth centuries, when charcoal was used for smelting, the virgin forests of America provided cheap fuel at almost the same time that the supply was being exhausted in England. When the possibility of using anthracite coal for smelting was discovered in the nineteenth century, the existence of iron and coal in close proximity was again most advantageous to American smelters. The rapidly growing manufactures and population provided an expanding market which was partially protected by tariffs.

Before the close of the Revolution iron was smelted from bog iron in all the thirteen colonies except Georgia. Bog iron was gradually supplemented by iron from the rich magnetic ore belt extending from the Berkshires in Massachusetts and the Salisbury district in Connecticut across the Hudson through Orange County, New York, and into Morris County, New Jersey. Slowly the smelting industry pushed westward. By 1810 iron making had extended up the Susquehanna, into the Juniata Valley, up the Lehigh; farther south it had crossed the mountains into Tennessee and Kentucky, where a considerable quantity of high-grade ore was later produced in an agrarian slave economy. The Census of 1810 reported 153 furnaces producing 53,908 tons of iron. The production of iron was also stimulated by the embargo and the War of 1812, but suffered a severe setback in the years immediately following. The Census of 1820 gives little information of value, but in the following decades the industry grew up in western Pennsylvania and the Ohio Valley, extending by 1860 as far as the region of Lake Superior, where smelting was carried on in northern Michigan and near Detroit. The use of mineral fuel after 1840, revived the smelting of iron east of the Alleghenies, especially in Pennsylvania and those points in New Jersey and New York reached by canal.

In the colonial period and the early decades of the nineteenth century iron products were likely to be made in the same little smelting mill that produced the raw material, or else the iron was smelted to be sold to nearby blacksmiths. Thus household utensils and the few metal tools in use were generally either custom-made or turned out on a very small scale. It was not until the 'twenties that specialization in metal products developed to any great extent, and even then the foundries and factories generally remained close to the source of supply. The use of the steam engine in water transportation after 1808 favored specialization in this type of ironwork and brought into being engine works on such important arteries of traffic as the Hudson, Delaware, and Ohio, although for many years engines were made only to order. With the advent of railroads, locomotives were built at many machine shops, but by 1860 their construction tended to concentrate at Philadelphia, the home of the Baldwin and Norris plants (founded in 1832 and 1834, respectively), and at Paterson, New Jersey. With the increased demand for new kinds of metal goods, rolling mills, which in the early years had been devoted chiefly to rolling and slitting nail plates, turned their attention to other products such as iron rails and tires. In the 'fifties the iron straps used for railroads were gradually discarded for the heavy solid iron rail, a transition which brought into existence a specialized form of the industry centered in eastern Pennsylvania. The iron industry, from mining to the finished article, was stimulated by the growing use of this metal for textile and other machinery which the Industrial Revolution was creating. Although the Industrial Revolution was to provide the greatest impetus for the development of the metal industries, the contemporary revolution in agriculture in the early years probably was responsible for the first important market for ironware, and the hundreds of factories turning out plows and other agricultural machinery laid the foundations for the rapidly developing industry. Until about 1859, as Professor Hunter has pointed out, "the manufacture of iron was controlled and conditioned by the needs and requirements of a pioneer agricultural population, which were met to a large extent by forges and rolling mills without the mediation of manufactories of finished iron products. The principal function of the manufacturers of wrought iron was to supply the country iron workers, blacksmiths by profession or necessity, with bar iron to be shaped to meet the needs of farmer, wagoner and mill owner. . . . In the period which followed the iron manufacturer gradually ceased to serve the agricultural population directly. The demand for iron came increasingly from industries engaged in the production of finished iron goods and the machinery of industry and commerce. . . . The agricultural era gave way to what might be termed the *industrial era*."[7]

One of the earliest of the metal industries to become specialized was the making of stoves. At first the plates were cast at the furnaces and assembled by the merchants, but eventually the whole process was carried on in the same establishment. The use of anthracite coal greatly increased the demand for the iron range, and by 1850 the annual production was over 300,000

[7] L. C. Hunter, "Influence of the Market upon Techniques in the Iron Industry in Western Pennsylvania to 1860," *Journal of Economic and Business History*, I, 241–281 (1929).

stoves, valued at around $6,000,000. These were manufactured chiefly in Philadelphia, New York, Albany, Cincinnati, Providence, and Pittsburgh.

For the smaller metal products, in some of which steel and iron were used, the center of manufacturing was New England. Iron axes, springs, bolts, wire, firearms, and clocks were largely made there. The factory system brought into being the manufacture of textile machinery, half of which in 1860 was constructed in Massachusetts. Likewise half of the edge tools and three-fourths of the cutlery produced in the country in that year came from New England, chiefly Connecticut. Berlin became a center for tinware and the Naugatuck Valley for brassware. The manufacture of sewing machines, the output of which reached 110,000 in 1860, was divided principally among the Singer factory at New York, the Wheeler and Wilson Company of Bridgeport, and the Grover and Baker Company of Boston.

PROCESSING OF FOODSTUFFS

The processing of foodstuffs, particularly the grinding of flour and the packing of meat, had been a household industry from the earliest colonial times. A gristmill was ordinarily one of the first forms of manufacturing outside the home to be found in a frontier community. Although gristmills, as Clark has pointed out, were "relatively smaller employers of labor than were sawmills and iron furnaces, and their owners were to a less extent industrialists, nevertheless they employed considerable capital and in the aggregate played an equally important part in the economic life of the community."[8] One reason for the smaller number of men employed was the early improvement in machinery. In the late eighteenth century Oliver Evans had perfected devices by which every step of milling from cleaning to barreling could be done by mechanical means. It is possible, as one student has suggested, that this may have been the first instance of an uninterrupted process of machine manufacturing from raw material to the finished product in the history of industry. By the end of the century mills existed which could turn 100,000 bushels of grain a year into flour. With the increasing population and the exportation of foodstuffs along with the invention of the reaper and other agricultural machinery, the milling of flour grew in importance. At the same time the wheat belt moved across the Alleghenies and was followed by the wheat processors, who set up their mills in Chicago, St. Louis, and the principal centers of the Ohio Valley.

Colonial farmers had found a market for their surplus meat in the coast towns, the West Indies, and other foreign countries. In the succeeding years the growing cities and the plantations of the South provided additional

[8] Victor S. Clark, *History of Manufactures in the United States*, I, 180.

markets. Meat packing in earlier times was essentially a seasonal industry. At certain periods it required a considerable labor supply, and also banking and shipping facilities. This forced its concentration in large centers where such facilities could be supplied. These centers were at first the seaport towns, but the packers followed the frontier and by 1850 Cincinnati was the chief center, packing 27 per cent of the meat products of the West. Also growing in importance were Louisville, Chicago, and St. Louis. Meat was preserved in the earlier years principally by salt, but by the middle of the nineteenth century the method of sterilizing by heat and enclosing in airtight receptacles was widely used. Meat packing had additional importance because of the numerous by-products—glue from hoofs; oils, candles, and soaps from the fats; bristles from hair, and fertilizers from other parts. Until the Civil War most meat packing was still done at home, but factory packing had made such headway that with the stimulation of the war it soon became the leading American industry in value of products.

Space forbids further treatment of the processing of foodstuffs. A word, however, may be added regarding the important distillery industry. The growth of the farming population in the West led to the decline of rum as the national drink and the substitution of whisky distilled from rye or corn. The chief center of the industry in 1810 was Pennsylvania, but it soon shifted to New York and Ohio. By 1850 Cincinnati was the largest whisky market in the world, and factories were capable of producing 2,000,000 gallons a year. Although whisky maintained its preeminence until well past the middle of the century, there was an increased production and use of malt beverages.

Distribution of Industry

The location of American industries was determined by chance in some cases, but more commonly by economic factors. The Northeast asserted her leadership in manufacturing in colonial times and continued to hold first rank. New England, with poor soil for agriculture but gifted with an abundance of water power, an active commerce, and a thrifty, energetic, closely settled population, was especially fitted for manufacturing, though she lacked raw materials. The Middle Atlantic States were favored by more varied mineral resources, by direct routes to the interior, and by a greater supply of capital and labor, but were handicapped by competing agriculture and the constant draining off of her population to the west. Nevertheless, important centers for textiles and other manufactures arose near the water power furnished by the Mohawk and the Hudson, and in such cities as New York, Newark, Paterson, Philadelphia, Rochester, and Pittsburgh, which were located on routes of travel or accessible to coal and iron. The early years of the century also gave promise of considerable manufacturing in the Piedmont regions of Virginia and the Carolinas, but the absorbing interest in agriculture prevented any great development until after the Civil War, although such successful enterprises as Gregg's cotton mills at Graniteville, South Carolina, and the Tredegar iron works at Richmond proved that this handicap might be overcome. Far more important than the South was the region of the Ohio River, where, prior to 1860, considerable manufacturing existed. Pittsburgh specialized in many forms of ironware; Cincinnati, until 1850 the only town west of the Alleghenies with a population of 100,000, was a great center for meat packing and the manufacture of machinery, clothing, and other commodities; Louisville produced cordage, bagging, and clothing, and Chicago was developing large milling and packing interests. This region produced flour, lumber, agricultural implements, meat and the by-products of the packing industry, cordage, bagging, and distilled liquors. The products of New England and the middle states in general were of a type requiring detailed manufacturing with finer mechanisms and involving higher labor costs. Thus textiles, boots and shoes, rubber goods, clothing, glassware, pottery, and cutlery were centered here. The following figures from the Census of 1860 give a comparison of the sections in manufacturing:

MANUFACTURING BY SECTIONS, 1860[9]

Sections	Number of Establishments	Capital Invested	Average Number of Laborers	Annual Value of Products
New England	20,671	$ 257,477,783	391,836	$ 468,599,287
Middle states	53,387	435,061,964	546,243	802,338,392
Western states	36,785	194,212,543	209,909	384,606,530
Southern states	20,631	95,975,185	110,721	155,531,281
Pacific states	8,777	23,380,334	50,204	71,229,989
Territories	282	3,747,906	2,333	3,556,197
Total	140,533	$1,009,855,715	1,311,246	$1,885,861,676

INFLUENCE OF TRANSPORTATION ON MANUFACTURING

The location of the early manufacturing plants was dependent not only on access to water power but on transportation facilities as well. The development of manufactures went hand in hand with the development of cheaper and more rapid means of transportation. Until overland routes were opened up, the settlers kept close to the coast line or the numerous rivers which cut inland in a northerly or northwesterly direction, and it was on the coast or along these rivers that the first tiny manufacturing plants were to be found. Many of the early industries were concerned with shipbuilding,

[9] Eighth Census, *Manufactures*, III, 725.

another factor that determined location. As the westward movement progressed and the various trans-Allegheny routes came into use, industrial life frequently made its appearance at key points on the rivers, such as Pittsburgh, Cincinnati, Louisville, and St. Louis. At such points factories were established to build ships and engines, and to manufacture cordage and other necessities in navigation, as well as nails, kitchen utensils, and furniture for the passing immigrant. As the newcomers filled up the surrounding country there also appeared packing plants, mills, breweries, and distilleries, where the products of the settlers could be turned into less bulky form for shipment. In a similar manner, points like Wheeling on the Cumberland road were given a start toward an industrial life, as were other towns, like Lexington, close to but not on the main line of travel. Although overland transportation was severely limited until the advent of canals and railroads, the improvement of wagon roads and the building of turnpikes were an important stimulus to both industry and commerce. About the middle of the seventeenth century two Irish tinsmiths, William and Edward Pattison, had settled in Berlin, Connecticut, and commenced to peddle their manufactured wares from house to house. As they prospered, others imitated them, until Connecticut became the center not only of tin manufacture but of brass products, clocks, and other small but desirable commodities; other New England towns manufactured cheap jewelry and novelties for the peddlers. Each spring New England capitalists and manufacturers supplied their agents with a stock of goods, and the agents set out on horseback, returning with their profits in the fall. The coming of the turnpike enabled the peddler to extend his operations, establish depots and operatives at distant points from which he might replenish his wares, and cover effectively almost every accessible settlement. "I have seen them," said Timothy Dwight, "on the peninsula of Cape Cod, and in the neighborhood of Lake Erie; distant from each other more than six hundred miles. They make their way to Detroit, four hundred miles farther; to Canada, to Kentucky; and, if I mistake not, to New Orleans and St. Louis." [10]

With the completion of the Hudson and Lake Champlain Canal in 1823, and the more important Erie Canal two years later, a mania for canal building ensued which opened up new and quicker routes from east to west, vitally affecting the growth of manufacturing. The fall in freight rates made it possible for eastern manufacturers to get their wares into the hands of the frontiersmen at prices within reach, and for the Westerner to ship his iron, lead, wool, leather, flour, and meat back east cheaply enough to find a market. The cheaper canal rates tended (1) to discourage the growth of the finer types of manufacturing on the frontier and to give added impetus to the growth of such industries in the Northeast, and (2) to

[10] Timothy Dwight, *Travels in New England and New York* (1823), II, 54.

stimulate production in the West and discourage manufacturing, other than putting frontier products—meat, leather, grain, and iron into shape for transportation. The more regular deliveries and the better information obtainable in regard to markets made it possible to conduct business on a surer foundation and a larger scale. As manufacturing towns had grown up on the rivers, the canals in a similar manner brought into existence manufacturing cities like Rochester or greatly stimulated industrial life in such terminal cities as New York, Buffalo, Philadelphia, and Pittsburgh. Even before the advent of railroads artificial water routes had so supplemented river navigation that it was possible to tap the resources of most of the settled regions.

The tendencies in manufacturing set in motion by the canals were further accentuated by the rapid building of railroads after 1840. Inland rates, which had dropped from eight cents a ton-mile to five cents on the completion of the Erie Canal, dropped still further, to one cent a ton-mile; transportation east and west was now as practical as from north to south. Industry was no longer dependent upon the seasons, for goods could be shipped in the winter months; hence the necessity of closed mills, idle workmen, and unproductive capital because of inability to move goods was largely eliminated. Railroads could be built more cheaply than canals, and to many points impossible of access by the latter, all of which tended to reduce the final cost of manufactured products. The railroads quickened the settlement of the frontier and the consequent increase in population created new and greater markets; they also made it possible for different sections to specialize in the occupations favorable to them. Although for some years railroad building absorbed most of the available capital and thus impeded manufacturing other than that concerned in railroad supplies, the setback was temporary.[11]

SELECTED READINGS

Clark, V. S., *History of Manufactures in the United States, 1607–1860*, Chaps. XI–XXI.

Tryon, R. M., *Household Manufacture in the United States, 1640–1860*, Chaps. VII, VIII.

Keir, Malcolm, *Manufacturing*, Chaps. III–VII.

Callender, G. S., *Selections from the Economic History of the United States, 1765–1860*, Chap. IX.

Bogart, E. L., and Thompson, C. M., *Readings in the Economic History of the United States*, Chaps. VIII, IX.

Flügel, F., and Faulkner, H. U., *Readings in the Economic and Social History of the United States*, Chaps. II, VIII.

[11] Economists have also pointed out the influence of transportation on labor organization. Greatly extended market areas brought severer competition among employers which resulted in wage cuts and speeded the organization of labor.

14.

Internal Transportation
and Communication to 1860

☆ ☆

SIGNIFICANCE IN AMERICAN HISTORY

THE ever-westward movement of population and the rapid conquest of a continent have made the matter of transportation one of the most vital problems which has faced both government and people since our history began. As the first settlers along the seacoast were dependent upon ocean transportation to market their raw materials in Europe and obtain manufactured products in return, so later waves of advancing settlers were in like manner dependent upon rivers, roads, canals, and railways in disposing of their products. Especially was the question acute in an essentially agricultural community, like that of the United States before the Civil War, where the commodities to be transported were likely to be bulky and in some cases perishable.

Not only was the economic life of the new settlements dependent largely upon transportation, but their location and existence were in many cases determined by it. The first settlements were usually made on rivers or harbors, and the advance inland followed the numerous rivers which ran into the Atlantic and provided the easiest facilities for transportation. As the best land was taken up along the rivers, the new settlers were forced to occupy the back country and to get to the rivers by crude roads. These roads often followed existing trails, for the paths of the deer and buffalo in their quest of water became the trails of the Indian hunters and the wagon roads and railroads of the white man.[1]

Where rivers met the ocean and formed good harbors, where one river ran into another, or where trails connected with rivers, particularly at the

[1] "The New York Central and the Lake Shore follow the old Lake Shore Trail; the Pennsylvania follows the old Mahoning Trail; the Toledo and Ohio Central follows the Monongahela Trail; the Baltimore and Ohio follows the Great or Big Trail; another Pennsylvania line follows the Moravia-Scioto-Beaver Trail; the Hocking Valley, the Sandusky-Richmond Trail; the Norfolk and Western follows the Scioto Trail; the Cincinnati, Hamilton and Dayton follows the Miami Trail; the Lake Erie and Wheeling, the Muskingum Trail." B. H. Meyer (ed.), *Transportation in the United States, 1860*, p. 6.

head of navigation, there were the strategic points at which towns and cities sprang up. After 1850 railroad building went on so rapidly that railroads often preceded the settlers and, like the rivers in earlier years, pointed to inevitable routes. Gradual improvements in transportation weakened economic sectionalism and in turn political sectionalism. When our national government was founded, the trip from Boston to New York by the fastest stage route required a week; today one can go from New York City to Los Angeles, California, in less than seventeen hours. Railroads bound the East and West together at the time of the Civil War, and have contributed greatly to the specialization of industry in certain sections and the mutual interdependence of economic groups and geographic sections.

PROBLEMS OF AMERICAN TRANSPORTATION

Two great transportation problems have faced the American people. The first was that of bringing the bulky agricultural products to the markets. Except for farmers who lived on or near navigable rivers, this was never adequately solved until the coming of the railroads. Moreover, while farmers might float their corn or cotton down the river, the difficulties of bringing back return cargoes of manufactured goods were not met until the river steamboat appeared.

Even after the steamboat had greatly facilitated river commerce, there remained the problem of those who lived far from water transportation. Although the United States is unusually well supplied with national waterways, a glance at the map will show that most of her rivers run generally from north to south. The population on the other hand has usually moved from east to west; hence the real transportation needs were for facilities which would allow an east-west movement rather than one from north to south. A survey of the history of American internal transportation makes this clear. The first important highways were in most cases roads reaching westward into the back country from the seacoast or from rivers. In some cases they were designed to connect the headwaters of navigable rivers running into the Atlantic or into the Mississippi, thus establishing a route westward. This was also true of most of the canals. With the coming of the railroads this problem was solved, for a railroad could free itself from the river valleys and cut westward at will, except where its route might be determined by mountain passes. Reference to a railroad map (p. 505) will establish the fact that with a few exceptions the important trunk lines run from east to west. A glance at a highway map or a map of air routes will also illustrate this point.

Improvements in transportation facilities before the Civil War fall roughly into three groups: (1) turnpikes and improved roads, (2) canals and improved rivers, and (3) railroads. Simultaneously came the introduction and rapid development of the river steamboat, an important feature of the transportation history of these years. Throughout this period, as in earlier and later years, the movement for better transportation facilities was impelled by certain fundamental motives. Among them were the demands of farmers for better transportation to market their products, demands that were supported by the inhabitants of coast towns who desired cheaper foodstuffs and by exporters who wanted larger amounts of commodities at cheaper prices. At the same time importers and eastern manufacturers hoped to widen their markets. When transportation facilities were privately built there was the hope of dividends and always the lure of speculation, for a turnpike, canal, or railroad was bound to affect the value of adjacent land. The building of transportation facilities inevitably went hand in hand with land speculation.

THE TURNPIKE ERA

At the opening of the national period the main towns along the seacoast were connected by roads of a most rudimentary type, constructed before the technique of modern roadbuilding was understood. Choked with mud in the spring, thick with dust in the summer, and heavy with snow in the winter, the overland routes were fraught with the most arduous labor and hardship, frequently with real danger. The risk was increased by the fact that until long after the Revolution there were no bridges over the principal rivers. In addition there were trails leading westward. During the French and Indian War Braddock cut a road across the Alleghenies from Cumberland, Maryland, to Pittsburgh, the route of the later National Road, and General Forbes cut one across Pennsylvania, the route of the subsequent Lincoln Highway. Settlers in western Virginia and North Carolina had blazed a trail to the Cumberland Gap and then northward to the Ohio, and traders in New York had opened the Mohawk Trail westward to the Genesee Valley and Lake Erie. As yet, however, these were little more than trails that provided routes for westward-moving settlers and the pack trains of fur traders.

In the 1790's an intense interest developed in improved transportation facilities, particularly in the building of turnpikes. This seems to have been caused primarily by the rapid westward movement and by the increased prosperity and growing foreign commerce resulting from the European wars. The inadequacy of the existing roads, built largely for local needs, and the need for better-constructed highways designed for through traffic, became more evident.

The lead in the movement for better roads was taken by private individuals, who organized companies and issued stock in order to build turnpikes, roads supported by tolls levied on everyone using them. The first turnpike constructed in America was the one from Philadelphia to Lancaster, a distance of 66 miles; it was built between 1792 and 1794 at a cost of $465,000. The optimism of those who had crowded to subscribe to the shares of the Philadelphia and Lancaster Turnpike Company was more than warranted. So successful was the road that a mania for building turnpikes spread over the whole country. In the next thirty years 86 companies were chartered in Pennsylvania; by 1832 that state had built about 2200 miles of roads at a cost ranging from $900 to $7000 a mile. By 1810, 20 turnpike companies had been chartered in New Hampshire, 26 in Vermont, and upwards of 180 in New England as a whole. New York by 1811 had chartered 137 companies whose combined capital was $7,500,000 and which constructed about 1400 miles of road; Connecticut built nearly 800 miles. The rivalry of cities for the western trade spurred on construction and led Baltimore to charter three roads leading west. The construction of toll bridges followed the building of the toll roads and was financed and supported in the same manner. While these turnpikes are not to be compared in construction with more modern roads, some of them were well built. Francis Baily wrote in 1797: "There is, at present, but one turnpike-road on the continent, which is between Lancaster and Philadelphia, a distance of sixty-six miles, and is a masterpiece of its kind; it is paved with stone the whole way, and overlaid with gravel; so that it is never obstructed during the most severe seasons."[2] Hard-surfaced roads of the macadam type were in use in New England before they had been perfected in England.

The value of new roads was clearly demonstrated, but the cost of transporting goods by land was still enormous. The freight per ton from Philadelphia to Pittsburgh by an all-land route was $125, and the average through the country for general merchandise, according to McMaster, was $10 per ton per hundred miles, making it out of the question to transport such bulky articles as grain and flour more than 150 miles. (At this time, the freight on a ton coming from Europe was 40 shillings.) These rates were kept high not only by poor roads but by high tolls. The average toll in New England was 12½ cents per wagon for each two miles. In New Jersey it was one cent per mile for each horse; the Pennsylvania rates varied according to the width of tire and number of horses. Nor did improved roads solve the problem of passenger transportation. Travel on the new turnpikes was faster and more comfortable, but the time consumed was still great and the average cost was 6 cents a mile.

[2] Francis Baily, *Journal of a Tour in Unsettled Parts of North America in 1796 and 1797*, p. 107.

THE GALLATIN PLAN

Both the high cost of travel and the success of the new turnpikes contributed to the demand for federal aid in the transportation problem. Loose constructionists, ardent nationalists, and those who might benefit financially believed that ample power for such aid was given in the Constitution under the "general welfare" clause as well as in Article I, Section VII, which gave the national government power to establish post offices and post roads and to regulate interstate commerce. Strict constructionists considered this interpretation too broad and their group was augmented by those who claimed that it was unfair to tax the whole country for the benefit of certain sections.

The discussion brought forth on April 4, 1808, the famous report on internal improvements made by Albert Gallatin at the request of Congress. Gallatin pointed out that in more developed countries where capital was plentiful transportation facilities could be built by private initiative without direct aid from the government. In America, however, this was largely prevented by the high cost of labor and the unusual demand for capital. Federal aid, he argued, was advisable since improved transportation would unite the country, provide an important aid in military defense, raise the value of western land, and contribute to the economic development. He urged that the peninsulas jutting into the Atlantic be cut by canals across Cape Cod, across New Jersey, and between the Delaware and the Chesapeake. Further communication north and south should be provided by a great turnpike running from Maine to Georgia. East and west transportation might be improved by building roads that would join the headwaters of certain eastern rivers with the headwaters of other rivers running into the Ohio. He suggested that one method of paying for this might be the sale of public lands.

THE CUMBERLAND ROAD

The chief result of the demand for internal improvements at the expense of the national government during these early years was the Cumberland Road. Ohio was admitted to the Union under an agreement whereby federal lands sold within her borders were exempt from taxation for five years; in return the federal government was to appropriate 5 per cent of the proceeds from the sale of such lands for the building of roads, three-fifths of which was to be expended within the state and two-fifths in building a road over the mountains to connect it with the East. Similar agreements were later made with Indiana, Illinois, and Missouri. This allowed even the strict-construction Republicans a loophole, and during Jefferson's administration, on March 29, 1806, Congress authorized the building of such a road. The first contract, however, was not signed until 1811, and the first stretch of 130 miles to Wheeling, West Virginia, was not completed until 1818. The road was continued almost due west through Zanesville, Columbus, and Springfield, Ohio; Richmond, Indianapolis, and Terre Haute, Indiana; to Vandalia, Illinois; it reached Columbus in 1833 and Vandalia in 1852. The road to Wheeling was especially well built: "Its numerous and stately stone bridges, with handsome stone arches, its iron mile posts, and it old iron gates, attest the skill of the workmen engaged in its construction, and to this day remain enduring monuments of its grandeur and solidity."[3] The road was supported by western Congressmen, whose influence went far in bringing about the passing of more than thirty Acts for its construction and maintenance between 1806 and 1838. It cost the federal government $6,821,200.

(From Faulkner's *Economic History of the United States*, by permission of the Macmillan Company.)

THE NATIONAL PIKE.

Until the coming of railroads the 834 miles of the "National Pike" provided one of the chief avenues to the West. "As many as twenty four-horse coaches have been counted in line at the time on the road, and large, broad-wheeled wagons, covered with white canvas stretched over bows laden with merchandise and drawn by six Conestoga horses, were visible all the day long at every point, and many times until late in the evening, besides innumerable caravans of horses, mules, cattle, hogs and sheep. It looked more like the leading avenue of a great city than a road through rural districts."[4]

The Cumberland Road not only furnished a great highway for emigration, but reduced transportation costs between Baltimore and the Ohio and brought great prosperity to the regions through which it ran. Communication between east and west was quickened by the Great Western Mail which followed it and by the express coaches of the rival transportation companies which developed incredible speed. So beneficial was the road that numerous local turnpikes were projected which it was hoped the

[3] T. B. Searight, *The Old Pike*, p. 16.
[4] *Ibid.*, p. 16.

national government would sponsor. No less than 111 surveys and plans for roads, canals, railroads, and river improvements were before Congress in 1830 when Jackson called a halt by his veto of the Maysville Road Bill (for a proposed turnpike from Maysville to Lexington, 60 miles in length, entirely in the state of Kentucky), in which he held it to be unconstitutional for the government to use money for such enterprises confined wholly to individual states. This veto contributed much to throwing future internal improvements into state hands.

The mania for turnpikes died down as the nation turned to canals, but there has never been a time in our history when there has not been continuous roadbuilding as the country has expanded. During the 'fifties, for example, interest blazed up again in a fever for building plank roads, and several thousand miles were constructed. These were built by laying parallel stringers on the ground about four feet apart, and nailing planks across them eight feet long and three or four inches thick. At a cost of $1200 to $1500 a mile these roads were relatively inexpensive, but they wore out quickly and were soon forgotten in the railroad boom of the 1850's.

THE RIVER STEAMBOAT

While turnpike projects were being pushed with feverish haste, experiments were being made with the steam engine that were destined to give longer life and renewed importance to river traffic. A number of American engineers, including Oliver Evans, John Fitch, James Rumsey, John Stevens, and others, had been experimenting with the steam engine in water transportation and had successfully propelled vessels, but it was left to Robert Fulton to make steam navigation commercially successful. After many discouragements, but with the backing of Chancellor Livingston, Fulton in 1807 built the *Clermont,* a 160-ton side-wheeler, which he navigated to Albany, a distance of 150 miles, in 32 hours. "My steamboat voyage to Albany and back," said Fulton in a letter, "has turned out rather more favorably than I had calculated. The distance from New York to Albany is one hundred and fifty miles. I ran it up in thirty-two hours, and down in thirty. I had a light breeze against me the whole way, both going and coming; and the voyage has been performed wholly by the power of the steam-engine. I overtook many sloops and schooners beating to windward, and parted with them. The power of propelling boats by steam is now fully proved. The morning I left New York there were not perhaps thirty persons in the city who believed that the boat would ever move one mile an hour or be of the least utility; and, while we were putting off from the wharf, which was crowded with spectators, I heard a number of sarcastic remarks. This is the way in which ignorant men compliment what they call philosophers and projectors."

Fulton's epochal voyage in 1807 inaugurated a revolution, not only in river traffic but in ocean commerce as well. He and Livingston immediately obtained a monopoly of the waters of New York State for twenty years, and soon afterward a similar monopoly of the waters of the lower Mississippi in the territory of New Orleans. Several steamboats were in operation on the Hudson before the two men established a shipyard at Pittsburgh in 1811 and launched the *Orleans,* the first steamboat on the Ohio. This boat descended the Ohio and Mississippi in the winter of 1812, but could not return against the swift current. It was three years (May, 1815) before a steamboat succeeded in ascending the rivers from New Orleans to Louisville, a feat accomplished in twenty-five days by Henry Shreve, the greatest of the western navigators.

The development of steam navigation was held up temporarily until the monopolies in New York and Louisiana were broken by the Supreme Court decision in Gibbons *v.* Ogden (1824), which held that river transportation could not be monopolized by any one state, but that the regulation of interstate traffic came under the powers of Congress. The success of the steamboat was demonstrated by the fact that the time from New Orleans to Pittsburgh was soon reduced from 100 to 30 days. By the 1850's the fastest steamboats were making the upstream journey from New Orleans to Louisville in less than five days. Freight and passenger rates were cut to a fraction of their former cost. Profits, nevertheless, were high and river steamboats were built rapidly. It is believed that in the late 'forties the steamboat tonnage on the western rivers was greater than that of the entire British Empire. Profiting from her position, New Orleans during the 1830's grew more rapidly in population and wealth than any city in the country.

The early experiments had been made in the East, but it was upon the western waters that the river steamboat was to play its greatest rôle. In 1816 Shreve, throwing precedents aside, used a flat-bottomed keel boat as his model, placed the engine on deck with the cylinders in a horizontal position, and built a second deck over the first. This flat-bottomed model was particularly suited to overcome the danger of river navigation, and it was the forerunner of those speedy and gorgeous palaces that plied between the western ports in the golden days of river navigation.

The loss of large numbers of steamboats because of bars and snags led to the appropriation between 1822 and 1860 of over $3,000,000 by the national government for bettering traffic conditions on the Mississippi, Ohio, Missouri, and Arkansas Rivers. The commerce of the Mississippi Valley in

1852 was estimated at $653,976,000, a large proportion of which was made possible by the steamboat, which not only aided in the marketing of bulky foodstuffs and cotton, but thereby stimulated a more rapid settlement of the region.

THE ERA OF CANAL BUILDING

The river steamboat was an immense boon to the river towns, but it did not, of course, solve the problem of land transportation. Nor did it contribute much to the movement of goods from east to west, for the great rivers of the continent run in a northerly-southerly direction. The "National Pike," as it was gradually opened, helped materially in the east-west movement of goods, but the costs of transportation were still too high to allow the extensive handling of trans-Allegheny freight. The population in the regions tributary to the Ohio was estimated in 1800 at 400,000 and was increasing rapidly; the population of Ohio, Indiana, Illinois, Michigan, Wisconsin, and Iowa increased from 50,240 in 1800 to 792,719 in 1820 and 2,967,840 in 1840. The center of population in 1800 was eighteen miles west of Baltimore; by 1840 it was near the center of West Virginia, and by 1850 had almost reached the Ohio River in the western part of that state. As this population was entirely agricultural, its products had to find a market either east of the Alleghenies or in foreign countries. The route to either market was roundabout and hazardous, for products went down the tributaries of the Mississippi to its mouth, where they were transshipped by sailing vessels to their destination. This route served the needs of the southwestern cotton planters fairly well, but it failed to meet those of the farmers north of the Ohio, although as years went by these farmers found an increasing market for their products in the plantations of the South. Better communication with the East was essential.

As the limitations of the roads became evident, attention was drawn more and more to artificial waterways as a possible solution. The distinct success of James Brindley in England in constructing the Bridgewater Canal (opened in 1761) and in other later projects had stimulated great activity in that country in canal building, which was reflected here in continually increasing interest. The Erie Canal was the most notable artificial waterway built in this country, but it was by no means the first. A number of short canals were built; others were projected or started, only to be abandoned or completed years later. Virginia, for example, authorized and constructed a seven-mile canal between Richmond and Westham as early as 1785. The Dismal Swamp Canal, authorized by Virginia and North Carolina, was begun in 1787 and completed in 1794. The first important artificial waterway in New England was the Middlesex Canal, thirty miles long and extending from the Merrimac to the Charles in Massachusetts; it was begun in 1795 and completed in 1808. Long before the Erie Canal was begun the superiority of canals over turnpikes was demonstrated. The chief advantage lay in the fact that a horse could drag through dead water a load fifty times heavier than on land. Against this advantage was the greater cost of building canals and the greater difficulty of surmounting changing levels. In the North freezing weather temporarily closed canals to traffic and in all parts of the country washouts often rendered them useless.

The Erie Canal

The great era of canal building may be said to have been inaugurated by the Erie Canal. No one contributed more to arousing interest in this project than Elkanah Watson, a member of the first commission appointed in 1792 to explore and lay out a possible route. In 1788 he had clearly seen the possibilities of such a canal:

In contemplating the situation of Ft. Stanwix, at the head of the Bateaux Navigation on the Mohawk River, . . . I am led to think this station will, in time, become an emporium of commerce between Albany and the vast western world above. . . .

Should the Little Falls ever be locked,—the obstructions in the Mohawk River removed,—and the canal between said river and Wood Creek at this place, formed, so as to unite the waters running east, with those running west; and other canals made, and obstructions removed at Fort Oswego,—who can reasonably doubt but that by such operations the state of New York have it within their power by a grand stroke of policy, to divert the future trade of Lake Ontario, and the Great Lakes above, from Alexandria and Quebec to Albany and New York.[5]

There followed twenty-five years of agitation, with unsuccessful efforts to obtain help from the national government and from Ohio and Indiana; finally in 1817, urged on by Governor Clinton, New York undertook the work alone. The chief engineer of the Erie Canal was Benjamin Wright, but the mechanical genius who circumvented so many difficulties was Canvass White, a young man who had walked two thousand miles along the towpaths of England studying every detail of canal construction there. White was the exception, for many of the engineers in the early days of canal building in America had never even seen a canal before they commenced to construct one. Fifteen miles of waterway between the towns of Utica and Rome were opened in 1819, and on October 26, 1825, cannon

[5] Elkanah Watson, *History of the Rise, Progress and Existing Condition of the Western Canals in the State of New York,* etc. (1820), p. 15.

stationed at intervals along the canal announced from Buffalo to Albany the opening of the entire length and the departure of the first boats. Some weeks later, from the decks of the *Seneca Chief,* which had headed the procession of vessels, Governor Clinton poured the contents of a cask filled with water from Lake Erie into New York Harbor to signify the wedding of the waters.

As originally built, the Erie Canal was 363 miles long. It was constructed at an average cost of $20,000 a mile, the total amounting to approximately

(From Faulkner's *Economic History of the United States,* by permission of the Macmillan Company.)

THE ERIE CANAL.

$7,000,000. Typical of other canals of the period, the Erie was 30 feet wide and 4 feet deep and could accommodate 30-ton barges. It followed the Mohawk to Rome, and thence westward through the present cities of Syracuse, Rochester, and Lockport to Buffalo by way of the Tonawanda and Niagara Rivers. Subsidiary canals connected it with Lakes Ontario, Champlain, and Seneca. Eventually New York had 906 miles of artificial waterways.

The success of the Erie was immediate. Tolls exceeded the interest charge before it was finished, and during the first nine years amountd to $8,500,-000—more than the initial cost. Nineteen thousand boats and rafts passed West Troy in the Erie and Champlain Canals during 1826. The first and greatest effect of "Clinton's ditch" was in providing an all-water route to the West, thus furnishing an outlet for the bulky products of the interior. Freight from Buffalo to New York dropped from $100 to $15 per ton, and the time from 20 days to 8. Farm produce of western New York doubled in value and that of the states north of the Ohio was increased; this carried in its wake a corresponding rise in land values. If the Old Northwest was mightily stimulated, the regions immediately adjoining this "great blood vessel of the state" fairly boomed. Utica, Syracuse, and Rochester became thriving towns, and the terminals—Buffalo, Albany, and New York—took on new life. The last-named city doubled its population between 1820 and

1830 and took from Philadelphia its leadership as the first American sea-port. The Lake cities of Buffalo, Cleveland, Detroit, and Chicago entered a period of rapid growth and began to rival Pittsburgh, Cincinnati, St. Louis, and New Orleans, as the produce of the western farmers was drawn through the northern route. To a large portion of the United States the Erie Canal opened a period of unprecedented prosperity. Passenger packets made the distance from Albany to Buffalo in four and a half days, and over this route passed a continually increasing stream of western immigrants. The Old Northwest seemed firmly bound to New York through the Erie, for the distance to the sea was shorter this way than through either the Mississippi or the St. Lawrence Valleys.

OTHER EASTERN CANALS

The success of the Erie Canal and the consequent prosperity enjoyed by New York led to similar projects in many other states. Pennsylvania, fearful lest her western trade be drawn off to New York, was first caught in the mania for canal building, and rapidly constructed (1826–1834) a system of canals and portages from Philadelphia to Pittsburgh, following the Susquehanna, Juniata, Conemaugh, and Allegheny Rivers. A horse railroad led from Philadelphia to Columbia on the Susquehanna where the canal began; from here the route was along the east bank of the Susquehanna and the west bank of the Juniata to Hollidaysburg. The mountains between Hollidaysburg and Johnstown were crossed by a portage railway 33½ miles long, upon the inclined planes of which it was possible to raise a boat 1399 feet in less than ten miles and lower it 1171 feet. The Pennsylvania Canal with its connecting railways was 394 miles long, and was constructed at a cost of over $10,000,000. Although state-owned, the government did not operate either cars or boats; it simply charged a toll for their use. To build this route to the West it had been necessary to surmount an altitude of almost 2300 feet as against a rise of 566 feet on the Erie Canal. Not so satisfactory as the Erie, this route was yet successful in its purpose and through it a share of the western trade reached Philadelphia.

Other canals were built in Pennsylvania, some subsidiary to the Pennsylvania Canal and others designed to float down the anthracite coal deposits of the Wyoming Valley. Two artificial waterways were cut across New Jersey and used chiefly to transport coal. The Delaware and Raritan Canal, built between 1834 and 1838 at a cost of $4,735,353, extended from Bordentown on the Delaware to New Brunswick on the Raritan. The Morris Canal, designed to connect the Hudson with the Delaware, was opened in 1836 and led from Jersey City through Newark, Dover, Hackettstown, and Washington, to Phillipsburg on the Delaware. The old plan of a waterway from the Chesapeake to the Delaware was revived, the Delaware and Chesapeake Canal, 13½ miles long, being completed in 1829.

Not to be outdone by their northern neighbors, the citizens of Maryland and Virginia took up with renewed vigor an old plan to connect the eastern coast and the Ohio River by means of a canal running along the Potomac. The Potomac Company, with Washington as its first president, had been incorporated in 1785, but it was not until 1828 that the Chesapeake and Ohio Canal was commenced. Originally planned to extend from Georgetown, as its eastern terminal, to Cumberland, and thence by a tunnel across the range to the Youghiogheny, it was never pushed farther than Cumberland. It was completed in 1850 after many discouraging setbacks, at a cost of $11,000,000, of which $7,000,000 was contributed by the state of Maryland, $1,500,000 by the terminal cities, and $1,000,000 by the United States government. The Chesapeake and Ohio Canal was unsuccessful, due largely to the fact that it did not cross the mountains and to the bitter opposition and competition of the Baltimore and Ohio Railroad, which was built simultaneously over the same route.

CANALS IN THE MIDDLE WEST

The success of the Erie Canal stimulated interest also in the Middle West, and projects were immediately formulated to connect the Ohio with Lake Erie and thus provide a continuous inland waterway from New York to New Orleans. In 1825 Ohio authorized the building of two canals, one, known as the Ohio and Erie, to extend from Portsmouth on the Ohio along the course of the Scioto, Muskingum, Tuscarawas, and Cuyahoga to Cleveland; the other, the Miami and Erie, to extend from Cincinnati through Middletown, Dayton, and Defiance to Toledo, following the course of the Miami and Maumee Rivers. The latter was practically completed in 1829. Governor Clinton, the "father of the Erie Canal," turned the first spadeful for the Ohio and Erie. It was finished in 1833, so that Ohio by that date had over 400 miles of navigable canals. By 1850 this had extended to over 1000 miles.

Indiana, caught with the same enthusiasm for internal improvements, commenced in 1832 (completed in 1843) the Wabash and Erie, which connected Lake Erie with the Ohio River. The route led through the Miami and Erie to Defiance, entered Indiana in Allen County, and then went southwest along the Wabash to Terre Haute and south through Worthington and Petersburg to Evansville on the Ohio. Indiana also built the White Water Canal from Hagerstown, Wayne County, mostly along the White Water River, to Lawrenceburg on the Ohio. Illinois, still sparsely settled, built the Illinois and Michigan Canal (1836–1848), connecting Lake

Michigan with the Mississippi by an artificial waterway from Chicago to La Salle, the head of navigation on the Illinois. Wisconsin attempted to join Green Bay, an arm of Lake Michigan, with the Mississippi by means of a canal between the Fox and Wisconsin Rivers, but the project was not completed until 1856. Lakes Huron and Superior were connected in 1855 by a canal around St. Mary's Falls. Constructed originally by Michigan, it was later turned over to the United States government and has become one of the most important artificial waterways in the world. Navigation on the Ohio was furthered by a short canal around the falls at Louisville. Canal mileage in the United States was estimated at 1270 in 1830, 3320 in 1840, and 3700 in 1850.

EFFECT OF THE PANIC OF 1837

Most of the canals had been built by the several states. Constitutional objections had tied the hands of the national government, although considerable aid was rendered by donations of public lands and by the purchase of stock, as in the case of the Chesapeake and Ohio. Private capital was inadequate, but the credit of the states in the prosperous days of the late 'twenties and early 'thirties seemed inexhaustible. Land speculators and bona fide settlers encouraged expenditures out of all proportion to the existing wealth and population of the states, and wrote into the state constitutions of the period directions "to encourage internal improvements within the state." Rivalries between states and cities contributed to the mania. State debts, which had amounted to only $12,790,728 in 1820, increased to $66,482,186 in 1835, to over $170,000,000 in 1838, and to $200,000,-000 in 1840, practically all of which had been incurred for banks, roads, canals, and railroads. A good share of the money for canals had been borrowed from England. The confidence placed in the United States Bank, the high standing of our national credit, the high interest rates on American securities—combined with ignorance of conditions here—easily induced Europeans to buy American stocks and bonds.[6] Only seven states (Connecticut, Delaware, Georgia, New Hampshire, North Carolina, Rhode Island, and Vermont) had not contracted debts for these purposes. Much of this work had been undertaken in an era of enthusiasm without adequate knowledge of difficulties and costs. The projects were speculative and in some cases unnecessary. Furthermore, in spite of the grandiose expectations of canal enthusiasts, the canals remained largely local in their commercial significance. In 1840 only one-seventh of the freight carried on the New York canals originated outside the state.

---

[6] See R. C. McGrane, "Some Aspects of American State Debts in the 'Forties," *American Historical Review*, Vol. XXXVIII, No. 4, pp. 673–686 (July, 1933), and his *Foreign Bondholders and American State Debts* (1935).

PRINCIPAL CANALS IN 1840

Scale of Miles
0   50   100   200

This too rapid investment in internal improvements, especially canals, contributed largely to the panic of 1837, and when the bubble was pricked in that year most of the states found themselves unable to pay interest or continue the work. Several of them, including Mississippi, Louisiana, Maryland, Pennsylvania, Indiana, and Michigan, repudiated their debts. Nearly all sold out their improvements to private concerns and ceased to aid public improvements, and the people, going to the opposite extreme, now forbade in the new state constitutions the use of government credit for such purposes. Consequently, private individuals and corporations shouldered the work during the era of railroad building which was just dawning.

SIGNIFICANCE OF RAILROADS

The full flush of prosperity for canals had scarcely been reached before they were challenged by a new form of transportation. Simultaneously with the success of steam-driven boats, the idea had come to engineers that a steam engine might also be used to propel wheeled vehicles. Oliver Evans in 1804 had put his steamboat on wheels and driven it through the streets of Philadelphia, and in 1820 John Stevens, on his estate at Hoboken, New Jersey, had built a little narrow-gauge railroad upon which he ran a locomotive and cars with himself a passenger. When in October, 1829, George Stephenson's *Rocket* pulled a train weighing thirteen tons on the Liverpool and Manchester Railroad at an average speed of fifteen miles an hour, the practicability of steam railroads was clearly demonstrated. The advantages of railroads over canals were eventually realized. They were cheaper to construct, and transportation over them was more rapid. Moreover, they were not confined to comparatively low districts on account of water supply or subject to the expense and delay of locks; they could be laid to reach almost any part of the country, even to the back doors of factories. They were not seriously affected by change of seasons, droughts, floods, or freezing; all sections could benefit at all times. The rivers ran mostly north and south, but the new railroads could strike directly west. Where railroads did follow in general the course of rivers, there were opportunities for short cuts which appreciably reduced the distance between points. The effect of the railroads in opening up the West, in providing transportation for western products, in stimulating eastern manufacturing, in speeding labor organization (note, p. 268), in binding the sections together, in disseminating information and education to remote sections, provides a story intertwined with every phase of our economic, social, and political life.

EARLY AMERICAN RAILROADS

"England," says Dunbar, "had been building railways for nearly two hundred years, had made iron rails since 1738 and steam locomotives since 1804."[7] Real progress came there after 1829. In America wooden rails for local roads to move iron and stone had been used in various places early in the century. The best known of these were the three-mile road from Quincy, Massachusetts, to Neponset, opened in 1827, and the Mauch Chunk Railway in Pennsylvania completed in the same year. The first railroads designed for passenger service were those built to supplement the canal system, such as the road from Philadelphia to Columbia and from Hollidaysburg to Johnstown.

The first spadeful of earth for the track of the Baltimore and Ohio was turned on July 4, 1828, by Charles Carroll of Carrollton, the last surviving signer of the Declaration of Independence. This was the first railroad in the modern sense in America; the first division of it, thirteen miles long, was opened in 1830. Even the builders of this road were not sufficiently convinced of the value of steam, and the motive power for the first vehicles was sails or horse power. On a trial trip in 1830 Peter Cooper's engine, *Tom Thumb,* made the thirteen miles from Baltimore to Ellicott's Mills in an hour, and the management turned definitely to steam.

The first attempt to run a steam railroad locomotive in this country (barring the demonstration by Stevens) was made in 1829 on the Carbondale and Honesdale Railroad (now part of the Delaware and Hudson), but the nine-horsepower *Stourbridge Lion,* imported from England and set up here, was found too heavy for the rails and trestles of the road and was discarded. Meanwhile a charter had been granted for a road from Charleston to Hamburg, South Carolina, and over this line in 1830 the *Best Friend of Charleston,* the first locomotive made in America for regular and practical use, was put in operation; it attained a speed of 30 miles an hour when traveling alone, and from 16 to 21 miles with four loaded cars. When this line was completed to Hamburg in 1833 it covered 136 miles and was the longest railroad at that time in the world. In 1826 the New York legislature granted a charter to the Mohawk and Hudson Railroad Company, the earliest forerunner of the New York Central. Construction was started in 1830, and in 1831 the *De Witt Clinton* on a trial trip made the seventeen miles from Albany to Schenectady in an hour. The first link in the present Pennsylvania system, a strip of road connecting Philadelphia with the Susquehanna, was completed in 1834.

[7] Seymour Dunbar, *History of Travel in America,* III, 906.

The practicability of the new transportation having been established, the nation turned to railroads to settle the great problem of intercourse with the same enthusiasm which a few years previously it had shown toward canals. Some railroads were built, as in the case of the Boston and Lowell, primarily to carry specific manufactured commodities to the seacoast, others because of a general desire to improve transportation; but everywhere was the hope that almost any village, if it could be touched by the magic influence of the rails, might duplicate the astounding development of a Syracuse or Buffalo. By 1860 more than 30,000 miles had been built.

The rivalry of the seaboard cities in their hope of tapping the western region sprang up anew, and such cities as Boston, Charleston, Savannah, and Mobile, which had been excluded from the race during the canal-building period, joined with the rest in projecting gigantic plans for routes into the interior. As the years went by the railroads passed from the stage in which they were built merely as feeders for canals and connecting links between rivers and artificial waterways, and great trunk lines dependent upon themselves alone were gradually constructed. Before 1850 only one line of railroad had been completed between the tidewater and the great interior basins of the country, but a passenger on it, as he crossed New York, was carried by sixteen different companies. Freight was restricted by the payment of tolls and by frequent transfers due to different-gauge roads. The first consolidation on this road, the New York Central, was effected in 1853, after which this route took its place as one of the two great railroad systems leading to the interior. This was also the year that saw the first rail service from New York to Chicago. Between 1850 and the opening of the Civil War eight other great lines were completed between the seaboard and the western system of lakes and rivers. The last link of a road from Boston to Ogdensburg, New York, was completed in 1850. The next year the New York and Erie, a rival route to the New York Central, was completed to Dunkirk on Lake Erie. By 1852 the Pennsylvania Railroad, planned to connect Philadelphia with Harrisburg, Petersburg, and Cleveland, had reached Pittsburgh. Farther south, the Baltimore and Ohio, reaching Wheeling in 1853, proved victorious over the Chesapeake and Ohio Canal and has since been the main artery by which western produce has reached Baltimore.

Similar activity was evident in the South. In 1850 the Western and Atlantic Railroad of Georgia reached the Tennessee River and, with the opening of the Nashville and Chattanooga in 1854, connected Atlanta with the river and rail system of the Northwest and became the distributing agency for western grain and meat in the eastern cotton belt. By 1858 the Central Virginia, running west from Richmond, and the Southside Railroad, running west from Petersburg, had extended to a connection with the Memphis and Charleston and the Nashville and Chattanooga. The Memphis and Charleston reached the Mississippi in 1859. Efforts of the eastern seaboard cities to tap the Mississippi Valley were centralized inevitably at Chattanooga because of the superior topography of that location. From here railroads branched southward to touch the Gulf at Mobile, westward to the Mississippi at Memphis, and northward into the Old Northwest.

As the products of the Southwest, which had formerly flowed through New Orleans and Mobile, began to be diverted eastward, the merchants of the Mississippi and Gulf ports were stirred to action. The citizens of Mobile organized the Mobile and Ohio which, with the aid of federal land grants, reached Cairo, Illinois, in 1859, and in the same year New Orleans opened connection with Jackson, Tennessee, by building the New Orleans, Jackson and Great Northern. In the meantime, the Illinois Central, also bolstered by gifts of federal land, had bridged the gap between Cairo and Chicago. Between 1850 and 1860 about 8000 miles of railroad were built in the Southwest and that region had rail connections not only with the Atlantic coast but with the Ohio Valley. These herculean efforts saved much of their earlier traffic for the Gulf ports, but relatively their position declined. The new railroads between New York, Philadelphia, Baltimore, and other northern ports and the Northwest not only spurred the economic life of the Ohio Valley but tended more and more to drain the western products eastward. The bands of steel which held these two sections together did much to hold the Northwest to the Union at the time of the Civil War.

By the opening of the Civil War the region east of the Alleghenies was equipped with a skeleton railroad system which was to grow rapidly in the years to come. As the primary passes of the Alleghenies were penetrated and the original tracks of the great railway system east of the Mississippi were laid down, the chief seaboard cities established connections with the West and the flow of commerce between these sections was immensely speeded.

PROBLEMS OF EARLY RAILROAD BUILDING

Because steam locomotion was in its infancy, the early American railroad builders, like the early canal builders, had to meet and solve innumerable problems. The decades of the 'forties and 'fifties were preeminently years of experimentation. Some ideas were obtained from England, but different conditions, such as long-distance passenger traffic and bulkier freight, soon made it apparent that development in the two countries would not be closely parallel.

Problems of track construction, gauge, friction of the wheels on the rails, bridges, brakes, coupling apparatus, safety devices, lighting and heating, all had to be worked out. Although decades passed before they were finally mastered, astonishing progress was made from the start. The first rails consisted of strips of iron laid longitudinally upon wooden beams attached

RAILROADS IN 1860

MANHATTAN DRAFTING CO. INC., N.Y.

to ties. These iron strips had the unfortunate faculty of coming loose and curling up, sometimes protruding through the floor of the coach and making it necessary for the engineer to stop the train and mend the track. It was not until the early 'fifties that iron rails came extensively into use. There was no uniform gauge at first, the distance between the rails ranging in width from four feet three inches on the Delaware and Hudson to six feet on the Delaware, Lackawanna, and Western. This lack of uniformity increased expenses in shipping freight and eventually necessitated the relaying of large portions of the roadbed. The early engines were not equipped with cabs until after 1842. Wood furnished the fuel for both engines and heating, and, until coal came into use, the destruction caused by escaping sparks that started forest fires and ignited the wooden coaches, to say nothing of their effect upon the passengers' clothing, was a serious problem. Although passenger coaches during the first twenty-five years of railroad history were the last word in discomfort, they as well as the engines were usually brightly painted, highly ornate, and emblazoned with some high-sounding name. The early trains averaged only about fifteen miles an hour, but they marked a new era in speed of transportation. The first passenger coaches were little more than the bodies of stagecoaches equipped with wheels adapted to the tracks. Gradually they were lengthened to cars more nearly resembling the modern type, with openings at each end and with seats in two rows separated by an aisle. The original brakes were identical in principle with those used in stagecoaches—blocks of hard wood brought into contact with the wheels by levers operated by foot power.

Inadequate and flimsy construction characterized most of the American railroads before the Civil War. As the roadbeds began to wear out and a greater strain was put upon them by the introduction of heavier rolling stock, accidents became increasingly frequent. Complications were often caused by the failure to fence off the right of way. During the decade of the 'fifties and even later, a railroad passenger literally took his life in his hands. The day of the air brake, the automatic coupler, the block system of signals, and scientifically constructed roadbeds was still in the future. An accident was considered an "act of God" rather than negligence on the part of the railroad. The departure and arrival of trains were matters of pure conjecture, and time-tables were hardly taken seriously until the 'forties. Nor was there any uniformity in rates or fares. In the late 'forties passenger fares ranged from 1.5 cents a mile in New York to 5.35 cents in Mississippi, and freight from 4 cents a ton-mile in Vermont to 24.39 cents in Mississippi. Charges depended largely on existing competition.

FINANCING THE EARLY RAILROADS

Hardly less important than the problems of engineering were those connected with raising sufficient funds to construct the 30,000 miles of railroad in operation before the Civil War. Railroad promoters had financial difficulties from the start, difficulties which were not lessened by the fact that the new railroads must necessarily come into competition with turnpikes, plank roads, canals, and interests vested in these enterprises.[8] There was the funda-

---

[8] A leading argument against railroads in these early years held that they were more monopolistic than turnpikes or canals. Benjamin Wright, engineer of the Erie Canal, wrote in a letter appended to a congressional document: "I consider a long line of railroad . . . as being odious in this country, as a monopoly of the carrying, which it necessarily must be. A canal, on the contrary, is open to any man who builds a boat." House Ex. Doc. No. 18, 1831–32, 22nd Cong., 1st Sess., I, 174.

mental difficulty inherent in the problem of financing a railroad in new unsettled country where an adequate return on the investment could be realized
only by the expected growth of the area. Such a condition does not offer
the prospective investor an immediate return; he has only a speculative
possibility of future income if people move to the sections tapped by the
road. While investments in railroads in the more thickly populated East
frequently paid large dividends, the prospect of returns on the projected
railways in the more sparsely settled West and South was uncertain. In
any case, the investor might wait years before dividends came in. In spite
of these difficulties, over $1,250,000,000 was invested in railroads between
1830 and 1860. Much of this was obtained from abroad, where financiers
had already forgotten their unfortunate experiences in the panic of 1837
and the repudiations incidental thereto, and were willing to speculate
again on the economic possibilities of the New World. Some capital was
drawn from New England from accumulated capital released by the
declining whaling industry; this was to be augmented in the years to come
by a similar decline in shipping. Merchants and farmers in the terminal
cities and along the routes subscribed, often influenced not so much by
the desire for dividends as by the expectation of profit from increased business and the rise in land values.

Where private capital was insufficient, city, state, county, and national
aid was freely given. Except in Massachusetts, where loans were extended
to certain early railroads, little state aid was given in New England. Elsewhere the situation was quite different. Pennsylvania, Michigan, South Carolina, and Georgia undertook to finance their first railroads. Georgia, in fact,
not only built a railroad from Atlanta to Chattanooga herself but continued to
operate it until 1870. New York loaned $6,000,000 to the New York and
Erie to help build a railroad across the southern section of the state. Maryland purchased $3,000,000 of Baltimore and Ohio stock; Virginia subscribed
three-fifths of the stock of many railroads and by 1860 had contributed
some $21,000,000. Illinois appropriated $8,000,000 for various internal improvements; Ohio passed a law in 1837 by which she loaned her credit in
6 per cent stock to the amount of one-third the stock in any railroad enterprise, provided the company secured the other two-thirds; railroad corporations in Indiana were allowed to issue scrip in payment for labor or purchased material. Although the exact amount is unknown, it is probable that
the aid extended by counties and towns exceeded that of the states. In Kentucky, for example, the "local debt" for railroads amounted in 1871 to over
$13,700,000. County contributions in Wisconsin in 1874 were estimated at
over $8,500,000. Towns and counties in Iowa had contributed $7,000,000 by
1856. What these funds amounted to in actual mileage may be estimated

by the cost of construction, which in the 1850's varied from $25,000 to $50,000 a mile.

Constitutional scruples held back federal aid to railroad construction for some time. The widespread demand for railroad transportation and the inability of the western states to finance the new projects, however, made such aid inevitable. It began in 1850 with a grant of over 2,500,000 acres of public land to the state of Illinois, the land lying in alternate sections along the projected route of the Illinois Central. This grant was turned over by the state to the railroad with the reservation that 7 per cent of the company's gross earnings be reserved for the state. In similar manner lavish gifts were made to Mississippi, Missouri, Michigan, Wisconsin, Minnesota, Iowa, Arkansas, Alabama, Florida, and Louisiana, amounting by 1861 to approximately $31,000,000. As it was to the advantage of the railroads to dispose of the public lands to provide cash for themselves and to increase the population along their routes, these grants had a part in speeding settlement as well as in promoting railroad construction. This was particularly evident in the case of the Illinois Central which worked energetically to bring immigrants to its region. Although the effort to bring about government regulation of railroads did not come until the 1870's, some faint beginnings are to be found in these early years when the states were so generous in extending aid. Some states attempted to limit charges, to put a ceiling on dividends, and to reserve the right to purchase the railroad after a certain date. But these efforts accomplished little for the time being.

STREET RAILWAYS

The increasing concentration of the population in cities developed in the fifth decade of the century a distinctly urban passenger problem. From the beginning it had been necessary in some cases to run railroads over city streets, but these were not street railways in the proper sense. The idea of the sunken rail which would not obstruct wheeled traffic had to be developed before such roads could be practical. The first vehicle used for periodic transportation of the city population was the omnibus, a modification of the stagecoach. In the 'fifties the sunken rail came into use, and from then until the days of the electric tramways various types of horse cars, some of which had two stories, handled the demands of city traffic as best they could.

TRANSPORTATION IN THE TRANS-MISSISSIPPI WEST

A glance at the railroad map (p. 288) makes it clear that railroad construction prior to 1860 was largely limited to the region east of the Mississippi. Except for a few prongs of steel extending westward from St. Louis and other points along the river and a few tiny railroads in California, the trans-Mississippi West was as yet dependent upon rivers and dirt roads. Despite these inadequate facilities this vast region was not devoid of a lively commerce. From the early years of the century fur traders working out of St. Louis had covered the valleys of the upper Mississippi and Missouri and had floated their pelts down the rivers to make St. Louis the great fur center of the nation. Moreover, these traders had discovered the routes followed in later years by the immigrants along the Oregon, California and Santa Fé trails and subsequently by the first transcontinental railroads.

Long before the first covered wagons started for Oregon or California in the early 'forties, an active commerce had developed over the Santa Fé trail. In 1821 a trading party setting out from the Missouri took their way to Santa Fé over the route now generally followed by the Atchison, Topeka and Santa Fé and found there a ready market for their goods. It was discovered that it was actually cheaper to transport goods up the Missouri to Independence and from there by pack train or freight wagon to Santa Fé than to bring them up through Mexico from Vera Cruz. This opened the Spanish Southwest to American traders and in the succeeding years there was a continuous movement of textiles, cutlery, and other commodities to Santa Fé where they were exchanged for furs, mules, and gold and silver bullion. Measured by modern standards the Santa Fé trade was not large. In only one year, 1843, when the eastern goods sent southward amounted to $450,000, did its value exceed $250,000. But the importance of the trade was greater than its value. It inflamed the national imagination and aroused interest in the Southwest years before the annexation of Texas. "The Santa Fé trail," says Paxson, "was the first beaten path thrust in advance of the western frontier."

With the discovery of gold in California in 1848 the whole history of trans-Mississippi transportation took on new life. Stage traffic from Independence to Santa Fé was begun in 1849 and in the same year a monthly mail to Salt Lake City was established. Although steamship and clipper communication between the east coast and California either around the Horn or by way of Panama was exceedingly brisk throughout the 'fifties, it was not until 1858 that the federal government awarded to John Butterfield a contract to carry mail overland from Memphis and St. Louis to California. In the fall of that year Butterfield started a semi-weekly passenger and mail service through Preston, El Paso, and Fort Yuma to the Pacific coast which made the trip in about 25 days. Others followed, including the famous firm of Russell, Majors and Waddell, which traveled over other routes and developed a large freight and passenger service. This was an extensive business in the early 'sixties; the above firm was reputed to have had 6250 wagons and 75,000 oxen in the freight business alone. In 1860 William H. Russell organized the pony express which by relays of horseback riders carried mail from St. Joseph, Missouri, to Sacramento, California, in about ten days. It was probably the fastest transportation of its kind yet known, but it brought financial ruin to Russell, Majors and Waddell. The bankrupt firm was bought in by Ben Holladay in 1862 and in turn sold by him to Wells, Fargo & Company who controlled much of this traffic until the first transcontinental railroad was completed. The pony express ended with the coming of the first transcontinental telegraph line in 1861.

DEVELOPMENT OF EXPRESS TRANSPORTATION

The entrance of Wells, Fargo & Company into western transportation gives some indication of the early development of transportation. The founder of express transportation was William Francis Harnden, a former conductor and ticket agent on the Boston and Worcester. Taking his cue from the methods by which gold and silver were transferred, Harnden in 1839 conceived the idea that a similar business might be developed in the rapid and safe transportation of small packages and valuable papers. Harnden himself carried the first express in a carpetbag between New York and Boston, but the business grew so rapidly that he took in a partner; the firm of Harnden & Company's Express was founded in 1840. Agents were hired, the business was extended in 1841 to include Philadelphia and Albany, and European agencies were opened to look after the transportation of immigrants. Harnden's success brought Alvin Adams into the field, and a rival express business was begun between New York and Boston. With Ephraim Farnsworth as a partner, Adams & Company was founded; by 1843 their business extended as far west as St. Louis and New Orleans. In 1854 Harnden & Company was merged with the new Adams Express Company, leaving the latter supreme in the Northeast for the time being. In the meantime, Henry Wells, Harnden's agent at Albany, had left Harnden and formed Wells, Fargo & Company, which by 1845 connected the East with Chicago, Cincinnati, and St. Louis. In that year Wells, Fargo sold out to the American Express and moved to the Pacific coast. It was here, curiously enough, that the express service, scarcely more than a decade after its birth, achieved its greatest triumph, when Wells, Fargo & Company carried the mail and gold of the 'forty-niners, and where, according to Samuel Bowles, "the first three establishments set up in a mining town were a restaurant, a billiard saloon, and a Wells & Fargo office." [9]

[9] Samuel Bowles, *Our New West*, p. 347.

COMMUNICATION BY TELEGRAPH

Samuel F. B. Morse (1791–1872), trained as an artist, and professor of the literature of the arts of design in New York University, evolved the idea of the electromagnetic telegraph in 1832. Three years afterward the first crude instrument was constructed, and by 1837 the apparatus was practical. Although his invention was repeatedly demonstrated and undoubtedly contained immense future possibilities, it was impossible to interest private entrepreneurs. Forced to seek government aid, Morse and his friends besieged Congress for six years before that body in 1843 finally appropriated $30,000 for the construction of a line from Baltimore to Washington. This line was completed by May of the following year in time to transmit to the Capital information from the Whig and Democratic conventions which met in Baltimore that spring. A private company was then formed, and with great difficulty funds were obtained for a line from Philadelphia to Newark. It was opened in 1846 and was later extended to Jersey City from which point messages were transmitted to New York by ferry.

The practicability of the telegraph once established, its extension was rapid. Ezra Cornell, who had been associated with Morse in constructing the first line and had demonstrated the superiority of the overhead wire, became the organizing genius of the rapid expansion which set in. In comparison to a railroad the cost of construction per mile was less, and the problems to be met were fewer. In 1846–1847 New York was connected with Boston, Albany, and Buffalo, and in the next year with Cleveland, Toledo, Detroit, and Chicago. Although forced to meet such new conditions as severe plain and mountain storms as well as hostile Indians, the Western Union, spurred on by government subsidies, extended its lines to the Pacific in 1861. In that year 50,000 miles of telegraph lines were in operation.

The rapid development of telegraphy was due in part to the close relations established early between railroads and the new invention. Railroads needed telegraphy to operate their roads efficiently and telegraph companies needed the railroad right of way to put up their lines. The possibilities of telegraphy once demonstrated, its usefulness in underseas communication was quickly realized. Cyrus Field completed the first transatlantic cable in 1858, but transmission was not successful until the cable was relaid in 1866.

SELECTED READINGS

MacGill, C. E., *et al.*, *History of Transportation in the United States Before 1860*, Chaps. II–XI, XVII.

Hulbert, A. B., *Paths of Inland Commerce.*

Harlow, A. F., *Old Towpaths*, Chaps. VI ff.

Gates, P. W., *The Illinois Central Railroad and Its Colonization Work*, Chaps. II, V, VI.

Callender, G. S., *Selections from the Economic History of the United States*, Chaps. VII, VIII.

Flügel, F., and Faulkner, H. U., *Readings in the Economic and Social History of the United States*, Chap. X.

15

Population and Labor

POPULATION: INCREASE AND DISTRIBUTION

A STUDY of population statistics for the first seventy years of our history reveals three outstanding tendencies, quite normal under the circumstances: (1) a rapid increase; (2) a westward migration; and (3) a concentration in cities. The total population of the nation in 1790 was probably under four million, while that given in the Census of 1860 was 31,443,321.

POPULATION OF THE UNITED STATES TO 1860[1]

Year	White	Colored	Total
1790	3,172,006	757,208	3,929,214
1800	4,306,446	1,002,037	5,308,483
1810	5,862,073	1,377,808	7,239,881
1820	7,866,797	1,771,656	9,638,453
1830	10,537,378	2,328,642	12,866,020
1840	14,195,805	2,873,648	17,069,453
1850	19,553,068	3,638,808	23,191,876
1860	26,922,537	4,441,830	31,443,321[a]

[a] Including Indians, Japanese, Chinese, and all others, who numbered 78,954.

Until after 1820 most of this growth was attributable to the natural increase in a new land where large families were economically profitable. Said the Swedish traveler, Peter Kalm, who toured America about 1750: "It does not seem difficult to find out the reasons, why people multiply faster here than in Europe. As soon as a person is old enough he may marry in these provinces without any fear of poverty. There is such an amount of good ground yet uncultivated, that a new-married man can, without difficulty, get a spot of ground, where he may comfortably subsist with his wife and children. The taxes are very low, and he need not be under any concern on their account."[2]

The conditions favoring large families which Kalm had observed in the late colonial period continued as long as this country remained preeminently

[1] *U.S. Census, 1910*, I, 127.
[2] A. B. Benson (ed.), *Peter Kalm's Travels in North America* (2 vols., 1937), p. 211.

an agrarian nation. In addition to the natural growth of population there was an immigration amounting to over 5,000,000 people between 1820 and 1860. Not only did the normal increase of births over deaths and the additions from immigration speed the population growth, but the effects of the Industrial Revolution and the expansion of commerce created new wealth and new possibilities of employment in trade and industry, and so provided a source of livelihood for additional people. The population growth during each decade was about 34 per cent, the population almost doubling every twenty years.

Even more striking than the increase in actual numbers was the distribution. In 1790 over 94 per cent lived on the Atlantic slope of the thirteen original colonies, with less than a quarter of a million west of the Alleghenies. By 1820 the proportion had distinctly changed. The census of that year showed about 73 per cent living on the Atlantic slope and 27 per cent west of the mountains. The southern group of states was still the most populous, but New York could boast of the greatest population of any single state. The population beyond the mountains now outnumbered that of New England. The ratio of increase had fallen in each of the Atlantic states with the exception of Connecticut and South Carolina, where it had progressed a fraction of 1 per cent. During the decade 1810 to 1820 New York added 413,000 to her numbers, more than any other state; Ohio came next, with 351,000. But the ratio of increase had been greatest in the new western states; one eastern state, Delaware, had remained practically stationary. In the thirty years from 1790 to 1820 the seaboard states had contributed almost two and one half millions to the population of the West. The Census of 1850 revealed that almost half of the population (45 per cent) now lived west of the Alleghenies. Professor Channing has pointed out [3] that in the thirty years from 1820 to 1850, the number of inhabitants of the region west of the Appalachians more than doubled by five millions, while the population of the seaboard states, notwithstanding the immigration from Europe, failed to double by two millions. Assuming that the population should double by natural reproduction in thirty years, it seems probable, he believes, that during these three decades the East contributed at least four million to the population of the West. [4]

The South furnished the largest proportion of this western migration. Two-fifths of the inhabitants of South Carolina, one-third of those of Virginia and North Carolina, and nearly one-quarter of those of Georgia emigrated west of the mountains to form almost the entire population of the

[3] Edward Channing, *History of the United States,* V, 49.

[4] Between 1820 and 1830 the population increased 32.5 per cent and the settled area 24.4 per cent; between 1830 and 1840 the figures were 32.5 and 27.6 per cent, respectively.

Old Southwest and the predominating element in the Old Northwest. A continual stream of New Englanders moved toward the west, sometimes pausing for a time in Vermont or western New York, but in most cases pushing on eventually to the new country and giving a distinct New England tone to the northern tier of counties in Ohio and Indiana. There was also a large movement from the middle states into the Northwest, in actual numbers greater than that from New England.

In addition to this movement across the mountains, there was the exodus, particularly in New England, from the farms to the cities. Both of them must have placed a severe strain upon the rural population, and both are illuminating in any attempt to study the social and economic cross-currents of life in the seaboard states during the first half of the nineteenth century. The causes of the cityward migration were many, chiefly attributable to the Industrial Revolution—the growth of the factory system, the development of internal transportation, and the economic processes which took people from the farm and allowed them to live by manufacturing, commerce, trade, or finance. The population of the seaboard cities was largely augmented after 1820 by immigrants, many of whom were ill adapted by training for farm life and went no farther. The development of the means of communication by canals and later by railroads allowed a greater distribution of agricultural produce and an expanded foreign commerce, leading to the growth of cities at collecting and transfer points. The market for agricultural products speeded the westward movement, which in turn added to the population of important points on the routes of travel. The competition of western agriculture became so keen as to discourage eastern farmers, especially in the less fertile regions, and to accentuate a movement toward the cities which the growth of manufacturing favored. In 1780 there were only five towns of over 8000 population—Philadelphia, New York, Boston, Charleston, and Baltimore, containing 2.7 per cent of the population of the country. Of these, Philadelphia alone had over 20,000. The Census of 1840 showed 44 cities over 8000, with New York, now the largest, containing 312,710. By 1860 there were 141 towns of over 8000, comprising 16.1 per cent of the population. In that year New York, as now constituted,[5] had a population of about 1,175,-000; Philadelphia, 566,000; and Baltimore, 212,000.

By 1810 New York City had forged to the front and after the completion of the Erie Canal speedily became the great American metropolis, acting as a shipping center for a large part of the western produce. The city was forced to meet the competition of other seaboard cities and even of New Orleans for the products of the rich grain section of the Great Lakes, but her excellent harbor and strategic geographic position, aided by canals and then

[5] The population of New York as then constituted was 813,669 (Borough of Manhattan).

GROWTH OF CITY POPULATION, 1780–1860

Year	Number of Cities Having a Population of					Percentage of Total Population in Cities
	8000 or Over	8000 to 20,000	20,000 to 75,000	75,000 to 250,000	250,000 or Over	
1780	5	4	1	. .	. .	2.7
1790	6	4	2	. .	. .	3.3
1800	6	1	5	. .	. .	4.0
1810	11	6	3	2	. .	4.9
1820	13	7	4	2	. .	4.9
1830	26	19	4	3	. .	6.7
1840	44	28	11	4	1	8.5
1850	85	56	21	6	2	12.5
1860	141	96	35	7	3	16.1

railroads, won unquestioned supremacy for her. Philadelphia and Baltimore, leading colonial towns that were favored by rich agricultural and mineral hinterlands, sought, by building competing systems of canals, to tap the western areas and draw to themselves a share of the produce, but their success was indifferent until the advent of railroads. Boston, a normal center for trade east of the Connecticut River and aided by a hinterland of thrifty and resourceful people, had played an important rôle in the great maritime days of the Republic, but as Americans turned their interests from the sea to the development of the West she was severely handicapped by her geographic position. Her commercial importance was now overshadowed by that of New York, and only the coming of the Industrial Revolution served to support her continued development as a trading center. A crescent of satellite textile, leather, and metal towns, including the thriving cities of Nashua, Lowell, Waltham, Lynn, Worcester, New Bedford, and Fall River, grew up behind her to bring a new era of prosperity. As New England turned to manufacturing, colonial towns like Providence, New London, Hartford, and New Haven became important cities, and hundreds of obscure villages grew into thriving towns or small cities. "In 1840," says Bidwell, "it would have been difficult to find 50 out of 479 townships in Southern New England which did not have at least one manufacturing village clustered around a cotton or a woolen mill, an iron furnace, a chair factory or a carriage shop, or some other representative of the hundred miscellaneous branches of manufacturing which had grown up in haphazard fashion in every part of these three states."[6] Although the early factories were small, they were widely dispersed, and the growth of the factory system was accompanied by a growth of urban population. Only three towns in New England in 1810 boasted over 10,000

[6] P. W. Bidwell, "The Agricultural Revolution in New England," *American Historical Review*, Vol. XXVI, No. 4, P. 686 (1921).

inhabitants—Boston, Providence, and New Haven, with a combined population of 56,000—whereas in 1860 there were twenty-six such cities with a population of 682,000.

Pittsburgh, located at the head of navigation on the Ohio where East met West, in a position to tap vast regions, and furthermore in the midst of a rich coal and iron district, became a city of note as early as 1800. The situation of Cincinnati and Louisville on the same river insured their future. St. Louis collected the commerce of the Missouri and upper Mississippi, and Mobile and New Orleans were the shipping points on the Gulf. Chicago, Detroit, Cleveland, Buffalo, the shipping ports of the Great Lakes, had begun by 1860 to show the promise of their subsequent greatness and to foretell the relative decline of the Ohio river towns. At other points too numerous to mention, natural advantages or fortuitous circumstances led to urban growth.

In the South, however, many of the cities, such as Williamsburg, Charleston, and Savannah, went back absolutely or relatively. The drain of population westward, the shift of the center of cotton production, the natural outlet of cotton culture across the mountains, the drawing of western produce to Baltimore and Philadelphia rather than to the southern seaports, and the lack of manufacturing development—all contributed to the relatively small growth of urban life in the South Atlantic States. South of Mason and Dixon's line there were in 1860 only 27 towns or cities with a population above 4000.

IMMIGRATION BEFORE 1860

The preliminary report of the Eighth Census estimated from a "survey of the irregular data previous to 1819" that from 1790 to 1800 about 50,000 Europeans arrived here, from 1800 to 1810 about 70,000, and from 1810 to the end of 1820 about 114,000. To determine the actual settlers, a deduction of 14.5 per cent from these figures should be made for transients. After 1819 official records were kept which are approximately correct. Immigration up to 1825 amounted to less than 10,000 a year, but gradually increased thereafter until by 1832 about 60,000 annually were coming to our shores, an increase probably due to the revolutionary disturbances of the period. This swelled to 79,000 in 1837, only to be cut in half the next year by the panic. The flow of immigration again increased to over 100,000 in 1842, to be reduced again in the next year by the financial depression. The five years from 1845 to 1850 showed a tremendous gain, because of the severe winters of 1845 and 1846 on the Continent, the subsequent spring floods which affected agriculture adversely, the potato famine of 1845 and 1846 in Ireland, and the revolutions of 1848 and 1849. Never before or since, in fact, has the number of immigrants been so great in proportion to the American population.

Economic and political influences abroad were not alone in driving hundreds of thousands to the New World; the discovery of gold in California lured many more. Immigration amounted to 427,833 in 1854 but dropped in the next year to less than half that number; in 1860 it amounted to only 153,640. This decline has been attributed to the Crimean War and troubles

IMMIGRATION INTO THE UNITED STATES 1820–1860.[7]

in India, which absorbed some of the excess population and increased the demand for agricultural and manufactured goods. The Civil War at first affected immigration adversely, but the war prosperity, combined with the allurements of the Homestead Act, renewed the flow of alien settlers. The great majority of immigrants prior to 1860 came from the British Isles, especially Ireland, and from Germany. The five leading occupations as stated by male immigrants during these years were: laborers, 872,317; farmers, 764,837; mechanics, 407,524; merchants, 231,852; and miners, 39,967. In 1860 there were about four million foreign-born settlers in the United States.

As regards distribution it is possible to speak only in general terms. At least five-sixths of the Irish immigrants remained east of the Appalachians, most of them in the cities, where they formed the bulk of the unskilled labor. On the other hand, the German immigrant of this period was more likely to be a farmer, and at least half of them took up lands west of the mountains,

[7] Eighth Census, 1860, *Preliminary Report,* pp. 12 ff.

not a few on the Wisconsin and Texas frontiers. The large majority of the Scandinavians pushed west to find homes in Illinois, Wisconsin, or Minnesota. Perhaps two-thirds of the English, Scotch, and Welsh stayed in the Northeast, the remaining third moving westward.

The influx of this tremendous horde of immigrants could not but have an important effect upon the social and economic life of the period. As the older cities doubled in size between 1840 and 1860 and scores of new ones sprang into existence, there appeared in the larger centers slum conditions hardly duplicated in later years. Pauperism increased rapidly, and the standard of living of the working classes was pushed steadily downward as real wages declined.[8] Tempting as it is to expatiate upon the "good old days," the fact remains that the two decades preceding the Civil War stand out as one of the most discouraging periods that the American wage earner has ever experienced. Not all of his troubles during these years was due to increased immigration, but it was an important factor.

LIFE IN TOWN AND COUNTRY

The second quarter of the century witnessed the beginning of revolutionary changes in the everyday life of the people. By that time the Industrial Revolution had progressed sufficiently so that many articles formerly made at home could now be bought more cheaply. In the more thickly settled regions of the Northeast domestic manufacture largely gave way to factory processes. This tendency brought greater specialization of work on the part of the men and more leisure for the women. Eventually it took many men and women away from agriculture and into factory work. Improved and factory-made machinery simplified and to some extent made agricultural labor easier, but most of the changes in actual living condition came of necessity first to the city dwellers. After the 'twenties, candles as a means of lighting slowly gave way to oil and, in the larger cities, to gas. Street lighting by gas was adopted in Boston in 1822, in New York in 1823, and in Philadelphia in 1837. Anthracite coal had been known to exist in the Wyoming Valley since 1762, and in the Lehigh Valley since 1791, and shipments had been made to Philadelphia as early as 1805; but it was not used for home heating until 1815. Its extensive use was delayed by the difficulties of transportation and the expense of installing grates and stoves. Canals and railroads solved the first problem, and the increasing cost of wood in the large cities made the solution of the second inevitable. By 1825 wood had been replaced by coal in a large number of homes in New York and Philadelphia, and in the Northeast during the succeeding years kitchen fireplaces were closed up and iron ranges

---

[8] See tables in N. J. Ware, *The Industrial Worker, 1840–1860*, pp. 27 ff.

put in their place, while fireplaces in other parts of the house gave way to iron stoves. The drudgery of housekeeping was also lightened by the substitution of tinware for much of the older and heavier iron and copper, a boon brought to the housewife by the ubiquitous Yankee peddler.

The problem of water supply was naturally a pressing one in the growing cities. Until well into the century, most of the water for city dwellers was obtained from cisterns, house pumps, or various community pumps scattered throughout the city. After 1799 water from the Schuylkill River was raised by steam pumps to a reservoir and distributed through log pipes to a small part of Philadelphia. This system was improved and extended in 1822 by the opening of the Fairmount Waterworks, which conveyed the water by iron pipes through the entire city. Wooden pipes carried water to lower New York up to 1842,[9] when the aqueducts were finished and Croton water was brought to the city. By that year all the larger cities were supplied by artificial means.

Problems of urban transportation were attacked first in New York City, where an omnibus line was established before 1828, running between Wall Street and Greenwich Village. The first omnibus in Philadelphia appeared in 1831.[10]

While the conveniences of life were increasing, some advance was also made in providing for public safety. The old and inefficient night watch which lit the lamps, cried out the hours of the night, and gave the alarm for fires was superseded in 1845 by an organization of day and night watchmen more nearly approximating our police force of today. As a matter of fact, the modern police system extends back hardly more than ninety years. Up to the decade of the 'fifties organized fire fighting had been carried on by volunteer groups—at their best enthusiastic and efficient, but at their worst little better than gangs of city toughs more interested in fighting a rival gang than in extinguishing a fire. This decade saw the beginning of the end of the volunteer fire department in the larger cities.

Of great influence in stimulating the economic and social life of the people was the Act of 1845 which introduced cheap postage. The charge on letters weighing not over a half ounce and going less than three hundred miles was now five cents; over that limit it was ten cents, with an additional charge for extra weight. Further reductions were made in 1851, when a half-

---

[9] The first effort to supply New York with water from a central reservoir was undertaken by the Manhattan Water Company, a concern created by a legislative bill proposed by Aaron Burr in 1799. In reality this company was a banking corporation disguised as a water company and was created to compete with Hamilton's Bank of New York. As a natural result the company took little interest in the water project, but was successful as a bank; it continues in existence today as the Bank of Manhattan.

[10] Above, p. 291.

ounce letter prepaid would be carried 3000 miles for three cents, or, if not prepaid, for five cents; for 3000 miles and over, the respective rates were six and twelve cents. By 1840 the penny newspaper had made its appearance upon the streets, competing newspapers had commenced their keen rivalry for news, and the mass of Americans, from the unskilled laborer to the powerful capitalist, became the slave of the daily paper—an institution purporting to exist to carry news, but usually spreading propaganda for some interest, political or economic. The news-spreading function of the papers and their ability to keep the people cognizant of what was happening in the world at large were made possible by the invention of the telegraph and its introduction after 1844. The effect of the invention of the steamboat and the steam railway was also considerable in promoting travel, in breaking up intellectual isolation, and in modifying intellectual provincialism to a slight extent.

As a whole, the American people during these early decades were not given to spending much for amusements. De Tocqueville remarked that people who spent every weekday making money and every Sunday in going to church "have nothing to invite the muse of comedy." [11] Other European visitors spoke of the haste and intense application of Americans to business, to the neglect of amusements. Possibly the Puritan antecedents of many may have accounted for the neglect in some cases, but the conquest of a continent in less than a century left little time for anything but work. Quilting parties, husking bees, house raisings, and church affairs continued to afford opportunities for social life in the rural districts; occasionally in the East a traveling group of actors gave a performance. On the frontier the social and economic life of colonial days was duplicated again and again as the line advanced. In the South the social life had changed little since colonial days. Visits back and forth on the plantations and occasionally a winter season in the city provided a change for the women, and hunting parties and horse racing gave amusement to the men. In the cities the period from the 'thirties to the 'fifties was the golden age of the lyceum. Public lectures on all kinds of subjects were very popular; it was a time when curiosity about anything unusual was highly developed, and exhibitions in phrenology, mesmerism, and the like drew great crowds. The theater, however, was in its infancy here, and an American school of actors had not yet risen. Foreign artists appeared and were welcomed in New York and Philadelphia, the centers of what drama there was; but the crowds were apparently drawn by curiosity rather than by any understanding of the dramatic art.

The culture of the three decades prior to the Civil War may have been crude and chaotic, but it was exceedingly alive and virile. It was an age of

[11] Alexis De Tocqueville, *Democracy in America*, II, Chap. XIX.

idealism, of humanitarianism, and of reform, in which rapid strides were made toward a better civilization. These years have been called the "hot-air period" of American history, and there were doubtless many cranks and false prophets; but this was also the era of Dorothea Dix, Samuel G. Howe, Elizabeth Cady Stanton, Robert Owen, and Horace Mann. It was also the era of Melville, Hawthorne, Thoreau, Emerson, Whitman, Webster and Lincoln—to name only the most outstanding of a host of geniuses who were molding American life.

CONDITIONS OF LABOR

Scarcity of skilled labor is a normal condition in a new country. As a consequence the status of the American wage earner relative to that of similar workers in the industrial nations of western Europe was fairly high, at least until the decade of the 'forties. Victor Clark estimates that the wages of unskilled labor in this country were between one-third and one-half higher than in Great Britain and those of skilled workers somewhat less. While the lot of the skilled laborer was tolerable, the unskilled laborer, although commanding greater wages than in Europe, barely made ends meet. His pay averaged about half that of skilled labor. Two shillings at the time of the Revolution was a day's pay; this increased to about 90 cents a day in 1800 and $1.00 in 1825, and remained around this point for many years, even during the activity of canal and railroad building. His condition at the opening of the century is gloomily pictured by McMaster:

Sand sprinkled on the floor did duty as a carpet. There was no glass on his table, there was no china in his cupboard, there were no prints on his wall. What a stove was he did not know, coal he had never seen, matches he had never heard of. . . . He rarely tasted fresh meat as often as once in a week, and paid for it a much higher price than his posterity. . . .

If the food of an artisan would now be thought coarse, his clothes would be thought abominable. A pair of yellow buckskin or leathern breeches, a checked shirt, a red flannel jacket, a rusty felt hat cocked up at the corners, shoes of neat's-skin set off with huge buckles of brass, and a leathern apron, comprised his scanty wardrobe. The leather he smeared with grease to keep it soft and flexible.[12]

Farm hands received from $7.00 to $15.00 a month, with board, depending upon season and locality; the general average tended from the lower to the higher figure as time went on. Without board, the compensation of agricultural laborers rose from 50 cents a day at the opening of the century to $1.50 and even $2.00 by 1860.[13] The wages of skilled labor, both agricultural

[12] J. B. McMaster, History of the People of the United States, I, 96–97.
[13] P. W. Bidwell and J. I. Falconer, History of Agriculture in the Northern United States, 1620–1860, pp. 275–277, 495.

and industrial, ran from $1.00 to $2.00 a day, although they often went much higher.

Factory workers also commanded higher wages than in Europe. Neverthe-less, between 1830 and 1860 in Massachusetts, where wages were highest, men earned $5.00 a week, children between $1.00 and $2.00, and women from $1.75 to $2.00 a week, the latter figures including board. Wages were lower in Pennsylvania and the southern states.

In comparison with modern wage scales the above compensations seem small indeed. But wage scales, of course, have no meaning except in relation to prices. During the 'thirties men could obtain board and room for from $1.75 to $2.00 a week; for women the cost ran from $1.25 to $1.50. As both were earning double this amount a margin of half their salary was left for other expenses. This might be enough for single men or women, even enough for them to save something; but it was inadequate to support a family unless more than one member was working. In other words, the situation was not unlike that of the average wage earner today.

Foreign travelers were particularly impressed with the lack of poverty and with the opportunities which they believed existed for the wage earner. Said the Irishman, Thomas Mooney, in 1850: "The lowest wages going in the United States for a labourer's day's work is seventy cents, or about three shillings British money. This would be eighteen shillings for a week; and you can obtain good board, lodging and washing for a little less than ten British shillings, or two and a half dollars a week. So that you will be able to save seven or eight shillings a week to buy a farm, which farm you can buy for five shillings an acre. . . . Remember that, if you please, you can, as soon as you get a regular employment, save the price of an acre and a half of the finest land in the world every week, and in less than a year you will have money enough to start for the west, and take up an eighty-acre farm which will be your own forever." [14]

As is often the case, Mooney's deductions looked better on paper than in reality. In actual practice few immigrant wage earners escaped to the frontier by this route. With enthusiasm if not accuracy, another traveler asserted: "Pauperism, the gaunt and hideous spectre, which has extended its desolating march over Asia and Europe, destroying its victims by thousands, even in the midst of luxury and wealth, has never yet carried its ravages into the United States; this is a blessing of which it is to be feared that few appreciate the magnitude, and which is, of itself, a preponderating weight in the balance of national happiness. . . . It is a fact no less surprising than pleasing to record, that, during two years spent in traveling through every part of the

[14] Thomas Mooney, *Nine Years in America* (1850), p. 37.

Union, I have only once been asked for alms."[15] That grim poverty existed, particularly in the cities and notably in the 'forties and 'fifties, we have ample evidence.

One fact that can be stated with certainty is that the introduction of the factory system was not attended with the extreme horrors which accompanied the change in England. In America most of the cloth had either been purchased from Europe or been made by women on the farm as part of their household duties. The factory system therefore threw few men out of labor, and the factories for many years had to compete for labor with the more alluring prospects of independence on a frontier farm. Moreover, the early textile mills in New England were largely cotton mills; up to that time cotton had not been manufactured to any great extent at home. Hence no large group of hand operatives was thrown out of employment. The early operatives in these mills were ordinarily girls or unmarried women who looked upon the chance of earning money and at the same time escaping from the drudgery and dependency of farm life as an opportunity rather than a misfortune, especially as working in the mills meant no loss of social standing. Many of the early mill owners were men of humanitarian instincts who, partly from desire and partly from necessity, made efforts to provide comfortable boarding houses, to safeguard the morals of their employees and, through donations of money for churches and libraries, to stimulate high aspirations. European observers were amazed at the high caliber of the factory girls and their comfortable living conditions. To Anthony Trollope, Lowell seemed "the realization of a commercial utopia" where the operatives were "taken in, as it were, to a philanthropical manufacturing college, and then looked after and regulated more as girls and lads at a great seminary, than as hands by whose industry profit is to be made out of capital."[16]

Harriet Martineau, writing of conditions as she saw them at Waltham in 1835, describes the life of the factory operatives:

I visited the corporate factory-establishment at Waltham, within a few miles of Boston. The Waltham Mills were at work before those of Lowell were set up. The establishment is for the spinning and weaving of cotton alone, and the construction of the requisite machinery. Five hundred persons were employed at the time of my visit. The girls earn two, and some three, dollars a-week, besides their board. The little children earn one dollar a-week. Most of the girls live in the houses provided by the corporation, which accommodate from six to eight each. When sisters come to the mill, it is a common practice for them to bring their mother to keep house for them and some of their companions, in a dwelling

---

[15] Charles A. Murray, *Travels in North America* (1839), II, 297.
[16] Anthony Trollope, *North America* (1864), pp. 245, 247.

built by their own earnings. In this case, they save enough out of their board to clothe themselves, and have their two or three dollars a-week to spare. Some have thus cleared off mortgages from their fathers' farms; others have educated the hope of the family at college; and many are rapidly accumulating an independence. I saw a whole street of houses built with the earnings of the girls; some with piazzas, and green venetian blinds; and all neat and sufficiently spacious.

The factory people built the church, which stands conspicuous on the green in the midst of the place. The minister's salary (eight hundred dollars last year) is raised by a tax on the pews. The corporation gave them a building for a lyceum, which they have furnished with a good library, and where they have lectures every winter,—the best that money can procure. The girls have, in many instances, private libraries of some merit and value.

The managers of the various factory establishments keep the wages as nearly equal as possible, and then let the girls freely shift about from one to another. When a girl comes to the overseer to inform him of her intention of working at the mill, he welcomes her, and asks her how long she means to stay. It may be six months, or a year, or five years, or for life. She declares what she considers herself fit for, and sets to work accordingly. If she finds that she cannot work so as to keep up with the companion appointed to her, or to please her employer or herself, she comes to the overseer, and volunteers to pick cotton, or sweep the rooms, or undertake some other service that she can perform.

The people work about seventy hours per week, on the average. The time of work varies with the length of the days, the wages continuing the same. All look like well-dressed young ladies. The health is good; or rather, (as this is too much to be said about health anywhere in the United States), it is no worse than it is elsewhere.

These facts speak for themselves. There is no need to enlarge on the pleasure of an acquaintance with the operative classes of the United States.[17]

This rosy picture of Miss Martineau's did not tell the whole story. While the condition of American operatives during the Industrial Revolution was undoubtedly much better than in Europe, it was not enviable. A paternalism in which the operatives lived in company houses, spent their earnings in company stores, worshiped in company churches, and had to submit to excessive supervision of their private lives would be considered intolerable today, and the long hours would tax the strength of even the hardiest farm girl. Nominal wages at the opening of the Industrial Revolution, it is true, gradually rose, but real wages fell. As in England, the increase of wealth due to machinery went largely into the hands of the capitalist class. The early mills were in most cases unsanitary and unhealthy places in which to work. Hours of labor were excessively long. According to Professor Ely: "The length of actual labor [1832] varied from twelve to fifteen hours. The New

[17] Harriet Martineau, *Society in America* (1837), II, 57–59.

England mills generally ran thirteen hours, but one mill in Connecticut ran fourteen hours, while the length of actual labor in another mill in the same State, the Eagle Mill at Griswold, was fifteen hours and ten minutes. The regulations at Paterson, New Jersey, required women and children to be at work at half-past four in the morning." [18] A committee of the Massachusetts Legislature, investigating the hours of labor of children in factories as affecting their education, reported in 1825: "It appears however that the time of employment is generally twelve or thirteen hours each day, excepting the Sabbath," and naïvely added, "which leaves little opportunity for daily instruction." [19] As late as 1845 the average hours of labor in the Lowell mills varied from eleven hours and twenty-four minutes in January to thirteen hours and thirty-one minutes in April, practically from sun to sun. An observer in Lowell in 1846 describes the hours of labor:

The operatives work thirteen hours a day in the summer time, and from daylight to dark in the winter. At half past four in the morning the factory bell rings, and at five the girls must be in the mills. A clerk, placed as a watch, observes those who are a few minutes behind the time, and effectual means are taken to stimulate to punctuality. This is the morning commencement of the industrial discipline—(should we not rather say industrial tyranny?) which is established in these Associations of this moral and Christian community. At seven the girls are allowed thirty minutes for breakfast, and at noon thirty minutes more for dinner, except during the first quarter of the year, when the time is extended to forty-five minutes. [20]

Children were at first not used in the Massachusetts mills to the extent that they were in England. The need of gathering workers together from the surrounding country and building quarters and boarding houses involved special problems with children. Nevertheless, as time went on the evil became widespread and was unchecked by law. This was particularly so in Rhode Island, southern New England, and elsewhere where it was common practice for manufacturers to contract for the labor of whole families rather than of individual adults. A report of a convention of New England mechanics and workingmen held at Boston in 1832 estimated that the children employed in manufactories constituted about two-fifths of the total number of workers. The *Mechanics' Free Press* for August 21, 1830, prints the following statement regarding children in the Philadelphia factories:

It is a well-known fact, that the principal part of the helps in cotton factories consists of boys and girls, we may safely say from six to seventeen years of age, and are confined to steady employment during the longest days of the year, from

---

[18] R. T. Ely, *Labor Movement in America*, p. 49.
[19] J. R. Commons, *et al.* (eds.), *Documentary History of American Industrial Society*, V, 59.
[20] *Ibid.*, VII, 132–133. From *The Harbinger*, Nov. 14, 1846, p. 366.

daylight until dark, allowing, at the outside, one hour and a half per day [for meals] . . . and that too with a small sum, that is hardly sufficient to support nature, while they [the employers] on the other hand are rolling in wealth of[f] the vitals of these poor children every day. We noticed the observations of our Pawtucket friend in your number of June 19, 1830, lamenting the grievances of the children employed in those factories. We think his observations very correct, with regard to their being brought up as ignorant as Arabs of the Desert; for we are confident that not more than one-sixth of the boys and girl employed in such factories are capable of reading or writing their own name. We have known many instances where parents who are capable of giving their children a trifling education one at a time, deprived of that opportunity by their employer's threats, that if they did take one child from their employ, (a short time for school) such family must leave the employment—and we have even known these threats put in execution. . . .[21]

While conditions for large groups of workers were relatively good during the early years of the Industrial Revolution, the situation changed notably in the 'forties. Immigration increased rapidly in that decade, crowding the cities and bringing a competition among laborers which speedily brought wage reductions. Beginning with the panic of 1837, practically every trade experienced radical reductions at a time when the cost of living, especially in the cities, was increasing. Horace Greeley estimated that the cost of provisions in New York City rose 50 per cent between 1843 and 1850, and in 1851 he estimated a minimum weekly budget for a family of five at $10.37. Yet at that time carpenters, plasterers, and bricklayers were averaging around $10 a week, and the majority of painters, hatters, cabinetmakers, and other skilled workmen were getting $4, $5, and $6 a week. One reformer estimated in 1845 that one person in seven in New York City was a pauper. All of this existed at a time when the housing problem in the cities was desperate, for the cities were flooded with immigrants more rapidly than houses could be built. Almost the only tinge of light in an otherwise black picture was the fact that the agitation for a shorter working day had cut down the work day in some mills to as low as eleven hours.

In the textile mills of New England and elsewhere conditions grew worse in the 'forties as wages were reduced and employers bound themselves more closely together by agreements as to wages, hours, and black lists, and extended their paternalism to intolerable lengths. Labor agents of textile manufacturers were still scouring the back country of New England for farm girls, but the "golden age" of the girl operative had passed. By 1850, says Ware, "the white-gowned girls who marched to welcome Presidents, who talked so intelligently to foreign visitors, who wrote poetry and stories filled

[21] *Ibid.*, V, 61–62.

with classical allusions, were no longer found in the cotton mills. They had been driven out by a prolonged and fruitless struggle to protect their standards."[22] They had also been driven out by the flood of Irish immigrants who were rapidly becoming a new labor force in the New England mills. Labor papers as well as reformers constantly and correctly complained that the condition of workers was growing worse, and resented the optimistic comments of foreign visitors.

EARLY LABOR ORGANIZATIONS

Three factors are chiefly responsible for the development of labor organizations in America—the coming of the Industrial Revolution, the concentration of labor in urban areas, and the changing economic position of the worker. Prior to the advent of the factory system most manufactured goods were produced in the home or small shop, and the products were the result of well-trained and skilled work. The typical workman learned his trade by serving as an apprentice, gained experience by working for wages for some years as a journeyman, and finished his career as a master workman. A laboring class, in the sense of people who spent their lives working for wages as employees, hardly existed in the colonial period. With the coming of machinery and the factory system this situation began to change. As machinery took the place of hand tools, the long training of the skilled craftsman became less necessary. The workman learned to run a machine rather than to produce by hand. Not only this, but he learned to handle just one type of machine, for specialization became characteristic of the new type of production. Moreover, the new machinery was expensive. Only the man with capital could afford to own it, and the worker must seek its owner if he wanted a job. Although hand production continued for many decades after the invention of machinery, the ability of machines to produce more cheaply doomed it in the end.

The necessity for the worker to seek the machine and to sell his services for wages created for the first time in this country a large wage-earning class. This tendency was undoubtedly speeded during the latter part of the eighteenth century and the early years of the nineteenth by the domination of the merchant-capitalist. He was the central figure in the nation's economic life during these years. He was essentially a wholesaler, an importer and exporter, who bought where it was cheapest and sold where he could secure the best prices. Sometimes he financed the individual worker or the small shop; often he expanded his business into manufacturing for himself. In

---

[22] The degradation of the worker during this period has been effectively discussed by N. J. Ware, *The Industrial Worker, 1840–1860*, particularly in Chaps. IV and VII. See also Vera Shlakman, *Economic History of a Factory Town*, Chaps. V and VI.

any event, he increased competition among manufacturers, forced prices down, and speeded the separation of master workmen and their employees. In this bitter competition for markets, and under the goad of the merchant-capitalist, employers saw no way of reducing prices except through lower wages and longer hours.

Under this pressure associations of master employers, hitherto chiefly interested in training apprentices and maintaining standards of workmanship and products, shifted their interests to reducing costs and increasing profits. Workingmen in turn slowly began to organize for their own protection. Short-lived local craft organizations appeared in the 1780's and more permanent unions in the 1790's. The Philadelphia shoemakers, for example, organized in 1792 and the New York printers established the Typographical Society in 1794. These societies were purely local, although organizations in the same trade were sometimes established in other cities and there was communication between them. Like unions in later years, these early organizations were primarily interested in obtaining higher wages, shorter hours, and better working conditions through collective bargaining, but they were also interested in sick and funeral benefits.

Although this early labor movement developed slowly and was localized in a few of the larger towns, it is interesting to note that even this early most of the techniques of later labor struggles were discovered and used. *Collective bargaining* was employed as early as 1799 by the Philadelphia shoemakers to effect a compromise in a wage dispute and was continually resorted to by many unions thereafter. *Strikes,* although not common, were recorded as early as 1786 when the printers of Philadelphia struck against their employers. *Walking delegates,* or *business agents* as they are usually called today, were appointed to see that agreements were lived up to. The *closed shop* goes back to 1794 when the Philadelphia shoemakers compelled each employer to hire only union members. Strikers often instigated *boycotts* against a firm which they were fighting, and on numerous occasions established control over apprenticeship to safeguard both their own wages and the quality of workmanship. The New York Typographical Society, for instance, complained in 1809, that "a superabuandance of learners, runaway apprentices and half-way journeymen as well as adults who had served less than half-time at their trade, had a depressing effect upon the wages of full-fledged workers." On the other hand, *employers' associations* were organized early for the purpose of protecting their own interests and opposing unions.

One of the most difficult problems faced by labor organizations was that of legal status. Under the English common law any combination of workmen formed to raise wages was a conspiracy against the public welfare. In the absence of statute law governing this point in America, the problem arose as to whether the English common law applied in this country. Between 1806 and 1815 six separate conspiracy trials were held, four of which were decided against the workers. Certain of the trials seemed to transcend the question at issue and to involve the political philosophy of Federalists and Republicans, with advocates of the Federalists upholding the English common law and Republicans insisting that it had no standing here. In such an economic, political, and class conflict, the court rooms were not without bias. Said the Federalist judge in the first trial: "In every point of view, this measure [the strike] is pregnant with public mischief and private injury, . . . tends to demoralize the workmen, . . . destroy the trade of the city, and leaves the pockets of the whole community to the discretion of the concerned. . . . A combination of workmen to raise their wages may be considered from a two-fold point of view: one is to benefit themselves, . . . the other is to injure those who do not join their society. The rule of law condemns both." [23] As time went on, however, the courts shifted their attention from the question as to whether a union of workers was a conspiracy to the means employed by labor to obtain its ends. The right of workers to join unions was finally recognized in a famous decision in 1842,[24] but for many years strikes, boycotts, and other labor weapons were subjects of legal action.

If any date can be set for the origin of the American labor movement, as we understand such a movement today, it is 1827 when the Philadelphia carpenters struck for a ten-hour day. They were immediately joined by the painters, glaziers, and bricklayers, and with this as a nucleus a Mechanics' Union of Trade Associations was organized which eventually included fifteen unions. Following the lead of Philadelphia, local unions sprang up in the leading cities, both on the eastern seacoast and in the Middle West, and more than a dozen city trade associations, like the Mechanics' Union of Trade Associations, appeared. Not only did this movement toward city-wide organization develop, but at least five unions—shoemakers, comb makers, carpenters, hand-loom weavers, and printers—established national organizations. The first national convention of labor representatives was held in 1834. This enlargement of union organization until it finally reached national proportions was made possible by increased population, growing urbanization, improved transportation facilities, and wider competition.

Labor organizations in America, it will be noted, began not in the factories but among the skilled workers in the trades. These men had spent years in acquiring their skills and they represented the more highly trained and alert group of workers. Their demands went beyond shorter hours and better

[23] J. R. Commons, *et al.* (eds.), *A Documentary History of American Industrial Society,* III, 230–233.

[24] Commonwealth *v.* Hunt, 4 Metcalf 111 (1842).

working conditions to include free schools, abolition of imprisonment for debt, restriction of child labor, mechanics' lien laws, equal taxation, direct election of public officials, and various other political and economic reforms.[25] In these they were often joined by reformers of various kinds and by workers and middle-class people unaffiliated with union organizations. So wide, in fact, was the reform program of these early unions that it could be achieved only through political action. Such action was now possible because of the wide extension of the suffrage in the new or revised state constitutions. In 1828 the Mechanics' Union of Trade Associations in Philadelphia proposed to the several unions in that city that they join in nominating candidates "to represent the interests of the working classes." This they did, and several of their candidates backed by the Jacksonian and other parties were elected. Other cities followed Philadelphia's example. In at least fifteen states local labor parties were formed and fifty labor papers founded. The strength of labor's first political effort was in the Northeast.

This first excursion into labor politics was brief and the results were local and temporary. The workers were new at the game of politics and confused by the skillful attacks of the old parties, and by 1832 the movement had virtually disappeared. Likewise this first wave of labor organization largely disintegrated with the panic of 1837. This temporary collapse of the labor movement left the field open to politicians and reformers of various kinds who hoped to rally labor to their reform schemes. The reforms advocated in the 'twenties were revived in the 'forties and new ones proposed. Of particular interest to labor as well as to other large elements in the country were the various projects for cooperative living advocated during these years. Utopian socialism had been brought to America in the 1820's by Robert Owen, who tried his experiment at New Harmony, Indiana. His project collapsed, but renewed interest was apparent in the late 'thirties and early 'forties after Horace Greeley and Albert Brisbane gave wide publicity to the cooperative organization advocated by the Frenchman, Charles Fourier. Unlike Owen, who stressed the overwhelming importance of environment on the character of human beings, Fourier emphasized the economy and efficiency that would result if mankind were organized into groups of from 300 to 1800 people (phalanxes) living in a central building (phalanstery), the group being to a large extent economically self-sufficing. Scores if not hundreds of "communities" of one kind or another were established in this country between 1820 and 1850, the most famous being Brook Farm, near Boston, where many of the best-known New England intellectuals resided at various times.

[25] Other reforms sometimes advocated by one group of labor or another included temperance, abolition of lotteries, abolition of capital punishment, abolition of monopolies, prohibition of private banks, abolition of compulsory military service and votes for women.

Through the influence of George Henry Evans, who had been prominent in the labor movement in New York, labor was also drawn closely into the activities of the "Agrarian League" and the land reform movement. Evans' program called for ending the sale of public land to companies and speculators and apportioning it in small amounts to actual settlers without charge. His agitation caught the attention of many in the dark days following the panic of 1837 and undoubtedly hastened the Homestead Act of 1862. Of more immediate value to labor than Evans' program was the progress toward a ten-hour day. What was left of organized labor after the panic made this an essential demand. Government employees obtained a ten-hour day in 1840, and gradually in the late 'forties and early 'fifties a few of the states began to pass ten-hour Acts, in some cases only for women and children. Although the efforts of organized labor during these years to improve the political and economic life of the worker seem slight, they were by no means fruitless. Many reforms which they advocated were eventually achieved; in this their cooperation played a part. The ten-hour day, for example, was widely accepted by the opening of the Civil War; this was only one type of legislation that labor had advocated. The important part labor played in the agitation for free public education has been admitted but probably not fully recognized. Almost all of the needed changes advocated during this great era of reform were part of the labor program.

During the 'fifties labor shifted from a policy of generally advocating reform to one of "old-line unionism." Discovery of gold in California, the rapid building of railroads, and other developments brought prosperity and higher prices. Labor responded by taking on new life and organizing new locals and new national unions. The Typographical Union founded a national organization in 1850, the Stone Cutters in 1853, the Hat Finishers in 1854, and the Moulders' International Union and the National Union of Machinists and Blacksmiths in 1857. Not only was unionization rapidly extended but it was organized upon a more practical, businesslike, solid basis. The panic of 1857 hit organization another blow, but this time labor was in a better position than it had been before to meet an economic depression.

SELECTED READINGS

Channing, E., *A History of the United States*, Vol. V, Chap. II.
Fairchild, H. P., *Immigration*, Chap. IV.
Stephenson, G. M., *History of American Immigration*, Chaps. I–XII.
Hansen, M. L., *The Atlantic Migration*, XI–XII.
Commons, J. R., *et al.* (eds.), *History of Labor in the United States*, Vol. I, pp. 169–230.

Beard, Mary, *A Short History of the American Labor Movement,* Chaps. I–VI.

Ware, N. J., *The Industrial Worker, 1840–1860,* Chaps. X–XV.

Bogart, E. L., and Thompson, C. M., *Readings in the Economic History of the United States,* Chap. XVI.

Flügel, F., and Faulkner, H. U., *Readings in the Economic and Social History of the United States,* pp. 251–259, 397–412.

16.

Economic Causes of the
Civil War

☆ ☆

Growth of Sectionalism

The fact that the political controversies preceding southern secession centered largely around the question of the further extension of the slave system and that one important result of the Civil War was the end of chattel slavery has often led historians to overemphasize this factor. That slavery was one of the main causes leading to the conflict of arms, no one will deny. That it was the "single cause," as Rhodes once asserted,[1] is an interpretation hardly warranted by facts. The Civil War was essentially a conflict of economic sections. It was by no means the first sectional conflict in our history, nor was it to be the last. During the War of 1812, New England leaders, for example, talked of secession at the time of the Hartford Convention. Twenty years later the South Carolina legislature passed an Ordinance of Nullification declaring the Tariff Acts of 1828 and 1832 not binding on the people of that state. The conflict of economic interests between the North and South had become so acute by 1860 that secession might have resulted without the complication of slavery.

The basic conflict between the two sections lay in the fact that the South was primarily agricultural and the North was becoming increasingly industrial. It was a friction between a plantation economy and a rising industrial capitalism. The agricultural life of colonial times, founded on the plantation system and perpetuated by the introduction of cotton, tended to make the South an agricultural and exporting section with little manufacturing. On the other hand, the North was steadily developing a commercial and manufacturing life. The opposition of interests first made itself felt on the question of the tariff. In the wave of nationalism following the War of 1812, southern leaders combined with northern in passing the protective tariff

[1] J. F. Rhodes, *Lectures on the Civil War.* p. 2.

317

of 1816; but by 1824 their attitude changed, and they vigorously opposed this and succeeding tariffs. The western states, desiring to build up a home market, had supported the tariffs of 1816, 1824, 1828, and 1832, but the growth of the southern market for their products made them inclined to shift their attitude. The doctrine of nullification, or state sovereignty, which had been earlier set forth by Kentucky in protest against the Alien and Sedition Acts and by New England in opposition to the War of 1812, was now reaffirmed by South Carolina against the "tariff of abominations" of 1828 and the tariff of 1832; the doctrine was never lost sight of and finally resulted in actual secession. The compromise tariff of 1833 registered a victory for the South, and her representatives, with the aid of the West, were able to prevent the adoption of the protective principle on a large scale until the Morrill Bill of 1861.

A similar battle was waged over the banking and currency system. The South in general, as a debtor region with a lack of liquid capital, favored easy banking laws and an expanded currency. In alliance with the frontier West she managed to destroy the Second Bank of the United States and to determine the banking system from 1836 until secession.

The South was victorious over the North not only in regard to tariff, currency, and banking, but also with respect to the public land policy and western expansion. Southern agriculture, tied up as it was with cotton and slavery, needed room for rapid expansion. Northern manufacturers, on the other hand, desired a more concentrated population and hence opposed measures which might encourage migration to the West. The South favored rapid sale of western lands in large tracts at low prices, while the North advocated smaller and more restricted sales at higher prices. These conflicting views resulted in a compromise in 1841, a preemption bill which provided for sales to actual settlers at a very low price. In actual practice, however, the southern planter found this law liberal enough for his needs, and in the 'fifties he vigorously opposed further liberalization of the land laws on the grounds that it would benefit the small white farmer and promote the rapid extension of free territory.

The same differences were to be seen in opinions on territorial expansion. Cotton production as practiced under slavery needed a constant supply of fresh land, and the demand for new slave territory was literally pushed on by its own weight. Furthermore, as the North began to surpass the South in population and wealth, it became more essential to the South to maintain a number of Senators sufficient to control the Senate and protect her interests. Southern leadership had largely favored the acquisition of Louisiana, Florida, Texas, and the lands won from Mexico, as well as the conspiracies to annex

Cuba. Opponents of the Mexican War were against expansion of the slave power rather than extension of territory.[2]

As long as the states of the Northwest found a market for their agricultural products in the South, they were inclined to support that section; but the building of canals and railroads eventually provided the trans-Appalachian states north of the Ohio with both an eastern and a European market. Quite as important, however, in linking the Old Northwest with the eastern seaboard states rather than with the South was the promise of free homesteads made by the Republican party. The alliance in the Republican party of 1860 of eastern manufacturers seeking high tariffs and western farmers demanding free lands was to the Southerner an unholy and malicious plot, and it meant the eventual defeat of the South. Southern leaders saw the issue clearly. Jefferson Davis openly declared that it was not the dictates of humanity or the desire to benefit the slaves that impelled the free-soil agitators to oppose the further extension of slavery. "Not at all. . . . It is that you may have an opportunity of cheating us that you want to limit slave territory within circumscribed bounds. It is that you may have a majority in the Congress of the United States and convert the government into an engine of northern aggrandizement. It is that your section may grow in power and prosperity upon treasures unjustly taken from the South, like the vampire bloated and gorged with the blood which it has secretly sucked from its victim. . . . You desire to weaken the political power of the southern states; and why? Because you want, by an unjust system of legislation, to promote the industry of the New England states, at the expense of the people of the South and their industry."[3]

SOUTHERN ECONOMY

The words of Jefferson Davis reflect with a fair degree of accuracy the attitude of the great majority of the cotton, tobacco, rice, and sugar planters of the South. Although, as we have seen,[4] the great mass of southern whites were small farmers, it was the plantation lords who dominated the economic, social, and political life of the South. "There was never in America," asserts Dodd, "a more perfect oligarchy of business men than that which ruled in the time of Jefferson Davis and Alexander Stephens."[5] These were the men whose opinions were followed in the South. They believed that the economic

[2] J. D. P. Fuller, "The Slavery Question and the Movement to Acquire Mexico, 1846–1848," *Mississippi Valley Historical Review*, XXI, 31–48 (June, 1934), argues convincingly, on the other hand, that many Southerners opposed annexation because the region was not suitable for slavery.

[3] Quoted by C. and M. Beard, *Rise of American Civilization*, II, 5–6.

[4] Above, pp. 66, 68.

[5] W. E. Dodd, *The Cotton Kingdom*, p. 121.

troubles of their section were the result of northern domination and that their problems could be solved only by political independence. It was the same belief that led plantation owners to favor independence from Great Britain in 1776. That the power of northern capitalism bore heavily upon them there can be no question. But that independence would have solved their problem is more than doubtful.

There is something inherent in a plantation economy that puts it in a dependent position in a capitalist world. Except under a system of highly regulated central control unknown in the nineteenth century, southern plantation owners had no more control over national production or prices than the wheat farmer in the 1920's. The price of cotton was determined by the world market. If it was sufficiently high so that a profit was realized, there was a tendency to increase production. In the South this meant investment of profits in land and slaves. If prices were low and the year's crop was sold at a loss, the planter had to borrow to carry himself until the next year, and he pledged his future crop as security for the loan. In either case he was left without liquid capital. It was easy under such a situation to fall into debt and to be overcharged by the bankers who lent him money and the commission men who marketed his crop. He began with no control over prices or total production and ended by dependence upon those who financed his operations.

How this operated in the pre-war South is easy to describe. To meet the expense of raising his crop the planter borrowed from his factor [6] at interest rates of from 8 to 12 per cent, pledging his future crop. If there was a surplus, the factor sold it at the prevailing price, charging a commission of from one-half of one per cent to 2.5 per cent. Hauling, storage, freight, weighing, and insurance cost an additional 2.5 to 4 per cent. To protect himself against loss it was customary for the factor to stipulate a minimum number of bales to be delivered and to make a penalty charge for failure. This, with other conditions, tended toward overproduction and resulting low prices.

The funds which financed this production came largely from British and northern banks. Payments were made in 120-day New York drafts or 60-day sterling bills of exchange which were discounted by southern banks. If there was a demand for these drafts or for sterling exchange in New York, the discount rates favored the planter. If there was little demand, he was at a disadvantage. Moreover, the price of cotton was inevitably influenced by exchange rates. This hazard was particularly acute during the panic of 1857 when exchange rates dropped, cotton buying slowed down, and the price of cotton fell. The South lost heavily during that year in a situation over which she had no control. This panic brought home more clearly than ever before

[6] In this case, a combination of banker's representative and commission merchant.

the fact that New York had become a bottleneck through which flowed the greater part of the financial transactions of the South and that southern prosperity might be dependent upon the condition of the money market in that city.

One important effect of the investment of a large proportion of southern wealth in land and slaves for the production of commercial crops was the one-sided economic life which it produced. Although many slaves became skilled mechanics, slave labor as a whole was too ignorant for large-scale industrial development. Whether it was or was not fitted for industry, the fact remains that the slave owner believed his labor was more profitable when expended in agriculture. Skilled white mechanics in general avoided the South. Although water power and cotton were both at hand, there was little liquid capital to invest in manufacturing, and the planter preferred to send his products to the mills of New England or Europe. The great industrial progress which encompassed the North in the two decades before the war largely passed by the South. Except in cotton manufacturing and iron founding, development was trivial.

COTTON MANUFACTURING IN NEW ENGLAND AND THE SOUTH, 1840–1850

	Census	Plants	Capital	Operatives
Southern states	1840	248	$ 4,331,078	6,642
	1850	166	7,256,056	10,043
New England	1840	674	34,931,399	46,834
	1850	564	53,832,430	61,893

The paucity of industrial development in the southern states was only too well illustrated after the war broke out, when the Confederacy found itself hopelessly dependent upon the outside for the simplest manufactured products. The planters of the Southwest even imported their corn and bacon from north of the Ohio in order to devote their whole plantation to cotton. The one-sidedness of southern economic life is thus pessimistically described by Helper, who produced the most scathing indictment to come from the pen of a Southerner:

In one way or another we are more or less subservient to the North every day of our lives. In infancy we are swaddled in Northern muslin; in childhood we are humored with Northern gewgaws; in youth we are instructed out of Northern books; at the age of maturity we sow our "wild oats" on Northern soil; in middle life we exhaust our wealth, energies and talents in the dishonorable vocation of entailing our dependence on our children and on our children's children, and, to the neglect of our own interests and the interests of those around us, in giving aid and succor to every department of Northern power; in the decline of life we remedy our eye-sight with Northern spectacles, and support our infirmities with Northern canes; in old age we are drugged with Northern physic; and, finally, when we die, our inanimate bodies, shrouded in Northern cambric, are stretched upon the bier, borne to the grave in a Northern carriage, entombed with a Northern spade, and memorized with a Northern slab.[7]

Lack of space forces us to leave to economic textbooks the arguments pro and con as to whether a region should specialize on the type production for which it is best fitted or whether it should attempt to develop a well-rounded and self-sufficient economic life. The South was preeminently fitted to produce certain subtropical staples, which she did, at the same time purchasing her manufactured commodities from Europe and the North and considerable foodstuffs from the Old Northwest. Conditions being what they were, it was quite unlikely that she would or could have done otherwise.

Nevertheless, the situation proved detrimental to the South. Whether the Southerners sold their staples at a good or poor price, they ordinarily bought their manufactured goods at a high price. For this they blamed the tariff. The effects of the tariff upon the South were probably less bad than was generally believed. She won the tariff fight in 1833 and except for brief periods the rates continued downward until the Civil War. Certainly, after 1857[8] tariff rates were low. More valid, perhaps, was the resentment of Southerners over the fact that, as an importing section, they paid a disproportionate amount in taxation to support the federal government. They argued correctly that a shift of policy from indirect to direct taxation would bring larger contributions from the North and so bear more equitably upon the whole country.

More detrimental to the South than the tariff was the costly system through which she purchased her manufactured commodities. Manufactured goods from the North were financed by northern bankers, brought to the South in northern ships, and distributed by northern jobbers or middlemen. Between the South and Europe there was little direct trade. A large proportion of southern cotton was shipped to New York and then to Europe. The return cargoes of manufactured goods went to northern ports and were then distributed throughout the South in the coastwise trade. This "cotton triangle" involved higher transportation costs and added commissions to middlemen. There is no doubt that the South would have benefited by the development of direct trade with Europe. There is great doubt, on the other hand, that the elimination of all tariffs would have greatly changed the existing trade

[7] H. R. Helper, *The Impending Crisis of the South*, pp. 22–23. Helper was a middle-class Southerner from North Carolina who believed that slavery was ruining the South both economically and socially. His famous book, based largely on the Census of 1850, was and still is considered by Southerners a strongly biased picture. See his biography in the *Dictionary of American Biography*.

[8] Richard Hofstadter, "The Tariff Issue and the Civil War," *American Historical Review*, XLIV, 50–55 (Oct., 1938).

routes or the system of distributing imported commodities. But Southerners believed that it would, and this fact is important in understanding their discontent.

Development of Slavery

Although the rivalry of economic interests was fundamental in explaining the Civil War, it is impossible to escape the important part played by the slave system. In the first place, slavery accentuated the economic differences between the South on the one hand and the North and the Northwest on the other, and, in the second place, the political means whereby the South sought to protect herself from the growing strength of her economic rivals became closely related with the extension of slavery. It is for these reasons, as well as the fact that the economic life of the South was strongly colored by the slave system, that the development and effects of slavery should be studied closely.

Slavery, which had flourished in the colonial South, was on the defensive at the close of the Revolution. Losses incurred by the planters in the War of Independence, the exhaustion of the soil in the coast states, and the influx of white settlers from the North into these regions all tended to to make the system less profitable. These influences, augmented by the Revolutionary theories unfavorable to slavery, led many Southerners to question its economic and moral basis, but it was still firmly intrenched in 1781 in the rice and indigo fields of the Carolinas and Georgia, although its hold on the tobacco plantations had been weakened. The factors which contributed beyond all others to revive an apparently dying institution were the introduction of Sea Island cotton and the invention of the cotton gin (1793) simultaneously with the coming of the Industrial Revolution. The first gave the planters of the coast regions an opportunity to recoup their waning fortunes, the latter made it possible to raise profitably the inland short-fibered variety; and both led to the rapid extension of cotton culture into the uplands and westward.

In cotton the South found a crop that apparently paid with slave labor, for the requisite conditions necessary to make it profitable seemed ideally combined. The first of these was simplicity of operation; slavery thrives under a one-crop system of agriculture, the methods of which can be learned and mechanically repeated year after year. Cotton is a comparatively easy plant to raise, and the labor of the Negro could be adapted to it. Few tools and little equipment were needed, so that small loss was sustained even from inefficient labor. Cotton culture extends over three-fourths of the year, and in its production, more than in that of many other staples, it was possible to give employment to women and children, thus obtaining the maximum return from an entire family.

Still another advantage was the fact that the slaves could be more compactly massed in raising cotton than in raising many other products. A single laborer could work only three acres of rice and only five to ten acres of cotton, while he might cultivate thirty or forty acres of corn, a significant fact when it is appreciated that the labor of slaves is usually secured only under compulsion and that constant supervision is necessary. Supervision, moreover, was expensive. "To diminish the inducement for overdriving," says Professor Phillips, "the method of paying the overseers by crop shares, which commonly prevailed in the colonial period, was generally replaced in the nineteenth century by that of fixed salaries." [9] An overseer's salary in 1863 was about $1300, a considerable amount of cash. The comparatively high cost of white overseers contributed as much as anything in shifting slave labor largely to cotton plantations.

A further condition necessary to the profitable employment of slave labor is cheapness and ease of subsistence. The expenditure for shelter, fuel, and clothing was naturally not great in the warm climate of the cotton belt. The slave's chief food was bacon and corn; consequently some corn was usually raised on the plantation to provide food for slaves and hogs, although in later years considerable corn and pork were obtained from the states north of the Ohio. The cost of maintaining a slave ranged from $15 a year under the most favorable conditions to from $30 to $40 on the border states; the average was about $20 a year.

Important also in fastening slavery on the South was the abundance of unoccupied land in the West. Slave labor, incompetent and ignorant as it was, condemned the cotton planter to a one-crop system. Although cotton was less destructive to the soil than other staples, especially tobacco, its uninterrupted growth without the use of fertilizer meant the wearing out of the soil. As land was cheaper than slaves, the tendency was to "butcher the land" by planting crops of cotton until it was exhausted, and then pushing on to new and fertile fields and repeating the process. This procedure was aided by the fact that most of the land was suitable for cotton. Thus slavery was dependent on a one-crop economy, which in turn, under the agricultural methods pursued, depended on the opening up of new lands. These facts explain in part the rapid westward advance of the cotton planter and the apparently insatiable hunger of the slaveholder for new land. They also explain why it was possible even with declining cotton prices and inefficient labor to continue to raise cotton at a profit. Until the fresh cheap land was exhausted, slavery seemed able to hold its own against the competition of free labor.

The southern states during the first half-century produced about seven-eighths of the world's cotton supply. The demand for it was steady and

[9] Ulrich B. Phillips, *American Negro Slavery* (1918), p. 281.

increasing. Whoever had slaves or could buy them turned more and more to raising cotton. DeBow estimated in 1850 that 2,500,000 of the 3,204,313 slaves were engaged in agriculture, and of these 72.6 per cent (1,815,000) were employed on cotton.[10] As the cotton planter pushed westward into the fertile lowlands of Alabama and Mississippi and a continually greater area was put under cultivation, the demand for slaves increased.[11] The wealthy planters were able to obtain the choicest lands, thus driving the poor whites to the small and less fertile farms where they raised food crops; these farmers would not or could not compete with slave labor, carried on as it was upon the big plantations. Not only were the efforts of the poor native whites largely withdrawn from cotton raising, but the labor situation in the South repelled the immigrant. The slaveholding states contained 378,205 foreign-born in 1850, the non-slave states 1,866,397; this constituted 3.91 per cent and 13.89 per cent, respectively, of the aggregate population of the sections.

The demand for slaves was met by natural increase and by importation from Africa, though the latter was illegal after 1808. There was also considerable internal slave trade. The surplus Negroes in the border states and the eastern Carolinas were shipped south to be sold to the cotton planters of the new states. The natural increase of the slave population on the cotton plantations was very slight; on the sugar plantations of Louisiana it was less than the waste of life. On the other hand, the border states developed a hardy type of Negro, longer lived and more prolific, so that the population increase on the Virginia farms amounted frequently to 20 per cent. With the growing demand for Negroes there was a corresponding rise in the price. The average value of slaves in 1798 has been estimated at about $200; in 1815, at $250; in 1840, at $500; and in 1860, at $700. "Prime field hands," however, who sold for $200 in 1780 brought from $350 to $500 in 1800, $700 to $1000 in 1818, $1200 to $1800 and $2000 in 1860.[12] The increase was not steady, but varied with periods of prosperity and depression, which in turn were dependent on the price of cotton.

Not only was it now possible for the border states of Virginia, Maryland, and Kentucky to get rid of their surplus laborers, but it became more and more profitable for the slaveholders there to raise Negroes to "sell south."

[10] J. D. B. DeBow, *Statistical View of the United States . . . Being a compendium of the Seventh Census* (1854), p. 94, note.

[11] The approximate Negro population, 1740–1860, is as follows. The estimate is taken from *The South in the Building of the Nation,* V, 111, note.

1740	140,000	1820	1,777,000
1776	300,000	1830	2,328,000
1790	750,000	1840	2,873,000
1800	1,002,000	1850	3,638,000
1810	1,380,000	1860	4,441,000

[12] *Ibid.,* V, 127.

Professor Dew of William and Mary College asserted in 1832 that Virginia was "a *negro* raising State for other States; she produces enough for her own supply, and six thousand for sale,"[13] and Olmsted estimated that in the ten years preceding 1860 the annual export of Negroes from the border states was about 25,000. Negroes formed 50 per cent of the population of Virginia in 1782 and only 37 per cent in 1860. Regarding this aspect of the slave trade the fact should be emphasized that there was little if any intentional breeding for the slave trade. Certain sections where the land had deteriorated and where slavery had become unprofitable found themselves with a surplus of Negroes. Hard pressed economically, masters were forced to dispose of their slaves in the southern market, often against their own wishes. The accompanying figures presented by Cairnes illustrate the constant draining off of slaves from the border states by the internal trade, as well as the decline of the system in the northern states.

PERCENTAGE INCREASE OF POPULATION IN THE DECADE ENDING 1850[14]

State	Whites	Slaves
Virginia	20.77	5.21
Maryland	31.34	0.70
Kentucky	28.99	15.75
Arkansas	110.16	136.26
Mississippi	65.13	58.74
Louisiana	61.23	45.32

To explain adequately the importance which southern leaders attached to the slave system, one further point should be emphasized. Southern wealth was invested primarily in cotton, land, and slaves. The value of cotton declined especially in the 'forties as greater quantities were thrown upon the market (see p. 351), and the value of the land simultaneously decreased under the wasteful methods then employed. Regions could be seen in the Southwest which in less than fifty years had advanced from a howling wilderness to a profitable agricultural economy, and then had declined to uninhabited wastes.[15] While cotton and land values declined, the price of slaves continued to mount. Thus, the one form of southern wealth that became more valuable as the years passed was investment in slaves. Under such circumstances it is not surprising that the Southerner placed an exaggerated value on this form of property, and that the perpetuation of the slave system seemed essential to southern prosperity.

[13] Thomas R. Dew, in *The Pro-Slavery Argument* (1852), p. 359.

[14] John E. Cairnes, *The Slave Power* (2nd ed., enlarged, 1863), p. 130.

[15] See above, p. 193; also F. L. Paxson, *History of the American Frontier*, p. 206, and G. S. Callender, *Selections from the Economic History of the United States*, pp. 765–767.

Threshing in the Age of Horse Power.

An Early McCormick Reaper—Probably the Second Type Invented by Him.

Haying by Hand and Horse Power.

Slaughter House in 1860. Meatpacking Had Already Become an Important American Industry.

Early Gold Mining in California. One Miner Is Rocking the Cradle While His Partner Brings the Results of His Diggings from a Nearby Stream.

Drake's First Oil Well, 1859. Depth, 69½ feet; Production, 20 Barrels a Day.

A River Steamboat Taking on Wood.

Model of John Fitch's First Steamboat.

South Street, New York, in 1855.

The Bettmann

U. S. M. Steam Ship *Atlantic*. Typical Transatlantic Steamship of the Middle
Nineteenth Century. Lithograph by N. Currier.

Photo by Brown Brothers

Immigrants Arriving. A Drawing Made in 1851.

New England Factory Workers—"Bell Time." Drawing by Winslow Homer.

Yankee Peddler. An Important Phase of Early American Commerce.

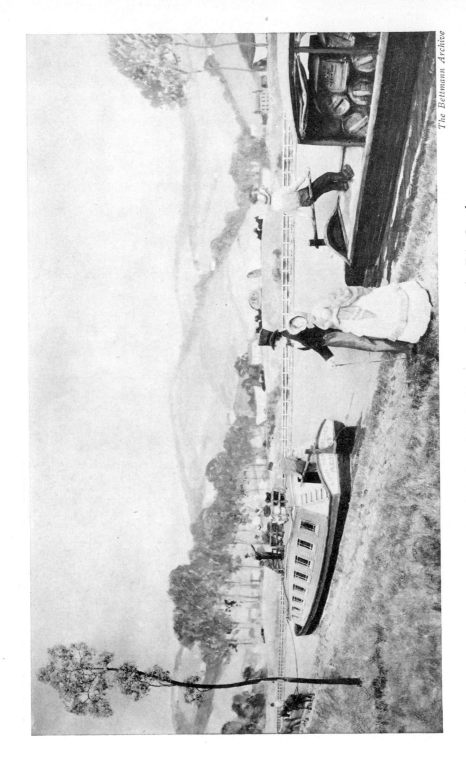

A Modern Painting of Early Transportation on the Erie Canal.

Some southern economists went even further and asserted that land values in the older states were dependent upon the institution of slavery. "It is, in truth, the slave labor in Virginia," said Professor Dew, "which gives value to her soil and her habitations;—eject from the State the whole slave population, and we risk nothing in the prediction, that on the day in which it shall be accomplished, the worn soils of Virginia would not bear the paltry price of the government lands in the West, and the Old Dominion will be a waste howling wilderness." [16]

The decade before the war saw both the maximum expansion of slavery and the early indications of its decline. Of the 12,000,000 people (in round numbers) in fifteen slave states, 4,000,000 were slaves. The production of cotton, the great staple of the South, was closely tied up with the institution, and the border states, whose land was exhausted or not adaptable to cotton, were unwittingly joined to the system as breeding grounds for slaves. At the same time, it was evident that the progress of slave labor was practically at a standstill in most of the South and was actually declining on the Atlantic seaboard and in the border states. Throughout the South white farmers and free laborers were increasing faster than slaves. The more rapid growth of the white population presaged even in the South an approaching struggle between white and slave labor, a contest in which slavery would be at an increasing disadvantage as the better land was absorbed.

Slavery in the South

The census in 1860 gave the white population of the slave states at 8,099,-760 and the slaves at 3,953,580. The slaves were owned by only 384,000 whites, of whom 107,957 owned more than ten slaves, 10,781 owned fifty or more, and 1733 owned one hundred or more. At least 6,000,000 southern whites were not interested directly in slave ownership. Nevertheless, the fact that the great staple upon which the wealth and prosperity of the South depended was raised largely by slaves under a plantation system gave the institution an importance which the number of slaveholders would not seem to warrant. The slaveholding aristocracy produced able politicians who so molded opinion in the South that when the break came in 1860 the great majority of whites were behind the secession movement. There is no better example in modern history of a handful of the ruling class so shaping public opinion as to bring on a war to preserve an institution which benefited themselves alone.

As three-fourths of the slaves were engaged directly in agriculture and most of them in the production of cotton, the typical life of the slave was

[16] Thomas R. Dew, in *The Pro-Slavery Argument*, p. 358.

life on the plantation. The most intelligent and trusted Negroes, often those with a mixture of white blood, were employed as household servants. On the plantation there were often Negro carpenters, blacksmiths, and drivers, but the great mass of slaves—men, women, and children—were occupied in the fields. The owner was usually his own overseer on the smaller plantations, but on the larger he was forced to turn over the direct management to hired white overseers. These were in turn assisted by drivers, trusty Negroes who set the pace or supervised small groups. Work on a plantation was carried on in one of three ways: by the task system, in which a definite amount of work for the day was assigned to each slave according to his ability; by the gang system, in which a good driver set the pace and the rest followed; or simply by setting the slave to work with no incentive but the fear of the lash. Absentee ownership was not widely prevalent in the South, but where it existed it was a great curse, involving as it did the employment of a hired overseer. Good overseers were scarce. Ordinarily of the poor-white class, they were not recognized as the social equals of their employers; often they were working temporarily as overseers to obtain money to become slave owners themselves. They were but one step removed from the professional slave dealer, who socially was decidedly under the ban. As the overseer was judged chiefly by his ability to produce a large crop, the typical overseer was likely to drive the slaves to the limit and to abuse the land more than an owner who directly supervised his plantation. Where the plantation was supervised by the owner, and especially on small plantations, the condition of the slaves was likely to be better.

Speaking broadly, the economic condition of a slave was not far above that of a well-kept farm animal of the present day. Likewise, it was not far different from that of the poorer laborers of the North. House servants inherited the cast-off clothing of the master's family and had enough to eat, but few comforts. The field hands worked usually from sunrise to sunset, cooked their own meals, and were lodged in cabins to the rear of the plantation, where furniture and cleanliness were notable by their absence. The ordinary food was corn bread and bacon. More humane masters sometimes allowed the slaves to cultivate a small garden patch and to keep a few chickens or a pig, varied their diet at times, and gave them holidays and presents. The more intelligent owners and those whose plantations were conducted most scientifically exerted great care with respect to the sanitation and health of the slaves and made some provision for their amusement and spiritual welfare. While teaching the Negro to read and write was forbidden in five states in the belief that it made him discontented, religious instruction was often given. Although he undoubtedly delighted in religious expression, any attempt to inculcate, through religious teaching, habits of honesty and chastity in men and women who did not own their own bodies or the fruit of their labors was not easy. A marriage ceremony was often performed, although none of the states recognized slave marriage by law.

The abolition literature of the time gave much attention to the cruelties practiced upon the slaves. In a system in which absolute ownership of certain human beings rests in others, and labor is rendered chiefly because of fear of the lash, flogging naturally existed and wanton cruelty was sometimes perpetrated. It was not, however, the general practice, certainly not with the house servants. Conditions were worst on the sugar plantations of Louisiana, the rice fields of Georgia and South Carolina, and the large cotton plantations of the lower South, where gangs of slaves worked under the direction of white overseers whom Patrick Henry described as "the most abject, degraded, unprincipled race." Certain other forms of cruelty which went with the system, in particular the separation of families and their disposal on the auction block, were more often seen in the border states, where slaves were sold for the southern market. On the other hand, there were many estates whose slaves were comparatively happy and contented, where kindly relations existed between master and slave, and where the economic condition of the Negro was undoubtedly better than after emancipation. Manumission was restricted as dangerous, but many masters set their slaves free. The incomplete figures of the Census of 1860 put the number of slaves manumitted in that year at 3018, a ratio of one to every 1309 slaves. In that year there were about 262,000 free Negroes in the slave states. With regard to the whole question of the treatment of slaves, Professor Phillips' comment seems reasonable. "The theory of rigid coercion, and complete exploitation," he says, "was as strange to the bulk of the planters as the doctrine and practice of moderation was to those who viewed the régime from afar and with the mind's eye." [17]

Economic Advantages and Disadvantages of Slavery

The advantages of slave labor, which had been questioned before the introduction of cotton culture, were more and more reaffirmed as the century progressed. It was maintained that the absolute ownership of the workmen by the employer was advantageous to the latter because it allowed him to enjoy the entire fruit of the product of labor, to organize his labor force as he thought best, and to control his workmen through his single will to a definite end. The control of the full time of men, women, and children seemed to be the last word in the elimination of waste power. After the

[17] Ulrich B. Phillips, *American Negro Slavery*, pp. 293–294.

initial purchase, in case this was necessary, the only expense was to keep the slave healthy and strong. It was furthermore sincerely believed that Negro labor under slavery was the only kind that could be employed in the unhealthy work on the rice fields. While some enlightened Southerners believed that cotton could be raised with free labor, the great majority were convinced that only by means of slaves could large-scale cotton production be carried on; in fact, cotton culture seemed providentially designed to enhance the advantages of slave labor. Southern writers argued, not without grounds in some localities, that the slave in the South was better housed, better fed, and happier than the free unskilled laborer in either Europe or the northern states. Not only was the slave better off, they contended, but the master and his family, freed from the necessity for manual work, could devote their abilities to the amenities of life and to intellectual development, a contention certainly borne out in the case of the eight or ten thousand families who were able to live in luxury on the labor of Negroes. As attacks upon slavery grew stronger, the institution was defended upon the authority of Scripture, upon the theory of the inferiority of the colored race which doomed it to economic dependence, and finally, as necessary to the safety of the whites, for Southerners declared that the revolt in Haiti and spasmodic disturbances in this country plainly showed what would happen to the future civilization of the South if the slaves were freed.[18]

The advantages of slave labor were more apparent than real. In the first place, the labor was given reluctantly and without interest. There was small incentive to increase production, for this meant a greater expectation on the part of the owner; therefore, the slave tended to hide his true ability and to render less labor than he was capable of. The continued supervision of the overseer and the fear of the lash were necessary to produce results. The hired overseer was expensive as regards both salary and methods, for his business was to turn out a big crop, and this he was tempted to do (especially when cotton profits were large) to the detriment of both land and slaves. The labor of the Negro slave not only was often reluctant, but it was essentially unskillful. Not far removed from African barbarism, with small incentive for intellectual growth, and with his character brutalized by the system under which he lived, it is little wonder that the slave produced ignorant and wasteful labor. He could use only the simplest tools, and ordinarily it was difficult to train him to use machinery. The average slave lacked versatility and had to be given the simplest tasks and kept at work on operations constantly repeated. Furthermore, although the cost of clothing and feeding a slave was small—from $15 to $40 a year—when to this is added the

---

[18] For further contemporary arguments, see C. F. McCay in *Eighty Years' Progress*, pp. 119 ff., and Thomas R. Dew in *The Pro-Slavery Argument*.

interest on capital, depreciation, taxation, and insurance against sickness, flight, and death, the yearly expense for an able-bodied slave was not far from $135. Slaves were hired out in Georgia before the war at from $140 to $150 a year, but afterward, under a system of free labor, Negroes could be obtained for $120 a year with board.

As a whole, the weight of evidence points to the fact that slave labor under the conditions present just before the Civil War was economically unsound. Certain plantations efficiently managed and located on excellent land made good profits, and they did so despite slave labor, high interest rates, factors' commissions, and a generally disadvantageous economic system. When all the conditions were favorable, reasonable profits could be made. But all the conditions were rarely favorable and the average plantation operated on so close a margin that it was lucky in many years if it could show even a slight profit.[19] One thing is certain—the general prosperity of cotton production under the plantation system was declining in the years before the war, and slave labor was one of the contributing causes, not alone because it was inefficient, but also because of the increasing price of slaves.

Operating as he did under numerous handicaps, the cotton planter discovered a partial outlet in an unlimited extent of extremely fertile soil. Consequently, as already pointed out,[20] the planter, fortified with the wealth of the South, appropriated the richest land, used it up, and traveled on to new land. Whatever the immediate gains might be, the eventual effect was bound to be disastrous and out of all proportion to the gains. The extent of unused and exhausted land was very great in the seaboard states, almost resembling the havoc wrought by an invading army. Dickens, who was strongly anti-slavery, asserted in 1842 that the soil between Fredericksburg and Richmond had been "exhausted by the system of employing a great amount of slave-labour in forcing crops without strengthening the land, and it is now little better than a sandy desert overgrown with trees." He continues, with a touch of exaggeration, "In this district, as in all others where slavery sets brooding . . . there is an air of ruin and decay abroad which is inseparable from the system." [21] The accompanying table shows the relationship between developed and undeveloped land. The proportion of the latter was great in the South, for only the best land could be made to pay.

Under such conditions it is quite likely that the exhaustion of new land might in itself have forced a reorganization of the southern economy and

[19] Some typical examples are given in Louis Hacker, *The Triumph of American Capitalism,* pp. 318–320, taken from R. B. Flanders, *Plantation Slavery in Georgia,* pp. 221–223, and C. S. Sydnor, *Slavery in Mississippi,* pp. 196–197.

[20] Above, pp. 181 ff.

[21] Charles Dickens, *American Notes* (1842), Chap. IX, p. 51.

AGRICULTURAL DEVELOPMENT IN FREE AND SLAVE STATES [22]

	Free States and Territories	Border States (Ill., Md., Ky. and Mo.)	Slave States
Improved land, acres	88,730,678	17,547,885	56,832,157
Unimproved land, acres	72,983,311	27,474,315	143,644,192
Total quantity, acres . . .	161,713,989	45,022,200	200,476,349
Cash value	$4,091,818,132	$702,518,382	$1,850,708,493
Average value per acre	$25.30	$15.60	$9.28
Agricultural implements, value . .	$ 142,077,802	$ 21,068,903	$ 82,971,436
Livestock, value	574,067,208	133,484,109	381,778,598
Agricultural capital	4,807,963,142	857,071,394	2,315,458,529

doomed the slave system.[23] Such a situation, however, had not become acute by 1860. There was still plenty of land upon which to expand and the development of railroads was opening up still more. The problem was whether cotton culture on fresh lands could overcome all the handicaps including slavery. As Louis Hacker has well put it:

The pinch came, however, when reduction of rent cost by transference to new areas of operations was not sufficient. For while prices of necessaries needed for farm and home were going up, and the price of cotton was fluctuating critically, the price of field hands was also advancing. Why was this? It was due to the fact that superior methods of organization and their locations in new planting regions made it possible for lower South farmers to tempt away the slaves from the interior, the Border States, and the tidewater. That is to say, by the late 1850's, with scarcity in the available unfree labor supply, slave prices were based on their productivity under ideal conditions. To a large company of Southern planters, therefore, it was of the utmost importance that this form of capital costs also be reduced; and it could be done only by the legal reopening of the oversea slave traffic. The heart of the southern program was to be found at this point.[24]

THE DILEMMA OF THE SOUTH

By the 1850's the full effect of a plantation economy concentrating on one crop and operated by slave labor was apparent. The characteristic tendency of commercial planting regions to stress maximum current money income, to expand recklessly, and to live extravagantly when income was high, had prevented the accumulation of liquid capital and kept the South in an

[22] Ezra C. Seaman, *Essays on the Progress of Nations* (2nd series, 1868), p. 572.

[23] C. W. Ramsdell, "The Natural Limits of Slave Expansion," *Mississippi Valley Historical Review*, XVI, 151–171 (Sept., 1929).

[24] Louis M. Hacker, *The Triumph of American Capitalism* (Simon and Schuster), pp. 281–282.

inferior economic position. "That the South in general," says Lewis C. Gray, "and particularly the lower South, was continuously a debtor region was partly due to the requirements for new capital on account of the exigencies of expansion. But the relative poverty of the South, as compared with the North, was largely the result of a system of rural economy characterized by extravagance both in production and consumption, a system which concentrated a large proportion of the money income in the hands of a relatively small proportion of the population." [25]

In brief, a situation had developed in which the commercial and financial life of the section was directed and controlled from the outside. Charges for commercial services were high; interest rates were exorbitant. At the same time, the cost of labor, the chief expense in raising cotton, was mounting as the price of slaves increased. During the 1850's, moreover, the price of cotton fluctuated in the neighborhood of 10 to 13 cents a pound, a price high enough to insure profits for the well-managed plantation on the richer soil, but only a precarious living and a debtor status for the great majority of planters.

It should also be added that the concentration of wealth in the hands of the large plantation owners was producing detrimental social as well as economic effects. Particularly to be noted was the deteriorating effect on the small farmer. Unable to compete in raising cotton with slaves on the richer lowlands and unable to resist the prices offered for his land by the rich plantation owners, he was gradually driven to the less desirable locations. Typical of what was going on all over the South was the process described by a southern observer, quoted in a country newspaper. "The cotton-growing portion of the valley of the Mississippi, the very garden of the Union, is year by year being wrested from the hands of the small farmer and delivered over to the great capitalists. The white yeoman, the class which has contributed more of the blood and devotion, and good sense and enterprise which have made this country what it is than any other, are either forced into the sandy pine-hills or are driven West to clear and prepare the soil for the army of Negroes and Negro-drivers which forever presses on their heels, to make their industry unprofitable, and their life intolerable." [26]

Keen-minded Southerners were well aware of the economically disadvantageous situation in which their section found itself and there were no lack of remedies offered. Many students of agriculture condemned the extravagance and wastefulness of the existing plantation system and urged

[25] L. C. Gray, *History of Agriculture in the Southern United States to 1850*, I, 460.

[26] Quoted by F. L. Olmsted, *A Journey in the Back Country* (1860, reprinted 1907), Chap. VIII, pp. 329–330 (1860 ed.), and also in G. S. Callender, *Selections from the Economic History of the United States*, p. 767.

a greater degree of self-sufficiency for the plantations. This would enable the farmer to avoid making heavy purchases of food and equipment from the outside, reduce the necessity of borrowing money, and still allow him to raise large amounts of cotton. "We cannot compete," said one advocate of better methods, "with the planters of Alabama and Mississippi, in a wild and destructive system, by which even they have sunk under embarrassment and ruin, with all their advantages of soil and climate. We can make up for our inferior soil and climate only by a superior system of husbandry. While they are exhausting their soil and preventing the natural increase of their slaves by a reckless system of pushing and driving, let us improve the fertility of the one, by resting and manuring it, and increase the number of the other, by moderate working and by providing everything necessary for their health and comfort." [27]

Other reformers urged escape from economic dependence by developing manufacturing in the South. Raw materials, they pointed out, existed in abundance and a labor supply might be obtained either from slaves or poor whites. "As long as we are tributaries," said a writer in the *Charleston Mercury*, "dependent on foreign labor and skill for food, clothing and countless necessaries of life, we are in thraldom." [28] Under the whip of widespread propaganda some progress toward manufacturing was made during the 'forties and 'fifties, but lack of liquid capital, competent managers, and trained labor, as well as other handicaps, prevented its rapid development. In 1860 the South contributed only 8 per cent of the country's $1,886,-000,000 of manufactures.

The disastrous effects of the panic of 1857 emphasized particularly the desirability of direct trade with Europe. Despite encouragement given by the southern states, efforts to develop a southern-owned merchant marine and direct trade with other nations proved unsuccessful. Much greater success was attained in internal improvements. As in the North, southern states, counties, and towns were lavish in their contributions for the building of railroads. The state of Georgia, for example, built and operated a railroad from Atlanta to the border near Chattanooga. By 1860 the South had constructed over 9500 miles (about one-third of the nation's total) at a cost of about $237,000,000, raised almost entirely in that section.

For the purpose of discussing and publicizing the various schemes to improve the economic position of the South, more than twelve commercial conventions were held between 1837 and 1860 in the southern states. Some of these conventions reflected little more than the ambitions of certain cities

[27] Address of General George McDuffie before the State Agricultural Society of South Carolina in 1840. Quoted by L. C. Gray, *History of Agriculture*, I, 460.
[28] *Niles Weekly Register*, April 19, 1845.

SLAVERY AFTER THE
MISSOURI COMPROMISE

- States entirely Free
- States undergoing Gradual Emancipation
- Area Free by Ordinance of 1787
- Area Free by Missouri Compromise
- Slave Area

Dates indicate when freedom
was granted, or when gradual
abolition began.

MANHATTAN DRAFTING CO. INC. N.Y.

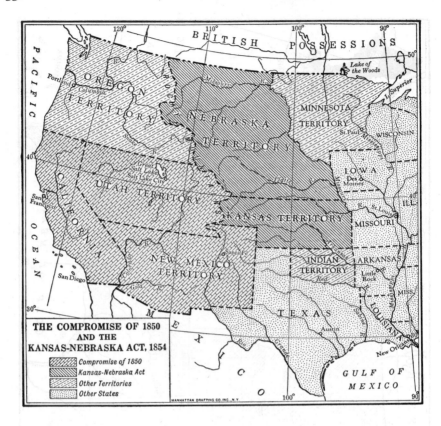

THE COMPROMISE OF 1850
AND THE
KANSAS-NEBRASKA ACT, 1854

Compromise of 1850
Kansas-Nebraska Act
Other Territories
Other States

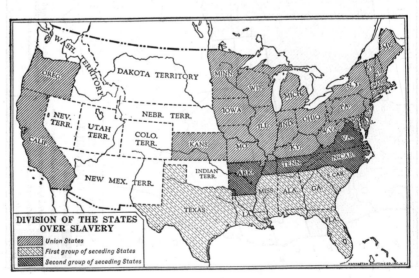

DIVISION OF THE STATES
OVER SLAVERY

Union States
First group of seceding States
Second group of seceding States

to promote their own interests or of fire-eating politicians to attack northern oppression. As a whole, however, they represented an effort to face
the economic problems of the South. Speakers repeatedly urged the development of manufacturing, the establishment of direct trade with Europe,
the abolition of the tariff, a Pacific railroad built by southern capital, and
internal improvements constructed with federal aid. Frequent demands,
particularly in the later years, were made for the revival of the African
slave trade in order to reduce the cost of plantation labor. The South was
by no means unanimously for this last. Slave owners in the border states who
sold their excess Negroes south and the great plantation owners who made
profits under the existing system had no interest in reopening the slave
trade. It was the small and middle-class planter who needed cheaper labor
that backed this demand. It was this group, in fact, that was most vocal
against what it believed to be northern oppression.

The South may have accomplished little in revising or improving her
economic status in the decades preceding the Civil War, but she was preeminently successful in defending her interests in the political arena. The
small southern oligarchy which dominated the economic, political, and
social life of the South also gained control of the federal government. During the thirty-two years between the election of Jackson and Lincoln, it controlled the Presidency and the Senate for twenty-four years, the Supreme
Court for twenty-six years, and the House of Representatives for twenty-two
years. During these years it reduced the tariff until it was no longer a heavy
burden. It revoked the subsidies to the merchant marine which had enabled northern shipowners to meet the intensified competition of Great
Britain. It kept federal subsidies for internal improvements under control
except where they were of direct benefit to the South. It had been the chief
influence in precipitating the war with Mexico which added large areas to
the plantation domain.

Against a rising anti-slavery movement southern politicians opened to
slavery in the Compromise of 1850 all the region obtained from Mexico
except California. Four years later in the Kansas-Nebraska bill they repealed the Missouri Compromise and opened to popular sovereignty the
great territories of Kansas and Nebraska. Finally, in the Dred Scott case
(1857), a Democratic states' rights Supreme Court declared the Missouri
Compromise unconstitutional by denying the authority of Congress to
legislate concerning slave property in the territories. Fearful that a westward movement of small farmers would create new areas hostile to slavery,
the South had enough influence to prevent the final enactment of the
Homestead Act until after secession.

These "amazing acts of mastery," as the Beards describe them, "—legislative, executive, judicial—committed by the federal government in the decade between 1850 and 1860 changed the whole political climate of America." They were accomplished not by the southern oligarchy alone, but by southern Democrats in alliance with those of the North and Northwest. By the end of the 'fifties many influences were at work to weaken this alliance. First of all was the rising anti-slavery movement in the North. Its chief strength was exerted not toward emancipation but rather in opposing the further extension of the slave system. Its backing came from the small farmers of the North and Northwest who looked forward to the extension of small farms freed from the rivalry of the plantation system. This opposition became stronger in the 'fifties as immigration flowed into the Old Northwest under the stimulus of improved transportation facilities and the new lands opened up by the Illinois Central Railroad.

In the second place, the economic and political bonds between the South and the Old Northwest, which had kept the Democrats in power for so long, were ready to snap by 1860. The agricultural produce of the regions north of the Ohio, which for decades had supported the plantations of the southern Mississippi Valley, now moved toward the Atlantic seaports as the trans-Allegheny railroads penetrated the Northwest. A desperate effort to save the old trade routes was made by lavish land grants to the Illinois Central, but it failed. As the outlet for the produce of the Northwest shifted to the Northeast and to Europe, the Northwest became more sympathetic toward a tariff system which would promote industrial cities and enlarge the eastern market. A southern writer in De Bow's Review had seen this clearly as early as 1847: "A contest has been going on between the North and South not limited to slavery or no slavery—to abolition or no abolition, nor to the politics of either whigs or democrats as such, but a contest for the wealth and commerce of the great valley of the Mississippi—a contest tendered by our Northern brethren, whether the growing commerce of the great West shall be thrown upon New Orleans or given to the Atlantic cities."

This new economic alignment was quickly reflected in politics. In the middle 'fifties the new Republican party sought to integrate the dissatisfaction with the Democratic party as controlled by southern plantation owners. By opposing the extension of slavery it drew to itself both anti-slavery idealists who were against slavery on principle and the small farmers who sought the extension of free agriculture. By favoring donation of public lands and a transcontinental railroad it won the adherence of prospective western settlers. By advocating a higher tariff it held out a beckoning hand to the rising industrial interests of the East. The strength of the platform was evident in 1856 and even more so in 1860. Together with a split in the

Democratic party in 1860, the platform carried the Republicans to victory. The victory was by no means complete—the Republicans had won the Presidency, but the Democrats still had control of Congress. Nevertheless, the slaveholding South interpreted the results of 1860 as portending the doom of her national control. There remained only political and economic submission or secession. She chose the latter. In the light of history this decision was a mistake. But there was no question that, as Seward put it, the issues involved an "irrepressible conflict." The economic forces unloosed by the Industrial Revolution were finding full play and were beating irresistibly upon the one-sided and somewhat static civilization of the South. At such a time in world history there could be but one result—a victory for free labor, *laissez faire,* and industrialization.

SELECTED READINGS

Phillips, U. B., *Life and Labor in the Old South,* Chaps. XI–XV.
Phillips, U. B., *American Negro Slavery,* Chaps. XI–XX.
Channing, E., *History of the United States,* Vol. V, Chap. V.
Dodd, W. E., *The Cotton Kingdom.*
Hacker, L. M., *The Triumph of American Capitalism,* Chaps. XXI–XXIII.
Gray, L. C., *History of Agriculture in the Southern United States to 1860,* Vol. I, Chaps. XX–XXIV.
Callender, G. S., *Selections from the Economic History of the United States, 1765–1860,* Chap. XV.
Flügel, F., and Faulkner, H. U., *Readings in the Economic and Social History of the United States,* pp. 413–447.

17.

The Civil War

THE SIGNIFICANCE OF THE CIVIL WAR

Whether we approach the Civil War from the point of view of economic, political, or social history, it is difficult to overemphasize its significance. It marks a definite break midway in the development of the nation. Its effects upon our industrial, financial, and commercial history were profound and will be developed in succeeding chapters. In the long story of the American worker this war not only marked the end of chattel slavery but speeded the national integration of the organized labor movement. In it the great sectional conflict based upon economic interests reached its climax. Economic sectionalism has remained, but no part of the country has since been strong enough to resort to arms. Politically the war for southern independence established the ultimate supremacy of the federal government. It also marked a division point in American social history. The great reform movement which characterized the decades of the 'thirties, 'forties, and 'fifties finally burned itself out in the slavery issue, and it was another half century before the nation again turned seriously to the quest for social justice.

A comparison of resources makes it clear that the South was bound to lose in a long war. The total population of the eleven seceding states was 9,000,-000, of which 3,500,000 were slaves; the population of the states remaining in the Union numbered over 22,000,000, and their labor force was recruited by continued immigration during the war. Of the real property of the nation estimated in 1860 at about $16,000,000,000, the South, including slaves valued at $2,000,000,000, had about one-third. Of the $3,736,000,000 wealth produced in 1859, the seceding states accounted for about one-fourth. Quite as important in considering the superiority of the North in fighting a long war was the fact that she controlled over 90 per cent of the manufacturing industry. If this was not sufficient, her possession of the merchant marine and the Navy enabled her to import needed supplies. The South based her hopes primarily upon two factors: first, the fact that she was engaged in a defensive war on her own territory which would help to neutralize the disparity in men and resources; and second, the importance of her cotton production which she believed would finance the struggle and bring foreign interference in her behalf. The first hope was rendered futile by overwhelming northern superiority. The second failed because of the North's blockade of southern ports and Europe's failure to interfere. Only the incredible inefficiency and mismanagement of the federal government prevented an earlier end to the conflict.

DEPRESSION OF 1861

The first economic effect of the Civil War was to throw the North and West into a severe panic. At the outbreak of the war the agricultural South owed northern merchants close to $300,000,000, practically all of which was a total loss. Uncertainty as to the future and the forebodings incident to the beginning of the war brought about a wave of retrenchment and economy, and the banks were caught with cash reserves far too small to meet such an emergency. All of these factors united in bringing on the depression of 1861. The Dun reports listed in 1861 nearly 6000 failures of northern firms for sums of $5000 or more (a larger number than in the panic year of 1857), and probably 6990 more failures for sums under that amount.[1] The northern banks in general were able to maintain specie payment until the latter part of December, 1861, when they were forced to suspend, followed almost at once by the federal government. In the South, except in New Orleans, suspension occurred immediately after the opening of the war and continued until the end. The wild-cat banks in the West were especially hard hit, not only because of their methods of banking, but also because of their more intimate relations with the South. In Illinois, 89 out of 110 banks failed, while in Wisconsin 39 and in Indiana 27 went under.

REVIVAL OF AGRICULTURAL PROSPERITY

The depression of 1861 gave way in the following spring to a revival of prosperity in the North and West. Although thousands of farmers were drawn into the Union Army and thousands more deserted agriculture for the mines of the Far West, the effect was offset by the work of women in the fields, by the influx of immigrants from Europe, and by the use of labor-saving machinery. The eastern farmers, finding that they could not compete in certain crops with the Westerner, emigrated in large numbers to take up lands in the West, a movement stimulated after 1862 by the Homestead Act,[2] which granted 160 acres free to almost anyone who would live on them for five years. Immigrants flocked from abroad during the five

[1] Emerson D. Fite, *Social and Industrial Conditions in the North During the Civil War,* pp. 105–106.

[2] See Chap. 18.

years to take advantage of this Act or to settle on the areas made available by the large railroad grants; upon arrival in New York, 45,000 declared their intention of continuing to Illinois, and 23,000 to Wisconsin.[3] There was also a considerable exodus to the western farmlands from the harassed border states. Never was such interest displayed in labor-saving farm machinery, now the center of attention at county fairs. The number of mowers manufactured increased from 20,000 in 1861 to 70,000 in 1865, and a similar story could be told of horse rakes, grain drills, threshers, and other improved machinery.

Not only were the crops saved, but there was considerable increase in agricultural production. The wheat crop was greater during the war than at any time previous. Corn production, although it fell off slightly for the country as a whole, showed a remarkable increase in the western states. More hogs were put on the market than before the war; wool production rose from 40,000,000 to 140,000,000 pounds, and the number of sheep from 16,000,000 to 32,000,000.

The principal factors which brought about this agricultural prosperity were (1) the necessity of feeding and clothing an army which at the close of the war numbered a million men; (2) the increasing population of the country as a whole; (3) the prosperity of the North which enabled a greater expenditure for farm products; (4) the rapidly growing manufacturers which employed increasing numbers in non-agricultural pursuits; (5) the stimulation of high prices which came from an expanding paper currency; and (6) the heavy demand from foreign countries, especially England, where the harvests of 1860, 1861, and 1862 had been below normal. As regards this last, it was freely asserted during the war, and with much foundation in fact, that the food supplies of the North and West were influential in preserving the neutrality of Great Britain.[4] When England had to choose between cotton and wheat there could be only one logical decision.

MANUFACTURING IN THE NORTH

Manufacturing, stimulated by war needs and liberally protected by tariff Acts passed at every session of Congress, prospered enormously during the last three years of the war. Although the record is stained with the usual story of the sale of inferior goods to the government at high prices, of speculation, of lobbying, and of the amassing of fortunes by the so-called "shoddy aristocracy" out of the needs of the soldiers and the exigencies of war, it is still a significant fact that the period marked a notable advance in American manufacturing. There had been a wide extension of the factory system in the Northeast during the previous half century, but it was the

[3] Emerson D. Fite, *Social and Industrial Conditions*, p. 11.
[4] Below, p. 352.

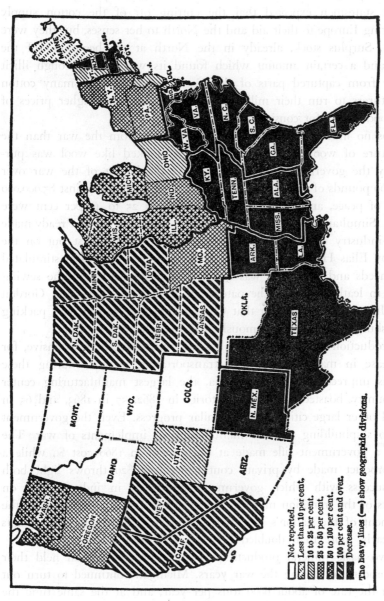

PERCENTAGE OF INCREASE OF ALL FARM PROPERTY, BY STATES, 1860–1870.[5]

5 From the *Statistical Atlas of the United States* (1924).

Civil War that actually was responsible for the Industrial Revolution. In only one important industry, cotton manufacturing, did production decline. Southern statesmen expected that the cutting off of the cotton supply would bring Europe to their aid and the North to her senses, but they were mistaken. Surplus stock, already in the North at the beginning of the conflict, and a certain amount which found its way there through illicit traffic or from captured parts of the Confederacy, enabled many cotton manufacturers to run their mills on part time, and the higher prices of cotton goods made for considerable profits.

Perhaps no industry received a greater impetus from the war than the manufacture of woolen cloth. Anything that looked like wool was purchased by the government for uniforms. At the height of the war over 200,000,000 pounds of wool per year were being woven, as against 85,000,000 in times of peace, and annual dividends of from 25 to 40 per cent were frequent. Simultaneously came the rapid development of the ready-made clothing industry made possible by the sewing machine first put on the market by Elias Howe in 1849. The leather industry was also stimulated by war needs and it in turn was aided by the application of the sewing machine to leather through the patents of Lyman R. Blake and Gordon McKay. It was during the war that Chicago took the lead in pork packing and Pittsburgh increased enormously the manufacture of iron.

The production of machinery of all kinds must have been extensive, for the increase in manufacturing and transportation facilities during these years was unprecedented. Philadelphia, the largest manufacturing center in the country, boasted of 58 new factories in 1862, 57 in 1863, and 65 in 1864, and other large cities showed similar progress. Even the government went into shipbuilding and the manufacture of implements of war. The fact that a government rifle made at Springfield in 1860 cost $9 while a similar product made by private contractors cost $20 throws light both on the success with which government embarked in industry and on the profits of the munition makers. The war apparently contributed to the development of the nation's inventive genius, for the number of patents issued yearly more than doubled between 1860 and 1866.

The two basic mineral products, coal and iron, more than held their own in production during the war years. Michigan continued to turn out copper at the rate of about 6000 tons per year, and at the same time the copper industry in California was developing rapidly. The striking of oil in 1859 on the Drake farm at Titusville, Venango County, Pennsylvania, was the beginning of a great industry which went through the first stages of its development during the war. Thousands of wells were soon bored along Oil Creek in Pennsylvania, as well as near Wheeling, West Virginia, and in Ohio. By 1862 production amounted to 128,000,000 gallons.

Coincident with the excitement in the oil fields was the speculation in the cities, where 1100 oil companies with a capital stock of $600,000,000 sold $90,000,000 worth of securities. The production of petroleum was not only the most important of the new industries developed during the war, but by 1865 it had become an appreciable item in our foreign trade. The value of the petroleum exported rose from nothing in 1860 to almost $16,000,000 in 1865, when it ranked sixth in our exports.

In 1859 the famous Comstock Lode of gold and silver was discovered in Nevada, and the Gregory Lode of gold in Colorado; these mines and others must have produced at least $8,000,000 worth of the precious metals during the war. The rush for the mining towns, which commenced in 1859 with the announcement of the discovery of new deposits, continued during the war years. The population of Colorado jumped from 32,227 in 1860 to about 100,000 in 1864. The year 1863 alone brought over 30,000 to Idaho. Virginia City, Nevada, grew from nothing to 18,000 in a short time, and the population of the state grew from 6857 in 1860 to 42,491 in 1870. The overland routes during the summer months were marked by a continuous stream of prairie schooners. One traveler on the Kansas route in 1863 testified to meeting on a sixteen-day journey an average of 500 wagons a day. In 1864 Omaha, the great point of exodus, saw 75,000 emigrants pass through toward the golden west.

LABOR AND THE COST OF LIVING

Reserving until a later chapter the discussion of the methods by which the Union government financed the war,[6] let us discuss here merely the cost of living, particularly as it affected the wage earner. The successive issues of legal tender notes (greenbacks) and of short-term treasury notes, which filled the country with a paper money fluctuating in value, tended, along with the increased demand for commodities, to drive prices up. According to the "Aldrich Report," [7] the relative course, measured in currency and in gold, of wholesale prices and of money wages was as follows:

Year	Prices in Currency	Prices in Gold	Money Wages in Currency	Money Wages in Gold
1860	100.0	100.0	100.0	100.0
1861	100.6	100.6	100.8	100.8
1862	117.8	114.9	102.9	100.4
1863	148.6	102.4	110.5	76.2
1864	190.5	122.5	125.6	80.8
1865	216.8	100.3	143.1	66.2

[6] Below, Chap. 25.

[7] Senate Reports, 52d Congress, 2d Session, 1892–1893 (special session, March 4, 1893), Vol. III, Part I, pp. 9, 13, 14, 99.

Labor, which had enjoyed fair wages in the years immediately preceding the war, was hard put to it to make ends meet in the face of the rapidly rising cost of living. It has been estimated that the cost of sixty articles of prime necessity, aggregated according to quantities of such articles consumed, increased 125 per cent during the four years of the war.

The whole problem of determining real wages during the Civil War is an exceedingly difficult one, as is the effort to compare wages during the war with scales which preceded it. The suspension of specie payments immediately eliminated gold from ordinary trade and put prices on the basis of greenbacks, and the value of the latter apparently fluctuated not according to the amount issued or the prosperity of the North, but rather according to confidence in the success of the northern cause. A victory of the North pushed the value of the greenbacks up; a defeat sent it skidding. When to this is added the fluctuating value of gold, the unreliability of price estimates is apparent.

While commodities measured in paper money doubled in price, wages lagged behind. During the first two years of the war, wages in paper money had advanced only about 10 per cent over the average for 1860, but prices (in currency) had increased nearly 50 per cent. This big jump in prices came in 1863, and the winter of 1863 and 1864 saw both the beginning of trade unionism on a large scale and numerous desperately fought strikes. Up to this time any rise in wages had been staved off by capital by means of labor-saving machinery, by the employment of women and children, by the systematic importation of cheap European labor, and by Negro strikebreakers; but capital was now forced to give in, and wages generally went up. During the war 800,000 immigrants entered the United States, a number sufficiently large to fill a big part of the gap which the war had made in the country's labor force. While it would be an exaggeration to say that the Union Army was an army of boys, it is true that a remarkably large number of the recruits were too young to have entered industry; this fact and the heavy immigration explain the slight disturbance in the labor market and the failure of wages to rise materially until 1863. Professor Fite believes that the average advance in wages during the war amounted to 60 per cent, a point which left the laborer worse off at its conclusion than he had been in 1860.[3]

Those most severely affected by the rising cost of living were, as usual, the professional classes, particularly clergymen and teachers, government employees, and women. The pay of soldiers remained at $13 a month until July 20, 1864, when it was advanced to $16. Many of the most efficient government officials in civil occupations were forced to sever their connections

---

[3] Emerson D. Fite, *Social and Industrial Conditions*, p. 185, note.

with the government because of low pay. Women, especially seamstresses, were apparently not able to hold the mailed fist over their employers as did the men, and in 1865 the average wage of women working for contractors on army clothing was $1.54 a week. The low wages of women in the industrial world were sometimes eked out by soldiers' wages, a part of which was often sent home, by military bounties, and by charitable aid given to soldiers' families. The increased buying capacity of the nation during the last years of the war, the sale of luxuries, and the prosperity of popular amusement enterprises demonstrate, on the other hand, that labor shared to some extent in the flush times.[9] Some light is thrown both on the rapid advance in manufacturing and on the demand for labor by the census figures of 1870, which place the increase in the number of industrial establishments for the decade at 252,148, an advance of 79.6 per cent and the greatest for any decade in our history. The number of wage earners in industrial establishments advanced from 1,311,246 to 2,053,996, an increase of 56.6 per cent which was not equaled even during the decade of the First World War.

NORTHERN CAPITAL

Although labor maintained itself with difficulty, capital found itself in a most flourishing position. Before the war the millionaires of the country might have been counted on the fingers of both hands; at its conclusion there were scores. War taxation favored the larger industry; and the process of consolidation, so marked in subsequent years, had its beginning during the war in the union of various telegraph lines and transportation companies. The American Telegraph Company and the United States Telegraph Company, the last important rivals of the Western Union, were acquired by the latter in 1866, giving it control of 75,000 miles of telegraph lines. In like manner, numerous smaller railroad companies in various parts of the country were brought under a single direction. The tendency toward centralized control of railroads was emphasized, no doubt, by the increased need of transportation facilities occasioned by the war and by the rivalry of different cities to be termini or collecting points for produce. The conduct of the war was hampered by the frequent transference of freight necessitated by the many little independent systems with different-gauge tracks and different types of rolling stock. The Pennsylvania, Lehigh, Erie, and most of the important roads absorbed the minor companies just before, during, or immediately after the war, and laid the foundations of the great railroad systems of today. Of particular importance was the acquisition by the Pennsylvania system of the Pittsburgh, Fort Wayne and Chicago, thus

[9] For the further history of labor during the war, see below, Chap. 22.

completing the first through-connection under single ownership between Lake Michigan and the seacoast.

In addition to the consolidation of various units, the war witnessed considerable activity in railroad building. The longest railroad constructed during the war was the Atlantic and Great Western, now part of the Erie system, which ran from Salamanca, New York, to Cincinnati, Ohio. By means of the Erie in the east and the Ohio and Mississippi in the west, it linked New York and St. Louis with a one-gauge railroad. This road, constructed at the rate of a mile a day by European capital and imported labor, demonstrated both the tireless business energy of the nation and the faith of northern and European financiers in the future, whatever might be the fate of the conflict. By giving New York the first single-gauge track extending west to the Mississippi, it afforded her a distinct advantage over rival eastern seaports. Important also was the Philadelphia and Erie, completed in 1864, which connected the new oil fields with Philadelphia. Massachusetts, hoping to save part of the western trade, in 1863 took up the unfinished work on the Hoosac tunnel of the Troy and Greenfield, and pushed to completion the connection between Albany and Boston. Other pieces of railroad construction were completed or planned, including the laying of the first rails for the Union Pacific, the first of the transcontinental lines to be built. Never were the railroads so prosperous. The Erie, the Hudson River, the Cleveland and Pittsburgh, and the Illinois Central, none of which had ever paid dividends, were paying 8 per cent or over by the end of the war, and many railroads sought to camouflage their real earnings by stock dividends. Capital was fully alive to its power and possibilities. The value of monopoly was understood, and the railroads began to tighten their grip on the coal producers in the anthracite region. In the cities, capitalists were indefatigable in planning street railway monopolies and pressing for long-term franchises in the legislatures. In twenty-seven cities street cars appeared for the first time.

Although the cost of building almost doubled, the decline in construction for the whole country was very slight, a striking difference from conditions during the First World War. In cities like Philadelphia, Chicago, and San Francisco, where population was rapidly mounting, or in cities like Lynn and Springfield, Massachusetts, where industry was immensely stimulated by war needs, there was extensive building. The Capitol at Washington was completed during the war, as were many state and municipal buildings. "On every street and avenue," said the Chicago *Tribune* on October 8, 1863, "one sees new buildings going up, immense stone, brick, and iron business blocks, marble palaces and new residences; everywhere the grading of streets, the building of sewers, the laying of water and gas pipes, are all in progress at the same time."

SOCIAL ACTIVITIES IN THE NORTH

The unprecedented war prosperity plunged many of those who benefited into a riot of extravagance and pursuit of pleasure. More charitable observers might attribute this to an attempt to forget the horrors of war and to keep up a brave front, but the true explanation was the accumulation of sudden wealth in the hands of those unused to it. The race tracks were crowded and stakes offered on a scale never before seen. Athletics were enthusiastically patronized, and the leading actors played to packed houses. The most expensive jewelry, clothing, and furniture found the readiest sale.

To picture the life of those who remained at home in the North as a mad scramble for wealth to be spent in extravagant living while the "boys in blue" were fighting and dying for the Union would be far from correct; high living was largely confined to certain classes and to the cities. Furthermore, if the Northerner was whole-hearted in his spending, he was also whole-hearted in his giving. At least fifteen colleges were founded during the 'sixties, including Vassar, the first institution of collegiate rank exclusively for women, the Massachusetts Institute of Technology, Cornell, Lehigh, Swarthmore, Bates, and the state universities of Kansas and Minnesota. Private benefactors contributed heavily to endowment funds and financed new buildings in most of the already existing institutions. Voluntary contributions of at least $5,000,000 to education are recorded. That the minds of the national legislators were turned to educational needs, even during the terrible strain of war, is demonstrated by the Morrill Act of July 2, 1862, by which the national government gave to each state 30,000 acres of public land for each of its Senators and Congressmen, the income from which was to be devoted to mechanical and agricultural schools, provision for military training to be made in their curricula.

Sanitary and welfare work among the soldiers, taken care of in subsequent wars by the Red Cross and other organizations, was consolidated chiefly under two bodies—the United States Sanitary Commission and the United States Christian Commission. The former, approved by the government to supplement the medical department of the Army, affiliated the local societies engaged in soldier welfare work. Through their instrumentality clothing, bandages, medicines, food, and tobacco to the value of $25,000,000 were distributed to the soldiers. The Commission's most important service was that rendered on the battlefield and in the actual campaign, but the other phases of its work were very valuable. These included twenty-five soldiers' homes maintained in the leading cities, where passing soldiers might find meals and lodging; agencies to advise and help soldiers in regard to back pay, bounties, and pensions; convalescent hospitals; the publishing of a hospital directory; and innumerable other measures to make the soldier's lot easier. Newspapers collected funds for the Commission; huge sanitary fairs were held in the large cities; theaters contributed from their receipts, as did public service utilities; school children gave entertainments and contributed their pennies. The spiritual welfare of the soldiers (in addition to the work of the regular chaplains) was taken care of by the United States Christian Commission, which sent clergymen and Bibles as well as hospital supplies and food.

Larger than the amounts given for soldiers welfare work were the donations and bounties to the dependent families of the soldiers, made by the state, county, and local authorities and by individuals. The Provost Marshal General of the United States estimated that $600,000,000 was distributed by national, state, and local authorities in bounties, and $100,000,000 more by individuals. Probably half of this found its way back to the dependent families. Municipalities contributed generously to the support of needy relatives, Philadelphia having at one time 9000 on its list at an annual expenditure of $600,000. Considerable sums were also raised in the North for the support of Negroes and southern refugees, and for the relief of the starving cotton operatives in Lancashire. The story of this whole-hearted generosity and sacrifice goes far to offset the more sordid details of war speculation, profiteering, and extravagance.

"KING COTTON"

To no small extent the South rested her hope of success upon the world's need of cotton. Said Senator James H. Hammond of South Carolina in a famous speech in 1858: "Without firing a gun, without drawing a sword, should they make war on us, we could bring the whole world to our feet. . . . What would happen if no cotton was furnished for three years? I will not stop to depict what every one can imagine, but this is certain: England would topple headlong and carry the whole civilized world with her save the south. No, you dare not to make war on cotton. No Power on the earth dares to make war upon it. Cotton *is* King."[10] This was the slogan that so powerfully affected southern economic thinking.

That events did not bear out these sanguine hopes was due to two chief causes: first, to a surplus of cotton on hand, resulting from overproduction; and second, to the European need of northern wheat. The decade 1840 to 1850 was one of overproduction, but during the next decade both planters and manufacturers "enjoyed a period of unexampled prosperity."[11] In

---

[10] Quoted by James A. B. Scherer, *Cotton as a World Power*, p. 239.
[11] James L. Watkins, *Production and Price of Cotton for One Hundred Years*, U. S. Dept. of Agriculture Bulletin No. 9, Miscellaneous Series (1895).

1860 a record crop was produced, "which the southern planter marketed with unusual haste on account of the threats of trouble, England taking 1,650,000 bales before the war broke out. The British market was glutted to such an extent that many of the mills actually shut down in 1861 and prices remained practically stationary. The blockade, when it came, was laughed at as a paper blockade; and indeed it seemed to be so, for it is estimated that 3,127,568 bales were exported during the year ending August 31, 1861. Mill owners, it was reported, even longed for an effective blockade to relieve the glut of the market." [12] The blockade saved English middlemen from actual bankruptcy. The North also had stock, and "in the first year the American mills ran on two-thirds time, the next year on from one-quarter to one-half time, in these two years consuming cotton that remained over from the heavy purchases of 1860." [13] Thus the cutting off of the supply of cotton was at first a benefit to cotton manufacturers, for it enabled them to dispose of their surplus stock and to keep up prices. When the mills in the North lowered production, operatives readily found

AVERAGE ANNUAL PRICES FOR MIDDLING UPLANDS, 1790–1940.[14]

employment in war industries. In England there was unemployment and great distress among factory operatives, but they realized that in the terrific struggle in America was being fought their battle as free laborers, and they stood stanchly by the side of the North, opposing any recognition

[12] James A. B. Scherer, *Cotton as a World Power*, p. 265.

[13] Emerson D. Fite, *Social and Industrial Conditions*, p. 86.

[14] M. B. Hammond, *The Cotton Industry*, Appendix I; *Statistical Abstract, 1921*, p. 878; *ibid., 1940*, p. 729. The prices up to 1921 are those that obtained on the New York market; after that year they are the general average prices in the chief cotton markets throughout the country.

of the Confederacy by the British government. The North realized the value of their good will, and showed appreciation by fitting out three ships with relief supplies for the Lancashire sufferers. In any event, northern mills were obtaining considerable supplies of southern cotton toward the end of the war as the northern armies occupied larger areas of the South (table, p. 354), and Great Britain was developing sources of raw cotton in other parts of the world.

A second deterrent to English aid to the Confederacy was her dependence upon northern wheat because of poor crops at home from 1860 to 1862. England, says S. J. Chapman, "was helpless in the matter of the cotton supply. Interference would probably have proved futile; for America lay far away, and any action to bring in cotton might conceivably have operated in keeping back corn." [15] This fact was plainly pointed out in Parliament at the time. Professor Fite, in summing up the balancing of British interests between wheat and cotton in the Civil War, says: "At this distance it may safely be concluded that while the need of grain would not have prevented England from defending herself from a war of aggression by the United States, it was doubtless one of the factors, and an important one, in preventing aggressive demonstrations by England in favor of the Confederacy and against the United States." [16]

Whether the need for American wheat actually kept England neutral it is difficult to say. A recent student of Civil War diplomacy believes that it was not so much wheat *per se* that kept her neutral as the desire for war profits.[17] Great Britain, he points out, could obtain plenty of wheat elsewhere. She bought wheat from the United States, first, because it was cheaper and more convenient to purchase it here, and second, because she could exchange arms and ammunition for it. For the moment at least, Britain's economic interests seemed more closely identified with the North than with the South.

THE SOUTHERN BLOCKADE

The effect of the war upon the North had been to accentuate existing economic tendencies. In the South the whole economic life was turned upside down. In the ante-bellum days the South had been a great agricultural region, with tobacco and cotton as the staple crops; these two commodities had been exchanged in the North and in Europe for manufactured goods. With his wealth tied up in cotton and slaves, the southern planter im-

[15] S. J. Chapman, *The Cotton Industry and Trade* (London, 1905), p. 66.
[16] Emerson D. Fite, *Social and Industrial Conditions,* p. 21. See also L. B. Schmidt, "The Influence of Wheat and Cotton on Anglo-American Relations During the War," *Iowa Journal of History and Politics* (July, 1918).
[17] F. W. Owsley, *King Cotton Diplomacy*, pp. 567 ff.

ported much of his foodstuffs from the states north of the Ohio. The very life of the South depended upon external trade. The first effect of the war was to break up this trade. Northern as well as southern statesmen realized that "cotton is king," and at the beginning of the war an iron ring was thrown around the South, growing tighter each year as the Union Armies pushed south and east, and as the Navy grew more efficient until finally it literally strangled the Confederacy into submission. The blockade acted detrimentally upon the South in three ways. In the first place, it cut off the outlet for her cotton and tobacco; and without a market it was impossible to establish commercial credit abroad with which to purchase supplies. The loss of markets and credit undermined the whole economic structure. Second, the blockade prevented the importing of the many kinds of manufactured goods upon which the agricultural South was dependent. Third, it forced slave labor into unaccustomed occupations and resulted in a tremendous decline in the value of both land and slaves.

The South strove heroically to counteract the effects of the blockade. Arms, ammunition, shoes, blankets, medicines, and various luxuries were shipped from Europe to various ports in the West Indies; from there low-built, lead-colored side-wheeled steamers slipped into the ports of Wilmington, Charleston, Savannah, Mobile, or Galveston. The profits were enormous and attracted a disproportionate amount of capital; £30,000 each way was a not uncommon profit on a voyage. Although captures were frequent and the chances of success grew smaller as the war drew to a conclusion, the fact that two successful voyages compensated the owners for total loss on a third made blockade running still a good gamble. Even the state governments invested in companies operating blockade runners. The North Atlantic blockading squadron reported the names of fifty runners captured between August 1, 1863, and September 30, 1864, but a large volume of business must have been carried on if southern sources are to be believed. According to the Secretary of the Treasury of the Confederate States, forty-three runners entered the ports of Wilmington and Charleston in May and June of 1864.

The temptation of excessive profits from certain types of imports was more than the patriotism of some could stand, and the Confederate government finally passed an Act (February 6, 1864) forbidding the importation of such luxuries as wines, spirits, laces, carpets, toys, furniture, and jewelry. By later laws the government sought to control for its own use a certain amount of space in incoming and outgoing boats. It is impossible to determine accurately the amount of goods exported and imported by blockade runners. In 1862, 1863, and 1864 the exportation of cotton to Europe was probably less than one-tenth that of the pre-war years. The comparatively small amount exported reached its destination either through the medium of blockade runners or by way of Matamoras, Mexico, to which point considerable cotton was taken overland through Texas.

Southern cotton found its way to the markets of the North by other routes than those of the blockade runner. The first policy of the Confederate government was to prevent any cotton whatsoever from reaching the North, on the theory that its lack would bring the war to a speedy conclusion; and in furtherance of this policy it passed an Act on May 21, 1861, prohibiting exportation of cotton except through seaports. This plan broke down under the exigencies of the situation, and contraband trade in the staple was carried on all through the war. There were times when the Confederate armies were provided with food obtained in exchange for cotton. This widespread illicit trade was a source of demoralization to civilians and officers of both North and South, and brought numerous protests from commanders in the field to their respective governments. The overland cotton trade to the North during the years 1862 to 1865[18] amounted to about 1,108,000 bales, an amount larger than that obtained by Great Britain from blockade runners. This trade was more essential to the South than to the North, of course, and helped to prolong the war. The accompanying table shows the cotton movement at New Orleans, the principal port of the Confederacy.

RECEIPTS AND SHIPMENTS OF COTTON FROM NEW ORLEANS DURING THE WAR[19] (in bales)

Year	Receipts	Total Exports	Export to Liverpool	Export to Havre	Export to New York	Export to Boston
1859–60	2,235,448	2,214,296	1,348,163	303,157	62,936	131,648
1860–61	1,849,312	1,015,852	1,074,131	384,938	29,539	94,307
1861–62	38,880	27,678	1,312	472	4,116	109
1862–63	22,078	23,750	2,070	1,849	17,859	1,418
1863–64	131,044	128,130	1,155	4,023	109,149	12,793
1864–65	271,015	192,315	31,326	5,952	144,190	15,993

MANUFACTURING IN THE SOUTH

The amount of cotton run through the blockade or smuggled through the lines, and the manufactured goods and gold received in return, softened but slightly the grip of the iron ring. The one-sided civilization of the South put the Confederate states at a decided disadvantage. Manufacturing concerns were comparatively few, and many of those existing were destroyed by the Union Armies. Up to the opening of the war practically all

[18] Freedom of trade was restored in May, 1865.
[19] M. B. Hammond, *The Cotton Industry*, p. 263.

the machinery had been imported, and the rich coal and iron deposits of the South had scarcely been tapped. It is true that cotton to the value of $7,000,000 was spun in the South in 1860 and that cotton manufacturers, although handicapped by depreciating machinery, continued production during the war and made extensive profits. Nevertheless, most of the large-scale manufacturing was carried on by the Confederate government itself, which took over and operated factories producing whisky, salt, guns, small arms, gunpowder, and other munitions of war. After the first two years of the war when the factories were in practical operation, the Confederate armies did not suffer for these essentials. Except for immediate war needs, manufacturing production as a whole declined.

In general, there was a reversion to hand industry. The hand looms and spinning wheels were brought out and much of the clothing and shoes for civilian and soldier were plantation-made. The sacrifice and painstaking labor of the women of the South who worked at these unaccustomed tasks were as heroic as the labor of the slaves was faithful, and both were in bright contrast to the speculation and extravagance all too evident in such cities as Charleston, Mobile, and Richmond. This rapid return to household production was like turning the hands of civilization backward, an undoing of the Industrial Revolution. The development of war manufacturing was severely handicapped by the lack of surplus capital. Previously most of the excess wealth had been invested in land and slaves, and much of the liquid capital on hand during the war years was attracted almost exclusively to blockade running, where profits were enormous. "Fifty or sixty millions of dollars," complained the president of a manufacturers' convention in Augusta in 1864, "have gone into blockade-running, while scarcely a new dollar has gone into manufacturing." [20] Speculation, in fact, was as widespread in the South as in the North, and with greater damage to her cause. "The passion for speculation," asserted President Davis in 1863, "has seduced citizens of all classes from a determined prosecution of the war to a sordid effort to amass money." [21]

AGRICULTURAL PRODUCTION AND THE COST OF LIVING

There was a decided reluctance on the part of many planters to substitute grain crops and meat production for cotton, but this became more and more necessary as the war progressed. In this respect an agricultural revolution was to a certain extent temporarily brought about by the war. The cotton crop of 1862 was only a little over one-quarter that of 1861, and that

[20] Quoted by J. F. Rhodes, *History of the United States*, V, 396, from the Augusta *Chronicle* May 26, 1864.
[21] *Ibid.*, V, 424, from *Official Records*, Vol. XXX, Part I, p. 212.

of 1864 only about one-eighth, while the production of cereals, especially corn, increased yearly. Nevertheless, the price of bread and meat, measured in gold, mounted steadily, and in many parts of the South there was a distressing lack of food at various times, a lack that was especially acute in 1864. The pinch was greatest in the cities, for the farmer could worry along somehow. "Meal is the only food now obtainable except by the rich," commented an observer in Richmond on February 23, 1864, and he added: "We look for a healthy year, everything being so cleanly consumed that no garbage or filth can accumulate." [22] In the early months of 1864, when one dollar of gold was worth $22 in Confederate money, flour sold in Richmond at $300 a barrel Confederate money, and shoes at $150 a pair. There were bread riots in Atlanta, Mobile, and other places.

The food scarcity was caused not so much by absolute lack as by poor distribution, for there was no failure of crops during the war. There were over 6000 miles of railroad in the southern states, sufficient at that time to distribute the food under normal conditions. But the rolling stock and rails wore out rapidly under the severe strain to which they were subjected by war needs, and it was impossible to replace them. The government used the iron mills for other work, and commandeered much of the rolling stock for military purposes. Necessarily, all but the main lines were abandoned. The result was that corn sold in Virginia for fifteen times its price in Georgia. The Union forces eventually obtained control of a large portion of the southern railways, thus further reducing the food supply. Sherman's sixty-mile swath of destruction in Georgia and the desolation left by Sheridan in the Shenandoah Valley added to the woe of the South and the scarcity of provisions.

Financing the Confederacy

When the war broke out the southern states were in debt both to the North and to Europe, and it was thus almost impossible to obtain further credit from the outside. Of surplus capital there was little. There was some metallic currency, of course, but it was difficult for the government to secure possession of it, and specie payment was suspended almost immediately after the outbreak of the struggle. In addition to taxation, the Confederate government endeavored up to 1863 to support itself by bond issues and fiat money in the form of treasury notes. Of the latter, close to one billion dollars were issued. With only the credit of a rebel government behind them, they speedily depreciated in value until on February 17, 1864, the Confederate Congress passed an Act providing for either the compulsory funding of these notes into 4 per cent bonds, or the exchange of all notes

[22] J. B. Jones, *A Rebel War Clerk's Diary at the Confederate Capitol*, II, 186.

under $100 for new notes at the rate of three dollars' worth of the old for two of the new.[23] This amounted to virtual repudiation and drove the people to primitive methods of barter during the final months of the war. The situation was made more hopeless by the state, municipal, and corporation issues of paper which passed as currency.

A $15,000,000 loan, floated in Europe early in 1863 by the French firm of Erlanger & Company, and secured by cotton purchased by the Confederate government, was designed to supply the specie with which to purchase naval and military supplies in Europe. Although the bonds maintained a surprisingly high value, the actual return to the South was slight; $5,000,-000 was expended on vessels that were never delivered, $6,000,000 in attempting to keep the market price of the bonds higher, another million in the three semi-annual drawings for redemption of bonds. Considering these expenditures, says Professor Schwab, and the fact that "the government had to go heavily into debt at home and wrecked the currency in order to gain the necessary cotton on which to base the foreign loan, the net gain from the loan sinks to an insignificant sum."[24] On their return from Europe, the Confederate agents reported to the Richmond government that "the loan was unsuccessful as a source of revenue, but very successful as a political demonstration." Professor Schwab says that "as late as September 7, 1864, the London *Times* considered the holders of the cotton bonds better off than those of Federal securities."[25]

In 1863 the Confederate Congress, realizing that the financial system was weakened beyond repair, passed a law providing for a levy of one-tenth on agricultural products and authorized any officer of the Army to seize such property within certain limits. Without specie, without credit abroad, with her foreign trade cut off, and with a virtually worthless paper currency, the South was forced to levy on agricultural products. It was the agricultural resources freely given or forcibly taken that provided the chief strength of the rebellion.

[23] G. C. Eggleston in *A Rebel's Recollections* (p. 84) quotes a friend as saying: "Before the war I went to market with the money in my pocket, and brought back my purchases in a basket; now I take the money in the basket, and bring the things home in my pocket." By the end of 1864 there were probably over one billion dollars in treasury notes in circulation, "but the issues grew so enormously," says Rhodes (*History*, V, p. 344), "that apparently no exact account of them was made public; it is even possible that the treasury department itself did not know the amount afloat." One gold dollar, according to a table given by Schwab (p. 167), would purchase 61 Confederate paper dollars. These figures, of course, do not seem impressive when compared to the inflation following World War I in central and eastern Europe. See J. C. Schwarb, "The Confederate Foreign Loan: An Episode in the Financial History of the Civil War," *Yale Review*, I (1893).

[24] *Ibid.*, p. 185.

[25] *Ibid.*, p. 183. He goes on to give the reasons for this optimism; it was largely due to the idea of investors that cotton for redeeming the bonds was certain to be forthcoming, and that there would be no repudiation of the debt.

ECONOMIC EFFECTS OF THE CIVIL WAR

In contrast to its effect in the North, the Civil War did not bring in its wake financial prosperity or a period of booming business for the South. Instead of inaugurating a new epoch of unprecedented expansion, it marked a period of destruction in which the old economic life was torn up by the roots. It is true that the fiat money made it a heyday for the speculator, that some fortunes were made by blockade runners, by merchants, and others in the cities, and that for those who had gold there was plenty of the best to be obtained, at least during the earlier years of the war. To the average Southerner the war meant the sacrifice of luxuries and many necessities, in addition to the distress and bitterness entailed by the disastrous outcome; to the economy of the South it meant destruction and chaos, and eventually a fresh start. In summarizing the war Woodrow Wilson said truly: "On the part of the North it was a wonderful display of spirit and power, a splendid revelation of national strength and coherency, a capital proof of quick, organic vitality throughout the great democratic body politic. . . . But its material resources for the stupendous tasks never lacked or were doubted; they even increased while it spent them. On the part of the South, on the other hand, the great struggle was maintained by sheer spirit and devotion, in spite of constantly diminishing resources and constantly waning hope. Her whole strength was put forth, her resources spent, exhausted, annihilated; and yet with such concentration of energy that for more than three years she seemed as fully equal to the contest as the North itself. And all for a belated principle of government, an outgrown economy, an impossible purpose." [26]

In the economic history of the United States the Civil War was extremely important. In the South it put an end to Negro slavery and, to a large extent, to the plantation system. In the North it speeded the Industrial Revolution and the development of capitalism by the prosperity which it brought to industry. The secession of the states'-rights agrarian representatives of the South opened the way for protective tariff legislation and for a more rapid development of the West through the Homestead Act and large railroad grants. The exigencies of war needs brought inflation and new types of paper currency; it brought a new effort on the part of the federal government through the National Bank Act to extend its influence in the banking activities of the nation, and an aggressive move to build a transcontinental railway—all of which were to have an important influence in later history. But, above all, the federal government passed from the control of the agrarian slavocracy of the South to that of the rising industrial plutocracy of the North. [27]

[26] Woodrow Wilson, *Division and Reunion* (rev. ed., 1898), p. 239.

[27] These and other effects of the conflict will be developed more fully in succeeding chapters

SELECTED READINGS

Schwab, J. C., *The Confederate States of America,* Chaps. IX–XII.

Dewey, D. R., *Financial History of the United States,* Chaps. XII, XIII.

Fite, E. D., *Social and Industrial Conditions in the North During the Civil War.*

Rhodes, J. F., *History of the United States,* Vol. V, Chaps. XXVII, XXVIII.

Randall, James G., *The Civil War and Reconstruction,* Chaps. XXVII, XXVIII.

Cole, A. C., *The Irrepressible Conflict,* Chaps. XIV, XV.

Owsley, F. L., *King Cotton Diplomacy,* Chaps. V, XIX.

Jones, J. B., *A Rebel War Clerk's Diary,* Chaps. XXIX, XXX.

Flügel, F., and Faulkner, H. U., *Readings in the Economic and Social History of the United States,* pp. 447–483.

18

The Last Frontier

THE TRANS-MISSISSIPPI ADVANCE

THE population of the United States according to the Census of 1860 was approximately 31,443,000. By that year the region bordering the west bank of the Mississippi had been admitted to statehood: Minnesota (1858), Iowa (1846), Missouri (1821), Arkansas (1836), and Louisiana (1812). West of that tier of states only three areas had sufficient population for admission: Texas, with 602,000 in 1860, Oregon with 52,000, and California with 380,000. By the 1860's two frontiers had been established—an eastward-moving one along the Pacific coast and a westward-moving one extending unevenly along the 97th meridian. The latter fringe of settlement ran southward through central Minnesota and Iowa, through eastern Kansas, and along the western boundary of Arkansas, and then bulged westward to include a large area of eastern Texas. In the region between this line and the fringe of settlement along the west coast lay approximately half the territory of the United States, but in 1860 this area contained only one per cent of the population. This intervening territory was America's "last frontier."

More than two centuries had elapsed between the founding of the first permanent white settlement within the boundary of the present United States and the extension of the frontier line west to the 97th meridian. The rest of the nation was largely occupied in the three decades 1870–1890. It was peopled by miners, ranchers, and farmers, lured by discoveries of rich deposits of minerals and by opportunities to exploit free grass and to open fertile farming areas. The process was speeded by favorable land laws, by a rapidly increasing immigration, and particularly by the building of the great transcontinental railroads, the invention of barbed wire, and the quantity production of windmills.

THE MINERS' FRONTIER

The search for minerals, which had played such a major rôle in the early exploration and settlement of the American continent, again became an important influence in the settlement of the "last frontier." Missionary activity and ranching had brought the first permanent white occupation of California. But the handful of Spaniards were quickly submerged in the flood of gold seekers who overran the country in 1849 and created from it an American state in 1850. Only a small percentage of the " 'forty-niners" actually acquired wealth from the metal, but a large number remained to exploit the possibilities in commerce, agriculture, and lumber. With thousands of white settlers in California and a scattered population of farmers and trappers in Oregon, America's possession of the Pacific coast was beyond dispute.

Some beginning of actual settlement had already been made in this vast region by Mormons around the Salt Lake basin, and by Spanish ranchers pushing north from Mexico. The discovery of gold in California was of course followed by the activities of numerous prospecting parties in many parts of the Rockies. Rumors that the precious metal was to be found in the Pike's Peak region were confirmed in 1859, and that year saw a great exodus to what later became the state of Colorado. Professional prospectors and miners of the West hastened to the scene, their ranks augmented by thousands from the East who had felt the pinch of the depression following the panic of 1857. "Pike's Peak or bust," was the motto of the " 'fifty-niners," and not far from 100,000 reached Colorado during the rush of the first year. Although half returned "Busted! By Gosh!" those who remained laid the foundations of a new state eventually admitted in 1876. The Colorado deposits, unfortunately for the early gold seekers, were embedded in quartz lodes that required heavy machinery and large capital for working; hence they could not be developed immediately. Although agriculture now surpasses in importance the products of the mines, for decades minerals played a leading rôle in the development of the state. The mines at Leadville have yielded over $300,000,000 worth of silver and those at Cripple Creek a similar amount of gold.

The rush which laid the foundations of Colorado was but one of a series of booms which planted mining camps on many a lonely creek and forbidding hillside in the Rockies. Small deposits of gold had brought about the founding of Carson City in 1858 at the extreme western part of the Territory of Utah, close to the California border line and near the old overland route from Salt Lake City to San Francisco. The discovery of the famous Comstock Lode in the next year on the eastern slope of Mt. Davidson, not far from Lake Tahoe, brought an influx of immigrants who transformed the region into the Territory of Nevada (formerly part of the Territory of Utah) in 1861 and into a state three years later. The great silver deposits were easily accessible, located as they were on the main route to

California, and Carson Valley was speedily entered from both the west and the east. From 1860 to 1890 the Comstock Lode yielded $340,000,000 worth of silver, and was the economic backbone of the region during those years. The yield declined rapidly after 1890, seriously affecting the prosperity of the state; however, new discoveries of gold, silver, and copper in 1906 and the following years at Tonopah, Goldfield, and other places renewed industry and brought a fresh influx of population. Copper was not mined in large quantities until after 1908, but today its annual production has a value double that of all other minerals produced in the state.[1]

Handicapped by climate and inaccessibility, the western part of the Territory of New Mexico (now Arizona) was prospected slowly, and individual miners found it difficult to operate successfully. Mining companies, however, with laborers recruited from California, opened up a few deserted shafts near the old Spanish town of Tucson soon after the Gadsden Purchase was consummated. The Civil War closed the Tucson mines for the time being, but further discoveries in 1862 and 1863 along the left bank of the Colorado near Bill Williams' Creek brought a new outburst of gold enthusiasm. Arizona was made a territory in 1863 (a state in 1912), but for over ten years after territorial government was set up troubles with the Apaches made mining a dangerous occupation. Gold and silver, which drew the first prospectors to Arizona, have since become a small part of her mineral production. She now leads the Union in copper production.

Just as the influx of gold diggers had brought sufficient population to create the new Territories of Colorado, Nevada, and Arizona, so discoveries of the precious metal led to the organization of Idaho Territory in 1863. The Territory of Washington had already been separated from the Oregon Territory in 1853, because of the inconvenience of administering the distant settlements on Puget Sound, but Washington was not admitted as a state until 1889. In 1860 gold was discovered on the reservation of the Nez Percé Indians near the juncture of the Clearwater and Snake Rivers. "To attempt to restrain these miners," reported the Superintendent of Indian Affairs, "would be like attempting to restrain the whirlwind," and in the next year thousands poured into these river valleys; the town of Lewiston sprang up as a center. The discoveries here were followed by others on the Salmon River, at Boisé, and in the Owyhee district, south of the great bend of the Snake. The trappers of the Hudson's Bay and the American Fur Companies first roamed over this country, and the farmers who followed McLoughlin and Whitman were the first serious settlers; but it was the gold seekers of '61 and '62 who gave Washington new life and founded Idaho. As gold had brought in 1861 the

---

[1] Fortunately Samuel L. Clemens (Mark Twain) went to Nevada in 1861 and in *Roughing It* (1871) has given to posterity unforgettable descriptions of the boom days in Virginia City.

development of the region which is now western Idaho, so new discoveries in 1863 gave birth to Alder Gulch, to Virginia City, and to a new group of mines in eastern Idaho between Beaver Head River and Madison River. Ten thousand came to Virginia City in 1864 and the same year saw the founding of Helena, "the last of the boom towns of the period." Such an ingress of miners to these points caused the cutting away of northeastern Idaho into the Territory of Montana in 1864, and the organization of Wyoming Territory in 1868. The discovery of gold in 1882 at Coeur d'Alene brought a new rush to Idaho; but the production of gold relative to that of other metals has not been large. Her next-door neighbor, Montana, produces copper in the Butte region in an amount which is surpassed only by Arizona and Utah (1937).

The decade of the 'sixties saw the Rockies at least partially occupied from Mexico to the Canadian border, with most of the population scattered on the mining claims which dotted the hillsides and valleys or gathered into the raw towns which had sprung up near the more valuable deposits. Frederick L. Paxson, historian of the frontier, has caught the spirit of the picturesque but demoralizing life of the mining frontier:

The shifting population which inhabited the new territories invites and at the same time defies description. It was made up chiefly of young men. Respectable women were not unknown, but were so few in number as to have little measurable influence upon social life. In many towns they were in the minority, even among their set, since the easily won wealth of the camps attracted dissolute women who cannot be numbered but who must be imagined. The social tone of the various camps was determined by the preponderance of men, the absence of regular labor, and the speculative fever which was the justification of their existence. The political tone was determined by the nature of the population, the character of the industry, and the remoteness from a seat of government. Combined, these factors produced a type of life the like of which America had never known, and whose picturesque qualities have blinded the thoughtless into believing that it was romantic. It was at best a hard, bitter struggle, with the dark places only accentuated by the tinsel of gambling and adventure.

A single street meandering along a valley, with one-story huts flanking it in irregular rows, was the typical mining camp. The saloon and the general store, sometimes combined, were its representative institutions. Deep ruts along the streets bore witness to the heavy wheels of the freighters, while horses loosely tied to all available posts at once revealed the regular means of locomotion, and by the careless way they were left about showed that this sort of property was not likely to be stolen. The mining population centering here lived a life of contrasts. The desolation and loneliness of prospecting and working claims alternated with the excitement of coming to town. Few decent beings habitually lived in the towns. The resident population expected to live off the miners, either in way of trade or worse. The bar, the gambling house, the dance hall have been made too common in description to need further account. In the reaction against loneliness, the extremes of drunkenness, debauchery, and murder were only too frequent in these places of amusement.[2]

Yet upon such unpromising foundations were laid the beginnings of many of our far-western states. The search for minerals brought the first important white migration to the present California, Nevada, Arizona, New Mexico, Colorado, Idaho, and Montana.

THE RANCHERS' FRONTIER

Between the eastern frontier line and the mining settlements of the West there stretched from Texas to Manitoba a vast territory of rolling land. Grass-covered but lacking in rainfall, this country was believed by many to be unfit for cultivation and unlikely ever to be occupied. It was in the 1860's that it was found that cattle not only could withstand the severe winters of northern Nebraska but would thrive on the pasturage of wild grass there. This discovery opened the country almost immediately to cattlemen and ranchers, who occupied it for the next two decades until driven aside by the advancing frontier of farmers.

Since the days of the Spaniards cattle had been bred on the Texas plains, and, exposed to the weather and running free on the wide ranges, a sturdy stock had developed. Heretofore there had been little incentive for ranchers to market their cattle, for the farmer of the Mississippi Valley and the Atlantic coast had easily been able to supply the local need. Moreover, a slowly developing southern market had been cut off by the Civil War, leaving the Texas range overstocked at the end of the conflict. But the rapidly growing population of the East and the railroads advancing to the very doors of the cattle ranch now offered both a market and the means of transportation, opportunities quickly taken advantage of by the Texas cattlemen. At the same time the slaughter of the buffalo had made way for the cattle. Without the buffalo, which provided subsistence for them, the plains Indians were rendered helpless and easily pushed back into reservations useless even for the grazing of cattle.

In the spring the cattle were rounded up and divided among the owners according to existing customs and laws. The yearling steers were separated from the rest, branded, and then started on the long trail north to Kansas, Nebraska, or Wyoming, to be fattened for the market; the remainder were turned back upon the range to multiply. At Abilene, Kansas, on the newly built Kansas Pacific, and at Dodge City on the Atchison, Topeka and Santa

[2] F. L. Paxson, *The Last American Frontier* (1910), pp. 170–172.

Fé there grew up during the 'seventies the greatest of the early cattle towns. At Ogallala, Nebraska, there was another great cattle center, and 400 miles northwest of there, at Miles City, Montana, still another great center developed for the Northwest. On their arrival at these points the herds were usually fattened for the market and then sold for immediate slaughter or for shipment to the stockyards of Kansas City, Milwaukee, or Chicago. As time went on and competition became keener, thought was given to experimental breeding and to the production of the most profitable type for this method of disposal. Stock growers' associations appeared for mutual protection against lawbreakers and thieves and to guard as best they could against the contamination of their herds by Texas fever, hoof and mouth disease, and other ailments.

The ranchers' frontier lasted about two decades, from the late 'sixties to the late 'eighties. It was characterized by the long drives which sent some 4,000,-000 Texas cattle northward to be slaughtered or to stock the northern ranges, and by the rapid spread of cattle ranches over the vast area of unenclosed government land. It was also characterized by large profits resulting from an expanding market and low overhead costs. Chiefly responsible for the latter was the opportunity to graze cattle free on government land. By 1890 the great drives were a thing of the past. Transient as this period was, the hard but romantic life of the cowboy has become immortalized as part of our history through Theodore Roosevelt's association with the cow country, the novels of Owen Wister and others, and the pictures of Frederic Remington. The "dime novel" and the moving picture have made it a part of American folklore.

Production of cattle for the market has continued as an important industry of the Great Plains, but the characteristics of the ranchers' last frontier are gone. Of all the factors which put an end to the open range and the long drive, the most important was the advancing farmers' frontier. This in turn, as we shall see, was speeded by the building of the transcontinental railroads and their subsidiaries. The railroads which had made the ranchers' frontier possible contributed to hasten its end. Railroads may have brought the farmer to the frontier, but it was the invention of barbed wire which really enabled him to take possession and hold the land against the range cattle. In the end it also helped the cattlemen. Under the severe competition the scrub stock and the longhorn had to give way to better breeds which required more care. The new stock could not fend for itself but had to be enclosed. As the ranchers witnessed the farmers' frontier eating into the open range, the more far-sighted hastened to enclose land. Much of this enclosure was illegal; the estimates of it in 1888 run as high as 8,000,000 acres. The increasing inroads of both farmers and ranchers on the public land soon changed the economic picture of the West. The shift of the cattle industry from the open range to the pasture was also hastened by the appearance of cattle diseases and the quarantine laws passed by northern states against southern cattle. Two other factors tended to stabilize the industry under the new conditions: the severe winters of the early 'eighties which destroyed many cattle, and the overexpansion during this period which brought collapse and ruin to many cattlemen.

Short as was the life of the ranchers' frontier, it left definite influences upon our history. Above all, it helped to open to settlement the vast area between the 100th meridian and the Rockies. The clamor of both ranchers and farmers for more land forced the opening of Oklahoma to settlement. With the growth of the ranchers' frontier, the packing industry moved westward to center in Chicago, St. Louis, Kansas City, and Omaha, where it quickly became a monopoly in the hands of Armour, Hammond, Morris, and Swift. Packing and refrigeration processes were forced upon the industry by the transportation factor. With these problems solved, the exportation of meat became increasingly important. The conflict between the cattlemen on the one hand and the packers and railroads on the other for the profits of the industry contributed to the economic and political controversies of the time and to the rising tide of agrarian unrest.

THE FARMERS' FRONTIER

Pressing rapidly on the heels of the ranchers came the vanguard of farmers who succeeded by 1890 in virtually closing the American frontier. Many factors explain the rapid occupation of this vast area. First of all were the land laws. The long agitation for free land finally achieved its objective. The first bill was passed in 1860 and vetoed by Buchanan, but a second, sponsored by the Republican party in the election of that year, was signed by Lincoln on May 20, 1862. The Homestead Act granted a quarter section (160 acres) free to the head of a family or to a person over twenty-one who was a citizen of the United States or who had filed his intention of becoming one. Residence of five years was required; good faith was to be evidenced by cultivation. After six months,[3] however, the entry might be commuted by the payment of $1.25 an acre. Later amendments have further liberalized the Act by permitting Union veterans of the Civil War and the veterans of all succeeding wars to count the time served in the Army against the five-year required residence period.

Other Acts which followed tended either to liberalize the Homestead Act or to make other land available at low cost. The Timber and Stone Act of

---

[3] Raised to fourteen months in 1891.

1878 opened to citizens at the appraisal value, but in no case at less than $2.50 an acre, 160 acres of public lands valuable chiefly for timber and stone and unfit for cultivation at the date of sale. The Dawes Act of 1887 provided for individual instead of tribal ownership of small amounts of land by the Indians and has thus opened up large areas of reservations to settlers. An Act passed in 1909 provided for enlarged homesteads of 320 acres of non-irrigable land where dry farming was necessary, one-fourth of which had to be cultivated in two years. In 1912 the five-year residence was reduced to three, and an Act to allow 640 acres for stock raising further liberalized the system in 1916.

The Homestead Act of 1862 has often been described as opening a great new era in the history of our national land policy. In a sense this is true, although free land was obtainable in the colonial period [4] and by special Acts in later years. Upon closer examination, however, the significance of the Act tends to diminish. First of all, the Homestead Act was superimposed on the old laws and was later restricted by new ones. The Preemption Act of 1841, allowing a person to buy choice lands by preemption, continued in effect until 1891. The old system of sale by auction and cash was still in existence, as, for example, in the Timber and Stone Act. Moreover, much of the best land had been given away and was not available for free homestead occupation. Through the Morrill grant for agricultural colleges and other legislation to foster education over 200,000,000 acres had been given away by 1930. Between 1850 and 1871 another 200,000,000 acres were given to aid in the building of railroads, although this was later reduced to 137,000,000 when the railroads failed to meet the requirements of the law. Much of the land obtained by treaties with the Indians was reserved for sale rather than for free distribution. The government likewise held for sale the alternate sections which it had reserved in the railroad grants. Since the railroad and educational grants, as well as much of the best land owned by the government, could be obtained only by purchase, the homesteader on the Great Plains was often forced to take second best lands and those at a distance from transportation facilities. It is not surprising, therefore, to find that up to 1890 only 48,225,736 acres were granted under the Homestead Act to 372,659 families, and only about one-third of these claims were finally proved. It is doubtful if more than 1,000,000 people out of a population increase of 30,000,000 between 1860 and 1890 actually profited from this Act.[5] Interestingly enough it was in the years after 1890 that the greatest expansion under the Homestead Act took place.

[4] Above, p. 54.

[5] The limitations of the Homestead Act are clearly shown in P. W. Gates, "The Homestead Act in an Incongruous Land System," *American Historical Review,* Vol. XLI, No. 4, pp. 652–681 (July, 1936), and in F. A. Shannon, "The Homestead Act and the Labor Surplus," *ibid.,* pp. 637–651.

From 1862 to 1926 the government issued patents for approximately 226,159,-000 acres.

Not only were the homestead laws limited in their benefits, but their intention was often frustrated by evasion and misuse. Their intention may have been to provide free land for migrant settlers and to cover the West with small freeholds, but the results were often far different. At one time it was possible for a settler to secure 1120 acres of land—160 acres under the Homestead Act, 160 acres under the old Preemption Act, 160 acres under the Stone and Timber Act, and 640 acres of desert land. By collusion with individuals it was a simple matter for mining and lumber companies to secure immense holdings by violating the intent, if not the letter, of the law. This was done through the privilege of commuting, a feature of the Homestead Act which allowed the homesteader at any time after six months of filing his claim to obtain his land by paying $1.25 or $2.50 an acre for it. Thus in six months large corporations acting through their agents might, at a small cost, obtain lands worth many times the amount paid. It is estimated that from 1881 to 1904, 23 per cent of the land transferred from government to private ownership under the Homestead Acts was obtained by commuting. In North Dakota during the first decade of the present century more acres were commuted than were obtained by five years' residence.[6] An agent of the land office asserted that "actual inspection of hundreds of commuted homesteads shows that not one in a hundred is ever occupied as a home after commutation." [7]

The situation respecting the public lands became so notorious that in 1879 Congress appointed a commission to examine and report on the land system, but the suggested reforms were ignored. Until the rise of the conservation movement about 1901 only the courageous stand of Arthur and Cleveland can be taken as real evidence of a national desire to enforce the existing laws. A new Public Land Commission appointed by Roosevelt submitted elaborate reports and suggested salutary reforms along the same line as the previous commission, but again little was done. The policy of the government as regards public land has remained essentially as before, and (according to the National Conservation Commission of 1909) is far from subserving the best interests of the nation.

Not only is our land policy open to the criticism that the laws have been criminally evaded and negligently enforced, but the wisdom of the whole system itself has been questioned. Has it been to the best interests of the nation to give away its heritage of land so rapidly and so freely that it has encouraged wasteful methods of farming, glutted the market with foodstuffs, and decreased the value of the agricultural lands in the East? On the other hand,

[6] B. H. Hibbard, *A History of the Public Land Policies* (1924), p. 387.
[7] Quoted in *ibid.*, p. 389.

farms have been provided for many settlers from the East and for multitudes drawn from Europe by the prospect of free land. The policy has enormously stimulated the rapid occupation of the trans-Mississippi country and the founding of new commonwealths. This, in fact, was the main purpose of the Homestead Act, and the intention was that settlement should proceed under a democratic system. The Public Land Commission said of the Act, "It protects the government, it fills the state with homes, it builds up communities and lessens the chances of social and civil disorder by giving ownership of the soil, in small tracts, to the occupants thereof." These hopes were but partly realized. Ownership of small tracts, as originally contemplated, was often frustrated by the fraudulent evasion of the Acts; the result was large holdings and landless workers. Moreover, it is doubtful if free land under the Homestead Act ever played an important part as a "safety valve" for labor. The last three decades of the nineteenth century were years of discontent and strife among eastern wage earners and of acute economic and political unrest in the agricultural West.

Quite as potent as the Homestead Act in promoting the advance of the farming frontier was the construction of the transcontinental railways. After

(From Faulkner's *Economic History of the United States,* by permission of The Macmillan Company.)

WESTWARD MOVEMENT OF THE CENTER OF POPULATION.

exhaustive government surveys, twenty years of agitation, and arduous labor, the last spike in the roadbed connecting the Union Pacific and the Central Pacific was driven on May 10, 1869, at Ogden, Utah, and the first railway across the continent was completed. Other transcontinental lines were authorized in the 'sixties, and the years from the close of the war until the panic of 1873 were characterized by feverish railroad building which was renewed with the revival of business after 1878. Under the direction of Henry Villard, the Northern Pacific was completed in 1883, and the same year saw the linking of the Atchison, Topeka, and Santa Fé and the Southern Pacific in a southern route to California. In 1882 the Texas Pacific and the Southern Pacific met at El Paso and connections were thus made between the Pacific and New Orleans or St. Louis. By the middle 'eighties there were at least four main routes to the Pacific, and such roads as the Kansas Pacific, completed to Denver in 1870, and the Chicago, Burlington, and Quincy, completed to the same point in 1882, opened up much additional territory to immigrants. The Union Pacific had been looked upon as a national project and had been aided lavishly by the government, a policy which until 1871 was generally followed with other prospective western roads. Approximately 137,000,000 acres have been granted by the national government to states or to private corporations for internal improvements, of which the larger part has gone to the transcontinental roads. In fact, all the western roads mentioned in this paragraph were recipients of large public land donations, except the Chicago, Burlington, and Quincy. These grants included a right of way and alternate sections on each side of the track, ranging from five sections per mile to as high as forty for the Union Pacific. The remaining sections were reserved by the government for later sale.

Whether the land belonged to the railroads or the government, it was essential for the railroads to populate it. Their literature and advertisements were printed in many languages and distributed over the eastern states and Europe. Agencies were established in Europe and America, and their representatives carried on propaganda wherever the field seemed ripe. In the East veterans' organizations were canvassed for likely immigrants, and influential men were obtained to lead groups of Scandinavians to the Northwest. Transportation rates were reduced, reception houses established, and liberal credit inducements offered for the purchase of land. The roads which were particularly active in this work, such as the Northern Pacific, overlooked few known methods of encouraging immigration. In a debate on the admission of the Dakotas in 1884, Benjamin Harrison correctly observed: "Conditions of emigration have changed. The emigrant who is seeking a home in the West does not now use as his vehicle a pack-train, a Conestoga wagon, or even a broad-horn. The great bulk of the people who have gone into Dakota have gone upon the steam-car, many of them within sight of the home which they were to take up under the homestead laws of the United States . . . whereas in the case of the state of Indiana it was thirty years after the admission of that state into the Union before a single line of railroad was built in its territory." [8]

[8] 48th Cong., 2nd Sess., *Congressional Record,* Vol. XVI, Part I, p. 109 (Dec. 9, 1884).

Important as were the Homestead Acts and the railroads, there were other significant factors in the rapid settlement of the Great Plains. The more permanent problem facing the farmer who settled in the region between the 98th meridian and the Rockies was the inadequate rainfall. In this section, says its greatest historian, "the scarcity of moisture is the subject that furnishes the greatest amount of thought and talk; in fact, it is the crux of the whole problem of conquering the Great Plains." [9] Its history has been largely determined by the search for water. Efforts to solve this problem extend from the dug wells of the first pioneers to the great irrigation projects of the federal government at Boulder Dam and Grand Coulee. They include experiments in dry farming and the importation and adaptation of drought-resisting wheat and corn. For the average prairie farmer, however, the supply of water depended on pumping up the ground water with a windmill; hence the development of quantity production of small metal windmills went hand in hand with frontier expansion into the Great Plains. Adapted to the almost continuous delivery of small amounts of water, the windmill was perhaps the most important mechanical aid in the occupation of this area.

Without the windmill the settlement of the prairies might have been indefinitely delayed; without barbed wire the plains might still be in possession of the cowboy and the roaming herds of cattle. Until the 'sixties, fencing material was primarily wooden rails, rocks, and hedge growth. This was sufficient until the pioneer left the timbered region and moved into the prairies. At first he avoided the open land, although it was often more fertile; when he finally struck into it he tried frantically to find substitutes for the old fencing materials. Solution of the problem came in the middle 'seventies when patents for practical barbed wire were taken out by two Illinois farmers, Joseph F. Glidden and Jacob Haish. Never did inventors find a more receptive market. The production and sale of barbed wire which amounted to 10,000 pounds in 1874 jumped to 80,500,000 six years later. Quantity production reduced the price from $20 a hundred pounds in 1874 to a low mark of $1.80 a hundred in 1897.

The way was now open for rapid expansion. Said an old settler in Texas: "It was not until about 1875 that the black lands really became available for agricultural purposes. The development of those lands had lagged for lack of the means of fencing them at moderate cost. They were so far from timber as to make rail fences out of the question. The want was supplied by the Glidden barbed wire, which, beginning about 1875, was shipped into the state, not by the carload but by the trainload. After that immigrants ceased to stop in East Texas, and the black lands came into their own." [10] Ranchers

[9] W. P. Webb, *The Great Plains* (1931), p. 322.
[10] *Ibid.*, p. 317.

might descend upon the outlying farms and cut the wire to pieces, but it was a losing battle. Barbed wire not only enabled the farmers to win the battle but it forced the ranchers to change the methods of their own industry.[11] "It was barbed wire," says Webb, "and not the railroads or the homestead law that made it possible for the farmers to resume, or at least accelerate, their march across the prairies and onto the plains. Even the fertile Prairie Plains were but sparsely settled until after the advent of barbed wire."[12]

A phase of the occupation of the last frontier, upon which it is unnecessary to enter in detail, is the dispossession of the Indians. Until 1861 the trans-Mississippi Indians were generally on friendly terms with the United States, notwithstanding the fact that their lands were continually traversed by surveyors and miners. Driven to desperation by the obvious fact that the end was near, the Indians made their last stand against encroaching civilization. The Sioux uprising in 1862 was followed by that of the Cheyenne and other tribes in the 'sixties, and the Indian struggle culminated in the Sioux war of 1876 and the defeat of their chieftain, Sitting Bull. In the elimination of the western Indian, it is only fair to say that the outstanding feature was not the treachery of the red man, but rather the ruthless greed of the white invader backed by the regular Army whose rifles gave way on the plains to the more deadly six-shooter. A subsequent chapter of this long-drawn-out tragedy was written in 1887 in the Dawes Act, in which the government sought to hasten the Indians' acceptance of the white man's civilization by abolishing the tribal ownership of land and allotting to the head of each family a quarter section of 160 acres, an eighth section to single adults and orphans, and a sixteenth to each dependent child. To protect the new owner, the right to mortgage or dispose of the land was withheld for twenty-five years, and it was to be tax-free for that period. The Dawes Act carried with it the right of citizenship for those Indians who voluntarily left their tribes and took up homesteads under its provisions. It has failed to solve the problem of the Indian, but it has been instrumental in opening much land to white settlers.

End of the Frontier

By 1890 the frontier (technically, a region with more than two and less than six people per square mile) had vanished. Most of the good arable land had been taken up by that time. The farmers' frontier had met and expropriated much of the ranchers' cow country and now reached the mining country in the mountains. Fertile farming land to the west of the Sierras on the Pacific coast was now yielding more than the precious metal ever had.

[11] Above, p. 365.
[12] W. P. Webb, *The Great Plains*, p. 317.

In 1904 the government still owned 700,000,000 acres of land, but most of it was valueless except for dry farming, irrigation, or drainage projects. Economically this great region between the Mississippi and the mountains is primarily agricultural, the newly populated territories separating roughly into the wheat country of Montana and the Dakotas; the corn belt of Kansas, Iowa, and Nebraska; and the cotton fields and grazing lands of Texas. Occupation and economic development were followed by admission to statehood —North Dakota, South Dakota, Montana, and Washington in 1889, and Idaho and Wyoming in 1890. The abandonment of polygamy by the Mormon church in 1890 paved the way for the admission of Utah in 1896; Oklahoma became a state in 1907, and New Mexico and Arizona in 1912.

With the passing of the frontier a new era in American history began. More than any other factor, the existence of a large area of unoccupied land and a constantly moving frontier had differentiated the underlying economic conditions of the United States from those of western Europe. The frontier had provided an outlet for restless groups from the East and a home for millions of immigrants from Europe. It had shaped the content and direction of foreign trade and the type and location of domestic industry. It had laid its mark on our monetary system and our railroad history. Not only had it been of primary importance in our economic history but it had reacted upon our social and political development and gone far to mold American psychology and American philosophy.

Historians and economists in recent years have been greatly interested in pointing out the influence of the frontier and in predicting the changes which may follow its disappearance. A word of caution, however, should be interjected. Good free land might be gone, but after 1890 there was still a large amount of inferior land which, with modern methods, might be made productive, and an abundance of cheap land was still obtainable;[13] and for those who still desired high-grade free land, it was possible, as thousands did, to emigrate to Canada. The twentieth-century immigrant might have to pay for his land, but he might also escape many of the hardships of the earlier settlers. Nevertheless, as the twentieth century swings into the fifth decade, certain effects of the passing of the frontier seem evident. An impetus has been given to conservation, reclamation, and scientific agriculture. Manufacturing is becoming less a simple supplement to extractive industry; rather, by greater use of improved machinery it is carrying its processes further. Commerce, which was early concerned with the exportation of agricultural and of raw or semi-manufactured products, and the importation of manufactured goods, has gradually become concerned with the importation of

[13] As already pointed out, three times as much land was patented under the Homestead Act after 1890 as before.

agricultural commodities and of raw materials and the exportation of manu-factured goods, thus laying the foundations for an economic imperialism similar to that of western Europe. What effect the passing of free land will have upon the growth of the tenant system, upon the development of or-ganized labor, and upon the growth of class consciousness it is too early to predict; but it is obvious that it portends a new group of economic and social problems whose solution will tax the best intelligence of the next century.[14]

SELECTED READINGS

Paxson, F. L., *History of the American Frontier,* Chaps. XLVII, XLVIII, L–LIX.

Osgood, E. S., *The Day of the Cattleman,* Chaps. IV and V.

Webb, W. P., *The Great Plains,* Chaps. V–VIII.

Gates, P. W., "The Homestead Law in an Incongruous Land System," *American Historical Review,* Vol. XLI, pp. 652–681 (July, 1936).

Hedges, J. B., "The Colonization Work of the Northern Pacific," *Mississippi Valley Historical Review,* Vol. XIII, pp. 311–342 (Dec., 1926).

Flügel, F., and Faulkner, H. U., *Readings in the Economic and Social History of the United States,* pp. 741–764.

[14] C. W. Wright, "The Disappearance of Free Land in Our Economic Development," *American Economic Review,* Vol. XVI, No. 1, Supplement (March, 1926), pp. 265–271, reprinted in F. Flügel and H. U. Faulkner, *Readings,* pp. 758–764.

19

The Agrarian Revolution

Agriculture Development, 1860–1910

So significant has been the industrial advance since 1860 that it has obscured an agricultural development quite as momentous. The half century from 1860 to 1910 witnessed an agrarian revolution which included both the introduction of agricultural machinery and the increased adoption of scientific farming. It saw the rapid growth of government interest and aid to agriculture and a widespread movement toward agricultural education. Spurred on by the Homestead Act, by migration from Europe, and by all the influences which have advanced our frontier, the agricultural domain was pushed westward until most of the usable land was preempted. The entire population of the United States in 1860 was 30 million, but in 1910 there were 50 million living on farms and in villages supported by agriculture, and the number of farms had grown from 2 million in 1860 to 6 million in 1910. During this half century over 500 million acres of new land had been brought under cultivation, an area almost as large as that of western Europe, providing new homes for millions of people, freight for railroads, and food for the increasing industrial classes in Europe and America.

This development was, perhaps, too rapid, for it drove the prices of foodstuffs down to a point in many cases below the cost of production. It was accompanied by circumstances which brought hardship and discontent to the farmers and which were reflected in political and economic unrest. The end of the frontier, however, eventually stimulated interest in conservation, in irrigation projects, and in scientific farming. With rising prices for products and land values from 1896 to 1920, and with better roads, electric trolleys, automobiles, and farm machinery, the economic condition of the farmer improved and rural life became more satisfying. Nevertheless, these years saw a constant increase in urban population and manufacturing, and a relative decline in agricultural population and wealth.

Agrarian Discontent

Although the period since the Civil War was one of great agricultural expansion, it was not one of uninterrupted prosperity. On the contrary, the period from 1867 to 1897 was one of uncertainty and discontent. During the flush period of the war when prices soared as the result of greater demand for foodstuffs and an inflated currency, many farmers extended their operations by increasing their holdings and equipment. Ex-soldiers, tradesmen, and mechanics, encouraged by the Homestead Act and railroad propaganda, hastened to take up land; but all of them usually lacked equipment and tools, and the land was mortgaged to provide for the necessary equipment. All went well until the inflated war prices collapsed. The government's policy of calling in some of the greenbacks and ultimately raising the paper currency to a parity with gold put the farmers at a disadvantage, for the American farmer was predominantly a debtor and consequently was injured by a decline in the general price level. Unable to meet his interest payments, which continued at the old rate while prices fell and the value of money increased, he was often forced to see his mortgage foreclosed and the results of years of labor wiped out; he had the option of going into industry, entering the ranks of the tenant farmer or agricultural laborer, or again moving on to the frontier.

It was not only the problem of deflation and the lack of adequate credit facilities which harassed the farmer, but the fact that he found himself at a disadvantage in his relations with the rapidly developing railroad and industrial monopolies. The railroads upon which he was dependent for marketing his products were often careless and inefficient, discriminating in their favors to industries at the expense of the agricultural sections. Where there was no discrimination, freight rates were still needlessly high because of dividend payments on heavily watered stock. Throughout the last decades of the nineteenth century, the development of big business and monopolies proceeded rapidly. "Never in our history," said the Greenbackers in prefacing their platform in 1884, "have the banks, the land-grant railroads, and other monopolies been more insolent in their demands for further privilege—still more class legislation. In this emergency the dominant parties are arrayed against the people and are the abject tools of corporate monopolies." While the prices of farm commodities declined, those of manufactured products, dominated by monopoly practices, remained high or did not decline proportionately. Monopolies in meat packing and other processing industries were often able to hold the prices of farm commodities artificially low while they profited by the high prices charged to consumers. Moreover, the holders of patent monopolies on such essential farm commodities as barbed wire or well machinery were often able to harass and overcharge the farmer.[1] At the same time the farmer felt that an undue share of the profits was taken by the

---

[1] Earl W. Hayter, "The Western Farmers and the Drivewell Patent Controversy," *Agricultural History*, XVI, 16–28 (Jan., 1942).

middlemen and by the speculators on the grain and cotton exchanges. While he bore the hardships of a lonely and arduous frontier life, eastern capitalists deprived him of the profits of his toil. "There are three great crops raised in Nebraska," said one of the farmers' papers in 1890. "One is a crop of corn, one a crop of freight rates, and one a crop of interest. One is produced by the farmers who by sweat and toil farm the land. The other two are produced by men who sit in their offices and behind their bank counters and farm the farmers." [2]

This feeling of bitterness over an exploitation which, in fact, existed, was particularly strong in the sections where the pinch was greatest, particularly on the wheat farms of the West. Minor elements in the prevailing unrest in that region were the conflict between the land-hungry pioneer farmers and the cattle raisers, and the fraudulent methods employed by individuals and companies in obtaining large blocks of land. But the trans-Mississippi West was not the only section that suffered from declining prices and the exploitation of railroads, monopolies, and middlemen. In the South the situation was equally discouraging. Here the whole economic structure had crashed with the Civil War, and a new economy was being painfully reconstructed on the ruins. Bankrupt planters, ignorant colored labor, and declining cotton prices were the elements from which the new system must be erected. In the Northeast, deflation and western competition severely affected the agricultural interests, accentuated the movement to the cities, and increased the area of deserted farms. Throughout the country the general decline in land values was a factor in the agrarian discontent; for the American farmer, it must be remembered, is a land speculator as well as an agriculturist. Added to all this was the high tariff of the Civil War, continued during the years of peace, which aided the manufacturing interests and at the same time increased the cost of living and jeopardized the foreign market for foodstuffs.

The farmers fought back against economic tendencies and specific grievances, and for three decades after the Civil War the agrarian sections were in an almost continuous condition of revolt. This revolt took the form of political pressure exerted through farmers' organizations and political parties, and various cooperative efforts in the field of business in an attempt to help themselves. It was directed against their chief difficulties—monetary deflation, railroad abuses, and monopoly practices. From the late 1860's until the end of the century the farmers fought bitterly the deflationary policies of the federal government. They organized the Greenback party in an effort to bring about inflation by fiat paper money, and the Populist party to achieve the same end by restoring free and unlimited coinage of gold and silver at 16 to 1. Both parties directed their attacks against monopolies as well as against

[2] *Farmers' Alliance*, August 23, 1890. Quoted by John Hicks, *The Populist Revolt*, p. 83.

deflation. The first great farmers' organization of the West, the Patrons of Husbandry, exerted its greatest influence in promoting state legislation to control railroad abuses. Although the farmers' revolt failed to bring inflation it was very influential, as we shall see,[3] in inaugurating anti-monopoly and anti-railroad legislation in the states and eventually in the federal government. It also resulted in the Federal Reserve Act, the Federal Farm Loan Act, and other legislation to improve the credit facilities of the farmer.[4]

In addition to political pressure, the farmers sought relief by entering the field of business for themselves. Examples of these attempts are cooperative buying and selling organizations, and farmers' insurance companies, promoted by the Grangers, the Farmers' Alliance, and, more recently, by state legislation in the Dakotas, and by federal legislation. The movement has been notably strong in the control of grain elevators, 4000 of which, it is estimated, are owned by 400,000 farmers. It appears to be the almost unanimous opinion of agricultural experts that consolidation of interests on the part of the farmers is essential to their prosperity. This point of view was eventually given official sanction in the Agricultural Marketing Act of 1929.[5] It should also be noted here that many laws to promote agricultural education and scientific agriculture have been passed during the past decades. For them to have the desired results requires both government aid and personal initiative, and both have been forthcoming.

After recovery from the panic of 1893, agricultural conditions improved as a result of currency inflation and the fact that the demand for agricultural products was catching up with the supply. The first two decades of the new century were years of expansion and prosperity when new buildings, fresh equipment, and improved roads demonstrated even to the casual observer that a better day had come. The total value of crops in 1899 was $2,998,704,-000; in 1909 it was $5,487,000,000. The value of all farm property, including land, increased from $20,440,000,000 in 1900 to $40,991,000,000 in 1910, about 100.5 per cent. The value of the land alone increased from an average of $15.57 per acre in 1900 to $32.40 in 1910, or 108.1 per cent, an increase greater than that in all previous years since the discovery of America. World War I with its inflated prices brought even greater prosperity, but no group felt the subsequent depression more keenly than the farmer.[6]

[3] The fight for inflation will be discussed more fully in Chap. 25, that for railroad legislation in Chap. 23, and that for monopoly control in Chap. 21.

[4] Below, pp. 389–390.

[5] Below, pp. 629–630.

[6] The average value of farm land per acre increased to $57.36 in 1920, decreasing to $35.40 by 1930; the estimated gross income from farms increased to $13,566,000,000 in 1920, decreasing to $9,414,000,000 in 1930; the value of all farm property increased to $77,924,000,-000 in 1920, decreasing to $57,246,000,000 in 1930. *Statistical Abstract, 1933*, pp. 535, 565.

MECHANIZATION OF THE FARM

Virgin soil and scarcity of labor, the two forces which heretofore had directed the development of farm machinery, continued to be operative after the Civil War. The first great improvements in the plow, reaper, and thresher had already demonstrated their practicability before 1860, but it was not until the war period that the last two inventions came into wide use. When the federal government mobilized the largest army that the world had yet seen, those who remained on the farm turned of necessity to labor-saving machinery. The rapid adoption of farm machinery was also encouraged by the fact that the type of country occupied during these years was adaptable to large-scale farming and to machine operation. It is therefore correct to say that the agricultural revolution in America, as far as machinery is concerned, came in the half century after 1860.

The climate in the wheat regions of the Middle West necessitated rapid harvesting when the crop was ripe, and the amount planted was dependent upon the farmer's ability to harvest before the grain spoiled. Consequently the attention of inventors was directed most of all toward methods to speed up harvesting. Already in 1858 C. W. and W. W. Marsh had patented the "Marsh harvester," a reaping machine which, by means of an endless apron, delivered the grain upon a table where two men could bind it. This reaper almost doubled the amount of grain that could be harvested in a given time. Even more important was John F. Appleby's invention in 1878 of a "twine binder," a machine which took the place of the crude and unsatisfactory wire binders in use, and increased eightfold the speed in harvesting. "The invention of the twine binder, therefore," says Professor Carver, "by increasing the amount which a farmer could harvest, increased by that precise amount the quantity which he could profitably grow. In other words, it was the twine binder more than any other single machine or implement that enabled the country to increase its production of grain, especially wheat, during this period. The per capita production of the country as a whole increased from about 5.6 bushels in 1860 to 9.2 bushels in 1880."[7] Further improvements were made by the addition of a bundle carrier and, in dry climates, of a header. On the great wheat farms of the West are now to be found "combines" drawn by a score or more horses or propelled by gasoline tractors which cut, thresh, clean, sack, and weigh the grain without the touch of human hands.

Improvements in machinery for planting and cultivating appeared simultaneously with those for harvesting. During this period there came into use

[7] T. N. Carver, *Principles of Rural Economics*, p. 99.

the straddle-row cultivator, the sulky plow, spring-tooth sulky harrows of various types, and seeders that plant, cover, and fertilize at the same time. This type of agricultural machinery, which helped to speed up the process of planting and thus put it on a par with harvesting, was rapidly adopted after 1875 in the Red River wheat country and the Far West. The lister, which plows and plants the seed at the same time, was introduced in 1880. The mowing machine has been perfected, and improvements in haying have included the spring-tooth sulky rake and machines for loading, stacking, and baling. Hand shelling of corn gave way after 1850 to machine shelling. The failure of the hay crop several times in the 'eighties, when the dairying industry was being rapidly developed, directed attention to corn raising, and the combined work of many inventors resulted in a machine with which one man can cut and bind from six to ten acres a day. This enables the farmer to cut his fodder corn green with the juice still in the stock and store it in the silo for winter food, whereas before he was often forced to leave it standing in the fields to dry.

The first stage in the mechanization of the farm was the general displacement of men by horses as the motive power for agricultural energy. This commenced long before the Civil War but developed most rapidly between 1860 and 1910. It was accompanied by a tremendous increase in the number of draft animals on the farm. The substitution of horsepower for manpower, however, had hardly begun before manufacturers of farm machinery were considering the possibility of substituting mechanical power for that of animals. On the large prairie farms experiments were soon being made with steam tractors for planting and preparing the land. By 1905 the gasoline engine had been made sufficiently practical and was so obviously superior to either steam or horsepower that it rapidly replaced both on large farms. Almost as revolutionary in its effects has been the use of the gasoline truck and pleasure car, which have brought the farmer into closer touch with urban life and thus facilitated both marketing and purchasing. Not only the automobile but gasoline pumping and lighting outfits have helped to bring the advantages of the city to the farmer and to decrease household drudgery. Where the farm is close to an electric supply, much of the smaller indoor machinery, such as milk separators, churns, and washing machines, are operated by electricity.

As a result of the mechanization of agriculture, the value of farm machinery in this country more than doubled between 1860 and 1890 and between 1890 and 1930 increased from $500,000,000 to $3,600,000,000. It is estimated that the amount of power used on farms increased eight times between 1900 and 1935. One of the important effects of this mechanization was the increased productivity of farm labor; the best estimates indicate an increased productivity per worker of about 400 per cent. One effect of this has been the creation of greater wealth. Some of this wealth has undoubtedly remained in the hands of the farmer, who has thus been enabled to buy machinery and improve his economic condition, but at the same time, mechanization has had a tendency to concentrate wealth in the hands of the proprietor class who are in a position to buy expensive machinery. This can be seen in the relative increase of agricultural laborers in the leading cereal states even before the turn of the century.

SEVEN LEADING CEREAL STATES
(Illinois, Iowa, Kansas, Nebraska, Minnesota, North and South Dakota)

	1880	1900	Percentage of Increase
Proprietors (owners or tenants) . . .	836,967	1,073,911	28
Agricultural laborers	363,233	631,740	74

In the country as a whole, the percentage of increase for the two classes was about the same, because of the growth of tenant farming in the South. The man with capital was obviously at an advantage in the cereal states, where expensive machinery was becoming the order of the day. As a result, the poorer farmer was reduced to the status of a tenant or an agricultural laborer. The rise of a constantly growing landless agricultural proletariat has been the most unfortunate concomitant of the agricultural revolution, and has become characteristic of America as well as Europe.

Summarizing, we may say that machinery on the farm has (1) released men for other work; (2) increased the production of agricultural products and the output per capita; (3) eliminated much of the drudgery from farm life; (4) allowed the cultivation for other purposes of many acres which had hitherto been used to produce fodder for horses; (5) enlarged the real income of proprietors. On the other hand, the new machinery has undoubtedly (6) increased relatively the landless agricultural laborer by making it more difficult for the man without capital to engage in agriculture; and (7) contributed to bring about the great overproduction of agricultural commodities characteristic of the period after World War I.

SCIENTIFIC FARMING

The mechanization of agriculture is but one aspect of a developing interest in scientific farming which has been evident in recent decades. Scientific farming, it will be remembered, began in England during the eighteenth century, but the abundance of unoccupied land and rich virgin soil as well as the scarcity of labor held back its development in the United

States. There were a few gentlemen farmers—among them, Washington, Jefferson, Livingston, and Clay—who sought through experimentation to improve methods, and there were agricultural societies and county fairs that attempted to distribute information and encourage better agriculture.[8] But the typical American farmer continued to "butcher" his land and neglect his livestock, following the careless methods of earlier years. During the last decades of the nineteenth century, however, certain factors were beginning to operate which inevitably aroused greater interest in scientific agriculture. Better transportation facilities made it possible to enlarge markets and gave an impetus to the improvement of the quality of the product. Declining prices during much of this period produced greater competition which in turn developed improved and cheaper methods of farming. The gradual disappearance of unoccupied arable land also heightened the interest in scientific farming.

Although private initiative, expressed through individual farmers, farm papers, and farm organizations, has continued to urge scientific methods, it has been chiefly the federal and state governments which have stimulated it. Unlike the great industrialists, the small individualistic farmer has little capital and operates on too small a scale to finance experimental research. If such research is to be done, it must be undertaken largely by government agencies.

Since the 1860's the American farmer has not lacked aid from either the state or the national government. This is attributable to three reasons. In the first place, the fundamental importance of agriculture has always been recognized. Although the estimated annual value of agricultural products averaged (1919–1929) only about 11 billion dollars and that of manufactured products 60 billion dollars, more than half of the important manufacturing industries—for example, slaughtering and meat packing, milling, the production of cotton and woolen cloth, boots and shoes, and many others—are dependent upon agriculture. Farm products are also an important, in some sections the most important, item of railroad freight. Agriculture still remains the foundation of much of our economic life. In the second place, during most of our history the farmer has exerted a potent influence on the legislative branch of the government. As late as 1880, 49 per cent of the gainfully employed population was engaged in agriculture; although this had fallen off in 1910 to 32.5, and in 1930 to 21.4 per cent,[9] the fact that the industrial population is largely centralized has given the farmer special weight in the upper house, where southern and western Senators are naturally very susceptible to the demands of agriculture. The so-called "agricultural bloc"

---

[8] Above, Chap. 11.

[9] Figures for 1880 included those engaged in lumbering and fishing. *Statistical Abstract, 1930*, p. 60; Census, 1930, *Population*, V, 39.

in the House has been quick to coalesce when the farmers' interests are at stake. In the third place, the policy of *laissez faire,* so strong during the first decades of the Industrial Revolution, has been gradually breaking down, and nowhere has this change of attitude been more apparent than in the relations of the government to agriculture. This has been due not alone to the political strength of the farmer, but to the realization of the economic importance of agriculture, of the farmer's handicaps in dealing with other economic groups, and of his consequent special need of protection. Consequently, government aid has taken three forms: first, research and education; second, protection by legislation against other groups; and third, help in reclamation and irrigation.

Some mention has already been made of government aid to education and the scientific study of agricultural problems. The work of the schools and experiment stations is augmented and to a certain extent directed by the activities of the Department of Agriculture. George Washington as President recommended a governmental board, but it was not until 1839 that Congress voted $1000 to the Commissioner of Patents for the "collection of agricultural statistics and other agricultural purposes." In 1862 these activities were removed from the Patent Office and a Commissioner of Agriculture was created to direct a bureau whose duty was "to acquire and diffuse among the people of the United States useful information on subjects connected with agriculture in the most general and comprehensive sense of the word, and to procure, propagate, and distribute among the people new and valuable seeds and plants." In 1889 this bureau was elevated to the rank of the other departments, and its head made a secretary and a member of the Cabinet.

The educational and research activities of the Department of Agriculture have extended into many fields and gradually been divided into separate bureaus. The Bureau of Animal Industry has charge of meat inspection and animal quarantine. It has done remarkable work in studying and checking such animal diseases as cattle fever, pleuro-pneumonia, and hoof and mouth disease. The Bureau of Plant Industry is engaged in combating plant disease, in studying better agricultural methods and plant acclimatization, in distributing seed, and in similar activities. More than 30,000 new plants have been brought into the country, notably Kaffir corn, durum wheat, and drought-proof alfalfa. Closely allied to the last-named Bureau is the Bureau of Entomology and Plant Quarantine, which studies insects and thus directs the work of combating pests and of introducing beneficial insects. Campaigns have been waged against the Hessian fly, the gypsy and browntail moth, the boll weevil, the corn borer, the Japanese beetle and the Mediterranean fruit-fly.[10] The Bureau of Agricultural Chemistry and Engineering investigates

[10] *Yearbook of Agriculture, 1930,* pp. 50–60.

the chemical and physical properties of soils, fertilizers, and agricultural products and conducts research in farm machinery and equipment.

Other Bureaus or divisions concentrate on the study and preservation of trees, on the problems of the dairy industry, on marketing problems, agricultural credits, home economics, and the collection and publishing of agricultural statistics. In fact, it would be difficult to find any phase of agriculture in which the Department of Agriculture is not active in giving serious study and sound advice. Moreover, other departments of the government are contributing to agriculture. For example, the Department of Commerce now makes the investigations in meteorology, climatology, and seismology formerly carried on by the Weather Bureau of the Department of Agriculture.

On a much smaller scale most of the states, through departments of agriculture, financial appropriations, and protective legislation, have sought to aid agriculture after the manner of the federal government. Some have gone to the extent of offering subsidies to encourage the production of certain agricultural products; for example, Kansas has tried to promote the growing of beet sugar. Perhaps the crowning example of state resources applied to the interests of the farmer was the North Dakota legislature's sanction in 1919 of the complete program of the Farmer's Non-Partisan Political League, which called among other things for state-owned flour mills and terminal elevators, a state-owned and -operated bank, and state loans to home builders and land purchasers. Opposition of eastern financial interests, the agricultural depression after 1920, and political reaction within the state largely ended these experiments.

Scientific farming, of course, has been given tremendous impetus by agricultural education, and this in turn has received its greatest stimulus from the federal and state governments. The decade of the 'fifties saw a rapidly growing interest in agricultural education which found vent in the establishment of several state agricultural schools. Impetus to the movement was given by the passage of the Morrill Act in 1862. Introduced by Justin S. Morrill in 1857 and vetoed by President Buchanan, it was brought up again during the war and passed. The Act provided that 30,000 acres of public land be given to each state for each Senator and Representative in Congress, the funds from the sale of these lands to be accumulated and the interest used to support, endow, and maintain "at least one college where the leading object shall be, without excluding other scientific and classical studies, and including military tactics, to teach such branches of learning as are related to agriculture and the mechanic arts, in such manner as the legislatures of the states may, respectively, prescribe, in order to promote the liberal and practical education of the industrial classes in the several pursuits and professions of life." This first "land-grant" Act constituted the greatest single piece of legislation ever passed in the interest of agricultural education, and under its provisions institutions were gradually established in each of the states and in Hawaii and Puerto Rico. In some states the agricultural or mechanical schools are attached to the state universities or other colleges. In Massachusetts, the income was divided to help found two schools, the Massachusetts Agricultural College [11] and the Massachusetts Institute of Technology. There were 68 land-grant colleges teaching agriculture in 1916. The Morrill Act has been extended by subsequent legislation, notably in 1890 and in 1907, when additional appropriations were voted to increase to $50,000 the annual income of each school subsidized by the government. The Hatch Act of 1887, which provided funds for experiment stations in the various state colleges, turned the attention of these schools to investigation as well as to teaching.

Almost as valuable as the actual instruction given in the colleges is the diffusion of information among those not regularly attending. The scope of the agricultural colleges has been extended to include special short-term winter courses and extension work. The latter is carried on by correspondence, by publications, by lectures, by itinerant schools sometimes conducted in special trains, by farmers' institutes, and by cooperation with farmers' organizations wherever possible. The value of this work was recognized by Congress in the Smith-Lever Extension Act of 1914; under its provisions $480,000 was appropriated, to be divided equally among the states, and an additional $600,000 was granted, to be increased annually by $500,000 until 1923, when the annual appropriation by the national government for this purpose would amount to $4,500,000.

Agricultural education is carried on by the United States Department of Agriculture, which is engaged in the twofold task of experimentation and dissemination of information. The latter is accomplished by means of more than a dozen publications, among which are the *Yearbook of Agriculture,* the *Farmer's Bulletin,* the *Journal of Agricultural Research,* the *Monthly Crop Reporter,* and the *Weekly News Letter.* The state agricultural departments, which exist in most of the states, function in a somewhat similar way. The educational influence of the county and state fairs is still potent. Hundreds of agricultural societies have grown up to promote knowledge and spread information on almost every conceivable phase of plant and animal culture. One or more of their organs or of the general farm journals, of which nearly 500 are published, reach almost every farmer. Several of these have a circulation of over 500,000. Agricultural instruction, aided by federal funds first granted in the Smith-Hughes Act of 1917, is gradually being introduced into high schools, and in several states it is required in the rural schools. Both federal and state departments of agriculture conduct regular

[11] Now the Massachusetts State College at Amherst.

educational programs by radio. While the channels for the diffusion of scientific agricultural information are many, it is a discouraging fact that as yet only a small percentage of the farmers are seriously influenced in their daily work by the information thus available.

So much attention has been given to the part played by the federal government in agricultural education and research that it is easy to overlook the work of the experiment stations in the land-grant colleges. The United States surpasses every other nation in the extent of her agricultural research and most of it is done in these experiment stations.

The first agricultural experiment station in this country was established under the direction of Professor W. O. Atwater in 1875 at Wesleyan University, Middletown, Connecticut, through appropriations of the state and donations by Orange Judd, proprietor of the *American Agriculturist*. The notable work accomplished here encouraged Congress to pass the Hatch Act of 1887. Under its terms experiment stations have been established in each of the states, where scientists often specialize on some problem connected with their particular section—for example, diseases and improvement of the cotton plant in Alabama and the pineapple in Florida, the proper feeding of cattle in Texas, new varieties of sugar cane in Louisiana, rust-resisting wheat in Minnesota, and diseases of potatoes in Vermont. Agricultural research has increased the annual value of crops by hundreds of millions, but there is still much to be done in this direction. The average yield of wheat per acre in America is only half that of England, Germany, or Holland, although the fields in those countries have been cultivated for centuries. Again it should be pointed out that we fail to equal western Europe in yield per acre not because less is known here of scientific agricultural methods, but because our uppermost interest is to produce more per unit of labor rather than per acre.

Especially interesting have been the effects on scientific agriculture of the pressure of the population on land. As the arable land was occupied, settlers pressed westward into the semi-arid country between the region of adequate rainfall and the Rockies. This movement was stimulated by a series of wet years in the early 'eighties. In later years, when normal weather returned, a partial solution for the lack of rainfall was provided in dry farming. The principles of dry farming call for plowing the land deep after harvest, disking deep after each rainfall, pulverizing the top soil and keeping it free from weeds, and in alternate years tilling through the summer without raising a crop—all of them expedients to lessen evaporation. To aid in this type of farming the Department of Agriculture has imported drought-resisting species of wheat, corn, and other plants from the dry regions of Asia and Africa. Dry farming has opened up a great deal of land to agriculture, but

it has also helped to destroy much land. Heavy winds have blown away
millions of acres of top soil and rendered the land utterly useless for agriculture.

IRRIGATION AND RECLAMATION

As the farmer pushed into the Great Plains and the foothills of the Rockies
it became increasingly clear that his primary problem was lack of water.
Cheap metal windmills and dry farming offered only partial solutions. From
the early settlement days there was the continuous hope that much could be
accomplished by irrigation. Although the federal government was giving
away 160 acres of fertile land under the Homestead Act, under the Desert
Land Act in 1877 it authorized the purchase of 640 acres at $1.25 per acre
(25 cents down and $1 within three years) on condition that a certain
amount be irrigated within three years. A holding of this size might
be necessary for dry farming, but irrigation was better adapted to a small
acreage intensively cultivated. In any event, this legislation accomplished
little except to stimulate land frauds. But propaganda for irrigation through
federal aid continued unabated during the late 'eighties and the 'nineties. In
1888 Congress provided for an irrigation survey and in 1894 passed the
Carey Act. Under it the states in the arid region might appropriate 1,000,-
000 acres of public land and authorize irrigation through private enterprise;
but they had to reserve authority to pass on the plans submitted and on the
charges for water rates. The land was sold at 50 cents an acre, and the water
rights of these irrigation projects averaged from $30 to $40 an acre, paid
for usually in ten annual installments; the irrigation companies retained
control of reservoirs, dams, and other equipment until full payment had
been made, when it was turned over to the landowners.

Artificial irrigation, however, proceeded slowly, chiefly because of the
large amount of capital required. This meant that when the country finally
committed itself to large-scale projects, only the federal government could
command the necessary resources. Federal participation finally came in
the Reclamation Act of 1902, which provided for the setting aside of
proceeds from the sale of public lands in sixteen designated states, to be used
as a fund for irrigation projects. When money is available, the Secretary
of the Interior may award contracts for such works. The farmers, who have
taken up the land either by purchase or under the Homestead Act, defray
the cost of the work by annual payments, thus perpetuating the fund.
Under this Act and subsequent appropriations over $300,000,000 has been
spent in the examination, construction, and operation of projects for the reclamation of arid regions and over 3,000,000 acres by this means brought under production. Completion of the score or more projects now under construc-

tion, including the Grand Coulee, will bring the irrigated area to 10,000,000 acres. Among the most notable of the irrigation projects are the Roosevelt Dam in Arizona, the Arrowrock Dam in Idaho, the Elephant Butte Dam in New Mexico, and the Boulder Dam on the Colorado River.

Although considerable valuable farm land has been reclaimed in this way, too much cannot be expected from this in the future. Only limited areas of the Grand Plains—probably not more than one-sixteenth—are located where water is available. This water the federal government is rapidly conserving and putting to use. The cheap electric power provided by a dam may in the end prove as valuable as the irrigation projects.

THE BATTLE FOR ECONOMIC EQUALITY

Faced with overproduction and declining prices, the farmers during the last four decades of the nineteenth century kept up a ceaseless struggle to restore their earlier economic position. Their battle against railroad abuses culminated in state and federal regulation and their fight against monopoly prices brought state and federal legislation. Their struggle for inflation and fair interest rates, on the other hand, made little progress up to 1890. Probably the Populist platform of 1892 comes as close as anything to stating the farmers' program at the end of the century. Among its important economic demands were a flexible currency divorced from any banking control; loans at 2 per cent interest; free and unlimited coinage of gold and silver at 16 to 1; a graduated income tax; postal savings banks; government ownership of railroads, telegraph, and telephones; a secret ballot; direct election of Senators, and the initiative and referendum. There was also an undercurrent of opposition to monopoly. This program (most of which has long since been attained) was considered essential to reestablish economic and political equality. The story of the conflict as it related to railroads, trusts, and currency will be told in succeeding chapters. It is sufficient here to note only one aspect of it, the effort to obtain improved credit facilities.

Since the West was developed on borrowed money, it has normally always been a debtor region. When in need of capital it has been forced to borrow from eastern money lenders, often at exorbitant rates of interest. While 5 and 6 per cent were the usual rates on eastern farm mortgages, farmers in the West were paying from 7 to 10 and sometimes as high as 12 per cent. This was due in part to the greater risks involved in frontier loans and in part to the inadequate banking facilities in the West. Although the situation improved after 1900 as more banks were established in that section and as insurance companies extended their investments in farm mortgages, the general credit situation continued to be disadvantageous for the farmer.

The natural reaction of the debtor farmer was to demand a monetary and banking system that would provide cheap and easy money. This explains the western farmers' opposition to the First and Second United States Banks, their opposition after the Civil War to greenback contraction, and

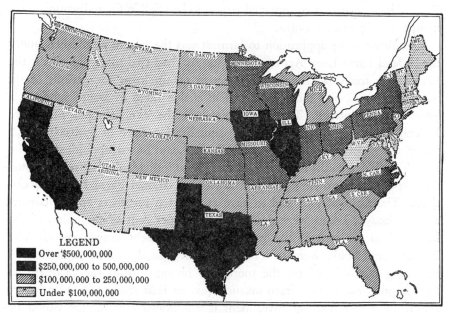

LEGEND
Over $500,000,000
$250,000,000 to 500,000,000
$100,000,000 to 250,000,000
Under $100,000,000

GROSS FARM INCOME BY STATES, 1939.

Rental and benefit payments are not included in the income shown on the map. *Statistical Abstracts, 1940,* p. 670.

their advocacy of free and unlimited coinage of gold and silver at 16 to 1. It also explains their demand for more liberal banking laws.

Although the farmers had complained of the inadequate credit facilities for decades, other groups took little interest until after 1900. A Country Life Commission appointed by Theodore Roosevelt in that year called attention to the need for better credit facilities, and the National Monetary Commission familiarized this country with the farm mortgage systems of Europe. Republicans, Progressives, and Democrats all promised action in their platforms in 1912. The existing national bank system, established in 1863, was criticized specifically by the farmer on two grounds: first, that it did not adequately serve small communities because the minimum capital required was too great; and second, that it encouraged the flow of accumulated capital from the country to the city where it was used for industry or speculation. The Federal Reserve System, inaugurated by a Democratic administration in 1913, was expected to be of particular aid to the agricultural class in the greater facilities it afforded for the expansion of the currency when needed, and the more rapid movement of funds from one section of the country to another. Under this Act national banks were for the first time permitted to lend money on farm mortgages. Furthermore, agricultural paper running six months could be rediscounted at the Federal Reserve bank, whereas commercial paper, to be eligible for rediscount, must mature within three months.

More direct in its application to farmers was the system established under the Federal Farm Loan Act of 1916. This Act had two main objectives; the first was to make it easier for farmers to obtain loans for periods of six months or more, and the second was to enable them to secure funds at a lower rate of interest. The Act authorized the establishment of twelve Federal Land banks, with an initial capitalization fixed at $750,000 each,[12] under the supervision of a Federal Farm Loan Board appointed by the President. These banks did not lend directly to individuals, but rediscounted for cooperative borrowing groups known as "National Farm Loan Associations." These associations had to have at least ten members and to borrow at least $20,000. Loans were not to exceed 50 per cent of the value of the land and 20 per cent of the value of the permanent improvements. The Federal Land banks were to secure funds beyond the initial capitalization by selling bonds based on the mortgages obtained from the farmers. As these bonds were exempt from taxation (except inheritance taxes) and were considered a safe form of investment it was hoped that money would be easily forthcoming to lend to farmers at low rates of interest. The Federal Farm Loan Act also created Joint-stock Land banks (subsequently liquidated under the Farm Credit Act of 1933), similar to the Federal Land banks, to be incorporated by private individuals; they obtained funds by selling first-mortgage, tax-exempt farm-loan bonds on the market. These banks could deal directly with the farmer instead of through associations.

Even the credit facilities provided by the legislation just described did not prove entirely satisfactory. Emphasis had been placed on long-term credits, but in the early 'twenties farmers also realized their need for better facilities for short-term borrowing. These were provided by the Agricultural Credits Act of 1923, which established twelve Federal Intermediate Credit banks (as adjuncts to the existing Federal Land banks). They do not deal with individual borrowers or lend directly on land security, but are banks for rediscount of agricultural and livestock paper for periods of six months to three years. Five millions of capital for these banks was furnished by the United States Treasury.

[12] Subscription was open to the public, but so little interest was shown that the federal government was forced to subscribe $8,891,270 of the $9,000,000 necessary for the twelve banks.

Under this legislation the farmer was now able to borrow money at reasonable rates of interest for any length of time. He was on the road to freedom from the loan shark and had virtually achieved the demands of the earlier Populists. Nevertheless, the entire agricultural credit structure was reorganized, extended, and liberalized, as we shall see, by the Farm Credits Act of 1933,[13] for by this time it was clear that more than easy credit was necessary to save farmers from bankruptcy.

RECENT AGRICULTURAL TENDENCIES

Speaking broadly, the history of American agriculture until about 1890 was chiefly the story of the westward movement and the continuous opening of new land for speculation and production. In detail this story has been modified by the invention of new machinery, by the necessary adaptation of crops to new soil, and by the gradual shifting of production to new regions whose superiority severely handicapped older communities. The placing of large areas of new land under cultivation was in turn attended by a decline in agricultural prices and by the production of a surplus for export.

With the opening of the twentieth century, American agriculture entered a new period in its history, radically different from the old. As most of the land immediately available for farming had been preempted by 1900, further additions to arable land have come from dry farming, from irrigation or drainage, or from putting into use woodland or other unimproved land on the farm. While the farm area increased by 15,000,000 acres a year for the thirty years previous to 1900, the increase from 1900 to 1910 was only 4,000,000 acres a year, or 4.8 per cent. The decade 1910 to 1920, however, showed an increase of 8.8 per cent in farm acreage and of 5.1 per cent in improved land; this can be accounted for by the unusual stimulus of the war. The percentage of the land area of the United States included in farms increased throughout our history up to 1920, when it reached 50.2; by 1925 it had decreased to 48.6, but by 1930 it reached 51.8. There was also an actual decline after 1920 in the number of farms (from 6,448,343 in 1920 to 6,288,648 in 1930), a phenomenon caused chiefly by scarcity of labor, consolidation of farms due to the introduction of new machinery, and the boll weevil.

Until 1910 American agriculture was still extensive in its nature and there was no hesitancy in sacrificing land to labor. The farmer resembled the miner who took out riches from the soil without giving anything in return. The increasing value of farm products and of land has turned the farmer to more intensive agriculture. This movement seemed well under way dur-

[13] Below, p. 655.

ing the first decade of the century but was not so pronounced during the next ten years when the demands of the First World War opened new land to cultivation. Nevertheless, large areas of corn, barley, and buckwheat have been turned over to more intensive crops, and the increasing use of fertilizer demonstrates more careful husbandry. While the production percentages in the 1920 Census did not keep pace with the increase in the acreage devoted to many of the products, this may not by any means mean less intensive farming. In view of the poorer land brought under cultivation, it may mean just the opposite.

Of all the influences which affected American agriculture in the half century after the Civil War, none was more important than foreign trade. Agriculture cannot move beyond the self-sufficing stage unless there is a market for its surplus. For the American farmer this market was provided during the last half of the nineteenth century and the early years of the twentieth in the rapidly growing cities of western Europe. Agricultural exports increased more or less steadily from 1860 until around the turn of the century, when the high point was reached. Fifteen years later they were artificially stimulated by the First World War. The peak year for corn exports was in 1897, when 212,000,000 bushels were exported; for wheat, in 1901, with 239,000,000 bushels exported. Meat and meat products, which had been relatively insignificant as exports before the Civil War, soon ranked third in importance, with a value of $179,000,000 in 1900. The effect of this on Europe was to disorganize the agricultural structure and to speed industrialization. As one Austrian economist has suggested, this flow of agricultural produce had an effect upon the economy of the Old World comparable to that produced by the flow of gold and silver after the discovery of America. For America, this market speeded the advancing frontier, the occupation of new land, the flow of immigration, and the improvement and enlargement of transportation and marketing facilities. At the same time the agricultural surplus helped to pay the unequal balance of trade between Europe and America and made possible large-scale borrowing from Europe. This in turn enabled the development of industry in America, artificially stimulated by a protective tariff system. When the export of agricultural commodities began to decline after 1900 she had become sufficiently urbanized to take up the slack. It was not the decline of the European market between 1900 and 1915 that injured the American farmer, it was the artificial revival of that market during the First World War and its decline in the 1920's.

An outstanding factor in agricultural life has been the decided movement toward the cities; neither rural population nor farm production has advanced as rapidly as the increase in urban population. As late as 1910 the urban population (that is, those living in towns of 2500 or more) was still in the minority (45.8 per cent); but in 1920 it had mounted to 51.4 per cent, and in 1930 to 56.2 per cent. On the whole this tendency has been for the best. As one government statistician aptly puts it: A century or more ago some four-fifths of the population was engaged in agriculture, which means that most of the people had to give their time to producing practically bare necessities. Ever since, there has been a rapid decline in this proportion, representing the freeing of larger and larger numbers to produce commodities and services of a less essential character, thus raising the standard of living. This shift has been due largely to advances in the productivity of agriculture itself, resulting in part from the opening up of better lands, but much more from improvements in methods of production." [14] To this statement should be added the obvious fact that many activities formerly performed on the farm have been transferred to the town or city.

Agriculture has steadily lost ground in percentage of population, of gainfully employed, and of national wealth. The proportion of our population thus engaged is now smaller than in most of the countries of the world. Argentina, Belgium, Holland, Switzerland, England and Wales, and (somewhat surprisingly) Australia are the only countries reporting a lower proportion in the years since the First World War.[15] Truly, the United States has become an industrialized nation.

POPULATION AND AGRICULTURE[16]

	1880	1900	1910	1920	1930
Rural population[a] (in millions)	32,950	39,313	41,637	42,437	44,637
Percentage rural	65.0	51.7	45.3	40.1	36.4
Percentage of increase over preceding census .	..	9.5	5.9	1.9	2.6
Percentage of increase of population as a whole over preceding census	30.1	20.7	21.0	14.9	7.7
Acres of improved land per capita of total population	5.7	5.5	5.2	4.8	4.3

[a] Defined in this table as population outside incorporated places.

The rapid occupation of the West under the stimulus of the Homestead Act and the building of the transcontinental railroads increased the production of foodstuffs beyond normal needs, and from the end of the Civil War until the late 'nineties American agriculture suffered from overproduction. Toward the end of the century the demand for foodstuffs began

[14] *Commerce Yearbook, 1932*, I, 31.
[15] *Ibid.*, II, 662–664.
[16] *Ibid.*, I, 132, 133.

to overtake the supply, and from then until the opening of World War I the farmers enjoyed their first real period of prosperity since the Civil War. A hectic boom period characterized the World War years, and then came deflation and depression. This depression has persisted in spite of the fact that the volume of agricultural products in general during the 'twenties showed an increase over the pre-war years.

The natural result of many of these factors was a sudden and enormous rise in land values during the first two decades of the twentieth century. Between 1900 and 1920 the value of farm lands and crops increased more than fourfold, and the prices of farm products nearly threefold (value changes due only in part to the rise in the price level), although the mass of crop production during the same period increased less than 50 per cent. The deflation of the post-war years wiped out part of this advance, but the figures for 1930 still showed a decided gain over those for 1910.[17]

Since 1900 there has been an increase in tenancy, but not so marked as during the final decades of the last century. In the raising of those products that require expensive machinery, and on those lands whose value has risen rapidly, tenancy has increased because of the inability of the poor man to meet such expenses. On the other hand, it should be pointed out that the growth of tenancy may be an encouraging sign, for to many men tenancy is a step toward ultimate ownership.[18]

PERCENTAGE OF ALL FARMS OPERATED BY TENANTS, 1880–1930 [19]

	1880	1890	1900	1910	1920	1925	1930
United States	26	28	35	37	38	39	42
New England	9	9	9	8	7	6	6
Middle Atlantic	19	22	25	22	21	16	15
East North Central	20	23	26	27	28	26	27
West North Central	21	24	30	31	34	38	40
South Atlantic	36	38	44	46	47	44	48
East South Central	37	38	48	51	50	50	56
West South Central	35	39	49	53	53	59	62
Mountain.	7	7	12	11	15	22	24
Pacific	17	15	20	17	20	16	18

[17] The agricultural depression of the 1920's and 1930's will be discussed in Chap. 28.

[18] Some observers think that farming in the future is to be like industry, a business carried on by large corporations with hired labor working at the height of the season in night and day shifts as in factories. This counsel of despair comes from those who do not see how agriculture as a whole can carry the marginal farmer who does not and seemingly will not treat farming as a business enterprise. Henry Ford's experimental farm is based on the idea of the industrialization of agriculture. The tendency is clearly toward larger farms in the black cotton belt and in the grain-growing areas, but division of labor cannot take place to any extent.

[19] Yearbook of Agriculture, 1930, p. 1008; Statistical Abstract, 1933, p. 548.

The Northeast.—Influences which were at work even before the Civil War to modify agricultural conditions in the Northeast have since been active in an increasingly greater degree. A century ago New England and the Middle Atlantic States were agriculturally self-sufficient. Today New England imports 80 per cent of her food. Competition of western products made possible through the development of transportation facilities, and the growth of industrial life, have radically altered the nature of agricultural products. Raising livestock for wool and meat has given place to dairying and to vegetable and fruit growing. The most fertile lands in New England are the rich bottom lands of the Connecticut Valley, largely given over to onions and tobacco, and the Aroostock Valley in Maine, where one-tenth of the potatoes sold in the country are raised. Where this type of farming is impossible, the competition of the West has often forced the poorer land out of cultivation. In New England between 1860 and 1910 farm land under cultivation decreased by over 5,000,000 acres, or 42 per cent, resulting in the thousands of deserted farms to be seen in this section. During these years cattle decreased from 56 to 20 per 100 of the population, and sheep from 60 to 4. Although the number of farms in New England has continued to decline during the decade 1920–1930, there appears to be no diminution in the agricultural products of the region. While rural population declined relatively, the whole population increased by 110 per cent. The richer soil in New York, Pennsylvania, and New Jersey has kept a greater amount of land under cultivation than in New England, but there has been the same transition to vegetables, dairy products, and fruit. This is due to the nearby and ever-increasing urban market.

The South.—Before the Civil War the South was almost entirely agricultural, engaged in raising some foodstuffs but dependent chiefly upon the great staple, cotton, which was produced on large plantations by the labor of Negro slaves. The war and the freeing of the slaves changed the system. The products remained the same, but the manner of production was altered. Ruined by the war, the great planter had neither resources nor equipment to continue the old plantation under a wage system. Some manner of livelihood, however, had to be found for him and for the new freeman. The result was the gradual breaking up of the large holdings into small farms ranging from 20 to 50 acres, which are operated by Negroes, usually as sharecroppers or tenant farmers. While in some cases (about one-fourth) cash rentals are paid, in most the farms are let out under a system by which the owner furnishes the tools and sometimes the seeds and a mule, and in return takes one-half of the corn and cotton raised.

The effect of this system has been almost as destructive to the soil as that of the old plantation system. There was actually less improved land in the South Atlantic division in 1900 than in 1860. Not only has this tenant farming been ruinous to the soil, but it has tended to perpetuate the one-crop system. The owner of the land or the local merchant who provides tools and supplies and in return takes a lien on the future crop insists that it be cotton, because that is the most salable product. It is, in fact, the crop which the Negro has been trained for generations to raise, and the simplicity of its production, as in slave days, fits in with the stage of his agricultural advancement. While it might be an overstatement to say that slavery in the South was followed by a period of serfdom in which the Negro was held in bondage by being constantly in debt to the landowner or cotton factor, it would not be far from the truth. This has been a normal evolution in society—a development made inevitable after the war by the economic situation and the intellectual status of the Negro at that time. At the height of the tenant farm system, conditions were thus described by a government expert:

The agricultural land of the cotton States has little sale. Merchants will not accept it as security for debt unless they are compelled to do so when crop, mules, cattle, and other personal property are insufficient. This is one reason why mortgages on Southern farm land are so few. . . . The blacks prefer a tenancy to selling their labor for wages and in some regions, at least, the white owners who cultivate their farms find that only the inferior laborers can be hired, because the superior ones prefer tenancies. As the planters become independent of merchants, they are unfriendly to these tenancies, but, in some instances, have to grant very small ones, in order to hold the services of the blacks, who, under such circumstances, work for wages during a part of the year on the plantation cultivated by their landlord. If the white landlords arrive at independence from debt before the black tenants do, as it may be assumed that they will, if either class is to improve, it seems likely that the blacks will see a service for wages encroaching upon the tenant system. . . .

. . . The plantation owners, most of whom are landlords, often live in towns, having abandoned their plantations to irresponsible tenants who care to work only indifferently and for a bare subsistence of the poorest sort. A tenant whose crop by chance more than suffices to meet his obligations, will pick enough cotton to discharge his debts to the landlord and the merchant and abandon the remainder, knowing that he can live on the next crop until it is harvested. . . . The merchant who has a lien on his share of the crop pays his taxes, buries his wife or child, buys him a mule if he needs one, and feeds and clothes him and his family to the extent that his improvidence and laziness are allowed credit.[20]

[20] G. H. Holmes, *Annals of the American Academy of Political and Social Science,* IV, 267 ff. (Sept., 1893). See also his article on "Tenancy in the South," reprinted in T. N. Carver's *Selected Readings in Rural Economics,* pp. 494, 495.

In considering southern agriculture it should be remembered that thousands of poor whites as well as the Negro have fallen victims to the system of sharecropping. The Negro, in fact, during recent decades has shown greater ability than the white to push up from this status. It is estimated that nearly 200,000 Negroes own their own farms, aggregating 20,000,000 acres and valued at over $500,000,000. But the tenant system for both blacks and whites is still predominant (it actually increased during the 'thirties),

PRODUCTION OF COTTON IN THE UNITED STATES BY 500-POUND BALES, 1865–1939 [21]

with the yield per acre discouragingly small and the average annual income of the tenant farmer only about $150. The methods are still crude and wasteful, and so little cereal and meat is raised that this agricultural region still imports foodstuffs. The salvation of the southern farmer has been the usually steady demand and the high price paid for cotton. The cotton crop increased from 3,841,000 bales (500 pounds) in 1860 to 14,828,000 in 1929, the South still producing from 60 to 65 per cent of the world's yield. This supremacy has recently been challenged by the northward advance of the boll weevil, but this has not been an unmixed curse, for it has forced certain sections to turn from one staple to diversified farming.

The center of cotton production continues to be west of the Alleghenies,

[21] *Statistical Abstract, 1940,* p. 698.

with Texas the largest producer. The center of tobacco culture, on the other hand, has moved back east of the mountains, with North Carolina far in the lead of the producing states. Sweet potatoes, peanuts, pecans, garden vegetables for the northern market, and semi-tropical fruit are now being grown in rapidly increasing amounts, bringing new prosperity to Georgia, Florida, and the Gulf states. There has also been a considerable development of truck farming and dairying near industrial centers for the local market. The potential agricultural possibilities of the South are enormous, and many students believe that the greatest agricultural progress in the future will come south of the Ohio and Mason and Dixon's line.

The Upper Mississippi Valley.—By 1890 the frontier line of farms had pushed west until practically all the arable land was occupied. In this great region between the Alleghenies and the Rockies has arisen the most productive agricultural area in the world. Its chief products are corn, wheat, and livestock. The central states from Ohio to Iowa were found well adapted to corn, and its production has laid the foundation for the raising of hogs, cattle, and poultry. While the center of corn production has to a certain extent remained fixed since 1860,[22] the center of wheat has moved steadily west. In 1860 most of the wheat was grown east of the Mississippi, but by 1939 almost 50 per cent was raised in the five states of Kansas, North Dakota, Oklahoma, Montana, and Washington. The westward advance was accelerated by certain inventions in flour manufacture, notably the "middlings purifier" of La Croix and the substitution of rollers for stones in crushing the grain. These inventions allowed the production of fine white flour from the hard spring wheat, the type best grown on the Minnesota and Dakota prairies. Under the liberal policy of the government large claims were staked out, and often through actual fraud immense farms were built up where the soil was worked for wheat alone by the wonderful new machinery. These "bonanza farms" of a thousand acres or more not only wore out the soil but glutted the market with wheat and drove prices down.

The growing value of farm land (particularly marked from 1900 to 1920) which has necessitated more intensive cultivation, the wearing out of the land, and the immigration of farmers into the Northwest have all helped to break up the large holdings and in many cases to substitute other kinds of agriculture. In Wisconsin, where twenty years ago wheat was the chief product, the farmers have turned to other cereals, to livestock, and particularly to dairying; this state leads all others in the value of dairy products. In 1929 she produced 60 per cent of the cheese made in this country.

---

[22] In 1859 over 70 per cent of the corn was raised in Illinois, Ohio, Missouri, Indiana, Kentucky, Tennessee, Iowa, Virginia, Alabama, and Georgia. In 1929 some 67 per cent was raised in the ten states of Iowa, Illinois, Nebraska, Indiana, Ohio, Missouri, South Dakota, Kansas, Texas, and Kentucky (listed in the order of their importance).

Though not so well situated, Minnesota has taken from Wisconsin the lead in the production of butter. By 1929 over half the nation's creamery butter was produced in Minnesota, Iowa, Wisconsin, Nebraska, and Ohio. At the same time, the competition of Canadian wheat is turning the attention of Dakota farmers to dairy products. As the reaper and binder have made possible the great wheat farms of the West, so have the Babcock tester and the power churn and mixer made possible the rapid expansion in butter and cheese production.

The Far West.—It was the gold stampede of 1849 that first brought large numbers to the Pacific coast, but the great wealth of this region was destined to be agricultural. The agricultural income of California today far outstrips her combined income from oil and mining, and the production cost more than triples that of the motion picture industry. With the exception of Texas, she surpasses all the other states in the value of her agricultural products. She produces nearly one-half of the country's fresh fruit, about 95 per cent of its dried fruit, a third of its truck crops, and nearly a third of its canned fruits and vegetables. Only the scarcity of water prevents an even greater production from this incredibly fertile soil. Although California supports a large dairy industry, made possible by the large production of tame hay and the rapidly increasing population, her chief agricultural products are fruits of both the subtropical and temperate varieties, and vegetables. In the Imperial Valley of southeastern California, in the Great Central Valley that stretches northward for hundreds of miles, and along the seacoast there have developed great farms where highly specialized commercial agriculture is carried on. If the future of agriculture is to resemble the "factory in the field," the future is already in evidence here. Huge farms, manned by migrant labor and often, as in large-scale business, controlled by the banks, are the general pattern. Two per cent of California's farms, it is estimated, control one-fourth of the acreage, produce nearly one-third of the crop value, and pay more than one-third of the bill for hired labor. Large-scale agriculture has been typical of this region since the days of the Mexican ranches. It has come down through the huge wheat fields which characterized California in the 'seventies and 'eighties and remains in the more recent development of fruit growing and truck farming. The seasonal and migrant agricultural labor which has received so much attention in recent years has been a serious economic and social problem in California since the earliest days.

In Oregon and Washington, where there is a greater variety of climate, agriculture is not specialized; fruit, wheat, dairy products, and wool are all produced in considerable quantities. Farther east the valleys and foothills of the Cordilleras, which hitherto had been supposed unarable, have been brought under cultivation by dry farming or irrigation. The introduction of durum wheat, Kaffir corn, and a different type of alfalfa, all suitable to dry soil or cold climate, has helped to vegetate these regions. Huge irrigation projects now in the process of construction will undoubtedly considerably increase the productive area.

SELECTED READINGS

Sanford, A. H., *The Story of Agriculture in the United States,* Chaps. XVIII-XXIX.

Everett, E. E., "American Agriculture—the First 300 Years," *Yearbook of Agriculture, 1940,* pp. 221–276.

Hammond, M. B., *The Cotton Industry,* Chaps. IV–VI.

Buck, S. J., *The Granger Movement,* Chaps. I–III, VIII–IX.

Flügel, F., and Faulkner, H. U., *Readings in the Economic and Social History of the United States,* Chap. XVII.

20.

Development of the
Industrial Revolution

Growth of Industry

Although the factory system in America obtained its first real foothold during the period of the embargo and the War of 1812 and in the mills which sprang up in the succeeding years, nevertheless it seems safe to say that "until about the year 1850, the bulk of general manufacturing done in the United States was carried on in the shop and the household, by the labor of the family or individual proprietors, with apprentice assistants, as contrasted with the present system of factory labor, compensated by wages, and assisted by power."[1] Since 1850 our economic life has been revolutionized as we followed in the wake of western Europe in substituting factory-made products for those made by hand labor. The development of the factory system has been continuous, but the process was immensely hastened by the demands of the Civil War. If the War of 1812 introduced the factory system, the Civil War effected an Industrial Revolution, and it is this development of the Industrial Revolution which was the outstanding feature of American economic life in the half century since 1860.

More and more America turned to factory-made goods and to large-scale industry, and Americans occupied themselves increasingly with manufacturing. Until the decade of the 'eighties agriculture was the principal source of wealth, but the Census of 1890 showed that manufacturing had forged to the front, and ten years later the value of manufactured products was more than double that of agricultural.

The increasing value of manufactured over agricultural products is reflected in the concentration of population. The Census of 1920 reported, for the first time in our history, the urban population (those living in towns of 2500 or over) as more than the rural, the percentages being 51.4 and 48.6, respectively. The percentage of people living in towns of over 8000 increased from 16.1 in 1860 to 43.8 in 1920. In 1930 the percentage of the

---

[1] Twelfth Census, VII, liii.

COMPARISON OF THE VALUE OF AGRICULTURAL AND MANUFACTURED PRODUCTS[2]

Value of Products	1889	1899	1909	1919
Agricultural	$2,460,107,000	$ 4,717,076,000	$ 8,498,311,000	$23,783,200,000
Manufactured (including those based on agriculture) . . .	9,372,379,000	11,406,927,000	20,672,052,000	62,418,079,000

urban population was 56.2 and that of towns of 8000 or more was 49.1 per cent. While the population from 1850 to 1900 trebled (from 23,192,000 to 75,995,000) and the products of agriculture nearly trebled ($1,600,000,000 to $4,717,070,000), the value of manufactures increased eleven-fold ($1,019,107,-000 to $11,406,927,000). From 1859 to 1914 the value of American manufactures increased eighteen-fold, and from 1859 to 1919 thirty-three-fold. Naturally this increase stands out when a comparison is made with foreign nations. M. G. Mulhall, in his *Industries and Wealth of Nations* (1896), shows how the United States, which had ranked fifth in the value of manufactured products in 1840 and fourth in 1860, had taken first place in 1894. At that time she produced twice as much as Great Britain and half as much as all Europe together.

The Census of Manufactures in 1909 gave the value of manufactured products as over $20,000,000,000. This figure may be compared with the Census of 1907 in Great Britain, which reported $8,000,000,000 for that nation, and with the estimate for Germany in 1913, which reported between $11,000,000,000 and $12,000,000,000. The United States, however, consumed a larger proportion of her manufactured goods at home than either of these nations, although there was a great actual increase in exports. In the normal years before the First World War, while Great Britain exported one-fourth, we exported less than one-tenth of our manufactured products, a proportion changed temporarily by the war.

Manufacturing was progressing favorably in the 'fifties when the panic of 1857 halted its development. The impetus to production given by the Civil War increased the number of establishments 79.6 per cent during the decade of the 'sixties, and the number of wage earners 56.6—the largest relative advances in any decade in our history. The severe panic of 1873 again retarded manufacturing, especially in the founding of new establish-

[2] *Statistical Abstract, 1921,* pp. 862, 868. This table has not been continued in the *Statistical Abstract* for recent years, but the gross farm income of all crops including government payments for 1939 is estimated at $9,769,000,000 (*Statistical Abstract, 1940,* p. 668). The decline since 1919 represents the deflation from the prices of the First World War. The value of the products for all industry in 1937 was approximately $61,000,000,000 (*ibid.,* p. 805).

ments, but before the decade had run its course recovery set in and a healthy progress was evident. The 'eighties showed the largest increase in manufacturing up to 1909 in capital invested and in wages paid, the growth during the decade amounting to 133.8 per cent for the former, and 99.5 for the latter. Despite the depressing effect of the panic of 1893 on industry, figures for 1899 evidenced substantial gains. They pale into insignificance, however, before the enormous strides in the twentieth century, the second decade of which, including as it did the period of the First World War, surpassed all others in our history in percentage of increase in capital, wages, and value of products. This increase was, of course, partly discounted by the decrease in the purchasing power of the dollar.[3] While capital, wages, and value of products advanced 95, 158, and 157 per cent respectively from 1914 to 1919, the number of wage earners increased only 29.3 and the number of establishments only 5.2 per cent. More detailed statistics on the development of manufactures over a period of eighty-eight years is given in the tables on page 404.

In a study of the development of manufacturing it is interesting to note the changes in the rank and importance of various industries. In 1860 the first four groups in value of products were dependent upon either agriculture or lumbering, while in 1914 four and in 1919 three groups (including the first) out of the first six were still dependent upon these sources. Although manufacturing from agricultural raw materials predominated, iron and steel manufacture had advanced by 1914 from fifth place to second; and foundry and machine-shop products, which in 1860 were included with crude iron and steel, ranked fourth as a separate division. Two new groups appeared among the first ten—car construction and repairs, and automobiles, both transportation products. Even among the great manufacturing groups the rank is not static, and no list long remains the same. For instance, between 1900 and 1914 automobile manufacture became so important that it was separated from machine-shop products and was in the eighth place. By 1929 it ranked first, exclusive of bodies and parts, but it dropped to second place in 1937. The products of the industry standing twenty-fifth in rank in 1914 (silk goods, including throwsters) had a higher value ($254,011,000) than those of the industry ranking first in 1860.

In these tables, the industries are arranged according to value of products, not always a satisfactory measure of the importance of a given industry "because only a part of this value is actually created within the industry. Another part, and often a much larger one, is contributed by the value of the materials used."[4] Statistics for both cost of materials and value of prod-

[3] Below, p. 586.
[4] Census of Manufactures, 1929, I, 35.

MANUFACTURES: SUMMARY, 1849 TO 1937 [5]

	Number of Establishments (in Thousands)	Percentage of Increase or Decrease (—)	Wage Earners (Average for the Year) (in Thousands)	Percentage of Increase or Decrease (—)	Wages (in Millions of Dollars)	Percentage of Increase or Decrease (—)	Cost of Material Supplies, Fuel, and Power (in Millions of Dollars)	Percentage of Increase or Decrease (—)	Value of Products (in Millions of Dollars)	Percentage of Increase or Decrease (—)	Value Added by Manufacture (in Millions of Dollars)	Percentage of Increase or Decrease (—)
Factories and hand and neighborhood industries:												
1849	123		957		237		555		1,019		464	
1859	140	14.1	1,311	37.0	379	60.0	1,032	85.8	1,886	85.1	854	84.1
1869	252	79.6	2,054	56.6	620	63.8	1,991	93.0	3,386	79.5	1,395	63.3
1879	254	0.7	2,733	33.0	948	52.8	3,397	70.6	5,370	58.6	1,973	41.4
1889	355	40.0	4,252	55.6	1,891	99.5	5,162	52.0	9,372	74.5	4,210	113.4
1899	512	44.1	5,306	24.8	2,321	22.7	7,344	42.3	13,000	38.7	5,656	34.3
Factories, excluding hand and neighborhood industries and establishments with products valued at less than $500:												
1899	205		4,510		1,895		6,441		11,103		4,662	
1909	265	29.3	6,273	39.1	3,210	69.3	11,876	84.3	20,068	80.7	8,191	75.6
1919	210	— 20.7	8,431	34.4	9,673	201.3	36,283	205.5	60,053	199.2	23,770	190.1
1929	207	— 1.4	8,380	— 0.6	10,910	12.7	37,441	3.1	68,178	13.5	30,737	29.3
1937	167	— 19.3	8,569	2.2	10,112	— 7.3	35,539	— 5.0	60,713	— 10.9	25,174	— 18.0

[5] *Census of Manufactures, 1937*, Part I, pp. 18 f. Percentages since 1899 determined by the author.

RANK OF LEADING INDUSTRIES, 1860, 1914, AND 1929 [6]

Rank	1860 Industry	1860 Value of Products (in Thousands)	1914 Industry	1914 Value of Products (in Thousands)	1929 Industry	1929 Value of Products (in Thousands)
1	Flour and meal	$248,580	Slaughtering and meat packing	$1,651,965	Motor vehicles	$3,722,793
2	Cotton goods	115,726	Iron and steel, steel works, and rolling mills	918,665	Meat packing, wholesale	3,434,634
3	Lumber planed and sawed	104,928	Flour-mill and gristmill products	877,680	Iron and steel, steel works, and rolling mills	3,365,789
4	Boots and shoes	91,889	Foundry and machine-shop products	866,545	Foundry and machine-shop products	2,791,462
5	Iron founding and machinery	88,618	Lumber and timber products	715,310	Petroleum refining	2,639,665
6	Clothing, including furnishing	88,095	Cotton goods	676,569	Electric machinery	2,300,916
7	Leather, including morocco and patent leather	75,698	Cars and general shop construction and repairs by steam railroad companies	510,041	Printing and publishing, newspapers, and periodicals	1,738,299
8	Woolen goods, including yarn, etc.	65,706	Automobiles	503,230	Clothing, women's	1,709,581
9	Liquors	56,588	Boots and shoes	501,760	Motor vehicles, bodies and parts	1,537,930
10	Steam engines	46,757	Printing and publishing, newspapers, and periodicals	495,906	Bread and bakery products	1,526,111
11	Iron, cast	36,638	Bread and other products	491,893	Cotton goods	1,524,177
12	Iron, forged, rolled, and wrought	36,537	Clothing, women's	437,888	Lumber and timber products	1,273,472
13	Provisions (beef, pork, etc.)	31,986	Clothing, men's	458,211	Car and general construction and repairs, steam railroads	1,184,435
14	Printing (book, job, etc.)	31,063	Smelting and refining copper	444,022	Cigars and cigarettes	1,066,909
15	Carriages	26,849	Liquors, malt	442,149	Flour and other grain-mill products	1,060,269

[6] Figures for 1860 compiled from Census of 1860, volume on *Manufactures*; for 1914, from *Abstract of Census of Manufactures, 1914*, Table 220, pp. 516 ff; for 1929, from *Abstract of Census of Manufactures, 1929*, I, 21, 35.

RELATIVE IMPORTANCE OF LEADING INDUSTRIES FOR THE UNITED STATES, 1937[7]

	Number of Establishments	Wage Earners		Cost of Materials, Fuel Purchased, Energy, and Contract Work		Value of Products		Value Added by Manufacture	
		Average for the Year	Rank	Amount in Thousands of Dollars	Rank	Amount in Thousands of Dollars	Rank	Amount in Thousands of Dollars	Rank
All industries	166,794	8,569,231		35,539,333		60,712,872		25,173,530	
Steel work and rolling mills	6,410	479,342	1	1,833,745	4	3,330,491	1	1,496,747	1
Motor vehicles	131	194,527	8	2,394,269	1	3,069,219	2	701,949	5
Meat packing, wholesale	1,160	127,477	15	2,386,090	2	2,787,358	3	401,267	13
Petroleum refining	365	83,182	22	2,064,307	3	2,546,746	4	482,439	10
Motor vehicles, bodies and parts	936	284,814	4	1,275,073	5	2,080,018	5	804,945	4
Electrical machinery, apparatus and supplies	1,435	257,660	5	642,867	10	1,622,098	6	979,232	3
Bread and bakery products	17,193	239,388	6	727,022	7	1,426,163	7	699,141	6
Printing and publishing, newspapers and periodicals	9,244	135,215	14	393,021	18	1,396,031	8	1,003,010	2
Cigarettes	34	26,149	70	771,522	6	968,927	9	197,405	30
Cotton woven goods	677	336,104	2	525,947	13	967,110	10	441,163	12
Machinery not otherwise classified	2,298	146,712	11	375,647	20	964,151	11	588,504	7
Paper	647	110,809	17	567,449	11	957,940	12	390,491	15
Chemicals not otherwise classified	601	78,951	25	455,062	16	932,750	13	477,688	11
Flour and other grain-mill products	2,238	26,390	69	722,711	8	856,310	14	133,600	41
Lumber and timber products	7,647	323,948	3	345,800	24	848,481	15	502,681	9

[7] *Ibid., 1937*, pp. 34-36.

ucts include a large amount of duplication because of the use of the products of some establishments as materials by others. The value added by manufacture gives a more accurate idea of the importance of the industry; most significant of all, particularly since unemployment became so widespread, is the average number of wage earners employed. In these tables the Census of 1937 has been used rather than more recent figures because this was the last census taken under approximately normal conditions before the Second World War. Changes between 1929 and 1937 in the relative value of the first fifteen industries have not been important. Paper and chemicals entered this group and boots and shoes returned to it. Cigarette manufacturing had been separated from cigars in the census, but nevertheless had advanced from fourteenth to ninth place.

The remarkable expansion in manufacturing has been attended by a corresponding growth in economic independence. During the colonial period and the years before the Civil War we were largely dependent upon Europe for much of the better class of manufactured goods; our exports consisted of our surplus of food and raw materials. The high tariff walls, and the influx of immigration from Europe that provided cheap labor, made it possible to exploit our unsurpassed mineral and agricultural wealth. Practically anything we need now can be manufactured at home; the First World War broke even the great chemical monopoly of the Germans. Imports now consist to a large extent of luxuries, tropical fruits, rubber, sugar, coffee, and manufactured goods involving hand labor. An indefinite blockade which cut us off from the rest of the world would not seriously interfere with our ability to live and carry on the economic functions, at least after we developed certain synthetic products such as rubber.

CAUSES OF THE GROWTH OF MANUFACTURE

Undoubtedly a strong impetus was given to the growth of manufacturing by the imperative needs of the Civil War and by the stimulation of high prices resulting from war demands and the printing of fiat money. The real causes of the long upward swing are more fundamental. The United States became a great manufacturing nation first of all because of her unsurpassed natural resources. Rich agricultural products, such as livestock and cotton, have formed the basis of some of her most important manufacturing industries; and iron, coal, oil, copper, and other minerals have been obtainable in large quantities. In addition to raw materials, manufacturing is dependent upon labor and a market. Labor was secured by the natural rapid increase of population in an undeveloped country and by millions of immigrants, many of whom were unfitted by training and environment for other than factory work. American manufacturers could not look to the older countries for a large market, but had to build one at home in competition with foreign markets. Such a market was partially supplied by the continued growth of the population, but particularly by the needs of the great agricultural South and West. During the three decades 1900–1930 the domestic market was increasingly supplemented by a growing export trade as the United States embarked aggressively upon a program of extending her foreign commerce and investment.

The high tariffs which the Civil War inaugurated have become a fixture in our system and have undoubtedly stimulated manufacturing, both by the large profits allowed to well-established industries and by the protection given to infant enterprises. That the United States would have experienced a marvelous development of manufacture without a protective tariff there is no reason to doubt, but it is equally evident that high tariff walls have considerably speeded the growth of certain industries. Under Republican and Democratic administrations alike, the government's great aim has ordinarily been to promote industrial prosperity.

In contrast to the system of high protective tariffs, the internal policy of the government has been largely *laissez faire*. The lack of government interference during the period of great growth undoubtedly imparted a spirit of confidence amounting sometimes to recklessness on the part of the organizer. Even after attempts to exercise control were made in 1887 and 1890, for a long time they met with slight success. Manufacturing has also been aided by the freedom of interstate commerce, a factor which was instrumental in the acceptance of the Constitution and amply justified it. "The mainland of the United States is the largest area in the civilized world which is thus unrestricted by customs, excises, or national prejudice, and its population possesses, because of its great collective wealth, a larger consuming capacity than that of any other nation." [8] "It is the enjoyment of free-trade and protection at the same time," said James G. Blaine, "which has contributed to the unexampled development and marvelous prosperity of the United States." [9] Both have undoubtedly helped, particularly the latter. The newness and freedom of the country have reacted upon the character of both capitalists and laborers. The former have generally been inventive, resourceful, ready to take risks and to seize whatever advantages offered; the latter have developed a mobility unknown elsewhere, and have been freer to desert the old hand processes for the new machinery than in older countries where there were fewer opportunities for change.

[8] *Twelfth Census of the United States*, VII, lvii.

[9] James G. Blaine, *Twenty Years of Congress*, I, 211. Unfortunately this freedom of interstate trade has been significantly modified in recent years by state legislation generally upheld by the Supreme Court. See below, p. 518.

Without transportation facilities, manufacturing, other than purely local, would be well-nigh impossible. The 26,000 miles of navigable rivers, the Great Lakes, the roads, and the canals helped in the early years of the introduction of the factory system, but it was not until the construction of a network of railways that large-scale manufacturing became practicable. More recently the railroad facilities have been augmented by the enlarging of some of the old canals, and by the invention of the automobile and the resulting highway construction. Manufacturing and transportation have helped to create wealth which has been constantly available for reinvestment in similar projects.

As the Industrial Revolution has progressed, new inventions have made possible many new manufacturing industries which have been stimulated by the purchasing power of the American consumer. Among these important industries may be mentioned the manufacture of transportation equipment; electrical supplies used for telephone, telegraph, radio, lighting, and household equipment; bicycles, and automobiles. The distribution of these and many other products has been aided by the development of advertising and salesmanship on a large scale, and has been stimulated, of course, by the relatively high wage scale of American workmen.

In discussing the causes for the development of manufacturing the application of science to industry, particularly in recent years, cannot be overemphasized. No longer do large industries depend upon the findings of individual inventors or scientists working independently; rather they support staffs of research workers whose business is to discover methods of producing a better product more cheaply or to develop an entirely new one. Thus research chemists in the rubber industry were able in fifteen years to quadruple the life of an automobile tire and to lower the price of tires. Less successful has been the effort to apply science to labor. "Scientific management" through studies of the most efficient type of operation, tools, and factory layout has likewise reduced costs, but in many cases labor has largely paid for it by the "speed-up" and the "stretch-out."

Any discussion of the causes of the development of American manufacturing would be incomplete without mentioning the part played by the entrepreneurs, who often were neither scientists nor, strictly speaking, manufacturers or industrialists. These were men like Andrew Carnegie in steel, Philip D. Armour in slaughtering and meat packing, John D. Rockefeller in oil refining, and J. P. Morgan in finance. Through their skill in integration, finance, or salesmanship these men were able to create great enterprises which reduced manufacturing costs, created new markets, and stimulated industrial development. Far more numerous were the small manufacturers who were often a combination of engineer, inventor or scientist, and business man, and who were the original entrepreneurs or builders of American manufacturing.

CHARACTERISTICS OF AMERICAN MANUFACTURING

The manufacturing industry in America has been influenced in its development by several factors which make it differ from the European system. Foremost among these is the scarcity of labor, prevalent during most of our history, and inevitably directing the inventive genius of the nation to the creation of labor-saving machinery. American products are preeminently machine-made, not hand-made, a characteristic not wholly favoring quality, since the substitution of machine for hand products has meant a certain sacrifice of the artistic, the delicate, and the beautiful for the sake of large-scale production. With certain notable exceptions, such as shoes and automobiles, it would probably be correct to say that European consumption goods are generally finer in quality and more artistic than ours, whereas our production goods (machinery, etc.) are generally finer than theirs.

Scarcity of labor also helped to develop earlier in America than in any other country the standardization of machinery and parts, permitting the rapid production of complicated mechanisms in large quantities, each part of which is made separately, the whole being assembled later. This enables easy replacement of parts and keeps down expenses in running machinery.

Another characteristic attributable partly to the scarcity of labor and partly to the character of the raw materials (particularly true in earlier years), is that much of our manufacturing produces small changes, and the value added by manufacture forms a relatively small proportion of the total value of the product. "Thus the slaughtering and meat-packing industry," said the *Census of Manufactures,* "which ranks first (1914) in gross value of products, and the flour-mill and gristmill industry, which ranks third in that respect, both hold a comparatively low rank in regard to number of wage earners and value added by manufacture." [10] This form of manufacturing is likely to be located close to the supply, whereas more complicated forms, like the metal and textile industries of New England, are often far from the raw material. The dependence of many of our leading manufactured products upon agriculture should again be emphasized. Of the fifteen leading industries summarized in the table of industries for 1937, at least five are directly dependent on agriculture.

Closely allied with the scarcity of labor has been the enthusiastic adoption of any power other than hand; most of our factories are operated by

[10] *Abstract of the Census of Manufactures, 1914,* p. 27.

steam, water, or electricity. Since 1870 mechanical power in the United States has increased from 2,346,000 horsepower to 42,931,000 in 1929. Whereas in 1870 the horsepower contributed by waterfalls and steam was about equal, the tendency during the next four decades was definitely toward steam. With the development of electricity and the increasing cost of coal there has been a swing back to water power. As electrical engineers have perfected the means for transporting power over long distances, it has been possible to manufacture electricity by water power rather than by coal, and manufacturers have found it advantageous to purchase power from hydroelectrical companies or to build their own power stations.[11] The development of electricity for manufacturing as well as for lighting and other purposes has been an important aspect of the recent history both of manufacturing and of the electrical industry. The extent of electrification of factory power equipment has grown from 33 per cent in 1914 to 74 per cent in 1929, and is constantly increasing. "Practically all of the increase in factory power equipment since 1914 has been in electric motors operated by current from central stations."[12]

Some note has already been made of an outstanding characteristic of American manufacturing—freedom from tradition. Our rapid development may be traced to some extent to the freedom from inherited ideas, leaving our industries unhampered to seek the best and quickest way. The surviving influences of guild regulation and the medieval legislation of town and nation were not felt. Furthermore, American labor is intelligent, quick to comprehend and to adopt new methods. Environment has made the American a jack-of-all-trades and has nurtured his inventive genius. Nowhere have new methods of machine production been more enthusiastically sought. Liberal patent laws have aided; the 276 patents granted in the decade 1790–1800 grew to 6480 in the decade 1840–1850, to 25,200 in the decade 1850–1860, to 85,910 in the ten years 1860–1870, and to 234,956 in the decade 1890–1900. In 1911 the total number of patents issued since 1790 reached the million mark. In the single year of 1932 the number issued and reissued amounted to 56,856. In a typical year more than 70,000 patents are applied for and over 40,000 granted. The greatest manufacturing plants now maintain laboratories devoted exclusively to the development of new devices and improvements. The mere recitation of some of the great patents issued in the field of electricity or gas engines would provide a thumb-nail sketch of the recent development of American manufacture and of technical advancement.

[11] C. O. Ruggles, "Problems in the Development of a Super-Power System," *Harvard Business Review*, II, 161 ff.; reprinted in part in F. Flügel and H. U. Faulkner, *Readings*, pp. 501–511.

[12] *Commerce Yearbook, 1930*, I, 268.

WESTWARD MOVEMENT OF MANUFACTURING

Like population and agriculture, the movement of manufactures has been steadily westward. A map published in the Twelfth Census [13] shows the center of manufacturing in 1850 (computed upon the gross value of products) near the center of Pennsylvania, 41 miles northwest of Harrisburg. In 1860, 1870, and 1880 it moved to western Pennsylvania, and by 1890 nearly to the center of Ohio, a few miles southwest of Canton; the next census shows a further progress westward to a point southeast of Mansfield. During the half century from 1850 to 1890 the westward movement of the center of manufacturing was 225 miles, and the westward movement of the center of population 243 miles, indicating the close relationship of the two movements.

The westward movement of manufacture has been caused primarily by the filling up of the West, which has provided labor and a market, and secondarily by the desire to be near raw materials. It has been retarded by the scarcity of labor in the new communities and by the concentration of capital in the older ones. It has likewise been forced to wait upon the development of transportation facilities. Although manufacturing has lagged behind both agriculture and population in the westward advance, it has usually followed the raw material as fast as labor could be obtained. Thus flour milling moved west from the coast rivers to Rochester on the Erie Canal, then to Chicago, and finally to Minneapolis and Kansas City. The meat-packing industry had its trans-Allegheny beginnings about 1816 at Cincinnati, but it moved to Chicago and Kansas City. Lumbering is an excellent example of an industry forced to follow the source of supply. The Northeast originally furnished most of the lumber, but at present it is obtained largely from the Northwest and South. As in the case of milling and meat packing, the manufacture of agricultural machinery moved westward. Most of the factories shifted from their original home in central New York to Illinois and Wisconsin, following both the hickory forest and the farmer. In a similar manner, the present century has shown a tendency for the cotton industry to shift toward the source. In 1880, for instance, the Carolinas and Georgia used only 8.4 per cent (133,000 bales) of the cotton consumed for manufactures, but in 1929 they used 59.2 per cent (4,203,000 bales). The number of spindles in the cotton-growing states increased fortyfold during this half-century. In many cases capital has set up industry close to the raw materials and has imported labor to handle it. Thus slaves were formerly imported to raise tobacco and cotton; and each year now lumberers are shipped to the lumber camps during the cutting season. It should,

[13] Twelfth Census of the United States, *Statistical Atlas*, plate No. 179.

however, be pointed out that the recent development of textile manufacturing in the South has been due not alone to nearness to raw material but also to the existence of a supply of cheap labor.

LOCALIZATION OF INDUSTRY

Although the center of manufacture has moved westward, this tendency has been hampered as well as aided by the many influences making for localization. The Twelfth Census has ably summed up the general causes for the localization of industry as follows: (1) nearness to materials, (2) nearness to markets, (3) nearness to water power, (4) a favorable climate, (5) supply of labor, (6) capital available for investment in manufactures, and (7) the momentum of an early start. Any one of these, or a combination of several, explains the location of most of our manufacturing.[14]

The nearness to materials explains the concentration of milling in the Twin Cities and Kansas City; of meat packing in Chicago, Omaha, and Kansas City; of furniture at Grand Rapids; of fruit and vegetable canning in California, central New York, and Baltimore; of fish canning in Oregon and on the New England coast; and of tobacco in North Carolina. It also explains, in part, the recent migration of many cotton mills to the South.

The nearness to market is an influential factor in the localization of industry, especially in the production of bulky and heavy articles. Four of the eight states ranking highest in value of manufactured products—New York, Pennsylvania, Illinois, Michigan, Ohio, New Jersey, California, and Massachusetts—are in the Northeast; they contributed (1937) approximately 50 per cent. The other area of industrial concentration is in the well-populated region of the East North Central States of Ohio, Indiana, Illinois, Michigan, and Wisconsin. The localization of the manufacture of such luxuries as jewelry at Providence, silk at Paterson, and furs at New York, and the localization in the Northeast of factories producing certain high-grade necessities is due to the fact either that originally the primary market was east of the Alleghenies or that the principal market remains there. Transportation costs, especially before the days of railroads and automobiles, were naturally a powerful factor in locating industries in thickly populated communities or on rivers and highways leading directly thereto.

Before the introduction of the steam engine, manufacturing was largely dependent upon water or hand power. The preeminence of New England and eastern New York as manufacturing communities is in no small degree due to the water power furnished by the Hudson, the Mohawk, the Con-

[14] Twelfth Census, VII, *Manufacturing*, Part I, pp. ccx–ccxiv; also in F. Fügel and H. U. Faulkner, *Readings*, pp. 495–503.

necticut, the Housatonic, the Merrimac, and scores of other streams. Industries like cotton and wool, founded in the early days on water power, have continued to depend upon it. In New England this has been partially due to the distance from the coal supply. The utilization of coal has made manufacturing in many districts independent of water power, and has caused the centering of many industries near the coal fields; as a result the horsepower generated by coal has until recently increased with greater rapidity than that obtained from water. As already pointed out, however, the ability to transport electric power over long distances (whether manufactured by coal or water power) has had a tendency to minimize the importance of both sources of power in determining the location of industry.

Along with water power, a favorable climate has helped to determine the geographic position of the textiles. High humidity and an even temperature have fitted Fall River and New Bedford for cotton manufacturing. The invigorating air of the North is infinitely more suitable for labor than the enervating climate of many parts of the South, and seems to be a permanent factor that tends toward the industrial development of the North.

Industries naturally tend to establish themselves where there is a supply of labor. While American labor is undoubtedly more mobile than that of other nations, the expense of moving and the attachment to home and friends tend to keep it relatively fixed. The decline of the merchant marine and the meager profits from agriculture freed much labor in New England for manufacturing, a supply augmented by women and children coming in from the farms. Immigrants who were factory workers at home drifted to the factory towns to swell the available labor force. An industry of a certain type draws skilled labor in that particular line, thus giving a further impetus to the establishment of new factories. As an industry becomes concentrated, future skilled labor must be trained in this center, an influence which keeps it from spreading. Two-thirds of women's clothing is made in New York State, three-fourths of the plated ware in Connecticut, and almost all of the carpets in Philadelphia, Thompsonville (Connecticut), and Yonkers and Amsterdam (New York). Industries employing women and children often follow those that employ men; thus textile mills are often set up in foundry and mining towns. It is easier to move capital than labor, and the human factor must always remain vital in the establishment of an industry.

In recent years most large enterprises have secured their capital from the great financial centers. This, however, is usually a second stage. Before financiers step in to reorganize or enlarge a manufacturing plant, the industry has ordinarily been established by the enterprise and capital of local business men, illustrating "the tendency of a town to own itself in the early stages of its industrial life.[15] Outside capital can be attracted more easily to a prosperous town and to an industry in which local people have invested. The rapid rise of textiles in New Bedford and other New England cities was due in part to the capital set free by the decline of whaling and the merchant marine. Fall River is an excellent illustration of a town which has specialized in one industry, the control of which has largely been retained in the community.

The momentum of an early start can be given as a leading cause for the localization of industry. It has been said that if the population of New England were suddenly wiped out it would be doubtful if its future would be other than that of a summer resort, its natural advantages for manufacturing as against its disadvantages being so slight. Johnstown and Gloversville, New York, the greatest glove center in America, originally drew glovers because they were advantageously located to make use of deer skins. As skilled labor gravitated there it has continued to produce leather, kid, and cloth gloves. An early carpet factory in Amsterdam, a few miles to the south, has drawn to it skilled weavers who have made it the second largest carpet city in the country. The chance settlement of a skilled shoemaker at Lynn in 1750 made it the leading shoe town and kept it so, notwithstanding its distance from the source of raw materials. A similar early settlement of jewelers in Providence made it a center in that industry. The habit of industrial imitation is great, for the average man has not the courage to be an industrial pioneer; with skilled labor at hand and successful industries already in operation, he is likely to follow the line of least resistance. Most industries, of course, are influenced not by one but by several of these factors. Thus the development of silk manufacturing in Paterson, New Jersey, was due to an early start, to the existence of skilled labor, to the special qualities of water required, and to this industry's need for certain climatic conditions. What has been said of industry in general is true to a limited extent of the concentration in certain districts of the great cities of middlemen, such as stock brokers, textile wholesalers, fur merchants, and others.

The Northeast (New England, New York, Pennsylvania, and New Jersey) from the beginning of our industrial history has been the most important manufacturing region, the value of her products in 1937 amounting to 35.7 per cent of the total. Almost all of the factors which influence localization have been operative here—markets, labor, capital, transportation facilities, and the impetus of an early start. The streams of New England and the coal of Pennsylvania provided ample power. In cer-

[15] Twelfth Census, VII, *Manufacturers*, Part I, pp. ccxi–ccxii.

tain raw materials alone was this section handicapped. In the small-scale industries of the early years a sufficiency of raw materials such as iron, wool, and hides could be found at home, but later these had to be imported to a large extent. The other advantages, however, not only preserved to this region its supremacy in many types of metal, leather, and textile manufacturing, but created cotton mills and sugar refineries, the raw materials for which are entirely imported. The Northeast surpasses all other sections in the value of output per person, the percentage of people engaged in manufacturing, and the number and variety of such enterprises.

Of the eight states which lead in the value of manufactured products, New York, Pennsylvania, New Jersey, and Massachusetts are in this region. The five most valuable manufactured products of New York State in 1937 were printing and publishing, women's clothing, men's clothing, foundry and machine-shop products, and bread and bakery products. In Pennsylvania (1937) steel works and rolling mills were by far the chief industry, followed by foundry and machine-shop products, electrical machinery, silk and rayon manufactures, and meat packing. The principal industries of New Jersey were the smelting and refining of copper, petroleum refining, chemicals, electrical machinery, and paints. Turning to New England, we find Massachusetts primarily interested in textiles, boots and shoes, and electrical machinery and apparatus. The remainder of the New England States, like Massachusetts, excel in textiles and also in the manufacture of smaller metal products. Connecticut leads in the production of brass, bronze, and copper objects, clocks, firearms, and silverware; and Rhode Island, until recently, in jewelry. The distance from raw materials has turned the Northeast to the manufacture of smaller commodities in which the labor cost is higher, the transportation cost lower, and the value added by manufacture greater.

The Middle West (East North Central and West North Central States) had to wait upon immigration and settlement before sufficient labor and capital could be accumulated for manufacturing. The wealth of raw materials, both agricultural and mineral, destined this section to an industrial future. As the greatest corn country in the world, she has naturally created a slaughtering and meat-packing industry and has drawn manufacturers of vehicles and farm machinery. The bituminous coal of Ohio, Illinois, and Michigan provided power; the iron of Ohio, Missouri, and the Lake Superior region of Minnesota furnished raw materials for foundries, and petroleum formed the foundation of other industries. In this section are located Illinois, Ohio, and Michigan, the third, fourth, and fifth states respectively in the value of manufactured products in 1937. At this date the most important manufactured products in point of value were: Illinois, meat packing;

Ohio, steel works and rolling mills; Michigan, motor vehicles; Wisconsin, paper; Missouri, motor vehicles; Iowa, meat packing.

The economic life and the manufactures of the Pacific States are founded primarily upon agriculture and lumbering. In both Washington and Oregon the preponderant industry is lumber and timber products; flour and other grain-mill products and meat packing are important. California leads the Union in canning and preserving fruits and vegetables, although her leading industry in point of value is petroleum refining, a recent development. Shipbuilding, which in each of these states ranked among the first five industries in 1919, sank to a position of relative unimportance in the 1920's, only to be revived during the Second World War.

It is customary to think of the eight Mountain States as interested fundamentally in the extraction of minerals, and of their manufactures as closely connected with smelting and refining. This impression is not borne out by the facts, for the value of the agricultural products of these states is nearly double that of the mineral. The chief industry (1937) in value of products in Idaho was lumber and timber products; in Colorado, meat packing; in Nevada, planing-mill and other wood products. It is interesting to note that one of the chief industries in the Mountain States is car and general shop construction and repairs by steam railroads. In Arizona the industry first in value of products is the smelting and refining of copper; in Utah the smelting and refining of lead, and in Wyoming and Montana the refining of petroleum.

In the South (East South Central and West South Central States) the Civil War ended forever the popular belief that the future of that section lay wholly in agriculture. Without capital, the great plantations were broken up to be tilled by tenant farmers; the remnants of the planter class pursued their fortunes in the cities. It was not until the decade of the 'eighties that manufacturing made much headway. By that time the South had recovered sufficiently to accumulate local capital, and northern investors began to pause in their exploitation of the West to see the latent possibilities in the South. This section was still and probably always will be primarily agricultural; but the great crops of cotton and tobacco needed preparation before marketing, and the cheap labor available from the Negroes and "poor whites" made it likely that factories would be set up close to the raw materials. Until recent years her lumber and mineral resources had scarcely been tapped, but both have provided inviting fields for outside capital.

The most spectacular development which any southern industry has experienced occurred in lumbering. The interest of the South in forest products goes back to colonial days, but her important position dates only recently from the partial depletion of the northern forests. In 1869 the northeastern states produced 35.7 per cent and the Lake states 28.2 per cent of the lumber cut in the United States, and ten years later these two regions still produced 60 per cent of the total, although the Lake states were now in the lead. By 1899 the southern states (including the Carolinas and Virginia) had taken the lead, and continued to hold it until 1930, when the Pacific States assumed first rank. Southern production still amounts

to over one-third of the total cut. Even more important is the extent of employment offered; in nine of these eleven states the lumber industry ranked either first or second, and in two third, in the number of wage earners.

Since 1880 New England's monopoly in the manufacture of cotton has been broken by the southern states, in particular by North and South Carolina. Nearness to the source of raw materials and cheap labor, combined with increased taxation and labor difficulties in New England, have been the chief causes. This southern movement forced the New England manufacturer to turn his attention to the production of the finer grades of cloth and has left the coarser grades of sheeting and ducks to the South. In 1880 there were less than 500,000 spindles in North Carolina, South Carolina, and Georgia, with a product valued at scarcely $13,000,000, while there were over 8,500,000 spindles in New England. By 1910 over half of the raw cotton was manufactured in the South. As notable as the increase in cotton manufacture has been the development in the utilization of the by-products. Cottonseed, formerly thrown away, is now fed to cattle or manufactured into cooking oil; the value of cottonseed products rose from $12,000,000 in the 'eighties to $265,000,000 in 1929.

Abundant supplies of coal, iron, and copper in Tennessee and Alabama led to the establishment, especially in Alabama, of extensive iron and steel works. The production of pig iron in Alabama increased from 347,000 tons in 1880 to 2,598,000 in 1937. The city of Birmingham grew from 3000 to 268,000 in 1940, and is one of the steel centers of the United States. More recently the discovery of oil wells in Texas and Louisiana has laid the foundations of a new industry and a new prosperity.

The value of southern manufactured products has increased from $338,-791,898 in 1880 to $9,916,000,000 in 1939; nevertheless, the southern states in 1939 produced but 17.5 per cent of the total manufactures of the nation, measured in terms of value. The future must necessarily see a further industrial development in the South, but it will be handicapped by unskilled labor, an enervating climate, and the superior possibilities of agriculture.

SUMMARY OF MANUFACTURERS BY GEOGRAPHIC SECTIONS, 1939 [16]

	Number of Establishments	Wage Earners (Average Number)	In Millions of Dollars				Percentage of Total Value of Products
			Wages	Cost of Materials, Containers, Fuel, and Power	Value Added by Manufacture	Value of Products	
New England	16,135	952,873	1,024	2,459	2,430	4,889	8.6
Middle Atlantic	56,300	2,249,683	2,689	8,667	7,370	16,037	28.2
East North Central . .	40,419	2,196,388	2,951	9,778	7,775	17,553	30.9
West North Central . .	14,947	382,354	428	2,453	1,363	3,816	6.7
South Atlantic	17,316	986,526	826	3,153	2,237	5,390	9.5
East South Central . .	7,279	357,827	291	1,130	828	1,959	3.5
West South Central . .	10,021	262,585	238	1,735	832	2,567	4.5
Mountain	4,011	69,339	82	545	275	820	1.4
Pacific	17,816	429,667	561	2,198	1,601	3,798	6.7
Total for the United States	184,244	7,887,242	9,090	32,118	24,711	56,829	100.0

BASIC INDUSTRIES

The basic industries in the United States coincide closely with the basic needs of the people—food, clothing, and metals for machinery, transportation, [17] and other uses.

Manufacture of Food.—When the position of the United States as a food-producing nation is taken into account, it is not at all surprising to find

[16] Preliminary report, *Census of Manufactures.*
[17] The development of the automobile industry is discussed below, pp. 508 ff., 621 ff.

that of the eight industries in 1937 whose output is valued at over one billion dollars per year, two are foodstuffs; meat packing, wholesale, ranks third, and bread and other bakery products ranks seventh. A glance at the table on page 405 will show that the relative importance of the manufacture of foodstuff was even greater in earlier decades. Of the group of industries as rated by the Census of Manufactures of 1937, food and kindred products stood first in value of products. The slaughtering of animals, the preserving of food, and even the grinding of grain were at one time largely household industries. The entrance of women into industry and professions, the multifarious activities of the modern housewife, the increasing scarcity of household servants, the growth of urban life, and the cheapness of manufactured products have all tended to take the preparation of food, at least in the processing stages, out of the home. Baker's bread, prepared breakfast food, and canned meat, vegetables, fruit, fish, and milk are all indications of this tendency.

Much of this manufacturing, it is true, is of a simple kind and has depended for its development rather on increased production of foodstuffs than on new inventions. Nevertheless, the invention of modern methods of refrigeration in the 'seventies immensely stimulated cattle raising and the transportation of fresh meats, and the roller process of making flour permitted the utilization of spring wheat and so put under cultivation the wheat fields of the Dakotas, Montana, and Minnesota. Innumerable patents have made possible the use of old staples in new forms. In like manner, manufacturing processes have introduced new but valuable foods, such as cottonseed oil and peanut butter. The total value of food and kindred products amounted in 1937 to $11,265,610,000, of which $3,354,242,000 was added by manufacture; food products then contributed about 17 per cent of the total value of the manufactures of the country.

Americans consume more meat per capita than any other people. In value of products, meat packing has ranked first, second, or third for over forty years, although 85 per cent of this value is in raw materials, and less than 2 per cent is added by manufacture. The industry, as before suggested, has followed the westward movement of the corn belt. From 1816 to 1860 its center was in Cincinnati and the cities of Ohio, but has now shifted west to Chicago, St. Louis, Omaha, and Kansas City. In addition to the introduction of refrigeration and canning, the industry has profited by the utilization of an ever-increasing number of by-products which are now the chief source of profit. No part of the animal is wasted; fertilizer, leather, glue, wool, and many other products are derived therefrom. The packing industry has grown from 259 establishments in 1859, the value of whose output was $29,441,000, to 1160 in 1937, with products valued at almost three billion. According to value in 1937, the chief animal products besides meat are butter, cheese, and condensed and evaporated milk, valued at over $900,000,000, and ice cream, valued at almost 300 million.

In 1919 the lead in the manufacturing of vegetable food was held by flour-mill and gristmill products, which then ranked sixth in value of products; by 1937, however, they had dropped to fourteenth place, and were surpassed by bread and other bakery products, which ranked seventh. The value added to bakery products by manufacture is over half the total value, while for flour and other grain mills it is less than one-fifth. Both industries are carried on in every state in the Union, but bread and bakery products are manufactured chiefly where the population is densest, while the center of flour milling has shifted west as the great wheat fields of the prairies have been opened up. New York in 1937 had regained first place in flour- and other grain-mill products, followed by Kansas, Minnesota, Texas, and Missouri. The manufacture of confectionery, whose output was valued in 1937 at over 300 millions, centered chiefly in Illinois, New York, Massachusetts, and Pennsylvania. The canning and preserving industry is well distributed throughout the United States, Nevada and South Dakota being the only states not represented by one or more establishments in 1939. Nevertheless, the Pacific States are far in the lead in the total value of the products, followed by the Middle Atlantic and the East North Central groups. The revival of the brewing and distilling industry, after the repeal of the Eighteenth Amendment, occurred on the whole in the regions in which this industry was formerly established. The Census of 1937 gives the value of distilled liquors manufactured as $113,102,000, malt liquors as $537,105,000, and wines as $42,732,000.

Few manufacturing industries have undergone more radical changes in the past half century than the food industries. This has been particularly noticeable in recent years in the retail food field. The development of urban life has made it impractical to purchase food in large quantities and has hastened the decline of baking, canning, preserving, and other forms of food preservation in the home. As a result, bread and other bakery products have now advanced to seventh place in value of products (see p. 406), and flour and butter are largely retailed in small quantities. The market for canned fruit, vegetables, and meat has grown tremendously. The retailer now handles chiefly package goods in small units, and industries that manufacture cartons and cans have developed to large proportions.

Textiles, Shoes, and Clothing.—The textile industry is largely concerned with the manufacture of cloth and clothing. In 1937 it ranked as third among the great groups of industries, with a total product valued at $7,061,609,000; only food products and iron and steel products outranked it. Textile manufacturing was carried on in over 20,600 mills with an average of more than 1,800,000 wage earners. Textiles increased in value more than sixfold in the last half of the nineteenth century, and in amount of produce tenfold. The general causes for this are the same as those that affected other manufactures—an increasing market and labor supply, an abundance of raw material in the case of cotton, and a high protective tariff. While the present value of manufactured textiles is enormous, we normally still import considerable quantities of high-grade silks and woolens.

Before 1860 cotton was the chief textile manufactured; it was the first American industry to be brought into the factory. In that year there were 572 mills in New England, 540 in the middle states, 159 in the South, and 22 in the West, their total production being valued at $115,600,000. The abnormal demand for woolens during the Civil War and the interruption in the supply of raw materials pushed cotton back temporarily. It was not until 1900 that cotton again attained first rank which it has held since that time. The value of cotton manufactures in 1937 was given as $1,274,294,000 and that for woolen as $826,801,000. Despite its leadership among textiles, cotton has declined in relative importance with the increased use of silk and rayon. This was particularly true after 1929. Nevertheless, in recent years the textile industry as a whole has appeared to be regaining some of its lost ground. The United States ranks second among the nations in the manufacture of textiles, being surpassed only by Great Britain; our position is due chiefly to the fact that we are the only great cotton-manufacturing nation whose raw material is available at home.

The movement of cotton manufacturing toward the source of supply has already been mentioned. New England's 572 establishments of 1860 had decreased to 259 in 1929, chiefly through consolidations, although the number of active spindles had increased from 3,859,000 to 12,537,000; but the South's 159 mills of 1860 had increased to 821 in 1929, and the spindles from 561,000 to 18,541,000. The cotton-growing states process about three-fifths of the cotton manufactured in the United States, although the better grades of cloth are still made in New England.

The great competition in cotton manufacturing has brought astounding progress since 1860. Although the fundamental patents were taken out before the Civil War, notable achievements, particularly in labor-saving devices, have been made since then, so revolutionary that the large concerns have been forced to replace their machinery two or three times. Among the most famous of the improvements are the ring spinner, the Northrop loom, the Barber warp-tying machine, and the automatic seamless knitting machine. The first three have doubled the production per operative. The ring spinner does not turn out as even or soft a thread as the old mule spinner, but its greater production speed has won it an assured place in American mills, where labor is costlier and scarcer. The Northrop loom is almost human in its ability to stop if the warp breaks or the shuttle gets out of place, and in inserting the colored warps at the proper time. The Barber machine ties the ends of the threads together, and the Bronson knitting machine knits stockings complete in every detail.

Although the Civil War temporarily set back cotton manufacturing, it gave the woolen industry an impetus that firmly established it. The value of woolens manufactured in 1850 was less than $50,000,000, whereas the combined manufactured value of woolen products in 1937 was $826,801,-799. The tendency toward consolidation has been marked in this industry, as is shown by the fact that the number of establishments in operation declined from 3208 in 1869 to 704 in 1937.

Because of special conditions the American manufacturer has until recently carried out all the processes of manufacture in a single plant, carding the short fiber for woolens, combing the long fiber for worsteds, spinning the thread, weaving the cloth, and dyeing it. In Europe, on the other hand, different plants have specialized in these processes and thus skilled labor has been concentrated on certain phases. This partially accounts for the frequent superiority of British woolens. Our manufacturers lead the field in the grade and variety of flannels and blankets, but their greatest output in quantity consists of the cheaper woolens that are consumed by the wholesale clothing houses. The manufacture of worsteds dates from about 1870 and is rapidly growing at the expense of other woolens, but expansion has been retarded by the greater amount of skill and labor necessary for its production. The development of woolen machinery has been less rapid than that of cotton, and the inventions have been mostly English in their origin, as is also the machinery itself.

The most spectacular advance in the woolen branch of textiles in America has occurred in the manufacture of carpets. Until after the Civil War carpets were largely hand woven. Most of the inventions have been the work of Americans, who have made the United States the greatest carpet-producing nation in the world and the products the finest obtainable, except the handloom rugs of the Orient, of which we imported over four million dollars' worth in 1937. The prosperity and wealth of the nation have enabled a high domestic consumption. We produced 65,346,000 square yards of carpets and rugs in 1937. Factory production of carpets began in 1841 when Erastus B. Bigelow of Boston adapted the power loom to the weaving of ingrain carpets and a few years later to the weaving of Wiltons and Brussels. His work was supplemented in 1864 by Smith & Skinner of Yonkers, who applied the power loom to Axminsters. The value of manufactured carpets and rugs rose from $7,857,000 in 1860 to $182,187,000 in 1937. The 105 mills operating in that year were located chiefly in New York, Pennsylvania, and Massachusetts.

In hosiery and knit goods the United States also leads the world. Hosiery was knit in the home until 1832, when Egbert Egberts at Cohoes, New York, successfully applied the principles of knitting by power; thereafter the manufacture of hosiery gradually shifted to the factory. Owing to the variety of products, the tendency toward comparatively small mills with moderate capital has been marked in this industry. The number of establishments increased from 197 in 1860 to 1821 in 1937, and the value of the products from $7,280,000 to $659,974,000. The industry is centered in Pennsylvania and New York.

The most remarkable advance in textiles in America has been made in the silk industry. This is the more astonishing because this industry has been built up on raw material which must be imported from a great distance and in competition with the long-established and well-equipped mills of France. The success has been due to tariff protection, to the enterprise of manufacturers, and to the nation's wealth, which has created a market. With these favoring factors but against great odds, the value of silk products grew from $6,608,000 in 1860 to $404,734,000 in 1937 (the latter figure including both rayon and silk); the output is larger than that of any other nation, and over 90 per cent is for domestic consumption. The value of rayon, or synthetic silk, manufactured now exceeds that of pure silk. John Ryle of Paterson, New Jersey, and the Cheneys of South Manchester, Connecticut, founded the industry when they began the manufacture of thread and ribbons; they branched out eventually into piece goods. Paterson is now the center of the silk and rayon industry, with Pennsylvania, New Jersey, New York, Connecticut, and Massachusetts the principal producing states.

Following closely upon the heels of textile development came that of ready-made clothing. This was stimulated by the demands of the Civil War and made possible by the invention of the sewing machine. Labor was provided by women and children and by the steady influx of foreigners, first the Irish, and after 1876 the Russian Jews. The application of factory methods to ready-made clothing is comparatively new; until recently the industry has been cursed by sweatshop methods under which operatives worked for a miserable pittance in their own homes, often in the most unhealthy surroundings. Considerations of humanity, of public health, and of business have gradually eliminated sweatshop clothing both voluntarily and through legal means. Some modern clothing factories are as up to date as any in other industries, though much clothing is still manufactured in small factories hardly better than sweat shops. The value of men's ready-made clothing increased from $80,830,000 in 1860 to $618,197,000 in 1937, and of women's from $7,181,000 to $1,213,202,000.[18] New York City is far in the lead in both branches, but her production is augmented by that of other metropolitan centers such as Chicago, Philadelphia, Rochester, and Baltimore. Recently a new clothing center has developed in Los Angeles.

Until 1845 shoemaking was a hand trade usually carried on in the home. The change to the factory began in that year with the invention of the leather roller which hastened the preparation of hides. Then came the Blanchard lasting machine which could turn out lasts of standardized sizes. Soon J. B. Nichols, a Lynn shoemaker, adapted Howe's sewing machine to the sewing of uppers, and just before the Civil War Lyman B. Blake invented the McKay machine for sewing the uppers to the soles. Shoe machinery is among the most ingenious in the world; an average factory uses sixty kinds of machines. A peculiarity of the industry is the control of the most important patents by a single company, the United Shoe Machinery Company, who lease the principal machines and are paid a royalty upon each pair of shoes manufactured.[19]

"The American shoe of today is the standard production of the world," says the Census of 1910. The Census of Manufacturers of 1937 credits the industry with 1080 establishments whose product is valued at $768,327,303, and which employ 215,000 wage earners. It is estimated that the American people spend $1,000,000,000 a year for footwear and average three pairs per capita annually. The centers of manufacturing are in the vicinity of Boston, New York and St. Louis. The boots and shoes produced in three New England states—Maine, Massachusetts, and New Hampshire—represented over one-third of the total for the United States, and Massachusetts still holds first rank among the states, with New York second, and Missouri third.

Iron and Steel.—It is impossible to overestimate the importance of iron and steel in modern life. We live in an age of machinery which rests upon iron and steel, as do our transportation system and our large structures. In steel rails, railroad coaches, automobiles, and an infinite variety of tools and machinery, the basic metal enters intimately into our everyday life. The rapid rise in output is accounted for chiefly by the increased demand, by the substitution of coke for anthracite coal in smelting, and by revo-

---

[18] *Census of Manufactures, 1937,* pp. 387, 419. These figures do not include certain minor items otherwise classified.

[19] The United Shoe Machinery Company was prosecuted by the government on the grounds that their "tying clause," which requires that one machine shall be used in conjunction with another, was in violation of the Clayton Act, a contention upheld in 1922 by the Supreme Court. United Shoe Machinery Corp. *et al. v.* U. S., 258 U. S. 451.

lutionary inventions which have facilitated and cheapened production.

Iron and steel and their products rank first among the leading industries of the United States, with 6410 steel works or rolling mills and total products valued at $3,330,000,000, over one-twentieth of the value of the nation's manufactured goods. This group includes many industries, such as blast furnaces, steel works, rolling mills, and other iron and steel manufacturing; but it excludes machinery, transportation equipment on land and water, and railroad repair shops, each of which forms a separate division in the census.

The manufacture of iron and steel falls into two divisions: the production of pig iron and its conversion into commercial iron and steel. Until after the Civil War, steel was a rare commodity that was used chiefly in cutlery and the finer grade of tools. Iron was the chief metal in use, and until 1839, when anthracite coal was introduced, it was for the most part smelted with charcoal. After the Civil War, bituminous coal, chiefly in the form of coke, was introduced in smelting, a factor that enabled the industry to distribute itself so widely that in 1880 iron was manufactured in thirty states. The greatest event in the history of iron and steel occurred in 1856 when two Englishmen, Henry Bessemer and Robert Mushet, invented a method, known as the Bessemer process, by which a blast of cold air is forced through the molten pig iron to oxidize the foreign substances; after this such quantities of carbon and other elements may be introduced as will make the desired quality of steel. The Bessemer process was first used in this country at Wyandotte, Michigan, in 1864. By cheapening production it made the use of steel universal and relegated iron to a position of comparative unimportance.[20]

The Bessemer process has its limitations. It is not suitable for ore of high phosphorus content, and this has led to its being supplanted by the open-hearth, or Martin, process, which enables the use of lower-grade ores. Because the ore in the Lake Superior region was high-grade, the Bessemer method was widely used until 1906, when 12,000,000 tons were manufactured by that process, but since then it has been superseded by the open-hearth method. Of the 50,568,000 tons of steel produced in 1937, the Bessemer process turned out only 3,450,000.

With greater production and better smelting methods there have appeared other improvements. The furnaces have doubled in size and tripled in heating capacity since 1850; the average output of 50 tons a day per furnace in 1870 has increased to a capacity of over 450 tons a day (1929). The mechanical progress of the industry is illustrated by the following description:

[20] Steel rails, cheaper and more durable than iron, influenced transportation tremendously.

The bulk of the domestic iron ore used in the United States is not touched by the hand of man from the time it leaves the mine until it is converted into forms for sale, as rails, structural shapes, wire rods, sheets, merchant bars, etc., and in many of the operations the ore is dug by power shovels, or "milled" through chutes, so that even in mining but little hand labor is necessary. Lifted from its bed by dippers on power shovels, ore is loaded into railway cars or directed through "mills" into chutes, or mined by pick and shovels and shot into mine tram cars. The cars run to pockets feeding skips, which are raised by power and automatically dumped into waiting railway cars, except when climatic conditions, stagnant trade, or the desirability of discontinuing operations require that ore be stocked for future shipment. Where necessary the ore passes through intermediate crushers to reduce the size of the pieces; but in crushing, stocking or reloading, man directs the movement of machinery and touches but little of the ore.

Railway cars, with their loads of iron ore, convey it to blast furnaces, or, as is the custom with most Lake Superior ores, to docks provided with pockets, into which the ore drops through the opened bottoms of the cars, while spouts connecting with the dock pockets deliver the ore by gravity into holds of the vessels specially constructed for the iron ore trade. At the end of the vessel's trip, mechanical devices remove the ore and deposit it in cars or on stock piles. . . .

When the furnace is reached to which the ore is consigned, the railway cars are run onto "car dumpers" which turn the cars over to discharge their contents into pits from which the ore is carried by cable or tramways to stock piles; or the cars drop their contents into the furnace supply bins. From the bins, whether fed direct from cars or from stock piles, the ore is chuted to scale charging cars which feed to skip cars. These skip cars, which also receive the fuel and fluxing material, are elevated to the furnace top and automatically discharge their contents.[21]

IRON AND STEEL INDUSTRY, 1869–1937 [22]

Year	Number of Establishments	Average Number of Wage Earners	Capital	Value of Products
1869	808	77,555	$ 121,772,000	$ 207,209,000
1879	792	140,798	209,905,000	296,558,000
1889	719	171,181	414,045,000	478,688,000
1899	668	222,490	513,392,000	803,968,000
1909	654	278,505	1,492,316,000	1,377,152,000
1919	695	416,748	3,458,935,000	3,623,369,000
1929	591	419,534	. . . .	4,137,214,000
1937	410	359,630	. . . .	3,330,491,000

[21] A. O. Backert (ed.), *The A B C of Iron and Steel* (4th ed., 1921), chap. i, by John Birkinbine, "Iron Ore and Mining Operations," p. 1.

[22] *Census of Manufacturers, 1921*, p. 360; *ibid., 1929*, I, 223; *ibid., 1937*, p. 977. These figures are for "blast furnaces and steel works and rolling mills" only; they exclude many iron and steel products of higher value that are made in thousands of establishments.

The steel, once made, is strengthened and cast into the desired forms by forging, pressing, and rolling.

The chief centers of pig iron production are (1) Pennsylvania and Ohio, (2) Illinois, and (3) Tennessee and Alabama, all located close to the Lake Superior or Allegheny fields. An abundance of raw material and an expanding market have enabled the United States to produce (1937) 35.4 per cent of the world's pig iron and 38.6 per cent of the world's steel.

Other Basic Manufacturing.—Although the chief emphasis in the preceding discussion has been on the production of iron and steel, the importance of the non-ferrous metals and their alloys in our industrial system should not be underestimated. These metals include copper, lead, aluminum, zinc, tin, gold, and silver. The total value of their products in 1937 ran to over $2,783,000,000. Their importance in the manufacture of intricate machinery, electrical apparatus, and small metal goods is obvious. In war time they rank second only to steel, and of them copper, lead, and aluminum are by all odds the most important.

The manufacture of electric supplies is another industry which depends on metals—copper, lead, zinc, and aluminum, as well as steel. Although the telegraph was in use in the 'forties and the telephone in the 'eighties, the general development of the industry has taken place during the past forty years. The electrification of railroads and the spectacular development of radio and household appliances have enormously stimulated this industry. In point of value electric machinery and appliances took sixth place in both 1929 and 1937, the value of electrical manufactures amounting to $1,622,000,-000 in 1937. The application of electricity to telegraphy, telephony, wireless communication, lighting, motors, and motion pictures has influenced economic and social life more powerfully than any group of mechanical inventions since those which ushered in the Industrial Revolution.

The birth of the petroleum industry, it will be remembered, took place during the Civil War.[23] So important was this product as a lubricant and illuminant that within six years after the boring of the first well it ranked sixth in American exports. The industry developed steadily as petroleum replaced other illuminants, but its great era of expansion waited upon the invention of the internal combustion engine and the Diesel engine. The hundred-million barrel mark in production was reached in 1895, but with the invention of the automobile around the turn of the century this figure jumped to five hundred million in 1917 and one billion in 1923. The Census of 1937 ranked petroleum refining as fourth in point of value with an output valued at $2,546,746,000. By that time the United States was producing approximately two-thirds of the world's supply; the chief centers were in

[23] Above, p. 344.

Texas, California, and Oklahoma. The history of the industry has been complicated by chaotic overproduction, by monopoly in refining, and later by government control. So essential has petroleum become for transportation and domestic heating that a threatened curtailment of supply caused rationing on the east coast and in Washington and Oregon in 1942. To the numerous uses of petroleum in America the Second World War added the manufacture of synthetic rubber.

SELECTED READINGS

Clark, V. S., *History of Manufactures in the United States,* Vol. II, Chaps. I, VI, XIII, XIV; Vol. III, Chaps. I, XXII.

Twelfth Census of the United States, Vol. VII, Chap. II.

Ise, John, *United States Oil Policy,* Chaps. II–V, XII–XVIII.

Wolfe, H. and R., *Rubber: A Story of Glory and Greed,* pp. 421–506.

Clemen, R. A., *The American Livestock and Meat Industry,* Chaps. VIII–XXI.

Kennedy, E. D., *The Automobile Industry,* Chaps. I–VI.

Flügel, F., and Faulkner, H. U., *Readings in the Economic and Social History of the United States,* Chap. XIII.

21

Consolidation of Business

☆ ☆

THE CULMINATION OF LAISSEZ FAIRE

THE half century following the Civil War saw both the culmination of the economic philosophy of *laissez faire* and the reaction against it. All the processes of the American Industrial Revolution were immensely speeded up by the war; but in the rapidly growing industrial and agricultural life unbridled freedom and competition reigned supreme. The *laissez faire* doctrine of Adam Smith and his successors had been accepted as final by the great majority of Americans in the years immediately following the war, and a fitting capstone had been put upon the theories by the first section of the fourteenth amendment.[1] Although this had supposedly been incorporated in the Constitution to protect the Negro, the increasing pressure of corporations upon the courts eventually led to an interpretation which went far to restrain the interference of state legislatures in the operation of business. To the rising capitalist and, in fact, to the average citizen, it seemed not only unnecessary, but bad economics, to regulate private capital. Capital should be aided, not impeded, in the development of the vast natural resources of which, it was believed, there was a sufficiency for all—a theory that was given practical application through the control of the federal government by the business interests during most of the period after 1860. This point of view was further strengthened by the pioneer individualism of a frontier people who demanded the utmost freedom of action. As a consequence, competition and *laissez faire* were the order of the day. These were the years when millions of acres were given to the railroads and charters bestowed with a free hand. The most valuable of the oil, lumber, and metal lands were occupied under federal land Acts, bought in, or obtained by fraud. Although there was indeed plenty for all, victory went to the strongest and the most unscrupulous. The same was true in the struggle for markets. The home

---

[1] "No State shall make or enforce any law which shall abridge the privileges or immunities of citizens of the United States; nor shall any State deprive any person of life, liberty, or property without due process of law; nor deny to any person within its jurisdiction the equal protection of the laws." See below, p. 497.

market, which had been freely supplied with manufactured goods from abroad during the early decades of the century, was buying 89 per cent of its manufactured commodities from domestic producers by 1860, and 97 per cent by 1900. In the struggle for these resources and markets legislatures were bribed, the people robbed,[2] all sorts of illegal methods used, and even armed force resorted to upon occasion. As late as 1910 a well-known British journalist aptly likened the United States to "an enormously rich country overrun by a horde of robber barons, and very inadequately policed by the central government and by certain local vigilant societies."[3]

In a famous passage written in 1776, Adam Smith made the assertion: "Every individual is continually exerting himself to find out the most advantageous employment for whatever capital he can command. It is his own advantage, indeed, and not that of society, which he has in view. But the study of his own advantage naturally, or rather necessarily, leads him to prefer that employment which is most advantageous to society."[4] This roseate prediction made at the dawn of the Industrial Revolution as to the beneficial results of *laissez faire* upon the welfare of society was hardly borne out in the decades following the Civil War. Unbridled competition as it developed not only destroyed many manufacturers but in the end brought consolidation which often worked harm both to producers of raw materials and to consumers. With unrestrained competition and *laissez faire*, however, came evils which to a certain extent applied their own curb. The public reacted against the wasteful exploitation of the country's resources and the illegal methods so commonly used, and cutthroat competition was so disastrous that some way out had to be found. Business consolidation and government regulation have been the inevitable outcome.

GROWTH OF BUSINESS CONSOLIDATION

The years before the Civil War saw the golden age of the small manufacturing business, the period when the typical concern was owned by a single entrepreneur, a family, or a small handful of stockholders. Since the 'seventies the tendency has been to consolidate. Economists at opposite ends of the scale of economic thought have agreed that the consolidation of smaller units into larger is an inevitable result of the conditions brought about by the Industrial Revolution. Whether this trend is inevitable or not, it has without doubt been

[2] M. N. Orfield, *Federal Land Grants to the States with Special Reference to Minnesota,* Bulletin of the University of Minnesota (1915), shows how the public lands, forests, and mineral wealth of one richly endowed state passed into private hands.

[3] William Archer, "The American Cheap Magazine," *Fortnightly Review,* LXXXVII, 930 (1910).

[4] Adam Smith, *Wealth of Nations,* Book IV, Chap. II, fourth paragraph.

very marked in our economic life. Most of the witnesses appearing before the Industrial Commission in 1899 believed that "competition so vigorous that profits of nearly all competing establishments were destroyed"[5] was the chief motivating force for business combinations, and this appears to have been the immediate cause which led many to unite to escape being driven to the wall. The bitter rate wars of the railroads during the early 'seventies had driven fares and rates between competitive points below the cost of transportation. Competition was so excessive in the refining of sugar, for example, that eighteen out of about forty refineries had failed before consolidation was begun. Added to the losses from price cutting were the inherent losses of competition due to costs of advertising and salesmen, and the many disadvantages which a small industry must suffer in comparison with a large one in utilizing by-products, securing the best management, and bargaining with labor, bankers, and transportation companies. The desire to eliminate needless costs went hand in hand with the eagerness to reap greater profits, which were particularly available when the business, as in the case of the Standard Oil, was large enough to effect a monopoly.

While these were the immediate causes, certain results of the Industrial Revolution made big business possible. The invention of labor-saving machinery made large-scale production profitable, the heavy fixed investment in expensive machinery and apparatus discouraged competition, and the very growth in the size of the nation and of its business tended, as in the case of the railroads, to inevitable consolidation. Gradually smaller inventions, such as the typewriter, adding machine, and many other appliances, contributed necessary elements to the age of big business. This development was greatly aided by the adoption of the corporate form, under which most large industrial units were organized. Likewise it should be remembered that concentration was a characteristic of the nineteenth century. It was to be seen not only in business, but also in labor in the formation of unions, and in the political world in the unification of Italy and Germany.

Laissez faire may have dominated American economic policy during the last half of the nineteenth century, but there was one notable exception to its sway. Under the influence of her developing industry the United States committed herself in 1861 to a system of high protective tariffs which in general she has maintained ever since. This deviation from *laissez faire* seems also to have aided in the development of big business and monopoly. Henry O. Havemeyer, president of the Sugar Trust at the time of its formation, asserted that "the tariff is the mother of trusts," and there were few who disputed him. Although many monopolies, such as the Standard Oil Trust and the American Tobacco Trust, owed little or nothing to the tariff, there were

[5] *Preliminary Report of the Industrial Commission*, p. 9.

others, like the Sugar Trust, that did. In any event the tariff allowed monopoly profits.

"A calculation of the flat averages of the returns from all the leading industrial lines for which figures are given since 1850," assert Jenks and Clark, "gives almost startling demonstration of industrial concentration in the United States during the past two generations. Such a calculation shows that in thirteen leading lines of industry in the United States, the average manufacturing plant in the sixty years from 1850 to 1910 multiplied its capital by more than thirty-nine, its number of wage earners by nearly seven and the value of its output by more than nineteen."[6] This tendency continues to be an outsanding feature of American industry, as can be seen in the accompanying table. By 1923 the census had ceased to tabulate data for establishments whose annual output was less than $5000. From 1914 to 1929, small establishments doing a business of $5000 to $20,000 declined in relative numbers from 48.9 per cent to 32.9, while all the larger units increased; in percentage of wage earners these small units decreased from 6.0 to 2.3, and in value of products, from 3.7 to 1.1. It is interesting to compare these figures with those for establishments doing a business of one billion dollars or over, which showed enormous increases. Although in 1929 this class constituted only 5.6 per cent of the total, it employed 58.3 of the workers and produced 69.2 of the value of products.

ADVANTAGES AND DISADVANTAGES OF THE CORPORATE FORM

As the size of the business unit increased and competition became more reckless and exacting, the old-fashioned methods of conducting a business by means of individual ownership or partnership became inadequate. The funds needed for buildings, equipment, and stocks were too great for individuals to supply, and the risk was too great to be undertaken singly. As a consequence, the corporate form of business was adopted after the Civil War to suit the new needs. Before that time it was used chiefly in the formation of banks, the building of turnpikes and railroads, or the launching of some project necessary for the public good, perhaps of such magnitude that the risks had to be widely distributed. It was generally looked upon as a dangerous and undemocratic form associated with the idea of monopoly, and one to be carefully supervised. In New York, for example, state incorporation under general laws was not permitted until the constitution of 1846.

A corporation, according to an excellent definition, is "a voluntary autonomous association formed for the private advantage of its members, which acts with compulsory unity and is authorized by the state for the accomplish-

[6] Jeremiah W. Jenks, and Walter E. Clark, *The Trust Problem* (7th ed., 1917), p. 17.

Manufactures: Establishments Classified by Value of Products 1914–1929 [7]

Class of Establishments According to Value of Products	Establishments		Wage Earners		Value of Products	
	Number	Per Cent Distribution	Average Number	Per Cent Distribution	Amount	Per Cent Distribution
$5,000 and over[a]						
1929	210,959	100.0	8,838,743	100.0	$70,434,863,443	100.0
1925	187,390	100.0	8,384,261	100.0	62,713,713,730	100.0
1921	196,267	100.0	6,946,570	99.4[a]	43,653,282,833	99.7[a]
1919	214,383	100.0	9,000,059	99.5[a]	62,041,795,316	99.8[a]
1914	177,110	100.0	6,896,190	98.2[a]	23,987,860,617	99.1[a]
$5,000 to $20,000						
1929	69,423	32.0	202,958	2.3	771,417,436	1.1
1925	55,876	29.8	156,373	1.9	628,373,403	1.0
1921	71,075	36.2	224,852	3.2	782,977,433	1.8
1919	79,699	37.2	227,977	2.5	866,086,290	1.4
1914	86,587	48.9	423,829	6.0	893,459,166	3.7
$20,000 to $100,000						
1929	75,225	35.7	693,155	7.8	3,587,697,276	5.1
1925	68,951	36.8	660,309	7.9	3,272,196,872	5.0
1921	72,251	36.8	746,024	10.0	3,330,350,409	7.6
1919	75,627	35.3	773,701	8.6	3,487,756,280	5.6
1914	56,557	31.9	995,743	14.2	2,540,949,405	10.5
$100,000 to $500,000						
1929	44,153	20.9	1,672,983	18.9	10,023,771,653	14.2
1925	42,209	22.5	1,675,911	20.0	9,576,090,022	15.3
1921	38,027	19.4	1,629,573	23.3	8,405,758,540	19.2
1919	39,477	18.4	1,712,854	18.9	8,929,364,110	14.4
1914[b]	30,147	17.0	3,000,612	42.7	8,759,391,117	36.2
$500,000 to $1,000,000						
1929	10,395	4.9	1,121,547	12.7	7,294,860,945	10.4
1925	9,771	5.2	1,131,439	13.5	6,870,112,293	11.0
1921	7,581	3.9	966,559	13.8	5,296,720,583	12.1
1919	9,197	4.2	1,112,815	12.3	6,457,485,019	10.4
1914[b]						
$1,000,000 and over						
1929	11,763	5.6	5,148,100	58.3	48,757,116,133	69.2
1925	10,583	5.7	4,760,229	56.7	42,366,941,140	67.5
1921	7,333	3.7	3,379,562	48.4	25,837,475,868	59.0
1919	10,413	4.9	5,172,712	57.2	42,301,103,617	68.0
1914	3,819	2.2	2,476,006	35.3	11,794,060,929	48.7

[a] Small percentages for establishments doing a business less than $5000 omitted.
[b] Figures include data for two groups, $100,000 to $1,000,000.

ment of some public good." [8] In other words, a corporation is an organization or association created by law under a charter which authorizes it to do certain things. Although not a person, a corporation is an artificial being which like a person may carry on business, break the law, sue and be sued. It has many

[7] *Statistical Abstract, 1933*, p. 693.
[8] L. H. Haney, *Business Organization and Combination*, p. 82. A more famous definition is that of Chief Justice Marshall in the Dartmouth College case: "A corporation is an artificial

advantages which explain its almost universal adoption. (1) It makes easier the raising of large amounts of capital. Under the terms of the charter, corporations are allowed to capitalize their holdings and issue stock. This stock may be bought by many persons who often contribute comparatively small amounts to build up a great business. Thus the American Telephone and Telegraph Company boasts of over 630,000 stockholders, the General Motors Corporation of more than 214,000, and the Pennsylvania Railroad of 209,000.[9] A corporation may also borrow money and issue bonds, thus giving it access to large resources of capital. (2) By owning corporate stocks, many people may share in the development of the country and in the profits of the largest concerns often managed by men of great ability, without themselves contributing anything but money. (3) The risk of the stockholders is limited by the law of the state. (4) The shares may usually be bought and sold, thus allowing a person voluntarily to enter or leave a concern as his private interests dictate. (5) The corporation has great advantages in that it is not disrupted by the death or retirement of its members.

On the other hand, the corporate form has disadvantages. Where the number of stockholders is large and scattered, it is impossible for them to exercise any real control over their delegated agents, the directors elected at the annual meetings. The irresponsibility of the directors is accentuated by the legal attitude that a corporation is a separate legal person and that the directors are the agents of the corporation and not of the stockholders, thus making it useless for a stockholder or a minority to sue a director or his agents for loss incurred through fraud or negligence. The lack of control of the stockholders over their directors has often encouraged the latter to use their position to promote personal interests or to indulge in speculative management, fraudulent promotions, and overcapitalization, which have in the end worked havoc to the stockholders, who are not inclined to inquire too closely as long as dividends are unimpaired. From the point of view of the investor the numerous stock and bond issues so common to corporations are confusing, and only an expert can work out their true valuation. From the broader outlook of public policy, corporations seem to promote monopoly, for stock ownership facilitates interlocking directorates and interlocking ownerships. Whatever its disadvantages may be, however, the corporation has become the dominant form of business organization today. Although in

---

being, invisible, intangible, and existing only in contemplation of law. Being the mere creature of law, it possesses only those properties which the charter of its creation confers upon it, either expressly, or as incidental to its very existence. . . . Among the most important are immortality, and, if the expression may be allowed, individuality; properties, by which a perpetual succession of many persons are considered as the same, and may act as a single individual." Dartmouth College v. Woodward, Vol. IV, Wheaton's Reports, 518, p. 636.

[9] These are figures for 1940.

1919 corporations numbered only 31.5 per cent of the total establishments, they employed 86 per cent of the wage earners and produced 87.7 per cent of the total value of the products.[10] There is plenty of evidence to show that their relative importance has increased during the last two decades.

EVOLUTION OF CONCENTRATION

While some large concerns have achieved their size by internal growth and natural expansion, many more have come to their present greatness through the consolidation of industries engaged in the production of similar commodities. Attempts like those of the salt producers in western Virginia after 1830 to restrict output and thus control prices had been made before the Civil War, but it was not until after the panic of 1873 that the movement toward consolidation became important. The periods through which the consolidation movement has passed can be divided roughly according to the forms which it has taken: (1) pools, (2) trusts, (3) holding companies, (4) amalgamations and mergers, and (5) "community of interest."

Pools.—Pools appeared after the panic of 1873 and the movement continued until about 1887. A pool is an organization of business units whose members seek to control prices by apportioning the available business in some way. This form was especially popular among the railroads, for the bitter rivalry between competitive points was fast leading to ruin. Although forbidden in the Interstate Commerce Act of 1887, the practice was continued, especially in the South, where the transportation of cotton was for a long time apportioned and the freight rates fixed by common consent. In addition to traffic pools there have been "output" pools, illustrated by the agreement between the powder manufacturers in 1886 which sought to eliminate "ill-regulated and unauthorized competition" by mutual understanding in regard to output and price. Informal apportionment of business among different units of the same industry undoubtedly still persists to some extent. Another form of pool is that in which territory and market are allotted. A typical example was the agreement entered into in 1902 between the Imperial Tobacco Company of Great Britain and the American Tobacco Company, giving the former exclusive control of the British Isles, and the latter control of the United States, her colonies, and Cuba; a new corporation, the British-American Tobacco Company, Limited, was to handle the business in the rest of the world. A more recent marketing pool was made shortly after the First World War when the British Marconi Company and the Radio Corporation of America

---

[10] *Abstract of the Census of Manufactures, 1919,* Table 195, p. 340. Classification according to ownership was omitted between 1919 and 1925.

attempted to divide between them the radio business of the world. Still another type of pool occurs when a certain part of profits or income is deposited with a central body to be distributed later.

Trusts.—Pools in railroads were declared illegal in 1887 by the Interstate Commerce Act, and again in 1897 by the Supreme Court in the case against the Trans-Missouri Freight Association. Pooling was deserted beginning in 1887 in favor of a new form of understanding which appeared to be legal and at the same time much more efficient. From that year until 1897 the trust was the most favored form of combination. A trust is a form of organization in which the stockholders under a trust agreement deposit with a board of trustees a controlling portion of their stock and receive trust certificates in return. Unlike a pool this is no mere federation; it is an actual consolidation of interests. It is a case of using the old legal idea of a trusteeship to create a monopoly, and was introduced as early as 1879 and 1882 by the Standard Oil Company. This was followed by the formation in 1887 of the "Whisky Trust" (Distillers' and Cattle Feeders' Trust), the "Sugar Trust" (Sugar Refineries Company), the "Lead Trust," the "Cotton-oil Trust" and by many others in succeeding years. The trust form, which gave absolute power to the trustees, created a monopoly, opposition to which produced anti-trust laws on the part of various states in 1889 and later, and the Sherman Anti-trust Act on the part of the national government in 1890. The early prosecutions by the federal courts under the Sherman Act were generally unsuccessful, but the dissolution of the North River Sugar Refining Company by the New York Court of Appeals in 1890 and of the Standard Oil Trust by the Ohio courts in 1892 put a decided damper upon this method of consolidation. Interestingly enough, these cases were decided on the grounds that the creation of a trust had violated rights granted in the charter and not on the grounds that monopolies had been created.[11] In any event the decisions were accepted by the corporations. Moreover, the panic of 1893 and the succeeding years of depression held up for the time being further aggressive moves toward consolidation.

Holding Companies.—The anti-trust legislation led to the adoption of a new form of consolidation, namely, the holding company. This was the form used during the greatest period of business consolidation, the years from 1897 to 1904. A holding company is an organization created to dominate other corporations by owning or controlling a portion of their stocks. Although this device had been employed before this time by the Pennsylvania Company and the American Bell Telephone Company, it was now adopted rapidly, the Standard Oil, as with the trust form, again taking the lead. The move-

[11] H. R. Seager and C. A. Gulick, Jr., *Trust and Corporation Problems* (1929), pp. 51–55.

ment toward the holding company was greatly facilitated by the complacent laws of a number of states, particularly New Jersey, West Virginia, Delaware, and Maine, which permitted the organization of pure finance corporations under a general statute allowing the widest powers to these corporations. Their obligations were so slight that merely the maintenance of a dummy office and the submission of a meager annual report complied with the law. New Jersey, because of her position, was able to outbid the other states, and the providing of head offices to which directors might journey from New York to hold their annual meetings became an important industry in Jersey City. Between 1897 and 1904 over $6,000,000,000 worth of securities were marketed; in 1897 alone, new corporations were organized with a nominal capital of $3,512,000,000, of which at least one-fourth was "water." In 1904 John Moody listed 318 greater or lesser industrial trusts representing consolidations of nearly 5300 distinct plants and capitalized at over seven billions, of which 236 (with five-sixths of the capital) had been incorporated since January 1, 1898, 170 of them under New Jersey law.[12] In fact, most of the great corporations of today were formed during those years, including what for many years was the greatest of them all—the United States Steel Corporation.

This huge holding company, with its eleven constituent companies, controlling some 170 subsidiary concerns, was the handiwork of J. P. Morgan and Elbert H. Gary and in a sense marked the climax of the trust movement. The underlying impetus for its organization was the bitter competition in the iron and steel business and Andrew Carnegie's threat of even keener warfare in the future. Carnegie, anxious to retire, finally succeeded in unloading his vast steel properties upon Morgan, who merged them with a number of steel concerns in which he was already interested, and certain others that were brought in, the whole constituting the United States Steel Corporation. The actual value of the tangible property of this new corporation was estimated by the Commissioner of Corporations at $682,000,000; yet it was capitalized at $1,402,846,000, of which $510,205,000 represented preferred stock, and $508,227,000 common.[13] Obviously all of the common stock and an appreciable share of the preferred represented "water," but so powerful and

[12] John Moody, *The Truth About the Trusts* (1904), p. 486. Seven of the greater trusts which he lists—the Amalgamated Copper Company (1899), the American Sugar Refining Company (1891), the American Smelting and Refining Company (1899), the Consolidated Tobacco Company (1901), the Standard Oil Company (1899), the U. S. Steel Corporation (1901), and the International Mercantile Marine Company (1902)—boasted an aggregate capital of over $2,500,000,000; with a single exception they were all formed after 1898, and all were incorporated under New Jersey law.

[13] *Report of the Commissioner of Corporations on the Steel Industry* (1911), Part I, pp. xvii–xxiv; also in F. Flügel and H. U. Faulkner, *Readings*, pp. 566–573.

so successful was the enterprise that with the exception of three years it paid dividends on its common stock until 1932. From the point of view of promotors and original investors it has proved one of the most successful of the great consolidations.

Mere size, as many investors discovered, did not necessarily mean profits. Such consolidations as the International Mercantile Marine Company and the United States Shipbuilding Company [14] brought losses rather than gains, and the speed with which consolidation proceeded filled the market with what Morgan called "undigested securities." By 1904, most of the important industries had been consolidated to a greater or lesser extent, and for the time being there were few remaining fields to conquer. Furthermore, when the holding company constituted a monopoly its position was no safer than that of the trust. In 1904 the Roosevelt administration secured the conviction and dissolution of the Northern Securties Company, an organization formed to hold the stock of the three great railroads tapping the Northwest. The courts affirmed that while a holding company was legal under the laws of the incorporating states, it was illegal when the obvious intent was to effect a monopoly. In the same tenor subsequent decisions dissolved the Standard Oil and American Tobacco holding companies.

Mergers and "Community of Interest."—The holding company is still the most significant type of corporate organization in the United States and in recent years it has been carried to new refinements by means of "voting trusts," investment trusts, and pyramided holding companies (below, pp. 610 ff.). Nevertheless, other methods of consolidation have supplemented it. Amalgamation and merger or the outright purchase of one organization by another is one method. Likewise anti-trust laws have stimulated new methods of achieving monopoly through "community of interest," usually through the purchase of stock by individuals, holding companies, corporations, investment trusts, or "voting trusts." One company can buy a sufficient quantity of another company's stock to make its influence felt, and directors of one company may thus sit on another's board. True, the Clayton Act forbids interlocking directorates in competitive companies engaged in interstate business whose capital, surplus, and undivided profits aggregate more than $1,000,000; but even here the same persons, as stockholders, may exercise great influence through "dummy" directors. So extensive was the "community of interest" in the oil companies that the dissolution of the trust in 1892 and of the holding company in 1911 made practically no difference. The railroads have been under the questioning eye of the people for so long that they especially have resorted to consolidation through "community of interest." To such an

[14] H. R. Seager and C. A. Gulick, Jr., *Trust and Corporation Problems*, Chap. XII.

extent has the purchase of stock been consummated between the railroads that it is comparatively easy to divide them into eight or ten different groups according to their controlling financial interests, a situation which has almost eliminated competition in the sections served by these systems.

THE STANDARD OIL COMPANY

The history of the oil business is of particular significance in the study of industrial combinations, for the rise and progress of the Standard Oil Company illustrates practically every phase in the development and methods of monopoly under American conditions. Successful drilling for oil commenced in 1859 in the vicinity of Titusville, Pennsylvania, after the discovery of the Drake well. While the business of drilling wells and refining oil expanded rapidly during the war, the production in 1865 was behind the demand and the whole industry was severely handicapped by lack of transportation facilities and efficient refining machinery. The fact that transportation was the great problem and the chief expense of the expanding oil industry made it quite evident to the most able men in the business that success would come to the large concern with enough capital to install the best machinery for large-scale production and sufficient output to force favorable railroad rates. In 1867, while the industry was still in its infancy, John D. Rockefeller united the refineries of William Rockefeller & Co., Rockefeller and Andrews, Rockefeller & Co., S. V. Harkness, and H. M. Flagler into the firm of Rockefeller, Andrews & Flagler. "The cause leading to its formation," he said, "was the desire to unite our skill and capital in order to carry on a business of some magnitude and importance in place of the small business that each separately had theretofore carried on." [15] Further capital was needed, and in 1870 the company was reorganized into the Standard Oil Company of Ohio, with a capital of $1,000,000 and a refining capacity in its Cleveland plant of about 600 barrels a day. This amounted, however, to only 4 per cent of the oil refined in the United States, and the Standard plant was not even then the largest in the country.

Up to 1879 competition among oil men had been largely in production. In the succeeding years it was a competition for transportation facilities and favorable rates, a bitter war which left the Standard Oil Company in complete control. This victory may be attributed largely to the business acumen of Rockefeller and his associates, to favorable freight rates, and to the unscrupulous and illegal methods to which these men resorted to destroy competition and win favorable concessions from railroads and legislatures. Their desire to secure cheap transportation rates was aided by the railroads (chiefly

---

[15] *Preliminary Report of the Industrial Commission*, p. 95.

the Erie, the New York Central, and the Pennsylvania, which were in competition for the oil business); in keeping with the policy of the time, the roads lowered their rates at competitive points and to promising concerns. In all the dickering with the railroads, no group of refiners was so successful as Standard Oil. Its favorable location at Cleveland was, to be sure, a factor in this success, since it freed the concern from complete dependence on the railroads by affording water transportation to the seaboard by way of the Great Lakes.

The most notorious of the rate agreements was made through the South Improvement Company chartered by the Pennsylvania legislature in 1871 with the widest powers, including authority "to construct and operate any work, or works, public or private, designed to include, increase, facilitate, or develop trade, travel, or the transportation of freight, livestock, passengers, or any traffic by land or water, from or to any part of the United States." [16] This company, 900 of whose 2000 shares were held by Rockefeller and his close associates, made contracts with the Pennsylvania, the New York Central, and the Erie, whereby it agreed to ship 45 per cent of all the oil transported by it over the first-named railroad and to divide the remainder between the other two roads. In return the railroads agreed to allow rebates on all petroleum shipped by the company and to charge all others the full rates, and in addition to furnish the South Improvement Company waybills of all petroleum and its products transported over their lines. Each road also agreed "at all times to cooperate, as far as it legally may, with the party hereto of the first part against loss by injury or competition, to the end that the party hereto of the first part may keep up a remunerative, and so a full and regular business, and to that end shall lower or raise the gross rates of transportation over its railroads and connections, as far as it legally may, for such times and to such extent as may be necessary to overcome such competition." The South Improvement Company aroused such a storm of opposition that its charter was revoked after three months, but, nevertheless, rebates and favorable discriminations were continued. The Standard Oil gradually extended its operations to include the ownership of pipe lines; by 1879 it controlled from 90 to 95 per cent of the oil refined and was able in turn to dictate its rates to the roads. The "Hepburn Committee," reporting to the New York legislature in January, 1880, said:

It owns and controls the pipe lines of the producing regions that connect with the railroads. It controls both ends of these roads. It ships 95 per cent of all oil. . . . It dictates terms and rates to the railroads. It has bought out and frozen out refiners all over the country. By means of the superior facilities for transportation which it thus possessed, it could overbid in the producing re-

[16] *Ibid.*, p. 608. The charter of the South Improvement Company is given on p. 607, and the contract with the Pennsylvania on p. 610.

gions and undersell in the markets of the world. Thus it has gone on buying out and freezing out all opposition, until it has absorbed and monopolized this great traffic, this great production which ranks second on the list of exports of our country. The parties whom they have driven to the wall have had ample capital, and equal ability in the prosecution of their business in all things save their ability to acquire facilities for transportation.[17]

In order to dominate the situation more completely, the Standard Oil Company of Ohio worked out a scheme in 1882 by which the stock holdings of fourteen companies and the majority of holdings in twenty-six others were placed in the hands of nine trustees having irrevocable powers of attorney. The stockholders received trust certificates in return. The par value of these certificates amounted to $70,000,000, of which $46,000,000 was owned by the nine trustees who dictated the policies of the constituent companies. The public in general had no difficulty in understanding the purpose of this new organization. A wave of state anti-monopoly legislation followed and the courts of Ohio in 1890 broke up the Standard Oil Trust into twenty constituent companies. Trust certificates were replaced by proportionate shares of stock in the new companies.

In 1899 a second attempt was made to bring the entire properties under single control by the formation of the Standard Oil Company of New Jersey, a holding company as well as an operating company, formed with the intention of transferring to it the stock of the different corporations so that in time one concern might own and direct the whole industry. The new company's position as a holding company was gravely imperiled by the decision in the Northern Securities case (1904) [18] and was finally made untenable by the Supreme Court order of dissolution in 1911.[19] The business since then has been carried on by corporations chartered by the several states, which usually act harmoniously and exercise a dominant influence through a "community of interest" brought about by the ownership by certain individuals of controlling stock in the several companies. By 1904 Standard Oil controlled about 85 per cent of the domestic and 90 per cent of the export trade. Its earning capacity had increased from $8,000,000 in 1882 to $57,459,356 in 1905, and dividends from 5¼ per cent in 1882 to 30 per cent in 1898. In recent years the company has stretched into foreign fields, notably in Latin America, Rumania, and Persia. Increased demand for oil for motor traffic has added impetus to production and stimulated the formation of many new and powerful companies, such as the Texas, the Gulf, and the Shell Companies, which have effectively undermined the almost complete monopoly enjoyed thirty

[17] New York Assembly Document No. 38, 1880.
[18] Below, p. 450.
[19] Below, p. 451.

years ago by the Standard Oil groups. The latter, however, continue to be dominant in the transportation and refining of oil and still far overshadow their rivals.[20]

Combinations and Monopolies

The discussion so far has been largely concerned with the combination movement and the various forms it has taken. It should be remembered, however, that a pool, a holding company, or even a trust may be organized without effecting a monopoly. But the desire for a monopoly and its advantages has ordinarily been in the minds of the organizers, for a virtual monopoly may be brought about by controlling an important percentage of the product. So obvious was it that the trusts were organized to eliminate competition and to control products that the term "trust" has been commonly used in America to designate any large combination which approaches a monopoly, and it is sometimes even applied indiscriminately to any big business.

There are a number of different kinds of monopolies with which we are familiar. There may be *personal* monopolies in which an individual possessing special talent or knowledge may be able to drive out competitors. There are *legal* monopolies: public, such as the post office in America, or private, such as those based on patents, copyrights, or franchises. Another important group is the *natural* monopoly of situation or organization, as illustrated by a street railway, gas works, or anthracite coal mines. *Labor* monopolies resulting from combinations of skilled laborers often control the labor supply. But of special interest to us here are the *capitalist* monopolies or monopolies of organization which, by the concentration of large aggregations of capital and the unification of a sufficient number of production units, have been able to exercise a monopoly.

Even a cursory consideration of these types brings home the fact that certain forms of monopoly are inevitable and that others are encouraged for the sake of the public welfare. Personal talent or a steam railway is often an inevitable monopoly. A government post office system and a franchise creating a street railway may be monopolies established for the public good; broad social welfare is considered in the granting of patents. On the other hand, capitalist monopolies and monopolies of labor lead at once into controversial fields. But even here modern conditions prevent us from taking too dogmatic an attitude. The cost of erecting a sugar refinery or a steel mill is so great that free competition is almost automatically cut off, and labor's

[20] For a brief review of Standard Oil history, see H. R. Seager and C. A. Gulick, Jr., *Trust and Corporation Problems,* Chaps. VI and VII, and H. W. Laidler, *Concentration of Control in American Industry,* Chap. II.

prefectly laudable determination to secure better conditions through a stronger bargaining organization cannot be condemned too hastily.

CAPITALIST MONOPOLIES—ADVANTAGES AND DISADVANTAGES

Large-scale monopolistic production has always had its strong advocates as well as its critics. The former have emphasized in particular the savings in both production and marketing. As to production, they hold that the large resources make it possible to use only the best-located plants and the most efficient machinery, especially in slack times; that large-scale production allows more complete utilization of by-products and economies in the division of labor; that it permits the specialization of production at the different plants; that administrative expenses can be saved by the elimination of duplicated high-salaried positions and at the same time the best talent in the field can be secured; that research can be pursued on a larger scale; that waste and ineffective methods can be more easily detected through careful comparison of different plants that produce the same article; and that there is greater strength in dealing with labor. As to marketing, it is maintained that expenses are reduced by the elimination of salesmen and advertising, by the elimination of cross-freights, since orders can be filled from the nearest plants, and by the development of greater strength in the export business. The argument is also advanced that control of the market price of both a raw commodity and the finished article helps to stabilize prices and production and thus exerts a healthy influence upon economic life. During periods of rapid monopolistic development, the evils of competition were always emphasized and the motto "competition is the death of trade" was kept well to the front.[21]

On the other hand, it is argued that while a monopoly may manufacture more cheaply, the savings are not passed on to the consumer, for a monopoly is usually formed to enhance profits, and there is conclusive evidence that in many cases the public has been gouged by unwarranted charges. It was the belief of the Industrial Commission in 1902, after a most exhaustive study, "that in most cases the combination has exerted an appreciable power over prices and in practically all cases it has increased the margin between raw materials and finished products. Since there is reason to believe that the cost of production over a period of years has lessened, the conclusion is inevitable that the combinations have been able to increase their profits."[22] A little earlier, Professor Jenks had come to the conclusion that "the fact that the power to increase the margin temporarily at least, somewhat arbitrarily, and the fact

---

[21] A. J. Eddy, the leading proponent of trade associations, epitomized this by the caption, "Competition is War, and 'War is Hell,'" across the title page of his book, *The New Competition* (1914).

[22] *Final Report of the Industrial Commission*, XIX, 621.

that the margin has been increased in specific cases, seems to be clearly established." [23] While the price to the consumer has often been raised, the producers of the raw materials, such as cattlemen, sugar raisers, and others, have suffered from the lack of competition among buyers. Furthermore, monopoly has often resulted in inefficient and careless service to the consumer, and he has been forced to accept what was given him. Whatever might be the gains of monopoly from a purely scientific point of view, it was quite obvious that both the producer of the raw material and the consumer of the finished product were pretty much at the mercy of the manufacturer if the manufacturing processes constituted a monopoly.

In a comparison of the advantages and disadvantages, it should be pointed out that many of the alleged advantages of monopolies are similarly applicable to any large-scale industry where there is no monopoly. Steady consolidation of business has gone far, and there is every reason to believe that in most industries the process will continue. Nevertheless, monopoly as such has generally been distrusted as both an economic and a social evil, and persistent efforts either to restore competition or to control the inevitable monopolies have been undertaken through legislative means.

EARLY ANTI-TRUST MOVEMENT

Notwithstanding the dominance of *laissez faire* and the enthusiasm with which business consolidation proceeded, there developed a strong opposition to the movement. This came first from the deep-seated antipathy to monopoly inherited from the old English common-law conception, a dislike which was undoubtedly stimulated by the misfortunes of those whose means of livelihood were injured by the new consolidations. Second, there was fear that the country's natural resources would be brought under the control of a few irresponsible men. By 1873 six corporations owned most of the anthracite coal deposits of Pennsylvania and the transportation facilities to carry the coal out, and in the succeeding years much of the bituminous field was appropriated. By 1882 thirty-nine refineries of the Standard Oil controlled 90 per cent of the product. "A small number of men," said Henry Demarest Lloyd (1894), "are obtaining the power to forbid any but themselves to supply the people with fire in nearly every form known to modern life and industry, from matches to locomotives and electricity. They control our hard coal and much of the soft, and stoves, furnaces, and steam and hot-water heaters; the governors on steam boilers and the boilers; gas and gas-fixtures, natural gas and gas-pipes, electric lighting, and all the appurtenances. You cannot free yourself by changing from electricity to gas, or from the gas of the city

[23] Jeremiah W. Jenks, *Trusts and Industrial Combinations,* Department of Labor Bulletin, No. 29, July, 1900, p. 765.

to the gas of the fields. If you fly from kerosene to candles, you are still under the ban." [24] By 1904 most of the great products of the country were in the control of big combinations, so large as to constitute monopolies.

Not only were the people disturbed over the appropriation and consolidation of the resources of the country, but they were thoroughly aroused over the dishonest methods of competition which in many cases had brought success by open evasion of the law. The concern that did not want to join the trust was throttled by every unfair means known, among the least vicious of which was the obtaining of special railroad rebates, a practice which as much as anything else made possible the success of Standard Oil. Not only was there evasion of the law, there was tampering with the government; the unwholesome influence of big business upon politics was evidenced by the free distribution of railroad passes and still more by activities at election time. The supreme court of Michigan undoubtedly expressed the current feeling when it said in a case involving the Diamond Match Company, one of the most notorious of the trusts during the period: "Indeed, it is doubtful if free government can long exist in a country where such enormous amounts of money are allowed to be accumulated in the vaults of corporations, to be used at discretion in controlling the property and business of the country against the interest of the public and that of the people, for the personal gain and aggrandizement of a few individuals." [25]

Moreover, the financial practices incident to consolidation, the watering of stocks, the paying of enormous commissions to lawyers and banking houses, had helped to fleece the general public. And, finally, labor has found it more difficult to deal with the increased power of consolidated capital and has been among the severest critics of the trusts. Typical of this power was the United States Steel Corporation, which for more than thirty years prevented large-scale labor organization in its mills, and through its influence as the dominant concern in the industry also prevented organization in other companies.

This rapid growth of monopoly and the irresponsible use of the power which went with it were viewed with concern by many of the most thoughtful. Among the literature calling attention to defects in the economic life of the time, three widely read books stand out preeminently. Henry George in 1879 published his *Progress and Poverty*, in which he advocated a single tax on land values as one solution for the problem of monopoly. Edward Bellamy's *Looking Backward* (1887), by glorifying the socialist state, pointed to another solution; and Henry Demarest Lloyd's *Wealth Against Commonwealth* (1894) was the ablest and most effective attack ever delivered against trusts. The opposition which developed had already made itself felt in politi-

[24] H. D. Lloyd, *Wealth Against Commonwealth*, pp. 9–10.
[25] Richardson *v.* Buhl *et al.*, 77 Michigan State Reports 658.

cal channels. Further grants to railroad corporations and monopolies had been opposed by both the major parties in 1872. The Greenbackers in 1880 and the Anti-Monopolists in 1884 had called for government action to prevent or control monopolies, and this was true in 1888 of the platforms of the four leading parties—the Republican, Democratic, Prohibition, and Union Labor. Although monopolies were already presumably banned under the common law, twenty-seven states and territories by the close of 1890 had passed laws intended to prevent or destroy them, and fifteen states had incorporated provisions in their constitutions for the same purpose. In that year the federal government also took action.

THE SHERMAN ANTI-TRUST ACT

By 1890 public opinion had become so aroused over the subject of monopolies that federal legislation was demanded to supplement state laws. Investigations undertaken in 1888 by a committee of the House of Representatives [26] and by a committee of the Senate of the State of New York [27] offered little in the shape of constructive suggestion but confirmed current beliefs as to the evils of monopolies. President Harrison in his message of December, 1889, urged legislation against trusts which partook of the nature of conspiracies.[28] A number of anti-trust bills were introduced in the Senate in 1888, but two years of discussion ensued before a bill was eventually passed; its enactment was in no small measure due to the willingness of conservative Republican Senators to trade their votes to secure a simultaneous enactment of the McKinley tariff.

The Sherman Anti-trust Act of 1890 [29] contained eight sections; the principle and theory of the Act, however, appear in the following:

"Sec. 1.—Every contract, combination in the form of trust or otherwise, or conspiracy, in restraint of trade or commerce among the several States, or with foreign nations, is hereby declared to be illegal. . . .

"Sec. 2.—Every person who shall monopolize or attempt to monopolize or combine or conspire with any other person or persons to monopolize any part of the trade or commerce among the several States, or with foreign nations, shall be deemed guilty of a misdemeanor. . . ."

[26] *Report of Investigation of Trusts*, House Reports, 50th Cong., 1st Sess., 1887–88, Vol. IX, Serial Number 3112.

[27] *Report of the Senate Committee of General Laws on Investigation Relative to Trusts*, March 6, 1888.

[28] Richardson, *Messages and Papers of the Presidents*, IX, 43.

[29] 26 Stat. 209. The texts of this Act and the other federal anti-trust Acts mentioned in this chapter are to be found in Jeremiah W. Jenks and Walter E. Clark, *The Trust Problem*, in "Appendix F: Federal Trust Legislation in the United States." The various sections of the Appendix contain much valuable source material. See also F. Flügel and H. U. Faulkner, *Readings*, pp. 541 ff.

Fines and imprisonment were provided for violation, and the injured person might recover three times the damages sustained. The several circuit courts of the United States were invested with jurisdiction to prevent or restrain violations of the Act, and the Attorney General was directed to institute proceedings in equity against such violations.

The Sherman Act was looked upon by many as an unnecessary blow at legitimate business and as futile opposition to an inevitable economic development. The committee who framed it maintained truly, however, that the bill was simply a restating of the usual English common-law principles and their extension to America. The Act did not attempt to define "contract, combination, or conspiracy in restraint of trade"; it was purposely drawn in general terms for the courts to interpret, the intention being that no business legitimately carried on need fear interference.

Senator Cullom called the Sherman Act "one of the most important enactments ever passed by Congress," but it was decidedly ineffective for a long while. This was due chiefly to three reasons—first, the economic depression in the succeeding years deferred further large-scale consolidation for some time; second, the general terms in which the bill was stated required much legal interpretation to be effective; and third, the federal government evinced lack of interest in enforcing it. The panic of 1893 temporarily crippled business and made both national and state governments loath to increase their burdens. The political weakness of the Harrison administration, followed by the necessary affiliations of Cleveland with eastern capitalists during his second term, prevented aggressive legislation; and under McKinley the combination movement went on merrily, with little apparent desire on the part of the administration to interfere. Down to 1901 the government had instituted eighteen suits, but with discouraging lack of success. The spirit of *laissez faire* and the economic tendency during the period toward consolidation, combined with the difficulties of handling the technical questions involved in the trust and corporate form, hindered decisive and clear-cut judicial action. The futility of the Sherman Act seemed indisputable when in 1895 the Supreme Court refused to dissolve the American Sugar Refining Company (which had just acquired four competing Pennsylvania plants, thus enabling it to control over 95 per cent of the sugar refined) on the ground that the Sherman law was applicable only to monopoly in restraint of trade and that the mere purchase of sugar refineries or the refining of sugar was not commerce in the strict constitutional sense.[30] This almost incredible decision was considerably weakened, however, four years later in the Addyston Pipe case, when the Court held that, although the members of the pool manufactured pipe, their agreements were concerned with buying and

[30] U. S. *v.* E. C. Knight Company, 156 U. S. 1.

selling across state lines, and in this case were illegal.[31] Although this case made it possible to accomplish something under the Sherman Act, we must agree with Professor Jenks when he says, "A study of these statues and of the decisions of our courts of last resort which have been made under them will show that they have had comparatively little, practically no, effect, as regards the trend of our industrial development." [32]

While the Sherman Act had little influence upon business consolidation, it is the irony of fate that capital has succeeded in using it effectively against labor unions. The Pullman strike of 1894 was broken by the government acting through the courts, when the latter held the actions of the union a conspiracy in restraint of interstate commerce and issued an injunction to desist.[33] In the famous Danbury hatters' case members of a labor union were held financially responsible under the Sherman Act to the full amount of their individual property for losses to business occasioned by an interstate boycott.[34] Certain courts actually went so far as to question the legality of trade unions *per se*, holding them, because of their restrictive rules and practices, as illegal combinations both at common law and under the Sherman Anti-trust Act.[35] In the Clayton Act of 1914, as we shall see, Congress tried to exempt labor unions from the application of the anti-trust Acts just as it tried more effectively to control business, but in neither case were its efforts crowned with notable success.

The Muckrakers and the Revival of Anti-trust Activities

The tremendous revival of the combination movement in the prosperous years immediately following the Spanish-American War, coincident with the abuses and the high-handed disregard of public welfare as evidenced by the large corporate interests, brought a logical reaction. Beginning with the publication in 1903–1904 of Ida M. Tarbell's "History of the Standard Oil Company" in *McClure's Magazine,* there ensued a period in which many of the worst features of our economic and social life were aired before the public. Lincoln Steffens's *Shame of the Cities* (1904) exposed the rottenness of many of the local governments; Thomas Lawson's "Frenzied Finance," published in *Everybody's Magazine* (1905–1906), showed Wall Street at its worst; Upton Sinclair in *The Jungle* (1906) revealed the horrible filth and misery of the workers in the meat-packing industry; Charles Edward Russell excoriated

[31] Addyston Pipe and Steel Co. *v.* U. S., 175 U. S. 211 (1899).

[32] J. W. Jenks, *The Trust Problem* (rev. ed., 1905), p. 218.

[33] *In re* Debs, 158 U. S. 564 (1894). See H. R. Seager and C. A. Gulick, Jr., *Trust and Corporation Problems*, pp. 374 ff.

[34] Loewe *v.* Lawlor, 235 U. S. 522 (1915).

[35] Kealy *v.* Faulkner, 18 Ohio Superior and Common Pleas Decision 498 (1908); Hitchman Coal and Coke Co. *v.* Mitchell, 202 Fed. 512 (1912).

the "beef trust" in *Everybody's* in articles entitled "The Greatest Trust in the World"; Winston Churchill in *Coniston* (1906) drew a picture of the subservience of the state legislatures to the railroads; other phases of the railroad problems were handled by Ray Stannard Baker in a series, "The Railroads on Trial," in *McClure's;* and B. J. Hendrick in the same magazine laid bare the illegal and crooked practice of the insurance companies in "The Story of Life Insurance" (1907). Other books and numerous magazine articles enlarged upon the lawlessness and greed of big business and the venality of politicians. In the campaigns of 1896, 1900, and 1904 the Democrats directed part of their artillery against the trusts.

Some of this "muckraking" was undoubtedly exaggerated, but most of it, unfortunately, was only too true. Whether exaggerated or not, it helped to stimulate a healthy reaction for reform, a movement in which President Theodore Roosevelt took the lead. On a campaign speaking tour in 1902 he attacked the trusts, and in the next year Congress passed three Acts to control big business more effectively. The first of these, known as the Expediting Act, gave preference to federal suits brought under the Interstate Commerce Act and the Sherman Anti-trust Act. The second was the Elkins Anti-rebate Act, which aimed to clarify the law and eliminate one of the worst practices of the railroads. The third created a Department of Commerce and Labor with a subsidiary Bureau of Corporations to make "diligent investigation into the organization, conduct, and management of corporations." In the same year the President directed his Attorney General to institute proceedings against the Northern Securities Company, a New Jersey holding corporation designed to create a transportation monopoly in the Northwest by controlling the stock of the Great Northern, the Northern Pacific, and the Chicago, Burlington, and Quincy. The successful issue of this suit [36] in 1904 showed that the Sherman Act might not be a useless reed in the hands of an aggressive administration. Under Roosevelt sixteen civil suits and eighteen criminal suits were prosecuted with considerable success, and under Taft the effort to enforce the Sherman Act was carried on even more aggressively. The Pure Food Law of 1906 marked a distinct step forward in the policy of government intervention to protect the welfare of the public, while the more comprehensive Act of 1907 aimed especially to bring the meat-packing business under supervision.

DISSOLUTION OF THE STANDARD OIL COMPANY AND THE AMERICAN TOBACCO COMPANY

The Taft administration believed that legitimate business might go on undisturbed and a solution to the trust problem be found by the voluntary fed-

[36] U. S. *v.* Northern Securities *et al.*, 120 Fed. Rep. 721; 193 U. S. 197.

eral incorporation of concerns, their charters to be approved by a projected corporation commission, with power reserved to Congress to revoke such charters. A bill to this effect was introduced, but public interest was never sufficient to push it through. As a consequence, the government continued to press the prosecutions already commenced, and succeeded in obtaining two notable decisions in 1911. The first of these, against the Standard Oil Company of New Jersey,[37] had been in the courts more than four years. The defendant argued that the Standard Oil companies were the natural products of the growth of a single business, that they had never competed with one another and consequently could not have conspired or combined in restraint of trade. Both the circuit and Supreme courts, however, affirmed the government's contention that the concerns had so conspired by many and devious methods to build up a monopoly. The dissolution was carried out by apportioning shares in the various constituent concerns pro rata to the stockholders of the holding company.

The case of the American Tobacco Company[38] was more complicated because the organization was not merely a holding company but an actual manufacturing concern, and one which was engaged in making a number of products, including chewing and smoking tobacco, snuff, little cigars, cigarettes, and tin foil. The court attempted to restore competition by creating separate companies in each line; for example, the manufacture of smoking tobacco was divided among four companies, cigarettes among three concerns, plug tobacco among four, and tin foil between two. A proportionate distribution of stock in the new companies was made, corresponding to the holdings in the old. Each new company was enjoined from cooperating with, or holding stock in, another company.

Two interesting facts stand out in regard to these decisions. The first is that the dissolutions failed in their purpose. In form there was competition, in reality there was little. The distribution of stock created simply a community of interest among the various concerns which appeared to work as harmoniously together as when under a single management. The increase in value of Standard Oil stocks after the dissolution showed that no detrimental results were feared. After more than thirty years of operation and numerous court dissolutions and interpretations, the Sherman Anti-trust Act appeared to have failed utterly in its purpose of preventing monopoly and restraint. The second point to be noted was the interpretation given to the Act by the two decisions. The Trans-Missouri Freight case decision (1897)[39] had refused to see any

[37] U. S. v. Standard Oil Company of New Jersey et al., 152 Fed. Rep. 290; 173 Fed. Rep. 177; 221 U. S. 1.

[38] U. S. v. American Tobacco Co. et al., 164 Fed. Rep. 700; 221 U. S. 106.

[39] U. S. v. Trans-Missouri Freight Association, 53 Fed. Rep. 440; 58 Fed. Rep. 58; 166 U. S. 290.

difference between reasonable and unreasonable combinations in restraint of trade, but the judges in the two decisions in 1911 professed to see a difference and maintained that the only restraint of trade which was intended by the law was that which monopolizes or attempts to monopolize. In other words, they introduced the so-called "rule of reason" and tried to differentiate between "good trusts" and "bad trusts." Many believed the "rule of reason" was an unwarranted interpretation and that it simply weakened the Act. It certainly made further consideration of trust cases by the courts more complicated.

DEMOCRATS AND THE TRUSTS—THE CLAYTON ACT AND THE FEDERAL TRADE COMMISSION

For years the Democratic party had assailed the Republicans as the friends and allies of the trusts. In their platform of 1912 the Democrats demanded that the Sherman Act be made more stringent in order to restore free competition. Their candidate, Woodrow Wilson, in a remarkable series of campaign speeches, emphasized what he called "The New Freedom." While claiming not to be one of those who think that competition can be established by law against a world-wide economic tendency, he still believed that much of our old, free cooperative life could be restored. Without condemning big business as such, he laid the destruction of competition to the trusts. "American industry is not free, as it once was free," he said. "American enterprise is not free; the man with only a little capital is finding it harder to get into the field, more and more impossible to compete with the big fellow. Why? Because the laws of this country do not prevent the strong from crushing the weak." [40] To restore, if possible, some of the old competition appeared to be the purpose of the new administration, and it was obvious that after years of criticism some legislation would be passed.

If any added impetus was necessary to bring further anti-trust legislation, it was furnished during the early months of the Wilson administration by the amazing revelations of the activities of the New York, New Haven and Hartford Railroad, under the direction of J. P. Morgan, William Rockefeller, Charles S. Mellen, and others, to effect a monopoly of transportation in New England. With reckless improvidence they had used the credit of the New Haven to gain control of the Boston and Maine, the Boston and Albany, and the New York, Ontario and Western; they had then bought up competing trolley lines, and finally gained virtual control of most of the water transportation to and from New England. The details of the many transactions by which this monopoly was attained revealed not only "a

[40] Woodrow Wilson, *The New Freedom*, p. 15.

loose, extravagant and an improvident management," [41] but corruption of legislatures, subsidizing of the press, the retention of powerful political bosses as attorneys who did no legitimate legal work, fictitious sales of stocks to boost market prices, payment of unitemized vouchers, dishonest use of corporate funds, and, in the words of the Interstate Commerce Commission, the erection of a web of entangling alliances "seemingly planned, created, and manipulated by lawyers expressly retained for the purpose of concealment or deception." [42] As this story came out through the government prosecutions, even the most naïve citizen could see that the demand for further anti-trust and railroad legislation had some foundation.

In his campaign speeches Wilson affirmed that the trouble with the Sherman Act was that it was not definite enough and needed a more careful statement of unlawful practices, so that legitimate business might better know when it was within the law. These ideas Congress sought to embody in the Clayton Anti-trust Act of 1914.[43] The following are the chief provisions:

1. The Act forbids (a) any person to discriminate in price, either directly or indirectly, between purchasers of commodities whenever such discrimination lessens competition or tends to create monopoly, (b) a manufacturer to sell his goods to a dealer under conditions requiring the latter not to handle the products of competitors—a hit at the so-called "tying" agreements.

2. Corporations were forbidden to acquire stock in another concern where the effect was substantially to lessen competition. The holding of stock solely for investment was allowed.

3. Interlocking directorates were forbidden in concerns engaged in interstate commerce whose capital, surplus, and undivided profits aggregated more than $1,000,000, if such concerns were competitors.

4. It was made unlawful in the case of banks for one person to serve as director or officer in another if the deposits, capital surplus, and undivided profits of any of the institutions exceeded $5,000,000.

5. Labor unions and farmers' organizations were specifically declared not to be conspiracies in restraint of trade.

A few days earlier a Federal Trade Commission of five members had been created,[44] whose business it was to investigate persons or corporations (except interstate carriers and banks) subject to the anti-trust laws, and present reports of its activities. It was also granted power to issue orders requiring the cessation of illegal practices, and if these were not obeyed it was

[41] *Interstate Commerce Commission Reports*, XXXI, 34.
[42] *Ibid.*, XXXI, 31. Excerpts in F. Flügel and H. U. Faulkner, *Readings*, pp. 577–583.
[43] 38 Stat. 730; reproduced in part in F. Flügel and H. U. Faulkner, *Readings*, pp. 543–547.
[44] 38 Stat. 717; quoted in part in F. Flügel and H. U. Faulkner, *Readings*, pp. 547–551.

to apply for federal action to the circuit court of appeals in the district where the alleged offense was committed. The commission took over the work of the old Bureau of Corporations and was designed to act for corporations along somewhat the same line as the Interstate Commerce Commission has done for interstate carriers.

In order that Americans might compete on more equal terms with great foreign concerns, the anti-trust laws were modified in 1918. The Webb Export Act stated that nothing in the Sherman Act was to be construed as making "illegal an association entered into for the sole purpose of engaging in export trade and actually engaged solely in such trade," providing this association was not party to any attempt to restrain competition or control prices within the country. Furthermore, the Clayton Act under the same condition was not to be construed as forbidding the "acquisition or ownership by any corporation of the whole or any part of the stock or other capital of any corporation organized solely for the purpose of engaging in export trade." There seems to be little doubt that the Webb Export Act has stimulated both foreign trade and combination at home.[45]

THE MONEY TRUST

No discussion of business consolidation would be complete without reference to the concentration of banking power. Parallel with the rapid but extensive consolidation of business has gone that of the banking interests. The increasing wealth of the country naturally enlarged the size of the banks, and the greater demands of their customers necessitated growth and consolidation in order to meet them. By the opening of the twentieth century, however, this concentration was so vast that there was a firmly grounded conviction among many that a small group controlled the financial resources of the land, lending and withholding funds where they pleased, thus holding in the hollow of their hands the fate of many businesses.

We have already seen how the important lines of railroads through interlocking directorates and stockholdings were in the power of six influential groups dominated by a score of men. It was now asserted that the same men controlled the banking facilities. Around the Morgan-Rockefeller interests, wrote John Moody in 1904,

or what must ultimately become one greater group, all other smaller groups of capitalists congregate. They are all allied and intertwined by their various mutual interests. For instance, the Pennsylvania Railroad interests are on the one hand allied with the Vanderbilts and on the other with the Rockefellers. The Vanderbilts are closely allied with the Morgan group, and both the Pennsylvania and

[45] L. T. Fournier, "The Purposes and Results of the Webb-Pomerene Law," *American Economic Review*, XXII, 18–33 (March, 1932).

the Vanderbilt interests have recently become the dominating factors in the Reading system, a former Morgan road and the most important part of the anthracite coal combine which has always been dominated by the Morgan people. . . . Viewed as a whole, we find the dominating influences in the Trust to be made up of an intricate network of large and small capitalists, many allied to one another by ties of more or less importance, but all being appendages to or parts of the greater groups, which are themselves dependent on and allied with the two mammoth, or Rockefeller and Morgan groups. These two mammoth groups jointly . . . constitute the heart of the business and commercial life of the nation.[46]

The concentration of capital was promoted by the fact that the Rockefeller and Morgan interests worked through banks which they controlled; thus the National City Bank, for some years the greatest of American banking institutions,[47] became the Rockefeller bank, while the Morgans controlled the First National, The Bankers' Trust, and others. Wall Street and the insurance companies formed a community of interest in the joint direction of the great trust companies; hence the influence of Wall Street became dominant in the vast lending operations of the insurance companies.

The general belief was fully confirmed in the report of the Pujo Committee (1913), which pointed out that the concentration of control of money and credit had been effected chiefly through consolidations of competitive or potentially competitive banks and trust companies; through interlocking directorates and stockholdings; through the influence of the powerful banking houses, banks, and trust companies brought to bear on insurance companies, railroads, and producing and trading companies; and finally through partnership arrangements between a few of the leading banking houses in the purchase of security issues, which had the effect of virtually destroying competition. The committee named J. P. Morgan & Co., the First National Bank of New York, and the National City Bank as the most powerful banking units, and placed their combined assets in New York City, as controlled through seven subsidiary banks, at over $2,000,000,000. In addition to the interests named, the committee believed that Lee Higginson & Co., Kidder, Peabody & Co., and Kuhn, Loeb & Co. were the principal banking agencies through which the corporate enterprises of the United States obtained capital for their operations. Four allied financial institutions in New York City, it affirmed, held 341 directorships in banks and in transportation, public utility, and insurance companies, whose aggregate resources were $22,245,000,000.

[46] John Moody, *The Truth About the Trusts,* p. 493.
[47] Through numerous consolidations, the Chase National Bank in 1930 finally surpassed the National City Bank in size. See pp. 612–613.

If by a "money trust" is meant an established and well-defined identity and community of interest between a few leaders of finance which has been created and is held together through stockholdings, interlocking directorates, and other forms of domination over banks, trust companies, railroads, public service, and industrial corporations, and which has resulted in a vast and growing concentration of control of money and credit in the hands of a comparatively few men— your committee has no hesitation in asserting as a result of its investigation that this condition, largely developed within the past five years, exists in this country today.[48]

While it was true that to a considerable extent this growth and consolidation followed natural economic laws—as is illustrated by the consolidation of financial power in other countries—at the same time there was a real danger in a situation in which the economic lifeblood of the nation was controlled by a small group of men using their power for private ends. The report of the committee contained a number of recommendations in regard to bettering the banking facilities, breaking up concentration, and supervising the stock exchange. Some of the best of these have been incorporated in the law creating the Federal Reserve System, the adoption of which was undoubtedly furthered by this investigation; in the Clayton Act, which forbade interlocking directorates in large banks, and in the Esch-Cummins bill, which empowered the Interstate Commerce Commission to supervise plans and security issues in the reorganization of interstate railroads. The laws, however, have probably had little, if any, real effect in preventing the consolidation of capital.

By 1914 the problem of monopoly had been studied and discussed from almost every angle. For more than a quarter of a century both the state and federal governments had experimented with legislation designed to prevent or check monopolies not operating under government permission. Nevertheless, the nation was to see during the post-war boom one of the most intensive and widespread .eras of consolidation it had yet experienced. The subsequent history of this consolidation and the public's more recent attitude on this subject will be presented in a later chapter.

SELECTED READINGS

Jenks, J. W., and Clark, W. E., *The Trust Problem,* Chaps. III–V, IX, XIII–XV.
Seager, H. R., and Gulick, C. A., Jr., *Trust and Corporation Problems,* Chaps. V, VIII–XV.

---

[48] Report of the Committee Appointed to Investigate the Concentration of Control of Money and Credit, 62nd Congress, 3rd Sess., p. 130; quoted by Chester A. Phillips, *Readings in Money and Banking* (1916), p. 606. See also F. Flügel and H. U. Faulkner, *Readings,* pp. 597–600.

Haney, L. H., *Business Organization and Combination,* Chaps. VI–XVI, XXIII–XXVII.

Ripley, W. Z., *Trusts, Pools, and Corporations,* Introduction.

Faulkner, H. U., *The Quest for Social Justice,* Chap. II.

Flügel, F., and Faulkner, H. U., *Readings in the Economic and Social History of the United States,* Chap. XIV.

22

The Labor Movement
to 1914

Background of Labor Organization

Our economic history from the earliest colonial days has been characterized by a "labor problem"; but a "labor movement"—that is, an organized continued effort on the part of wage earners to better their standard of living—necessarily waited upon conditions arising from the growth in population, the rapid increase in manufacturing, and the concentration of population in cities. These effects of the Industrial Revolution were delayed in this country for many reasons—scarcity of labor, lack of liquid capital, abundance of rich unoccupied farming land—all tending to direct the energies of the people into rural occupations and delay the era of manufacturing and urban life.[1]

Nevertheless, population grew rapidly, almost doubling every twenty years. The percentage of the total population living in cities of 8000 or over increased slowly before 1840 and then more rapidly; only 8.5 per cent of the people lived in such cities in 1841, but by 1860 the percentage had risen to 16.1 and by 1930 to 49.1. The years of most rapid growth as shown in the accompanying table correspond closely with the period of greatest activity on the part of labor. If the word urban is used, as it is in the Fourteenth Census, to designate places of 2500 inhabitants or over, it is found that, in 1920, 51.4 per cent of the population lived in urban territory, as compared with 28.6 per cent in 1880.

Although the growth of the urban population has been nation-wide, it has been most notable in the manufacturing sections; in 1920 more than two-thirds was contained in three geographic sections—the New England, the Middle Atlantic, and the East North Central States. Rhode Island and Massachusetts each showed over 90 per cent living in towns, New York over 80 per cent, and New Jersey over 70 per cent. The three sections noted above turned out almost three-quarters of the manufactured products of

[1] Above, pp. 249 ff.

GROWTH OF CITY POPULATION [2]

Year	Total Population	Places of 8000 Inhabitants or Over		
		Population	Number of Places	Per Cent of Population
1790	3,929,214	131,472	6	3.3
1800	5,308,483	210,873	6	4.0
1820	9,638,453	475,135	13	4.9
1840	17,069,453	1,453,994	44	8.5
1860	31,443,321	5,072,256	141	16.1
1880	50,155,783	11,365,698	285	22.7
1900	75,994,575	25,018,335	547	32.0
1920	105,710,620	46,307,640	924	43.8
1930	122,775,046	60,333,452	1208	49.1
1940	131,669,275	64,896,083	1323	49.3

the nation, reckoned in terms of value. The Census of 1849 recorded 957,000 wage earners producing commodities to the value of $1,019,000,000; that of 1889 showed 4,252,000, whose products were valued at $9,372,000,000; the figures for 1914 placed the wage earners at 7,036,000 and the value of the products at $24,246,000,000; those for 1919, at 8,998,000 and $62,418,000,000; and those for 1929 at 8,839,000 and $70,435,000,000.

The rise of a class of wage earners and their concentration in urban communities are the fundamental factors leading to the growth of the labor movement. The increase in manufacturing after the Civil War developed larger business units, usually under the corporate form. This accretion in the power of capital stirred the wage earners to action, especially those skilled workers whose occupations were imperiled by the invention of new machinery. The passing of the small industry in which a close personal relationship could be maintained between employer and employee, and its replacement by the corporation with its thousands of owners scattered throughout the country, tended to a lack of understanding between labor and capital.

If the new machinery and the growth of mighty business units affected the wage earner detrimentally, they also contained the elements of his salvation. Big factories brought the workers together in cities where they could mingle with their fellows, exchange their ideas more readily, and combine more easily for resistance. Improvements in paper manufacture and printing made it possible to spread their program, develop loyalty, and weld the local organizations more firmly together. An aggressive labor press, as it developed, not only contributed to the education of the worker in the problems involved, but in like manner made capital conversant with

[2] Fifteenth Census, 1930, Vol. I, Population, p. 9.

the aims of labor. The whole movement was accelerated by the diffusion of knowledge through our democratic system of education and was integrated by the development of railways and more rapid methods of communication.

Finally, the conditions under which labor worked provided a real impetus to the development of an organized movement. The truck system of payment, company stores, long hours, low pay, unsanitary conditions of work, the sweatshop evil, the unconscionable exploitation of women and children, the incredibly degrading rules in practice in many establishments, lack of effective labor legislation, and inability to obtain justice in the courts— these and many other aspects of the problem which existed in the decades following the Civil War help to make clear the need of such organizations as the Knights of Labor and the American Federation of Labor.[3]

Effect of the Civil War on Labor

Organized labor, as we have already pointed out, had a history extending back half a century before the Civil War.[4] Until the 1850's, however, organization was largely local and on a relatively small scale. The Civil War gave a distinct impetus to the American labor movement. The struggle resulted in a deeper consideration of economic and social matters, for the question of the liberation of the slaves could hardly be discussed without also involving the status of northern labor, especially when economists of the South maintained that the condition of a southern slave was preferable to that of a northern wage earner—a contention which, considering hours and factory conditions, was not without point. The increasing cost of living brought on by the war was not met by a parallel rise in wages, for a steady influx of immigrants and the adoption of labor-saving machinery helped to meet the scarcity of labor. Especially irritating to labor was an Act of July 4, 1864, which enabled agents of employers to engage foreign laborers under a contract in which their transportation was to be paid by future wages.

War tariffs and war contracts brought a sudden accumulation of wealth in the hands of a few men and at the same time accentuated the sharp contrast between rich and poor. On the one hand was a growing power in the hands of capital, and on the other a misgiving concerning the likelihood of a glutted labor market when the soldiers returned; both factors strengthened the determination of labor to keep wages up after they commenced to ascend during the last two years of the war. Numerous local unions and at least ten national unions sprang into existence between 1863 and 1866.

[3] See excerpts from *Report of the Committee of the Senate upon the Relations Between Labor and Capital* (1885), in F. Flügel and H. U. Faulkner, *Readings,* pp. 816–829.

[4] Above, pp. 311 ff.

The first of the great railroad brotherhoods, the Brotherhood of Locomotive Engineers, was organized at Detroit in 1863 as the "Brotherhood of the Footboard"; their example was followed in 1869 by the founding of the Brotherhood of Locomotive Firemen. By 1870 there were in existence no less than thirty-two national trade unions, and each important city had its trade assembly, its labor press, and its workingmen's library.

THE KNIGHTS OF LABOR AND ITS FORERUNNERS

Before the impetus given by the Civil War had spent itself, at least one notable attempt had been made to bring all labor together in a single organization. Under the leadership of W. H. Sylvis, and on the basis of the city assemblies of trade unions, the National Labor Union was organized; it held seven annual conventions, beginning in 1866, and at the height of its power had a membership of 600,000. The idea that the future of the wage earner lay in cooperative enterprises rather than in militant trade unionism was strongly held and numerous experiments were made. The National Labor Union, among other things, advocated Chinese exclusion, the eight-hour day, and the establishment of a government bureau of labor. Another notable development immediately after the war was the growth of the Knights of St. Crispin,[5] founded in Milwaukee in 1867 and especially strong in the shoe-trade centers of Massachusetts. It throve from 1868 to 1870, when it became the "undoubted foremost trade organization of the world." [6] Participation in politics and the depression following the panic of 1873 smashed both of these groups as they did many others. The period 1873–1880 was characterized by business demoralization, unemployment, and desperate and usually unsuccessful strikes sometimes accompanied by violence and crime [7]—notably the great railroad strike of 1877 [8]—all of which left the labor movement disintegrated and to some extent discredited. Only 18 per cent of the national trade unions survived these years.

During this discouraging period labor turned whole-heartedly to political action and to secret organizations. One of these was destined to play an important rôle in the recuperative years of the early 'eighties. In 1869 Uriah S. Stevens, a Philadelphia garment marker, and six fellow craftsmen organized the Noble Order of the Knights of Labor. The high idealism of Stevens was written into the constitution and upheld by Terence V. Powderly, who succeeded him as Grand Master. Taking their motto from

[5] So called after St. Crispin, the patron saint of shoemakers.
[6] G. E. McNeill, *The Labor Movement*, p. 200.
[7] The deeds of the "Mollie Maguires" in the anthracite coal regions of Pennsylvania illustrate the extreme of labor lawlessness during this period. See James F. Rhodes, *History of the United States from Hayes to McKinley, 1877–1896*, pp. 52–87.
[8] *Appletons' Annual Cyclopaedia, 1877*, pp. 423–432.

Solon, they affirmed, "That is the most perfect government in which an injury to one is the concern of all." The set of instructions given to every initiate into the order read: "Labor is noble and holy. To defend it from degradation; to divest it of the evils to body, mind, and estate which ignorance and greed have imposed; to rescue the toiler from the grip of the selfish—is a work worthy of the noblest and best of our race. . . . We mean no conflict with legitimate enterprise, no antagonism to necessary capital; but men, in their haste and greed, blinded by self-interests, overlook the interests of others, and sometimes violate the rights of those they deem helpless. We mean to uphold the dignity of labor, to affirm the nobility of all who earn their bread by the sweat of their brows. We mean to create a healthy public opinion on the subject of labor (the only creator of values) and the justice of its receiving a full, just share of the values or capital it has created. We shall, with all our strength, support laws made to harmonize the interests of labor and capital, and also those laws which tend to lighten the exhaustiveness of toil. To pause in his toil, to devote [himself] to his own interests, to gather a knowledge of the world's commerce, to unite, combine and cooperate in the great army of peace and industry, to nourish and cherish, build and develop, the temple he lives in, is the highest and noblest duty of man to himself, to his fellow-man and to his Creator." [9] In other words, their aim was to secure to the wage earner the fullest enjoyment of the wealth he creates, and leisure for the development of his intellectual, moral, and social faculties. They favored the eight-hour day, a tax on incomes and inheritances, postal savings banks, workingmen's compensation for injuries received through lack of necessary safeguards, and the appropriation by the community of the unearned increment on land. That the socialism strong in Europe at that time had made some progress here is seen in their advocacy of the public ownership of such utilities as railways, gas plants, and waterworks. In addition they urged private cooperative organizations of workingmen to handle the production and distribution of goods. The leaders and a minority of the order felt "that strikes are deplorable in their effect and contrary to the best interests of the order," and that success lay in "agitation, education and organization." "Without organization," said Powderly, "we cannot accomplish anything; through it, we hope to forever banish that curse of modern civilization—wage slavery." [10]

The order was secret at first; even the name was unknown. It was designated by five asterisks and usually spoken of as the "Five Stars." Growth was slow in the beginning. In 1869 only eleven tailors comprised the

[9] C. D. Wright, "Historical Sketch of the Knights of Labor," *Quarterly Journal of Economics*, pp. 142–143 (Jan., 1887). See also F. Flügel and H. U. Faulkner, *Readings*, pp. 793–798.

[10] Speech before the annual convention in Pittsburgh, 1880.

membership of Assembly No. 1, and in 1873 there were only six assemblies, all in Philadelphia. Two years later the organization had grown to eighty assemblies in the city and vicinity, and in 1875 a national convention was called at Tyrone, Pennsylvania, and an invitation extended to other labor organizations to join them. By 1883 the membership was 52,000; but within three years it had jumped to 700,000, and at the height of its career numbered close to a million. Widespread, though unwarranted, distrust of the organization led the Knights in 1881 to abolish its secret character. In make-up it resembled a "grand national union of industrial workers" rather than a federation of craft unions as exemplified later in the American Federation of Labor. Composed of both national trade unions and local assemblies, its composition was heterogeneous. Only three-fourths of its members needed to be wage earners, a rule which gave access to all types of reformers; many of the assemblies were composed of women and unskilled laborers. Under such conditions strong divergence of opinion as to policies was bound to arise. Two main factions appeared, one favoring reform through political channels and the other advocating direct action. The latter group proved the more powerful and embarked the Knights in an aggressive campaign to raise the standard of living, thus involving them in many severe strikes. The most notable and successful of these was the one directed against the Gould railway system in 1885 which wrung concessions from the most powerful capitalist of the day. Writing in 1886 of the Knights of Labor, Professor Ely described them as "the most powerful and the most remarkable labor organization of modern times . . . established on truly scientific principles which involved either an intuitive perception of the nature of industrial progress, or a wonderful acquaintance with the laws of economic society." [11]

But the year 1886, which marked the height of their power, marked also the beginning of their downfall. Unsuccessful strikes in that year undermined their prestige and alienated public sympathy; [12] factional differences prevented united action; inadequate leadership handicapped them; [13] political activity hurt them; overcentralization of power created suspicion; but more than all else, the rising opposition of a new organization, the American Federation of Labor, proved their undoing. The decline of the order after 1888 was as rapid as had been its growth. Its brief but spectacular

[11] R. T. Ely, *Labor Movement in America*, p. 75.

[12] The Haymarket riot of 1886, with the attendant bomb-throwing, also alienated public sympathy from the labor movement, although neither the Knights of Labor nor the American Federation of Labor had any connection with the anarchists who were responsible.

[13] This weakness is particularly emphasized in N. J. Ware, *The Labor Movement in the United States, 1860–1895* (1929). A more favorable impression of Powderly will be found in his autobiography, *The Path I Trod*, edited by H. J. Carman, Henry David, and P. N. Guthrie (1940).

career, however, was not without results. Many weak unions had been reorganized and put on their feet through affiliation with the Knights, and others had been founded. A standing Committee of Labor was established by the House of Representatives in 1883, and in the following year a national Bureau of Labor was created to gather expert information. At the same time a rather thorough investigation by a Senate committee was undertaken in 1883.[14] Even President Cleveland, who little understood the significance of the labor disputes which filled his first administration, in 1886 sent to Congress the first presidential message devoted to labor, in which he advocated the creation of a board of labor commissioners to act as official arbiters in labor disputes. Congress followed his suggestion half-heartedly in 1888 by enacting a law for the settlement of railway disputes by arbitration, provided both parties were willing.

THE AMERICAN FEDERATION OF LABOR

The origin of the American Federation of Labor dates from 1881, when a joint call for a convention was issued by the Knights of Industry, an organization strong in the Middle West, and the Amalgamated Labor Union, an offshoot of the Knights of Labor. This convention called a second, which met at Pittsburgh in the same year and formed a union which was reorganized at Columbus in 1886 as the American Federation of Labor. Although the early platforms of the Federation embodied such demands as a protective tariff, anti-contract immigration, the abolition of conspiracy laws as applied to trade unions, and compulsory education, the trend of its policy has been quite consistently away from direct political action to unionism pure and simple. In this it differed radically from the Knights of Labor.

The American Federation, as its name implies, was distinctly a federation of craft and industrial unions rather than a "one big union" affair, and its policy has been one of distinct liberality toward the autonomy of its constituent groups. In 1941 it was composed of the following elements:

1. National and International Unions, of which there were 106, comprising 33,000 local unions.
2. Local Trade and Federal Unions, composed of seven or more wage earners whose trade and calling are not organized and who are not members of any body affiliated with the Federation. There were 1517 such unions in 1941.

[14] *Report of the Committee of the Senate upon the Relations Between Labor and Capital* (1885). Excerpts from this report are to be found in F. Flügel and H. U. Faulkner, *Readings,* pp. 816–832.

3. Forty-nine State Federations (including Puerto Rico), with which the labor groups inside the several states are directed to join.

4. City Central Bodies, numbering 793, to which the locals are expected to ally themselves, but whose powers are limited by the American Federation and the various national trade unions.

5. The National and International Unions are grouped more or less roughly into departments, according to the line of work followed, as the Building Trades Department, Metal Trades Department, Railroad Employees Department, and Union Label Trades Department. Local Department Councils to the number of 712 supervise more locally the work of the departments. Each of the four departments has its separate set of officers.

The officers of the Federation consist of a president, fifteen vice presidents, and a secretary-treasurer, who are elected at the annual convention and form a powerful executive body. The National and International Unions have virtual self-government, but the power of the local union is distinctly circumscribed. By a per capita tax on all of the members, ample funds are obtained to carry on the work of the Federation, whose executive offices are in its own building in Washington.

The growth of the American Federation was slow for a number of years, its membership in 1890 numbering only 100,000, and 278,000 in 1898. By 1900 this had grown to 548,000; by 1904 to 1,676,000 and by 1914 to 2,000,000. The years from 1898 to 1904 were, perhaps, the most successful which the A. F. of L. has experienced, years which one labor historian has called the "heroic" days of unionism,[15] a period in which idealism, self-sacrifice, and driving energy made organized labor an important factor in American economic life. It was also a period in which organized labor received wide recognition from employers, one which another historian has called a "honeymoon period of capital and labor." [16]

Not only did membership increase rapidly, but a helping hand was extended from such middle-class organizations as the National Consumers' League (organized 1898), the National Civic Federation (1901), the National Child Labor Committee (1904), and the American Association for Labor Legislation (1906), all committed to collective bargaining, and, in the case of the last two, to far-reaching social legislation. "It was the harvest," said Gompers, "of the years of organizing work which was beginning to bear fruit." [17] These successful years, however, brought a stiffening of the lines of battle on the part of capital, and progress during the next decade

[15] L. L. Lorwin, *The American Federation of Labor*, p. 59, note.
[16] Selig Perlman in J. R. Commons *et al.*, *History of Labor in the United States*, II, 524.
[17] Samuel Gompers, *Seventy Years of Life and Labor* (1925), II, 105.

was not so rapid.[18] This growing opposition to labor development was headed by the National Association of Manufactures (founded 1895) and its subsidiary organizations such as the American Anti-Boycott Association which financed the legal battles in the Danbury Hatters' case and the Buck Stove and Range case. It was characterized by the extension and perfection of a technique for fighting labor which included the use of the injunction, the "yellow-dog contract," and the labor spy. Internally labor itself was weakened by the perpetual battle between those favoring industrial organization and those committed to craft unions, and between those favoring a distinct labor party and those who would continue the accepted political policy of the A. F. of L. A second period of rapid growth occurred during the First World War when the membership doubled from approximately 2,020,000 in 1914 to 4,078,000 in 1920, and a third great period of expansion occurred during the years of the New Deal.[19]

Although built primarily upon the basis of craft unions, certain large industrial unions like the United Mine Workers, the Western, Federation of Miners, and the International Union of Brewery Workers affiliated without materially changing the complexion of the larger organization. On the other hand, certain important groups, notably the Railway Brotherhoods, have constantly refused to affiliate with the Federation. In recent years, as we shall see later, there have been important defections from the ranks of the A. F. of L. and a powerful rival organization has appeared.

POLICIES OF THE AMERICAN FEDERATION OF LABOR

Broadly speaking, the purpose of the American Federation of Labor has been: (1) to agitate all questions looking toward the benefit of the working classes, in order to bring about the enactment of favorable measures and the repeal of oppressive laws in both state and national legislatures; (2) to use all possible means to remedy abuses under which the wage earner works and to uphold him in his just rights and privileges; and (3) to promote close and thorough organization to insure such results. More definitely, it has attempted to raise the standard of living by fighting for shorter hours, higher wages, and better working conditions. At the same time it has sought to protect its members by benefit and insurance schemes and by pushing union labor products.

The policies of the labor unions and the measure of success they have won during the past forty years have been to no small degree due to the

[18] See H. U. Faulkner, *Quest for Social Justice*, Chap. III, and F. Flügel and H. U. Faulkner, *Readings*, pp. 808–812.
[19] Below, pp. 668 ff.

leaders. During these formative years American labor on the whole was fortunate in its leadership, and the long tenure of office which the best officials have had shows a realization of this fact on the part of the rank and file. Perhaps the most brilliant was John Mitchell (1870–1919). Starting work in the coal mines at thirteen, he joined the United Mine Workers of America on its organization in 1890 and nine years later, at the age of twenty-nine, was its president. Although there were only 43,000 members when he rose to power, so skillfully did he direct their uphill fight that he lived to see a membership of 400,000, probably the largest trade union of his time. At the age of thirty-two he led the miners through the spectacular and successful coal strike of 1902 in such superb fashion that his prestige became national. The most famous of the labor leaders and the most valuable in his services to the wage earner was Samuel Gompers. Born in London in 1850 of Dutch-Jewish parentage, he emigrated to America at the age of thirteen and soon after joined as an apprentice the first cigar makers' union organized in New York. An active worker in the founding of both the American Federation and the Cigar Makers' International Union, he became president of the former in 1882, and with the exception of one year (1894) was annually reelected until his death. Scores of other able leaders could be mentioned—the Railway Brotherhoods have been particularly productive of them—men whose contributions to the organization and integration of the 100 or more national and international unions are well known in the labor world.

These men, trained in the rough school of experience, have developed a hard-headed and practical, but at the same time aggressive, policy. Whatever may have been their attitude as to ultimate ends, they refused to allow any dreams of a millennium to stand in the way of fighting for what small gains could be attained at the moment. "We are all practical men," said Adolph Strasser, president of the Cigar Makers' Union, before a Senate committee in 1883. "We have no ultimate ends. We are going on from day to day. We are fighting only for immediate objects—objects that can be realized in a few years." [20] Samuel Gompers' insistence upon rather strict adherence to a policy of organization based on national craft or trade unions, upon frugality in money matters, and upon avoidance of radical economic theories enabled him with considerable success to bring the pressure of organized labor to bear on such practical demands as the eight-hour day, the Saturday half holiday, federal child labor legislation, the restriction of immigration and alien contract labor, and workingmen's compensation. In

[20] *Report of the Committee of the Senate upon the Relations Between Capital and Labor*, I, 460.

brief, American labor under the leadership of Gompers and the A. F. of L. largely reverted to the type of old-line unionism followed in Great Britain for many decades after the collapse of Chartism.

While pleased with whatever can be obtained peaceably, the American Federation of Labor has not hesitated to back its constituent unions in the fierce warfare of strikes and boycotts. Ordinarily a local is forbidden to strike without the consent of the national, but, that consent once given, the national is responsible for the successful outcome. With the growth of the Federation has come a corresponding increase of strikes and lockouts, rather than a diminution, notwithstanding the improved methods for settling disputes adopted by many of the leading unions. The two chief ends hoped for in recent strikes have been wage increases and recognition of the union; it is interesting to note that the proportion of strikes attributable to the latter has constantly increased. Three-fifths of the strikes called in 1881, for example, were for higher wages and only one-sixteenth for recognition of the union, while in 1905 less than one-third were for higher pay and about an equal proportion for union recognition.[21] By means of the boycott the unions have attempted to put their stamp of disapproval upon the products of certain employers hostile to organized labor, as in the case of the Buck Stove and Range Company of St. Louis, and Daniel Loewe, hat manufacturer of Danbury, Connecticut. What amounts to an indirect boycott is the appeal to all friends of labor to use only goods bearing a union label. Other methods by which labor has sought to protect itself are infinite. Regulations are demanded regarding hours of work, relations of union to non-union men in the shop, use of non-union materials, number of helpers and apprentices, and many other matters of daily importance about which it seems advisable to have a definite understanding.

The most fundamental desire of the wage earner is for some sense of security as regards his work and wages. This, along with the growing strength of trade unionism, has brought a rapid development in collective bargaining. John Mitchell believed that "the hope of future peace in the industrial world lies in the trade agreement," [22] and it must be admitted that where given a fair trial collective bargaining has proved the most hopeful factor in lessening the possibility of serious labor strife. The trade agreement as it developed ranged from the simplest type to the more complicated forms taken by the International Typographical Union in its dealing with the American Newspaper Publishers' Association and the elaborate ones in the organized ready-made clothing industry. Some employers have be-

---

[21] *Twenty-First Annual Report of the Commissioner of Labor, 1906, Strikes and Lockouts* (1907), p. 32. See also F. Flügel and H. U. Faulkner, *Readings*, pp. 832–835.

[22] John Mitchell, *Organized Labor* (1903), p. 347.

come so enthusiastic over the stabilizing influence of these agreements that they are actually reconciled to the closed shop.

INDUSTRIAL UNIONISM AND THE I.W.W.

Although craft unionism was undoubtedly in the ascendant from the 1880's until the late 1930's, it did not occupy the entire stage even in the early years. Industrial unionism persisted in such groups as the United Mine Workers of America, where every workman from slate picker to engineer belongs to one union, in the International Longshoremen's Association, and in the rapidly developing clothing unions.[23]

For practical reasons, industrial unionism survived even in the days when skilled craftsmen predominated. It was the logical form for an industry which has workmen in many different trades, or an industry like mining, that is often isolated from great centers. Moreover, as we shall see later, it was practically the only type that could be successful in the new mass industries where labor-saving machinery was rapidly displacing skilled craftsmen.[24]

Militant industrial unionism never quite died out after the disintegration of the Knights of Labor, but it was not until 1905 that it seriously challenged the trade unions. A convention held in that year in Chicago under the influence of the Western Federation of Miners and the socialistically inclined American Labor Union, and dominated by such radicals as Eugene V. Debs, Daniel DeLeon, and William D. Haywood, founded the Industrial Workers of the World. Declaring that the "universal economic evils affecting the working class can be eradicated only by a universal working-class movement," they demanded the formation of "one great industrial union, embracing all industries, providing for craft autonomy locally, industrial autonomy internationally and wage class unity generally." "It must be founded on the class struggle," said the manifesto, "and its general administration must be conducted in harmony with the recognition of the irrepressible conflict between the capitalist class and the working class." A new preamble affixed to their constitution in 1908 asserted that "a struggle must go on until the workers of the world organize as a class, take possession of the earth and the machinery of production and abolish the wage system."[25] Believing in the class struggle, they advocated direct action as the means to victory. Direct action included such tactics as the general strike, boycott, and sabotage. Sabotage might be peaceful, merely soldiering on the job, or it might involve such violent tactics as destruction of property. Enmity to the

[23] Amalgamated Clothing Workers (men's clothing) and the International Ladies' Garment Workers' Union (women's clothing).
[24] Below, pp. 671 f.
[25] Quoted in P. F. Brissenden, *The I.W.W.*, Appendix II.

present order was fundamental in their philosophy, and their methods of warfare were those best suited to the moment. Their idea of a future state appears to have been much like that developd in Russia under Sovietism.

Their doctrines appealed to the great class of unorganized, unskilled workers generally, especially to certain groups of eastern factory operatives and to the migratory workers of the West who follow the harvest and cut the lumber. Although handicapped from the start by factional quarrels and overloaded with strong leaders, the I.W.W. from 1909 to 1917 was an aggressive organization. With great ability its agitators handled the Lawrence strike of 1912 and the Paterson strike of 1913, and kept the Northwest in a state of unrest. Their revolutionary language and violent methods eventually aroused the hostility of the public and inclined it to condone the lawless and extra-legal methods employed by communities in their efforts to rid themselves of this group. The opposition of the I.W.W. to the war in 1914 brought them into direct hostility to the government, which further curtailed their operations. Although its members at the height of its activity in 1917 probably did not number more than 75,000, the lack of numbers was counterbalanced by the enthusiasm and revolutionary ardor of its members. In the years after the war its members were largely absorbed in the Communist party.

Before going further it may be well to note briefly certain criticisms of labor unions. The hostility of the public to a revolutionary organization of the I.W.W. type is easily understandable. But the American Federation of Labor, and in more recent years, the Congress of Industrial Organizations, profess to be neither radical nor socialist, so that the attack proceeds from a different angle. Many critics have assailed labor unions on the grounds of "authorized practices that destroy efficiency, limit output, increase costs enormously, produce a labor monopoly,"[26] and this arraignment undoubtedly includes the chief counts brought against them. The unions are ac cused of so minutely prescribing the amount of work to be done by their members and the manner in which the job shall be carried on, and of so arbitrarily limiting membership, as to show an utter indifference to other workmen and to the public welfare amounting almost to a conspiracy against society. The classic examples of this evil, it is pointed out, are found in the building trade, one of the great basic industries, where regional disputes, limitation of output, and arbitrary rules of all kinds are sometimes carried to absurd and dangerous extremes. Labor has also been bitterly criticized because of certain unscrupulous leaders who have used their power to rob both workers and employers. Although this type of racketeer

[26] F. L. Bullard, "Labor Unions at the Danger Line," *Atlantic Monthly,* Vol. CXXVI, No. 6 (Dec., 1923).

is rare, enough of them have operated, particularly during the 1920's, to injure the reputation of a great and fundamentally honest movement.

LABOR AND POLITICS

As soon as the franchise was extended downward far enough to include the wage earners, it was inevitable that the demands of labor would become intertwined with politics. This was true of the first labor movement of the 1820's and 1830's, but inadequate facilities for communication, as well as the localization of manufacturing, prevented this first political effort from becoming national in scope. Workingmen's parties, nevertheless, were formed in New York State and workingmen's candidates presented themselves in Philadelphia, New England, and elsewhere. The depression following the panic of 1837 interrupted the political activities of labor, and until after the Civil War its efforts were directed along other channels.[27]

Although a Labor Reform party entered a presidential candidate in 1872, the radical labor vote during the next few years was absorbed in the Greenback party, which in 1878 coalesced with the Labor Reform group. The Greenback platform, in addition to its views on currency reform, included demands for the regulation of interstate commerce, a graduated income tax, prohibition of the importation of contract labor, and labor legislation. The support of the Greenbackers in 1880 and 1884 was drawn chiefly from the western farmers and eastern labor; the party disappeared in the election of 1888 and its place was taken by the Union Labor party which drew its vote chiefly from the West and South. The strongest and most radical of the early third parties was the Populist or People's party, which polled over a million votes in 1892 on a platform which included free coinage of silver, a graduated income tax, postal savings banks, and the government ownership of railways, telegraphs, and telephones. Their convention declared itself in sympathy "with organized workingmen to shorten hours of labor" and maintained that "the interests of rural and city labor are the same, their enemies identical." This effort to tie up the political interests of the farmer and city laborer, which extended even to the Farmer-Labor party of 1920, the Progressive party of 1924, and subsequent left-wing efforts, is one of the most persistent and interesting developments in American political history.

With the passing of the Populist party and the growing strength of the American Federation of Labor, organized labor has been less ready to embark officially in politics. Samuel Gompers during his thirty-five years of control persistently and successfully opposed the formation of a distinct labor party, and his successor, William Green, has pursued the same policy. Nevertheless, this policy of the Federation has been under the continued

[27] Above, pp. 314–315.

fire of the radicals, some of whom insist upon independent political action, while others would secure from that body its endorsement of socialism. Daniel DeLeon, the early intellectual leader of the labor group, attempted unsuccessfully in the 'eighties to induce both the Knights of Labor and the American Federation of Labor to join the nucleus of a Socialist party. Failing in this, he organized rival bodies[28] and became the dominant figure in the Socialist Labor party. This party, however, never became strong and was pushed into the background after 1898 by the Social Democratic party (later called the Socialist party) led by Eugene V. Debs and Victor Berger. Although the Socialist party undoubtedly received considerable backing from the liberal bourgeoisie, the large proportion of its votes must have come from labor. The fact that its popular standard-bearer, Debs, received over 901,000 votes in 1912 and 919,000 in 1920[29] shows that up to that time, in reality, a labor party was already in existence that might have become exceedingly powerful if it had officially received trade union support.

The failure to work through a distinct labor-party movement does not mean that the labor unions hesitate to throw their political influence where it may be of the most benefit. Holding the balance of power in numerous instances, they have been able to elect candidates friendly to labor, and by aggressive lobbying have influenced much labor legislation. Furthermore, the American Federation has not hesitated to take an official stand on issues involving political action; it has endorsed proposals for the initiative, the referendum, and the recall, the direct election of Senators, woman suffrage, government ownership or regulation of public utilities, restriction of immigration, the establishment of state and national labor bureaus and a national department of education, abolition of child labor, and all manner of legislation protecting the life, health, and future of the worker.

Although the "full dinner pail" argument which the Republicans have advanced to reconcile workmen to the Republican party has been powerful, labor in general has been inclined to divide its vote among opposing parties. When the Democratic organization in 1896 absorbed the Populist party and at the same time severely criticized the Supreme Court decision on the income tax and the use of the injunction, the appeal to labor was strong. In 1908 labor appealed to both conventions for an anti-injunction plank. The "Republican reactionists," said Gompers, "told Labor to go to Denver," where the Democrats were to meet.[30] There the Democratic party put itself on record as opposed to the use of injunctions in labor disputes, and after that Gompers and other leaders worked unofficially but openly for both

[28] First the Socialist Trade and Alliance, and years later the I.W.W.

[29] The votes in 1920 were cast for Debs in spite of the fact that he was in prison at the time for alleged violation of the Espionage Act.

[30] Samuel Gompers, *Seventy Years of Life and Labor*, II, 202.

Bryan and Wilson. Through the medium of this party two of their greatest legislative victories were obtained—the Adamson Act and the Clayton Act. In 1924 labor momentarily deserted its time-honored policy when the A. F. of L. officially endorsed its lifelong friend, La Follette, but it has since reaffirmed its earlier policy. Even in recent years this official neutrality has been maintained, although it is clear that labor as a whole has supported the Democratic party and the "New Deal."

LABOR AND THE COURTS

While the wage earner has been able to influence state and national legislatures and to make distinct progress in his dealings with his employer, his experience with the judiciary has not been so fortunate. Under the American system of checks and balances, in which a judiciary (by its very nature conservative and not representative of the working class) passes on the constitutionality of legislation, it is not at all surprising that progress has been slow. Labor has had to struggle not only against a conservative judiciary but also against legal theories and economic philosophies whose origin antedated the Industrial Revolution.

Labor unions had scarcely been formed before they were haled into court on the ground that, in the absence of a statute or legislation on the point, the old common law of England applied in America, and a combination of workmen to raise wages was a conspiracy against the public and, as such, illegal. Decisions during the first two decades of the nineteenth century were generally against the workmen, but gradually the attitude of the courts shifted. Mere combining was no longer taken as conspiracy, and the judiciary now directed its attention rather to the methods employed by the unions to gain their ends. For years, however, the right to strike, to boycott, and to picket was questioned in the courts.

The fifth amendment to the Constitution asserted that no one could be "deprived of life, liberty, or property without due process of law," and most of the state constitutions contain similar statements. The idea was again incorporated in the first section of the fourteenth amendment when the same restrictions were placed upon the states. Although Justice Holmes once asserted that this amendment did not write *laissez faire* or any other economic doctrine into the Constitution, his belief was not generally held by the sturdy exponents of that economic doctrine, who interpreted many labor laws as an infringement of liberty, an abridgment of contract, or class legislation. With such a background, it is not surprising that many labor laws have been declared unconstitutional. Legislation which has come under the ban of the courts at various times includes laws fixing the hours of labor engaged on public works, laws designed to protect the health of adult male workers by limiting the hours of labor in private industries, laws prohibiting the payment of wages in scrip or the enforced dealing at company stores, laws prohibiting the manufacture of such commodities as cigars in tenement houses, laws forbidding employers from holding back wages, workingmen's compensation laws, and minimum-wage laws. To many observers the courts have seemed to stretch their ingenuity to the limit to hamper organized labor. The use of picketing has been narrowly restricted;[31] laws to prevent an employer from discharging a man on account of membership in a union have been thrown out;[32] laws forbidding an employer to compel a worker to sign a non-union card ("yellow-dog contract") have been set aside;[33] and at the same time unions have been enjoined from inducing workers who have signed such a contract to join a union.[34] In fact, almost every type of social legislation or laws protecting union activities has at some time or other been held unconstitutional.

Notwithstanding the long list of adverse decisions, labor has been insistent in affirming the constitutionality of labor legislation under the police power given the state to look after the health and safety of the people. This power has been generally, although not always, upheld by the courts in the case of laws governing the hours and conditions of work of women, and the position of guardian which the state maintains toward children has allowed protective legislation for minors. In the case of adult males there has been much judicial interpretation. Where the laws have obviously been designed to protect the health and safety of the community, such as those limiting the hours of employment on public carriers, they have generally been upheld. In the case of laws governing hours of labor in private industries intended to protect not so much the safety of the public as the health and safety of the workers, the courts have been more dilatory. In 1895, for example, the Illinois supreme court declared unconstitutional an eight-hour day for women;[35] the Colorado supreme court in 1899 acted similarly on an eight-hour law for the smelting industry as "an unwarrantable interference with the right of both the employer and employee in making contracts";[36] the United States Supreme Court in 1905 declared the Lochner ten-hour law fixing the hours of work in bakeshops in New York as one which "reached and passed the limit of police power";[37] the New York supreme court in 1907 nullified a law prohibiting night work for women,[38]

[31] Truax *v.* Corrigan, 257 U. S. 312 (1921).
[32] Adair *v.* U. S., 208 U. S. 161 (1908).
[33] Coppage *v.* Kansas, 236 U. S. 1 (1915).
[34] Hichman Coal & Coke Co. *v.* Mitchell, 245 U. S. 229 (1917).
[35] Ritchie *v.* People, 155 Ill. 98 (1895).
[36] *In re* Morgan, 26 Colo. 415; 58 Pacific 1071 (1899).
[37] Lochner *v.* New York, 198 U. S. 45 (1905).
[38] People *v.* Williams, 189 N. Y. 131 (1907).

and as late as 1923 the United States Supreme Court declared a minimum wage law in the District of Columbia unconstitutional.[39]

Eventually through the insistence of progressive public sentiment there has been a reversal of earlier decisions, and there is now little doubt of the right of a state to regulate hours of labor under the police power.[40] Legislation respecting safety and sanitation in factories is now generally held to be constitutional, and the courts have come to be more liberal in rewriting the old common law and in placing more responsibility upon employers in case of accident. Less success has been experienced with laws aimed to control methods of wage payment.

The national government's control over interstate commerce has aroused hope that something might be accomplished here. In 1913 a separate Cabinet department was created for labor; in 1914 an effort was made in the Clayton Act to exempt labor unions from prosecution as conspiracies in restraint of trade; in 1915 the La Follette Seaman's Act went far to insure decent conditions for American sailors. The Adamson Act of 1916, which provided for a basic eight-hour day on interstate carriers, was a great victory and was upheld by the Supreme Court.[41] On the other hand, the Keating-Owen Bill, which was passed in 1916 to prohibit interstate commerce in the products of children under sixteen, was declared unconstitutional in 1918,[42] and an attempt in 1919 to accomplish the same object by the imposition of a 10 per cent tax on the net profits of factories employing children under fourteen years of age met the same fate (May 18, 1922).[43]

No judicial activity has been so bitterly opposed by labor as the use of the injunction in labor disputes.[44] Designed originally as a powerful weapon in the hand of the crown to be employed only rarely against threatened lawlessness and riotous outbreaks, in recent years in America it has come

---

[39] Adkins v. Children's Hospital, 261 U. S. 525 (1923).

[40] Holden v. Hardy, 169 U. S. 366 (1898); Bunting v. Oregon, 243 U. S. 240 (1917); Ritchie v. Wayman, 244 Ill. 509 (1910); People v. Charles Schweinler Press, 214 N. Y. 395 (1915).

[41] Wilson v. New, 243 U. S. 322 (1917).

[42] Hammer v. Dagenhart, 247 U. S. 251 (1918).

[43] Bailey v. Drexel Furniture Company, 259 U. S. 20 (1922).

[44] "An injunction," says Professor Watkins (*An Introduction to the Study of Labor Problems*, p. 324), "is an order issued by a court of equity for purpose of preventing injury to a person or property or of preserving the existing conditions until the final determination of rights." In theory it is an extraordinary expedient, to be used when property and personal rights are imperiled, and when there are no other remedies at law adequate to meet the emergency. A violation of an injunction is punished as contempt of court without jury trial and may involve fine or imprisonment. In earlier years the injunction was used by the courts only in extraordinary situations. In recent years it has become a common instrument in labor cases. The development of the free use of the injunction has a twofold significance. In the first place, it has enormously increased the power of the judiciary. In the second place, the original theory of the injunction has been strained greatly to fit labor cases, and has been developed chiefly as a weapon to be used against labor.

to be used quite commonly by the courts to limit the activity of labor during strikes. The imprisonment of Eugene V. Debs for violating a federal injunction during the Pullman strike of 1894, and the sentencing to prison of Gompers, Mitchell, and Morrison for ignoring the Buck Stove and Range injunction, are two striking incidents in the more or less free use made of this instrument. "Government by injunction" has been denounced as a one-sided and unjust use of power, and labor succeeded in writing into the Clayton Act of 1914 a clause which prohibits the use of restraining injunctions in cases between employers and employees "unless necessary to prevent irreparable injury to property, or to a property right, of the party making the application, for which injury there is no adequate remedy at law." As might be expected from the looseness of the phraseology of this prohibition, little actual change was effected. In 1932 a federal anti-injunction Act (Norris LaGuardia Act) again prohibited labor injunctions in federal courts as well as prohibiting the use of "yellow-dog contracts."

PROGRESS OF THE WAGE EARNERS

Although the income of the great majority of wage earners continues to be inadequate to maintain a proper standard of living, it is undoubtedly true that distinct progress has been made along certain lines vital to labor. During the Civil War prices rose faster than wages, but at its conclusion real wages were not far below the level of 1861. After the war, prices declined, but wages tended to remain near the point of 1865; between that year and 1890 real wages rose more than 100 per cent in industry and 70 per cent in agriculture. From 1897 to 1914 wages continued to advance, but hardly as rapidly as prices, with the result that during these years the wage earner actually lost ground as far as real wages were concerned. The same was true during the period of World War I, although from 1920 to 1929 there appears to have been a distinct advance in real wages.[45] The problem of labor income and real wages is, of course, significant, for it immediately raises the question whether labor is receiving its fair share in the increase of wealth due to the unprecedented productivity of the nation's industries.

On the other hand, it should be pointed out that real wages tell only part of the story of the condition of the working classes. It is possible for real wages to decline, as they probably did from 1897 to 1919, and for a group still to improve greatly its standard of living. Through public works and charity a certain portion of the national income may find its way back to the people as a whole; likewise, inventions of various kinds and labor-saving devices may become available for the masses through large-scale

[45] Below, pp. 586 ff., 599 f.

cheap production. Furthermore, social legislation may improve the conditions of work. Real progress, for example, was made in decreasing the length of the working day. Operatives in cotton mills in the 'forties sometimes worked thirteen and fourteen hours. By 1860 the average day for all labor was eleven hours—this after an agitation for a ten-hour day which extended

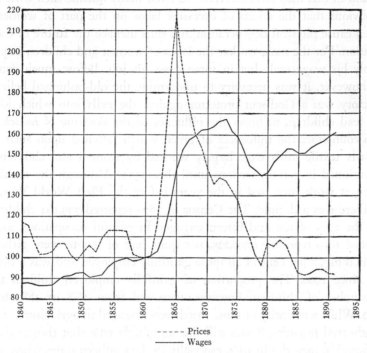

WAGES AND PRICES, 1840-1891. [46]

over thirty years. Though inadequate, the best figures obtainable for the period 1840–1890 are from the Aldrich Report; this gives the average in 1844 at eleven and one-half hours a day, in 1865 eleven, with a gradual reduction until 1890, when the average was ten hours. Since its organization the American Federation of Labor has steadily advocated the eight-hour day. This with a Saturday half holiday, making a forty-four-hour week, has been the great demand of labor. In some of the highly organized industries this has been achieved by the unions,[47] and in certain hazardous occupations by legal enactment. Beginning with Utah in 1896, thirty states by 1916 had placed an eight-hour day for miners upon the statute books. Some impetus was given to the movement by a law passed by Congress in 1892 providing

[46] Statistical Abstract, 1899, p. 92, and ibid., 1921, p. 854.

[47] In the 1930's, in an effort to check the evils of the speed-up and to spread the available work, a number of unions agitated for and obtained the six-hour day.

for an eight-hour day for government employees. During the First World War the labor shortage gave momentum to this demand, and a majority of trades using skilled labor worked under this schedule.

Organized labor and certain liberal middle-class organizations[48] have fought strenuously against the exploitation of the labor of women and children, and in this they have received aid from many outside their own ranks. It is obvious that the effects of excessive labor on the part of women and children cause physical degeneration and thus menace the future of the race and nation. For the male worker the labor of women and children imperiled not only his wage scale but in some cases his job. Before much could be done, however, it was necessary to undermine the old-fashioned belief that the factory was a God-sent protector against the evils into which idleness might lead children, to break the influence of the doctrine of *laissez faire,* and to counteract the influences of greed which fattened upon such labor. The early textile mills were largely worked by women and children, and this continued in certain sections until the 1930's. Although the number of children at work increased in the years before the First World War, relatively there was a decline. The Census of 1870 reported 739,164 children between the ages of ten and fifteen engaged in gainful occupations, and the Census of 1910 reported 1,990,225, not quite half of whom were girls. This amounted to 5.2 per cent of all those gainfully employed and was a decrease of 0.8 since 1900. The proportion of gainfully employed children to the total number of children, however, increased from 16.8 in 1880 to 18.8 in 1910. While a majority of those listed were engaged in agriculture or other non-industrial pursuits, it was still discouragingly true that thousands were to be found in factories in 1914, especially in the southern states where northern capital has built large textile mills. It is true that agricultural labor up to a certain extent may not be physically deleterious to a child of immature years, but this can hardly be said of factory or sweatshop work. Certainly the reports of conditions of child labor throughout the nation were bad enough during these years to shame the most callous government into action.[49]

Attempts to do away with child labor have taken the form of laws limiting the working hours, setting an age limit below which children may not be gainfully employed, prohibiting night work, and providing for compulsory education. Legislation in regard to child labor started in Massachusetts in 1836, when a law was passed regulating the instruction of children

---

[48] Such as the National Consumers League, founded in 1899, and the National Child Labor Committee (1904).

[49] See John Spargo, *The Bitter Cry of the Children* (1906); Mrs. John Van Vorst. *The Cry of the Children* (1908), and such government bulletins as "Child Labor in Canneries," *Child Labor Bulletin,* Vol. I, No. 4 (Feb., 1913).

employed in manufacturing establishments. In 1842 the working day for children under twelve was limited to ten hours (considered a great advance!), and acts of 1866 and 1867 forbade the employment of any child under sixteen for more than sixty hours a week. In 1873 the length of the school year was extended to twenty weeks and the age of attendance to twelve years, and ten years later all towns of more than 10,000 population were compelled to establish evening schools. A law of 1888 excluded children under thirteen from factories, workshops, and mercantile establishments, and those under fourteen except during vacation; other indoor work was forbidden children under thirteen unless they had attended school twenty weeks. The age of compulsory attendance was raised in 1889 to fourteen years and the school year to thirty weeks. In this hesitating manner Massachusetts, a state always in the forefront of labor legislation, has tackled the evil of child labor, and by much the same methods other states have taken up the problem. Although as late as 1914 six states (all in the South) had no laws making school attendance compulsory, all the states had some form of child labor legislation on the statute books by the 1930's. In 1914 the minimum age of lawful employment varied from twelve to fourteen years, depending on the economic background and the social consciousness of the states. New Mexico, for example, had no law except one prohibiting children under fourteen from working in mines; in Utah and Wyoming only mines and dangerous occupations were forbidden to children; and in four of the southern states there was no minimum age for employment in stores. With few exceptions, the states now limit the working day of a child under sixteen to eight hours, and the majority of the states and the District of Columbia prohibit night work. Laws of this nature, combined with vigorously enforced legislation for compulsory education and with appropriate penalties for infringement, are necessary to eliminate this curse. Child labor has been most common in the families of newly arrived immigrants and among the poor whites of certain sections of the South, where economic pressure was sufficient in many cases to cause the parents to cooperate with the employer in ignoring existing laws.[50]

Aroused by the agitation against child labor during the early years of the century, the federal government also engaged in the battle. In 1912 Congress added a Children's Bureau to the Department of Labor and at various times passed legislation to ban child labor in the District of Columbia. In 1916 and again in 1919, as we have pointed out, Congress attempted to curtail child labor throughout the nation, only to have the laws declared unconstitutional

[50] A summary of child-labor laws, as they existed in 1933 is given in Publication 197, *Child Labor Facts and Figures* (revised to October, 1933), published by the Children's Bureau of the Department of Labor.

by the Supreme Court.[51] To overcome this check, a constitutional amendment to permit the prohibition of child labor under eighteen was submitted to the states in 1924, but only twenty-eight had ratified it by the end of 1941. However, certain New Deal legislation, including the National Industrial Recovery Act, the Walsh Healey Government Contracts Act, and the Fair Labor Standards Act, has sought to accomplish this purpose.[52] Since the constitutionality of the last Act has been upheld, child labor in industry may be ended whether or not the amendment is ratified.

The factory system and other results of the Industrial Revolution have thrown open to women innumerable new opportunities to earn a livelihood. Many of the old home occupations, such as cloth making, soap making, and fruit and meat preserving, have passed to the factory and women have followed. Usually unorganized, often living at home and looking upon their work as temporary, they have been subject, like children, to economic exploitation. They have been particularly the victims of the "sweated industries," where work is contracted out to be done in the home. In recent years the number of women employed outside the home has increased faster than the total population, but the advance has come in middle-class occupational groups rather than among factory workers. Also noticeable is a relative decline in the number of women employed in such traditionally feminine occupations as waitresses, general servants, and seamstresses. The number of women engaged in manufacturing industries in 1914 was 1,500,-000 and in 1930 about 1,886,000.

The two great evils attendant upon the employment of women which legislation has attempted to mitigate are insufficient pay and physical injury, both of which may have deleterious effects extending to society as a whole. The feeling has gradually spread that women, like children, need the protection of the state, and especially that their physical well-being as mothers of future citizens is a concern of society. In certain of the states commissions have been instituted to study the cost of living and to decide upon minimum wage scales, which in some cases are compulsory. The first minimum wage law in the country was passed in Massachusetts in 1912. Although the First World War drew thousands of women into industry under supposedly advantageous circumstances, many students in close touch with labor conditions believe that the wages of women relative to those received by men were hardly bettered. Of 117 plants investigated in 1919 in New York State, 29 paid women less than $12 a week, and 69 less than $14.[53] The Consumers' League in 1919 claimed, on the basis of sta-

---

[51] Above, p. 475.

[52] Below, pp. 668, 675–676.

[53] *The Industrial Replacement of Men by Women.* Bulletin issued by the Industrial Commission of New York, March, 1919.

tistics compiled by the U. S. Bureau of Labor Statistics, that only one out of fourteen industries in New York City which employed large numbers of women paid a living wage.[54] While it is true that women are still underpaid in most occupations, the conditions under which they work have been bettered. Numerous laws improving factory conditions have been passed; practically all the states limit the hours of labor for women, and several have laws that prohibit night work.

Although the percentage of accidents among workmen is larger in the United States than in any of the great industrial nations, we have been the last to recognize that these accidents should be borne by industry rather than wholly by the workman. Until within the last few years the law worked on the theory that responsibility for an accident could be placed upon some person and he must bear the loss. This responsibility was almost always placed upon labor rather than capital, on the ground that the workman knew the risk he must run if he accepted a job, or that the accident was caused by contributory negligence on his part or that of a fellow worker. If the employer could prove that he had exercised reasonable precautions, he was ordinarily relieved of responsibility.

Eventually the point of view of society changed. It was realized that the old common law which might have fitted conditions before the Industrial Revolution was no longer adequate. Under modern conditions it became impossible to prove anyone's negligence in many accidents; obviously they were due to the inevitable risks of industry. In reality, industry was the guilty party, not the workman. Following in the footsteps of Germany (1884) and England (1897), various American states, beginning with Maryland in 1902, began to pass workingmen's compensation acts. The first compensation laws of Maryland (1902), Montana (1909), and New York (1910) were declared unconstitutional, but after 1911 laws were framed which stood the tests of the courts. By 1942 all the states but Mississippi, together with the territories of Alaska, Hawaii, and Puerto Rico had workingmen's compensation laws, as did the Philippine Islands, the District of Columbia, and the United States government for its civilian employees. Most of these laws, besides cutting away the old common-law defenses of the employer, provide (1) for the payment, in case of death or permanent disability, of a maximum amount in weekly allotments extending over a period of from 300 to 500 weeks, (2) in the case of temporary disability the payment of doctors' bills and for a certain period a percentage of the regular wages, and (3) in the case of certain specified industries the pay-

---

[54] *Survey*, April 17, 1920. The percentage for the entire state was even more striking. "Nineteen per cent of the workers received less than $11 a week, 71 per cent received less than $14, and 88 per cent received less than $16."

ment of a fixed lump sum. Usually agricultural laborers and domestic servants are excluded, as are commonly those employed in establishments that hire less than five men. Provisions for the payments required by the law are usually met by some form of insurance, either through state or private companies. It is now decidedly to the advantage of the employer as well as the employee to avoid accidents, and the salutary effect of these laws is increasingly evident. As a rule, their operation is supervised by special tribunals which pass on the claims for compensation. The widespread adoption of workingmen's compensation was probably the greatest legislative victory won by labor during the years just prior to the First World War.

Progress is evidenced not only by these laws protecting women and children and providing for workingmen's compensation, but also by other important pieces of social legislation designed to ameliorate conditions of work and to raise the standard of living of the wage earners. Their children have better milk as the result of city or state laws, playgrounds in the cities, medical inspection in the schools, and improved education. Better tenement house laws have improved their living quarters, and better-lighted and more sanitary factories, in part resulting from state legislation and in part from efforts on the part of management to achieve greater production, have made their working hours easier. Initial steps have been taken for mothers' pensions, and before 1914 there was active propaganda for sickness and unemployment insurance and for old age pensions.

IMMIGRATION

Closely allied with the labor problem but containing elements of significance to all phases of our political, social, and economic life, is the problem of immigration. Between 1860 and 1920 close to 28,500,000 foreigners sought our shores to enter our labor force permanently or temporarily, a number almost equal to the total population of the country in 1850. This incoming tide of labor as it rose and fell corresponded quite closely with the periods of prosperity and depression. Thus we find the peak years in 1873 with 459,803 arrivals, in 1882 with 788,922, in 1892 with 579,663, in 1907 with 1,285,349, and in 1914 with 1,218,420. While in actual numbers immigration increased in each decade up to the opening of the First World War, emigration and the normal growth of population kept the proportion of foreign-born to the whole population at about 14 per cent; it was slightly under this in 1860, and slightly over in 1910.

As before the Civil War, the hope of economic betterment or the desire for greater political and religious freedom has been the compelling motive in the minds of the immigrants themselves. Nevertheless, the impetus has been partially supplied from without. Professor Commons is of the opinion that "the desire to get cheap labor, to take in passenger fares, and to sell land have probably brought more immigrants than the hard conditions of Europe, Asia, and Africa have sent." [56] Capital seeking renewed supplies of

IMMIGRATION INTO THE UNITED STATES, 1860–1939.[55]

cheap labor and land-grant railroads desirous of peopling their territory and selling their real estate have cooperated with steamship companies in scouring Europe for prospective immigrants.[57] Until recent years, relatives and friends in America in at least one-fourth of the cases sent back the cost of transporation. Emigration ceased to be a hazardous undertaking limited to the strong and self-reliant. As emigration from Europe became easier, the type of immigrant changed. Up to 1896 Great Britain, Ireland, and Germany contributed the greater number—aggressive and forceful men, and often skilled artisans and farmers, not radically different in blood and characteristics from the people already here. During the decade 1851–1860 these three countries sent 88 per cent of the immigrants, while Austria-Hungary, Italy, Russia, and Poland sent .4 of one per cent. In 1891–1910 the above three northern European nations sent 31.6 per cent, while the four nations in southern and eastern Europe furnished over 50 per cent. By the latter date the "new immigration" constituted over four-fifths of the total. This flow from southeastern Europe brought a different type, hard-working

[55] *Statistical Abstract, 1921,* p. 883; *ibid., 1940,* p. 99.
[56] J. R. Commons, *Races and Immigrants in America,* p. 108.
[57] Above, p. 370.

and thrifty to be sure, but generally unskilled and accustomed to political and economic autocracy.

Opposition to immigration came from two sources: (1) a large part of organized and unorganized labor, who held that the continued inflow of cheap labor kept wages low and prevented a rise in the standard of living; and (2) many ardent Americans who believed that ideals and standards were being jeopardized by a too rapid addition to the "melting pot" of those who did not readily "melt." On the other hand, the advocates of comparatively easy immigration laws were represented until the First World War by capital, which argued that a continued supply of cheap labor was necessary to develop the nation's resources and to fill the jobs avoided by the native American. For this contention there was much to be said, for without doubt our economic structure has been reared to no small extent upon the rough labor of newly arrived immigrants. Yet it was a question whether tireless hunt for cheaper and cheaper labor was not bringing undesirable accessions to our shores more rapidly than they could be absorbed. That it is possible to maintain industry without fresh supplies of labor from abroad, even during periods of great demand, was proved during the First World War; the widespread unemployment in times of depression hardly bespeaks the need of a greater labor force. Cheap labor is usually the most expensive in the long run, and it is quite probable that the nation might profit more by being forced to develop greater efficiency in the labor that is here than by importing unskilled and consequently low-paid wage earners.

Until recently, whatever restrictions were put on immigration were due to the demands of labor. A number of Acts culminating in 1882 finally prohibited Chinese immigration, and subsequent agreements with Japan aimed at a similar exclusion of her citizens. With the Act of 1882 the first step in federal control of immigration was taken. It placed a head tax of fifty cents on those entering, excluded certain undesirable classes of aliens, and provided for cooperation between the states and the federal government in the enforcement of the Act. Under the influence of the Knights of Labor, laws were enacted in 1885 and 1889 prohibiting bringing over immigrants under contract to labor; these laws were generally evaded. The office which corresponds to the present Commissioner-General of Immigration was created in 1891. In the Acts of 1891, 1893, 1907, and 1917 the policy was developed to exclude those morally, mentally, and physically unfit, and those afflicted with physical and mental diseases; vagrants, paupers, anarchists, and contract laborers are also debarred. For bringing in immigrants illegally, steamship companies are liable to fine and to the necessity of returning them, nor may they encourage or solicit immigrants. In an effort to devise new methods of exclusion Congress enacted a literacy test but it was vetoed by Cleveland, Taft, and Wilson. Finally in 1917 such a test was passed over Wilson's veto. As a result of war conditions and because of apprehension that we might be deluged by an inflow from the war-torn nations of Europe, agitation for further restriction was strong at the conclusion of World War I. Not only labor but the general public, particularly many organizations who posed as super-patriotic, favored restriction, and the 1920's saw a determined and successful effort to restrict radically the flow of alien immigrants.[58]

SELECTED READINGS

Daugherty, C. R., *Labor Problems in American Industry,* Chaps. XVI–XVIII.

Lorwin, L. L., *The American Federation of Labor.*

Ware, N. J., *The Labor Movement in the United States,* Chaps. I–IX.

Brissenden, P. F., *The I.W.W., a Study in American Syndicalism,* Chaps. I–V.

Fitch, J. A., *The Causes of Industrial Unrest,* Chaps. II–V.

Parker, C. H., *The Casual Laborer and Other Essays,* Chaps. II–III.

Berman, Edward, *Labor and the Sherman Act.*

Faulkner, H. U., *The Quest for Social Justice,* Chap. III.

Flügel, F., and Faulkner, H. U., *Readings in the Economic and Social History of the United States,* Chap. XVIII.

[58] Below, pp. 636–637.

23

Development of Transportation and Communication, 1860–1914

Rapid Railroad Expansion

THE importance of railroad expansion in American history in the half century after 1860 can hardly be overestimated. Our industrial and agricultural development was dependent upon internal transportation, of which the major part was furnished by the railroad. The very settlement of large sections of the West was promoted by the railroads, built in many instances through unoccupied regions with the settlers following in their wake. In 1860 the railroad mileage amounted to 30,625, most of which had been constructed in the prosperous years preceding the panic of 1857. The effect of the Civil War upon the railroads was both disastrous and stimulating. While the rolling stock and other equipment in the South either depreciated or was destroyed, the war spurred the North to fresh construction.[1] It was during the midst of the conflict and partially as a war measure that the first transcontinental railroad was commenced. Most of the construction during the decade, however, came after 1865, the mileage in 1870 amounting to 52,922.

In the succeeding decades the increase was rapid and, except in periods of acute depression, continuous. Thirty-three thousand miles were built between 1867 and 1873, before the first great spurt had played itself out and the panic temporarily halted further construction. The panic of 1873 was itself partly attributable to overbuilding and overcapitalization of railroads. The period from 1860 to 1875 witnessed not only the construction of the first transcontinental line, but also the extension of five great railroads from the Atlantic seaboard to Chicago—the New York Central, the Pennsylvania, the Erie, the Baltimore and Ohio, and the Grand Trunk. After the recovery from the depression, the country entered another phenomenal period of railroad growth. The mileage in 1880, totaling 93,261, rose to 167,191 in 1890 —an increase of over 70,000 miles in one decade. The panic of 1893 again

---

[1] Above, p. 348.

Freight Transportation by Land—A Conestoga Wagon.

The "DeWitt Clinton"—First Railroad Train in New York.

Engines of the Civil War Days. Railroad Yards, City Point, Virginia, October 21, 1864.

Meeting of a Local Grange in the Early 1870's at the Height of the Agrarian Crusade.

Anti-Railroad Cartoon of the 1870's.

Wheat Threshing, Cheyenne County, Nebraska, About 1900.

Culver Service

Thirty Horses Pulling a Combine, Harvesting Wheat in the Northwest.

Communication on Lower Broadway, 1889.

New York's New Elevated Railroad, 1887.

America's New Labor Force—A Group of New Arrivals at Ellis Island Early
in the Twentieth Century.

Labor in the Textile Mills Was Largely Women and Children. Picture
Taken About 1900.

hampered construction, but it picked up in the prosperous years after 1898, and for twelve years thereafter new mileage averaged 5000 a year (2 per cent annual increase). Railroad miles in operation amounted in 1900 to 198,964; in 1910 to 249,992; and in 1920 to 263,821. This growth far exceeded that of

MILES OF RAILROAD IN OPERATION, 1850–1939.[2]

the population; since the Civil War the population has trebled, whereas railroad mileage has grown eightfold. In 1860 there was one mile of road to every 1087 people; in 1880 one mile to every 571, and in 1920 one mile to every 417. In 1914 the United States boasted of more mileage than all Europe, and more than one-third that of the entire world.

On the other hand, by 1914 the country seemed to have approached a point of saturation. While the average construction was over 3000 miles a year between 1910 and 1913, it declined rapidly thereafter until in 1920 only 314 miles were built. Between 1916 and 1920 more mileage was abandoned than built, and this tendency has continued to the present time.[3] Many causes have contributed: (1) the competition of gasoline motor traffic, (2) economies of war time, (3) low railroad profits and the precarious financial condition of many of the roads, which have suffered in the adjustments to

[2] *Statistical Abstract, 1940,* p. 424.
[3] Mileage, which reached the high point of 266,381 in 1916, dropped to 249,826 in 1938. Railroads reported the abandonment of 1299 miles in 1940 and 1509 miles in 1941, the tenth consecutive year that abandonment has exceeded 1000 miles.

higher costs, (4) the approach to the saturation point. During the decade 1920–1930 the weak roads exerted all their efforts to keep alive, while the prosperous companies improved their equipment rather than lengthened their lines.

The economic significance of railroads is far wider than merely that of transportation. It is impossible to gauge the social significance of facilities which have tended to break down rural isolation and link up the benefits of city and country. In our financial system railroad securities for decades were the most important single group and formed an integral part of the activities of the investment market and the credit world. In 1921 the railroads were capitalized (par value of stocks and bonds) at $21,891,450,785 and valued in 1920 by the Interstate Commerce Commission at $18,900,000,000. Ten years later the Commission set the valuation as of December 31, 1930, at $21,691,000,000, and the net book value at $23,518,000,000. It can be reasonably deduced from available figures that the capital tied up in rail transportation before the First World War constituted probably about one-tenth of the total wealth of the nation, estimated in 1912 at $187,739,071,090. In 1910 the railroads furnished employment to 1,700,000 persons, 4.4 per cent of the gainfully employed.

THE TRANSCONTINENTAL ROADS

The idea of a transcontinental railroad seems to have originated in the lure of Oriental trade, but the discovery of gold in California in 1848 and the rapid settlement of that region gave the idea great impetus and led Congress in 1853 to provide for a survey of possible routes from the Mississippi to the Pacific.[4] The exigencies of the Civil War, political and military as well as economic, led eventually to the construction of the first line. The Union Pacific Railroad Company was created by Congress in 1862 for the purpose of building a road from Nebraska west to California; and the Central Pacific, under the leadership of Leland Stanford, Collis P. Huntington, and other famous railroad men, was organized to build from the Pacific coast eastward to meet the Union Pacific. Both railroads were granted subsidies of $16,000 a mile for construction on the level country, $48,000 a mile through the mountain ranges, and $32,000 for the sections between the ranges, the government taking a second lien on the property. Land grants of alternate sections contiguous to the railroads were offered in addition. Stimulated by loans and land grants and urged on by the great popular interest, both roads built frantically toward each other in the hope of obtaining as much

---

[4] In the East it was the merchant, Asa Whitney, who spent many years in agitating for such a road; in the West it was Theodore D. Judah who surveyed routes and interested the Sacramento merchants, Stanford, Huntington, Crocker, and Hopkins, in the project. Both died before the road was actually begun.

of the subsidy as possible. Neither expense, hostile Indians, nor the severity of the mountain winters were permitted to hold up the work. Twenty thousand men were laying two miles of track a day in the concluding weeks of an effort which brought the two roads together at Promontory Point, Utah, on May 10, 1869, where Leland Stanford drove the last spike of California gold while telegraph wires received the taps of the hammer and transmitted them to a rejoicing nation. The joining of these roads brought to its culmination the greatest transportation project in American history since the completion of the Erie Canal.

Hardly less romantic in its conception, but less successful in its immediate realization, was the effort to construct the Northern Pacific. Chartered by Congress in 1864 and subsidized with land grants larger than the combined area of the six New England States, it was finally begun in 1867 through the financing of Jay Cooke & Company. Five hundred miles had been built when the road was thrown into receivership by the failure of Jay Cooke. Eventually aggressive construction was resumed and, largely through the genius of Henry Villard, backed by German capital, the road was completed in 1883. The Atchison, Topeka, and Santa Fé obtained from the national government in 1863 a grant of 6400 acres for every mile built; but construction did not begin until 1869 and had proceeded no farther than the eastern boundary of Colorado when it was stopped by the panic of 1873. Construction was resumed in 1880, following in general the old Santa Fé Trail, and in 1884 the tracks reached the Pacific coast. In 1878 James J. Hill, a man who later became one of the greatest of railway executives, but at that time an unknown storekeeper in St. Paul, interested influential Canadians in a bankrupt little two-hundred-mile railroad without any apparent future, known as the St. Paul and Pacific and described as "a streak of rust running through a desert." The Canadian capitalists were interested in the road only as a link in the freight operations of the Hudson's Bay Company between the Mississippi and Winnipeg, but under Hill's direction it was pushed to the Pacific and developed into the Great Northern system. In the meantime the group who had built the Central Pacific began to consolidate various little railroads running south out of San Francisco and during the 'seventies pushed them through Arizona and New Mexico to El Paso, Texas, where in 1882 communication with the East was secured. By the middle 'eighties the chief lines to the Pacific had been constructed.

Financing and Government Aid

Not the least interesting phase in the history of American railroads is the story of their early financing, which can be merely touched upon here. The urgent need for internal transportation, the remarkable success of the

Erie Canal, sectional rivalries, and the scarcity of private capital were chief among the causes leading the states to finance many of the early projects. State aid was overdone and was brought to a disastrous close by the panic of 1837, an event which prevented what might have been a normal development in this country of state-owned transportation facilities. Thereafter, although government aid was rendered, particularly in the case of the transcontinental roads, the financing and management of internal transportation have been largely in the hands of private capital.

An appreciable share of the yearly surplus of wealth has been invested in railroads. The fundamental fact that transportation was essential to the building up of the nation was apparent, and nowhere was the American willingness to speculate on the country's progress better seen. But before private capital went into railroads, the government was expected to do much to make the way easy. Railroads were built under charters voted by the state legislatures; all of them contained valuable rights and concessions and many were obtained by corrupt means. The right of eminent domain—that is, the power to lay out a road and condemn the land needed if impossible to obtain it otherwise—was invariably granted. In certain cases a monopoly or protection against competition was conferred, as were special banking privileges to aid in raising money. Tax exemption was permitted in some charters forever, in others for a stated period, and in still others until the dividends should reach a certain percentage. On the other hand, even in these free-and-easy early railroad charters, sections were sometimes inserted providing for a reduction in rates when the dividends exceeded a normal yield. The attitude of the legislatures and the public was that transportation should be encouraged by every possible means, and the charters reflected this attitude. The charter having been secured, the railroad was built by money or credit obtained through national, state, county, municipal, or private subscriptions. National aid was rendered by (1) tariff remission on rails, (2) land grants, and (3) direct financial aid. Almost 200,000,000 acres were originally granted, but this was reduced to 137,000,000 by forfeitures resulting from inability to meet the requirements of the law. These land grants included one-fourth of the states of Minnesota and Washington; one-fifth of Wisconsin, Iowa, Kansas, North Dakota, and Montana; one-seventh of Nebraska, one-eighth of California, and one-ninth of Louisiana. In all, 242,000 square miles, a region larger than Germany or France, was given to the railroads. Of the individual donations, the Northern Pacific received 44,-000,000 acres, the Southern Pacific 24,000,000, the Union Pacific 20,000,000, the Santa Fé system 17,000,000. National bonds to the amount of $64,623,512 were also issued on the security of second mortgages to help certain of the transcontinental lines—loans eventually almost entirely repaid.

Aid on the part of the various states were rendered chiefly by (1) subscriptions to the capital stock, a method resorted to by a number of states; (2) the loan of state credit by such methods as direct purchase of railroad

LAND GRANTS TO TRANSCONTINENTAL RAILROADS

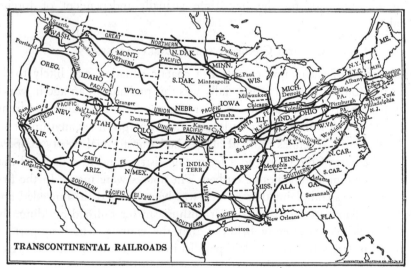

TRANSCONTINENTAL RAILROADS

bonds or endorsement of construction bonds; (3) state land grants; (4) bearing the expense of survey. Close to 55,000,000 acres were turned over by the states to transportation companies. Counties and municipalities followed the states in encouraging construction by subscribing for stock, by exchanging municipal or county bonds for railroad securities, or by actually donating money and land. In New York State 294 cities, towns, and villages contributed $29,978,206 to railroads, and 51 counties gave subsidies or amounts varying from $5000 to $3,000,000. In Massachusetts, 171 towns and cities had issued bonds to aid railroads up to 1871.[5] This public aid should not be forgotten in the subsequent discussion of railroad abuses and the demand for public regulation.

The sum total of these various aids, amounting in most cases to outright subsidies, was very large; nevertheless, private backing has been even greater. Two classes of speculators have purchased railroad securities—those buying for dividends and a market rise, and those buying to promote building through their own region. This latter group in their enthusiasm were glad to exchange labor, land, and money for stock which often proved worthless. A considerable amount of financing was done in Europe, where American transportation securities have been exceedingly popular. In 1907 over $6,000,000,000 of railroad stocks and bonds were held abroad, representing over one-fourth of the entire value of the roads at that time. Of this amount Great Britain owned $4,000,000,000, and Germany $1,000,000,000. In 1914 the *Wall Street Journal* estimated $3,400,000,000 worth of bonds, one-third of the outstanding railroad mortgage indebtedness, as held abroad; but the First World War brought many of these securities back to America, rendering our railroads for the first time virtually independent of foreign capital.

CHAOTIC CONDITIONS AND EARLY ABUSES

In a period of such rapid extension a chaotic situation was likely to develop, and abuses to creep in. Especially was this probable in an age in which business morality was at a low ebb. For some years the demand for transportation was so insistent that little attention was given to anything else; but by the early 'seventies railroad abuses had transformed hearty cooperation on the part of the people to a feeling of distrust and to a demand that the transportation companies be curbed. The abuses were many. In the first place, there was complaint that money was being wasted in unneeded and purely speculative enterprises. In their enthusiasm for railroad building, the American people apparently believed that the country could support an unlimited mileage. Roads were laid parallel in direct competition and driven into uninhabited country whose future was doubtful.

While some excuse might be made for overconstruction, none whatsoever can be discovered for the reckless graft practiced by the promoters through the medium of construction companies. These companies in them-

[5] The experience of a typical New England town with the coming of various new types of transportation facilities is told in Ellen E. Callahan, *Hadley: A Study of the Political Development of a Typical New England Town from the Official Records (1659–1930)*, in Smith College Studies in History, Vol. XVI, Nos. 1–2 (Oct., 1930–Jan., 1931).

selves were not necessarily bad. In fact, there was considerable justification for them, since the rapid extension of railroads in the South and West, where the promise of adequate returns was not sufficient to attract capital, made it necessary to build them through organizations willing to take land and railroad securities in payment. The trouble was that there was little or no competition in awarding the bids, for the construction companies were generally made up of the group who controlled the projected railroad and who voted to themselves, as members of the construction company, contracts to build the roads. As the future of the roads was uncertain, the temptation to take all the profits possible in construction was ever present, and some of the roads thus built were so heavily loaded with debt at the start that bankruptcy was inevitable. The cost of building the Central Pacific was $58,000,000, but a construction company was paid $120,000,000 for the work; the profits of building the Union Pacific were estimated at between forty and fifty millions.

The most famous of these companies was the Crédit Mobilier, formed to build the Union Pacific. To prevent any interference which might arise because of the aid received from the government, Oakes Ames, a representative from Massachusetts and prominent in the Crédit Mobilier, was given 343 shares of stock, to be distributed among Congressmen where they would "do the most good." Ames' activities resulted in an investigation which showed that he had sold stock below its actual value to a number of Congressmen to influence their votes, and that the trail of bribery reached as high as the Vice President. The exorbitant and reckless expenditures as exemplified by the construction companies were typical of methods in many channels of railroad finance, but it is only fair to say that some railroads condemned these practices.

Even more exasperating than the wasteful and irresponsible methods of construction were the reckless manipulations of the finances of the roads, once built. Railroad magnates of the early decades looked upon the whole matter as a private business for personal gain. Apparently no feeling of public responsibility swayed them, and their conception of common honesty was exceedingly flexible. The attitude is illustrated by the famous story about Cornelius Vanderbilt, perhaps the greatest of the early railroad builders, who is alleged to have replied to a remonstrance regarding the feelings of the public over an arbitrary act, "The public be damned." Men like Jay Gould and Daniel Drew controlled railroads not to serve the public, improve the property, and make legitimate profits, but to manipulate the stock to build their fortunes. No industry has suffered more from stock-watering than the railroads, for time and again an expanded capitalization was placed upon a road without an equivalent addition in actual equipment. This has been done chiefly to pay expenses which the roads did not want to carry under regular expenditures, and to camouflage earnings. In many cases the increasing valuation of the properties has soaked up the water, but in more cases watered stock lies like an inert weight upon the real earnings, and stockholders clamor for dividends that can be paid only by unreasonably high charges. It was estimated that of the $7,500,000,000 indebtedness of the railroads in 1883, as much as $2,000,000,000 represented water. In four years, 1868 to 1872, Erie stock was watered from $17,000,000 to $78,000,000 in market speculation. In 1897 only 29.9 per cent of the country's railroad stock paid dividends; in the prosperous year 1890 less than 50 per cent, and even in the war year 1918 only 58.09 per cent. In the words of Charles Francis Adams, Jr., a railroad president, "The system was, indeed, fairly honeycombed with jobbery and corruption." [6]

An abuse which struck at the very foundation of our democracy was the continued assault upon the integrity of the government by the railroad interests. The Crédit Mobilier scandal was notorious and famous because it implicated the highest legislators in the land, but similar activities on a smaller scale were common. Pressure upon legislators to grant favorable charters, and upon courts to interpret them broadly, was exerted by every means. The pass system in the height of its glory took care of many influential persons. The most powerful of the legislators were frequently employed as counsel at large salaries. Where this was not sufficient, many roads followed the example of the Erie, which in one year expended $700,000 as a corruption fund and for legal expenses, the amount being carried on the books as the "india-rubber account." The general attitude was much like that of the railroad magnate who was reported as saying that in Republican counties he was a Republican and in Democratic counties he was a Democrat, but everywhere he was for the railroad. The low political as well as low business morality of the period made corrupt practices possible, and the blame rests not alone with the roads.

More closely concerned with the general prosperity were the straits to which competition had reduced the railroads. Rate wars had lowered transportation costs between competitive points to ruinous figures. Passenger fares between Cleveland and Boston in August, 1876, were down to $6.50; cattle in the same year were carried from Chicago to New York for a dollar a carload. While the shippers at competitive points (especially where there was an option of water transportation) profited at the expense of the roads, the farmers suffered from the railroads' general practice of raising their tariffs at non-competitive points to recoup their losses. The same causes led to another form of discrimination equally galling, the

[6] C. F. Adams, Jr., *The Railroad Problem*, p. 126.

custom of charging more for a short haul than for a long. Still another unfair practice which was exceedingly prevalent was the granting of rebates
on freight charges. Where competition was bitter or the shipping concern
strong, substantial refunds were obtained. Thus the Standard Oil and other
large shippers procured rebates that gave them an advantage the smaller
organizations failed to obtain and, like the farmer, the smaller concerns
had to pay higher freight rates to make up for the losses of the railroads.
Cutthroat competition led eventually to the system of "pooling," by which
the available business was allotted proportionately at agreed rates. Although
the railroads broke the pooling agreements almost as soon as they were
made, the mere attempt to make them was looked upon as unfair, monopolistic, and contrary to the common law. A mere enumeration of the grievances against the railroads in the decade of the 'seventies enables one to
understand the strong reaction against them which culminated in the
"Granger movement." While many of these abuses have been eliminated
and others softened, the old distrust on the part of the public has never
entirely died out.[7]

THE GRANGER MOVEMENT AND THE RAILROADS

The first strong agitation against the railroads occurred in the early
'seventies among the farmers, especially those of the middle-western states
of Illinois, Minnesota, Iowa, and Wisconsin. This activity is known as the
"Granger movement," a name originating from the "Granges," or local
lodges, of the Patrons of Husbandry. The significance of the Grange lies
in the fact that through it the isolation of the farmer broke down to some
extent, and he was able to voice his grievances. "We are not enemies of
railroads," asserted the Grange, and "we wage no aggressive warfare against
any other interest whatever."[8] Whatever the Grangers may have said, they
counted the railroad abuses among their grievances; the first laws passed in
the agricultural states in an effort to control better or to regulate common
carriers were popularly known as "Granger laws," and the legal cases
arising from them, as the "Granger cases." The attack on the railroads,
which was waged fiercely from 1869 to 1875, was but one phase of a mighty
movement of agrarian unrest which was inaugurated by the Granger
movement and surged through the West until 1896.

Inasmuch as early legal decisions, such as that in the Dartmouth College
case, had interpreted a charter as a contract, the western states had been

[7] The *First Annual Report of the Interstate Commerce Commission*, reprinted in part in F.
Flügel and H. U. Faulkner, *Readings*, pp. 609–618, reviews in some detail the causes for the
passing of the Interstate Commerce Act of 1887.

[8] See excerpt from the *Seventh Session of the National Grange*, as given in *ibid.*, pp. 741–
744.

careful to insert in their constitutions provisions declaring that laws creating corporations might be altered or repealed, or to specify in the charters that railroad rates must be equal and reasonable. Backed by these specific rights and by the common-law conception that a business which was a public calling came under the regulatory power of the state, the representatives of the farmers passed laws in an attempt to control the railroads. The first act was passed in Illinois in 1869, and limited the roads to "just, reasonable, and uniform rates." In the new Illinois state constitution of 1870 the legislature was ordered to "pass laws to correct abuses and to prevent unjust discrimination and extortion in the rates of freight and passenger tariffs." Laws of 1871 attempted to do this by providing maximum fares and freight rates, by regulating warehouses and the transportation of grain, by establishing a board of railway and warehouse commissioners, and by providing for the enactment of a general railway incorporation act. Minnesota followed in the same year with laws fixing freight and passenger schedules and providing for a railroad commission. Iowa and Wisconsin passed similar acts in 1874, the latter state enacting the Potter law, the most radical of the Granger laws. During this decade the demand for the regulation of railroads spread, and there seems to be no doubt that the aggressive activity of the "Granger states" of the upper Mississippi Valley gave an impetus to the whole movement for control which in some states was not consummated until the next decade. Most of the states passed some kind of railroad legislation; and in practically all of the new or rewritten state constitutions of the decade, provisions were inserted making it the duty of the legislatures to regulate rates and prevent discrimination, and declaring the railroads public highways and the companies common carriers.

As a whole, the Granger laws sought (1) to establish, either by direct legislation or through a commission, schedules of maximum rates; (2) to prohibit a greater charge for a short haul than for a long one; (3) to preserve competition by forbidding the consolidation of parallel lines; and (4) to eliminate the evil of free passes for public officials. "Several of the principal features of American railroad legislation," says Professor Buck, "can be looked upon as primarily Granger in their origin."[9] Subsequent federal legislation sought to correct the same abuses against which the Granger states had legislated. Where railroad legislation was passed it was customary to set up commissions of experts. These were of two kinds: the strong commission, as in Illinois, with power to regulate rates and enforce the law; and the weaker commission, as in Massachusetts, with merely advisory powers and the duty of making reports to the legislature.

These first attempts to regulate the railroads were of course vigorously

⁸ S. J. Buck, *The Granger Movement*, p. 205.

opposed by the companies and immediately fought in the courts. In general, the railroad laws were attacked from two angles. It was maintained, first, that the exclusive power to regulate interstate commerce rested with Congress, and that, as the bulk of the commerce was interstate, the national government should legislate if it was necessary. Second, the effort to regulate rates was maintained to be contrary to that portion of Section I of the Fourteenth Amendment which declares, "No state shall make or enforce any law which shall abridge the privileges or immunities of citizens of the United States; nor shall any state deprive any person of life, liberty, or property, without due process of law; nor deny to any person within its jurisdiction the equal protection of the laws."

The first of the so-called "Granger cases" was that of Munn v. Illinois, decided by the Supreme Court in 1876 and involving the Illinois law of 1871, which declared grain elevators to be public warehouses and established maximum charges. The plaintiffs sued on the ground that (1) warehousing was not a public calling and the business was therefore not within the regulatory power of the state; (2) the fixing of rates deprived the owners of the power to establish higher rates and thus deprived them of their property without due process of law. They further maintained that if the courts did decide that their business was a public calling, it was the work of the judiciary and not the legislature to determine a fair charge. All of these contentions were thrown out by the decision of Chief Justice Waite, who held that this section of the Constitution did not invalidate the old English common law that was generally accepted when the amendment was passed. "Property," said he, "does become clothed with a public interest when used in a manner to make it of public consequence, and affect the community at large. When, therefore, one devotes his property to a use in which the public has an interest, he, in effect, grants to the public an interest in that use, and must submit to be controlled by the public for the common good." He further held that the fixing of rates was a legislative and not a judicial matter, asserting that "it has been customary from time immemorial for the legislature to declare what shall be reasonable compensation under such circumstances." [10]

The firm attitude of the court in the Munn case was maintained in the case of Peik v. the Chicago and Northwestern Railway Company, handed down in the same year. The contention of the railroads that state regulation was an infringement of interstate commerce (and thus unconstitutional), since most of the railroad traffic crosses state boundaries, was thrown out. Ignoring the effect of such laws upon those outside the state, the court declared that "until Congress acts in reference to the relations of this company

[10] Munn v. Illinois, 94 U. S. 113.

to interstate commerce, it is certainly within the power of Wisconsin to regulate its fares, etc., so far as they are of domestic concern." [11] The contention of the railroads that the courts and not the legislatures should fix charges was likewise dismissed. "Where property has been clothed with a public interest," said the Court, "the legislature may fix a limit to that which shall be in law reasonable for its use. This limit binds the courts as well as the people. If it has been improperly fixed, the legislature, not the courts, must be appealed to for the change." The decisions in the Munn and Peik cases were supposed to have settled the main points of constitutional law involved in railway regulation; hence it was a matter of surprise when, ten years later (1886), in the case of the Wabash, St. Louis, and Pacific Railway v. Illinois,[12] the Supreme Court reversed itself. The case arose over the violation of a law forbidding a greater charge for a short haul than for a long one, when it was discovered that railroad rates were higher on freight from Gilman to New York than from Peoria to New York, although the latter point was eighty-six miles farther away. The decision now held that no state could exercise any control over commerce beyond its limits. Three years later in the "Minnesota Rate case" [13] the railroads won the victory for which they had long struggled, when the Supreme Court took the stand that the reasonableness of rates was ultimately a judicial question. The Wabash and Minnesota cases made federal rather than state regulation the inevitable development.

DEVELOPMENT OF FEDERAL CONTROL

The Granger attack upon the railroads brought with it the demand for federal as well as state regulation. At the recommendation of President Grant in 1872 a committee was appointed under the chairmanship of William Windom of Minnesota which made a report [14] in 1874 advising government construction and extension of transportation facilities in order to reduce rates by making the government a competitor to private roads. The "Regan bill," aiming to abolish some of the worst abuses of the railroads, passed the House in 1878 but was not acted on in the Senate, and the question of railroad legislation lay dormant until 1885. In that year a Senate committee was appointed, headed by Shelby M. Cullom of Illinois, an indefatigable worker for railroad regulation. In its report the following year [15] it reviewed carefully the various methods by which a remedy for the situation might be found, and endorsed some form of federal regulation and control to obviate what seemed to it

[11] Peik v. Chicago and Northwestern Railroad Co., 94 U. S. 164.

[12] 118 U. S. 557.

[13] Chicago, Milwaukee, and St. Paul Railroad Company v. Minnesota. This decision was foretold in 1886 in the case of Stone v. Farmers' Loan and Trust Co.

[14] *The Windom Report*, Senate Report No. 307, 43rd Cong., 1st Sess.

[15] *The Cullom Report*, Senate Report No. 46, 49th Cong., 1st Sess., Vol. II.

the greatest evil, namely, "unjust discrimination between persons, places, commodities, or particular descriptions of traffic."

In 1887 federal regulation of railroads was inaugurated as a compromise between government ownership and unrestrained private operation. Although passed during the Cleveland administration, the Interstate Commerce Act was supported by both parties and backed by urban as well as agricultural groups. It (1) provided that all charges should be just and reasonable; (2) forbade personal discriminations in the form of special rates, rebates, or otherwise; (3) forbade discriminations between localities, classes of freight, and connecting lines; (4) forbade a greater charge for a short haul than for a long; (5) prohibited pooling; and (6) ordered that all rates and fares should be printed and publicly posted, and no advance be made except after ten days' notice. The administration of the law was placed in the hands of an Interstate Commerce Commission of five members, which was given power to collect data from the carriers, call witnesses, hear complaints, and render decisions. If the commissioners believed that the law was violated and the roads refused to abide by their decisions, it was their duty to institute proceedings in the circuit courts. They were required to submit annual reports to Congress.

The passage of the Interstate Commerce Act was strongly opposed by the railroad officials, who predicted dire results; and their continued opposition and evasion, aided by various judicial decisions, effectively pulled the teeth from the Act. The railroads successfully avoided giving full testimony until 1896, when the Commission eventually obtained compulsory power of investigation.[16] In 1897 the Supreme Court rendered the Commission virtually powerless when in the Maximum Freight Rate case it held "that the power to prescribe rates or fix any tariff is not among the powers granted to the Commission," thus limiting the latter's power over rates to deciding what was unfair, without the right to prescribe fair rates.[17] As if this was not enough, the Court cut the heart out of other sections of the act, notably Section 4 which forbade a greater charge for a short haul than a long one when made under "substantially similar circumstances." In the Alabama Midland Case the Court ordered that the words "substantially similar circumstances" be interpreted literally—an impossible thing to do.[18] The greatest weakness in the position of the Commission, however, was the fact that its decisions were not compulsory and that upon it rested the burden of initiating action in the courts. The attitude of the railroads and courts prevented the Interstate Commerce Act of 1887 from receiving a fair trial. Of sixteen rate

[16] Brown v. Walker, 161 U. S. 591.

[17] Interstate Commerce Commission v. Cincinnati, New Orleans, and Texas Pacific Railway Company, 167 U. S. 479.

[18] 168 U. S. 144.

cases appealed to the Supreme Court for enforcement between 1887 and 1905, fifteen were decided in favor of the carriers and only one sustained in part for the Commission. Abuses continued, and the Commission became little more than a bureau of statistics. Although some good work was done in securing rate publicity and in reducing the number of freight classifications, the Act was important chiefly in its educational value and in introducing federal legislation, the system which has been in effect until the present time.

That the Interstate Commerce Act of 1887 had achieved no solution of the problem was apparent to all. Both the letter and the spirit of the Act had been evaded, the Industrial Commission reporting in 1900 "that the railways still make discriminations between individuals, and perhaps to as great an extent as ever before." [19] The development of the Progressive movement in politics under the leadership of such men as Roosevelt and La Follette, however, meant a new effort to strengthen federal control.

The Elkins Act of 1903, aimed at the practice of rebates, declared deviation from published rates to be discrimination, and held both giver and receiver guilty. The Expediting Act of the same year gave preference in the circuit courts to cases arising under the Interstate Commerce Act of 1887 and the Sherman Anti-trust Act of 1890, on the theory that such cases were "of general public importance." An important amendment to the legislation of 1887 was the Hepburn Act of 1906, which enlarged the scope of the Interstate Commerce Act to include express and sleeping-car companies, pipe lines, switches, spurs, tracks, and terminal facilities. The Commission, now increased to seven, of whom only four could be of the same political party, was empowered to determine just and reasonable rates and to order the carrier to adhere to them, leaving to the latter the burden of initiating court action. The Act also instructed the Commission to prescribe methods of bookkeeping for the railroads, and made their adoption compulsory. To obviate a certain type of discrimination, railroads were forbidden to carry commodities which they had themselves produced, except timber and goods needed in the conduct of their business. Free passes were forbidden, and rates had to be published thirty days before change. Although the part of the Act respecting the right of railroads to carry commodities in which they had an interest has been largely nullified by court action, in general the court has limited itself to determining the legality of the Commission's orders rather than their wisdom or expediency. The Hepburn Act went far to obviate the faults of the Act of 1887, and since 1906 the Commission has been a responsible and powerful body.

In 1910 the Mann-Elkins Act was passed. It clarified the short- and long-haul clause of the Interstate Commerce Act and enlarged the powers of the Commission by granting to it the right to suspend for ten months the operation of a new scale of rates to allow time for an investigation. It set up a special Commerce Court to hear railroad cases arising from the Commission's activities; this was considered a much-needed innovation, for there was an obvious necessity for railroad cases to be tried by judges who were experts in such questions.[20] Of the subsequent minor legislation, mention may be made of the amendment of 1913 to the Interstate Commerce Act, requiring the Commission to report the value of all proprety owned or used by all the common carriers; and of the Newlands Act of 1913 (amending the Erdman Act of 1898), providing for voluntary settlement of railroad disputes. In 1916 in the Adamson Eight-hour Act the government entered into a new sphere of activity in regulating the hours of labor in interstate traffic.[21] During these same progressive years, several of the states, notably Iowa, California, and Wisconsin, moved aggressively to break the political power of the railroads by new legislation.

The opening of the First World War found the principle of government regulation firmly established and the railroad industry stabilized as never before. At the same time, inefficient management and the inevitable results of early excesses, coupled with dislike of government regulation, had helped to instill in many units of the industry a feeling of disquiet and uncertainty as to the future. Furthermore, railroad labor was becoming more restless and the public more exacting. All factors pointed to further developments in federal regulation when war broke out.

RAILROAD CONSOLIDATION

Parallel to the combination of capital in other lines of industry there also developed a consolidation of railroads. This took place primarily to insure greater efficiency, to eliminate competition, and to secure larger profits. It took two courses—that of uniting railroads to form a continuous line of travel, and that of consolidating the roads in a given geographic division. The first type of consolidation began before the Civil War and continued for many years. It is best exemplified by Vanderbilt's work in combining (1853) eleven little roads, which hitherto had most inefficiently handled the traffic between Albany and Buffalo, into the New York Central, and in adding five more roads to the system between 1855 and 1858.

As already noted, the late 'sixties and the decade of the 'seventies was a

---

[20] The Progressives in Congress distrusted the Commerce Court as a body of conservative judges biased in favor of the railroads, and discontinued it in 1912 by failing to appropriate funds for its maintenance.

[21] W. E. Dodd, *Woodrow Wilson and His Work* (1920), pp. 164, 189, 190.

period of disastrous and unbridled railroad competition. By this time the through lines had taken form and were fighting bitterly for traffic. As this competition bade fair to ruin the roads, repeated efforts to eliminate it were made by means of pools or traffic associations, which sought to apportion the available business arbitrarily among the roads at rates mutually agreed upon. Such methods proved inadequate because the railroads did not keep their own agreements, and they became illegal after the Interstate Commerce Act forbade "any contract, agreement, or combination . . . for the pooling of freights of different and competing railroads," a clause later upheld by the Supreme Court in the case against the Trans-Missouri Freight Association (1898), when the decision asserted that the agreements entered into by this association violated the Sherman Anti-trust Act of 1890 as agreements "in restraint of trade and commerce."

With pooling forbidden by law, the railroads, like other industries, turned again to consolidation to save themselves from the evils of too great competition. During the 'eighties, and again from 1898 to 1904, consolidation went on rapidly. By purchase, by lease, by the ownership of a majority of the stock, the larger railroads absorbed many of the smaller competing lines, which were thereafter often operated as separate but subsidiary companies. The period of rapid consolidation was brought to a halt in 1904 by the Supreme Court decision in the Northern Securities case. In 1901 the Harriman interests, which dominated the Union Pacific and the Southern Pacific, and the Morgan-Hill interests, which dominated the Great Northern, engaged in a battle royal for control of the Northern Pacific, which in turn controlled the Burlington system. Having driven Northern Pacific common from around $100 to $1000 in a few days, the giants discovered that the fight had reached a stalemate, whereupon they reconciled their differences and organized the Northern Securities Company, a holding company to acquire the stock of the Great Northern and the Northern Pacific and thus control the Burlington system. Such an organization meant the elimination of competition in the Northwest. Scarcely three months after its formation the reviving storm of anti-trust agitation broke upon it. The federal government instituted suit under the Sherman Act, and in 1904 the Supreme Court ordered its dissolution. "If Congress has not," said the Court, "by the words of this Act, described this and like cases, it would, we apprehend, be impossible to find words that would describe them." [22]

By the time this great era of railroad consolidation reached its climax in 1906, the division of ownership and territory had been pretty clearly laid down. Of the 228,000 miles of railroad in that year, about two-thirds were in the hands of seven groups. The Vanderbilt roads with over 22,500 miles

[22] Northern Securities Co. *v.* U. S., 193 U. S. 197.

controlled the northern routes from New York to Chicago; the Pennsylvania interests (20,000 miles) dominated the roads to the West emanating from Pennsylvania and Maryland; the Morgan roads (18,000 miles) and their affiliates dominated the Southeast; the Gould roads (almost 17,000 miles) and the Rock Island system (almost 15,000 miles) were powerful in the Mississippi Valley. Beyond the Mississippi the Hill roads with over 21,000 miles had a monopoly of the Northwest, and the Harriman roads dominated the central and southern transcontinental routes. Although two-thirds of the mileage by this time had been divided among seven groups, in reality consolidation was even more far-reaching. These seven groups, for example, controlled 85 per cent of railroad earnings. Moreover, certain of these groups were closely allied through the same banking interests, and through interlocking directorates and stock ownership in the same concerns. Although the situation was by no means static since new alignments and new shifts were made under the pressure of one or another group of railroad speculators, the picture had not changed essentially up to the opening of the First World War. "The working out of the higher strategy in railroad consolidation," comments a leading authority of that period, "was the most significant feature of American transportation history in the decade of 1910. Within this brief period what now promised to become more or less permanent financial and operating groups evolved out of the competitive chaos of the period of depression of 1893–1897." [23]

In the face of this tendency the government has been able to do little. The federal courts broke up the Northern Securities Company (1904), ordered the Union Pacific to dispose of its Southern Pacific stock (1912), and dissolved the New Haven monopoly in 1914. In the Panama Canal Act of 1912 Congress attempted to prevent the control of domestic water transportation by competing railroads, and in the Clayton Anti-trust Act of 1914 it forbade a corporation's acquiring, "directly or indirectly, the whole or any part of the stock or other share capital of another corporation engaged also in commerce, where the effect of such acquisition may be to substantially lessen competition between the corporation whose stock is acquired, and the corporation making the acquisition." The apparent futility of preventing an accomplished fact was recognized in the Transportation Act of 1920, which gave the Interstate Commerce Commission power to permit the carrier to acquire control by lease or purchase of another carrier in any manner which does not involve

---

[23] W. Z. Ripley, *Railroads: Finance and Organization* (1915), p. 459.

In 1921 Senator La Follette charged that twenty-five directors linked together 99 Class I roads, operating 211,280 miles, or 82 per cent of the country's transportation system, and that these were likewise closely allied with the leading equipment companies. The truth of these charges would support the belief that consolidation through community of interest has continued unabated. *Congressional Record,* March 14, 1921, with diagrams.

their consolidation into a single system of ownership and management. The Act went further when it empowered the Commission to prepare plans for the consolidation of the roads into a number of systems in which competition might "be preserved as fully as possible." [24]

RAILROAD SERVICE AND COSTS

A number of factors have prevented a more rapid advance in improvements to railroad rolling stock. The financial hardships, the elimination of competition through consolidation, and the fact that express companies and the government have taken over the responsibilities of handling the more exacting traffic have all contributed to delay this phase of development. Nevertheless, great progress has been made, but before it could come steel rails had to be substituted for iron, just as the solid iron had been substituted for the strips. The first steel rails were imported in 1863, and their manufacture was begun in 1865, impelled by the discovery of the Bessemer process. After that date much of the mileage was thus equipped. With better rails came more scientific roadbeds, and with heavier rolling stock, better bridges and other structures.

Perhaps the most notable advance in railroad operation since the opening of the present century has been the substitution of electricity for steam on certain of the lines. The pioneers were the New York Central, which began operating by electricity from the Grand Central Terminal in 1906, and the New York, New Haven and Hartford, which two years later inaugurated complete electric service from the same terminal to Stamford, Connecticut. The Norfolk and Western used electric power for heavy freight, and the Chicago, Milwaukee and Puget Sound for long-distance traffic. The electric engine was found to be cheaper, faster, cleaner, and much better adapted to the crowded conditions of enclosed city terminals, as well as more dependable in zero weather. Only the precarious financial condition of many roads and the outbreak of the First World War prevented more rapid electrification. In the post-war years, however, came a new era of improved service characterized by Diesel engines, streamlined cars, greater comfort, and faster speed.

Freight earnings are over three times as great as passenger earnings on American roads, and there are forty freight cars to one passenger car. A majority of the freight consists of heavy bulky products, such as coal, grain, timber, and petroleum, a factor of great influence in the development of rolling stock. In contrast to European equipment—which is light and small, designed to carry compact freight for short hauls—monster engines and large cars, built to carry heavy freight for long distances, have been the rule in America. Passenger coaches have followed this tendency in size, and our more

[24] Below, pp. 615 ff.

NETWORK OF RAILROADS
IN THE 1940's

MANHATTAN DRAFTING CO. INC., N.Y.

democratic customs have prevented the adoption of the European compart-
ment train. The tremendous weight of engines and cars has put a continually
increasing strain on roadbeds, but the abundance of raw materials has held
down the expense of keeping them in repair.

The comfort of passengers goes far beyond the dream of earlier travelers.
Better springs, heating and lighting facilities, Pullman day and sleeping
coaches and dining cars have all contributed to this. With the completion
of the South Station in Boston in 1898, an era of huge station construction
commenced, culminating in such beautiful and luxurious structures as the
Washington depot (completed 1907), the Pennsylvania Station in New
York (1910), and the Grand Central (1913)—marvelous combinations of
aesthetic qualities with utilitarian needs. Many safety devices have considerably eliminated the old danger for both passengers and workmen. Air brakes,
block signals, the automatic coupler, and steel cars have furthered safety.
Nevertheless, the loss of life on American railroads is great, and railroading
continues among the most hazardous occupations. In 1920 the roads reported 6958 killed and 168,309 injured in accidents; of employees 2578 were
killed and 149,414 injured; of trainmen, one in every 391 was killed and one
in every eleven was injured.[25]

Equitable and fair freight rates are essential in a country whose economic
life depends upon the transportation of large amounts of freight. Railroad
transportation is a business that ought to yield increasing returns, for the first
cost is highest, and with the growth of population business should automatically increase without proportionate new expenditure. This, of course, is
particularly true of a new and developing country like the United States. As
the population has grown and new industries have been begun, transportation has been stimulated, resulting in more efficient service, the use of improved machinery, and the construction of better roadbeds. These factors,
together with competition, kept freight rates on the decline until 1899, but
since then government regulation has been necessary to keep them as low as
possible. The average freight receipts per ton-mile measured in gold were
1.92 cents in 1867; .941 in 1890, and .724 in 1899. Since then they have increased—.766 in 1905, 1.069 in 1920, and 1.094 in 1928. By 1940 they had declined to .945. These changes, it should be noted, roughly followed the
changes in general prices during this period.

Passenger fares have not decreased to the same extent, but travelers have
benefited by improved service. The average revenue per passenger per mile
was 2.63 cents in 1871, 2.42 in 1883, 1.99 in 1898, and 1.94 in 1910. Fares were

[25] The figures for 1939 show an appreciable reduction in casualties. In that year the roads
reported 4492 killed and 28,144 injured; 536 employees were killed and 17,383 injured. By
the 'thirties passenger casualties were few and railroad travel had become the safest of any of
the important facilities.

increased during the First World War by the United States Railroad Commission, and in 1920 by the Interstate Commerce Commission. The average receipts per passenger per mile on Class I carriers was 2.76 cents in 1920 and 1.75 in 1940.

The old theory of charging "all that the traffic will bear" was modified first by the desire not to antagonize public opinion further, and later by government interference. The present rate-making policy as exemplified by the Transportation Act of 1920 is to allow rates high enough to give a fair return on the actual value of the porperty. Farmers, miners, and other producers of raw materials have been the great gainers from decreased freight rates, although the people as a whole have also profited.[26]

ELECTRIC RAILWAY TRANSPORTATION

The development of electric railways has taken place almost entirely in the last fifty years. The first practical overhead trolley line was built in Kansas City in 1884, and by 1888 there were thirteen electric railways with forty-eight miles of track in the United States. After 1890 progress was extremely rapid, when inventors like Charles J. Van Depoele, Stephen D. Field, Frank J. Sprague, and Elihu Thompson turned their genius to this field. At the same time financiers and entrepreneurs, such as Thomas F. Ryan, Charles T. Yerkes, and William L. Elkins, entered as enthusiastically and as ruthlessly upon the building of trolleys as the "robber barons" of half a century earlier had taken up the construction of steam railroads. As with railroads, an early glamour surrounded the electric trolleys, for a town's pretensions to cityhood depended upon possession of a street car system.

There were numerous street railways before 1890, but the motive power was chiefly animal and steam. Electricity was rapidly substituted. New York, Chicago, and Boston all had elevated systems by 1901, but not until the latter date was electricity first used on the New York elevated. Electricity not only greatly facilitated traffic on the railways but made it possible to build subways. Boston, the pioneer in American subways, completed her first unit in 1898, and New York began construction in 1900. By 1905 trains were running under the East River to Brooklyn and, three years later, under the North River to New Jersey. Single-track mileage of street and electrical railways amounted in 1920 to 47,705; since then it has dropped to 23,770 in 1937.

The electric railroads have supplied an important economic need made imperative by the growth of urban life. So far their chief business has been the transportation of passengers in thickly populated sections. Their freight possibilities, discouraged by the competition and hostility of the steam rail-

[26] For a discussion of railroads since 1914, see pp. 615 ff.

roads, have never been fully exploited. The type of traffic thus handled has had an important significance, social as well as economic. The trolley in its day helped to break down the isolation of country life, decrease its disadvantages, and improve the economic and cultural opportunities of regions near the cities, and it afforded greater opportunity for the city population to reach the country. In this way it has done more than anything else except the automobile to unite suburban and urban communities.

Electric railways under certain conditions and in certain areas have been able to compete with steam roads quite successfully for passenger traffic. Greater cheapness in construction and operation has made lower fares possible, and the ability to run single cars has allowed frequent service and thus greater facilities and convenience. Built ordinarily in densely populated regions, they have an advantage over a railroad which is forced to carry the burden of long stretches of thinly peopled country. Nevertheless, the history of electric railways has been checkered. The rising costs of fuel and equipment, combined with the constant introduction of improvements rendered necessary in many cases by municipal ordinances, have made operating more expensive. The habit of the five-cent fare, which had become grounded in custom and law, was difficult to break. High financing, over-optimism in construction, and the growth of gasoline motor traffic all added to the discomfiture of electric roads. Between 1900 and 1913 a considerable portion of the street railways passed through either financial reorganization or actual receivership. The attitude of the people in regard to street railways has been a repetition of their attitude toward the steam carriers—first a period of encouragement and aid through liberal franchises and stock subscriptions, then a period of dissatisfaction and criticism, in many cases justly deserved; and finally realization that the roads are an essential means of transportation that must be preserved and regulated for the benefit of the whole community. The competition of electric urban and interurban railways has been met by the railroads in two ways: first, by purchasing and operating the trolleys themselves, and second, by electrifying their own lines. The New Haven and the New York Central, both operating in congested regions, have used these methods.

THE AUTOMOBILE AND THE RENAISSANCE OF ROAD BUILDING

Of greater significance for the future than electric street railways was the gasoline-driven motor vehicle. After a century of experimentation, mostly with steam, practical cars were produced in 1893, but until 1903 the industry was in an experimental and unstable position. The early experimentation was done largely in Europe, where the automobile had been considerably developed before there was much interest in America; but at least one

American—George B. Selden, of Rochester, N. Y.—as early as 1877 had built a vehicle propelled by a gasoline engine, a patent for which he finally obtained in 1895. As the news of the "horseless carriages" reached America in the 'nineties, many tinkering mechanics like Charles E. Duryea, Ransom E. Olds, Elwood Haynes, and Henry Ford succeeded in putting together contraptions which would run, some of which were driven by electricity, by gasoline, by steam, by carbonic acid gas and alcohol.[27] The Selden patent failed to prevent a rapid development,[28] and after 1900 there ensued a period of intense competition in which the automobile was quickly made practical. The popularity of the automobile was undoubtedly increased by the improvement in design which took the engine from underneath and placed it in front, making the car look less like a horseless carriage, and by innumerable technical improvements which made it possible for persons without mechanical training to operate automobiles. Gasoline cars could be run in reverse by 1900 and by 1913 a practical self-starter had been invented. Furthermore, the price, under Ford's impetus, had been reduced by 1914 to a figure within the reach of at least the upper middle class. In that year the production of automobiles was about 569,000, the vehicles registered numbered 1,711,339, and the capital invested in manufacturing amounted to $407,730,000. The great expansion and the great influence of the motor car were to come in the next fifteen years.[29]

One of the most important effects of the automobile was the renaissance of road building, reminiscent of the turnpike era of the closing years of the eighteenth and the early years of the nineteenth centuries.[30] The bicycle craze of the 'nineties, the introduction of the rural free delivery in 1896, and finally the advent of the motor inaugurated a widespread movement for improved highways. Better-roads organizations were formed, culminating in 1910 in the American Association for Highway Improvement. The lead in the movement was taken by New Jersey in 1891 and quickly followed in the succeeding years by other states, particularly in the East. They began by making small contributions for the improvement of town and county roads, but gradually extended their appropriations and their supervision until by 1914 some of them had laid out trunk lines and were appropriating millions of dollars to improve and keep them in repair. Under the strain of motor traffic the old dirt, gravel, or "water-bound macadam"

---

[27] When the National Automobile Chamber of Commerce in 1925 determined to honor the American pioneers in the industry, it conferred medals upon John D. Maxwell, Edgar L. Apperson, A. L. Riker, John S. Clarke, Rollin H. White, H. H. Franklin, Charles Duryea, Charles B. King, Elwood Haynes, Alexander Winton, and R. E. Olds.

[28] W. Kaempffert, A Popular History of American Invention (1924), Chap. IV.

[29] Below, pp. 621 ff.

[30] Above, pp. 271 ff.

surfaces were found inadequate, and some form of bituminous macadam or bitulithic pavement was gradually substituted. Stretches of concrete also were being laid by 1914, a material used extensively in the new bridges which were laid simultaneously with the new roads. Roadways, whose economic significance had declined with the advent of railroads, by 1914 were rapidly achieving their erstwhile position of primary importance, but the great period of highway construction, like the great period of automobile expansion, was to come in the next fifteen years.

AVIATION

Although commercial aviation, which holds forth such great possibilities for the future, had made no progress in this country before the First World War, the science of aviation had sufficiently advanced to make its development possible, and American inventors were primarily responsible. Experiments in the construction of airplanes had been made in the 'nineties in England and France, but nothing came of them; the chief interest in aviation at the turn of the century concerned ballooning. The brilliant scientist of the Smithsonian Institution, Samuel P. Langley, was busy in the 'nineties devising steam-driven models which made successful flights, and finally by means of an appropriation by the War Department he built a man-size airplane which in 1903 his assistant, Charles M. Manly, tried twice unsuccessfully to fly over the Potomac. Langley claimed that the trouble was not with the airplane but with the failure to launch it properly, and his belief was in part vindicated in 1914 when Glenn Curtiss installed a more powerful engine and flew the plane successfully.

While the public press was still jeering over the failure of the Smithsonian scientists, two mechanics from Toledo, Ohio, Orville and Wilbur Wright, were making the first successful flights in the history of the world with a heavier-than-air machine carrying a man. These flights at Kitty Hawk on the lonely Carolina coast were the result of years of experimentation which were continued in secret until 1908, when the Wrights began their demonstration in Europe and America. Although enthusiasm was widespread, the advance during the next few years occurred chiefly in Europe. America, however, had one further contribution of importance to make before 1914 in the hydroaeroplane designed by Glenn E. Curtiss and flown by him over the Hudson in 1911. It was the military possibilities of the airplane in the First World War that gave aviation its first great impetus. The rapid development of commercial aviation came in the 'twenties and 'thirties.[31]

[31] For a further discussion of aviation, see below, pp. 623 ff.

Internal Water Transportation

It is estimated that there are 260 streams available in the United States for commercial transportation, with over 26,000 navigable miles. These streams together with the Great Lakes give this country the finest natural system of internal waterways available to any nation in the world. Despite this fact and the large annual federal grants for the improvement of river channels, the importance of internal waterways has declined since the advent of the railroads. Only upon the Great Lakes has the tendency been otherwise. While the tonnage carried by the railroads has increased enormously, river tonnage has shown an absolute as well as a relative falling off. This is true even of the Mississippi traffic. The high-water mark of river transportation for the lower Mississippi came in 1880, when over 1,000,000 tons were received and shipped at St. Louis from and for the lower Mississippi; the figure fell to 141,000 in 1905. Receipts and shipments at St. Louis to and from the upper Mississippi declined from 340,000 tons in 1870 to less than 70,000 in 1905. Cotton receipts by river at New Orleans were reduced from 1,087,000 bales in 1880 to 231,000 in 1906. On the Ohio, however, there has been an absolute increase because of coal shipments, but a relative decline.

What is true of rivers holds even more for canals. Of the 4633 miles of canals built in the United States before 1909, 2444, or over half, have been abandoned. Of all artificial waterways, the Erie Canal in New York State has been the most important, and the statistics for this canal are indicative of the general tendency. The annual tonnage carried on it increased to a high point of over 4,500,000 tons in 1889, only to decline to 2,000,000 in 1905 and to 891,000 tons in 1920; this, too, in spite of the fact that tolls were abolished in 1882 and the canal has been enlarged and improved since 1903.[32] The tonnage of the Erie Railroad in the same state increased by 1905 to over 30,000,000, and that of the New York Central to over 40,000,000. In 1853 the New York State canal system carried 81 per cent of the total traffic; in 1873 it carried 35 per cent, and in both 1907 and 1908 only 4 per cent. The traffic which waterways still carry is largely bulky and low-class freight—iron, coal, lumber, grain, and building materials. The Sault Ste. Marie connecting Lakes Superior and Huron, and in amount of tonnage carried the most important American canal, reported for the year 1908 iron ore as 59.6 per cent of its traffic, coal 23.9 per cent, and wheat 7.7 per cent. Over half the Mississippi River traffic and over three-fourths of that of the Ohio in recent years has been coal. The tonnage on the Monongahela,

[32] In recent years this has increased, the total freight for 1939 being 3,643,782 tons.

Allegheny, and Kanawha is similar. Nearly 90 per cent of the entire tonnage of the Chesapeake and Ohio Canal is coal.

The causes for the decline of water transportation in the United States are many. While ordinarily transportation by water is cheaper than by land, this advantage has been lost because of other factors. In the first place, American railroads have also been designed to handle large bulky traffic. As they were improved and enlarged, they have been able in many instances to lower their rates to a point approximately as low as those charged for water transportation. Where this has been impossible, the roads have obtained possession of the steamship lines and canals, and either operated or discontinued them. The speed of the railroads and their superiority in handling high-class freight have been influential in diverting traffic to them, for America as a nation likes speed. Their many branch lines touch an infinite number of points inaccessible to canals. Many of the early canals were unwisely located, others are too short to be used for through freight, and still others are built in regions where the original products, such as lumber, have become exhausted. The cost of transshipment often eats up the advantages that might accrue from cheaper rates. Furthermore, with the exception of the New York Barge Canal, the service and facilities of the canals have not been improved to meet the demands of present-day traffic. The difficulty of river navigation, owing to shifting sand, snags, and other impediments, to say nothing of winter freezing, has discouraged development. The large rivers, furthermore, flow in a southerly direction, whereas the bulk of the traffic moves east and west.

In spite of the decline in water traffic and the coming of the automobile and airplane, interest in canal and river transportation has revived in recent years, and persistent agitation in its behalf has developed. Any temporary inability of the railroads to handle freight, or an increase in rates, invariably turns the attention of shippers to water facilities. River towns, hoping for a brighter future, promote almost continuous propaganda for improved waterways. Considerable stimulus was given to the interest in artificial waterways by the building of the Panama Canal, the greatest transportation project which the federal government has yet embarked upon. The victorious battles which Colonel William C. Gorgas fought against tropical disease, and which Colonel George W. Goethals waged against almost insurmountable natural barriers to accomplish a dream of centuries, thrilled the American people, as well they might, and turned their attention again to canals. A little later the problem became tied up with the conservation movement, and in 1907 Roosevelt appointed an Inland Waterways Commission to survey the entire subject. The agitation resulted in the appropriation in 1911 of approximately $10,000,000 to improve navigation on the Ohio; it also resulted in the state of Illinois undertaking the first link in the projected "Lakes-to-Gulf Deep Waterway," and in a revival of the old scheme, first broached by Gallatin, for an intra-coastal waterway along the Atlantic coast. In 1909 a private company started a canal across Cape Cod which was completed in 1914. The most tangible result of this agitation, however, was the improvement and enlargement of the New York canal system, which involved 440 miles of improvement or new construction and the canalization of 350 miles of lakes and rivers. An initial appropriation of $101,000,000 was made in 1903, and New York again looked forward to the day when the products of the Great Lakes basin would pass over her waterways.

While river and canal traffic has diminished, that on the Great Lakes has increased. Here the ordinary advantages of water transportation are evident, and in addition long-distance conveyance is provided during a larger part of the year than is possible on canals; the cost of maintenance is smaller, too, than that of canals and rivers. This is seen in the freight rates, which in 1900 were 4.42 cents per bushel of wheat from Chicago to New York by lake and canal and 9.98 by railroad, and in 1920 were 14.60 and 16.68 cents respectively. Furthermore, the freight is especially suitable to water transportation, being composed almost entirely of bulky raw material. Anthracite and bituminous coal is transported north and west, and the return shipments are composed of flour, grain, iron ore from the Lake Superior mines, copper, and lumber. The tonnage of the Great Lakes trade increased from 467,-700 in 1860 to 2,595,062 in 1920. At the same time the tonnage of vessels passing through the Sault Ste. Marie Canal rose from 403,659 in 1860 to 68,240,000 in 1929.

TELEPHONY, TELEGRAPHY, AND WIRELESS

The closing years of the nineteenth century saw a rapid expansion in the use of the telephone, an invention of epoch-making significance in the history of communication. Although a number of experiments had been made in transmitting the human voice by electricity, not until 1876 did Alexander Graham Bell successfully carry on a conversation with his assistant, Thomas A. Watson, over a line which he had erected between Boston and Cambridgeport, Massachusetts. Bell's first patent, which was taken out in that year, marked the beginning of the telephone industry, largely American in its origin [33] and improvements; today this nation has approximately two-thirds of the telephones in the world. In 1880 there were 34,305 miles of telephone wires in the United States; in 1940 the American Tele-

[33] Bell himself was a Scotchman who came to America in early manhood.

phone and Telegraph Company, the huge holding company that controls most of the important American systems, reported about 89,000,000 miles under its direction. It boasted 855,000 telephones in 1900 and 9,172,000 in 1915, by which time the telephone had become standard equipment for a middle-class home. In 1940 it controlled over 17,000,000. Long-distance telephony began with the opening of a line between New York and Philadelphia in January, 1887, but it was not until 1915 that Bell spoke into an exact reproduction of his original instrument and was clearly heard by Watson in San Francisco. In the meantime the large research staff maintained by the American Telephone and Telegraph Company had developed technical improvements which were to make the next fifteen years a period of spectacular advance.

While telephony was revolutionizing our methods of communication, telegraphy also made important progress. Spurred on by the Civil War, a telegraph line was strung across the continent in 1862, and since that time the growth of telegraphy has been rapid. In 1937 there were in the United States 250,880 miles of telegraph lines, a substantial percentage of the world's telegraph service, over which about 206,987,000 telegrams were sent. Not only has the industry grown enormously, but numerous inventions have enabled it to expand in various ways. Beginning with J. B. Stearns' invention in 1872 of the duplex method by which two messages can be sent simultaneously in the same direction, the wires were further utilized by the discovery of the quadruplex system of transmitting four messages simultaneously, two each way, and later by multiplex telegraphy. Submarine telegraphic communication was achieved by Cyrus Field in 1858 after many unsuccessful efforts and has been in extensive use since 1866. The significance of cable communication is too obvious to need comment. Printing telegraphy has been developed, as exemplified in the stock ticker, and various forms of writing telegraphy have been put in operation. Practically all of the telegraph lines in the United States are privately owned, and 98 per cent are under control of two affiliated companies. The telegraph and cable business reached its high point about 1927. Since then it has suffered from telephone and wireless competition.

The most spectacular development in telegraphy came with wireless in the first decade of the present century. Many experimenters had worked on the principles underlying wireless, but it was left to the Italian, Guglielmo Marconi, to make it a practical thing. Marconi took out his first English patent in 1896 and gradually extended the range of his operations until in December of 1901 he caught at St. Johns, Newfoundland, the signal sent from Poldhu Station, Cornwall. By the opening of the First World War wireless installations had become standard equipment on every ship of any size, huge wireless stations were being erected, commercial wireless was an accomplished fact, and the way was open for the development of wireless telephony and radio.

THE POST OFFICE

One of the most important social and economic functions of government in modern times is the proper collection and distribution of mails. So important is this considered that any interference with the mails is a criminal offense. The great development of the postal system has occurred since 1860. The postal law of 1816, which was in effect until 1845, charged six cents for one piece of paper going not over thirty miles, prepayment being optional. In 1847 the rates were lowered and postage stamps of five- and ten-cent denominations introduced; prepayment was required. The rates were again reduced in 1861 to three cents per half ounce for distances under 3000 miles and in 1883 to two cents an ounce for all first-class mail. The registration of letters was begun in 1854, and during Lincoln's administration the free delivery of mail (1863), the railroad post office (1862), and the money-order system (1864) were instituted. Under McKinley in 1896 the rural free delivery was established, with 87 routes, the number of which had grown by 1939 to 32,839, covering 1,392,657 miles. In 1838 the country declared every railroad a mail route, but the post office pushed ahead and beyond the railroads, its operations in the sparsely settled West of the pioneer days forming a romantic and inspiring story. Always alert for new opportunities, the federal government began the transportation of mail by air in 1918 when Army planes carried the first mail from New York to Washington.[34]

In recent years the activities of the government have been extended into both the express and the banking businesses, although its entrance in both cases was bitterly fought by the interests affected. A postal-savings system was inaugurated in 1910 to provide absolute safety at low interest for the comparatively poor man. The interest of 2 per cent upon a full year's deposit was in fact so low that the amount placed was relatively small. Of more general use, the domestic parcel-post system, introduced in 1913 after successful operation in Europe, has been an immense blessing to the people, enabling as it does the transportation of small packages more rapidly, cheaply, and safely than does any other means. Some industries, the most notable of which are the great mail-order houses of Chicago, base the large bulk of their business upon its facilities. Again the farmer has been the great gainer. On the other hand, the federal government, presumably to promote the cultural and economic life of the nation, carries a great deal

[34] Below, p. 624.

of second-class mail, particularly newspapers and magazines, at much less than cost. While this objective is to some extent achieved, the policy also results in subsidizing advertising and the transportation of much material that degrades rather than elevates the cultural level—all at the expense of the taxpayers. Some indication of the development of the post office may be seen from the fact that the gross postal revenues increased from $8,518,-000 in 1860 to $745,955,000 in 1939, and the gross expenditures from $19,171,-000 to $784,550,000.

SELECTED READINGS

Moody, John, *The Railroad Builders.*
Riegel, R. E., *Story of Western Railroads,* Chaps. I–VIII.
Jones, Eliot, *Principles of Railway Transportation,* Chaps. X–XV (survey of legislation).
Daggett, Stuart, *Principles of Inland Transportation,* Chap. VI (street and interurban railroads).
Moulton, H. G., *Waterways vs. Railways,* Chaps. I–V, XV–XIX.
Faulkner, H. U., *The Quest for Social Justice,* Chap. VI.
Flügel, F., and Faulkner, H. U., *Readings in the Economic and Social History of the United States,* Chap. XV.

24.

Domestic and Foreign Commerce

Routes of and Barriers to Internal Commerce

As all sections of the country do not specialize in the growing or manufacturing of the same commodities, internal commerce is largely concerned with the distribution of commodities from the producing areas to consumers, wherever they may be. In earlier decades the routes followed mainly the rivers and canals. With the invention of the steam railroad and the automobile and the great improvement of roads the problem of mere physical distribution was largely solved. Since the general expansion of the population was essentially westward rather than north or south, artificial transportation facilities tended to follow the people; hence the chief routes of American commerce are east and west.

This general east-west movement is of course modified by sectional specialization and by the influence of metropolitan areas. The northeastern section of the country, for example, is largly concerned with manufacturing and the import-export trade. Foodstuffs or raw materials for manufacturing move from many sections toward this area to be processed or exported to the European or Latin-American market. Conversely, imports and manufactured goods move from the Northeast in all directions to supply consumers' needs. In the Old Northwest—that is, the states north of the Ohio and east of the Mississippi—is to be found the most self-sufficing section of the nation. Rich agricultural lands, abundant minerals, and intensive manufacturing make it possible for the population to buy largely at home. Despite this fact there is, of course, a steady stream of manufactured products, such as automobiles and steel, moving out and specialized products manufactured elsewhere coming in. From the earliest times the South has always specialized in the extractive industries—at first tobacco, later cotton and other agricultural products, and finally lumber and such minerals as iron and petroleum. Most of these extractive commodities are shipped northward to be processed; but local manufacturing, stimulated by importations of northern capital, has increased in the past forty years. This is also true of the Far West. A region chiefly concerned during the nineteenth century with agriculture and the extraction of minerals, this section has also developed manufacturing. The rapid growth of the population and the desire to save on freight rates led many eastern manufacturers to establish branch factories on the west coast. Nevertheless, a large proportion of the Far West's manufactured goods is imported from the East in exchange for fruit, vegetables, and other agricultural products.

A certain modification in these main routes of commerce, as earlier suggested, is inherent in the fact that the surplus products of a section tend to gather in a central point where they are warehoused, wholesaled, financed, and later distributed to other parts of the country. This concentration has resulted in "metropolitan areas" which largely dominate the economic life of a section. When the Federal Reserve System was created in 1913 the government divided the nation into twelve regions whose banking facilities centered in the cities of Boston, New York, Philadelphia, Richmond, Cleveland, Atlanta, Chicago, St. Louis, Dallas, Kansas City, Minneapolis, and San Francisco. These cities, in fact, are not only the financial centers but also the commercial centers of these areas. There are subsidiary metropolitan areas within the larger ones, but the center largely dominates commerce. Although a portion of a region's products are distributed and consumed in the immediate area, the surplus, usually the major part of the total, moves out of the area.

Economists have often stressed the advantage this country enjoys in freedom of interstate trade. The Constitution presumably insures this freedom, giving the federal government power to control interstate traffic. In recent years there has been, nevertheless, a growing tendency on the part of the states to find methods of evading the obvious purpose of the Constitution. The reasons are perfectly understandable and in some cases laudable—protection of the economic and physical well-being of the citizens. A state often establishes quarantines to protect the health of its people or to prevent the spread of insect pests or animal diseases. Sometimes the purpose is to check the evasion of taxation. Usually it is plainly an effort to prevent competition and to protect the economic interests of the citizens. Although this tendency toward interstate barriers has grown rapidly in the past fifteen years, it has not yet become a major problem. These barriers are chiefly used to interfere with the interstate movement of agricultural products. Thus the milk farmers of one state will induce the legislature to establish certain standards and requirements of inspection which cannot be met easily by another state. Similarly, the dairy farmers who produce butter will do everything possible to have state laws impede the sale of margarine. All types of ingenious regulations are devised to harass the merchant trucker from outside the state in order to aid the local truck farmer. Regulations regarding grading and labeling are often purposely designed to keep fruit, vegetables, or eggs from entering a particular commonwealth. Amendment XXI makes illegal the importation of intoxicating liquors into a state in violation of the laws of that state. Using this as a wedge, certain states have passed laws designed not to protect their inhabitants from the deleterious effects of alcoholic beverages but rather to help local brewers, distillers, or farmers. This has been achieved by requiring higher sales taxes on outside liquor, special licenses before an outside manufacturer can do business within the state, and other devices. Such practices often bring retaliatory measures until there develops a situation of state fighting state not unlike conditions during the period of the Articles of Confederation. Up to the present the Supreme Court has shown little interest or desire to stop this tendency.

Trends in Wholesale and Retail Selling

Internal commerce has been largely influenced during the past half century by the growth of the urban population and the improvement in transportation facilities. Increased urbanization has allowed more specialization in both wholesaling and retailing, and better transportation has had almost revolutionary effects upon rural buying. Population increase and concentration, for example, have made it possible for wholesalers to specialize in single commodities and has enabled the development of the grain, cotton, coffee, and other exchanges whose operations are patterned after those of the stock market. Here the buying and selling of raw materials tends to set the price for the commodity. Urbanization has enabled not only wholesalers to specialize, but retailers as well. Sections given over to the wholesaling or retailing of specific commodities are often found in large cities.

Specialization in retailing is the normal practice in urban communities where there is enough business to make it possible. Interestingly enough, one persistent trend has been contrary to specialized retailing—the continued existence and even growth of the department store. Originally the department store as developed by Alexander T. Stewart in New York in the 1860's and in succeeding years by John Wanamaker in New York and Marshall Field in Chicago was little more than a glorified country general store. The convenience, particularly for suburban buyers, of making all the purchases under one roof rather than going from one store to another was sufficient to make a place for the department store. The business of many of these stores became so large that their various departments could be conducted as efficiently and on as large a scale as the specialized store.

Rural buying at the end of the nineteenth century was largely done in the country general store which, like the city's glorified department store, carried almost everything that the community needed. The old-fashioned peddler who traveled from door to door still existed, but his number was declining. Two developments of the 1890's did much to change this picture, the introduction of the rural free delivery and the invention of the automobile. The first of these made possible the rapid expansion of the mail-order house. Montgomery, Ward & Company was founded in 1872 especially to sell to the Grangers; Sears, Roebuck & Company was founded in 1895. Both grew rapidly in the late 'nineties and again after the inauguration of the parcels post system in 1913. To the typical farmer and small-town American the mail-order purchase became as common as that from the country store. Revolutionary also was the automobile which considerably extended the farmer's purchasing radius. Before its advent the average farmer bought from his country store and from mail-order houses, with possibly one trip to the city each year, if he was prosperous. The automobile made it possible to run into the nearest town every Saturday afternoon for shopping, even if the town was fifty or more miles away.

The automobile gave another blow to the country store, already forced to reduce its business to a few necessities; it forced the mail-order houses to change their technique. To catch the farmer's business on his frequent trips to the city, the mail-order houses beginning in 1926 opened retail outlets in many of the small and medium-sized urban centers. This made it possible through carload shipments to cut prices even further for the farmer, and at the same time it gave the mail-order houses a chance to enlarge their business to include the urban as well as the rural buyer. The establishment of these chain outlets was in line with a development which had been going on for years. The first and greatest of the chains goes back to the founding of the great Atlantic & Pacific Tea Company in 1858 which by 1930 had approximately 1600 branches and an annual business of one billion dollars. The success of the A. & P. led to the founding of many other chains in the grocery and other fields. The Woolworth Five and Ten Cent chain started in 1879, the United Cigar Stories in 1892, and the Kresge system in 1897. In more recent years other successful chains have been built up, particularly in clothing, shoes, and drugs. Over fifty different lines of merchandise have been taken over by these chains and in some small towns they handle most of the retailing. In 1935 there were over 6000 different chains with 127,482 separate stores, and net sales of $7,550,-000,000. They handled over one-fifth of the total retail sales of the country.[1]

Advertising of one kind or other probably goes back to the days when

[1] *Statistical Abstract, 1940*, p. 879.

the first seller attempted to find a purchaser, but it waited upon the twentieth century to flower in its full glory. In the effort to sell commodities every human weakness and desire was exploited. If you had no interest in a commodity, you were made to desire it; if you already possessed it, you became convinced that yours was out of date and a new one was necessary; if you thought you were perfectly healthy, you were told about all the diseases you might have now or in the future, and so on. By suggestion, innuendo, or outright assertion one product was held up as superior to the next. The philosophy was largely based upon the old policy of *caveat emptor* —let the buyer beware. In the field of patent medicines and cosmetics this led to high-pressure advertising of commodities that were often absolutely worthless or harmful. A slight check was put on the sale of harmful medicines by the Pure Food and Drug Act of 1906, and a much stronger one by the Food, Drug, and Cosmetic Act of 1938. By the 1930's the advertising business had grown to tremendous proportions. Advertising agencies in 1935 reported a business of over $400,000,000 which of course did not include direct advertising, door-to-door canvassing, and innumerable other methods of pushing a commodity. Newspapers and magazines were obtaining from two to three times as great an income from advertisers as from readers, a fact which tended to make the typical newspaper essentially an organ for advertisers. The radio chains also were largely supported by advertising.

There is no intention in these pages to discount the valuable aspects of advertising in acquainting the consumer with the merits of a new product or the advantages of a particular product, or the aid it contributes in developing the mass production of a useful commodity. Advertising without doubt increases one's desire to buy and thus increases business. The difficulty is that it often stimulates a desire which the consumer can hardly afford. This dilemma was in part taken care of during the 'twenties and 'thirties by the tremendous expansion of installment buying—approximately 15 per cent of all goods were sold in this way. In recent years about 60 per cent of automobiles, 55 per cent of household appliances, and 50 per cent of furniture have been purchased on the installment plan. Credit is handled largely by small loan companies, by banks which have set up special departments in order to share in this lucrative business, and in some cases by the manufacturer, as for example General Motors, which has organized finance companies to finance sales.

Present Distribution of Goods

To trace and estimate the flow of goods in internal commerce is a rather difficult task. The Census of 1930 attempted to do this for the first time.

Fortunately, the year 1929 was used, a year which represented the highest volume of internal trade in our history. Beginning with raw materials obtained from agriculture, mining, and other extractive industries, and imports, valued together at about 21.7 billion dollars, the census reported that about 45 per cent of these materials (reckoned in value) went to some type of intermediate distributor (wholesaler), about one-third direct to manufacturers, and the remaining small portion to retailers or terminal buyers such as institutions, utilities, exporters, or ultimate consumers.[2] An examination of sales made by manufacturers, which amounted in 1929 to 69.6 billion dollars (more than three times the total value of goods received from primary sources), showed that 32 billion, nearly half the total, went to intermediary dealers, about 7.2 billion was sold direct to household and other terminal buyers such as public utilities, government institutions, transportation agencies, etc., 6.4 billion went direct to retail trade, and 3.1 billion was exported. It is interesting to note that a substantial part of the volume of manufacturers' sales to intermediaries is resold to other factories.

For the wholesalers, the total volume of sales was somewhat over 69 billion dollars, of which more than 27 billion went to retailers, 16 billion to manufacturers, 16 billion to other intermediaries and the rest to industries, institutions, exporters, or direct to consumers. Retail sales in 1929 amounted to 49 billion dollars, of which 44.4 billion represented sales to consumers, the remainder comprising certain sales to farmers, retailers, intermediaries, and manufacturers. This business was handled by 169,700 wholesale establishments and 1,543,000 retail stores. In breaking down the amount of retail sales we find that food accounted for over one-fifth of the total, automotive commodities about one-fifth, general merchandise, including department, dry goods, and variety sales, about one-seventh, and clothing about one-eleventh.

Estimates[3] place the total of these various sales, including 8.7 billion dollars paid for transportation, at 218.6 billion, and the total of purchases by all producing and selling agencies at 153 billion. The difference, 65.6 billion, represents the total cost of producing and distributing goods and is equal to the total amount paid by terminal buyers for finished goods. Of this, 87 per cent represents the costs of extracting or growing, manufacturing, storing, or selling, and 13 per cent (8.7 billion) the cost of transportation. It will be seen from these estimates that the total of all sales is more than three times the value of the finished goods purchased by terminal buyers.

[2] For the flow of goods through distribution channels, see Twentieth Century Fund, *Does Distribution Cost Too Much?* (1939), Chap. III.
[3] *Ibid.*, p. 67.

Estimates from these and other data indicate also that it costs about 50 per cent more to have goods distributed than it does to have them produced. This throws considerable light on the important rôle played by various types of distributors in our economic system. It also indicates how small the actual costs of raw material and labor often are in the total cost of a commodity.

The realization that costs often double or triple from the time a commodity leaves the factory until it finally reaches the consumer has led to repeated efforts to cut the costs of distribution. Although the prices charged by individual distributors for an individual commodity usually appear reasonable, the costs of the complicated structure bear heavily upon the consumer. Important as is the distributing and marketing agencies' rôle, there is widespread belief that distribution has become too complicated and costly and constitutes too large a proportion of the total cost of a commodity. This in part explains the rapid development of consumers' cooperatives since 1935.

CAUSES OF THE DEVELOPMENT OF FOREIGN COMMERCE

The foreign commerce of the United States has grown tremendously since 1860. By 1920 exports had increased twenty-fourfold and imports sixteenfold. In 1850 imports exceeded exports by $20,040,062, but in 1920 the excess of exports over imports was $2,880,114,000. During the same period per capita imports increased threefold, and per capita exports increased sevenfold. The reasons for this great development are not hard to find. First of all was the continued and rapid expansion of the settled area of the nation which opened to exploitation vast agricultural regions and new mineral resources. Along with this came the development of transportation facilities capable of handling commerce as it expanded. In the second place, the unsurpassed natural resources of America combined with a rapidly growing population and a high protective tariff were gradually changing her from a nation whose interests were essentially agricultural to one predominantly manufacturing. The basic result of a situation in which an abundance of raw material is combined with continually improving machinery is the production of a surplus of manufactured goods which seeks an outlet abroad as well as at home. American industry needed foreign markets, and as industry developed, it necessarily promoted foreign trade and the development of economic imperialism.

Along with this there was the rapid development of all types of facilities tending to stimulate foreign trade. These included the expansion of the internal transportation system, technical improvements in communication such as the invention of cables and the wireless and transatlantic telephones, and improvement in banking and credit facilities. The principle of the telegraph was put into operation in undersea cables after 1852, the year in which a short line was laid from Dover to Ostend. Chiefly through the efforts of Cyrus Field, a successful transatlantic cable was laid in 1866. By 1918 at least nine active cables connected North America with Europe, and the principal ports of the world were joined with 281,000 nautical miles of cable, enough to girdle the world thirteen times. Experiments by Heinrich Hertz in Germany after 1888, by Marconi in Italy, and by numerous inventors throughout the world perfected the wireless to such an extent that messages were sent across the Atlantic in 1903.[4] Within two decades after transoceanic wireless had been established, it was possible for anyone at small expense to receive by radio in his own home news flashes, stock quotations, and the commercial news of the day.

With the growth of foreign commerce has gone that of extended financial facilities. Some of our largest banks maintain branch offices in Europe, Asia, South America, and Africa which are able to furnish credit information, negotiate loans, issue bills of exchange, and in other ways aid commerce. In this connection the student of foreign commerce should keep in mind the aid continually given by various government facilities. This was particularly evident in the Department of Commerce under Secretary Hoover during the 1920's.

EXPORTS AND IMPORTS, 1860–1939[5]

Year	Exports of Merchandise	Exports of Merchandise and Specie	Imports of Merchandise	Imports of Merchandise and Specie	Excess of Total Exports or Imports[a]
1860 . .	$ 333,576,000	$ 400,122,000	$ 353,616,000	$ 362,166,000	$ 37,956,000
1900 . .	1,394,483,000	1,499,462,000	849,941,000	929,771,000	569,691,000
1920 . .	8,228,016,000	8,663,723,000	5,278,481,000	5,783,609,000	2,880,114,000
1929 . .	5,240,995,000	5,440,985,000	4,399,361,000	4,754,950,000	686,035,000
1932 . .	1,611,016,000	2,434,394,000	1,322,774,000	1,705,739,000	728,655,000
1939 . .	3,177,176,000	3,192,314,000	2,318,081,000	5,978,047,000	2,785,733,000

[a] All figures in this column are excess of exports except those for 1939. The excess of imports over exports is due to the heavy flow of American gold because of World War II.

Foreign trade, of course, cannot be carried on without commodities to export. During the last half of the nineteenth century, as in earlier years, American agricultural products supplied the chief commodities for the export trade—cotton to keep the textile mills of Europe humming and

[4] On December 12 and 13, 1901, Guglielmo Marconi with the aid of a kite at St. John's, Newfoundland, caught the signal sent from Poldhu Station, Cornwall.

[5] Statistical Abstract, 1921, Table 482, pp. 840–841, 854–855; ibid., 1940, pp. 488–489.

foodstuffs to feed the rapidly growing industrial population of western Europe. With the turn of the century, however, manufactured products began to supplement and finally to surpass the agricultural value. American ingenuity, protected by patents, had evolved numerous types of labor-saving machinery so epoch-making in their significance that they found a ready sale abroad. Of these may be mentioned agricultural implements, sewing machines, typewriters, and cash registers. The United States also led the world in the development of mass production, and the low cost of commodities thus produced, notably automobiles, provided goods for the export market. Foreign commerce, of course, originates and is stimulated by the needs of one part of the world for the products of another. As we have repeatedly emphasized, no nation has been more fortunately situated in respect to resources than the United States; she has been in a position to furnish raw materials and eventually manufactured products to other parts of the world on most advantageous terms.

Importation has increased along with exportation, although the excess of exports over imports has grown since 1860 out of proportion to the increase of either exports or imports. Importation has resulted primarily from the desire for certain commodities such as coffee and rubber which we do not produce, and from the necessity of taking in exchange some commodities classed as luxuries and many products of minute and skilled workmanship which the cheaper labor costs and more artistic training of foreign artisans have enabled them to produce. It should be remembered also that the excess of exports over imports in value is partially compensated for (1) by large sums paid to Europeans (especially before the First World War) for marine freight and insurance, (2) by dividends and interest paid to foreign stock and bond holders, (3) by money sent home by immigrants, and (4) by American travelers, who were reported in those years as spending about $350,000,000 annually.

GOVERNMENT AID TO COMMERCE

Although it is a normal function of government to promote the trade and prosperity of its people, the extent to which this is actually done is sometimes not realized. Even in the United States which, until recent years, was dominated by a *laissez-faire* theory as to the function of government, the government has been continually at work promoting commercial activity. This has been done chiefly through three methods: (1) construction and improvement of harbors, and measures to increase the safety of navigation, (2) efforts to make commerce more profitable, and (3) aids to the shipbuilding industry. Such aid originates in the first place from congressional legislation and is carried on either by bureaus of the executive departments or through independent agencies. This activity has been greatly extended since the rapid expansion of American commerce after the Spanish-American War, and especially since the division of the Department of Commerce and Labor into two executive divisions in 1913. A mere citation of the bureaus at present included under the Department of Commerce will give some idea of the extensive activity of that branch of the government: Coast and Geodetic Survey, to survey and chart the coasts; Bureau of Foreign and Domestic Commerce, to collect all data essential to the conduct of foreign and domestic trade; Bureau of Marine Inspection and Navigation, to administer the laws regarding the construction, equipment, and other matters pertaining to commercial vessels; Inland Waterways Corporation, to promote, encourage, and develop inland water transportation; Weather Bureau, to provide weather forecasts for air transport, shipping, and other interests; Civil Aeronautics Authority and Civil Aeronautics Administration, to supervise and encourage air transport; Foreign-trade Zones Board, to expedite and encourage foreign commerce in American ports of entry; there are also other bureaus designed to aid American business.[6] Of great value also are the various bulletins, reports, and statistical material on trade published by the Department of Commerce.

Since 1802, when the first federal appropriation was made for rivers and harbors, over one billion dollars has been expended. The amount spent in 1929 was close to $82,000,000. This work is recommended and supervised by the Corps of Engineers of the United States Army, but owing to the fact that the appropriations are influenced to a considerable extent by political logrolling, not all of this money has been spent wisely. Safety in navigation has been promoted by the Bureau of Lighthouses, now part of the work of the Coast Guard under the Treasury Department, by the Coast and Geodetic Survey, by the Bureau of Marine Inspection and Navigation, and by the Weather Bureau, already mentioned. The Coast Guard divides its work between the maintenance of lighthouses and other safety devices, the Life Saving Service, which maintains over 250 active stations to warn ships of impending danger and help those in distress, and the Revenue Cutter Service, which aims not only to enforce the revenue laws but to supplement the work of the Life Saving Service. Much of the work of the Coast and Geodetic Survey is supplemented by the Hydrographic Office of the Bureau of Navigation of the Navy Department, whose duty it is to provide accurate nautical charts, sailing directions, and manuals of instruction.

Efforts on the part of the government to make commerce more profitable have been exerted from the beginning of our history. Tonnage Acts have been passed favoring American ships, and treaties negotiated to secure

[6] Information as to government activities may be obtained from the *United States Government Manual,* published three times a year by the United States Information Service.

favorable treatment for American products. In addition to activities of the State, Treasury, and Post Office Departments and various subsidiary bureaus in providing valuable information, there was instituted in 1912 the Bureau of Foreign and Domestic Commerce under the Department of Commerce, whose business it is "to develop the various manufacturing industries of the United States and markets for their products at home and abroad, by gathering and publishing useful information, or by any other available method." Through special agents and commercial attachés in foreign countries and by means of cooperation with the consular service of the State Department, data covering conditions and commercial opportunities abroad are gathered and distributed. As already stated, the work of this Bureau, particularly that of the special agents and commercial attachés, was greatly expanded during the years Hoover was a member of the Department.

Special encouragement to foreign commerce was afforded in the Webb Export Act of April 10, 1918, which exempted associations entered into "for the sole purpose of engaging in export trade and actually so engaged" from the provisions of the Sherman Anti-trust Act, on condition that such associations did not enter into a conspiracy to control prices or restrain competition. Corporations desiring to acquire part or entire ownership of such foreign trading associations were exempted from the provisions of the Clayton Act. During the 1930's, as we shall see, the Roosevelt administration took even more far-reaching steps to promote foreign commerce by trade agreements, loans to Latin-American nations, and new facilities provided through the Export-Import Bank.[7]

The Merchant Marine

A merchant marine owned at home is not essential to an extensive foreign commerce. In fact, it may be cheaper to hire other nations to handle the carrying trade than to participate in it directly. On the other hand, there are certain advantages, particularly during time of war, which may warrant aggressive government encouragement to the maintenance of a merchant marine. The Civil War dealt our once famous merchant marine a blow from which it never recovered. Destruction by Confederate privateers and large sales abroad decreased the tonnage. Delay in adopting iron steam-driven ships gave British builders an advantage which they continued to hold. But more important than all else was the fact that more profitable investments in internal transportation and the exploitation of raw materials in the great industrial age which dawned after the war drew capital away from the sea. Lack of government interest helped complete the downfall of American shipping.[8]

[7] Below, p. 688.
[8] Above, pp. 242–243.

The five years following the Civil War showed a slight revival, but the forces tending to a decline continued operative. American shipping engaged in foreign trade and the fisheries, which amounted to 2,642,628 tons in 1870, dropped to 826,694 tons in 1900. In 1860 the percentage of imports and

TONNAGE OF THE UNITED STATES MERCHANT MARINE ENGAGED IN FOREIGN COMMERCE, 1789-1939.[9]

exports carried in American ships was 66.5, but this dropped in 1870 to 35.6, in 1880 to 13, in 1890 to 9.4, in 1900 to 7.1. The merchant marine had a loyal friend in Senator Frye of Maine, who in 1891 introduced bills to subsidize mail steamers, freight steamers, and sailing vessels; but the encouragement was insufficient and a subsequent bill introduced by him in 1901 and strongly supported by Senator Hanna, providing for a more liberal subsidy of $9,000,000 for thirty years, was defeated by the agricultural and manufacturing interests.

The La Follette Seamen's Act of 1915 was unjustly denounced by the shipping interests as the final blow at a declining merchant marine, but its backers claimed that it was a protection to American shipping and a simple act of justice to American seamen. Among other things it provided (1) that 75 per cent of the crew in American-owned and operated ships should understand any order given by the officers; (2) that 64 per cent of the deck crews employed on American ships should ultimately be able seamen, having passed physical and professional examinations; (3) that half wages should be paid the crew in every port; and (4) that the crew of any vessel touching at an American port might quit the service. Other pro-

[9] W. Bates, *American Marine*, p. 462 ff.; and *Statistical Abstract, 1940*, p. 463.

visions regarding hours of labor in ports and the safety of seamen were looked upon as marking a long forward step in the legal code governing marine operations.

There appears to be little or no evidence that this law providing decent

REGISTERED AND ENROLLED TONNAGE [10]

Year	Tonnage Registered in Foreign Trade	Tonnage Employed in Coastwise and Internal Trade	Proportion of Imports and Exports Carried in American Vessels by Value
	Tons	Tons	
1910	782,517	6,668,966	8.7
1914	1,066,288	6,818,363	9.7
1915	1,862,714	6,486,384	14.3
1916	2,185,008	6,244,550	16.3
1917	2,440,776	6,392,583	18.6
1918	3,599,213	6,282,474	21.9
1919	6,665,376	6,201,426	27.8
1920	9,924,694	6,357,706	43.0
1921	11,077,000	7,163,000	35.7
1925	8,151,000	9,216,000	33.0
1929	6,906,000	9,526,000	33.1
1932	5,071,000	10,728,000	35.6
1939	3,312,000	11,228,000	35.8[a]

[a] This figure is for 1935, the last available percentage as given in the *Statistical Abstract* for 1940.

treatment for American sailors has appreciably delayed the revival of the American merchant marine. In fact, indications were already evident that a revival was impending, which would have made progress without the artificial stimulation provided by the First World War. American manufacturers were able to produce steel plates cheaper than European, and there was surplus capital which might be enticed into the shipping industry. The elimination of the German merchant marine after the outbreak of war, and the rapid increase of exports due to war orders gave new stimulus to American shipyards.

Dependence upon European shipping from 1914 to 1916 demonstrated anew the need for a merchant marine, and in the latter year Congress approved the appointment of a United States Shipping Board to supervise ocean freight rates, prevent unjust combinations and excessive charges, and advise on methods to increase the merchant marine. When we entered the First World War the Shipping Board organized the Emergency Fleet Corporation, which bent all its efforts to turning out steel, wooden, and cement ships. Congress made $4,000,000,000 available for this work, and during the nineteen months of the war 875 vessels of 2,941,845 gross tons

[10] *Statistical Abstract, 1921*, p. 410; *1933*, pp. 377, 396; *1940*, pp. 463, 482.

were built. The 61 shipyards of 1917 with their 235 ways had increased by November, 1918, to 341 shipyards and 1284 launching ways, and the number of workmen had grown from 45,000 to 380,000.

A large proportion of the gross tonnage in 1920 was owned by the government, and the question of its future was one which Congress was called upon to decide. The bitter hostility of capital to government-owned transportation presaged the government's retirement from the ocean carrying trade, an end partially achieved in the Merchant Marine Act of 1920. This bill, known as the Jones Act, continued the United States Shipping Board and gave partial recognition to the principle of subsidies to American shipping by exempting companies from an excess profits tax up to a certain amount, and by providing for government loans for construction to the amount of $25,000,000 a year for five years, the sum to be obtained from the sale of government ships. In a number of other ways it sought to stabilize and aid the newborn merchant marine. However, the effects of the Jones Act in promoting American shipping were very slight, and subsequent amendments and legislation, notably that of May 23, 1928, sought to strengthen and liberalize it. Although outright subsidies were avoided, the principle was recognized in loans for various purposes, in payments for carrying mail, in tax exemption, and in government operation of ships at a loss. Discrimination in tonnage and customs rates was provided by the Act of 1920 but were opposed by the administration and eventually repudiated. On the other hand, foreign-owned ships were excluded from the coastwise trade altogether, government ships were disposed of at ridiculously low prices, and the government cooperated in many ways to encourage development. By 1929 the government had succeeded in selling its passenger liners on the Atlantic and Pacific to private operators, thus retiring from this shipping business.

In spite of this liberal policy and the definite effort on the part of the government to extend aid, the merchant marine declined relatively between the First and Second World Wars. Tonnage engaged in foreign trade dropped from 11,077,000 in 1921 to 3,312,000 in 1929, and the proportion of imports and exports carried in American bottoms from 42.7 per cent in 1920 to 35.8 in 1935.[11] The Shipping Board reported in 1927 that of $600,000,000 paid annually by shippers for freight, $480,000,000 went to foreign ships. Lloyd's register reported that for 1925 the tonnage constructed in America was less than one-eighth that built in Great Britain and Ireland, less than one-third that of Italy, and less than one-half that of Germany. In 1927 the Shipping Board reported that for every first-class merchant ship built in the United States since 1921, Great Britain had built 41, Germany 12, Italy 5, and France

[11] See table above, p. 529.

and Japan 4 each.[12] In that year the historic firm of William Cramp and Sons withdrew from shipbuilding because of lack of business. The failure of American shipping to advance was attributed by government officials to the greater cost of building and operating, but undoubtedly other factors were contributing causes, including the artificial economic situation of the industry, the rapidity and newness of its development, and the competition of other industries for capital. In spite of all of this, the artificial extension of the merchant marine had, by 1928, placed it second among the fleets of the world, with Great Britain first; the United States was followed by Japan, Italy, Germany, and France.[13]

Trend of Foreign Commerce, 1860–1930

The Civil War profoundly affected foreign commerce. The high tariffs it inaugurated stimulated manufacturing. The cutting off of the southern trade

Merchandise Imported and Exported, 1850–1939.[14]

forced northern producers to seek other markets, with the result that between 1860 and 1865 there was an actual increase in exports other than cotton. The war temporarily ruined the cotton business of the South, and the amount of cotton exported did not reach the pre-war level until 1875. This in turn cut down imports to the South. While the war ruined the merchant marine, it

[12] In 1929 only 128,976 gross tons of shipping were built, as compared with 3,880,639 in 1920.

[13] The merchant marine under the New Deal and in the Second World War is discussed below, pp. 667–668, 692.

[14] *Statistical Abstract, 1899*, p. 92; *ibid., 1921*, p. 854; and *ibid., 1940*, p. 487.

stimulated the building of transcontinental railroads and further aided commerce by the concentration of capital and the better banking system which was introduced in 1863.

From 1865 until 1920 the increase in imports and exports was irregular, but large in the long run. Between 1870 and 1890 the value of the annual imports of merchandise increased 118 per cent and that of the annual exports 74 per cent. The first decade of the century saw an increase of 25 per cent in the value of the exports and 83 per cent in that of the imports. The figures for the next decade are even more striking, but the increases in value must be discounted to a certain extent by the rise in prices, and by the fact that they represent an artificial stimulation caused by the First World War. The decline after 1929 was the result of the economic depression. To obtain a true conception of the growth of foreign commerce, the figures in the accompanying table should be compared with the amount of imports and exports of certain commodities rather than their value.

EXPORTS AND IMPORTS OF MERCHANDISE BY DECADES [15]

Year	Exports	Imports
1860	$ 333,576,157	$ 353,616,119
1870	392,771,768	453,958,408
1880	835,638,658	667,954,746
1890	857,828,684	789,310,409
1900	1,394,483,082	849,941,184
1910	1,744,984,720	1,556,947,430
1920	8,228,016,307	5,278,481,490
1930	3,843,181,000	3,060,908,000
1939	3,177,176,000	2,318,081,000

Up to 1890 the leading exports were agricultural, including wheat, corn, and meat products and such processed agricultural commodities as flour, glucose, cotton and vegetable oils, butter, and cheese. Agricultural products amounted to 79.4 per cent of the country's exports in 1870, 83.3 per cent in 1880, 74.5 per cent in 1890, and 60.9 per cent in 1900. Manufactures ranked next to agriculture in importance, followed by minerals, food products, and fisheries. Of individual commodities, exported grains took the lead, followed by cotton, meat and meat products, iron and steel, and mineral oil.

The percentages considered in connection with figures for valuation show a gradual decline in the relative importance of agricultural products in exports and an increase in that of partly or wholly manufactured commodities. Particularly is this to be noted during the last decade of the century. By far the greatest market was Great Britain, but there was a growing demand in

[15] Fiscal years until 1920. Compiled from *Statistical Abstract, 1921*, table 482, pp. 840–841, 854–855; *ibid., 1940*, p. 487.

all of the countries of northern Europe except Russia. Trade with southern Europe was stagnant; for South American trade, although the amount almost doubled between 1870 and 1900, the percentage of the total was less. Healthy progress was made in the Asian, Australian, and African markets. In 1870

DOMESTIC EXPORTS GROUPED ACCORDING TO SOURCES OF PRODUCTION [16]

	1870		1880		1890		1900	
	Value[a]	Per Cent	Value[a]	Per Cent	Value[a]	Per Cent	Value[a]	Per Cent
Agriculture . .	$361,188	79.35	$685,961	83.25	$629,821	74.51	$835,858	60.98
Manufactures .	68,280	15.00	102,856	12.48	151,102	17.87	433,852	31.65
Forests . . .	14,898	3.27	17,321	2.11	29,473	3.49	52,218	3.81
Mining . . .	5,026	1.10	5,863	.71	22,298	2.64	37,844	2.76
Fisheries . . .	2,836	.62	5,255	.64	7,458	.88	6,327	.46
Miscellaneous .	2,981	.66	6,689	.81	5,141	.61	4,665	.34
Total . . .	$455,209	100.00	$823,935	100.00	$845,293	100.00	$1,370,764	100.00

[a] In thousands of dollars.

the percentage of our total exports which went to Europe was 79.35, to North America 13.03, to South America 4.09, to Asia 2.07, to Oceanica .82, and to Africa .64. In 1900 Europe received 76.60 per cent, North America 13.45, South America 2.79, Asia 4.66, Oceanica 3.11, and Africa 1.79.

The figures for imports for 1870–1890 show foodstuffs, both in crude condition and partly manufactured, holding up well, and in the latter case actually increasing, with sugar as the leading single import. The group which advanced most rapidly was crude materials for use in manufacturing, including rubber, hides and skins, raw silks, and fibers. While Europe took 74.6 per cent of our exports, in 1900 she sent us only 51.8 per cent of our imports, most of which were in manufactured products. Relatively the import trade with North America declined greatly and that with South America increased slightly, while the imports from Asia, which had constituted 6.8 per cent of the total in 1870, advanced to 16.5 per cent in 1900.

By 1900 industrial development in the United States had advanced to the stage where there was an excess of manufactured products and minerals for export, and this, furthered by the impetus of the Spanish-American War, drove American capital and products into foreign markets. The same tendencies that were apparent in the last decade of the preceding century became more evident. Foodstuffs, which had led in exportation, gave place to manufactures. In 1900 all classes of foodstuffs constituted 39.80 per cent of our total exports; in 1910, only 21.58, with a decline in absolute value of nearly $177,-000,000. This decline is all the more marked because prices on the whole were

[16] *Monthly Summary of Commerce and Finance*, p. 3249 (April, 1903).

rising. It will be noticed that while the value of foodstuffs exported increased nearly fourfold from 1900 to 1920, their percentage of total exports decreased from 39.80 to 25.18. During these twenty years manufactured exports increased nearly ten times in value and from 35.38 to 51.52 in percentage of total exports. Crude materials for further use in manufacturing were relatively in the same position in 1929 as at the opening of the century. Up tc 1914 cotton, of which about two-thirds was exported annually, made up the bulk of this group and retained its position as the leading single American export. The decline of agricultural exports in comparison with manufactures is shown in the accompanying table.

EXPORTS OF UNITED STATES MERCHANDISE, BY ECONOMIC CLASSES [17]

	Total Exports	Percentage of Total Exports				
		Crude Materials	Crude Foodstuffs	Manufactured Foodstuffs	Semimanufactures	Finished Manufactures
1900	$1,370,764,000	24.81	16.48	23.32	11.18	24.20
1910	1,710,084,000	33.57	6.42	15.16	15.66	29.19
1915	2,716,178,000	21.77	11.66	16.74	13.10	29.73
1920	8,080,481,000	23.30	11.36	13.82	11.86	39.66
1925	4,818,722,000	29.51	6.60	11.90	13.73	38.26
1929	5,157,083,000	22.15	5.23	9.40	14.13	49.09
1932	1,576,151,000	32.60	5.67	9.65	12.48	39.60
1939	3,123,343,000	17.44	3.55	6.48	19.17	59.21

As American manufactured articles have been exported in larger amounts, other nations have endeavored to keep them out by keen competition and high tariff duties. Although in 1914 our European exports amounted to 63.37 per cent of the total they consisted chiefly of cotton, wheat, flour, meat products, and tobacco. An outlet for manufactured products had to be found in other quarters. North American countries, especially Canada, have furnished the chief new markets, and exports to them have shown both absolute and relative gains. The first two decades saw an intensified rivalry in the Far East, complicated by the entrance of Japan; but the United States, at least until 1930, was fortunate in obtaining her share of the Asiatic trade. Particularly noticeable also has been the advance in South and Central American commerce, part of which was a normal development and part promoted by World War I. The relative importance of our export markets as shown by the percentage of exports in 1929 was as follows: to Europe, 44.7; to North America, 26.6; to Asia, 12.3; to South America, 10.3; to Oceanica,

[17] Statistical Abstract, 1933, pp. 406, 411; ibid., 1941, p. 533.

3.7; and to Africa, 2.5. In contrast to our exports, more of our imports came from non-European countries. In 1929 less than one-third of our imports came from Europe and about the same amount from Asia; from North America came 22.3 per cent, and from South America, 14.5. From the latter we obtained coffee, which we are unable to raise at home, and from the Far East rubber and raw silk. At the same time our domestic supply of minerals, hides, chemicals, and tropical fruits was considerably augmented from these sources.

All this may be summed up by saying that in the years after the Civil War two-thirds of our exports were crude materials for use in manufacturing and more than four-fifths were crude materials and foodstuffs. By the end of the century this situation was changing rapidly and by the 1920's foodstuffs partly or wholly manufactured, manufactures for use in further manufacturing, and manufactures ready for consumption comprised more than three-fifths of all our exports. This meant that the United States was no longer chiefly a source of raw materials for the European market but was herself scouring the world for raw materials and for new markets for her manufactured goods.

ORGANIZATION OF FOREIGN TRADE

The general organization of foreign trade has changed considerably during the past century. During the early decades of the nineteenth century importers and exporters were likely to deal in many commodities, to own their own ships, and themselves to provide the necessary services. In contrast to this, foreign trade in recent years has become much more specialized. Importers or exporters are inclined to limit their activities to certain lines. Instead of owning their own ships, they employ brokers to secure space in the vessels of some line that goes to the region in which they are interested. This is also true of the typical manufacturer; he merely wholesales his product to the exporter, and he in turn secures shipping space and sells the commodity to foreign retailers. In other words, a commodity may be manufactured by one corporation, exported through the medium of a group of commission men and brokers, and shipped on boats owned by a separate corporation.

Along with this specialization of trade activities there has developed in certain fields a considerable integration of activities. For example, the United Fruit Company owns its own plantations, railroads, and ships, and wholesales its tropical fruit. Similarly, some of the great oil companies, like the Standard Oil, not only produce and refine their product but export it in their own tankers. Other concerns, such as General Motors, which do a large volume of export business, establish subsidiary corporations to handle their export trade through their own warehouses and distributing systems. The necessity of strengthening the position of American exporters, as we have already seen, led to the passage of the Exports Association Act (Webb Export Act) in 1918 to exempt organizations engaged in foreign trade from prosecution under the anti-trust Acts as long as their operations do not injure other Americans.[18]

TARIFF HISTORY SINCE 1860

The American system of high protective tariffs may be said to date from the Civil War. There had been protective tariffs, of course, before that time, but they had not been exorbitantly high and the tendency in the years immediately before the war was downward. The Act of 1857 reduced the maximum protection to 24 per cent, and the general level of duties was reduced to the lowest point since 1815. This policy of tariff reduction, which in general had been in vogue during the period from 1833 to 1861, was completely reversed with the Morrill tariff of 1861, which inaugurated the present high tariff system. The Morrill Act of 1861 was not passed as a war revenue measure, but it contributed in bringing on the conflict. Historians are far from unanimous as to the relative importance of southern fear and hatred of a high tariff in the rebellion, but there is a growing tendency to lay more emphasis upon it. This much seems evident. There was no widespread demand by manufacturers for a high tariff in 1860; Morrill himself admitted in later years that the tariff "was not asked for, and but coldly welcomed by manufacturers, who always and justly fear instability." [19] With the exception of the short period of the panic of 1857, the period from 1846 to 1861 was one of great economic prosperity. The Republicans, searching for issues to bind together the discordant elements in the North, evidently believed that the old Whig protectionists could be allied with the new Republicans if protectionism was offered them. The Morrill tariff with its high rates was introduced in the House of Representatives in the session of 1859–1860 and passed, but did not come before the Senate until the session of 1860–1861.

In the meantime the Republican convention met at Chicago, where high-protection industrialists and representatives of the frontier farmers demanding free homesteads jostled for recognition with the more idealistic free-soilers of '56 and '58. The Republicans went on record not only for free soil but for free homesteads and a protective tariff, and in the Middle Atlantic manufacturing states protection was the chief issue stressed. Curtin, Republican candidate for governor of Pennsylvania, did not even mention slavery in his

---

[18] For the discussion of foreign trade in later years, see below, pp. 646, 684 ff.

[19] Quoted by F. W. Taussig, *Tariff History of the United States* (7th ed.), p. 160; *Congressional Globe, 1869–1870*, p. 3295.

ratification speech but dwelt on "the vast heavings of the heart of Pennsylvania whose sons are pining for protection to their labor and dearest interests."[20] Between the time of the election and the inauguration of Lincoln the Senate acted favorably on the Morrill bill and the South had the most definite proof possible that the control of the government had passed from her own land-owning aristocracy to the rising plutocracy of the North. The Morrill tariff had hardly become law when Fort Sumter was fired upon. For the third time a high tariff played a part in an American rebellion.

The Civil War having begun, the Morrill tariff was not only retained, but there was no session of Congress which did not raise the rates. Money to carry on the war had to be obtained; war industries were demanding protection, and manufacturers were clamoring for higher rates to offset the vast system of internal excise taxes which were being levied. The most important of the war tariffs were those of 1862 and 1864. Earlier in 1862 an internal revenue bill had been passed and to compensate manufacturers added protection was granted. Under the guidance of strong protectionists and under the spur of war needs wholesale advances were again made in 1864. This latter Act, says Taussig, "was in many ways crude and ill-considered; it established protective duties more extreme than had been ventured on in any previous tariff act in our country's history," yet "five days in all were given by the two houses to this act, which was in its effects one of the most important financial measures ever passed in the United States."[21] Among other things, it brought the average level of duties up to 47 per cent. This legislation of 1864, hastily drawn and crude as it was, and denying no protectionist request, remained for decades the basis of the American tariff system.

These war tariffs, unscientific and exorbitant as they were, naturally laid themselves open to the criticism of tariff reformers in the post-bellum years. David A. Wells, Special Commissioner of the Revenue, and Secretary of the Treasury McCulloch united in 1867 in urging reduction, but their bill failed. The Act of 1870 aimed to reduce taxation, but the reductions affected almost entirely such purely revenue articles as tea, coffee, wines, and sugar. The growth of the Liberal Republican movement in 1872 which advocated a lower tariff was strong enough to bring a 10 per cent reduction just before the election of that year, but the panic of 1873, and the loss of revenue resulting therefrom, afforded an excuse to restore the earlier levels. Throughout these reconstruction years the high-tariff lobby defeated practically every effort at reform; prosperity, when it existed, was attributed to the tariff, and the burdens of taxation were lifted by reducing the internal excises.

For almost a decade no further important attempt at tariff reduction was

[20] Quoted and discussed by C. and M. Beard, *Rise of American Civilization*, II, 35.
[21] F. W. Taussig, *Tariff History of the United States*, pp. 167–168.

made. However, a treasury surplus of one hundred million in 1881 and 1882 led President Arthur to suggest a general overhauling. A strongly protective commission was appointed which advocated reductions averaging 25 per cent, but the resulting bill of 1883 lowered the general level only 5 per cent. From the close of the Civil War until the 'eighties neither political party in their official pronouncements was clear on the tariff. The tariff reform clubs and the northern tariff reformers were as likely to be Republican as Democratic, and Republicans, like President Arthur, had taken the initiative in urging action. But in 1887 President Cleveland made the tariff a party issue when he devoted his entire message to it. Pointing out the dangers of a continuing treasury surplus and declaring the existing tariff to be a "vicious, inequitable, and illogical source of unnecessary taxation," he demanded a general reduction. Following the President's lead, a bill was prepared under the direction of John G. Carlisle and passed the Democratic House. The Senate, on the other hand, passed a bill of its own, known as the Mills bill; but as neither could pass the other branch of Congress the matter waited upon the decision of the electorate in the campaign of 1888. For the first time in our history the tariff was the chief campaign issue and was given adequate discussion. Although Cleveland received a majority of the popular votes, Harrison won in the electoral college, and in 1890 the Republicans, after revising the House rules to prevent dilatory tactics on the part of their opponents, passed the McKinley bill, which raised the average level to 49.5 per cent. High duties were placed on the finer grades of woolens, cottons, linens, and clothing, and on iron, steel, glass, and tin plate. To propitiate the farmer, tariffs were imposed on agricultural products; and to take care of the surplus, the duty on sugar was removed and a bounty of two cents a pound placed on the domestic product in order to protect the Louisiana producers.

This tariff was so quickly reflected in the higher cost of living that the Democrats were given possession of the House in 1890, and of the Senate and the Chief Executive's office in 1892. For the first time since the Civil War that party had control of both the legislative and executive branches; and since the campaign of 1892 had been fought over the tariff, some change was inevitable. Cleveland immediately pressed Congress for action, but his efforts toward a healthy reduction were foiled by an active lobby supported by Democratic protectionists. After denouncing the Wilson-Gorman tariff of 1894 as an example of party perfidy and dishonor, he allowed it to become law without his signature. It did, nevertheless, put wool, copper, and lumber on the free list and lowered the average level to 39.9 per cent. The decreased revenue was to be made up by a tax of 2 per cent on incomes over $4000, a feature of the Act which was declared unconstitutional in 1895.[22]

[22] Pollock v. Farmers' Loan and Trust Company, 158 U S. 429.

The campaign of 1896 was fought over the question of currency, and in 1897 there appeared to be little interest in the tariff or demand for change. McKinley, however, scarcely entered the White House before he called a special session of Congress to revise the rates. The Wilson-Gorman bill was speedily wiped from the statute books and the Dingley Act substituted; the latter not only restored the McKinley rates but raised the average level to 57 per cent, imposing high duties on raw and manufactured wool and restoring hides to the dutiable list.

Of the general tariff Acts of the United States, the Dingley bill remained in force the longest. The deluge of prosperity which swept the country as it swung to the upgrade of a new business cycle in the years following the Spanish-American War gave it prestige with large groups, but this popularity was eventually undermined by the rising cost of living and the reviving anti-trust sentiment. The Republican platform of 1908 promised "revision" and the electorate interpreted the word as meaning downward. The disappointment which ensued after the Payne-Aldrich bill was passed in 1909 was a potent element in the Republican defeat in 1910 and the election of Wilson in 1912. President Taft in his Winona speech characterized the Payne-Aldrich Act as the best tariff bill the Republican party had ever passed, but this highly roseate view was not widely entertained.

Since the days of Cleveland the Democrats had bitterly denounced Republican high protectionism, and Wilson's victory made a new Act inevitable. A "competitive tariff" had been emphasized; hence the Underwood-Simmons bill of 1913 put iron, steel, raw wool, sugar (the latter in 1916), and certain agricultural products on the free list and made large reductions on cotton and woolen goods, but raised the rates on chemicals and other products. The reduction in revenue was taken care of by an income tax, now constitutional under the sixteenth amendment. Whatever may have been the official stand of the Democratic party, its two attempts at tariff making resulted in Acts which remained highly protective.

American tariffs in the making have been characterized by a most unscientific procedure of political give and take. The need of turning the question over to a group of experts was recognized in the creation of the Tariff Commission of 1882 and the Tariff Board of 1909. Neither of these were taken seriously by Congress, and the latter was legislated out of existence. In 1916 a new Tariff Commission of six members was created to investigate all questions with reference to tariffs and to submit reports to Congress. These tariff commissions, however "scientific" they are supposed to be, somehow take on a Republican complexion during a Republican administration and a Democratic complexion when that party is in power.

With the conclusion of the First World War and the return of the Republican party to power in 1920, a radical revision of the tariff was to be expected. Two factors were dominant in its making: first, the agricultural distress following the collapse of the war boom; and second, the voice of economic interests, using the nationalism kindled during the war to give force to their demands, and clamoring for protection of the industries stimulated by the war. To prevent post-war dumping and to meet the demands of the farmers, an "emergency" tariff was rushed through a special session of Congress (May 27, 1921); it imposed duties on wheat, corn, meat, wool, and sugar, and was to be kept on the statute books until a more detailed Act could be framed. The latter, known as the Fordney-McCumber tariff (passed September 19, 1922), not only returned to the high duties of 1909 and earlier tariffs, but surpassed them in the protection given. Agricultural products were protected to a high degree, although this was hardly needed and did not perceptibly affect the decline in prices. Hides, however, remained on the free list to offset the effects of the absence of a tariff on boots and shoes, an omission insisted upon by the farmers. The duties on manufactured goods were fully as high as those on agricultural products, and of more significance. The duties on iron and steel, omitted in 1912, were reimposed, and those on textiles, especially silk, were increased. In response to the demands mentioned above, the Act was particularly concerned with the so-called "war babies," especially with the chemical and dyestuff industries, and gave them ample protection. There was much talk during the passage of the Act about equalizing "the differences in costs of production in the United States and the competing foreign countries"; and in fear that foreign competition might possibly injure the American producer, the President was given power to raise or lower duties not exceeding 50 per cent upon recommendation of the Tariff Commission. This power and the extreme protection conferred by the tariff are the outstanding features of the Act.[23]

SELECTED READINGS

Twentieth Century Fund, *Does Distribution Cost Too Much?* Chaps. I–III.

Taylor, G. R., Bertis, E. L., and Waugh, F. V., *Barriers to Internal Trade in Farm Products.*

Zeis, P. M., *American Shipping Policy,* Chaps. I–XI.

Taussig, F. W., *Tariff History of the United States* (7th ed.), Part II.

Dietrich, Ethel, *World Trade,* Chaps. I–VI.

[23] For the tariff of 1930, see below, pp. 646–647.

☆ ☆

25

Financial History
Since 1860

☆ ☆

FINANCING THE CIVIL WAR

No phase of American economic history was more directly affected by the Civil War than public finance. The effects of this conflict upon the financial structure of our nation were, in fact, revolutionary in their scope. The needs of war financing enormously increased the rates of the protective tariff of 1861, created a new banking system, injected fiat paper money into the currency, and inaugurated a bitter half-century conflict between the currency inflationists and contractionists. The cost of the war was stupendous for that period, and much greater than was believed possible at the opening of the struggle. David A. Wells, Special Commissioner of Revenue, estimated in 1869 that the total war expenditure of the national government in the eight and a quarter years of the war and post-war period was $4,171,914,498.33. In addition, he pointed out, there should be reckoned the payment for pensions amounting to $2,000,000,000, and the further direct and indirect losses to Union and Confederate states of some $4,823,000,000. "These estimates, which are believed to be moderate and reasonable," said Wells, "show an aggregate destruction of wealth, or diversion of industry, which would have produced wealth, in the United States since 1861, approximating *nine* thousand *millions* of dollars. . . . It is three times as much as the slave property of the country was ever worth. It is a sum which at interest would yield to the end of time twice as much as the annual slave product of the South in its best estate."[1]

In four years the government expenditures amounted to more than during the whole previous history of the nation. In an effort to meet these expenses, Congress used every known device for obtaining revenue. Since the tariff had supplied most of the federal income up to that time, it was regarded as the most important source. A new tariff, framed largely by J. S. Morrill, was

[1] *Report of the Special Commissioner of the Revenue, 1869,* Executive Document No. 27, House of Representatives, 41st Cong., 2nd Sess., p. vi. Up to 1940 Civil War pensions amounted to over $8,000,000,000.

passed by the House in 1860 and accepted by the Senate on March 2, 1861, just before Lincoln's inauguration; it aimed to supplant the low rates of 1857 and restore the general level of the Walker tariff of 1846, the average rates of which were about 25 per cent. But the Morrill tariff did not produce the income anticipated, and legislation during succeeding years gradually raised the average of duties until in 1864 it reached 47 per cent.

The continued tariff increases had been enacted to balance in some degree the high internal taxes imposed upon a wide variety of manufactured articles and business transactions. The method of distributing the excises was likened by Wells to the advice given the Irishman at Donnybrook Fair: "Whenever you see a head, hit it; whenever you see a commodity, tax it." [2] By the end of the war the internal revenue was yielding twice as much as the tariff. Another form of taxation, a tax upon incomes, was levied for the first time in our history in 1861, when 3 per cent was imposed on incomes above $800. Increased in 1862 and 1865 until incomes between $600 and $5000 were taxed at 5 per cent and those above $5000 at 10 per cent, this tax yielded about $347,000,000 before it was abolished in 1872.

While taxes were levied with a free hand, a large proportion of the income derived therefrom was not received until the later period of the war. In the meantime the conflict was prosecuted upon borrowed money obtained first through the flotation of short-time loans and later, when it became evident that the war would not be over in a few months, by long-term borrowing. On September 1, 1865, the public debt reached its highest point; it amounted to $2,846,000,000, and was made up of many types of notes. In June, 1866, the "interest-bearing debt consisted of loans bearing five different rates of interest and maturing at nineteen different periods of time,[3] some payable in coin and some in currency. Eight-ninths of these were short-time notes.

One other method of financing the war expenses of the national government brought results which were to plague the country for decades. This was the issuance of paper money "on the credit of the United States." Treasury notes had been issued in times of stress earlier in our history, but they had been interest-bearing, had not been legal tender, had been issued for the most part in large denominations, and hence had had small circulation as currency. Other than these, no paper money had ever before been issued by the national government. Bank notes, supplied by some 1600 state banking institutions, and the metal coined by the United States Mint, together with the "old demand notes" issued in 1861,[4] made up the currency at the beginning of the war. The drain upon the metal in the Treasury occasioned the suspension of

---

[2] Quoted by F. W. Taussig, *Tariff History of the United States* (5th ed.), p. 164.

[3] D. R. Dewey, *Financial History of the United States* (10th ed.), p. 332.

[4] These notes, unlike the greenbacks, were receivable for customs duties and hence kept metal from flowing into the Treasury, thus hastening suspension of specie payment.

specie payments in December, 1861, first by the banks and soon afterward by the government. Metal currency was hoarded (except on the Pacific coast), and the issues of state banks were inadequate to meet the increased needs for a circulating medium. On February 25, 1862, an Act was passed authorizing an issue of $150,000,000 in notes on the credit of the United States, and making them legal tender. Supplementary Acts followed—altogether authorizing greenbacks to the extent of $450,000,000. They were legal payment for all debts public and private, except tariff duties and interest on the public debt. The colloquial term greenbacks originated from the green ink used in printing the backs of these notes. The greenbacks were supplemented by an authorization of $50,000,000 for fractional currency in denominations as low as three cents, to replace the subsidiary coins that, as the war went on, had been hoarded and withdrawn from circulation. On September 1, 1865, $433,-160,000 in United States notes was outstanding, besides $26,344,000 in fractional currency.[5] Other government obligations were also employed as currency, but were interest-bearing. The war left the country with the problem of fiat money still to settle, and the greenbacks became a burning issue, both legally and financially.

Although the resources of the nation were quite adequate to finance the war and Congress was quite willing to increase taxation, the handling of Civil War finances as a whole was inept. Salmon P. Chase, Secretary of the Treasury until June, 1864, based his policy on the experience in earlier American wars—"finance your war costs on borrowed funds, and increase your taxes only for the purpose of covering service on the newly incurred debt." Sumner calls the financial maneuvers of 1861–1862 a "simple record of temporary makeshifts,"[6] and, with the exception of the National Bank Acts, this description might well apply to the financial history of the whole Civil War. It is the opinion of most students that the weakest element in the financing of this war was the delay in applying effective taxation. Only slightly over one-quarter of the federal receipts during the four fiscal years 1862 through 1865 were obtained by this means.[7]

[5] Earlier efforts to replace small coins by people who had to make change had resulted in the use of stamps, old Spanish quarter dollars, bank bills cut in halves or quarters, and the issuance of tickets, due bills, and other forms of obligation by individuals, firms, banks, and even municipalities. These were called "shinplasters." Congress interfered with this private issuance of money and first authorized the use of postage stamps; later, to prevent the inconvenience of using gummed stamps as currency, it authorized the Post Office Department to issue postal currency in denominations of five to fifty cents. By May 27, 1863, over $20,000,000 had been placed in circulation.

[6] W. G. Sumner, *A History of American Currency* (1876), p. 197.

[7] Customs receipts for these four years were $305,360,451; internal revenue and income taxes, $356,846,136; and loans including treasury notes, $2,621,916,786. The ratio of loans to taxes decreased from $8.52 to $1 for 1861–1862 to $2.95 to $1 in 1864–1865. D. R. Dewey, *Financial History of the United States*, p. 299.

THE NATIONAL BANKING SYSTEM

After the Second Bank of the United States ceased to exist in 1836, the federal government withdrew from any supervision of the nation's banking until the creation of the National Banking system in 1863.[8] For a time it deposited its money in state-chartered banks and then established an "independent treasury system" through which it paid its own bills and received money due it. With the restraining hand of the government removed, these state banks flourished like a green bay tree. What paper money existed was in the form of bank notes circulated by the state banks. As far as paper money was concerned, the chaos was almost indescribable. In 1862 there were about 1600 banks established under the laws of the various states whose notes circulated at a discount varying with the confidence in the bank and the distance from the bank of issue. "It was estimated," said A. Barton Hepburn, "that there were 7000 kinds and denominations of notes, and fully 4000 spurious or altered varieties were reported."[9] It was difficult to estimate the value of the various notes, and the annoyances and losses attendant upon doing business with them can easily be imagined. It was in part to eliminate this chaotic paper currency that the National Banking system was established and it was one beneficial result of the war.

But the elimination of the state bank notes was not the only argument advanced for the creation of a national banking system. It was hoped that national banks would create a market for United States bonds, provide the country with a standardized paper currency, and tie up the financial interests more closely with the Union cause. The plan, in fact, had wide approval. A system of banks resting upon national rather than state authority, as Professor Dewey points out, "appealed to the growing feeling of nationalism; . . . it appealed to those who were jealous of the power of private corporations; it appealed to those who wished to relieve the government of distressing bargains, and who hoped the government would thus gain the ascendency in the control of capital; and finally it appealed to those who feared that further issues of United States notes would ultimately ruin both the government and private credit."[10]

The National Bank Act of 1863 (amended in 1864) granted charters to groups of not less than five stockholders (the amount of the capital stock being graduated for cities of different size) who must deposit with the

---

[8] Above, pp. 165 ff.

[9] A. Barton Hepburn, *History of Coinage and Currency in the United States*, p. 177. An interesting old book compiled to aid in detecting spurious notes and published in New York in 1863 is *Hodge's Bank Note Safeguard; giving facsimile descriptions of upwards of ten thousand bank notes, embracing every genuine note issued in the United States and Canada.*

[10] D. R. Dewey, *Financial History*, p. 321.

federal government federal bonds equal in amount to one-third of the bank's capital, not less than $30,000. In return the banks might receive bank notes up to 90 per cent of the current market value (not exceeding par) of the bonds. These notes were legal tender for all government dues except import duties and might be used by the government for all transactions except payment of principal and interest on the national debt. Numerous provisions, including reserve requirements, liability of stockholders, and strict national supervision, protected the depositor. Banks were slow in taking out charters, and in 1865 state bank issues were driven out by a 10 per cent tax. Supplementary legislation in 1900 liberalized the National Bank Act by permitting bank notes to be issued up to the full par value of the bonds; by reducing the capitalization of banks in cities of 3000 or under from $50,000 to $25,000; by refunding the existing national debt in thirty-year 2 per cent bonds; and by reducing the tax from 1 to ½ of one per cent per annum on all bonds yielding not over 2 per cent. The bank-note circulation, which reached $339,000,000 in 1873, declined to $168,000,000 in 1891 as the bonds fell due and were retired. Eventually further loans, issued to cover the Spanish-American War and other expenses, increased the note circulation by 1913 to $715,754,236, issued from 7473 national banks.[11]

RESULTS OF WAR FINANCING

In December, 1861, the northern banks, followed shortly after by the federal government, suspended specie payments. With the issuance of greenbacks, metallic money virtually disappeared. Under the impetus of Gresham's Law,[12] greenbacks, the cheapest money, became the standard of value for ordinary commercial transactions. It would be incorrect, however, to attribute the rise in prices during the war to the legal tender greenbacks alone. Contributing factors were the numerous short-term Treasury notes which passed almost like money, and the enlarged issues of state bank notes. The Civil War boom and the increased demand for commodities of all sorts likewise influenced the prices of certain commodities. But the issuance of nearly $450,000,000 worth of irredeemable paper money at a time when prices were already on the rise greatly emphasized the movement. Measured in terms of gold, the greenbacks, as will be seen from the accompanying graph, at no time during the war reached par; in the summer of 1864 they dropped as low as 39. The fluctuations in their value were caused partly by speculation and partly by varying confidence in the government's credit and do not necessarily approximate the rise of living costs.

[11] By January 30, 1939, the number of national banks had decreased to 5209. As a result of the New Deal currency legislation, national bank notes have been largely replaced by Federal Reserve notes.

[12] Above, p. 162 n.

While the government during the Civil War gained as an employer of labor from the issuing of the greenbacks, it lost in the long run from the rise in prices. It has been estimated that the cost of the war was increased by over $500,000,000 by the decline in value of legal tender money. Between 1860 and 1865 textiles quadrupled in price; groceries and flour doubled; meat, fuel, and rents increased over 50 per cent. At the same time real wages, especially for salaried men, lagged far behind.[13]

One of the legacies of Civil War finance was a thirty-year battle waged by the debtor groups, particularly the farmers, to prevent contraction and to maintain prices at the Civil War level during which many debts were contracted. Three factors were primarily responsible for the decline of prices in the post-war years. First of all was the cessation of the artificial demand for commodities produced by the war and accentuated by the disastrous panic of 1873. Second was the glut of foodstuffs, caused chiefly by the extreme rapidity with which the trans-Mississippi West was brought under cultivation. The third factor was the currency policy of the government which looked toward the contraction of the paper currency and the resumption of specie payment.

The last of these was probably the most important. The government was contracting its paper currency at a time when there was a growing need for more money in business, a situation which was accentuated after the war by the fact that the area in which United States money was current was increased to include the South, the Confederate currency being replaced by that of the United States. This situation continued even after contraction was stopped. After the resumption of specie payments in 1879 and the re-establishment of the gold standard, prices continued to decline here until 1896, along with a general decline in world prices measured in gold. While the production of gold during the 'seventies and 'eighties remained relatively about the same, the demand for it increased, owing to the adoption of the gold standard by many new and large countries and the rapid growth of gold-standard countries; this pushed up the price of gold and depressed the price of commodities.[14] The farmer fought bitterly and consistently against contraction. Any revolution in prices is bound to injure certain groups, and in this case it was the debtor farmer, chiefly in the West and South, particularly the Westerners who had pioneered during the war period of rising prices and who were now finding it increasingly difficult to carry their mortgages and pay the debts incurred in buying stock and machinery. Declining prices of foodstuffs and a contracting currency had brought real hardship, and the debtor farmer put forth every effort to maintain or restore the former prices through currency inflation.

[13] Above, pp. 345 ff.   [14] F. A. Fetter, *Modern Economic Problems* (1916), pp. 48–54, 74 ff.

The Greenback Movement

In its early stages the fight swung around the question of greenbacks. Three main problems in connection with the greenbacks pressed for settlement at the close of the war: (1) Had Congress the power under the Constitution to issue legal tender? (2) Should the existing issues be enlarged or contracted? and (3) Should specie payment be resumed? The first question was settled in 1871 by the Supreme Court in the case of Knox *v.* Lee [15] (overruling a previous decision in Hepburn *v.* Griswold, 1870),[16] when it affirmed that greenbacks could be presented to satisfy any debt contracted before the legal tender Acts were passed. The other questions reopened the conflict between inflationists and contractionists which has, to a certain extent, been ever present in our history. Before the constitutional questions were settled, the battle for inflation had started. The first move was to urge the payment in paper of both interest and principal upon all Civil War bonds unless the bond definitely specified gold. This plan, known as the "Ohio idea," was incorporated in the Democratic platform of 1868, but the election of Grant insured the payment of the debt in gold. Having lost this battle, the inflationists attempted not only to prevent the further contraction of the greenbacks, but even to increase the amount. In 1864, $400,000,000 was fixed as a maximum, with a further reserve of $50,000,000 to redeem a temporary loan. In 1866 the Treasury was authorized to retire the greenbacks, and Secretary McCulloch did withdraw about $77,000,000, reducing the volume to about $356,000,000 when in February, 1868, further contraction was suspended. This amount remained practically constant for nearly five years. In 1874 Congress fixed the maximum at $382,000,000. The Resumption Act (1875) provided for reducing the volume of United States notes to $300,000,000, but in 1878 the Greenbackers succeeded again in suspending further contraction. The amount then outstanding, $346,681,016, is the number of greenbacks still circulating today.

The fight now turned to the resumption of specie payments. The exchange of gold for paper by the government would bring the greenback to par, stabilize the currency, and raise the credit of the government. On the other hand, it was believed that this would further depress prices, and it was doubtful if gold in sufficient quantities could be obtained for the purpose. The defeat of the Republicans in the congressional election of 1874 caused that party to hasten through a Resumption Bill in the following year, calling

---

[15] Knox *v.* Lee, 12 Wallace 457.

[16] Hepburn *v.* Griswold, 8 Wallace 603. This decision is especially interesting inasmuch as it was delivered by Chief Justice Chase, who had been Secretary of the Treasury when greenbacks were first authorized, and who here passed adversely on the constitutionality of his own acts.

for the restoration of specie payments on January 1, 1879. This controversy over paper money, especially in its last phase, gave birth to a new political organization, the Independent National, or Greenback, party. Formed in 1876, it presented national tickets in three presidential campaigns and called

GOLD VALUE OF THE GREENBACK, 1862–1879

for a number of reforms radical for that day, particularly the redemption of war bonds in paper and the non-resumption of specie payments. Its greatest strength was exhibited in the congressional elections of 1878, when it polled over a million votes. This, however, was no indication of the strength of the movement, for both major parties were shot through with sentiment for inflation.

THE PANIC OF 1873

In the meantime the distress of the debtors had been accentuated and the greenback movement stimulated by the panic of 1873. The feverish industrial and agricultural activity in the North during the Civil War, aided by the rising prices, had inaugurated a period of unprecedented prosperity. Immense regions in the West had been opened up to agriculture, and the easy profits of war prosperity had been invested freely in fixed forms of capital, notably transportation facilities. The prosperity had been too rapid, the expenditures too lavish, to be healthy; and the decade of the 'seventies opened with underlying conditions far from encouraging. Enormous amounts of capital had been sunk in railroads to finance the 30,000 miles built between 1867 and 1873, from which small immediate returns could be expected. The opening of western lands had thrown older areas out of cultivation and decreased their value. Speculation and extravagance were rampant, and the business morality of politicians and capitalists, as witnessed by the Crédit Mobilier and the Black Friday scandals, left much to be desired. The failure in September, 1873, of the country's leading brokerage firm, Jay Cooke & Company, then engaged in building the Northern Pacific Railroad, precipitated the most severe panic in our history up to that time. This failure was followed by that of numerous banks, the closing of the Stock Exchange for ten days, and the partial suspension of specie payments. A period of severe retrenchment and depression ensued for several years, until sufficient capital was again accumulated for further advance.[17]

THE SILVER ISSUE

The administration's determination in 1879 to return to specie payment drove the inflationists to another expedient. If the value of the currency could not be forced down to the level of inconvertible paper, perhaps enough silver could be injected into the monetary system at an inflated ratio to achieve the same end. It will be recalled that in Acts of 1834 and 1837 the ratio of gold to silver, previously 15 to 1, had been changed to 16 to 1 (actually 15.98 to 1), the gold dollar thereafter containing 23.22 grains of pure gold and the silver dollar 371.25 grains of pure silver.[18] Since this overvalued gold slightly, silver, in accordance with Gresham's Law, disappeared and gold came into circulation. In 1873 the silver dollar was worth $1.02 in gold and it was no longer profitable to coin it. So scarce was silver and so long had it been since any had been presented to the mints for coinage that Congress in 1873 dropped the further minting of the standard silver dollar.[19] Far from a deep-dyed plot to demonetize silver, this Act, later denounced as the "Crime of '73," was merely legislative recognition of the fact that silver dollars were not being coined. A congressional committee composed of a majority of silver men bitterly denounced this Act three years later, pointing out that while silver possessed the function of money it always stood guard against any considerable rise in gold. "To divest either metal of the money function because temporarily out of use," it asserted, was "reckless and unwise. . . . As well might the commander of an army while battle was raging disband and discharge his reserves because they were not engaged at the front.

---

[17] For a further discussion of panics and business cycles in our history, see Chap. 29; and for two contemporary explanations, one American and one English, see F. Flügel and H. U. Faulkner, *Readings*, pp. 688–695.

[18] Standard weight was 25.8 grains of gold nine-tenths fine and 412.5 grains of silver nine-tenths fine.

[19] The coinage of subsidiary silver under the Act of 1853 was, of course, maintained and provision was made for a trade dollar.

As well might the master of a ship cut loose and scuttle his lifeboats because the sky was clear and the sea calm." [20]

Well might the inflationists grow bitter when they contemplated the legislation of 1873, for the situation in regard to silver changed rapidly after that date. Germany in 1871, and Holland and the Scandinavian peninsula from 1873 to 1875, adopted the gold standard, and the Latin Monetary Union (France, Switzerland, Belgium, Italy, and Greece) in 1873 limited the coinage of silver. This threw a large supply of bullion on the market, which was augmented by the discovery of large deposits in Nevada. The price of silver dropped so sharply that in 1876 it was worth ninety cents, with the prospect of further decline.

As silver grew cheaper, it was evident that if enough could be coined at the old ratio of 16 to 1, the working of Gresham's Law would drive out the gold and reduce the currency to the value of silver. The demonetization of silver was now called the "Crime of '73," and the debtor West and South, backed by the silver states, demanded that the government "do something for silver."

The silver sentiment had grown so strong by 1876 that a commission was appointed to study the currency problem, but before it presented its report Richard Bland of Missouri in 1877 offered a bill for the free and unlimited coinage of silver at the old ratio of 16 to 1. In the more conservative Senate the bill was toned down to limit the purchase of bullion to not less than $2,000,000 and not more than $4,000,000 a month, to be coined into silver dollars of 412.5 grains. That such a bill had wide backing there could be little doubt. Said the chairman of the resolutions committee at a mass meeting in Chicago: "We would in this matter arouse the slumbering consciousness of the President and his advisers to some apprehension of the fact that there is a thunderstorm brewing in the West, and that unless they have a care, somebody is likely to be hit by the lightning of public indignation, unless they concede the just demands of the people." [21] In spite of this sentiment, Hayes vetoed the bill, but it was quickly passed over his veto, and during the twelve years of its operation 378,166,000 silver dollars were coined. The Bland-Allison Act of 1878 provided for the issuing of silver certificates in amounts of ten dollars and upward upon the deposit of silver dollars; but the metal money proved unpopular in business centers, and in 1886 the denomination of the certificates was reduced to include one-, two-, and five-dollar bills.

To the great disappointment both of the silver interests and of inflationists the Bland-Allison Act failed to halt the decline in the value of silver or the

[20] F. Flügel and H. U. Faulkner, *Readings*, pp. 695–697.
[21] Quoted by C. R. Williams, *Life of Rutherford B. Hayes*, II, 120.

downward trend of prices. Nor was there any indication that silver would drive out gold in accordance with Gresham's Law. For this situation a number of factors were responsible. The nation was going through a period of tremendous industrial expansion; a larger amount of currency was necessary and the silver dollars and certificates were absorbed without difficulty. Moreover, there were several years during the 'eighties when the federal Treasury enjoyed a surplus. Part of this was stored in the Treasury and part was used to retire Civil War bonds. In either case the tendency was to reduce the circulating mediums and prevent inflation. Retirement of Civil War bonds reduced the bank-note circulation by $126,000,000 between 1886 and 1890. While one type of money was pushed into circulation another type was being withdrawn.

On the first of the year following the passing of the Bland-Allison Act the Treasury went back to specie payment. On January 2, 1879, Secretary Sherman had a slender supply of $140,000,000 in gold that had been accumulated with great difficulty, to meet the expected rush of holders of paper, but the soundness of the government's credit was demonstrated by the fact that only $125,000 was presented for gold, while $400,000 in gold was turned in for paper.

Although the Bland-Allison Act was in force for twelve years, it was unsatisfactory to both the inflationists and their opponents. The former looked upon it as simply an opening wedge to be pushed further if the purposes for which it had been passed failed to materialize. Prices of agricultural products continued to fall, and the distress of the debtor farmer who had borrowed on a fifty-cent dollar and must pay his debts with an eighty- or ninety-cent one, became keener. By 1889 the silver in the dollar had declined to seventy-two cents, and hope persisted that if more silver was forced into the currency, inflation would take place.

This was exactly what the gold advocates feared, and both President Arthur and President Cleveland urged the repeal of the Act, the latter pointing out to Congress that the continued coining of silver dollars would eventually increase the currency beyond the needs of business, after which the unnecessary portion would be hoarded and thus the gold gradually eliminated.

Notwithstanding the opposition of the Chief Executive and the Treasury Department, the pressure for more silver became so great that the Republican party, as a matter of political expediency and as a means of insuring the passage of the McKinley tariff, sponsored and passed the Sherman Silver Purchase Act in 1890. This bill required the Secretary of the Treasury to purchase 4,500,000 ounces of silver bullion a month and in payment for it to issue Treasury notes having full legal tender. These notes were to be redeemed in gold or silver at the discretion of the Secretary, "it being the established policy of the United States to maintain the two metals on a parity with each other," a provision later interpreted by the Executive as a promise to redeem all notes in gold. The amount of silver purchased under this Act was practically the entire output of the American mines and was almost double that required by the Bland-Allison Act; it amounted to $155,931,002 in the three years of its operation. This proved to be more than the currency could stand without endangering the gold standard. The only saving feature of the bill was the provision to purchase by ounces rather than by dollars, which meant that the amount of silver bought by the government would be kept at a uniform level. If the law had provided for purchase by dollars (as in the Bland-Allison Act) rather than by ounces, a decline in the value of silver would automatically have increased the coinage of that metal. Since the value of silver fell steadily during the life of the Act until it reached sixty cents in 1893, the significance of this provision is apparent.

THE PANIC OF 1893 AND THE ELECTION OF 1896

The decade of the 'nineties opened with the nation approaching the end of another business cycle. Railroad building during the 'eighties had been accompanied by inordinate speculation which had undermined supposedly strong organizations. Corporations on the verge of bankruptcy declared stock dividends and paid regular dividends out of capital. The failure of the Philadelphia and Reading and the National Cordage Company early in 1893 aroused the nation to its unhealthy industrial situation which had already been foretold by financial conditions in Europe. A reaction from the highly speculative years through which the country had just passed was inevitable, but the panic of 1893 was precipitated in part by the results of the presidential election of 1892, which presaged a modification of the government's tariff policy, and by the apprehension that the gold standard could not be maintained. Cleveland was elected that year on a Democratic platform committed to a reduction of the tariff, a prospect which manufacturers contemplated with dark forebodings. Cleveland himself believed in the gold standard, but his party was shot through with inflationary sentiment.[22]

From the point of view of those who would maintain the gold standard, the federal Treasury was in a precarious situation. This was due to a number of causes. The amount of silver purchased under the Sherman Act was too large to be readily absorbed, and by the operation of Gresham's Law gold began to be crowded out of circulation. The financial crisis in England

---

[22] Conflicting reasons for the panic advanced by contemporaries can be found in F. Flügel and H. U. Faulkner, *Readings*, pp. 710–717.

in 1890 brought about liquidation there, which resulted in a net loss of $68,000,000 in gold exported from the United States. The bumper wheat crop of 1891 coincident with a failure of European crops gave a temporary favorable balance of trade; but in 1893 the situation was reversed, with a net loss of $87,000,000 in gold exported. To complicate the difficulties of the Treasury Department, the surplus of the 'eighties had been wiped out by the extravagances of the Harrison administration and by the McKinley tariff of 1890, and a Treasury deficit was impending in 1893. An Act of 1882 which authorized the Secretary of the Treasury to suspend the issue of gold certificates whenever the amount of gold coin or bullion in the Treasury reserved for the redemption of United States notes fell below $100,000,000, tacitly recognized the existence of a reserve and set a minimum safety point. Subsequent Secretaries had not allowed the reserve to fall below this point, and so far it had been sufficient to maintain the gold standard even after the added strain imposed by the Sherman Silver Purchase Act of 1890. Wiping out the gold reserve would mean the suspension of specie payments or the substitution of silver for gold in the payment of paper presented under the Act of 1890. Either would mean the elimination of the gold standard and the cheapening of money. While this would have brought joy to the inflationists, the mere possibility paralyzed with fear the holders of fixed capital and business in general.

When Cleveland was inaugurated the reserve was $100,982,410, and on April 22, 1893, it fell below the $100,000,000 mark, recovered temporarily in July, and then declined until in November it reached $59,000,000. Failures of well-known concerns had already shaken public confidence in the business structure, and the decline of the reserve set in motion a period of the severest liquidation yet experienced. During 1893 over 600 banking institutions failed, and during the summer 74 railroad corporations owning 30,000 miles of road passed into the hands of receivers. By the end of the next year 194 roads operating 39,000 miles had failed, including the Philadelphia and Reading, the Erie, the Northern Pacific, and the Union Pacific. More than 15,000 commercial failures involving liabilities of $346,000,000 were recorded for 1893. The production of iron and coal declined, and to add to the general distress there was a poor corn crop in 1894 and a decreased demand on the part of Europe for wheat. Unemployment, strikes, discontent, and much actual suffering characterized the winters of 1893 and 1894, a period which encompassed the Pullman strike in Chicago and the marching of "Coxey's army."

Cleveland, a firm believer in the gold standard, was determined to maintain it at any cost. Absolutely convinced that the treasury's distress and the panic itself were "principally chargeable to Congressional legislation touching the purchase and coinage of silver," [23] he called a special session of Congress on August 1, 1893, and demanded repeal of the Sherman Silver Purchase Act. A bill to this effect passed the House with little delay, but the Senate held it up until October 30, when it was granted by a sectional vote, with the West and South aligned against the North and East. The repeal of the Sherman Act came too late to stave off the panic and the exhaustion of the gold reserve. In January, 1894, the Treasury sold $50,000,000 of 5 per cent ten-year bonds to obtain gold, and in November resorted to an additional loan of $50,000,000. The gold obtained in this way soon drained out, for there was nothing to prevent the man who lent gold one day from presenting paper and demanding it back the next day. Borrowing on these conditions seemed useless; and when in February, 1895, the Treasury found itself with a reserve of only $41,000,000—and that declining at the rate of $2,000,000 a day—Cleveland negotiated with J. P. Morgan and a group of bankers for a loan of 3,500,000 ounces of gold, to be paid for in 4 per cent United States bonds. It was agreed that half the gold should be obtained abroad and that the bankers would exert every influence to prevent its withdrawal until the contract had been fulfilled. Cleveland's action in borrowing privately from the bankers brought down upon him a storm of abuse, and when, a year later (January, 1896), a fourth loan was resorted to, it was offered to the public. Liquidation by this time had run its course; the loan was several times oversubscribed, and during the year the gold reserve in the Treasury continued to mount.

The efforts of the inflationists to expand the currency, continuously evident since the close of the Civil War, reached their climax in the campaign of 1896. Agricultural prices, which had been on the decline since the 'sixties, touched bottom in the early 'nineties. Wheat in 1894 sold at 49 cents, corn in 1896 at 21 cents; in Kansas and Nebraska it was cheaper to burn it for fuel than to sell it. Against this situation the Populist party made organized protest, and when in 1896 the Democratic farmers of the West and South, incensed by Cleveland's hard-money stand, drove the gold-standard Easterners from control of the party and nominated William Jennings Bryan as their standard-bearer, there ensued one of the hardest-fought and most significant political campaigns in our history. The chief issue of the campaign of 1896 was the free and unlimited coinage of silver at a ratio of 16 to 1, but behind this demand was thirty years of agrarian unrest and a cumulative protest against the currency and credit system and against railroads and other monopolies which had borne hard upon them. Their failure in this crusade left the federal government at the opening of the new century in the control of conservative eastern capitalism.

[23] Message on Silver, in F. Flügel and H. U. Faulkner, *Readings*, p. 707.

BULLION VALUE OF 371¼ GRAINS OF SILVER (CONTENTS OF ONE UNITED
STATES SILVER DOLLAR) IN TERMS OF GOLD AT THE ANNUAL AVERAGE PRICE
OF SILVER EACH YEAR, 1866–1930.[24]

THE CURRENCY ACT OF 1900 AND THE REVERSAL OF THE PRICE TREND

Although the campaign of 1896 settled the long controversy over bimetallism, the silver advocates were still so strong in the Senate that the gold
standard was not officially adopted until four years later. The Currency Act
of 1900 finally provided that the gold dollar of 25.8 grains nine-tenths fine
should be the unit of value and that all other forms of currency should be
maintained at parity with this dollar. To maintain this parity provisions were
made to keep a gold reserve of $150,000,000 in the Treasury. Other pro-
visions of the Act called for the retirement of the Treasury notes of 1890,
their replacement by silver certificates based on coined silver dollars, and the
liberalizing of the laws governing national banks.

At the time the Act was passed it was doubtful if in a severe crisis the
$150,000,000 gold reserve could withstand the pressure of the existing re-
deemable money, which then amounted to $346,000,000 of greenbacks,
$76,000,000 of silver (coined or bullion), every dollar of which was worth
only forty-seven cents in bullion, and the $331,000,000 of national bank notes
based entirely upon the credit of the United States. The machinery for
maintenance, though clumsy, proved efficient, and the gold dollar as pro-

[24] *Statistical Abstract, 1930,* p. 769.

vided in 1900 continued to be the unit of value until changed by the currency legislation of 1933 and 1934.[25]

Fortunately for the nation, new discoveries of gold in South Africa, the Yukon, and Alaska, as well as the development of new processes for extracting the precious metal from the ore, flooded the world with gold during these critical years. The average annual coinage of gold, which had been $67,185,000 in the years 1891–1900, increased during the following decade to $101,022,000. This, with additions to the supply of bank notes, increased the per capita circulation from $23.85 in 1893 to $33.86 in 1907 and $34.20 in 1911. This had the effect not alone of enabling the government to maintain the gold standard but also of reversing the downward trend of prices. From the low point of 1896 to 1914 the general price level increased 50 per cent. The demand for inflation subsided as a leading political and economic issue and the debtor farmer enjoyed one of his few periods of economic prosperity. Gold, interestingly enough, had helped to provide an inflation which for years many believed could most easily be obtained through silver.

THE PANIC OF 1907 AND THE MOVEMENT FOR BANKING REFORM

In the campaign of 1896 McKinley had been heralded as the "advance agent of prosperity." In truth, liquidation had about run its course, and he entered office on a returning wave of prosperity which advanced with but few interruptions until temporarily halted in 1907. The discovery of fresh deposits of gold, a succession of good harvests, the greater activity of American exporters in foreign fields, coincident with our embarkation upon a career as a colonial power, all served to stimulate business. Rising prices and confidence in the administration helped to promote rapid expansion and a great movement toward consolidation.

This prosperity continued with but slight interruption until 1907, when a brief and severe "bankers' panic" ensued. This panic was due chiefly to over-speculation in the large money centers and was the culmination of a long struggle between the rapidly rising trust companies acting as commercial banks under inadequate reserve requirements and the more conservative and rigidly regulated commercial banks.[26] It was precipitated by the action of the Knickerbocker Trust Company in closing its doors on October 22 to prevent a run on the bank. Many of the speculative ventures crashed, but efforts by the government and by leading capitalists did much to prevent the panic from becoming general. It was limited largely to the cities and its effects were not widespread, a fact which gave it the name of the "rich

[25] Below, pp. 656 ff.
[26] J. G. Smith, *The Development of Trust Companies in the United States* (1927), pp. 345–352.

man's panic." The panic of 1907 was laid by capital at the doors of the Roosevelt administration, whose meddling with business, it was claimed, had brought on the catastrophe. There was no basis for this charge; the fundamental and immediate cause was overexpansion and speculation by reckless and unscrupulous financiers, and inadequate banking facilities.

The panic served one good purpose in that it brought out clearly the defects of the national bank system. Although the national banks had marked a long step forward by providing relatively safe banking facilities and a standard bank note based on the credit of the national government, further improvements were necessary. Probably the chief criticism brought against the system was its lack of elasticity. The Currency Act of 1900 had extended the issue of bank notes from 90 per cent to the full face value of the bonds upon which they were issued, but in times of emergency this did not provide sufficient currency. More could be obtained only by purchasing additional bonds, a fact which tied up the whole question of paper money with the public debt and meant that the volume of national bank notes fluctuated with the monetary needs of the federal government and not with the currency needs of business. It was further maintained that the rigid reserve limits fixed by law made the credit facilities needlessly inelastic. Another great weakness of the national banking system was its inadequacy in providing credit facilities for the rural agricultural regions. The Currency Act of 1900 had reduced the minimum requirements for bank capital from $50,000 for cities of 6000 or less to $25,000 for towns of 3000 or less, but even this reduction did not promote the establishment of national banks in rural regions. Even when they did exist, their inability under the law to lend on real estate and their policy of extending commercial loans for 60 or 90 days did not fit the needs of the farmers. As a result, the rural communities were served, if banking facilities were available, largely by state banks whose interest rates were high and whose financial condition was often precarious. The agricultural interests also complained that the whole banking system encouraged the flow of funds from communities where they had been accumulated to the large financial centers, where they were used for speculative purposes rather than for the legitimate needs of agriculture and industry. The efficiency of the system was hampered by the cumbersome and expensive exchange and transfer system and the decentralization of the gold supply.

Profiting from the lessons of the panic, Congress in 1908 passed an emergency measure, known as the Aldrich-Vreeland Act, making temporary provision for the issue of bank notes upon approved securities of states, cities, towns, or municipalities, and upon commercial paper, and providing for the formation of associations of national banks for the purpose of issuing notes, the Act to be in force until June 30, 1914 (later extended another year).

The same bill also called for the appointment of a National Monetary Commission to study banking conditions and report to Congress.[27] Much popular interest was now aroused, and both major parties were pledged to some kind of reform. The report of the Commission was submitted in January, 1912, with specific recommendations known as the "Aldrich plan." This plan did not suit either political group; but President Wilson, having disposed of the tariff, next pressed for banking legislation which took form in the Federal Reserve Act of December 23, 1913.

THE FEDERAL RESERVE SYSTEM

The Act of 1913 (as amended in 1916 and in later years) did much to eliminate certain defects of the national banking system. It divided the country into twelve districts, and provided that a Federal Reserve bank was to be located in the principal banking city of each district—tacit recognition that the nation was fundamentally a group of economic sections rather than an agglomeration of states. The Federal Reserve cities decided upon were Boston, New York, Philadelphia, Cleveland, Richmond, Atlanta, Chicago, St. Louis, Minneapolis, Kansas City, Dallas, and San Francisco. Every national bank was required, and other banks were encouraged, to become members of the system by subscribing to the capital stock of the Federal Reserve bank in their district an amount equal to 6 per cent of their capital stock and surplus. In this manner each district Federal Reserve bank is owned by the various member banks scattered throughout the district. The district banks were to be governed by a board of nine members, six chosen by the member banks and three by the Federal Reserve Board.

To direct the whole system, a Federal Reserve Board was set up at Washington; it consisted of eight members, including the Secretary of the Treasury, the Comptroller of the Currency, and six members appointed by the President. This board was to exercise supervisory powers and determine the larger questions of policy. A Federal Advisory Council, composed of one representative from each Federal Reserve bank, was created to consult with the board and help in unifying and carrying out the policies decided upon.

The Federal Reserve banks do no direct banking with individuals or business houses. They are simply bankers' banks, central agents for the member banks. Their duties include the rediscount of commercial paper for the member banks in the district, the purchase and sale of bills of exchange, the granting of loans to member banks on government securities as collateral, and other similar banking operations; and, in addition, the issuing of Federal

[27] *The Report of the National Monetary Commission* (1912), pp. 6–9, gives in detail the weaknesses of the old national bank system. See F. Flügel and H. U. Faulkner, *Readings*, pp. 719–721.

Reserve notes. Furthermore the Reserve banks act as the fiscal agents of the government. Federal Reserve bank notes are issued, like national bank notes, upon the deposit of government bonds (also commercial paper since 1933), and were designed eventually to supplant the earlier notes. To provide a

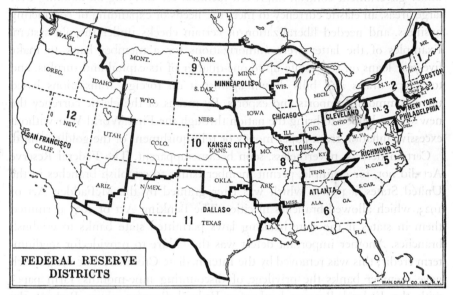

FEDERAL RESERVE
DISTRICTS

(From H. U. Faulkner and Tyler Kepner, *America, Its History and People,* Harper & Brothers.)

type of money which would expand and contract as needed, the Reserve banks were empowered to issue Federal Reserve notes on the security of short-term commercial paper. When this paper matures, the Federal Reserve bank (holder in due course) is paid largely with Federal Reserve notes. Hence the volume of these notes corresponds with the volume of commercial paper and the latter with the currency needs of business. Federal Reserve notes are receivable for taxes, customs, and all public dues, are obligations of the United States, and until 1933 were redeemable in gold on demand at the Treasury Department.

To safeguard the system, member banks were required (after 1917) to maintain with the district Federal Reserve bank 3 per cent of their time deposits and from 7 to 13 per cent of their demand deposits, depending on the population of the city. In turn the Federal Reserve banks were required to carry a 40 per cent reserve of gold (since 1933, gold certificates) against Federal Reserve notes outstanding, and a 35 per cent reserve of lawful money against deposits. Amendments to the original Act have made it profitable for the state banks and trust companies to become members; their number amounted on December 30, 1939, to 1175. At the same time this rapid extension has necessitated another amendment establishing branches of the Federal Reserve banks in a number of the larger cities.

The Federal Reserve system is generally conceded to mark a distinct advance over the old national bank system. It brought greater coordination under government control, improved facilities for carrying on banking over large areas, an elastic currency to meet the needs of expanding or contracting business, and needed liberalization of certain checks under the old system. Examples of the latter were authorizations for a member bank to make five-year loans on real estate up to one-quarter of its capital and surplus, and to accept drafts and bills drawn against it on foreign transactions based upon commodity imports and exports. By means of the elastic currency the new system helped to bring the nation through the First World War without excessive inflation from paper money or relinquishment of the gold standard.

Certain defects, nevertheless, soon became apparent. The Federal Reserve Act did not, for example, permit member banks to establish branches in the United States, a power which was later granted by the McFadden Act of 1923, which allowed branches in cities. The Banking Act of 1933 permitted them in states if the state banking laws permitted state banks to establish branches. Another important defect was the failure to provide for medium-term credit; this was removed by the Intermediate Credits Act of 1923, which gave member banks the privilege of discounting nine-months' farm paper with the Federal Reserve banks for Federal Reserve notes. Perhaps the worst abuse which developed was the growth of security affiliates, brought to an end by the Banking Act of 1933. The elimination of security affiliates, the required insurance of deposits up to $5000, and other needed improvements, as we shall see, were later achieved by the New Deal in the Banking Acts of 1933 and 1935.[28]

RECAPITULATION

An effort has been made in this chapter to trace the financial history of the United States since 1860 primarily as it concerned banking and currency. The history of taxation during these years, essentially a problem of tariff policy, has been treated elsewhere.[29] Even from this brief résumé certain facts stand out clearly. First of all was the influence of Civil War financing upon both banking and currency. This financing created the national banking system, and at the same time introduced national bank notes and eliminated state notes. Civil War needs also brought the greenbacks into existence. The elimination of the paper currency existing at the opening of the war and the creation of two new kinds brought a fundamental change in our currency.

The effects of the war were apparent long after it ended. Efforts to restore the war-time price level lay behind the battles of debtor farmers and other

[28] Below, pp. 659 f.   [29] Above, pp. 536 ff.

inflationists to prevent the resumption of specie payment, to expand the greenback circulation, and to restore the free and unlimited coinage of gold and silver at a ratio of 16 to 1. This attempt at inflation by means of the Bland-Allison and the Sherman Silver Purchase Acts added a large amount of silver or silver certificates to the currency system. This drive for inflation, it should be remembered, was interwoven with the whole American scene— economic, social, and political. It was in part a reaction against the decline of agriculture and the growing power of industrial capitalism. It was closely affected by the panics of 1873 and 1894 and it permeated political controversy for thirty years.

The long battle for inflation may have ended temporarily with the gold-standard Republicans in 1896, but the history of banking and currency reform and their interrelations did not. The national bank system was radically revised and improved by the Federal Reserve Act of 1913, and the currency system was changed by the addition of Federal Reserve bank notes and Federal Reserve notes. Although state-chartered banks continue, the system of nationally chartered banks goes back in direct lineage to the Act of 1863. In a similar manner the currency is a conglomerate of the various kinds of money introduced, mainly since the Civil War. Treasury reports in 1942 still showed the following types of money in circulation: gold certificates, silver dollars, silver certificates and Treasury notes of 1890 (based in part on the Bland-Allison and Sherman Silver Purchase Acts), subsidiary metal coins, United States notes (Civil War greenbacks), national bank notes, Federal Reserve bank notes, and Federal Reserve notes. Not even the important currency legislation of the New Deal has erased from our monetary system the imprint of the economic and political conflicts during the half century from the first greenback legislation in 1862 to the passage of the Federal Reserve Act in 1913. The more recent history of banking and currency will be discussed in a later chapter.[30]

SELECTED READINGS

Dewey, D. R., *Financial History of the United States*, Chaps. XII–XXII.

Shultz, W. J., and Caine, M. R., *Financial Development of the United States*, Chaps. XIII, XIV, XVI, XVIII, XX–V.

Hepburn, A. B., *A History of Currency in the United States*, Chaps. XI–XXV.

Willis, H. P., *The Federal Reserve*, Chaps. I–VIII.

Lauck, W. J., *The Causes for the Panic of 1893*.

Bogart, E. L., and Thompson, C. M., *Readings in the Economic History of the United States*, Chap. XX.

Flügel, F., and Faulkner, H. U., *Readings in the Economic and Social History of the United States*, Chap. XVI.

[30] Below, pp. 651–652, 657 ff.

26.

Economic Imperialism

The Old Imperialism

IMPERIALISM, that national policy which tends toward the extension of political, economic, and intellectual dominion over regions geographically situated beyond the national boundaries, is a phenomenon discernible from the earliest times in nations which have progressed to a position of wealth and power. In modern times the world has witnessed two distinct waves or outbursts of imperialism. The first of these, which we may designate as the Old Imperialism, commenced with the discovery of new trade routes to the East at the close of the fifteenth century and lasted until 1815, the end of the Second Hundred Years' War between France and England. Then ensued a lull in expansion, during which statesmen were little interested in extending their foreign dominions. The last third of the century, however, saw renewed interest and activity in foreign expansion on the part of many nations, a period inaugurated in England by Disraeli (1874–1880) and by the embarkation of France and Germany after 1880 upon new imperial efforts.

The Old Imperialism was influenced by mercantilism. It looked toward the founding of foreign settlements of colonists from the home country who were to set up little Spains, little Englands, and little Hollands throughout the world to serve as sources of raw materials and markets for home products. Under the impetus of the Old Imperialism, North and South America, Australia, and Siberia were conquered and peopled by Europeans, and settlements and trading posts were established in South Africa, India, the East Indies, and elsewhere.

If the Old Imperialism is defined as the acquisition of land which is actually settled by those who acquire it, American imperialism up to 1898 may be largely considered as such. Certainly until this time it was primarily agricultural rather than commercial or financial. The area of the United States in 1800 was 892,135 square miles, sufficient in the belief of most men to accommodate the needs of our population for an indefinite period. But the restless, land-hungry spirit of the pioneer was so intense that it was only three years later that the Louisiana Purchase of 885,000 square miles was consummated. Florida, containing 59,600 square miles, was purchased from Spain in 1819; Texas, a region of 389,000 square miles, was annexed in 1845; and the Oregon territory (285,000 square miles) was secured by treaty in 1845. The Mexican War, instigated for apparently little else than to confirm the annexation of Texas and to extend our boundaries to the Pacific, added 529,000 square miles, augmented in 1853 by the Gadsden Purchase of 30,000 square miles. In the case of Florida, Texas, and Oregon, settlers had gone ahead of acquisition,[1] but in general the acquisition of large stretches of land was made without any immediate expectation of use. This was true of Alaska, purchased in 1867 for $7,200,000; but in all cases white settlers speedily entered to dominate and occupy. The habit of imperialism was too easily formed. The prices paid were trivial in comparison to the value of the land, and where wars were fought they were neither sanguinary nor costly. The anti-imperialists were easily overrun by the frontiersmen or by the southern expansionists so generally in control of the national government before the Civil War. The Indian inhabitants were ruthlessly brushed aside; an inferior civilization in a sparsely occupied region inevitably gave way to an aggressive people possessed with energy and numbers to conquer, and resources to develop the land.

THE NEW IMPERIALISM

The new wave of imperialism which has swept over the world since 1870 has perhaps brought in its wake results more far-reaching than any other human event since the Industrial Revolution ushered in modern times. In fact, the New Imperialism is a direct result of the Industrial Revolution. Its causes are principally economic. The new inventions in machinery increased production so enormously that new markets had to be developed to dispose of the surplus products and the vast population of Africa and Asia came to be considered potential customers. Improvements in transportation and communication by land and sea were of inestimable value in speeding up this search for new markets. As the Industrial Revolution increased the population and hence the markets at home, and as new markets were discovered abroad, it was necessary to develop new sources of raw material. Those interested in manufacturing and commerce believed that such sources were safer when controlled by the home government. In addition to these economic factors, a third was equally important. With the tremendous increase in manufacturing and transportation, there followed accumulations

---

[1] True also of Utah, where the Mormons first settled while the Mexican War was in progress. In California there were probably fewer than 1000 immigrants from the United States when this war broke out.

of capital seeking investment. As the surplus of capital increased in Europe, interest rates declined and financiers were forced to go far afield for profitable investments. As a result, European capital was invested heavily abroad. British foreign investments in 1914 were estimated by Sir George Paish at about $20,000,000,000, approximately 23 per cent of the total capital investments of the nation.[2] British investments in India amounted to nearly $1,844,600,000, and in the United States before the First World War, close to $3,673,900,000. In 1912 France was estimated to have loaned abroad, chiefly in the Near East and Russia, over $8,000,000,000, amounting to 37 per cent of the total personal securities of the French; and Germany was estimated to have about $6,500,000,000 invested abroad at the beginning of that war. This money, invested in factories, mines, oil wells, railroads, and other public utilities, or loaned to foreign governments, had to be protected. It continually directed the eyes of capitalists and governments to foreign fields and served to weaken the independence of smaller powers as the wealthier nations gained economic control. It gave the tone to the New Imperialism, which was in reality financial imperialism. As in the sixteenth and seventeenth centuries the homeland sent out settlers to conquer and occupy, so now the capitalists of the nineteenth century sent out manufactured products and money. They were not interested in settlement, for the lands now exploited were often densely peopled.

In addition to the economic there were of course other motives: First, there was a sincere desire on the part of Christians to convert the followers of other religions—a course favored by imperialists of all kinds who realized that the missionaries were blazing the trails which the soldier and merchant were only too ready to follow. The nineteenth century witnessed a remarkable effort on the part of both Catholic and Protestant missionaries, who sometimes sought the protection of their government to facilitate their work in foreign fields. Second, the argument that the colonies might absorb the surplus population and products of Europe was frequently advanced. Between 1870 and 1900 Great Britain added to her possessions (exclusive of spheres of influence) about 5,000,000 square miles with an estimated population of 88,000,000; France added 3,500,000 square miles with a population of 37,000,000, and Germany 1,000,000 square miles with an estimated population of 14,000,000. Third, the whole movement was stimulated and condoned by the desire for national power and prestige. It is this intimate relation to national policy and to diplomacy, and to the competition in armies and navies, that forms part of the essential background of the world wars of the twentieth century.

[2] E. L. Bogart, *War Costs and Their Financing*, pp. 14–16.

The United States and the New Imperialism

Into this competition for extra-territorial possessions the United States entered—late, to be sure, but with vigor. Until 1898 there had been little reason for overseas expansion. Up to 1890 there had been free land suitable for settlement, and abundant opportunities for whatever free capital might be seeking investments. In fact, the usual scarcity of capital in a new country was so acute that European wealth to the extent of over $6,000,000,000 (more than half of which was British) was still invested here in 1910. But the Spanish-American War marked a turning point. From a position of inferiority in 1860 we had advanced to a position of great economic importance. Our population had increased 97 per cent between 1870 and 1900, and during the same period the annual production of wheat had increased from 236,000,-000 bushels to 522,000,000 bushels, corn from 1,094,000,000 to 2,105,000,000 bushels; cotton from 4,352,000 to 10,100,000 bales; petroleum from 221,000,000 to 2,672,000,000 gallons; coal from 29,000,000 to 241,000,000 tons, and pig iron from 1,665,000 to 13,789,000 tons.

The nation was rapidly demonstrating that its resources were the greatest of any single nation and that they were well in hand for exploitation. In amount of productive land the United States in 1900 was second only to Russia, and first in lands under actual cultivation. With her forest reserves of over 400,000,000 acres, second only to Russia, with 30 per cent of the world's iron, with more than half of the world's coal, and with ample copper, petroleum, and water power, she was well supplied with essential raw materials.[3] While approximately nine-tenths of the production was consumed at home, the tenth, which was exported and in 1898 amounted to $1,210,291,913, had become sufficient to make the matter of foreign markets important. By that year the necessity of calling upon Europe for continual loans to develop transportation and manufacturing was beginning to pass. Although the flow of capital was inward until the opening of the First World War, for the most part we financed our own operations and even accumulated a surplus for foreign investment. In comparison with present investments abroad, the amount thus placed in 1898 was small; yet even at that time it was undoubtedly a strong factor in hastening the war with Spain. Americans invested more than $50,000,000 in Cuban business before 1898, and our commerce with the island amounted to $100,000,000 annually, a fact which President Cleveland noted in his last message to Congress. Estimates of American capital invested abroad in that year place the figure at approximately $500,000,000, an amount which by 1914 had grown

[3] See Chap. I.

to between two and one-half and three billions. As with Europe, this export of capital flowed chiefly to the more backward nations.[4]

Although the Spanish-American War is generally considered as marking the definite embarkation of the United States upon a career of imperialism, a gradual development can be traced from a much earlier period.[5] The Monroe Doctrine in its stated intention—(1) to refrain from interference in European affairs, (2) to consider any attempt by the European powers to "extend their political system to any portion of either continent of America as endangering our peace and happiness," and (3) that the era of colonization in the Americas was over—seemed rather to be a reaffirmation of Washington's policy of isolation than any move toward foreign power. If any imperialism was furthered by it, not American but English economic imperialism was the gainer. Yet the Monroe Doctrine has so grown in importance and so broadened in interpretation that it eventually became a strong factor in American imperialism. It was an early indication of the region in which our interests would become keen and our financial imperialism make its start. In a sense it preserved "America for Americans." In combination with England's desertion of the Quadruple Alliance, it prevented further European conquests.

That the United States had every intention of upholding the Monroe Doctrine was demonstrated by the opposition to French expansion in Mexico during the Civil War. On the other hand, whatever foundations the Monroe Doctrine laid in the Latin-American republics for confidence in our friendliness and unselfishness were largely sacrificed by our wholesale annexations at the end of the Mexican War. The Latin-American came to look upon the Monroe Doctrine as a policy of keeping out Europeans from regions which we intended to dominate. Nevertheless, the ideal of closer relations between the American republics first conceived by Clay was kept alive, notably through the efforts of James G. Blaine and the Pan-American Congress of 1889. Cleveland's aggressive championship of the South American republic in the boundary line dispute between Great Britain and Venezuela was a continuation of the same policy.

In the meantime, political developments in the Pacific were following

---

[4] This was estimated by R. W. Dunn (*American Foreign Investments,* p. 2) at 185 million dollars in Mexico, 150 million in Canada, 50 million in Cuba, 10 million in Europe, 55 million in other Latin-American countries, 5 million in China and Japan, and 45 million in life insurance company guaranteed investments in Russia and elsewhere. This included investments in government bonds as well as in foreign corporations.

[5] "It is true," says John Bassett Moore, "that the expansion of 1898 involved, so far as concerns the Philippine Islands, the taking of a step geographically in advance of any that has been taken before; but so far as concerns the acquisition of new territory we were merely following a habit which had characterized our entire national existence." *Four Phases of American Development* (1912), pp. 147–148.

economic penetration. The conquest of California and the purchase of Alaska had definitely made the United States a Pacific power. Long before American settlers reached the western coast, Yankee sailors had built up a brisk trade with the Orient. Commodore Perry's famous voyage to Japan in 1854 was a natural sequel to our commercial interests, as was our eventual appearance in the Samoan Islands. American control of Hawaii was presaged as early as 1875, when a treaty of reciprocity was arranged, which stipulated that none of the territory should be leased or sold to any other power. Eventually American economic interests there became so powerful that they were able to instigate a rebellion against the autocratic native queen which was carried out with the active cooperation of the American minister and the presence of an American naval force. Cleveland refused to sanction acquisition by such methods, but the Americans in Hawaii would not return to the old régime. The matter hung fire until 1898, when McKinley's administration under the stress of war pushed through annexation.

THE SPANISH-AMERICAN WAR

The eyes of Americans had turned toward the control of Cuba for half a century before the Spanish-American War. Cuba occupied a strategic position controlling the entrance to the Gulf of Mexico. It would provide a natural extension for southern slavery, and its accession was a logical continuation of the policy which brought us Florida and the Southwest. American control of Cuba was a leading question from 1850 to 1861. "It is our destiny to have Cuba," said Stephen A. Douglas in 1858, "and it is folly to debate the question. It naturally belongs to the American continent."[6] With the overthrow of the slave-owning aristocracy in the Civil War, the matter of Cuban annexation became quiescent until the nation was sufficiently advanced for financial imperialism. This situation had arrived by 1898.

Although the Spanish-American War marked a turning point in American foreign policy characterized by a definite trend toward economic imperialism, the war itself was not caused primarily by economic interests. It is true that American investments in Cuba had become important by 1898 and that the sugar interests were anxious for the United States to bring peace to that harassed island. Nevertheless, American business in general, desirous of promoting the reviving business prosperity, opposed the war.[7] It was primarily a "newspaperman's war" promoted by the so-called "yellow press" which strengthened American sympathy for the Cuban revolutionists and disgust for the policies of Spanish misrule, at the same time

[6] Speech in New Orleans, December 6, 1858; given in *Life of Stephen A. Douglas*, by "A Member of the Western Bar" (1860), p. 184.
[7] J. W. Pratt, *Expansionists of 1898*, Chap. VII.

playing up every possible incident that might lead to a break with Spain. Behind the press was a small but powerful group led by Theodore Roosevelt, Lodge, Hay, and others, who were enamored with the philosophy of Captain Mahan and who welcomed the war as an opportunity for America to fulfill her "manifest destiny" in world affairs. They aimed, says Professor Pratt, "at no less than making the United States the indisputably dominant power in the western hemisphere, possessed of a great navy, owning and controlling an Isthmian Canal, holding naval bases in the Caribbean and the Pacific, and contesting, on at least even terms with the greatest powers, the naval and commercial supremacy of the Pacific Ocean and the Far East." [8]

The war left us with the Philippines, Puerto Rico, Guam, and the destiny of Cuba on our hands. The main problem we faced was the future of the Philippines. Annexation, it was evident, meant the subjugation of an alien race in a remote tropical region and the definite embarkation upon the uncertain path of imperialism. The implications of this step were clearly seen by a strong anti-imperialist minority who fought strenuously against annexation. They received some backing from tobacco, beet sugar, and other agricultural interests fearful of competition, and from labor leaders like Gompers who feared the menace of cheap Oriental labor. On the other hand a large section of the business interests were won over to the idea that retention of the Spanish islands in the Far East would mean a rapid expansion of American trade. The administration was at first uncertain, but President McKinley, finally convinced that the majority of voters favored territorial expansion, insisted on annexation. The treaty was ratified February 6, 1899, by a margin of only one vote more than the required two-thirds majority.

There could be no mistaking the significance of the annexation of the Philippines. Nevertheless, McKinley insisted that it was a purely altruistic decision. "The Philippines, like Cuba and Puerto Rico," said he in 1899, "were intrusted to our hands by the war, and to that great trust, under the providence of God and in the name of human progress and civilization, we are committed. . . . We could not discharge the responsibilities upon us until these colonies became ours, either by conquest or treaty. Our concern was not for territory or trade or empire, but for the people whose interests and destiny, without our willing it, had been put in our hands." [9] In more realistic terms Senator Beveridge a year later expressed the attitude of the victorious imperialists: "The Philippines are ours forever, 'territory belonging to the United States,' as the Constitution calls them. And just beyond

[8] J. W. Pratt, "The Large Policy of 1898," *Mississippi Valley Historical Review*, XIX, 223 (Sept., 1932).
[9] Speech in Boston, February 16, 1899. Boston *Herald*, Feb. 17, 1899, pp. 2–3.

the Philippines are China's illimitable markets. We will not retreat from either. We will not repudiate our duty in the archipelago. We will not abandon our opportunity in the Orient. We will not renounce our part in the mission of our race, trustee, under God, of the civilization of the world." [10]

CARIBBEAN PENETRATION

American penetration of the Caribbean has been motivated by two primary interests. The first is self-protection and involves the naval and air strategy of safeguarding the Panama Canal. The second is economic, the expansion of commerce and investments. These interests are obviously intertwined, and together they comprise the history of our relations in this region during the past forty-five years. Of the Caribbean Islands, Cuba is the most important and there American economic expansion has been the greatest. When war was declared against Spain, Congress in the Teller Resolution asserted that "the United States hereby disclaims any disposition or intention to exercise sovereignty, jurisdiction, or control over said Island, except for the pacification thereof, and asserts its determination, when that is accomplished, to leave the government and control of the Island to its people." In spite of this resolution, American soldiers were kept in Cuba until 1902 and before they returned Cuba was forced to incorporate in a treaty and in her constitution the provisions of the Platt Amendment. By this she agreed that she would not enter into any treaty with a foreign nation that might impair her independence, that she would not assume any public debt for which her ordinary revenues were inadequate, that she would consent to the intervention of the United States "for the preservation of Cuban independence, the maintenance of a government adequate for protection of life, property and individual liberty," and that she would lease or sell to the United States land sufficient for coaling and naval stations.

The Platt Amendment reduced Cuba to the status of an American protectorate. Under its provisions the United States has repeatedly intervened, usually to maintain the *status quo,* and under this close protection American financial interests have moved in to absorb much of her wealth. By the late 1920's American investments in Cuba were placed at $1,500,000,000 of which $600,000,000 was in sugar, $145,000,000 in public utilities, $120,000,000 in rails, $50,000,000 in mines, $20,000,000 in tobacco, $110,000,000 in government securities, and the rest distributed among hotel, mercantile, industrial, and other interests. [11] Much of this financial penetration centered in the National City Bank of New York, which directly controlled the General Sugar

---

[10] *Congressional Record,* January 9, 1900, 56th Congress, 1st Sess., Vol. XXXIII, Part I, p. 704.

[11] L. H. Jenks, *Our Cuban Colony,* pp. 299 ff. Other estimates give higher figures.

THE UNITED STATES IN THE CARIBBEAN

U.S. possessions shown in black or with heavy underlining

British possessions

⊕ U.S. naval bases and stations

.... French possessions

0   200   400   600 MILES

PANAMA CANAL & CANAL ZONE

(From H. U. Faulkner, Tyler Kepner, and Hall Bartlett, *The American Way of Life*, Harper & Brothers.)

Company, the Consolidated Railways, the immense sugar holdings of the Cuba Company, and many other Cuban corporations, and through its twenty-four banks financed the native planters. Under the impetus of this penetration Cuba has become a land of great sugar and tobacco plantations, owned abroad and worked by a landless Cuban proletariat whose prosperity is almost entirely dependent upon the American market, which in turn is dependent upon the American tariff.

In a situation of this kind it is clear that economic or political independence is a mere fiction. It is also doubtful if Cuba has profited economically from the turn of events since 1898. In any case President Franklin D. Roosevelt as part of his "good-neighbor policy" determined on a gesture of good will. A treaty with Cuba in 1934 ended the famous Platt Amendment and removed her from her position as technically a protectorate. In the same year a tariff treaty under the Trade Agreement Act [12] enlarged the American market for Cuban commodities.

The social and economic history of Puerto Rico since American annexation in 1898 has not been unlike that of Cuba. There has been a notable advance in the sanitary and educational facilities of the island, an improvement in transportation facilities, and the building of public works. The wealth of the island has increased, from $100,000,000 to $650,000,000 or more, but, as in Cuba, it has come under the control of American capital, the land has been consolidated into large sugar and tobacco plantations, and the small farmer has been reduced to the status of a landless proletarian. Experts have estimated that 60 per cent of the sugar production, 30 per cent of the fruit, 60 per cent of the railroads, and 50 per cent of the public utilities are absentee-owned. "There is no important source of wealth," they assert, "that is not partially in the hands of outsiders, and in some instances, such as steamships, outsiders control the entire business. Any estimate of Puerto Rico's dependence on absentees which places the total at less than 60 per cent of the island's wealth is certainly too low." [13] To complicate the situation even more, the island has become essentially a two-crop country dependent on the American market; and when that market collapses, as it did in 1929, the economic situation becomes intolerable. At the depth of the depression in 1930, 60 per cent of the population were unemployed. Free trade with the United States since 1902 has been an advantage to Puerto Rico, but the American tariff system, which also applies to the island, has kept the cost of living higher than it would be otherwise.

With the annexation of Puerto Rico and the establishment of a protectorate over Cuba it was inevitable that the old project of an interoceanic

[12] Below, pp. 686 ff.
[13] B. W. and J. F. Diffie. *Porto Rico: A Broken Pledge*, p. 135.

canal would assume new importance to the United States. If this country looked forward to the maintenance of an overseas empire, such a canal not only was necessary but its control by our government was essential. In preparation for this the Clayton-Bulwer Treaty (1850) with England was brushed aside by the new Hay-Pauncefote Treaty (1901), in which Great Britain removed all former restrictions on our building and fortifying the canal on condition that it be regulated by certain rules and that it be "free and open to the vessels of commerce and war of all nations observing these Rules, on terms of entire equality." After much debate Congress chose the Panama route rather than that through Nicaragua, and reached an understanding with the French Canal Company (which had recently been purchased by an American syndicate) to purchase its rights and equipment for $40,000,000 if negotiations with Colombia were successful in obtaining control of a zone around the proposed canal and the right to fortify it. This proposition was embodied in the Hay-Herran Treaty (1903), which was ratified by the United States Senate but failed of ratification by the Colombian Congress, notwithstanding pressure from the Province of Panama. Roosevelt, exasperated over the delay in his plans which he looked upon as simply an attempt to exact a higher price for the concession, listened willingly to rumors of a rebellion against Colombia by the discontented Panamanians, and when the revolution (fostered aggressively by agents of the French Canal Company) actually took place on November 3, 1903, he was careful to have battleships at hand to prevent Colombia from landing troops to put down the rebellion. Before it could be crushed, he recognized the new republic and by November 18 the Hay-Varilla Treaty had been signed in Washington. By this treaty the United States guaranteed the independence of Panama and agreed to pay $10,000,000 outright, and an annuity of $250,000 beginning nine years later, in return for a strip ten miles wide upon which to build the canal. Construction was finally started in 1906 and the canal completed in 1914. The Panama Canal not only put in the hands of the United States the shortest water route from the Atlantic to the Pacific,[14] but the conditions under which it was built and obtained made Panama virtually a protectorate of this country. With Panama an independent nation but dependent entirely upon the protection of the United States, it was natural that economic and political control should follow. As another gesture of the "good-neighbor" policy a new treaty with her was ratified in 1939; this cleared up certain inequities of the Hay-Varilla Treaty and, as with Cuba, removed her from being technically a protectorate.

[14] In 1855 a group of Americans had built a railroad across the Isthmus.

Climax of Imperialism

With the building of the Panama Canal the preservation of the United States' interests in Central America and the Caribbean became a matter of even greater concern. The unstable governments, continually changing through forcible political upheavals, endangered the constantly increasing investments of American financiers and the rapidly developing commerce. Inability to pay or repudiation of foreign debts made the interference of foreign creditor nations a constant danger. To meet the situation our government evolved a policy somewhat as follows: First, the Monroe Doctrine must be maintained, a position demonstrated in 1902 when Roosevelt insisted that the Venezuelan debt controversy be submitted to arbitration. Second, while our policy was opposed to European nations forcibly collecting claims, it admitted that the recalcitrant tropical countries must be required to meet their just debts. Third, where this was necessary or where our own financial interests were at stake, the policy of intervention and supervision might be adopted. In this manner a "Pax Americana" might be established in the Caribbean and this region made safe for American economic interests.

This policy, since known as the "Roosevelt Corollary" to the Monroe Doctrine, was first enunciated by Theodore Roosevelt in a message to Congress in 1904 and for two decades it dominated our relations with the small republics of the Caribbean and Central America.

If a nation [said Roosevelt] shows that it knows how to act with reasonable efficiency and decency in social and political matters, if it keeps order and pays its obligations, it need fear no interference from the United States. Chronic wrongdoing, or an impotence which results in a general loosening of the ties of civilized society, may in America, as elsewhere, ultimately require intervention by some civilized nation, and in the Western Hemisphere the adherence of the United States to the Monroe Doctrine may force the United States, however reluctantly, in flagrant cases of such wrongdoing or impotence, to the exercise of an international police power.

It was in Santo Domingo that the Roosevelt Corollary received its first practical application. Conditions there became so chaotic after the death of President Heureaux in 1899 that in 1904 the nation was bankrupt and unable to meet the interest on its debt. An executive arrangement was made in 1905 (later passed in treaty form in 1907) whereby the United States was to take over the administration of the customs houses and pay the Dominican government 45 per cent of the income for current expenses and 55 per cent for foreign claims. In 1908, Kuhn, Loeb & Company of New York refunded the debt of $20,000,000 under a treaty by which the United States was to collect the customs until the debt was paid. Furthermore, the public debt was not to be increased without the consent of the United States. Interference in the country's political life began in 1912, when Taft forced the resignation of a president, and culminated in the invasion of the Marines in 1916. From then until 1924, when the Marines were withdrawn, Santo Domingo remained under a military government conducted by the United States. In that year a new convention was drawn up validating earlier arrangements and extending the treaty of 1907 during the life of the bond issues, an arrangement which continued our control of Dominican finances and the power to intervene. In the meantime American interests had obtained complete control of the financial affairs of the country, one-third of the sugar industry, and other important economic gains.

In Santo Domingo the United States worked out a technique of imperialism which was soon to be applied in Haiti on the western part of the same island. With its 3,000,000 inhabitants, Haiti is the most thickly populated of the West Indies and probably the richest in natural resources. For a number of years American bankers had been interested in Haitian finances, and the First World War gave an opportunity for government intervention. Professing to believe that Germany had designs upon Haiti and determined that no European nation should assume control of Haitian customs in the hour of financial difficulty, American troops invaded the island, forced through a treaty, and, despite armed opposition by the natives, occupied the country for almost twenty years. The treaty of 1915 imposed much the same conditions as applied to Santo Domingo: American aid in the development of natural and commercial resources, American receivership of customs and supervision of expenditures, an American financial adviser, and no cession of any Haitian territory to any foreign nation.

Under this treaty Haiti definitely became a protectorate of the United States, with American officials directing the government under the protection of the Marines. The results were those ordinarily following American occupation. Finances were put on an orderly basis; the educational, sanitary, and transportation systems were improved, and peace was brought to the distracted island. At the same time financial control and economic penetration were pushed vigorously. In Haiti, as in other places where American political and military control was established, occupation was opposed and resented. It was also strongly criticized at home. Weary of the rôle of policeman, President Hoover in 1930 sent a commission to study the Haitian problem and in the next year most of the Marines were withdrawn. American control was ended by agreements in 1933, except for an American fiscal representative to direct the customs service and supervise other aspects of Haitian finance. In August, 1934, the last of the Marines departed.

With the construction of the Panama Canal, with American fruit interests active in Costa Rica and Honduras and virtually dominating the latter, the spread of American interests in Central America was inevitable. Nicaragua was the most important of the Central American states to encounter American penetration, and her possession of a second route for an interoceanic canal was the primary cause. On a number of occasions United States Marines had been landed in Nicaragua at the request of her government, even before our participation in the revolution of 1912. At this time (figures for 1913) the United States handled 35 per cent of the imports and purchased 56 per cent of the exports of the country. Following this interference, American bankers, with the unofficial sanction of the State Department (after a treaty providing for intervention had failed to pass the Senate), reorganized the finances of the little country, established a national bank, and assumed control of the principal industries. A treaty ratified by Nicaragua in 1914, and by the United States in 1916, provided that the latter should pay $3,000,000, receiving in return the exclusive right to build a canal on the Nicaraguan route, a ninety-nine year lease on three small islands, and a naval base on the Gulf of Fonseca.

With the signing of the Bryan-Chamorro Treaty the main objective as far as the United States government was concerned was achieved. Nevertheless, our State Department continued to take an active interest in aiding American bankers with the agreements of 1917 and 1920, which continued outside financial control until the middle 'twenties. In like manner the Coolidge administration felt it necessary to send the Marines back to Nicaragua during the revolutionary years after 1925 to protect American life and property, safeguard canal rights, and prevent foreign interference. The Marines did not leave again until 1933.

Although in January, 1916, President Wilson stated that "there is not a foot of territory belonging to any nation which this nation covets or desires," in the summer of that year sufficient inducements were offered to the Danish government to make it sell its possessions in the West Indies, known as the Virgin Islands. The purchase of these islands had no direct economic significance. It was essentially a matter of naval strategy to safeguard the routes to the canal. Whatever the objectives, it was clear that by the end of the First World War the Caribbean was virtually an "American lake." America's first "sphere of influence" had been achieved. Economic penetration, working hand in hand with political policy and naval exigency, had brought the acquisition of Puerto Rico, the Great and Little Corn Islands, the naval stations at Guantanamo, Cuba, at Mole St. Nicholas, Haiti, at

Samana Bay, Santo Domingo, and in the Gulf of Fonseca. It had brought the establishment of protectorates over five nations—Cuba, Panama, the Dominican Republic, Nicaragua, and Haiti—and of these Cuba and Panama were nations only by the grace of the United States. In all this the policy of the Roosevelt, Taft, and Wilson administrations had been virtually the same.

The most important exception to the hegemony of the United States in the region of the Caribbean and Central America was Mexico. Easy as it was to ride roughshod over the diminutive republics of Haiti and Nicaragua, the problem of Mexico was more difficult, and our relations with that nation have been exceedingly complicated since the revolution of 1910. Encouraged by thirty years of strong rule under Porfirio Diaz, United States oil drillers, silver miners, railroad builders, ranchers, and others had invested close to one billion dollars, and Europeans had interests aggregating half that amount. By 1910 approximately 80 per cent of investments in Mexican railroads were controlled by Americans, and 70 per cent of the oil was being taken out by American firms. During this period our government was under pressure to intervene for the protection of American capital, and at the same time European nations almost forced us either to look after their interests or to allow intervention on their part, an action hardly in keeping with the Roosevelt Corollary. The Mexican revolution, itself largely an agrarian revolt by an exploited peasantry against the inordinately large accumulations of land, was accompanied by much banditry and considerable loss to the investments of American citizens, and it was further complicated by the fact that European and American interests often pulled the strings behind the scenes which gave impetus to the revolutionary activity.

On two occasions (1914 and 1917) armed forces entered Mexico but withdrew; probably only the European war prevented further outside interference. Since 1917 the diplomatic problems of the two nations have swung chiefly around the economic interests of American investors as affected by the Mexican Constitution of that year. This Constitution nationalized church property, secularized the schools, promised varied legislation, and declared that the soil and subsoil of Mexico belonged to the Mexican people. In the future only Mexicans might acquire ownership of Mexican land, except that Mexico might grant the same right to foreigners on condition that they agree "to be considered Mexicans in respect to such property, and accordingly not to envoke the protection of their governments to the same, under penalty, in case of breach, of forfeiture." Under no condition might a foreigner acquire land within 100 kilometers from the frontier or 50 from the coast. Although this was not retroactive, it was bitterly opposed by American investors. Relations with Mexico improved greatly during the late 'twenties through the tact of Ambassador Dwight W. Morrow, but deteriorated again a decade later when, as a result of a dispute over labor conditions, the Mexican government in 1938 nationalized foreign oil properties but promised indemnification. The American government conceded the right of expropriation; hence this phase of our relations with Mexico has been largely concerned since 1938 with securing a fair appraisal and adequate indemnification. Generally speaking, the policy of the United States from Taft to Franklin D. Roosevelt has been to let the Mexicans work out their own salvation, but at the same time to exert pressure for more settled conditions and for protection of foreign interests.

THE FAR EAST

American economic interests in the Far East go back to the 1790's when American merchants found in China a market for furs and other commodities and a source of tea and other Oriental goods.[15] As far as the United States had any policy in the Far East during the nineteenth century, it was the desire to keep the field open for free and equal commercial opportunities for all nations. In the furtherance of this objective this country made numerous contributions, including our part in the opening of Japan in the 1850's, to foreign trade. This policy was continued and more definitely enunciated in the twentieth century as a result of the industrial development at home, the new spirit of economic imperialism, and three important developments in the Far East. The first was the annexation of the Philippines, which made the United States a power in that part of the world; the second was the phenomenal emergence of Japan as a powerful nation; the third was the imperialistic designs of Japan and the great European nations upon the integrity of China.

The Philippines, as we have seen, were annexed in 1899 despite strong opposition at home and the necessity of overcoming the armed resistance of the Filipinos. Although many motives contributed to this, the principal one seems to have been the hope of commercial expansion. Unlike American domination in Puerto Rico and certain other areas, American administration in the Philippines has been efficient, liberal, and interested in the welfare of the natives. Civil government with native participation was established in 1901, partial home rule in 1907, and virtual home rule in 1916 with the Jones Act. Trade was promoted by an Act of 1902 allowing Philippine commodities to enter the United States under a 25 per cent tariff reduction. Free importation was permitted in 1909, except that only a specified amount of sugar and tobacco could be brought in. Since 1913 there has been complete free trade.

From the beginning the Philippines have been a burden rather than an

[15] Above, p. 229.

asset. American trade with the islands increased—our exports from about $4,000,000 in 1901 to $83,400,000 in 1939, and imports from about $10,000,000 in 1900 to $92,000,000 in 1939. But this was by no means pure gain, for certain of the leading Philippine exports to the United States—sugar, tobacco, and coconut products—came into competition with American produce. Nor did the Philippines prove to be a fruitful field for investment. Total American investments in 1935 amounted to approximately $200,000,000, of which about one-sixth was in government bonds. The total was less than one-fifth the amount of capital that had flowed into Cuba. Moreover, it was difficult to see how ownership of the islands had contributed much to the development of the fabulous trade of the Orient. In any case a combination of three factors—Philippine demands for independence, the American farm bloc, and anti-imperialist Democrats—combined to bring passage of the Tydings-McDuffie Act of 1934, which granted Philippine independence after a period of ten years. But this was by no means all gain to the Filipinos. In return for eventual independence, immigration from the Philippines was to end and Philippine imports were to pay the regular American tariffs. Since the United States in 1934 took 87 per cent of Philippine exports, this was a high price. The greatest price was the danger of Japanese aggression and this, as it turned out, was paid before the United States retired from the islands.

American annexation of the Philippines was but one aspect of a great imperialistic movement which was to throw the Far East into a turmoil and which reached a climax in the Second World War. It began at the end of the Chinese-Japanese War in 1895, when Japan annexed Formosa and made Korea a sphere of influence. This was followed immediately by demands by France, Germany, Russia, and Great Britain upon China for long-term leases of important ports behind which they hoped to erect spheres of economic influence. In an effort to prevent China's economic resources from being grabbed by outside nations and to protect America's growing commerce, John Hay in September, 1899, addressed to the great powers interested in Far East exploitation essentially identical notes enunciating the now famous "open-door" policy. They requested that in its sphere of influence each nation give assurances (1) that all existing treaty ports and established interests in each sphere of influence would be unmolested, (2) that the Chinese tariffs and no others would be enforced and collected by Chinese officials, and (3) that no differentiation in port and railroad charges would be made between the citizens of any nation carrying on business. Russia declined; the others (except Italy) answered evasively; but Hay, ignoring the evasive replies, announced that in view of the favorable reception of his proposals, they would be regarded "as final and definitive."

This policy of encouraging China's economic integrity Hay in the following year augmented by the policy of maintaining her political integrity. When a group of Chinese nationalists reacted against foreign aggression in the Boxer Rebellion of 1900, he reaffirmed the open-door policy and insisted that the rebellion should not be an excuse for the annexation of territory. This policy of attempting to maintain the economic and political integrity of China has continued to be the official policy of the United States for the past four decades. Although the *status quo* was upset by the Russo-Japanese War in 1904–1905 and again by the First World War, the United States succeeded at the Washington conference in 1921 in reestablishing it temporarily. Not until the Japanese invasion of Manchuria in 1931 did it completely collapse.

Behind this policy and with the active aid of the State Department, American exporters and financiers have attempted aggressively to push their economic interests in China. On the whole, however, the roseate dreams of great commercial expansion have failed to materialize. It is true that American exports to China increased from $16,724,000 in 1900 to $138,455,000 in 1920, but they declined to $55,481,000 in 1936 on the eve of the war between Japan and China.[16] The China trade was but a tiny fraction of the total commerce of the United States. Efforts of American financiers to participate in the building of Chinese railroads were usually checkmated by the opposition of Japan and other nations, and difficulties were experienced in American participation in Chinese government loans. After thirty years of active effort, American investments in China in 1930 amounted to approximately $240,000,000, of which $155,000,000 was in business enterprises, $42,000,000 in securities and obligations of the Chinese government, and $43,000,000 in missions.[17]

Technique of Imperialism

Enough has been said in a general way to give some idea of the manner in which imperialism is pursued, and it may be wise to pause for a moment to emphasize this. The New Imperialism of the last forty years has generally been carried out by one of the following methods, or variations and combinations of them: (1) by means of military conquest, as in the case of the Boer War and the Spanish-American War; (2) by the appropriation, frequently by treaty consent from the natives, of certain regions not yet preempted by white men, as in large parts of Africa; (3) by means of lending money to weak or impoverished governments who eventually are unable to pay, after which the lending government steps in to enforce payment by

[16] The value of Chinese exports to this country in 1936 was $55,685,000.
[17] C. F. Remer, *Foreign Investments in China*, p. 328.

taking over the customs, appointing a financial adviser, or actually establishing a protectorate—excellent examples are England in Egypt and the United States in Nicaragua, Haiti, and Santo Domingo; (4) by economic penetration, followed by friction with the natives and demand by the settlers for intervention and protection on the part of the home country. Hawaii

FOREIGN TRADE OF CONTINENTAL UNITED STATES WITH ITS TERRITORIES AND POSSESSIONS.[18]

is an example of this last. The process of imperialism may be completed in one stroke, but it is more likely to run through various stages. The first may be missionary activity followed by economic penetration, which in turn may entail friction with the natives or danger to investments. Then may come intervention, with the establishment of a virtual protectorate. The last stage is actual annexation, but under modern conditions this is often unnecessary, for economic exploitation can be carried on quite as effectively in a protectorate, thus avoiding the expense and trouble of administration. This is notably true in Cuba, where American investments are greater than in all American colonies and protectorates combined.

While the technique of modern imperialism is obviously somewhat different from that of the seventeenth and eighteenth centuries, the underlying motive—economic benefit to the home or exploiting nation—is essentially the same. It should be pointed out, however, that the benefits have not been entirely one-sided. American imperialism has meant the loss of political and economic independence, but it has often, though not always, brought

[18] *Commerce Yearbook, 1930,* I, 88.

greater prosperity and better living conditions. Improved transportation facilities, better sanitation, an aggressive attack upon tropical diseases, an extension of educational facilities, and a more efficient and honest government have all followed in the wake of imperialism. Although this has not been due entirely to unselfish motives, the fact remains that the United States has assumed "the white man's burden" in a serious mood. That the policy of economic imperialism has progressed simultaneously with the rapid expansion of our commerce with these dependencies may be seen from the accompanying graph. This is also true of the expansion of American investments. It should be pointed out, however, that American foreign trade and investments have also expanded elsewhere in the world and in regions where there have been no political expansion and control. American economic investments in Japan, for example, amounted to $418,000,000 in 1933, more than twice those in China.

Retreat from Imperialism

An effort has been made in the preceding pages to trace the development of our economic imperialism during the early decades of the present century. This began in a definite and aggressive manner with the Spanish-American War. In the Far East it led to the annexation of the Philippines and to the development of the "open-door" policy in China. In Latin America it began with a protectorate over Cuba, the enunciation ·of the Roosevelt Corollary, and the rapid expansion of economic and political power. There it reached a climax in the capture of Vera Cruz (1914), the military occupation of Haiti (1915), Pershing's invasion of Mexico (1916), and the purchase of the Virgin Islands (1917).

Although there has been a rapid expansion of commerce and investments in certain areas, as a whole the experience has not been happy or in certain aspects successful. The Philippine Islands did not prove to be a steppingstone to "China's illimitable markets." It was impossible to achieve the "open-door" policy without war, and as the years passed the United States seemed unwilling to precipitate a Far Eastern conflict to maintain this policy. When war finally came, it was Japan rather than the United States that began it. In the Caribbean the Roosevelt Corollary, which would make the United States the policeman of Latin America and the collector of debts owed to American citizens, proved impractical. Too many Latin-American states were disturbed by revolution, and too many had defaulted on their bond issues, for any one nation to police them all. Furthermore, American industrialists were eager to extend their foreign markets and this could hardly be done without building up a spirit of good will among our southern neighbors. Finally, it was beginning to dawn on the

American people that colonies and dependencies were more likely to be a source of trouble and financial loss than of gain. In brief, economic imperialism as supported by the Roosevelt Corollary had turned sour, and there was little appetite for further adventures.

With this as a background, there began a retreat from the type of imperialism evident since the Spanish-American War. Legislation in 1934 provided for Philippine independence after ten years. In Latin America a "good-neighbor policy" was gradually substituted for the Roosevelt Corollary. Military intervention ceased in Santo Domingo in 1924; the Marines were withdrawn from Nicaragua in 1933 and from Haiti in 1934. Treaties with Cuba in 1934 and with Panama helped to lift these nations from their status of at least technical protectorates. The new policy was made clear in a series of Pan-American conferences promoted by the United States. At Montevideo in 1933 the United States took a definite stand against "the intervention of any state of the American continent in the internal affairs of another state" and at Lima in 1938 she officially abrogated the Roosevelt Corollary. Closer economic relations for the benefit of all were to be promoted by reciprocal trade agreements and similar methods rather than by armed intervention. In the darkening clouds of a second world war the government of the United States hoped also to change the Monroe Doctrine from a policy promoted by herself alone to one in which all the American nations would cooperate in upholding a mutual program of hemisphere defense.

SELECTED READINGS

Moon, P. T., *Imperialism and World Politics,* Chap. XVI.
Williams, B. H., *Economic Foreign Policy of the United States,* Chap. I.
Williams, B. H., *American Diplomacy,* Chaps. V–IX.
Bemis, S. F., *A Diplomatic History of the United States,* Chaps. XXVII–XXX, XXXV, XXXVIII–XL.
Stuart, G. H., *Latin America and the United States,* Chap. V.
Griswold, A. W., *The Far Eastern Policy of the United States,* Chaps. I, IV.
Perkins, Dexter, *Hands Off,* Chaps. VII, IX.
Flügel, F., and Faulkner, H. U., *Readings in the Economic and Social History of the United States,* Chap. XIX.

or Union Meeting
the Time of the
akmaker's Strike in
ew York in 1912.

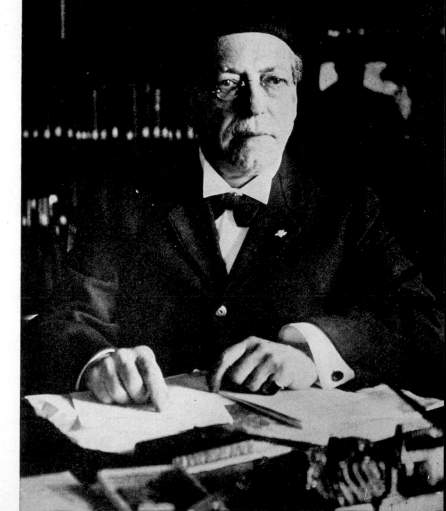

uel Gompers, Pres-
t of the American
eration of Labor,
5–1894, 1896–1924.

Culver

Train of the Camden and Amboy Railroad Reconstructing the Delaware and
Raritan Canal About 1866 at a Time When Canal Transportation
Was Declining.

Completion of the First Transcontinental Railroad at Promontory Point, Utah,
May 10, 1869.

Photo by Brown

Poster Advertising the Opening of the Union
Pacific Railroad.

Union Pacific's First Locomotive. It Was Brought to Omaha by Steamboat from St. Louis, June 5, 1865.

A Crack Pullman Train of the Early Twentieth Century Running Along the Bank of the Chesapeake and Ohio Canal.

Photo by Brown Brothers

City Transportation at the Turn of the Century.

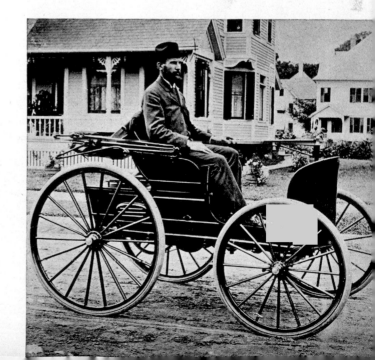

les Duryea in His First
Horseless Carriage.

Photo by Brown Brothers

The Wright Brothers' First Flight Near Kitty Hawk, North Carolina, December 17, 1903.

Black Maria—The First Moving Picture Studio Set Up by Edison for His Experiments.

Mechanized Agriculture—Twelve McCormick-Deering Sixteen-foot Threshers Cutting a Swath 192 Feet Wide and Capable of Cutting 640 Acres a Day.

Mechanized Agriculture—A Caterpillar Diesel Pulling a 14-foot Drill and a 14-foot Land Roller in Tandem.

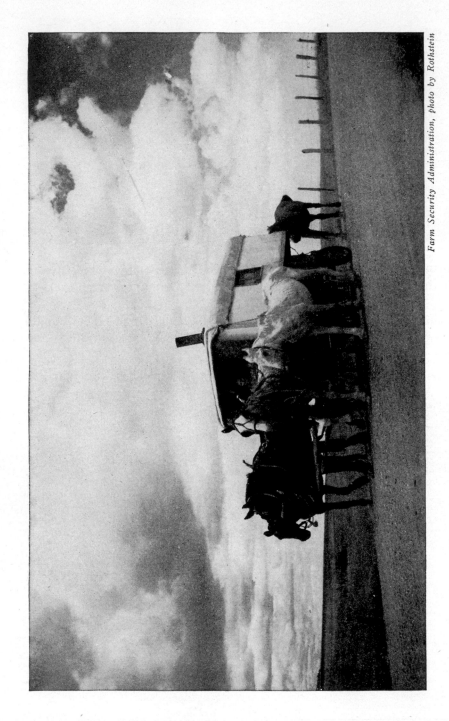

Farm Security Administration, photo by Rothstein

Displaced by Drought and Mechanical Agriculture, the Small Farmer Moves
on in Search of Work

27

America and the First
World War

ECONOMIC TRENDS ON THE EVE OF THE WAR—DECLINE OF LAISSEZ FAIRE

In the last eight chapters an effort was made to trace the economic development of the United States from the conclusion of the Civil War to 1914. The more important changes wrought in our economic life during that half century should now be obvious to any reader. With economic changes came a different attitude toward economic policy. Although federal and state aid had been granted at various times for internal improvements and industry had received aid from the protective tariff, America in general had been committed during these years to the economic doctrine of *laissez faire,* and faith in this doctrine was never stronger than in the hectic period of economic development following the Civil War. Although the 'eighties and 'nineties saw the golden age of *laissez faire,* the average citizen's naïve faith in it was already being undermined. Particularly had this faith been weakened by the long period of agrarian distress, by the resentment against railroad abuses, by the opposition of the small business man and manufacturer to the consolidation of industry and capital, and by the example of state control and social experiment in Europe. There was a growing feeling that America was no longer the land of opportunity and that uncontrolled *laissez faire* had benefited only a small group who had amassed the major share of the wealth and resources of the nation. The culmination of this discontent came in the first decade of the present century when Theodore Roosevelt, catching the prevailing feeling of unrest, led a vigorous campaign toward government regulation, a campaign which was duplicated in many of the states.

Preliminary shots had been fired in the Interstate Commerce Act of 1887 and the Sherman Anti-trust Act of 1890, which inaugurated a policy of government regulation that was widened and strengthened in the succeeding decades. But the extension of federal activities has not been confined simply to restraining harmful practices; the government definitely enlarged its own business interests in many ways, notably by embarking in the transportation business through the parcels post (1912) and in the banking business through the postal savings banks (1912). It sought to aid agriculture, industry, commerce, and labor, particularly through the Department of Agriculture, established in 1889, and the Department of Commerce and Labor, established in 1903 and separated in 1913.

In many ways the breakdown of *laissez faire* was more striking in state legislation than in that of the federal government. The leadership among the states was taken by Wisconsin under the inspiration of La Follette during 1900 to 1905, when that state became a veritable laboratory for social legislation, strengthening its railroad commission, establishing a public utility commission to regulate rates and determine valuation, and creating an industrial commission to enforce labor legislation and, finally, a tax commission to evolve a more equitable and scientific system of taxation. One of the most important of the Wisconsin laws was that providing for a personal income tax (1911) and her lead was followed by the federal government (1913) and eventually by many states.[1] In practically every state inheritance taxes have also been enacted. These new taxes, it should be pointed out, are a result of the mounting expenses of the government as well as of a change in the attitude of the people. It is unnecessary to review here the many types of labor legislation and other efforts toward social control characteristic of the first decade of the century or to point out how the demands for social control found their way into party platforms.[2] "Eminent economists," wrote Dr. Beard in 1914, "turned from free trade and *laissez faire* to consider some of the grievances of the working class, and many abandoned the time-honored discussions of 'economic theories,' in favor of legislative programs embracing the principles of state socialism to which Germany and England were already committed. . . . While none of the states went so far as to establish old-age pensions and general sickness and accident insurance, it was apparent from an examination of the legislation of the first decade of the twentieth century that they were well on the paths of nations like Germany, England and Australia."[3]

[1] Although an income tax had been imposed during the Civil War (above, p. 542), a second effort was declared unconstitutional in 1895. The income tax of 1913 was made possible by the sixteenth amendment adopted in that year. By 1940 thirty-two states and the District of Columbia were taxing both personal and corporate income. Two others (Connecticut and Pennsylvania) were taxing only corporate income. Delaware, New Hampshire, and West Virginia taxed personal income only.

[2] Above, Chap. XXII, and H. U. Faulkner, *Quest for Social Justice, 1898–1914;* the latter covers the subject in some detail.

[3] C. A. Beard, *Contemporary American History*, pp. 304–305.

CONSERVATION

An important aspect of the decline of *laissez faire* was the rather sudden interest aroused during these years in the problem of conservation. Blessed for three centuries with an apparently exhaustless supply of land and raw materials, the American people became prodigal of their heritage and wasteful in their habits. As population began to press seriously upon the land and the cost of raw materials increased, attention was drawn more and more to the conservation of the remaining resources. Investigations showed that our supplies of wood and minerals were not inexhaustible;[4] that in the mining of bituminous coal, one-fourth was left underground permanently lost, and in like manner at least half of the anthracite, while annually millions of gallons of mineral oils evaporated or were lost in pumping. Unscientific methods of lumbering were both denuding the nation of wood and releasing the floods to spread havoc, and soil eroded or was being robbed of its fertility without renewal. Not alone in the processes of production was waste to be found, but also in the use of the finished material. Furthermore, in no highly developed industrial nation was human life more lightly regarded than in the United States. Conservative estimates placed the deaths from industrial accidents at around 20,000 a year, with industrial injuries of greater or less importance at about 2,000,000.[5] For every 100,000 tons of coal mined it was claimed that one man was killed and several were injured. The Interstate Commerce Commission reported for the year 1919 over 2000 railroad employees killed and over 131,000 injured.

Although the conservation of material and human resources may take many forms, the "conservation movement" in America is generally considered to have commenced with the agitation of such men as Gifford Pinchot and Frederick Haynes Newell and to have been promoted by President Roosevelt, who called a famous conference of governors in 1908. The result was the appointment of forty state conservation committees and a national conservation committee, and much publicity for the whole subject. From it came a reaction against the wasteful exploitations of earlier years, a new interest in the more scientific and intelligent use of natural

---

[4] The consumption figures for a single issue of a great metropolitan newspaper furnish an excellent illustration of the rapid use of our natural resources. The Public Service Bureau of the Chicago *Tribune* gave "the approximate figures on the materials that are required to publish the Sunday edition of the Chicago *Tribune*" in 1924 as follows: "Standing timber, 54 acres; sulphur, 21 tons; coal, 665 tons; electric horsepower, 63,000; water, 18,200,000 gallons; limestone, 28 tons; paper, 800 tons." Mr. S. M. Williams of the New York *World* estimated (1924) 400 to 450 tons of newsprint paper as the average of the New York Sunday *World*, with coal consumption varying from 1400 to 1700 pounds of coal per ton of paper and approximately fifty acres of pulpwood (chiefly spruce and balsam) forests cut over.

[5] See C. R. Daugherty, *Labor Problems in American Industry*, Chap. V.

resources, particularly inland waterways, and new legislation to protect the public domain and the subsoil resources on public lands. It was found that under the liberal land laws large corporations had acquired, often by fraudulent methods, a large part of the mineral resources of the country. To prevent a similar fate for the water-power resources, the great power of the future, Roosevelt hastened to withdraw 148,346,925 acres from public entry. The efforts of public-spirited men to preserve some parts of the public lands for the nation as a whole were hampered by lack of congressional interest, by the opposition of private interests, and even by the corruption of high public officials, but progress was made.

Progress has been made also in the conservation of human resources, as can be seen by surveying the important social legislation passed since the opening of the century and by noting the various federal and state agencies, such as the Public Health Service of the Treasury Department[6] and the Women's and Children's Bureaus of the Department of Labor, set up to safeguard the physical welfare of the nation. It can be seen likewise in the more aggressive and definite attitude taken by the churches, Catholic and Protestant alike, on the subject of social and economic justice. Significant as is the conservation movement in the general story of the breakdown of *laissez faire,* it is ironical that it should appear in the years just before the First World War plunged the world into the greatest orgy of waste and destruction which history records up to that time.

INCOMES AND THE DISTRIBUTION OF WEALTH

The need for conservation and for a more scientific approach to the whole problem of the production and distribution of economic wealth is obvious when one attempts to survey the material well-being of the American people in the years before that war. The Census of 1900 placed the total wealth of the nation at approximately $88,500,000,000. This had certainly more than doubled by 1914 and with it had come an increase in per capita wealth. Significant increases are also to be noted during these years in the national income. No adequate statistics are available before 1909, but the best figures collected since then appear in the accompanying table. In examining the figures due consideration should be given to the inflation after 1914. When reduced to the price level of 1913, the purchasing power of the $61,000,000,000 national income in 1918, for example, would amount to but 38.8 billion dollars, and that of the per capita income of $586 would be only $372.

The figures in this table do not necessarily mean that the income of the average wage earner in terms of purchasing power was necessarily increasing.

[6] Transferred in 1939 to the Federal Security Agency.

NATIONAL INCOME, 1909-1918 [7]

Years	National Income (in billions)	Population (in millions)	Income per Capita (in dollars)
1909	28.8	90.37	319
1910	31.4	92.23	340
1911	31.2	93.81	333
1912	33.0	95.34	346
1913	34.4	97.28	354
1914	33.2	99.19	335
1915	36.0	100.43	358
1916	45.4	101.72	446
1917	53.9	103.06	523
1918	61.0	104.18	586

Economists in 1914 were generally agreed on two points: (1) that comparatively few adult workers earned wages which would secure a decent standard of living, and (2) that real wages had declined between 1900 and 1914.[8] It appears, however, that real wages increased in the following decade. Douglas, who has made the most intensive study of the period since 1890, believes that there was a gain of 19 per cent in the purchasing power of a full-time week's work in 1926 from that in the period 1890 to 1899, and holds that most groups of manual workers enjoyed a substantial increase in real wages in the decade following the war. On the other hand, he believes that most groups of non-manual workers, with the notable exception of teachers, experienced a real decline.[9] From another angle of the situation it appears that the share of the wage earners in the total national income increased slightly, if at all, during the 1920's.[10] Whatever the situation regarding real wages and the share of labor in the national income, there seems to be no question but that the standard of living improved rather steadily during the forty years prior to 1929. This was due primarily to two influences—new inventions that have made work easier and living more comfortable, and the large amount of social legislation that has gone far to protect the health, well-being, and working conditions of the wage earner and his family. His standard has indeed improved, but in most cases it remains, as in 1914, below a decent minimum. Furthermore, as a class, the American wage earner, owing to the disintegration of the organized labor

[7] *Income in the United States, Its Amount and Distribution, 1909–1919,* by the Staff of the National Bureau of Economic Research, Inc., 1921. This table is adapted from Tables 1, 9, and 11, in Vol. I, pp. 13, 64, and 68.

[8] For a summary of this, see H. U. Faulkner, *Quest for Social Justice,* p. 21 ff.; also P. H. Douglas, *Real Wages in the United States, 1890–1926,* p. 572; and W. J. Lauck and E. Sydenstricker, *Conditions of Labor in American Industries.*

[9] P. H. Douglas, *Real Wages,* Chap. XXII.

[10] *Recent Economic Changes,* II, 766–771.

movement in the post-war years,[11] was in a weaker position in 1932 than in 1914.

At least one other aspect of this problem must be discussed—the distribution of wealth. Although per capita income and per capita wealth are greater in the United States than in European countries, the distribution of

GENERAL PRICES AND PURCHASING POWER OF THE DOLLAR, 1900–1940.
(1926 = 100.)

(From P. F. Gemmill and R. H. Blodgett, *Economics: Principles & Problems,* Harper & Brothers.)

general wealth is not radically different, a striking and sobering fact when the greater resources, the newness of the country, and its democratic institutions are remembered. According to a careful study made in 1890, seven-eighths of the families held but one-eighth of the wealth, and one per cent of the people owned more than the remaining 99.[12] A decade later there appeared to be little change. A study of estates probated in five Wisconsin counties during 1900 revealed the fact that the poorest two-thirds of the population owned only 5 or 6 per cent of the wealth and the poorest four-fifths scarcely 10 per cent, while the richest one per cent owned half of the property probated. As these Wisconsin counties comprised rural communities and cities including Milwaukee, and as the findings agree with

[11] *See* below, pp. 630 ff.
[12] C. B. Spahr, *The Present Distribution of Wealth in the United States,* p. 65.

similar studies made at different periods in Massachusetts, they may be taken as typical.[13] They point inevitably to the fact that fully 80 per cent of the people lived on the margin of existence and that the wealth of the nation was largely owned by the remaining 20 per cent. Little had happened by 1914 or, for that matter, by 1940, to change this situation.[14]

Although the distribution of wealth is far more unequal than that of income, a study of income tax returns only serves to strengthen conclusions obtained from probate records. Taking the year 1920 as fairly indicative (for it included both the last months of the war inflation and the beginning of the subsequent depression), we find that even in this year of partially inflated wages 83 per cent of those over ten years of age gainfully employed did not receive an income amounting to $1000. Yet this was a period when government agencies were putting $2200 or over as a minimum comfort income for a family of five. Although it is extremely difficult, even with the force of government pressure, to secure accurate information on incomes, it appeared that in 1920 less than one per cent of the income receivers had close to 12 per cent of the national income and 10 per cent had 34 per cent. At the same time, whereas the incomes of those receiving between $1000 and $5000 amounted to 64.35 per cent of the total income reported, they paid only 15.43 per cent of the tax.[15]

Despite the discouraging facts revealed by a study of incomes and the distribution of wealth, the American people had never before made more rapid progress toward a better civilization than in the decade preceding the World War. Not alone was there a tremendous economic development on all fronts, but great progress was being made in the integration and regulation of economic life. The bitter attacks of the "muckrakers" upon the social, political, and economic ills of the day were but the symbol of the changed attitude of the nation, of its willingness to take sober stock of its resources, to modify the economic brigandage which had ushered in the new century, and to value more highly the scientific approach as the solution of many ills. The attack on the old order was carried on along the entire front. In the states by means of the initiative, referendum, and recall and improved city government an effort was made to rescue the government from exploiting private interests and return it to the people. The seventeenth amendment was aimed in the same direction in the federal government.

[13] W. I. King, *The Wealth and Income of the People of the United States*, pp. 72–87, 90–115.

[14] A study by the Federal Trade Commission of estates left between 1912 and 1923 showed that 80 per cent of decedents left estates valued at less than $500 and that more than 90 per cent of all estates amounted to less than $5000. About one per cent of the decedents owned more than 90 per cent of the wealth. P. H. Nystrom, *Economics of Consumption*, p. 152.

[15] For a statement on the distribution of income under the "New Deal," see below, p. 677.

An infinite variety of social legislation directed on the one hand against the slums, the exploitation of the labor of women and children, and the waste of life in industry, and on the other toward the improvement of the facilities for education, recreation, and health gave the tone to the new century. The pre-war years closed with four notable pieces of federal legislation—the Clayton Anti-trust Act, a new effort to prevent monopolies; the Federal Trade Commission Act, better to control big business; the Federal Reserve Act, to integrate more closely the nation's banking system; and the Underwood-Simmons Act, the most intelligent tariff Act since the Civil War.

Years of Neutrality

The famous Acts in the first year of the Wilson administration represented the climax of the reform movement of the early years of the century. The First World War, which engulfed Europe in the late summer of 1914 and three years later widened to include the United States, virtually ended for the time being the drive for social justice and ushered in a period of reaction. Few Americans who followed their newspapers with such intensity in 1914 had any realization of the far-reaching economic effects which the war would bring. For four years most of the European nations devoted their supreme efforts to the task of annihilation. Millions of workers were withdrawn from productive industry to indulge in an orgy of destruction which was to use up the accumulated wealth of decades. To the 7,450,000 men killed in battle must be added a greater number disabled or brought to an early death by wounds, and the fatalities to the civilian population because of disease and starvation. To the immediate cost of $186,000,000,000 must be added the subsequent payments for pensions, the cost of reconstruction, and other burdens too infinite to estimate. It piled up the debts of the warring nations to a figure which could be met only by repudiation; for two decades after the conflict the world was cursed by the problems of war debts and inflation. For the moment the war disorganized the financial, commercial, and industrial systems of the world. But even the expenditure of human life and material wealth was of little avail. The First World War was to prove but a preliminary struggle to an even greater world conflict.

The early effect of the First World War upon the United States was much like that experienced during the period of the French Revolution and the Napoleonic Wars. The years 1913 and 1914 found this country suffering from a minor depression which was accentuated by the economic disorganization of the first few months of the European conflict. Beginning in 1915, however, there ensued a five-year period of enormous industrial and agricultural expansion due in the first instance to increased European needs and later augmented by our participation in the war. As Europeans turned from peace-time pursuits the gap had to be filled elsewhere, and the United States, as she had done a century earlier, served as a source of raw materials and food supplies. Unlike her rôle in the Napoleonic Wars, this country, because of her industrial development, now played an important part as a producer of munitions. In the end, however, whatever gains she may have made from the woes of Europe were canceled by her own participation. The world again proved too small for the United States to escape being drawn into a world conflict.

Producers of metals and other minerals were naturally the first to feel the impetus. The production of iron ore increased from 41,439,000 long tons in 1914 to 75,288,000 in 1917; the production of copper from 1,150,137,000 pounds to 1,886,120,000 pounds, of zinc from 343,000 short tons to 584,600, of bituminous coal from 422,703,000 short tons to 551,790,000, and of petroleum from 265;762,000 barrels to 335,315,000. Agricultural prosperity soon followed as the demand for cotton, wool, leather, and lumber increased. Cotton, which was a drug on the market in 1915 at 8.5 cents a pound, rose to an average of 35.9 cents during 1920. The production of wheat, which had been 763,380,000 bushels in 1913, rose to 1,025,800,000 in 1915. Poor crops cut it in 1916 and 1917, but the output in both 1918 and 1919 was well over 900,000,000 bushels; the price of wheat rose from 97 cents in 1913 to $2.73 in 1920. The corn crop, which amounted to 2,445,988,000 bushels in 1913, was pushed up to 3,065,233,000 in 1917, a record up to that time. Not only was the production of metals and agricultural products stimulated, but many articles hitherto largely purchased abroad were manufactured here in increased quantities. Of these should be mentioned dyes, potash, chemicals, scientific instruments, and optical goods. The rapid development of the chemical industry, the most important of the "war babies," was, in fact, one of the most significant effects of the war upon American industry.

Since we were the largest producers of the chief raw materials and the most convenient source of foodstuffs, foreign purchases from us were extremely heavy during the war and immediately afterward. As a consequence, foreign commerce increased enormously, notwithstanding the activity of German submarines. For a decade preceding the war American exports had surpassed imports by between $450,000,000 and $500,000,000, a balance of trade which had been offset by the payment of interest and dividends on borrowed capital, by the payment of freight rates to European shippers, by the expenditures of American travelers, and by immigrant remittances. The excess of exports over imports, which had amounted to $435,800,000 in the year ending June 30, 1914, jumped to $3,567,800,000 in 1917. Exports, as will be seen from the accompanying table, considerably more than tripled between 1914 and 1920. As was natural, the great increase came in munitions and foodstuffs; thus the value of explosives exported rose from $6,272,197 in 1914 to $802,789,437 in 1917; of chemicals, dyes, drugs, etc., from $21,924,337 to $181,028,432; of iron and steel, from $251,480,677 to $1,133,746,188; of meat products, from $143,261,000 to $353,812,000; and of wheat, from $87,953,400 to $298,179,705. This excess of exports was made possible, of course, by this country's extensive loans to the Allies.

Even when the price inflation caused by the war is taken into consideration, the increase in foreign trade was enormous. It was due not alone to the war needs of Europe but also to an increase in trade with Latin America and Asia where the United States was able to fill the gap made by the elimination of Germany and the preoccupation of Great Britain. The excess of

FOREIGN TRADE OF THE UNITED STATES, 1914–1921[16] (IN MILLIONS OF DOLLARS)

Year[a]	Exports of Domestic Merchandise	Imports of Merchandise	Excess of Exports over Imports	Percentage of Agricultural Exports	Percentage of Manufactured Exports
1914	2,329.7	1,893.9	435.8	48	47
1915	2,716.2	1,674.2	1,042.0	54	43
1916	4,272.2	2,197.9	2,074.3	36	62
1917	6,227.2	2,659.4	3,567.8	32	66
1918	5,838.7	2,945.7	2,893.0	39	58
1919	7,749.8	3,904.4	3,845.4	53	45
1920	8,080.5	5,278.5	2,802.0	43	52
1921	4,378.9	2,509.1	1,869.8	48	46

[a] Fiscal years ending June 30 to 1918; thereafter calendar years.

exports over imports, along with the prosperity in this country and the destruction in Europe, helps to explain the shifting of the world's financial center to New York. For the first time in her history the United States became a creditor nation.

The rapid expansion of American commerce did not go on unhampered. Of the difficulties faced by the United States, inadequate shipping facilities was the most important. Unlike the Napoleonic era when this country had the second largest merchant fleet in the world, the year 1914 found her with a relatively small tonnage. In that year the tonnage of American vessels engaged in foreign trade amounted to a little over a million. The lack of a merchant marine was keenly felt, particularly as the great German steamship lines were driven from the sea at the very time when German submarines were destroying Allied tonnage faster than it could be replaced and

[16] Statistical Abstract, 1921, Table 482, pp. 840, 847, 849.

when considerable Allied tonnage was being withdrawn from commerce for strictly war purposes. The situation was acute, and as early as 1914 the federal government instituted an active policy for the stimulation of shipping. In that year the laws regarding registry and other matters were modified to allow foreign ships to seek refuge under the neutral flag of the United States, and an Act was passed creating a Bureau of War Risk Insurance in the Treasury Department to insure American vessels and cargoes if insurance could not be otherwise provided on reasonable terms.[17] Two years later (September 7, 1916), Congress authorized the appointment of a United States Shipping Board to promote the development of the merchant marine and to regulate shipping.

With Europe battling in a life-and-death struggle, it was unlikely that America could enjoy unmolested the profits of neutrality. As in the Napoleonic Wars, each side in the struggle was anxious to keep American products from reaching the other. To achieve this purpose both Great Britain and Germany violated neutral rights as they balanced their immediate needs against the displeasure and possible action of the United States. Great Britain, controlling the sea, blockaded German ports and arbitrarily extended the contraband list to include cotton, wool, leather, rubber, copper, and chemicals, which had formerly been free of seizure, and later included foodstuffs. She also enforced the theory of "ultimate destination" and seized cargoes bound for the neutral nations of Europe on the grounds that they were destined eventually for the Central Powers. On her part, Germany proclaimed the waters around the British Isles a "war zone" and embarked on a policy of unrestricted submarine warfare which resulted in the loss of American lives and property.

The causes which make for war are extremely complex, and their relative importance is often impossible to determine. Much emphasis has been given during the last two decades to the economic causes for our entry. American economic life, it is pointed out, had become geared more and more to the task of supplying essential war commodities, and these commodities, owing to Britain's control of the seas, had gone only to one side. It was Germany's interference with this commerce that provided the technical cause for our declaration of war on April 17, 1917. Moreover, private loans to the Allies amounted to $1,500,000,000 before our entry into the war, compared with $35,000,000 to Germany. America had a definite economic interest in the success of the Allies. But this is far from explaining our entry. Incredible blunders of German diplomacy and violations of neutral rights were alone sufficient to bring this country into the war without

---

[17] Extended by an Act of October, 1917, to include compensation to sailors and their dependents in case of death or disability.

the influence of other factors. American culture and traditions were based on those of Great Britain; her language and legal and constitutional institutions stemmed from the British Isles. Long before 1917 most Americans were convinced of the justice of the Allied cause; they interpreted it as a fight for civilization and liberal institutions. The decision could hardly be otherwise.

ECONOMIC MOBILIZATION

The policy of *laissez faire* which had been gradually crumbling during the first two decades of the century collapsed completely under the stress of war conditions. Economic life in America was so radically affected by the war even before this country entered the conflict that it was felt necessary for the government to interfere actively in private business; with our entrance, centralized supervision and direction of production and distribution were absolutely essential to effective participation. Government control, to an extent never before exercised here, was effected through federal boards, commissions, or corporations, endowed in some instances with very wide powers and sometimes aided by subordinate state or local bodies.

When the United States entered the conflict, the war had been in progress almost two and one-half years. European experience had made American leaders at least aware of the enormity and complexity of the problems of economic mobilization. Primarily, it was a task of integration and cooperation. It meant, first of all, a survey of resources, an estimate of needs, and then a shift of production from peace-time needs to those of war. Fortunately for this country, the rapid expansion of the industries producing metal and munitions for the Allies had laid a foundation for this shift of production. In the second place, it meant the establishment of central governing and purchasing boards to ration raw materials through priority rules, to direct purchasing at fair prices, and to bring some order out of the chaos of competition among manufacturers for raw materials, machinery, and labor. There were the problems of standardization, of profit control, of labor policies, of price fixing, of civilian needs, along with the necessity of speeding up war production as rapidly as possible. The government itself was also entering the field of production as in the case of nitrates and shipping. Other pressing problems included the development of more efficient transportation, greater production of food, and the financing of the war. For a nation of immense size, conditioned to individual rather than cooperative action, and with virtually no experience in this type of action, the task was one of almost superhuman proportions. Despite inevitable inefficiency, blunders, and failures in specific projects, the job as a whole was accomplished. During the year and a half of our participation in the war, the government maintained a continuous flow of food and munitions to the Allies, raised and armed over 4,000,000 men, transported 2,000,000 to Europe, and put 1,000,000 on the battle lines. In addition it financed the Allied nations during these months.

As the possibility of America's entrance into the war loomed larger, Congress was stirred to action. Legislation in August, 1916, authorized the creation of a United States Shipping Board to promote and regulate the merchant marine, and a Council of National Defense to supervise and integrate the defense program. It was not until October 11, 1916, barely six months before the declaration of war, that this Council, consisting of the Secretaries of War, Navy, Interior, Agriculture, Commerce, and Labor, was organized. At the same time an Advisory Commission of seven experts was set up to cover the fields of munitions and manufacturing, transportation, engineering and education, medicine and surgery, raw materials, supplies, and labor. From this Council and its Advisory Commission eventually evolved numerous subordinate committees or boards to deal with almost every important phase or problem affecting the war.

Of all the subdivisions created by the Council of National Defense, the most important was undoubtedly the War Industries Board. Its duties were wide, for it was to "act as a clearing-house for the war industry needs of the Government, and determine the most effective way of meeting them, and the best means and methods of increasing production. . . ."[18] So important was the work done by this Board under the able chairmanship of Bernard M. Baruch that the President in the spring of 1918 reorganized it, gave it enlarged powers, and made it an independent agency directly responsible to himself. Its work was grouped into functional divisions— conservation, priorities, price fixing, requirements, labor, and Allied purchasing. To aid these divisions the Board gradually organized fifty-seven sections of experts on particular industries who acted as a clearing house of information.

FOOD AND FUELS

As the stock of foodstuffs and fuels declined in the warring nations, the latter came to depend so much upon the United States for them that their production and conservation became a matter of extreme importance. By the Food Production Act and the Food and Fuel Control Act of August, 1917, the administration was given power to control "foods, feeds, fuel including fuel oil and natural gas, and fertilizer and fertilizer ingredients, tools, utensils, implements, machinery, and equipment required for the actual production of foods, feeds, and fuel." These Acts forbade hoarding,

---

[18] G. B. Clarkson, *Industrial America and the World War*, p. 37.

willful destruction, and discrimination or unfair practices in sale and distribution, and gave the President power under certain conditions to purchase, store, and sell wheat and other commodities. To administer them a National Food Administration, headed by Herbert Hoover, was organized.

Although Hoover preferred voluntary cooperation, it became necessary as the war continued to impose restrictions and use the power granted by Congress. By licensing the manufacture, storage, and distribution of food products, effectual regulations limiting the use of sugar, wheat, meat, butter, and other foods were imposed. The people as a whole were stimulated to self-denial and to the use of substitutes, and meatless and wheatless days were imposed to further this self-denial. While the consumer was urged to curtail, every means was used to stimulate farmers to greater production. Under the power to set prices the government in 1918 guaranteed a minimum of $2.26 per bushel for No. 1 northern spring wheat or its equivalent. A Food Administration Grain Cooperative was established whose functions were to purchase wheat and flour for the United States and her Allies and to maintain the guaranteed price. In similar manner a Sugar Equalization Board was established to buy raw sugar from producers at an agreed price and to supply refineries under arrangements to fix profits and stabilize prices.

The most acute shortage that developed during the war, both for civilian needs and for war industries, was in coal. Under the Fuel Administration, headed by Harry A. Garfield, almost every known means was used to overcome the difficulty. The problem was threefold—production, distribution, and rationing. To stimulate production, operators and miners were urged to eliminate waste and to introduce more efficient methods. The problem of distribution was met in part by introducing a zoning system which served consumers from the nearest mine and eliminated cross-hauls. To make the coal go as far as possible, unnecessary illumination and heating were curtailed and in April, 1918, a system of general rationing for domestic users was established. Control over the distribution of fuel oil was instituted in January of that year and was later extended to natural gas and gasoline.

WAR-TIME CONTROL OF TRANSPORTATION

Preliminary efforts to enlarge the American merchant marine before we entered the war have already been noted (p. 593). After our entrance the functions of the United States Shipping Board were enlarged to include supervision of the vast shipbuilding program, control of vessels under the jurisdiction of the government, and the training of men for service in the merchant marine. When we declared war Germany was sinking shipping faster than it could be built. Our problem was to reverse this situation and to keep supplies moving on the high seas. In April, 1917, the Shipping Board organized a subsidiary, the Emergency Fleet Corporation, with a capital of $50,000,000, to undertake the construction of merchant ships. In May Congress authorized the President to take over 600,000 tons of German shipping interned in American ports. In August the government commandeered all steel vessels in process of construction; this added 3,000,000,000 dead-weight tons. In October the President created a War Trade Board to regulate the import and export trade and thus better to conserve shipping for absolute war needs.

The Emergency Fleet Corporation did some of the most notable work of the war. With virtually unlimited funds made available by Congress, it bent all efforts to turning out steel, wood, and even concrete ships. It expanded old shipyards already working to capacity and built new ones. The largest of these, Hog Island at Philadelphia, had a capacity greater than that of Great Britain in any pre-war year. The 61 shipyards of 1917 and their 235 ways had increased by November, 1918, to 341 shipyards and 1284 launching ways, and the number of workmen from 45,000 to 380,000. During the nineteen months of the war 875 vessels were built, totaling over 2,941,000 tons. American tonnage engaged in foreign trade increased from 2,191,000 in 1916 to 11,082,000 in 1921.

Government regulation of the railroads has been the accepted policy since 1887, but it was only during the war that the experiment of government operation was tried. The inability of the railroads to cope successfully with the exigencies of war needs, and the absolute necessity of subordinating transportation facilities to the one purpose of winning the war, brought about this step. The position of the roads at the opening of the European conflict was far from strong. For fifteen years the costs of railroad operation in maintenance, materials, and labor had been increasing. On the other hand, attempts to gain higher rates had been unsuccessful until 1913. In 1910 certain of the roads petitioned for a 10 per cent advance in freight rates, but this was refused by the Interstate Commerce Commission, which based its decision on the prosperous year of 1910. Further efforts in 1913 and 1914 were partially successful, in that the Commission eventually permitted substantial increases, but these came too late to be of much immediate value. The year 1914 was disastrous to the railroads, and 1915 found one-sixth (42,000 miles) of the railroad system of the United States in the hands of receivers. The war brought temporary prosperity with the enormous stimulation of the freight business in 1915 and 1916. But the rising cost of materials and the greater expenditures for wages, necessitated partly by the Adamson Eight-hour Act of 1916,[19] absorbed much of the profits. The rail-

[19] Above, p. 475.

roads for some time had been buying little new equipment and their roll-ing stock was not sufficient to meet the pressure of war needs. It was in this predicament that the roads found themselves when the United States entered the war.

As a whole, the railroads did their best to rise to the occasion. Daniel Willard, president of the Baltimore and Ohio, was appointed as transporta-tion expert to the Advisory Commission of the Council of National Defense. Under his direction the railroad executives organized a Special Committee of National Defense which elected an executive committee of five, known as the Railroads' War Board. This Board opened offices in Washington and made every effort to cooperate with the government; but as the months went on there were increasing complications due to special Army needs, to the orders of the Priorities Boards, to lack of equipment, to the inability to force all the roads to follow the orders of the committee, to the impos-sibility of obtaining joint action among the competing roads, and to labor difficulties brought about by demands for higher wages and the departure of men to join the Army—all of which pointed to the breaking down of private control and the need for government operation. The Esch bill of May, 1917, gave the Interstate Commerce Commission power to regulate freight cars, and finally on December 26, 1917, upon the advice of the Inter-state Commerce Commission and after a thorough investigation of the sit-uation, President Wilson issued a proclamation providing for government operation two days later.

The President's proclamation was followed on March 21, 1918, by a Rail-road Control Act which provided (1) that each road taken over should re-ceive an annual payment not to exceed its average net operating income for the three years ending June 30, 1917; (2) that a revolving fund of $500,-000,000 should be created to finance the operation; (3) that the roads should be returned to their owners within one year and nine months following the ratification of the treaty of peace; (4) that each road should be returned "in substantially as good repair and in substantially as complete equipment as it was at the beginning of government control"; and (5) that the Inter-state Commerce Commission should be deprived of its power to suspend rates, but that it should retain most of its other powers. The Pullman and express companies were taken over, but not all of the short lines. William G. McAdoo, Secretary of the Treasury, was made Director General of the Railroads. Eventually the whole transportation system was handled through eight administrative divisions at Washington, and for operating purposes the country was divided into seven regional organizations. Over each district was a regional director and over each road a federal manager, the latter in some cases a former railroad president. In connection with the history of transportation control it should be added that in July, 1918, the government took over control of the telegraph and telephone systems and placed them under the direction of the Postmaster General; in November it assumed control of marine cables.

In dealing with labor the government found it necessary to take cognizance of the fact that railroad wages were not as high as those in other lines of work. In the absence of legislation to require railroad men to stay on the job, the only other course was to increase wages, which was done on the recommendation of a non-partisan board of adjustment. Increased rates were necessary, and on May 25, 1918, all classes of freight were raised 25 per cent, and passenger fares to three cents a mile.

The gains to the efficient prosecution of the war from government operation were many. Joint use of terminals, equipment, and repair shops; relief of congestion by arbitrary routing; better control of traffic at the source; more efficient handling of troops and war supplies; the elimination of duplicate passenger service, and the standardization of equipment in purchasing—all these aided in carrying on the war. On the other hand it was discovered, when the roads were returned to their original ownership on February 28, 1920, that the excess of operating costs over revenues for the twenty-six months of government control was about $900,000,000. How much of this was due, as alleged, to "wasteful government administration," how much to the exigencies of the situation in a war period of mounting costs, and how much to the previous run-down condition of the railroad system which had to be rectified, will never be known. Without entering upon a discussion of the efficiency of government operation, it must be said that it accomplished the purpose aimed at and was a necessary war measure. That the government erred in not increasing rates and fares proportionately to the advancing cost of materials and labor is generally conceded.

Labor During War Times

The greatest immediate effect of the First World War upon labor was to create a shortage which was felt even before our participation. The normal flow of immigration declined from an annual average of about 662,100 during the three years 1912–1914 to about 257,887 for 1915–1918. At the same time thousands of those engaged in industry were called home to serve in the European armies or joined the military forces here. The supply of labor was consequently falling off just at the time when there was an abnormal expansion in industry. After we entered the war the shortage was of course accentuated by the addition of over 4,000,000 men to our armed forces. This gap in the ranks of labor was partly filled by women— at least 1,000,000 entered industry during the war—but the shortage persisted. The government's chief method of meeting this problem was to expand the activities of the Employment Service of the Department of Labor. This organization, cooperating with state and local agencies, was able to some extent to coordinate the task of directing needed workers to defense jobs and decreasing labor turnover. The President in June, 1918, requested all employers engaged in war work to secure their workers through the Employment Service and in that year it placed over 10,000 workers a day.

As a natural consequence of this shortage the position of labor was at least temporarily strengthened. Wages were forced up and labor's increased buying power in turn abnormally stimulated industries which were not essential to the war but which further increased the labor shortage. While wages advanced rapidly until the early months of 1920, prices rose even more quickly so that real wages per hour or per piece tended to fall. It is doubtful if in the long run real wages were appreciably bettered by the war, but the fact that some workers were able to buy luxuries for perhaps the first time gave rise to the myth of the "silk-shirted worker." The aggregate earnings of labor, however, undoubtedly increased, but this was due to the larger volume of employment which the war made possible. The rise in the cost of living further stimulated the demand for higher pay, already inevitable because of lack of labor. The accompanying index numbers, compiled by the Department of Labor, give a general picture of the relations between wages and the cost of living during the war years.[20]

Year	Wages per Hour	Cost of Living	Real Wages
1913	100	100.0	100.0
1916	111	118.3	93.8
1917	128	142.4	89.9
1918	162	174.4	92.9
1919	184	188.3	97.7
1920	234	208.5	112.2

Led by Gompers and the Executive Committee, which declared that "this is labor's war," the American Federation of Labor threw itself wholeheartedly into the war, removing restrictions and suspending regulations inimical to efficiency, but demanding that the standard of living be not lowered. Gompers was placed upon the Advisory Committee of National Defense, and labor leaders were appointed to most of the war boards organized

[20] *Statistical Abstract, 1931,* p. 347. The figures on wages do not include agricultural labor. Other students have slightly modified these statistics, but in general they represent what happened. Beginning in 1920, it will be noticed, real wages increased and this trend continued throughout the decade.

by the government. In addition, numerous mediation committees were established by the various boards. Early in the war Gompers, as Chairman of the Committee on Labor of the Council of National Defense, called a conference of representatives of both employers and labor, at which both sides agreed not to take advantage of the emergency to press their demands in a way which would hinder the prosecution of the war. It was a sort of informal truce for the duration of the conflict, but, surprisingly enough, it worked fairly well. It did not, of course, end labor disputes or even prevent strikes.

Early in 1918, in an effort to consolidate the labor policies and the mediation work of the numerous labor boards and committees, the President appointed Secretary of Labor Wilson as Labor Administrator, and under him a War Labor Board and a War Labor Policies Board were established. The latter was to determine the general policies of the government toward hours, wages, and working conditions, and, as far as possible, the relations between capital and labor. The War Labor Board was a judicial body to which disputes between employers and employees could be submitted. Some fifteen hundred disputes were adjudicated by this Board; in a number of cases it prescribed the creation of shop committees and other means by which further controversies might be adjusted. Matters of wage adjustment on the railroads were handled, after government control was inaugurated, by a Railroad Wage Commission appointed by the railroad administration. By means of this machinery, by wage increases, and by the loyalty of both leaders and rank and file, labor disturbances were greatly reduced during the war.

Labor's contribution to the winning of the war resulted in the recognition in the peace treaty of certain specific rights for which it had long contended and the provision for a permanent organization to promote the international regulation of labor conditions. In accordance with the treaty, an international labor conference was held in Washington in 1919 which drew up a program to be recommended to the League of Nations.

In spite of this international recognition, the immediate effect of the war appeared detrimental to labor in the United States. Wages increased rapidly to be sure, but the cost of living more than kept pace with them.[21] Some of the most important losses, however, had little to do with wages or working conditions. The weakening of the Socialist party, which by 1912 had grown to sizable proportions, and the disintegration of the I.W.W. and other radical elements so necessary to the development of a healthy

[21] Bulletins of the U. S. Bureau of Labor Statistics, No. 274, *Union Scale of Wages and Hours of Labor, May, 15, 1919*, pp. 47–50, and No. 270, *Retail Prices 1913 to December 1919*, pp. 50–58.

labor movement, were a misfortune. The growth of intolerance and the decline of personal liberty were more prejudicial to labor than to other classes, and there was a relative economic decline for labor as other classes reaped the financial profits of the war.[22]

FINANCING THE FIRST WORLD WAR

Long before our entrance, heavy loans had been floated in America by the Entente governments, and with our declaration of war it was expected that these loans would be greatly increased. That the financial cost of our participation would be stupendous was obvious, and plans were at once formulated to meet the increased expenditures. Two general policies were advocated: one, that the cost of the war be paid immediately by taxation, thus meeting the entire expense to the government at once; the other, that loans be chiefly relied upon to meet the increasing burden. A compromise between these two policies seemed the most practical solution, as well as being in line with precedent, and hence was adopted. About one-third of

AGGREGATE EXPENDITURES AND FOREIGN LOANS OF THE UNITED STATES
GOVERNMENT, FISCAL YEARS 1917–1920 [23]

Year	Normal Net Expense	Net War Cost (Excess Above Estimated Normal Expenses)	
		Excess Army and Navy	Excess Interest, Pensions, etc.
1917	$ 659,860,650	$ 393,852,949	$ 2,690,164
1918	682,458,285	6,770,295,897	120,952,611
1919	691,858,252	10,917,817,469	379,367,891
1920	826,550,410	1,073,892,747	1,073,392,874
	$2,860,727,597	$19,155,859,062	$1,576,403,540

Year	Net War Cost (Excess Above Estimated Normal Expenses)		Loans to European Governments (Less Repayments)
	Special War Activities	Total War Cost	
1917	$ 33,060,510	$ 429,603,623	$ 885,000,000
1918	1,094,994,128	7,986,242,636	4,739,434,750
1919	2,487,710,885	13,784,896,245	3,470,280,265
1920	1,634,695,094	3,781,980,715	350,291,840
	$5,250,460,617	$25,982,723,219	$9,445,006,855

[22] In 1914 there were believed to be 7,508 millionaires in the United States; in 1917 there were 19,103.

[23] From Table 3, p. 21, of E. B. Rosa, "Expenditures and Revenues of the Federal Government," Annals of the American Academy of Political and Social Science, Vol. XCV, No. 184 (May, 1921).

the direct cost of the war was met by immediate taxation, and about two-thirds by loans.

The expenses of the federal government had not materially increased in the years before the war. The normal net expenses in 1916 ($674,230,020) were less than $35,000,000 in excess of those of 1910. But succeeding years saw a vast increase; within two years the federal government's interest charge alone had become greater than the entire cost of running the government before the war. The total direct cost of the war to the United States, including the nine and a half billions lent to the Allies, was about $35,500,000,000, an amount three times the total expenditures of the federal government during the first hundred years of its existence and close to $2,000,000 an hour for the duration of the war. The national debt, which amounted to only $1,000,000,000 before the war, jumped to the unprecedented total of $26,596,701,648 by the end of August, 1919.

To obtain these vast amounts spent at home and lent to the Allies, the government relied chiefly upon loans. Five bond issues were subscribed to by the people, in units of as low as $50 and with interest rates varying from $3\frac{1}{2}$ to $4\frac{1}{4}$ per cent. The first four issues were known as Liberty Loans; the fifth, floated after the armistice, was called the Victory Liberty Loan. At the height of war enthusiasm, almost $7,000,000,000 was subscribed in a single loan by over 22,000,000 people. In addition to the Victory and Liberty

UNITED STATES WAR LOANS [24]

Loan	Billions Asked	Subscribed	Allotted	Subscribers (Approximately)
First Liberty Loan	2	$ 3,035,226,850	$ 1,989,455,550	4,500,000
Second Liberty Loan	3	4,617,532,300	3,807,865,000	9,420,000
Third Liberty Loan	3	4,176,516,850	4,175,650,050	18,376,815
Fourth Liberty Loan	6	6,993,073,250	6,964,581,250	22,177,680
Victory Liberty Loan	4.5	5,249,980,300	4,497,818,750	12,000,000
Total	18.5	$24,072,329,550	$21,435,370,600	

Loans, war saving certificates of five dollars and war saving stamps of twenty-five cents were sold to a total of $1,000,000,000. The grand total of the loans floated in these two ways was close to $22,500,000,000.

Not alone was large-scale borrowing resorted to, but also new and heavier taxes were imposed. Contrary to the method pursued during the Civil War, the Democratic Congress, which had reduced the tariff in 1913, refused to consider import duties as an important source of revenue, and scarcely 5 per cent of the taxes for the war year of 1918 were derived from this

[24] The amounts subscribed and allotted are taken from the *Report of the Secretary of the Treasury, 1920*, tables on pp. 419 and 439.

source. On the other hand, a comprehensive scheme of taxation was inaugurated. The income tax levied by virtue of the sixteenth amendment in 1913 and increased in 1916, was further increased by the Act of October 3, 1917. Personal exemptions were reduced to $2000 and $1000 in the case of married and unmarried persons, and the rate was graduated from 6 per cent on the first $4000 above exemption to 67 per cent on incomes of over a million. In addition, this Act inaugurated (1) a war excess profits tax on the incomes of corporations, partnerships, and individuals ranging from 15 to 60 per cent, depending on the amount of capital invested in the business; (2) additional taxes upon liquors, beverages, and tobacco; (3) taxes on luxuries and amusements; (4) war taxes on facilities furnished by public utilities; (5) war taxes on instruments and documents of various kinds; and (6) an increase on estate taxes. The effect of these additions to taxation is shown by a comparison of the amounts raised by taxation immediately preceding and during the war, which were as follows: for the fiscal year ending June 30, 1914, $735,000,000; 1915, $692,000,000; 1916, $779,000,000; 1917, $1,118,000,000; 1918, $4,174,000,000; 1919, $4,648,000,000. Of the amount credited to internal revenue taxes, well over two-thirds came from the income and excess profits taxes. In spite of this heavy taxation, the public debt mounted to over 26.5 billion dollars in 1919. Of this, over one-third was made up of loans to foreign governments.

With reference to the monetary statistics of war time, it should again be emphasized that they must be interpreted with reference to the inflation of those years. As we have already pointed out, there was virtually no suspension of specie payments in the United States, but there was great inflation. This was due in the first place to the enormous amount of gold which was sent here to finance the purchase of war materials, and which eventually brought to this country almost half of the world's monetary supply of that metal. In the second place, the liberal policies of the Federal Reserve System in extending credit during the war and in assisting in the flotation of Liberty Loans tended toward inflation, as did the vast issue of government bonds which could be used as a reserve against bank note issue. Besides these factors, there was, as in all wars, a rise in commodity prices because of increased demand. Inflation, indeed, was as great as during the Civil War, but it differed in being due to a plethora of gold and the enormous extension of credit instead of to suspension of specie payments and the printing of fiat money.

Conclusion

In this chapter certain phases of America's economic reaction to the First World War have been recounted in some detail. This has been done for two reasons. In the first place, the economic effects were strongly felt in subsequent years. Despite all efforts to "return to normalcy" America could never quite go back to the economic conditions of the pre-war days. The tremendous industrial expansion of the war years left her with a productive capacity in certain fields far beyond her normal needs. This was particularly true in textiles, leather manufacturing, shipbuilding, and coal mining. The post-war deflation combined with competition from other commodities left these industries in a permanently weak condition. The rapid expansion of the merchant marine left the nation with a fleet of ocean carriers far beyond any possible need. A similar expansion of agricultural production left farmers, after the inevitable collapse, in a worse condition than followed the Civil War. Government control and operation of transportation facilities presented the problem of continued operation or return to private owners. In the end the properties were returned, but control was increased. Deflation of wages after the war brought labor struggles of greater proportions than the nation had yet seen. These and other effects will be discussed in the next chapter.

In the second place, it is evident that America's economic experience in the First World War provided the experience upon which she could build in the world conflict of the 1940's. The maze of boards, commissions, and committees set up to integrate the economic efforts of the Second World War may seem superficially to be quite different from those of the earlier struggle, but fundamentally they are engaged in the same effort and in much the same way. On the economic front Wilson's administration achieved its greatest success in industrial expansion and experienced its greatest failure in preventing price and wage inflation. It also failed to develop any policy for reconstruction. The success or failure in the present conflict and in the reconstruction period to follow will depend to no small extent upon the lessons learned from the experiences of the First World War.

SELECTED READINGS

Wright, C. W., *Economic History of the United States,* Chaps. XLII, XLIII.
Faulkner, H. U., *The Quest for Social Justice.*
Slosson, P. W., *The Great Crusade and After,* Chaps. I, II.
Noyes, A. D., *The War Period of American Finance,* Chaps. II–V.
Gompers, Samuel, *Seventy Years of Life and Labor,* Chap. XL.
Dixon, F. H., *Railroads and Government,* Chaps. VIII–XIV.
Clarkson, G. B., *Industrial America in the World War,* Chaps. XII–XXX.
Lorwin, L. L., *The American Federation of Labor,* Chap. VI.
Genung, A. B., "Agriculture in the World War Period," *Yearbook of Agriculture, 1940,* pp. 277–296.

28

The Great Illusion

Post-war Depression

THE business boom of the war period, with the accompanying inflation in prices and wages, was followed in the later months of 1920 and during the entire year of 1921 by a corresponding period of industrial stagnation and deflation. Just as the wave of prosperity had been the result of conditions in Europe, so the deflation was primarily the result of foreign influences. Exports and imports, which had reached unheard-of figures in 1918 and 1919, had declined radically by 1921. The warring nations, impoverished by the struggle, staggering under crushing debts, and with exchange rates decidedly against them, no longer had either the funds or the credit to make extensive purchases. This in itself would have held up American production sharply, but to it was added the failure of buying power to keep pace with prices. The average American who had spent freely during the war now reacted strongly against the high cost of living and began to retrench in preparation for the uncertain future. What amounted practically to a "buyers' strike" ensued.

With these adverse factors at work, the business cycle rapidly pursued its downward swing. Cancellation of orders or failure to book new ones reduced output and closed mills, causing reduced wages and unemployment. The depression, which had first appeared in the production of luxuries, especially the silk industry and certain phases of the rubber and automobile industry, soon became general. In only a few industries did business continue normal. Upon no group did the depression fall more heavily than upon the farmers. Encouraged by the war prices and the demand for foodstuffs, many had borrowed heavily to purchase land and equipment in order to increase production, only to be caught in a glutted market in which values were declining to a point below the cost of production. Wheat, which had sold for $2.15 a bushel in December, 1919, dropped to $1.44 in December, 1920; corn from $1.35 to $.68; oats from $.72 to $.47; and cotton from $.36 a pound to $.14. Labor, which had become accustomed to a higher standard of living, was loath to return to previous wage scales, and, where strongly organized, succeeded in maintaining most of what was gained during the war period. Nevertheless, the number of those actively employed declined almost one-third during the depression,[1] and the average hourly wage as reported by the National Industrial Conference Board was as follows: July, 1914, 24.3 cents; peak, 1920, 62.1; December, 1921, 48.2. Capital as a whole probably suffered less than any other group, although, as in previous panics, the small business man was hit hard. Mercantile and industrial insolvencies, which numbered 6451 with liabilities of $113,291,237 in 1919, increased in 1921 to 19,652 with liabilities of $627,401,883. Although bank failures reached 383 in 1921, with liabilities of almost $168,000,000, they were mainly rural banks with small capitalization and did not fundamentally endanger the general banking structure. The deflation, although severe, did not reach the proportions of a panic.

The natural effect of this industrial collapse upon prices was to force them downward. The decline included most commodities, being especially noticeable in foodstuffs and clothing, and least apparent in fuel and rent. The partial cessation of normal building during the war, which caused a shortage of living accommodations, and the high cost of building materials explain to some extent the failure of rents to decline. The explanation of the continued high cost of fuel is not so easy, but it was due among other factors to increased cost of labor and transportation and the continued high profits taken by capital. According to the United States Department of Labor, the average index number of wholesale prices of typical commodities, the figure for 1913 being taken as 100, was 272 in May, 1920; 148 in June, 1921; 150 in June, 1922; 153 in June, 1923.

By the end of 1922 deflation had run its course and industry was to a considerable extent adjusted to a peace basis. Increased work on the part of labor and caution on the part of capital placed economic life on a sounder basis and increased the demand for all kinds of commodities. Most of the principal industries were again working at close to capacity, the railroads reported record business, and unemployment had largely disappeared. Certain industries, particularly agriculture, failed to respond to the renewed prosperity, and the agricultural unrest remained an uncertain political and economic factor. That and the unsettled conditions abroad were in 1923 the chief adverse factors in what appeared to be the opening of a period of greater business activity and more normal conditions.

[1] W. I. King (*Employment Hours and Earnings in Prosperity and Depression*, pp. 29–31) believes that there were 4,000,000 unemployed in 1921. W. A. Berridge (*Business Cycles and Unemployment*, p. 59) believes that the unemployment situation in that year was almost twice as acute as in 1908 and at least twice as acute as in 1914–1915.

THE HECTIC 'TWENTIES

In retrospect the post-war depression seems a perfectly normal effect of the artificial expansion of the war years. More difficult is the problem of explaining the brevity of the depression and the intense business activity of the 1920's, a period in which the rest of the world was still suffering from the economic post-war recession. Although there was much that was artificial about the economic life of the 1920's, the fact remains that during the six years from 1923 until the stock market crash in the autumn of 1929 large groups of people and certain sections of the country enjoyed an era of prosperity approaching that of war time. A partial explanation may be found in the fact that while population gained approximately 12 per cent between 1920 and 1928, physical production increased 25 per cent, the productivity per worker increased by the same amount, and the national wealth at least twenty billions. Although the share of wage earners in the total national income increased only slightly, if at all, after 1920, real wages among certain groups showed a substantial advance. The decline in the birth rate, restriction of immigration, and increased application of science to business may also have helped in promoting this prosperity. To many economists it is this last that furnishes the fundamental explanation. "Since 1921," wrote Wesley C. Mitchell, surveying the work of the Committee on Economic Changes, "Americans have applied intelligence to the day's work more effectively than ever before. . . . The whole process of putting science into industry has been followed more intensively than before; it has been supplemented by tentative efforts to put science into business management, trade-union policy and Government administration."[2] It is an acceleration of earlier tendencies rather than structural change that provides the key to an understanding of the 1920's.

To be more specific, the foundation upon which this economic development apparently rested was the automobile, the great development of which came in the decade and a half from 1914 to 1929. It is estimated that nearly four million jobs were created directly or indirectly by the automobile, and that they probably supported from sixteen to twenty million people, the approximate increase in population between 1920 and 1930. Although an appreciable part of the income which went into automobiles was income which would normally have been expended for other commodities, thereby injuring other industries, the fact remains that enough new industry and wealth were created by the motor car to speed up the whole economic machine. Of the many by-products of the automobile industry which created work and stimulated industry, the most important perhaps was better roads,

[2] *Recent Economic Changes*, p. 862.

in the construction of which close to two billions of dollars a year were expended even in the depression years of 1930 and 1931. The radio, which had a phenomenal development in the half decade 1924–1929, contributed in a lesser degree to the prosperity of the twenties, as did the development of many electrical household appliances. To take care of this and the expansion of manufacturing, the production of electric power increased from 43.5 billion kilowatt-hours to approximately 96 billion in 1930.

The vast expenditures which made possible this boom era were undoubtedly stimulated by the development of "high-pressure" advertising and installment buying. Conservative estimates place the number of automobiles sold on installment in 1927 at around 60 per cent, but other estimates for various years are much higher.[3] Concerning installment buying, Seligman makes the conservative estimate of $4,875,000,000 as the total volume of retail installment sales for 1925.[4] These figures were to increase in subsequent years until 15 per cent of all goods were sold on the installment plan. By the end of the decade there was practically nothing, in the realm of either luxury or necessity, that could not be bought "on time."

Outside of the spectacular development of the automobile industry, the most striking aspect of the prosperous years of the mid-'twenties was the extraordinary building boom, probably the greatest in our history. Normal construction retarded during the war years had to be made good, high rents stimulated building, a rapid increase of surplus wealth made it possible, and modern improvements made even recent structures seem out of date. Building construction in 120 cities which had reached the high point of $919,000,000 in 1916 dropped to $373,000,000 in 1918 and rose to $1,172,000,000 in 1919, and finally to $3,399,000,000 in 1925, when the high point was reached.[5] Total building in that year amounted to somewhat over six billions. A good share of the building in cities (about one-third) was carried on in New York, where the sky line changed with amazing rapidity, and where the Empire State Building with its 86 stories towering 1248 feet into the sky was completed in 1931. In automobiles, new roads, new buildings, and electrical equipment was invested much of the wealth created in this country during the third decade.

Despite the fact that most people were mortgaging their future income through installment buying and spending a disproportionate share of their wages in the purchase and maintenance of automobiles, the fact remains that during the speculative and spendthrift period from 1914 to 1925 the number of savings accounts increased nearly fourfold, from 11 to 43 mil-

[3] E. R. A. Seligman, *The Economics of Installment Selling* (2 vols., 1927), I, 111, 117; II, 426; and *Recent Economic Changes*, I, 390 ff.

[4] E. R. A. Seligman, *The Economics of Installment Selling*, I, 117.

[5] Given by Bradstreet for 120 identical cities; *New International Year Book, 1930*, p. 118.

lions, and their amount from 8 to 23 billions. In addition to this it is notable that more than 25,500,000 ordinary life insurance policies and over 76,000,000 industrial policies were in force in the United States by the end of 1926, their total assets amounting to $12,500,000,000. The number of building and loan policies increased from 3,103,935 to 8,554,352 in the ten years up to 1924, when over 11,000,000 families owned their own homes.

Not all economists were willing to grant unreservedly that this decade was a period of prosperity.[6] Prosperity, if such it was, was exceedingly uneven, for it did not include all sections or all groups. Furthermore, coal mining, cotton manufacturing, shipbuilding, the shoe and leather business, and particularly agriculture were stagnant, or declining. The Middle Atlantic, the East North Central, and the Pacific States seemed prosperous; but New England, which suffered from the textile depression, and the South, the Middle West, and the Mountain sections, which suffered from the decline in agricultural prices, did not participate greatly in the economic boom. Even in the most prosperous of these years there was considerable unemployment, due in part to technological improvements. In Massachusetts, for example, the wage earners employed in manufacturing declined from the high of 757,100 in January, 1920, to 509,700 in July, 1928. These were not the only sour notes in the paean of self-congratulatory praise. Some students were quick to point out that, notwithstanding the increase in profits, in wages, and in the consumption of consumers' goods, practically no progress was being made in solving the problems of unemployment or economic and old age security; the mania for gambling and speculation was a warning signal to the experienced economic navigator. While trusting souls talked glibly of a "New Economic Era" from which panics and depressions were forever banished, and European observers came to America to study the causes of this prosperity, a few realists regarded dubiously the unsound structure being reared and looked forward with apprehension to its collapse.

RENEWAL OF BUSINESS CONSOLIDATION

In spite of state laws and federal enactments passed in the hope of maintaining free competition and protecting the consumer, the consolidation of American business continued with little interruption. The decade following the First World War, in fact, witnessed a most significant revival in business consolidation, comparable to that in the years 1897–1904. An intensive study recorded a steadily increasing number of mergers in manufacturing and mining, from 67 in 1923 to 221 in 1928, with the number of

[6] Stuart Chase, *Prosperity, Fact or Myth* (1930) shows clearly that there were two sides to the question.

merged or acquired concerns increasing correspondingly from 311 to 1038.[7]
In actual mergers the iron, steel, and machinery group took the lead, accounting for about one-fifth of all those in mining and manufacturing; but
there was hardly an industry which did not show a notable development
along this line. Important mergers took place in the automobile industry,
in the manufacture of food, in the moving picture industry, in banking,
and most conspicuously, perhaps, in the field of public utilities. Over 3700
utility companies disappeared during 1919–1927, including many municipally
operated concerns.[8] While thousands of concerns were going out of existence, the larger ones which remained were being rapidly welded together
into huge holding companies. "In 1915," asserts the Federal Trade Commission, "the 16 largest groups controlled about 22.8 per cent [generating
capacity of the country], while in 1925 the 16 largest interests consisting of
11 holding-company groups and five independent operating interests,
controlled approximately 53 per cent of the country's total."[9] Since 1925
this process of consolidation, chiefly through holding companies, has gone
on rapidly. The speed with which the nation's electric power resources
were consolidated brought the question of the effective control of this industry before the country as a problem of major importance, and the so-called
"power trust" became a political issue after 1928.[10]

In previous decades the consolidation of industry was closely identified
with the development of the corporate form of ownership. By 1929, however, this form was so typical of American business, both large and small,
that the process of consolidation was indicated in the census by a new classification of establishments according to type of management, whether independent or one of a number of plants under unified central control. "The
heightened industrial activity of the decade 1919 to 1929," said the census,
"was not accompanied by any material alteration in the size of manufacturing establishments in general. The changes which occurred for the most part
took other directions. Integration, for example, was accomplished not so
much by the concentration of more wage earners in individual plants as
by a common superstructure of ownership and control."[11]

The post-war movement toward business consolidation, as is obvious

[7] Willard Thorpe, in Recent Economic Changes, I, 184.

[8] Ibid., p. 187.

[9] Federal Trade Commission, Electric Power Industry: Supply of Electrical Equipment and
Competitive Conditions, 70th Cong., 1st Sess., Senate Doc. 46, p. 176. The figures of the
Federal Trade Commission are based on 1924 production. The Federal Power Commission,
reporting as late as 1936, asserted that 90 per cent of the electric generating capacity of the
utility industry (book value $13,000,000,000) was controlled by 57 companies. Of these,
twelve controlled 49.7 per cent and one of them, the Electric Bond and Share group, controlled 11.5 per cent.

[10] Below, p. 664.

[11] Census of Manufactures, 1929, I, 61.

enough, differed also from those of the past in several other aspects. Not only did it include new industries that had appeared since the last era of consolidation, but it also embraced a much larger field than it did prior to 1917; for example, it extended into the automobile industry, into the production of package foods, and into the realm of banking. There was likewise a rapid development of consolidation in retailing as well as in production. The growth of chain stores has been particularly notable in the drug, tobacco, and grocery fields, and the small merchant has come to feel the same competition from the large corporations as the small manufacturer faced for decades.[12] The Great Atlantic & Pacific Tea Company, for example, which had 5000 stores in 1922, had 17,500 by 1928, with an annual business of $750,000,000.

Space forbids a detailed treatment of consolidation in the various fields in which it operated, but special mention should be made of banking, where this trend was particularly evident. In 1921 the number of banks in the nation reached a peak of 30,812. Although the country's wealth and resources increased greatly, the number of banks ten years later had dropped to about 22,000. Of those that no longer existed, some had failed and others had merged with neighboring institutions. The trend toward consolidation was particularly evident in the large cities. The lead was taken during 1928–1930 by the three titans in New York, with the consolidation of the National City Bank and the Farmers' Loan and Trust Company, of the Guarantee Trust Company and the Bank of Commerce, and finally of the Chase National Bank and the Equitable Trust Company, making the Chase the largest bank in the world. While large-scale mergers were occurring among city banks, concentration of resources was also taking place through the development of chain banking. In California, where chain banking reached its greatest development, a huge holding company, the Trans-America Corporation, controlled the Bank of America of California and other large banks, which in turn had 500 chain banks spreading across the state.

What is the explanation for this extraordinary revival of consolidation during the decade of the 'twenties? In the first place, the rather widespread industrial prosperity from 1923 to 1929 stimulated the movement. In spite of the fact that many mergers take place to obviate bitter competition and precarious prices, it is in times of prosperity that consolidations are more common.[13] The spirit of confidence and the ease of floating security issues may in part explain this. In the second place, the artificial expansion of the war days left American industry in an overbuilt and overexpanded condition, and salvation was sought by this method. In the third place, the

---

[12] Flügel and H. U. Faulkner, *Readings,* pp. 600–607.
[13] Willard Thorpe, in *Recent Economic Changes,* I, 183–184.

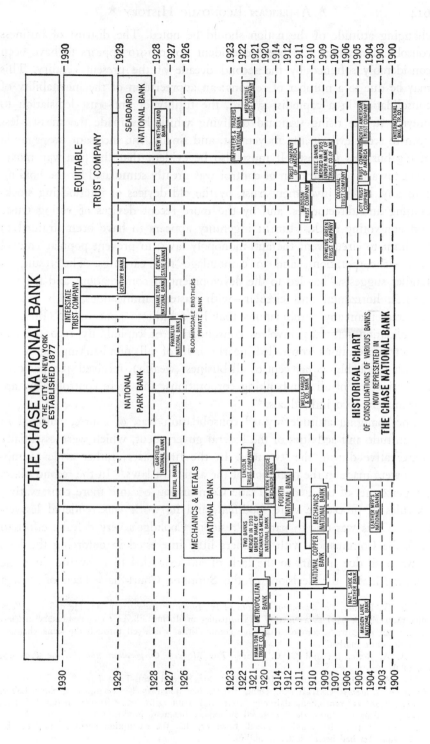

THE CHASE NATIONAL BANK
OF THE CITY OF NEW YORK
ESTABLISHED 1877

HISTORICAL CHART
OF CONSOLIDATIONS OF VARIOUS BANKS
NOW REPRESENTED IN
THE CHASE NATIONAL BANK

changing attitude of the nation should be noted. The distrust of business consolidation which had been so evident up to 1910 appears to have been considerably softened by the second decade of the present century. This may be due to a number of reasons: an appreciation of the inevitability of consolidation in a capitalist system, the futility of anti-trust legislation to prevent it, the rising standard of living which has made the masses less keen to scent evils in the movement, and finally, the incessant propaganda of big business interests. It must also be evident that the post-war movement toward concentration of control was greatly stimulated by the holding company, by the investment trust, by the old devices of interlocking stockholding and directorates, and by the more recent devices of voting trusts and non-voting stock. Human ingenuity appears to have been strained to the limit to circumvent the anti-monopoly laws, to prevent popular control of great corporations, and to camouflage real earnings. The result, as Laidler suggests, "has led to the development of combinations and trusts—vertical, horizontal and circular—with vaster ramifications, with greater resources than any combinations that have hitherto appeared." [14] Business consolidation naturally involves consolidation of capital. By 1930 the 200 largest corporations controlled nearly half of all non-banking corporate wealth (probably 38 per cent of all business wealth), received 43.2 per cent of the income of all non-banking corporations, and were controlled by approximately 2000 individuals. [15]

The changing attitude toward consolidation was, of course, reflected in the attitude and activities of the federal government, which were essentially conservative during the 'twenties. In the first place, rather wide exemptions were made in the operation of the anti-trust laws. [16] In the second place, the personnel of the Federal Trade Commission became more conservative, its rules of procedure were modified, and its work was rendered less effective. This was due in part to President Coolidge's very definite effort to pack the Commission with members little interested in enforcing the law. It was also due in part to the lack of aid extended to it by the Supreme Court. Finally, the decisions of the Supreme Court have been of such a

[14] H. W. Laidler, *Concentration of Control in American Industry,* p. 11. He defines a "circuler merger" (p. 444) as a "merger of companies producing allied or complementary articles, usually, but not always, composed of those commodities which sell through the same channels or to the same market."

[15] A. A. Berle, Jr., and G. C. Means, *The Modern Corporation and Private Property,* pp. 28 ff.

[16] G. A. Fernby, "Special Privilege Under Our Federal Anti-Trust Laws," *Annals of the American Academy,* CXLVII, 38, (Jan., 1930), has noted twelve exempted groups: Labor, farmers, planters, ranchmen, dairymen, nut and fruit growers, railroads, national banks, American steamship lines, those engaged in export business, producers of industrial alcohol, Philippine exporters. It should be noted, however, that the exemption extended to labor by the Clayton Act had been effectively nullified.

nature as to make public regulation of business increasingly difficult. Figuratively speaking, the lid was taken off in 1920 when, in the case against the United States Steel Company,[17] the Court refused to dissolve that corporation, holding that neither mere size, short of actual monopoly, nor the possession of potential power to restrain trade was necessarily a violation of the Sherman Act. The earlier theory that regulation might be achieved by extending the principle of public interest over a larger number of activities was scotched when in three decisions in two years the Court held that gasoline dealers in Tennessee, employment agencies in New Jersey, and ticket brokers in New York did not fall into the category of "public interest" enterprises.[18] The Court has also badly weakened effective regulation of public utilities, long recognized as vitally affecting the public interest, in a number of ways, but particularly by introducing into valuation cases the theory of "reproduction costs."[19] From a relatively simple and just method of determining rates, the Court has made the problem extremely difficult and complex, with the consumer always at a disadvantage. The Court also appears to have put its stamp of approval upon trade associations, although the activities of such associations often seem in contravention of the anti-trust laws.[20] "It is highly significant," remarks one student tersely, "that in recent years not a single adverse decision has been rendered requiring the dissolution of an actually functioning business merger."[21]

RAILROADS DURING THE POST-WAR PERIOD

One of the more important problems of reconstruction was the future of the railroads. Director-General McAdoo advised continued government operation for five years. Labor, on the other hand, strongly advocated government ownership and worked hard to popularize the "Plumb Plan," which called for the government purchase of the roads and their operation by a board of directors upon which the public, operating officers, and employees would be equally represented. The earnings, after operating expenses, maintenance, and liquidation of the purchase price had been taken care of, were to be divided between the government and the operating com-

[17] 251 U. S. 444.

[18] Williams v. Standard Oil Co. of La., Docket No. 64, U. S. Court, October Term 1928 (1929); Rupert Ribnick v. Andrew F. McBride, 277 U. S. 350 (1928); Tyson v. Banton, 273 U. S. 418 (1927). See D. M. Keezer and Stacy May, *Public Control of Business* (1930), pp. 108, 235; also H. S. Raushenbush, "Government Ownership and Control," *Annals of the American Academy*, Vol. CXLIX, Part I (May, 1930), p. 133.

[19] McCurdle v. Indianapolis Water Company, 272 U. S. 400 (1926).

[20] Maple Flooring Manufacturers Association v. U. S., 268 U. S. 563 (1925); Cement Manufacturers Protective Association v. U. S., 268 U. S. 588 (1925).

[21] M. W. Watkins, "The Sherman Act," *Quarterly Journal of Economics*, XLIII, 37 (Nov. 1928).

pany. This ingenious scheme might have gone far toward solving many difficult aspects of the railroad problem, but it was too much of an innovation in the conservative reaction following the war. Finally Congress was spurred to action by the President's threat to return the roads on March 1, 1920, whether Congress legislated or not.

The Transportation Act of February 28, 1920 (the Esch-Cummins Act), made up largely of amendments to the Interstate Commerce Act, is important as providing the law under which the roads operated during the post-war period. Among other provisions, it guaranteed the roads, for a period of six months after March 1, 1920, a net return equal to one-half the rental paid during government operation. The Interstate Commerce Commission was authorized to divide the country into rate districts, and in each of them to prescribe rates which "under honest, efficient, and economical management" would give a "fair return upon the aggregate value of the railroad property." The duty of appraising the property and determining a "fair return" was left to the Commission, but this was temporarily fixed for two years at 5½ per cent, with the addition of .5 of one per cent to provide for improvements and additions if the Commission thought best. In order that the weak roads might be preserved without the strong being permitted to reap too great profits, it was stipulated that any carrier receiving in any year a net income in excess of 6 per cent should turn over one-half of the excess to the Interstate Commerce Commission to be held as a revolving fund to be lent to the weak roads. The half retained by the carrier had to be placed in a reserve fund until the sum accumulated amounted to 5 per cent of the value of its property, after which the annual excess income might be used at will. In any year in which the income failed to reach 6 per cent, the reserve might be drawn on for dividends. The Commission was authorized to work out plans for the consolidation of the roads into not less than twenty nor more than thirty-five systems. At the same time it could permit pooling agreements subject to its supervision. It was given new power in regulating the capitalization of the roads and now had the right to prescribe minimum as well as maximum rates. Additional powers were conferred upon it in the control of rolling stock and the use of terminal facilities and in respect to the control of new road construction. Severe strikes in 1919 brought home to the public the importance of uninterrupted transportation, and in the hope of obviating strikes the Act created railroad boards of adjustment between one road or group of roads and employees, and in addition created a Railroad Labor Board of nine members, three representing the railroad employees, three representing the public, and three representing labor. From this somewhat lengthy description of the law it will be seen that the authority of the Commission, now increased to eleven members, was considerably augmented. More important than this, perhaps, was the evidence of a changing attitude on the part of the public toward the railroads. Up to this time the business of the Commission was essentially to protect the public from the railroads. By the Act of 1920 it also became the Commission's duty to see that the railroads received a fair return on the capital invested and that they were maintained as an essential part of our economic equipment. Although competition was to continue, the Act showed a realization of the fact that efficiency would be promoted by further consolidation of many railroad systems.

While many of the innovations introduced by the Transportation Act of 1920 were undeniably desirable, few of them were successfully applied. The Labor Board, unsatisfactory to management and labor alike, and powerless because its decisions were not binding, was abolished in 1926, and new experiments in labor mediation were tried.[22] Efforts by the Interstate Commerce Commission to enforce the recapture clause of the 1920 Act have been fruitless in spite of the fact that its constitutionality was upheld by the Supreme Court. Difficulties encountered in applying it, particularly after the O'Fallon decision in May, 1929,[23] and the relentless opposition of the more prosperous railroads led the Commission in 1930 to ask Congress to modify this part of the Act. This action, as we shall see, was taken in 1933.[24] Great difficulties likewise were met in carrying out the theory of the Act of 1920—that railroad consolidation to promote efficiency should be encouraged, but that at the same time competition, if possible, should be maintained. Although various plans were submitted to the Commission and studies made, it was not until December, 1929, that the Commission finally offered a tentative scheme of consolidation into twenty-one systems. Even

[22] The Watson-Parker bill (Railway Labor Act), which abolished the Labor Board, provided for a Board of Mediation to act in all controversies not settled within the individual roads by bipartisan boards of adjustment. In case of failure to adjust, the Board was to induce both parties to submit the case to a court of arbitration and if that failed the President was empowered to set up an emergency board to investigate and report. Although workers were not denied the right to strike, they were legally bound to accept the decision if they accepted arbitration. Failure of the railroads in many cases to set up bipartisan boards of adjustment and the desire to protect labor still further led Congress in 1934 to pass the Crosser-Dill Act, which established a new and smaller board of mediation, provided for a national railway adjustment board whose members were to be selected by carriers and labor organizations, and made possible the establishment of regional or system boards. The Act safeguards *bona fide* labor organizations by making it difficult for company unions to exist and it makes it practically obligatory to submit disputes to arbitration.

[23] In the O'Fallon decision (St. Louis and O'Fallon Railway Company *v.* United States, 279 U. S. 461) the Supreme Court annulled an order of the Interstate Commerce Commission which assessed the St. Louis and O'Fallon Railway Company for excess earnings on its valuations on the ground that it had not taken into consideration present as well as former prices in fixing a final valuation as a preliminary to recapture.

[24] Below, p. 666.

then little progress was made. The railroads found it difficult to agree on plans; the Commission had power only to suggest and approve, not to compel.

A survey of railroad statistics since 1920 gives conclusive evidence of the weakened position of the roads. While the investment in rolling stock and other equipment substantially increased and the burden of taxation grew heavier, freight revenue increased but slightly and passenger traffic declined by one-third. The cause for this decline was obviously the

RAILROADS DURING THE 'TWENTIES [25]

Year	Investment in Road and Equipment (in millions)	Freight Revenue (in millions)	Passenger Revenue (in millions)	Passengers Carried (in thousands)	Taxes (in millions)
1920	$19,849	$4,421	$1,305	1,269,913	$289
1925	23,231	4,648	1,065	901,963	366
1929	25,405	4,899	876	786,432	403

rapid development of private automobiles and motor busses; the failure of freight traffic to increase notably in a decade of prosperity was attributable to a similar development of freight trucks. Although domestic airplanes were carrying over 400,000 passengers by 1930, competition from this source was as yet a problem of the future. Competition from motor vehicles forced roads to abandon mileage and to curtail passenger service. The more progressive of them operated busses themselves; others streamlined their trains, installed air-conditioned cars, and attempted through greater luxury and speed to win back their passenger business. It was obvious that motor transportation was enjoying temporary advantages during the 'twenties because of the low burden of taxation and the lack of efficient regulation, but these advantages largely disappeared in the 'thirties.[26]

In spite of this new competition, the general situation of the more prosperous railroads appears to have been about as good in the years following as in those which preceded the First World War. It is true that the average return on investment for Class I railways was estimated at only 4.3 per cent for the seven years 1921–1927, but the better-managed and better-situated railroads actually made large profits during certain of these years. In the eight years 1920–1927, Class I railways and their subsidiaries spent close to six billion dollars for extensions, additions, and betterments. Until

[25] Interstate Commerce Commission, *Statistics of Railways in the United States* for 1922, 1930, 1931. See also H. G. Moulton and associates, *The American Transportation Problem*, pp. 28 ff.

[26] Below, p. 666.

the depression that began in 1929 there was a steady increase in total track mileage, although "first-track" mileage just about held its own. Furthermore, in 1929 the Pennsylvania, the Philadelphia and Reading, the Delaware, Lackawanna and Western, and several other railroads announced plans for electrification and many of these projects were completed in spite of the depression.

EXPANSION OF TRANSPORTATION FACILITIES

The revival of interest in the development of inland waterway transportation and in artificial waterways which took place in the first decade of the century has continued with little abatement. This is so despite the tremendous development of motor vehicle traffic and the fact that railroads have continued to improve their facilities and seem adequately equipped to handle normal demands. A partial explanation can be found in the fact that inland water transportation on the Great Lakes and the contributory canals has shown a notable increase, and in the current belief that water transportation is cheaper than rail and should be encouraged.[27] Likewise it is felt that since the United States has the finest inland waterways to be found in any nation in the world, they should be further developed. A great impetus has undoubtedly been given by the agricultural distress of the Middle West and by the conviction that cheaper all-water routes to foreign markets would help to remedy the situation.

Two projects have long been discussed: (1) the Lakes-to-the-Gulf Deep Waterway, which would follow the line of the Chicago Sanitary Drainage Canal, the Illinois and Michigan Canal, and the Mississippi River; and (2) the St. Lawrence Ship Canal. The first project, it was hoped, would restore the Mississippi traffic and provide a direct route from the Mississippi Valley to South American ports; the latter would connect the great agricultural regions of the Middle West with Europe by a direct all-water route.[28] The Lakes-to-the-Gulf Deep Waterway has had the endorsement of successive administrations since Theodore Roosevelt's, and has been aided

[27] In round numbers, the freight carried on the Sault Ste. Marie increased from 62,363,000 tons in 1910 to 92,622,000 in 1929, only to drop to 20,480,873 in 1932; tonnage on the Erie and other New York canals has a little more than held its own, increasing from an average of 3,328,000 (1906–1910) to 3,643,433 in 1932; the freight carried in 1929 through the Sault Ste. Marie alone was more than three times that carried through the Panama Canal. *Statistical Abstract, 1930*, pp. 435, 436, 442.

[28] A third project of much less importance has also received considerable publicity and, up to 1933, appropriations of over $40,000,000—the Intracoastal Waterway. This is a sheltered series of coastal waterways and canals planned to extend from Boston to Corpus Christi, Texas. A glance at the map (p. 620) will show the amount completed by the late 1930's. The project has no naval significance and at the present has no transportation importance except as a yacht route from the northern states to Florida and the Gulf ports, a type of traffic which has declined materially since 1929.

since 1917 by a succession of important legislative Acts and appropriations.[29]
This whole project has been entangled with the expensive problem of flood
control, but the political strength of those desiring both flood control and

**INTERNAL WATERWAYS
IN THE 1930's**

━ ━ ━ St. Lawrence Waterway Project
•••••• Lakes to Gulf Deep Water Way
▭▭▭▭ Canals and Intracoastal Water-
ways
━━━ Main Canalized Rivers

inland water routes appears great enough to achieve both objects. With the
opening in 1933 of the Illinois Waterway, which linked Lake Michigan,
the Illinois River, and the Mississippi by canal, the through route from the
Great Lakes to the Gulf was made available. In 1924 the federal government

[29] For a summary of this legislation, see J. C. Malin, *The United States After the World
War* (1930), Chap. XI.

went so far as to organize an Inland Waterways Corporation to carry on the operation of government-owned inland, canal, and coastwise water transportation, but particularly to demonstrate the practicability of water transportation on the upper Mississippi. An outstanding event of the year 1929 was the formal opening of the Ohio River Canalization, a project which had been under way for some fifty years and had cost $125,000,000. Both the Mississippi and the Ohio projects provided for a minimum depth of 9 feet.

The St. Lawrence Ship Canal project, which also included schemes for a great hydraulic development, met strong opposition in New York State, where over $200,000,000 had recently been invested in the Barge Canal (an enlargement and improvement of the old Erie Canal) and which demanded an all-American route. After various investigations had been made, Secretary Hoover recommended the St. Lawrence route as cheaper to construct, as a shorter route to northern Europe, and as providing greater savings to the shipper than the New York route. His advocacy of this project failed to accomplish much during his administration as President. His successor, President Franklin D. Roosevelt, in January, 1934, urged the Senate to ratify the treaty which would make possible the construction of this project, but the Senate failed to act. On the ground that it was necessary for the long-range defense needs of both Canada and the United States it was revived in 1941 in the form of an agreement (requiring only a majority approval of Congress) between the two nations. Up to the end of 1942 Congress had taken no action. Obviously the St. Lawrence project is tangled in politics and sectional interests which often obscure fundamental factors. That there would be a saving in mileage and possibly in freight between the Middle West and the ports of Europe over this route is conceded. From an engineering point of view it is practicable, and there is no doubt that the Middle West sincerely desires it. The project, however, would cost close to a billion dollars (including power projects) and many experts doubt whether it can be justified on purely economic grounds for many years to come.[30] It is doubtful if the savings in transportation would be commensurate with the initial cost and upkeep. The power developments, on the other hand, while not needed by Canada, would be advantageous to the northeastern section of the United States.

At the opening of the First World War the automobile was just passing out of the experimental stage. Its use was still largely confined to the wealthy and upper middle classes, the number of motor vehicles produced

[30] H. G. Moulton, C. S. Morgan, and A. L. Lee, *The St. Lawrence Navigation and Power Project* (1929). See also H. G. Moulton and associates, *The American Transportation Problem*, pp. 505–513.

in the United States in 1914 being 569,054, and the number registered 1,258,062. During the next fifteen years the motor car had its great era of expansion and became a pleasure and business vehicle for all classes of people. Production of passenger cars and trucks increased to 5,621,715 in 1929 and the number registered to 26,501,443.[31] This represented about five-sixths of the world's production, and about one automobile to every five people in the United States. While the automobile has undoubtedly affected the steam and interurban electric roads, even to the extent of causing the abandonment of several thousand miles of track, much of the business of the bus and motor truck is new, and these agencies are supplementing rather than supplanting the older facilities. For example, there are today in this country 45,000 communities with no important means of transportation other than the motor vehicle. The United States has become a nation on wheels.

The agitation for better roads which had been stimulated in the late 'eighties and early 'nineties by the bicycle craze was given increased impetus by the automobile, but the work done prior to World War I was largely in local and state hands.[32] Ignoring the constitutional limitations pointed out by Jackson in the Maysville Road veto,[33] the federal government reverted in 1916 to the old policy which had built the national pike. By the Rural Post Roads Act of 1916, supplemented by subsequent legislation, it has been aiding the states to build primary interstate roads and secondary connecting roads, the states contributing an amount equal to that given by the federal government. Under this stimulus some 108,000 miles of road had been improved by 1933 and the federal government was regularly appropriating $75,000,000 a year. Important as this federal help is in the improvement of highways, the amount appropriated is rather trivial in comparison to the expenditures for county and city roads which in 1930 ran somewhere between $2,500,000,000 and $3,000,000,000. In spite of this tremendous advance, little more than 20 per cent of the 3,000,000 miles of road in the United States are better than dirt roads. Nevertheless, the effect of the automobile and improved roads upon our economic, social, and intellectual history in stimulating economic life, in providing work and support for millions of people, in speeding up our civilization, in breaking down rural isolation, and in integrating social and intellectual development is almost beyond comprehension.

[31] Owing to the depression the production of motor vehicles dropped to 1,431,494 in 1932 and the automobile registrations to 24,136,879. The year 1933, however, showed a 45 per cent increase in production and an increase in registration. Motor vehicles registered in 1940 numbered 31,104,118.

[32] Above, pp. 508 ff.

[33] Above, p. 275.

To those old enough to remember pre-automobile days, many of the effects of the motor vehicle are obvious, but the significance may not be so clear to the present generation of college students. A study of transportation published in the early 'thirties comments that the diffusion of the automobile "within the population, vertically and horizontally, has been without precedent. It has increased the mobility of people in all classes of

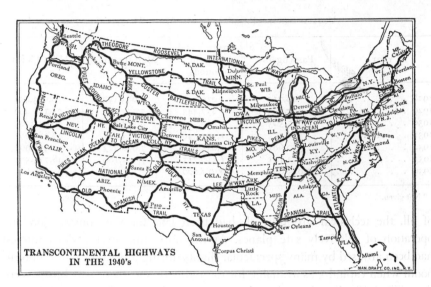

TRANSCONTINENTAL HIGHWAYS
IN THE 1940's

society, and given them a control over their own movements that could not have been foreseen thirty years ago. It is bringing into existence new and integrated transportation systems, both within local communities, which it is helping to transform into larger and more closely knit regional urban areas, and between more distant points. It has multiplied enormously man's potential personal contacts in remote communities, and with his fellow townsmen as well. It is an innovation that has been reshaping many phases of contemporary life."[34] When the saga of the motor car is finally written, it may well show that the coming of the motor vehicle inaugurated a second industrial and social revolution.

Although the development of the commercial airplane has been exceedingly rapid since 1919, air transport is still the least important of the forms of organized transportation available to the American public.[35] Contrary to the general belief, however, airplane development in this country has long since surpassed that abroad. For example, the annual aircraft production in the United States increased from 662 units in 1919 to 5306 in

[34] M. W. Willey, and S. A. Rice, *Communication Agencies and Social Life,* pp. 39–40.
[35] The early years of aviation history are described above, p. 510.

1929, only to fall to 2394 in 1931. On the other hand, there has been a continuous development of commercial air service which has gone on in spite of the depression of the 1930's.

A glance at a table of airplane statistics will show that the great period of American development began in 1929 and was particularly rapid from then until 1931. Certain obvious causes explain this sudden spurt. First

UNITED STATES PASSENGER AND MAIL TRAFFIC [36]

Year	Passengers	Express and Freight (pounds)	Mail (pounds)	Miles Flown
1928	49,713	216,644	4,063,173	10,673,450
1929	173,405	257,443	7,772,014	25,141,499
1930	417,505	468,571	8,513,675	36,945,203
1931	522,345	1,151,348	9,643,211	47,385,987
1932	540,681	1,033,970	7,908,723	50,932,967
1933	493,141	1,510,215	7,362,180	48,771,533
1939	2,045,021	10,912,000	a	99,976,000

a Not given.

of all, the technical groundwork had been laid for the construction and operation of relatively safe planes. At the same time tremendous interest had been aroused by many spectacular flights during a period of an economic boom when capital was available for the industry and there was business for the planes. Finally, there was the assistance of the government. This last cannot be overestimated. The United States was the chief customer of the manufacturers of aviation supplies. In 1931, for example, 812 of the 2394 planes produced were military units. Actual transportation by air was even more dependent upon government aid than was the manufacturing. The government became interested in aviation first in its military aspects and then in its commercial. In 1918 an experimental Air Mail Service was established jointly by the Post Office Department and the Army. This was soon abandoned, but in the following year the Post Office Department acting alone inaugurated a mail service between Chicago and Cleveland, which in 1924 was extended to transcontinental proportions. When a government service was finally established on a satisfactory basis, Congress suddenly reversed itself and virtually ordered the Post Office Department to cease carrying air mail and to contract the business to private concerns. The result has been the subsidization of American aviation chiefly by means of post office air contracts. This particular form of aid got out of bounds by 1934, and when charges of fraud and favoritism were

[36] Statistical Abstract, 1933, p. 371, for figures through 1932; Statistical Abstract, 1940, p. 457.

made, the government suddenly revoked its contracts, carried the mail itself for a few weeks, and then called for new bids.[37]

In the middle 'thirties aviation experienced a second period of rapid expansion and began to free itself from its utter dependence upon government subsidy. After 1934 its chief source of revenue was its passenger

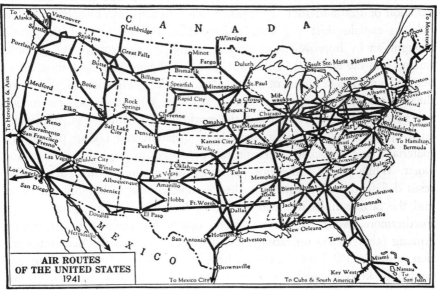

(From H. U. Faulkner and Tyler Kepner, *America, Its History and People,* Harper & Brothers.)

traffic. Beginning in 1938 the government received more from postal revenues than it paid to air mail carriers. In 1940 commercial passenger planes flew over 94,000,000 miles and carried 3,185,000 passengers over a nation equipped with 2600 airports and landing fields. This was about 10 per cent of the passengers carried on Pullman trains. Planes were carrying one-seventh of the first-class mail and one-fourth of the transcontinental mail. Commercial aviation was rapidly reaching maturity. Its expanding popularity was due primarily to the increasing speed and safety of air flights. By 1940 the time from New York to San Francisco had been cut to fifteen hours. In March, 1940, commercial air lines completed a full year without a fatal accident.[38]

[37] Estimates for 1932 put the various kinds of federal aid to air transports at $26,274,000, and contributions from passenger and postal carriers at not more than $15,000,000. In that year the government paid air mail carriers $19,938,123 but received only $6,016,280 in postal revenue.

[38] Matters of safety in interstate travel are supervised by the Department of Commerce under the Air Commerce Act of 1926; the Post Office Department has comprehensive powers over air mail carriers. Under the Air Mail Act of 1934 the Interstate Commerce Commission determines fair and reasonable rates for carrying air mail.

AGRICULTURE ON THE WANE

Just as the American farmer found himself confronted with a serious economic crisis in the years following the Napoleonic and Civil Wars, so also after the First World War he was again faced by a somewhat similar situation. While many other economic interests recovered rapidly after the deflation of 1920 and 1921, agriculture failed to respond. Two basic factors help to explain this: (1) overproduction in the markets of the world brought on by improved agricultural machinery, particularly the gasoline tractor, and the demands of the war, and (2) the world-wide falling off in demand and the deflation of prices after the war. The first of these produced a second agricultural revolution at a time when increased production was hardly necessary. The second, the world-wide deflation, was particularly hard upon agriculture, for in periods of deflation and falling prices, raw materials, and especially agricultural products, usually suffer first and worst. While wages and retail prices go down more slowly or possibly resist deflation, the bottom is knocked completely out of agricultural prices and the farmer finds his income out of line with that of other groups. Furthermore, while his income went down, his taxes were increasing. Among other factors operating against the farmer was the new immigration policy of the United States which cut the flow of immigration and tended to keep wages high, freight rates and handling costs which did not decline with the price of agricultural products, and dietary and style changes which led people to turn from meats and cereals to vegetables and fruit. Individualistic, the farmer adjusts himself less easily to new conditions. The war encouraged overexpansion and overemphasis upon the one-crop system, both of which proved ruinous in the post-war years. Finally, before any satisfactory adjustment was achieved, a second period of world-wide depression began in 1929.

In the sudden deflation at the conclusion of the war the price farmers received for corn in 1921 dropped to a third that of 1919; cotton, wheat, and hogs fell to half the 1919 figure, and cattle to almost half. The prices of most agricultural commodities recovered somewhat during 1923 to 1926, but they dropped again. With the decline in prices, the bankruptcy rate per 1000 farms jumped from 0.21 in 1920 to slightly over 1.20 for the years 1924–1926. In spite of this increase, the total farm mortgage debt rose by almost two billion dollars between 1920 and 1928, an increase of 19 per cent from 1920 to 1925 and a rise of one per cent from 1925 to 1928.[39] Under the circumstances a decline in land values was to be expected, but the

[39] The figures for the three years are $7,857,700,000 in 1920, $9,360,620,000 in 1925, and $9,468,526,000 in 1928.

drop in agricultural land values from $79,000,000,000 in 1920 to $58,000,000,-
000 in 1927 was staggering.[40] At the same time, the population on farms declined from 31,614,000 in 1920 to 30,169,000 in 1930, with a net movement
from farms during the decade of about 600,000 per year.[41] The accompanying
table of index numbers gives a rough idea of the agricultural problem in
pre- and post-war years.

INDEX NUMBERS OF FARM PRICES, PRICES PAID BY FARMERS, FARM WAGES, AND
TAXES, 1910-1929 (1910-1914 = 100)[42]

Date	Prices Received for Farm Products	Prices Paid by Farmers for Commodities Used in		Farm Wages Paid to Hired Labor	Taxes on Farm Property (1914=100)
		Living	Production		
1910	103	98	98	97	...
1911	95	100	103	97	...
1912	99	101	98	101	...
1913	100	100	102	104	...
1914	102	102	99	101	100
1915	100	107	104	102	102
1916	117	124	124	112	104
1917	176	147	151	140	106
1918	200	177	174	176	118
1919	209	210	192	206	130
1920	205	222	174	239	155
1921	116	161	141	150	217
1922	123	156	139	146	232
1923	134	160	141	166	246
1924	134	159	143	166	249
1925	147	164	147	168	250
1926	136	162	146	171	253
1927	131	159	145	170	258
1928	139	160	148	169	263
1929	138	158	147	170	267
1930	117	148	140	152	266
1931	80	126	122	116	...
1932	57	108	107	86	...
1933	63	109	108	80	...

It was inevitable that the agricultural depression would have reverbera-
tions in politics and would result in legislation. In May, 1921, Senators and
Representatives of both parties from the agricultural states organized the
"farm bloc" and led the movement for legislation. Thoroughgoing legislation, they asserted, was necessary not only to help remedy a very serious situation, but also to put the farmers on an equal status with other economic

[40] At the same time capital invested in corporations increased from $99,000,000,000 to
$134,000,000,000.

[41] Yearbook of Agriculture, 1934, p. 699. The figure 600,000 represents roughly the excess
of those leaving the farms over those arriving at farms from the cities.

[42] Ibid., 1932, p. 900; ibid., 1934, p. 706.

groups protected and favored by the federal government. The result of this agitation led to a considerable amount of legislation which can be roughly grouped under three heads.[43] In the first place, the various tariff measures, including the emergency tariff of 1921, the Fordney-McCumber tariff of 1922, and the Hawley-Smoot bill of 1930, all made an effort to protect agricultural commodities from foreign competition. While these tariffs undoubtedly helped to raise the prices on certain agricultural products, economists were pretty well agreed that they had no effect upon the prices of high-

FARM PRICES OF WHEAT AND INDEX OF RETAIL PRICES OF COMMODITIES FARMERS BUY.[44]

protein wheat, corn, barley, cotton, and other important commodities. A tariff on agricultural commodities of which there is a large surplus for export is not likely to be beneficial, particularly when a general high tariff policy may close just those markets where an agricultural surplus might be disposed of. The irony of helping an export industry, such as American agriculture, by a tariff was at last becoming evident even to Republican farm leaders, and this time-honored sop no longer satisfied them. The blind spot in the whole agricultural program of the 1920's was the failure of farm leaders

[43] A summary of this legislation from 1920 to 1928 is given in J. D. Black, *Agricultural Reform in the United States* (1929), pp. 69–73, and in C. C. Davis, "The Development of Agricultural Policy Since the End of the World War," *Yearbook of Agriculture, 1940*, pp. 297–326.

[44] "Farm prices of wheat rose more rapidly and higher during the war than did retail prices of commodities farmers buy. In 1920 and 1921, however, wheat prices fell more rapidly and, most of the years since the war, have remained below the prices of commodities farmers buy. Year-to-year changes in wheat prices are due largely to changes in world production but also depend upon whether the various classes of wheat in the United States are on a domestic or an export basis." *Yearbook of Agriculture, 1930*, p. 574.

to realize that the foreign market for agricultural products was permanently contracted and that the shift of the United States from a debtor to a creditor nation made the exportation of the agricultural surplus of less importance to the national welfare.

In the second place, a number of Acts were passed, designed to extend better credit to farmers and encourage them in cooperative efforts. These included the War Finance Corporation, revived in 1921 to finance the exportation of agricultural products and handle emergency agricultural credits, the Agricultural Credits Act of 1923,[45] and the Agricultural Marketing Act of 1929. These and other measures were designed to extend the work inaugurated by the Federal Farm Loan Act of 1916.

Valuable as these Acts might be, they did not effectively remedy the situation, and the more radical of the agricultural group pressed for a third type of legislation which would actually raise prices. This hope was incorporated in the McNary-Haugen bills, twice passed by Congress in 1927 and 1928 and vetoed both times by Coolidge. While the details of these bills differed somewhat, the general method to be employed was the same. The bills provided that a gigantic government corporation should purchase the chief agricultural products at a price which would yield a fair profit, and that the surplus should be sold abroad at what it would bring, the loss on the foreign sales to be assessed in the form of an equalization fee against every unit of the product sold by the producer. The net price to the producer would be the fixed price minus the equalization fee; the larger the surplus the larger the fee and the smaller the return to the farmer. As the producers of tobacco and cotton sold too great a proportion of these crops abroad to be much interested in the scheme, and as many products were sold abroad in only small quantities, the bill was a middle-western measure designed primarily to help the producers of wheat and hogs.

Both parties in 1928 pledged themselves to agricultural relief, and after the veto of the second McNary-Haugen bill the Hoover administration sanctioned the Agricultural Marketing Act of 1929, mentioned above. By this Act Congress appropriated $500,000,000 to be loaned by a Federal Farm Board to cooperative associations in the hope that this would promote orderly marketing and sound policies, and put the farmer in a position to deal more effectively with the whole problem of marketing. Although the Federal Farm Board encouraged cooperatives and through stabilization corporations attempted to prevent the decline of prices, the effect upon the

[45] This Act set up a Federal Intermediate Credit bank in each of the federal land bank districts, with a capitalization of $5,000,000 and the power to issue debentures to ten times that amount; the purpose was to extend personal and collateral credit for periods intermediate between the usual short-term commercial loan and the long-term obligations secured by land.

general agricultural situation was slight. The Board's career was short and disastrous, ending as it did with the Roosevelt legislation of 1933.

The body of agricultural legislation passed in the decade and a half after 1915 was considerable in amount and undoubtedly of substantial assistance to the farmers. It is of interest in our economic history because it

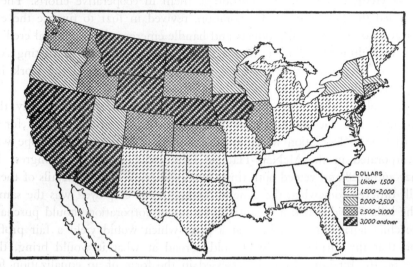

DOLLARS
Under 1,500
1,500-2,000
2,000-2,500
2,500-3,000
3,000 and over

ANNUAL GROSS INCOME PER FARM, 1924-1928 [46]

marked a change in policy. "Prior to 1913," says Malin, "United States agricultural policy was focused upon the problems of production. In that year a new departure was inaugurated which for the first time placed systematic emphasis upon the problems of marketing." [47] A revolution in distribution methods was obviously needed, and the Agricultural Marketing Act distinctly recognized the fact. All the assistance which the government could offer during the 'twenties, however, could not overcome the two most important handicaps under which the farmer suffered—overproduction and a world-wide economic depression which radically curtailed the market.

DECLINE OF ORGANIZED LABOR

Although the international position of labor was stronger after the First World War, the prosperity of American labor was decidedly checked and its unity broken after the conclusion of the conflict. The American Federation of Labor, proudly conscious of its war record, laid down at its annual convention in 1919 a "reconstruction program" which called for democracy in industry, abolition of unemployment, higher wages, shorter hours, equal

[46] *Yearbook of Agriculture, 1930,* p. 245.
[47] J. C. Malin, *The United States After the World War,* p. 247.

pay to women for equal work, abolition of child labor, the right of public employees to organize and bargain collectively, a curtailment of the power of the judiciary, government ownership of public and semi-public utilities, development and operation of water power, better federal and state regulation of corporations, absolute freedom of expression and association, extension of workmen's compensation, establishment of government employment agencies and the abolition of those conducted for private profit, the building of model homes by the government and aid in enabling workers to own their homes, and a two-year cessation of immigration.[48]

If labor had any idea that a grateful republic would be sympathetic to this program, it was doomed to speedy disillusionment. In the reaction which settled dismally upon the nation in the post-war years labor found itself attacked from many quarters and its power badly impaired. In the economic depression which inevitably followed in the wake of war expansion, all but the most powerfully organized workers experienced wage decreases. Strikes to prevent deflation or to secure higher wages were generally unsuccessful. The federal government broke up a bituminous coal strike in 1919 by obtaining a sweeping injunction authorized, according to the Attorney General, under the Lever Fuel and Food Control Act of 1917; a railroad shopmen's strike in 1919 collapsed through government opposition and the failure of labor to cooperate, and the steel strike in the same year was unsuccessful. The speed with which the hard-earned gains of labor were disappearing and the ease with which this was accomplished amazed Gompers, and he bitterly denounced the Bourbon policies of American industrialists. Inadequate labor leadership, however, was an important cause.[49] The steel strike of 1919, for example, was a strategic struggle in which the demands of labor were eminently fair, the sympathy of a large element of the public with them, and the chances for success at least even. A united front on the part of American labor might have seen a different outcome. In 1919 there were nine labor disturbances in each of which over 90,000 men were involved, and in that year over 4,000,000 men went on strike.[50] Most of the important conflicts terminated unsuccessfully for labor.

[48] *Monthly Labor Review*, Vol. VIII, No. 3, pp. 63–72 (March, 1919). See also F. Flügel and H. U. Faulkner, *Readings*, pp. 839–842.

[49] Aroused to action, the A. F. of L., for the first time in its history, officially supported a presidential candidate, La Follette, in 1924, whose consistent labor record could not be ignored. His defeat merely served to convince labor leaders of the correctness of their former policy, which, if possible, became more conservative than ever regarding political action.

[50] The number of strikes reported for the year was 3630. See *Monthly Labor Review*, July, 1929. The figures of workmen on strike since the First World War are interesting. The 4,160,348 in 1919 dropped to 1,463,054 in 1920 and to 1,099,247 in 1921, then rose in 1922 during the railroad strike to 1,612,562, but dropped to 756,584 in 1923 and then steadily downward to 329,592 in 1926. From 1927 to 1931 the annual average number of strikes was 763 and the annual average number of strikers involved was 275,000. See table in C. R. Daugherty, *Labor Problems in American Industry*, p. 356.

Labor was also experiencing losses in other directions. The depression and absorption of four million soldiers increased the competition for jobs; corporations, as they saw their profits decline, curtailed their welfare operations; public interest in social legislation declined, and the hand of the judiciary grew heavier. The courts, which during the war had complacently watched constitutional and human rights repeatedly violated, continued to countenance extra-legal proceedings, particularly those used to hinder the activities of labor radicals. At the same time, capital, taking a leaf from war experience, increased the use of the labor spy and the *agent provocateur,* and called repeatedly upon the state militia.

While organized labor grew weaker, organized capital became stronger. Manufacturers' associations devoted increased attention to combating labor and in many communities secured the close cooperation of Chambers of Commerce. This effort to break the power of labor and promote the "open shop" was euphemistically called the "American plan" and met with considerable success. A barrage of propaganda asserting that labor was to blame for the high cost of living helped to alienate the sympathy of the middle class so important to the labor movement.

Particularly detrimental to labor were the reactionary decisions of the state and federal judiciary. Federal child labor laws were declared unconstitutional in 1918 and 1922, and in 1923 a minimum-wage law for women in the District of Columbia fell under the ban of the court.[51] Not only was social legislation endangered, but the very existence of labor unions was jeopardized. The Supreme Court in the Danbury Hatters' case (1908, 1915) and in other decisions had held that labor unions and their individual members were responsible without limit for actions of union officers which they had in any way sanctioned; in 1915 it declared unconstitutional a state statute aimed to prevent an employer from forcing his employee to agree not to join a union during the latter's term of service ("yellow-dog contract"),[52] and it even upheld a decision that it was illegal to try to organize employees who signed a "yellow-dog contract." [53] It cut the heart out of the protection which Congress intended to give labor in the Clayton Act by declaring a secondary boycott illegal [54] and by permitting suit against an unincorporated union for violation of that Act.[55] Particularly dangerous to labor was the growing use of the injunction in labor disputes, a procedure which even the conservative A. F. of L. fought consistently and

---

[51] Above, p. 475.
[52] Coppage *v.* Kansas, 236 U. S. (1915).
[53] Hitchman Coal and Coke *v.* Mitchell *et al.,* 254 U. S. 229 (1917).
[54] Duplex Printing Press Company *v.* Deering *et al.,* 254 U. S. 443 (1921).
[55] United Mine Workers of America *v.* Coronado Coal and Coke Company, 259 U. S. 344 (1922).

bitterly. In theory labor still had the right to organize, to strike, to picket, and to boycott; but "in practice," says Morris Hillquit, "the rules have been hedged in by so many exceptions and weakened by so many modifications and departures that they have been reduced to the status of an abstract social philosophy rather than a statement of positive law." [56] A minor gain in the realm of judicial decisions, however, was registered. In 1920 Kansas passed an Act forbidding strikes in basic industries but created a Court of Industrial Relations to investigate and settle disputes and empowered the state to take over and operate any of the enumerated industries in which work was suspended in violation of the law. Bitterly opposed by labor leaders as violating what they believed to be their inalienable right to strike, the law, in several important sections, was declared unconstitutional in 1923.

Difficult as it was to counteract the decisions of a conservative judiciary, the activities of the *agent provocateur,* and the decline of public sympathy, organized labor now found its influence undermined in much subtler ways. One of the chief weapons used to disrupt the organized labor movement is the "company union." Prior to 1917 not more than a dozen important plants had introduced this system, but by 1927 there were hundreds, with a membership of over 1,400,000. The growth of company unions was particularly rapid in the railway industry after the collapse of the shopmen's strike in 1922, but it was also important in the metal trades and electrical manufacturing establishments. Another subtle weapon directed against organized labor was employee stock ownership. Although the promotion of this can be validated on the grounds that it improves morale, diminishes labor troubles and turnover, and develops a contented personnel, its chief effects appear to have been to weaken the organized labor movement, and consequently the power of labor. The leadership in the promotion of stock ownership in the utilities was taken by the American Telephone and Telegraph Company; in the industrial field by such concerns as the Eastman Kodak Company, United States Steel, and Bethlehem Steel; in the rails by the New York Central and the Pennsylvania, and in the oils by the Standard Oil Company. [57] Encouraged chiefly through installment purchases, the number of employee stockholders grew to well over a million, and certain devotees of "Pollyanna economics" extravagantly hailed it as an indication of an "economic revolution" by which the ownership of the nation's wealth was being accumulated in the hands of the wage earner. [58] That employee stock ownership undoubtedly acts as a palliative in the conflict between

[56] *New Leader* (Dec. 4, 1926).

[57] R. F. Foerster and E. N. Dietel, *Employee Stock Ownership in the United States* (1926), pp. 99 ff.

[58] T. N. Carver, *The Present Economic Revolution in the United States* (1925).

capital and labor is readily conceded, but even the most casual examination quickly dispels the dream that any economic millennium is being achieved through this medium.[59] A Federal Trade Commission investigation made in 1922 and covering a cross-section of American business found that employees comprised 7.5 per cent of the common stockholders of corporations in which they were employed, and 3.5 per cent of the preferred stockholders, but held only 1.5 per cent of the common stock and 1.9 of the preferred.[60] A later study made by the Industrial Relations Section of Princeton University found that only 4.26 per cent of the stock of twenty important companies which had vigorously encouraged employee stock ownership was actually owned by employees.[61] When it is realized that a large proportion of this stock is held by superintendents and by the salaried office and executive force, the actual share owned by labor appears even smaller. It should furthermore be pointed out that while the actual number of shareholders has increased, the technique whereby a small group may maintain control of an industry has been perfected.[62] The democratization of capital and of business has made little if any progress through employee stock ownership.

It is impossible for any student of labor to ignore the rapid development during the 1920's of a wide range of activities often grouped under the term "welfare capitalism." The impetus for this has often been the desire to paralyze unionization or to develop a more loyal, stable, and efficient working force. Combined with this there has frequently been a sincere humanitarian attempt to improve the lot of the worker. Among the most valid and helpful of these efforts has been the establishment of insurance and pension schemes. Various forms of group insurance (in addition to the compulsory workmen's compensation) have been widely established, covering disability and death. It was estimated in 1927 that group insurance had been taken out to the extent of $5,600,000,000 covering 4,700,-000 employees, one insurance company alone, the Metropolitan, having written it for 2500 firms and 815,000 workers.[63] Also worthy of attention is the development of employee pensions. A survey by the Pennsylvania Old Age Pension Commission in 1926 revealed the fact that at least 400 firms employing 4,000,000 workers had established pension plans, 88 per cent of which had been inaugurated in the past fifteen years.[64]

In addition to pensions and insurance, an infinite variety of welfare

[59] R. W. Dunn, *The Americanization of Labor* (1927), pp. 102 ff.

[60] Federal Trade Commission, *Report on National Wealth and Income* (1926).

[61] R. F. Foerster and E. N. Dietel, *Employee Stock Ownership;* and R. W. Dunn, *The Americanization of Labor,* p. 153.

[62] W. Z. Ripley, *Main Street and Wall Street* (1927).

[63] *Annals of the American Academy of Political and Social Science,* p. 32 (March, 1927).

[64] Abraham Epstein, *The Problem of Old Age Pensions in Industry* (1926), pp. 18–19.

projects have been devised. Anyone who looks over the literature on the subject, says one labor writer disgustedly,

. . . will find frequent references to service pin associations, swimming clubs, Boy Scouts, Camp Fire Girls, housing, company gardens, day nurseries, women's aid circles, soccer teams, booster clubs, minstrel shows and square deal societies. He will come upon employers who have organized for their workers—bands, bowling leagues, visiting nurses, mutual aid societies, legal assistance, dramatic clubs, thrift clubs, sewing circles and libraries. He will take note of Sunshine Committees, Christmas treats, cafeterias, clam bakes, plant song leaders, dispensaries, "dividend days," educational departments, "June walks," athletics and sports of every sort, churches, stores and cobbler shops, kindergartens, amusements and diversions by the dozen. If the worker is employed at the Endicott-Johnson shoe plant he will find himself the participant in "George F. Days" in honor of the "Big Boss." In any one of a score of factories he will belong to a committee designed to develop the "Babbitt Spirit," Mr. Babbitt being the owner of the concern. The worker may also be a member of a "flying squadron," a fellowship club, a savings committee, a suggestion league, an Americanization class, or a "cooperative" purchasing committee. He may find himself the recipient of a turkey at Christmas or a gold watch at the end of twenty-five years' non-strike service. He may have his instincts studied, his incentives tapped, his soul "psyched" by the appropriate department. He will be vocationally guided, time-studied, personally-developed, job-analyzed, and first-aided. He will be given "advice on vacation plans," and have phonograph music played to him while he works. (One writer discovered that in an iron foundry he visited it was arranged that the molders, presumably not members of the International Molders' Union, should eat their lunches in "a specially constructed rose garden equipped with canaries in cages.") There seems to be no limit to the varieties of camera clubs, cooperative plans, veterans' associations, brotherhood clubs, Bible classes, Greek letter fraternities, domestic science matrons, and even golf courses and club houses that certain corporations have provided one group or another of their employees during the last fifteen or twenty years. One company even provides its female workers with a "Dean of women, who supervises their work and play." [65]

This sort of thing undoubtedly has it value, but it also indicated that the initiative in improving the condition of labor was shifting from the laborer to the employer and that personal independence and initiative were rapidly being undermined. Obviously the organized labor movement was being outmaneuvered by the employer. The membership of the A. F. of L. dropped from the high point of 4,078,740 in 1920 to 2,803,966 in 1926, and up to 1933 it showed little aggressiveness in winning back lost members. These figures tell but a part of the story of the decline of organized labor. The

[65] R. W. Dunn, *The Americanization of Labor*, pp. 193–194.

Federation failed miserably in organizing the workers in the automobile factories and in the southern textile mills, it saw strong unions like those of the bituminous coal workers rapidly disintegrate, and it failed badly in making the Amalgamated Association of Iron, Steel and Tin workers a going concern. Gompers, who died in 1924, passed on his conservative policies to less able leaders, in whose hands they seemed for years to have degenerated into "do-nothingism." The skilled workers who comprise the largest portion of organized labor found their position improving with the decline of prices after World War I and the rising wave of prosperity following the depression of 1920, and were as conservative as their leaders. The more radical element in the ranks of labor who questioned the policies (or, perhaps, lack of them) of the leaders were bitterly assailed by the spokesmen of the Federation and denounced as radicals. By the end of the decade, however, there were indications that the dissatisfied minority, who realized the stagnant position of the organized labor movement, were rapidly increasing and were anxious to write a new chapter in American labor history.

Closely concerned with the history of American labor since the war has been the radical change in the immigration policy. For decades organized labor had been agitating for greater immigration restrictions, and since the 'eighties the laws had gradually tightened. Organized labor, fearful of a declining wage scale, was now joined by groups of many types who thought that further large-scale immigration was fraught with danger to American institutions. Nor did employers vigorously oppose restriction, for there was practically no labor shortage in the prosperous years of the middle 'twenties. Earlier Acts which had put every conceivable type of undesirable on the restricted list had failed to prevent large-scale immigration, and the restrictionists now turned to the quota system. In 1921 the so-called "quota law" was passed, limiting immigration in any year to 3 per cent of the number of each nationality in the United States according to the Census of 1910. This did not go far enough for ardent restrictionists, and in 1924 a new law was passed changing the quota to 2 per cent of any nationality residing here in 1890. Canadians and Mexicans were exempt, as were travelers, merchants, seamen, and officials; Japanese were debarred under the 1924 Act. This Act not only cut the quota of the 1921 Act in half,[66] but it also favored the "old immigration" from northern and western Europe at the expense of the "new immigration" from eastern and southern Europe.[67] The Immigration Act of 1924 also provided that the numerical quota scheme of 2 per cent of 1890 residents should remain

[66] The quota for 1923 was placed at 357,803, and that for 1924–1925 at 164,667.
[67] F. Flügel and H. U. Faulkner, *Readings*, pp. 865–868.

in force only until 1927, when a "national-origins" method should be applied. Government scientists were to attempt to find out the real origin of the American people as constituted in 1920, and then apportion the immigration among the nationalities, with the total quota immigration limited to 150,000 a year. So much opposition to this law developed that it did not go into effect until July, 1929.[68] Whatever may have been the weaknesses of the immigration legislation of the 1920's, it accomplished its objective—the radical curtailment of immigration. From 1927 until 1933 the number of immigrants declined each year. The years 1927 to 1935 saw more aliens leave this country than were admitted.

SELECTED READINGS

Slosson, P. W., *The Great Crusade and After.*

Chase, Stuart, *Prosperity, Fact or Myth.*

Laidler, H. W., *Concentration in American Industries,* Chap. XXIII.

Berle, A. A., Jr., and Means, G. C., *The Modern Corporation and Private Property,* Chaps. II–V.

Moulton, H. G., and associates, *The American Transportation Problem,* Chaps. XXI–XXXI.

Davis, C. C., "The Development of Agricultural Policy Since the End of the World War," *Yearbook of Agriculture, 1940,* pp. 297–326.

Lorwin, L. L., *The American Federation of Labor,* Chaps. VIII–X.

Perlman, Selig, and Taft, Philip, *History of Labor in the United States, 1896–1932,* Chaps. XXXVII–XLIV.

Williams, B. H., *Economic Foreign Policy of the United States.*

[68] Since July 1, 1929, the annual quota of any nationality for each fiscal year has been a number which bears the same ratio to 150,000 as the number of inhabitants in 1920 having that origin bears to the total number of inhabitants in continental United States in 1920. The 1929 law which gives American consuls power to refuse visas to all applicants who may become "public charges" over here helped to cut down immigration radically during the depression.

Economic Collapse

THE ECONOMIC CYCLE

THE decade of the 'twenties, which many believed had opened a new and never-ending era of prosperity, closed in the most complete economic collapse in American history. Depressions, of course, are not new phenomena; they have occurred intermittently in the United States, as they have in other parts of the capitalist world. American economic history, in fact, might quite logically be written around the story of the recurrent booms and slumps which have characterized our economic life. More than half of this economic life has been wasted in disastrous depression or characterized by overspending, extravagance, and waste of wealth. The crisis years of these cycles (1819, 1837, 1847, 1857, 1873, 1884, 1893, 1903, 1907, 1913, 1920, 1929) stand out as key dates. W. C. Mitchell, a leading American authority, states that ". . . the modern view is that crises are but one feature of recurrent 'business cycles.' . . . A crisis is expected to be followed by a depression, the depression by a revival, the revival by prosperity, and prosperity by a new crisis. Cycles of this sort can be traced for at least a century in America." [1]

As these facts became somewhat obvious, and as a new school of practical or "institutional" economics as distinguished from the older theoretical one emerged, much study was devoted to the problem of the "business cycle." Some economists or pseudo-economists went so far, in fact, as to organize commercial corporations purporting to inform business men, investors, and speculators as to the exact point reached in a cycle at a particular moment. The fact that past cycles had shown certain common tendencies made this seem plausible. A committee appointed by Secretary Hoover in 1921 thus describes the typical cycle:

If we begin the analysis when business is reviving, in general the characteristic features are increased volume of manufacturing, rising stock exchange prices followed by rising commodity prices, then by business expansion and increased

[1] W. C. Mitchell, *Business Cycles and Unemployment*, p. 5.

demand for credit from both business men and speculators. As the result of the advance of commodity prices, money rates stiffen and credit gradually becomes strained, and these conditions may be accompanied by a curtailment of credit for speculative purposes. Then stock exchange prices fall; for a while longer general business continues to increase unevenly, and transportation facilities are overburdened and deliveries are delayed, the apparent shortage of goods is intensified by speculative buying and duplication of orders by merchants and other buyers until credit expansion nears its limit. Public confidence is then shaken, resulting in widespread cancellation of orders if the cycle is extreme. This is always followed by liquidation of inventories and sharp and irregular fall of prices. During the period of depression, there is always more or less widespread unemployment.[2]

This brief but excellent description does not, of course, deal with the special causes or details of a particular cycle. As we glance back over the history of American panics we note that certain causes have been particularly characteristic of this country.[3] In almost every case depression in America has followed an overexpansion of transportation facilities and land speculation. Thus the panic of 1837 was preceded by a boom in canal building; the panics of 1857, 1873, and 1893, by overexpansion in railroad building; and the depression of the 1930's, by extensive automobile and road building. When good public lands were available speculation in them characterized every boom. Even after these were sold, there was tremendous speculation in city real estate and building construction in the boom of the 1920's.

While the direct cause of these recurrent cycles of prosperity and depression in the United States appears to be much the same, there are always some differences, for history never repeats itself in detail. The difficulty of determining all the factors in a complex economic phenomenon is sometimes increased by the fact that economists differ radically in the emphasis which they put on the various causes. Certain students stress the size of bank credits, others the price structure; still others interpret the business cycle as dependent upon distribution of income. Marxian socialists base their explanation upon the labor theory of values. Two leading American students, Veblen and Mitchell, center their explanation around the driving impetus of profits. "Profits," says Mitchell, "are the focus of economic activities in a business economy."[4] In the end, he says, the cycles rest upon "this crucial factor—the prospects of profit."[5] Whatever the causes, one

[2] *Business Cycles and Unemployment,* Report and Recommendations of a Committee of the President's Conference on Unemployment, pp. xii, xiii.
[3] See index under panics.
[4] *Encyclopaedia of the Social Sciences,* III, 102.
[5] W. C. Mitchell, *Business Cycles and Unemployment,* p. 5.

(From H. U. Faulkner, Tyler Kepner, and Hall Bartlett, *The American Way of Life*, Harper & Brothers.)

thing is clear—the lack of stability in our economic life. The only certain factor is continual change.

The terrific havoc wrought by depression, particularly in the years following 1929, has concentrated much attention upon causes and cures. Students with particular theories are inclined to the belief that the elimination of certain causes might solve the problem. For example, those who lay emphasis upon banking credit urge that a better control of banking might prevent depression, those who stress the influence of profits would modify the profit system, and so forth. In any case economists in general hold to the belief that scientific study may discern storm signals and thus forestall collapse, or that by means of regulated competition and social legislation depressions may be prevented or at least mitigated. Whatever "scientific" economics existed in the 'twenties failed utterly to prevent collapse. The Roosevelt administration after March, 1933, approached the problem through the method of regulated competition and social legislation.

CAUSES OF THE COLLAPSE OF 1929

Too short a period, perhaps, has elapsed since the decade of the 'twenties to permit the construction of a complete picture of the economic tendencies of that decade. Nevertheless, certain trends stand out. The prosperity of this period, such as it was, seems to have been in part a "carryover" from the war years. The war, which left Europe impoverished, failed radically to affect the American standard of living. After a brief post-war recession (1919–1921) prosperity returned to many lines of industry and to certain areas of the country. As we have already noted (pp. 608–609), the foundation of this prosperity was primarily the development of the automotive industry and the accompanying boom in road building. Secondly, it was characterized by a boom in urban construction resulting from the scarcity which developed during the war years. Greatly aided by these domestic factors and by an appreciable improvement in general conditions over much of the world, the United States moved into the prosperous years of the middle and later 'twenties. There was widespread demand, aided and abetted by installment buying, for new products, such as radios and household electric equipment. Favorable trade balances enlarged an already unprecedented abundance of gold and on this basis credit expanded and trade developed apace. Private loans on a large scale were made to Europe and South America and the proceeds were spent largely in this country.

While evidences of prosperity were sufficiently numerous to give the decade an appearance of a boom era, there were undoubtedly fundamental flaws in the business structure. Certain industries, notably coal mining, textiles, shipbuilding, railroad equipment and leather manufactures, failed to revive after the post-war depression. More important was the failure of agriculture to respond to the post-war economic recovery. Overexpansion during the war period, the slowing up of population growth, dietary changes of the American people, increased competition from other parts of the world, and the development of economic nationalism in Europe explain in part the condition of the American farmer. The time-honored rôle of American agriculture was twofold: first, to feed the rapidly increasing population of Europe, and second, to provide commodities to exchange with Europe for the capital necessary to develop a new nation. Other new countries were now helping to supply Europe, and as the United States shifted from a debtor to a creditor nation, her industry no longer needed foreign loans. What market the farmer still had in Europe was further curtailed by the exorbitantly high Fordney-McCumber (1922) and Hawley-Smoot (1930) tariffs, which prevented Europe from exchanging manufactured goods for agricultural commodities. Agriculture more definitely than ever was subordinated to industry. The per capita production of major agricultural products in the United States was certainly less in 1930 than in 1920, but relative to the world market demand there was overproduction.

Even in the industries which were prosperous during the 'twenties there were elements tending to undermine the economic structure. Most important, perhaps, was the fact that "there was an increase in the proportion of total income going to profits (including those left in the business) and a corresponding decrease in the relative proportion going to wages and salaries—this in spite of a very considerable increase in real wages, reckoned in terms of commodity buying power."[6] The obvious result of this was the tendency to pile up wealth where it would be used chiefly for the further expansion of industrial units rather than to place it in the hands of those who would use it to purchase manufactured commodities. In conjunction with this another alarming fact was observable: there was little or no upward trend in employment to match the growth of population. In certain industries, such as mining, railroads, and agriculture, the number of persons employed actually declined. Conservative estimates show that even in the boom years the average number of unemployed ran well above a million and a half.[7] In other words, there had been no increase in employment relative to the increase in capital equipment. Much of this was due to what was usually termed "technological unemployment." "Technological unemployment" has been more or less continuous since the Industrial Revolu-

[6] J. M. Clark, *Strategic Factors in Business Cycles*, p. 106.

[7] In the recession years of 1921, 1922, 1924, and 1927 unemployment estimates ran between two and four millions. See Leo Wolman, "Labor," in *Recent Economic Changes*, II, 478.

tion, but it is doubtful if it has ever been more acute than in the period since the First World War.

The domestic picture, consequently, showed continued depression in certain lines and overexpansion in others, accompanied by maldistribution of the profits of industry—conditions which made collapse inevitable. While the domestic situation displayed serious weaknesses those latent in the international economy also contributed largely to our economic collapse. Europe's impoverishment and the high American tariffs made it impossible for Europe to pay her loans to us either in gold or in commodities. Furthermore, the intense nationalism engendered by the war resulted in a new wave of high tariffs throughout Europe. Even England deserted her long-tried policy of free trade to protect her industries, and she was followed enthusiastically by her colonies. There was the tendency during the post-war years for the major portion of the world's gold to move to the United States, a phenomenon which tended to keep prices abnormally high here and to make more difficult the efforts of European governments to return to a gold basis. The economic distress of Europe reacted to create political instability there, this in turn created uncertainty in international finance, and the whole situation made for world economic insecurity.

Increase in stock market speculation is always characteristic of so-called "boom eras." The decade of the 'twenties was no exception. Deluded by the insane propaganda inculcating the belief that prosperity was permanent, at least a million people managed to save enough from their income to speculate in stocks. The influx of hundreds of thousands of new gamblers increased the demand for securities and naturally enhanced prices. The sight of these lambs crowding to be shorn was too much for the captains of industry and finance, and they hastened to print new securities to meet the insatiable demand, or split old stock to make it more easily purchasable. Upon the *bona fide* investor who had no desire to speculate but wanted chiefly to invest his savings, the bankers and bond houses "palmed off" foreign bonds and "guaranteed" real estate mortgages, some of which their own employee experts asserted were too risky to purchase. To catch what surplus funds still remained, banks and bond houses organized "investment trusts" which were often used to manipulate stocks owned by the sponsors of these trusts.

The easy money made in speculation as stock prices mounted stimulated increased interest until speculators talked little about actual values and thought only of future accretions. The traditional basis of judging the value of a stock was "ten times earnings." Some stocks in 1929 were selling at fifty times this, or more. The market, as one expert observed, was discounting not only the future but the hereafter. The speculative frenzy was also accentuated by the retirement of the federal war debt at the rate of $800,000,000 a year, which tended to increase the volume of free funds seeking reinvestment, and also by the disproportionately large amount of the national income which went to capital rather than labor. In the end speculation went to incredible lengths; stocks were selling from three to twenty times their book value, thousands abandoned all interest in their legitimate business in order to concentrate on speculation, and the stock exchange became the dominant topic of conversation at business and social gatherings. So frantic was speculation that, unlike previous cycles, the market price of stocks continued to mount for months after it was obvious that business was receding.

There could be only one end. It came on October 29, 1929.

The big gong had hardly sounded in the great hall of the Exchange at ten o'clock Tuesday morning before the storm broke in full force. Huge blocks of stock were thrown upon the market for what they would bring. . . . Not only were innumerable small traders being sold out, but big ones, too. . . . Again and again the specialist in a stock would find himself surrounded by brokers fighting to sell—and nobody at all even thinking of buying. . . . The scene on the floor was chaotic. . . . Within half an hour of the opening the volume of trading passed three million shares, by twelve o'clock it had passed eight million, by half-past one it had passed twelve million, and when the closing gong brought the day's madness to an end the gigantic record of 16,410,030 shares had been set; . . . the average prices of fifty leading stocks, as compiled by the New York *Times,* had fallen nearly forty points.[8]

THE COURSE OF THE DEPRESSION

The stock market crash of October, 1929, was but the beginning of an economic decline that continued with little interruption until the spring of 1933. Stock prices which had climbed to the most unwarranted heights now dropped to but a small fraction of their former quotations. From September, 1929, to January, 1933, according to the Dow-Jones index, thirty industrial stocks fell from an average of 364.9 to 62.7 dollars per share, a group of twenty public utilities dropped from 141.9 to 28.0 dollars per share, and twenty railroad stocks declined from an average of 180.0 to 28.1 dollars per share. The same story could be told of bank stocks and, as we shall see, of more tangible commodities. When the stock market decline finally hit bottom in July, 1933, some $74,000,000,000, or five-sixths of the September. 1929, value, had disappeared.

Prices of stocks were only a reflection of the business situation as a whole.

[8] F. L. Allen, *Only Yesterday,* pp. 333–334.

A general picture is given by the following index numbers compiled by the United States Bureau of Labor Statistics, using 1926 as a base year with an index number of 100:

	Wholesale Prices	Employment	Payrolls
1929 average	95.3	97.5	100.5
1930 "	86.4	84.7	81.3
1931 "	73.0	72.2	61.5
1932 "	64.8	60.1	41.6
1933 "	65.9	64.6	44.0

The above index numbers on employment when expressed in terms of human beings meant, according to estimates of the American Federation of Labor, that in October, 1930, there were approximately 4,639,000 unemployed; in October, 1931, the number rose to 7,778,000; in October, 1932, to 11,586,000, and early in 1933 to over 13,000,000. These estimates may possibly have been a trifle high, but when it is remembered that a goodly proportion of these unemployed were heads of families upon whose wages others were dependent, the number affected by unemployment ran into many millions more. A fair estimate of the number on public relief late in 1934 was 17,000,000. In addition to the millions thrown out of work, there were a larger number living on reduced incomes. The index numbers of payrolls given above show that the total paid in wages was more than cut in half during the first five years of the depression. As production rests primarily upon the purchasing power of the market it is not at all surprising to find business and industrial activity falling in proportion. One authority puts the nation's production in 1932 as more than 47 per cent below normal,[9] and it was to sink farther in the next few months. An estimate of the physical volume of trade, based on the clearing index of business of the Federal Reserve Bank of New York (1926 = 100), shows a drop from 103 in 1929 to 54 in January, 1933.[10]

In agriculture the situation was somewhat different. The general level of production, as the following figures show, did not change radically for the principal crops:

	Corn (bu.)	Wheat (bu.)	Cotton (bales)
1929	2,622,189,000	806,508,000	14,919,000
1930	2,081,048,000	850,965,000	14,243,000
1931	2,567,306,000	900,219,000	17,097,000
1932	2,908,145,000	726,863,000	12,727,000

[9] Leonard, Ayres, *The Economics of Recovery*, p. 5.
[10] C. A. Beard and G. H. E. Smith, *The Future Comes*, p. 9.

The income of the farmers, however, as we have already noted,[11] declined sharply during these years. Between 1929 and 1932 farm values, already severely deflated, suffered a further decline of 33 per cent and the farmers' gross income declined 57 per cent. When it is remembered that agriculture had been in the throes of a depression ever since the war these figures are extremely significant.

More striking, perhaps, than any of the figures yet given to illustrate the devastation wrought by the depression are those showing the decline in foreign trade:

	Exports (Millions of Dollars)	Imports (Millions of Dollars)
1929	5,241	4,399
1930	3,843	3,061
1931	2,424	2,091
1932	1,611	1,323

For this it is possible to find an abundance of reasons: the decline in purchasing power, not only in the United States but elsewhere in the markets of the world; the cessation after 1929 of American foreign loans which had provided funds for some of this international trade; the premium on the American dollar in international exchange, which discouraged the purchase of American goods; the high tariff policy of the United States, which brought retaliatory tariffs and special discriminations by license or quota devices against American goods. There is no doubt that the collapse in America brought on a depression in Europe which in turn intensified and deepened the economic decline here. Curtailment of American loans forced a similar procedure in England with a freezing of bank credits which ended in precipitating a banking collapse in Germany and Austria. Germany in 1931 defaulted on her war debt and President Hoover, to prevent a further world economic collapse, effected an agreement for the temporary suspension of intergovernmental debts and reparation payments. Shortly afterward Great Britain abandoned the gold standard for a managed currency and was followed by a number of other European countries; this put these nations at a temporary advantage in international commerce at the expense of the gold standard countries including the United States.

The uprising of the world against the American tariff system came after the Hawley-Smoot Act of 1930 which raised the already high duties of the Fordney-McCumber tariff of 1922. In the new tariff the average of all the schedules went up; one-third of the dutiable items were changed, 890 being

[11] Above, pp. 626 ff.

increased, including 50 transfers from the free to the dutiable list; 235 were lowered, including 75 transfers from the dutiable to the free list. Among the commodities removed from the free list were cement, hides, boots, and shoes. The average rate upon agricultural raw materials, according to a White House statement, was raised from 38.10 to 48.92 per cent, while the rate on other commodities was increased from 31.02 to 34.30 per cent.[12] The general average of the increase may not have been tremendously high, but the general effect appears to have been unfortunate in accelerating a trade decline and in arousing antagonism in other parts of the world. Some opposition developed among farmers and large manufacturers with surpluses to export; more from bankers with billions invested in foreign loans, the payment of which was largely dependent upon the export trade of the debtor nations; and more than a thousand economists petitioned the President not to sign the bill. President Hoover, however, insisted that the new tariff would improve the economic situation and that any striking defects might be eliminated by the flexible provision allowing him to make changes upon recommendation of the Tariff Commission, a provision retained from the previous tariff.[13]

Regarding the severity of the depression, statistics could be quoted almost without end. By 1934 most students agreed with Colonel Ayres who, in discussing the decline of production, maintained that "this depression has been far more severe than any of the 20 major depressions that we have experienced in this country since 1790."[14] On the other hand, there is little unanimity as to the reasons for the unique severity of this particular débâcle. One economist has suggested two reasons—the uneven decline in prices and the long-drawn-out series of crises in credit.[15] For various reasons already discussed, agricultural prices slumped rapidly, but the prices of manufactured commodities, influenced by wage agreements and monopoly practices, held up longer. The utter collapse of the buying power of millions of farmers curtailed radically the business of workers and manufacturers and accentuated the depression. The series of credit crises was due primarily to the weakness of the American banking system and the unsettlement of European finances which culminated in 1931 when Great Britain went off the gold standard. The fact that 6987 of our banks failed in the decade ending in 1930, to which were added 2294 failures in 1931 and 1456 in 1932, explains much.

[12] *Commerce Year Book, 1930,* p. 13. It is estimated that the average for the dutiable articles in the McKinley tariff was 48.39 per cent; in the Wilson-Gorman tariff, 41.29; in the Dingley bill, 46.49; in the Payne-Aldrich, 40.73; in the Fordney-McCumber, 38.24; and in the Hawley-Smoot Bill (based on imports for 1928), 41.57 per cent. *Ibid.,* pp. 437–438.

[13] F. W. Taussig, "The Tariff Act of 1930," *Quarterly Journal of Economics,* XIV, 1–21 (November, 1930).

[14] Leonard Ayres, *The Economics of Recovery,* p. 5.

[15] *Ibid.,* p. 5 ff.

Another explanation offered for the severity was the terrific public and private debt which had been built up out of all proportion to the national income.[16] Still another explanation was the large amount invested during the preceding years in such durable goods as automobiles whose replacement could be delayed, thus retarding recovery.[17] Another explanation frequently offered is the coincidence of much technological unemployment with the coming of the depression. To these may be added certain factors tending to accentuate the depression and delay recovery—world economic conditions; the increasing competition faced by the American farmer from other parts of the world; the collapse of the foreign market for industrial products, emphasized by the establishment of American factories in foreign countries to avoid their tariffs; the collapse of the foreign market as a place for safe investment; the continued concentration of wealth and income; the growing rigidity of the price system (due to increased business consolidation) and the failure of prices in certain lines to respond to deflation; and, finally, the difficulty of putting labor back to work because of labor-saving machinery. It looked as if American agriculture, industry, banking, and labor had indeed entered a new era, but not the dazzling "new era" predicted in the dreams of the inflated 'twenties.

EARLY EFFORTS TOWARD RECOVERY

The depression following the stock market crash of 1929 was not only the most severe in our history, but also the first one in which the federal government entered aggressively into the situation to alleviate conditions. During earlier panics the government did little except to safeguard its own credit and sit by until the storms blew over. This was partly because earlier generations did not know what to do, or because, dominated by a *laissez-faire* philosophy, they did not consider it the function of government to interfere in economic life to this extent. This does not mean that depressions did not eventually have an effect in speeding certain reform legislation, but it usually came after the event. The days had passed when a government could sit by calmly and let its people suffer without some gesture of help. Too many revolutions had taken place in the world during the previous decade as a result of economic conditions, and too great a change had occurred in the philosophy of governmental functions for any government to adopt a do-nothing policy.

Despite the fact that the Hoover administration prided itself on its adherence to *laissez faire* and glorified "rugged individualism," it made definite efforts to stay the economic collapse. This has given certain Republicans

---

[16] C. A. Beard and G. H. E. Smith, *The Future Comes*, p. 9.
[17] J. M. Clark, *Strategic Factors in Business Cycles*, p. 108.

who are sympathetic toward the "New Deal" an opportunity to claim Hoover as its originator. Be that as it may, after the stock market crash of 1929 the President called a series of conferences which resulted in the expenditure of many hundreds of millions of dollars by federal and state governments and private corporations. Under the authority of the Agricultural Marketing Act passed about four months before the crash,[18] the Federal Farm Board created a Grain Stabilization Corporation and a Cotton Stabilization Corporation whose purpose it was to raise the prices of those commodities. Beginning in 1930, both corporations went into the market and by actual purchase of these commodities, or of "futures" in them, succeeded for a brief period in maintaining their prices at levels slightly higher than the world market averages. Altogether almost half a billion was spent to support the prices of farm commodities, but the net result, except for a loss of some $148,000,000 to the American taxpayer, appears to have been nil. While the Federal Farm Board was frantically attempting to stay the decline of agricultural prices, the government, after Congress in 1931 passed a bonus bill over the President's veto, released almost a billion dollars[19] which offered temporary relief to needy veterans but utterly failed to prime the pump of economic recovery.

The continuance of the depression in conjunction with the coming presidential campaign led to a renewed effort in 1932 on the part of the Hoover administration to improve the economic situation. In January of that year Congress created the Reconstruction Finance Corporation (RFC), with a capital of $500,000,000 and power to incur debts to three times that amount. Originally designed to aid in financing agriculture, commerce, and industry, its scope was enlarged by a new Act passed in July, which authorized the lending of $1,800,000,000 to states, cities, and other government agencies for self-liquidating public projects and for direct relief. In addition, the federal government was authorized to spend $322,000,000 on public works; and a special Act provided for the creation of from eight to twelve banks with a capital of $5,000,000, each with a share in a government subsidy of $125,000,000, for the purpose of aiding in the building of homes. Under Roosevelt the functions of the RFC were extended even more widely, with the result that during the first year and a half of its operation it loaned about $3,000,000,000. The philosophy of the Hoover administration, it appeared, was to rehabilitate

---

[18] Above, pp. 629–630.

[19] The Bonus Bill of 1924 provided for service certificates which would mature in twenty years and against which a veteran might borrow up to 22½ per cent of the matured value. The Act of 1931 raised this to 50 per cent. In 1936 a new Bonus Act was passed over the President's veto; it provided for the redemption of the adjusted service certificates held by the government life insurance fund by means of exchanging them for 3 per cent bonds which in turn might be converted into cash.

the economic structure from the top down. This meant, of course, the ladling out of public credit to many blind and incapable leaders who had helped bring the nation to its unfortunate state. Nevertheless, there is no doubt that the RFC saved many a tottering bank, railroad, and insurance company from collapse, and in that way eased the strain in one of the most acute periods.

POLITICAL REACTIONS

That the economic depression would have its political reactions was perfectly obvious. Only one American President, James Monroe, ever politically survived a major economic depression, and he was probably saved only by the fact that there was no strong political party to oppose him. Hoover, as it turned out, was no exception to the rule. The congressional elections of 1930 wiped out the Republican majority in the House and cut their majority in the Senate to the slimmest margin. As the presidential election of 1932 approached, it became even clearer that the Hoover administration had no policy beyond an effort to cushion the depression—a policy which to most people seemed utterly inadequate.

Although the platforms of the two parties in 1932 were much alike and considerable attention was devoted during the campaign to the question of prohibition, there was only one real issue—the depression. Hoover and his spokesmen tried to convince the voters that the Republicans had accomplished all that could be done safely and that a Democratic victory would precipitate an even greater economic collapse. The Democratic candidate, Franklin D. Roosevelt, presented his views on economic problems in a series of speeches. He spoke in general terms but he implied that a change in policies would improve conditions. In brief, he promised a "New Deal." This was enough. The Democrats were overwhelmingly victorious not only in the national elections but also in state and local elections. For the first time since 1919 the Democratic party had control of both the legislative and executive branches. What the "New Deal" would mean in practice no one knew, but if the new administration had any real program with which to meet a major economic catastrophe, their opportunity had come.

SELECTED READINGS

Hacker, L. M., *American Problems of Today,* Chap. VII.

Mitchell, W. O., "Business Cycles," *Encyclopaedia of the Social Sciences,* Vol. III, pp. 92–106.

Shultz, W. J., and Caine, M. R., *Financial Development of the United States,* Chap. XXVII.

Dumond, D. L., *From Roosevelt to Roosevelt,* Chaps. XI, XII, XV.

Clark, J. M., *Strategic Factors in Business Cycles,* pp. 96–124.

30.

The New Deal

Beginnings of the New Deal

THE beginning of the year 1933 saw the most acute stage of the depression. General business had sunk to less than 60 per cent of normal, steel output during January was but 15 per cent of capacity, commodity prices had declined in that month to the lowest point since the beginning of the depression, and American exports for November, 1932 ($139,000,000), marked the lowest monthly total in thirty years. Estimates of the number of unemployed ran from 13,000,000 to over 17,000,000. Even more serious, possibly, was the fact that the credit and banking structure was rapidly crumbling to collapse. During 1932 over 1400 banks had failed, and the year opened with little confidence. The banking situation reached its climax on February 14, when leading banks in Detroit closed and the state of Michigan declared an eight-day banking moratorium. This action was quickly followed elsewhere until by March 2 there were 21 states, besides the District of Columbia, where either moratoria had been established or the banks were operating under special regulation. On the day of Roosevelt's inauguration New York and Illinois declared bank holidays which closed the stock and commodity markets in the country's greatest financial centers, New York City and Chicago.

In the face of this critical and unprecedented situation the new President acted with unexpected celerity. He immediately called Congress into special session for the purpose of passing relief legislation and on March 5 declared a nation-wide bank moratorium and placed an embargo on the withdrawal or transportation of gold and silver. When Congress met on March 9 there was prepared for it an Emergency Banking Act which confirmed the order and proclamation of the President and gave him emergency powers to regulate transactions in credit, currency, gold and silver, and foreign exchange. It empowered the Secretary of the Treasury to require deposit of all gold and gold certificates and authorized the Comptroller to appoint a conservator for any national bank in difficulty and for the reorganization of such banks. It provided that national and state banks which were members of the Federal

Reserve System might open under license, and it sought to strengthen the position of these banks by empowering the RFC to purchase their preferred stock or take it as collateral for loans. To help break the credit *impasse,* the note-issuing power of the Federal Reserve banks was enlarged. On March 13 the bank moratorium officially came to an end when banks which had obtained licenses were reopened.

Altogether, during the special session of the Seventy-third Congress, that body passed almost a score of major Acts dealing with various aspects of the economic situation, which roughly comprise what the nation came to term the "New Deal." In addition to the Emergency Banking Act Congress passed during March at least two others which should be noted. The first was a Beer and Wine Act that permitted, in states so desiring, the manufacture and sale of malt and vinous liquors having an alcoholic content of not more than 3.2 per cent by weight and 4 per cent by volume.[1] The second was an Act empowering the President to employ men in a Citizens' Civilian Conservation Corps to construct public works in connection with reforestation, flood control, and similar projects, in an effort to relieve unemployment among the younger men. During the first year over 300,000 enrolled in the Citizens' Conservation camps. A pet project of the administration, the Citizens' Conservation Corps was maintained as a permanent feature of the New Deal policy until Congress finally ended its appropriations in 1942.

A NEW DEAL FOR AGRICULTURE

The Acts of March, 1933, just mentioned were but the opening guns in the battle against depression. In that month the administration sent to Congress its program for agricultural relief, which was enacted in May as the Farm Relief and Inflation Act, better known as the Agricultural Adjustment Act. The theory behind this Act was simple enough: agriculture was suffering a depression because of low prices resulting from a surplus; eliminate the surplus, and prices would automatically rise and prosperity would return to agriculture. The administration proceeded to follow this formula with an enthusiasm which hardly envisaged the complexities of the agricultural situation. Under the authorization of this Act the Agricultural Adjustment Administration (AAA) moved to cut the surplus and raise the income of the farmers by three methods: (1) by cotton options under which cotton growers were to reduce their cotton acreage at least 30 per cent and for which they were given options to purchase an amount of cotton corresponding to the

[1] Congress had already in the closing days of the Hoover administration sent to the states an amendment repealing Amendment XVIII. Ratification of Amendment XXI (1933) placed the whole liquor problem, as far as the federal government was concerned, back where it had been before 1919.

amount they agreed not to raise, cotton which was still held by the former Federal Farm Board and which the option holders might sell if prices went up; (2) by "rental" or benefit payments under which the government gave bonuses for acreage temporarily taken out of cultivation; and (3) by marketing agreements which might eliminate waste and provide for more scientific marketing. The cost was to be paid by processing taxes levied on products manufactured from the basic commodities concerned. The object of the Act was to restore the farmers' buying power to its pre-war level.[2]

Under arrangements of this type the administration in 1933 obtained over 1,000,000 adjustment contracts from cotton growers, removed over 10,000,000 acres from cultivation, and practically doubled the income of the cotton growers over their 1932 returns. A somewhat similar result was obtained with the wheat crop; strenuous and partly successful efforts were made to improve the situation for the producers of hogs, corn, and tobacco; and some forty marketing agreements were made for various other agricultural commodities. This program seemed sufficiently successful to enlarge its operation in 1934 to include beef and dairy cattle, peanuts, rye, barley, flax, grain sorghums, sugar beets, and sugar cane; the tobacco and cotton curtailment programs were strengthened by special Acts. At the same time the government encouraged submarginal farmers to retire from commercial agriculture and attempted through trade agreements (reciprocal tariffs) to stimulate foreign trade in agricultural commodities.

No part of the New Deal program inspired more widespread criticism than that pertaining to agriculture. The whole idea of curtailing the production of foodstuffs while millions were on the point of starvation seemed to humanitarians like a scheme verging on insanity. An effort to promote a "scarcity economy" at a time when the opposite was needed seemed incredible. Furthermore, it largely shifted the burden to the hard-pressed consumer. Even from the point of view of scarcity economics, however, there was no clear-cut proof in the early months that the program was successful. Despite government efforts, the violation of acreage reduction contracts, favorable climatic conditions, and more intensive farming produced crops of cotton, corn, and hogs in 1933 not much below those of 1932. While the controlled crops were reduced, farmers turned to other crops. The sudden increase in the cost of foodstuffs brought consumer resistance, and the general rise in

---

[2] The policy was thus specifically stated in the Act:

"To establish and maintain such balance between the production and consumption of agricultural commodities, and such marketing conditions therefor, as will reestablish prices to farmers at a level that will give agricultural commodities a purchasing power with respect to articles that farmers buy, equivalent to the purchasing power of agricultural commodities in the base period. The base period in the case of all agricultural commodities except tobacco shall be the pre-war period, August, 1909–July, 1914. In the case of tobacco, the base period shall be the post-war period, August, 1919–July, 1929."

prices kept the purchasing power of the farmer's dollar about where it had been. Likewise, American curtailment stimulated foreign agricultural production. Nor were the prospects of increased foreign trade through reciprocal tariffs particularly bright for the farmers because in some cases such tariffs were bound to bring foreign agricultural products in greater competition with domestic products.

Despite these disadvantages there was no question as to the fact that the economic condition of the farmers rapidly improved. Early in 1935 the AAA noted that the purchasing power of units of farm products in 1934 averaged 73 per cent of the pre-war level, as compared with 55 per cent at the low point in March, 1933; that the purchasing power of the farmers' net income in 1934 was nearly 80 per cent of the pre-war level, as compared with 52 per cent in 1932; and that their per capita share of the national income was 80 per cent of the pre-war level, as compared with 60 per cent in 1932. Although some of this improvement was undoubtedly due to the government's agricultural program, part of it must have been attributable to the general economic improvement.

Whatever may have been the contributions of the Agricultural Adjustment Act, they were greatly curtailed when in January, 1936, the Supreme Court declared parts of the Act unconstitutional on the grounds that it invaded the reserved rights of the states and was an improper use of the taxing power. The strong probability that this might happen had led the government to canvass the possibilities of continuing agricultural relief in some other way, and the method decided upon was soil conservation. The drought of 1934 and the dust storms in the spring of 1935 called attention to the tragic results of soil destruction, and Congress recognized the problem by creating in 1933 a Soil Erosion Service and by enacting in 1935 the Soil Erosion Act. This legislation created the Soil Conservation Service, under the Secretary of Agriculture, to conduct soil erosion surveys and carry out preventive measures. The scope of this work was greatly enlarged after the AAA decision by the Soil Conservation and Domestic Allotment Act (1936), which appropriated $500,000,000 for the preservation and improvement of soil fertility, the promotion of the economic use and conservation of land, and the protection of rivers and harbors against soil erosion. For two years direct aid might be given to cooperating farmers, after which it was to be extended only to states that had adopted authorizing legislation and a conservation plan acceptable to the Secretary of Agriculture.

The Soil Conservation and Domestic Allotment Act was a makeshift. By 1938 the Supreme Court had become more sympathetic to New Deal policies and Congress determined to pass new agricultural legislation. The Agricultural Adjustment Act of 1938 retained certain features of the old

Acts and added new ones. Its primary aim, as in earlier Acts, was to establish "parity prices," that is, to maintain the prices of certain agricultural products (wheat, cotton, corn, tobacco, and rice) at a level in relation to the cost of commodities bought by farmers in 1909–1914.[3] This was to be achieved by the government setting a "parity price" each year for the commodity to be raised. If the price fell below this, the government would in part recompense the farmer for the difference between the actual price received and the "parity price." If production in any year was far beyond the amount set by the government, marketing quotas might be established if two-thirds of the farmers producing that commodity agreed. Such agreements would be enforced by penalty taxes for selling beyond the quota. In determining the amount of a commodity to be raised in a year, the Department of Agriculture was to include a surplus so that in case of drought or other emergency a sufficient quantity would always be on hand. This policy, a new feature of the Act, was expected to maintain an "ever-normal granary." Another new feature was the establishment of insurance on wheat. The maintenance of soil resources as provided in the Soil Conservation and Allotment Act was retained as a permanent policy.[4]

As its name suggests, the Farm Relief and Inflation Act (AAA) provided for an agricultural program far broader than merely increasing prices through crop curtailment. In addition to the broad inflationary powers, which will be discussed in the next section, the Act was designed to aid the farmers' credit situation by authorizing the Federal Land banks to issue $2,000,000,000 in 4 per cent bonds—the interest but not the principal to be guaranteed by the government—to refinance farm mortgages at an interest rate not to exceed 4½ per cent. To increase efficiency the President in 1933 consolidated the government's various agricultural credit agencies in the Farm Credit Administration. This consolidation, authorized under the Farm Credit Act (June, 1933), grouped the credit facilities into four divisions dealing with land banks, production credit, intermediate credit, and cooperative credit, and considerably enlarged existing facilities.

Even the wide ramifications of the federal agricultural credit facilities did not seem to cover the mortgage problem adequately; consequently three additional Acts were passed in 1934: (1) the Farm Mortgage Refinancing Act, creating a Federal Farm Mortgage Corporation to aid further in refinancing farm debts by guaranteeing as to both principal and interest federal bonds exchanged for consolidated farm loan bonds; (2) a Farm Mortgage Foreclosure Act, extending the authority of the Land Bank Commissioner to

[3] For tobacco the years 1919–1929 were to be used. See above, p. 653.
[4] Congress in 1940 appropriated $438,560,000 for conservation projects and $225,000,000 for parity payments on cotton, corn, rice and tobacco.

enable him to make loans to farmers for the purpose of enabling them to redeem farm properties owned by them prior to foreclosure; and (3) the Frazier-Lemke Bankruptcy Act, providing that in cases of bankruptcy the farmer might demand a "fair and reasonable" appraisal and might repurchase his property over a period of six years with interest at one per cent. If creditor or mortgagee objected to the settlement the farmer might retain the property for a period of five years at a reasonable rental, bankruptcy proceedings being halted. The Frazier-Lemke Act was declared unconstitutional in 1935 as a violation of the fifth amendment, but a similar Act shortening the retention period to three years was upheld in 1936.

A survey of the farm legislation passed during the five years 1933–1938 make clear certain facts. First of all, "economic planning" was carried further with respect to agriculture than to any other economic interest. The government took upon itself the responsibility of attempting to determine both production and prices as well as maintaining soil resources and handling most of the credit resources of the farmers. In the second place, this program was carried out at the expense of the consumer. Agriculture was to be a favored industry, with the taxpayer and consumer paying the bill. This, of course, did not disturb the farmer; he insisted that agriculture was now merely receiving protection as industry had long received it through the protective tariff. Finally, it should be noted that the government entered so definitely into the program of financing agriculture that by 1937 its agencies held about half of the long-term agricultural paper of the country. This was indeed a big step from the *laissez-faire* policies of a quarter century earlier.

CURRENCY AND CREDIT

In every major depression experienced by the United States there has been a strong demand for inflation. By 1933 the clamor became so insistent that it could not be denied. The arguments for inflation rested, of course, primarily upon the fact that the increased value of the dollar bore heavily upon the debtor class who compose the great majority of the population, and that restoration of currency values to the level at which the debts were contracted was necessary to restore equilibrium between debtor and creditor and thus halt the economic collapse. Mention has already been made of efforts to improve the credit situation in the Emergency Banking Act (p. 651) and in the Agricultural Adjustment Act (p. 652). The latter gave the President the power, if he desired to exercise it, (1) to require the Federal Reserve banks to expand their credit up to $3,000,000,000; (2) to issue United States notes secured solely on the credit of the United States up to $3,000,000,000, these notes to be used only to retire outstanding federal obligations but to be legal tender for all debts, public and private; (3) to devalue the gold dollar by as much as 50 per cent; and (4) to accept silver for six months up to $200,000,000, at a price not exceeding 50 cents an ounce, in payment of war debts due from foreign governments. This Act gave him power to inflate in almost any way he pleased. He could print more paper money, the old demand of the Greenbackers. He could buy more silver, the old cry of the silver group in the 1880's and 1890's.

Under the authority of these two Acts inflation may be said to have begun with Executive Orders of March 10, 1933, halting the export of gold except when licensed by the Treasury; of April 5, forbidding the hoarding of gold and gold certificates; and of April 19, forbidding the export of gold. The last is generally regarded as taking the nation off the gold standard. This was technically true, but as the gold was impounded in the Treasury it remained, in the words of economists, a "psychological reserve." This was made more definite by the Gold Repeal Joint Resolution of June 5 which canceled the gold clauses in public and private obligations, making debts payable in legal tender. A rise in prices in the spring and early summer of 1933 halted for the moment further tinkering with the currency, but their decline in the early autumn simultaneously with the marketing of summer crops revived agitation for inflation.

It was at this point that the administration decided to attempt inflation by reducing the gold content of the dollar. Beginning in September the Treasury was ordered to accept gold from producers for resale at the world price. When this did not secure the desired result, the President on October 22 announced that the Treasury would buy gold at a price determined by the RFC. Instead of the long-established legal price of $20.67 an ounce, the price was initially set at $31.36 and eventually raised to $34.45 (January 16, 1934). This operation was carried out in practice by giving sellers of gold more paper dollars for the same amount of gold than they had previously received. As long as the government could peg the price of gold in the open market it could theoretically devalue the dollar and raise prices. To the surprise of the advocates of this scheme, prices did not rise proportionately to the depreciation of the dollar; and on December 21 the President ordered the Treasury to purchase at 64½ cents an ounce all of the silver mined in the United States; this price was 21½ cents higher than that at which silver was then selling on the open market.

When the President inaugurated the gold purchase plan in October, 1933, he declared as his objective the desire "to make possible the payment of public and private debts more nearly at the price level at which they were incurred," and stated that he was "moving toward a managed currency." That he might have even more clear-cut authorization, he asked Congress in January, 1934, for legislation containing specific power to devalue the dollar to between 50 and 60 cents in terms of its former gold content, to manage the dollar within these limits, to impound in the Treasury the gold held in the Federal Reserve banks, to assure to the government the profits that might accrue from devaluing the dollar, and, finally, to use part of this profit to create a $2,000,000,000 fund to stabilize the dollar. Under the authority of this Act the value of the dollar was officially fixed in February at 59.06 per cent of its former (1900) value in terms of gold. Three months later it was discovered that while the gold content of the dollar had been reduced by law 40.94 per cent, wholesale commodity prices had risen only 22 per cent. At the insistent clamor of the silver advocates the administration consented to further legislation, and in June, 1934, the Silver Purchase Act was passed, the "ultimate objective" of which was to increase the use of silver in the nation's monetary stock until the proportions were one-quarter in silver to three-quarters in gold.

In the particular method it pursued to raise prices the administration appeared to have been influenced by the school of economists who hold that the price level of commodities is closely influenced by the gold content of the monetary medium. That such a relationship exists, no one will deny, but it proved to be no short cut to inflation. The fact that nine-tenths of the nation's business is conducted on bank credit rather than with money is a partial explanation for the failure of the government's inflation policy to raise prices to the extent expected. It also helps to explain the shift of inflationary efforts from currency to credit and is a clear indication of the necessity of repairing the credit system and the importance of extending credit. This process had begun, in fact, during the Hoover administration with the establishment of the Reconstruction Finance Corporation. The powers of the RFC, as we have seen, were extended under the Emergency Banking Act (p. 652) and again in June, 1934, when the Loans-to-Industry Act authorized direct loans to industrial organizations up to $580,000,000. The latter Act aroused considerable criticism on the ground that it was poor economy to attempt to save the weaker units in an already overbuilt industrial system, but the great need of keeping men at work was the important argument for the loans. A further effort to stabilize the credit situation, and at the same time save the small home owner, began in 1932 with the Home Loan Bank Act, which established federal banks to lend to private banks and building and loan associations on real estate mortgages. This was supplemented in 1933 by the Home Owner's Loan Act, setting up a corporation which could issue bonds up to $2,000,000,000 to refinance first mortgages on homes whose value did not exceed $20,000. Interest on the bonds was guaranteed and an amendment of 1934 extended this guarantee to the principal. The lending activities of this corporation lasted for three years, when they were taken over by the Federal Housing Administration, which also insured against losses from loans on real estate. Any discussion of inflationary possibilities through extension of credit would also include consideration of the credit facilities extended to agriculture through various channels (pp. 655–656).

The tragic shortcomings of the American banking system had been amply demonstrated, during both the boom years of the 'twenties and the depression years of the 'thirties. Reform of some sort would have been inevitable under any administration. That adopted by the Democrats was incorporated in two Acts, the Banking Act (Glass-Steagall Act) of June, 1933, and the Banking Act of 1935. The most widely discussed and perhaps the most important parts of the 1933 legislation were those which separated security affiliates from the parent banks in the Federal Reserve System and those which set up a Federal Deposit Insurance Corporation to provide insurance on deposits.[5] The provision requiring banks to relinquish their security affiliates confined them again to a strictly banking business, and the insurance scheme was devised to safeguard the almost defenseless depositor. Under the latter all Federal Reserve banks were required to insure, and state banks approved as solvent by the state banking authorities might participate. Other clauses in the Act restricted the use of Federal Reserve bank credit for stock market speculation, broadened the power of national banks to establish branch banks in those states that permitted branch banking, restrained national banks from dealing in the securities of foreign countries and other foreign securities, forbade private banks that conduct a business of underwriting and promoting the sale of securities from acting as banks of deposit, and established a quick liquidating procedure for the benefit of depositors in banks that had failed. There were many who wished that the Glass-Steagall Act had gone farther on the road of banking reform; nevertheless, it was an honest effort to rectify some of the worst abuses which had developed since the establishment of the Federal Reserve system in 1913.

In the Banking Act of 1935 an important effort was made to extend federal power over money and credit. Although the amount insurable under the Federal Deposit Insurance Corporation was reduced, the supervisory powers of that corporation were considerably extended. In the second place, the Federal Reserve Board was reorganized into a seven-member board by eliminating the Secretary of the Treasury and the Comptroller from ex-officio membership, in the hope of lessening political influence and making

---

[5] This Act provided for total insurance up to $10,000, 75 per cent between that sum and $50,000, and 50 per cent on sums over $50,000, but these provisions were not to go into effect until 1934. As an interim measure deposits up to $2500 were insured. The temporary provision was extended to 1935 when the original insurance features of the 1933 Act were discarded and a limit of $5000 was set to the amount insured.

it more impartial and disinterested. In the third place, the credit policy of the separate banks was transferred from their jurisdiction to that of a Federal Open Market Committee made up of the seven members of the Board and five regional representatives of the Reserve banks. In the fourth place, the Board may now vary within certain limits the reserve requirements of the member banks and may review every two weeks the rates charged by the Reserve banks, and it must give its approval to appointments for president and vice president of each Reserve bank. Finally, certain technical changes enlarged the credit facilities. The Federal Reserve banks, for example, may make advances to their members on any satisfactory security and member banks may make a larger volume of real estate loans. The latter provision is an acknowledgment of the fact that American commercial banks are also, to a considerable extent, savings banks.

The widespread popular resentment against the banks and security houses which had foisted securities of questionable value upon a gullible public also brought about, in May, 1933, the passage of the Sale of Securities Act which sought to protect prospective investors by affording them certain information regarding new securities sold in interstate commerce. Under this Act a concern offering securities was required to file detailed information with the Federal Trade Commission (later with a newly created commission, the Securities and Exchange Commission), and even after approval was granted by the Commission sellers might be held liable in civil or criminal suits for untrue statements. This was a preliminary to another Act, the Securities Exchange Act of June, 1934 (amended in 1936 to include unlisted securities), which provided for the regulation of securities exchanges and established a Securities and Exchange Commission to supervise them. Both Acts were bitterly opposed by the financial interests and in the second Act they succeeded in reducing the liability of underwriters, officers, and directors of the concerns issuing securities as originally provided in the Sale of Securities Act. Regulation of a somewhat similar type was extended to certain agricultural commodities in 1936 by the Commodity Exchange Act, which set up a Commodity Exchange Commission to regulate transactions on commodity futures exchanges, to limit or abolish short selling, and to curb manipulation. The general purpose of all these Acts was obviously to control speculation, eliminate dishonest manipulation, and protect the investor. To what extent this objective may be reached only experience can tell.

Industry and the New Deal

Perhaps the most important single piece of legislation during the first year of the Roosevelt administration was a two-year emergency measure known as the National Industrial Recovery Act (NIRA). The general purpose of the Act was to provide work for the millions of unemployed by putting into effect an extensive program of public works and by stimulating industry. Part of this, it was hoped, might be accomplished by a bond issue of $3,300,-000,000 to finance the construction of federal, state, and local projects to create employment, for which new taxes were provided. The other part of the Act gave the President and his administrators wide powers to promote self-regulation of industry under federal supervision, to curtail overproduction, increase wages, shorten hours of labor, and raise prices. To accomplish this the President was authorized to work out codes of fair competition which industry was to accept voluntarily but with which through a system of licensing the President might force compliance. Behind this Act was the theory that the efforts of the older anti-trust Acts to maintain unlimited competition had brought disaster and that in their place, at least temporarily, should be substituted an attempt to establish industrial cooperation under government control. Technically the anti-trust Acts were still in force; actually they were pushed in the background. "History," said the President, "probably will record the National Industrial Recovery Act as the most far-reaching legislation ever enacted by the American Congress."

To carry out this part of the NIRA a National Recovery Administration (NRA) was set up under the direction of General Hugh S. Johnson as administrator and Donald Richberg as general counsel. These men, with a staff of expert assistants in cooperation with representatives of industry and labor, drew up what were believed to be fair codes, held public hearings, and finally promulgated the codes over the President's signature. As several thousand industries were eligible for codification and the duration of the Act was only two years, the first problem was to decide whether it would be better to hammer out a few perfect codes for the basic industries or to formulate as many as possible as quickly as possible in the hope that defects could be eventually ironed out. The latter course was followed; but as a stopgap until separate codes could be drawn, a blanket agreement on hours and wages, known as the President's Reemployment Agreement, was promulgated in July. This blanket code banned child labor, established a working week of 35 hours for industrial workers and 40 for white-collar workers, and set minimum wages of 40 cents per hour for industry and from $12 to $15 per week for others depending on the size of the community. Employers who would adhere to this temporary agreement (to last six months but later extended to May 1, 1934) would receive the symbol of the Blue Eagle. In the meantime Washington took on a hectic atmosphere reminiscent of war days as representatives of industrial trade associations and labor unions flocked to the Capitol to participate in code-making. By May, 1934, almost a year after the Act was passed, more than 400 codes had been signed and hearings had been completed on an additional 300; it was estimated that about 20,000,000 workers were under the Blue Eagle.

No effort to codify and integrate industry on such a scale had ever before been made in America, and the difficulties were great. The desperate condition in which the nation found itself, however, created, at least in the early months, a willingness to cooperate in carrying the NIRA into effect. Nevertheless, there was criticism from the start. There were frequent charges that the codes were evaded ("chiseling") and that the interests of the consumer were ignored in making the codes. Unorganized and inadequately represented as this group was, their complaint had a strong basis in fact. But as the months went by, criticism also developed rapidly on the part of labor, which insisted that there had been widespread evasion of those parts of the codes applying to labor, especially of the spirit and intention of Section 7 (a) of the National Industrial Recovery Act, which guaranteed the right of labor to organize and be represented by persons of their own choosing (below, p. 668). In the end there was considerable opposition also from industry, particularly from the small manufacturer who felt that the codes favored the larger unit.[6] The barrage of criticism culminated in the textile strike of September, 1934, the resignation of Johnson, and the reorganization of the National Recovery Administration. In the face of the criticism the administration claimed that the NIRA had lifted the nation out of its economic slough and put it on the road to recovery. Many opponents, on the other hand, asserted that it had delayed recovery. This is one of those controversial problems the truth of which can never be ascertained. Certainly, as we shall see, labor gained important initial benefits, industry escaped temporarily from the anti-trust laws, and there was an improvement in the general economic situation. Only the consumer seemed lost in the shuffle.

Whatever may have been the gains or losses through the organization of industry under the NIRA, the whole question became largely academic when the Supreme Court in the Schechter case (May, 1935) held that the code-making provisions in the NIRA were an invalid transfer of the legislative power from Congress to the President and that the attempt to regulate industry in the manner prescribed was an improper use of the interstate commerce power. The result of the decision, which was unanimous, was to liquidate the NRA quickly. Despite the decision, Congress tried to maintain its principles in one of the nation's most demoralized industries. In the Bituminous Coal Conservation Act (1935) the mining of bituminous

---

[6] This point of view was stressed in the report by the National Recovery Review Board, created in February, 1934, which contended that the NRA was fostering monopoly and that codes were administered by monopolists to oppress small industrialists, distributors, and consumers.

coal was declared "affected with a national public interest" and a National Bituminous Coal Commission was set up to formulate a bituminous coal code and determine minimum wages and hours. Labor, as under the NIRA, was given the "right to organize and bargain collectively through representatives of their own choosing," and the Act was to be enforced by a 15 per cent excise tax imposed on the sale price at the mines, nine-tenths of which was to be returned to those producers who accepted the code. Without committing itself on the price-fixing clause, the Court in 1936 declared this Act unconstitutional, but early in 1937 Congress came back with new legislation (Vinson-Guffey Act) to regulate the industry, this time without the labor provisions.

It is clear from a study of the above legislation that during the early years of the New Deal the government was in a mood to soften the anti-trust legislation in order to restrain unbridled competition. This attitude was also evident in later legislation. The Robinson-Patman Act of 1936 made illegal the sale of goods where there was discrimination between individuals and localities or where the price was so low as to destroy competition or eliminate a competitor. This Act, which was obviously directed against chain stores, was expected to give relief to the local storekeeper. In the meantime various states had attempted to aid this group by legislation allowing agreements between manufacturers and their distributors or retailers which fixed minimum prices for trade-marked commodities. This was made national by the Miller-Tidings Act of 1937, which amended the Sherman Anti-trust Act.

Interestingly enough, the attitude of the administration toward monopoly appeared to change about 1938. Believing that the recession of 1937 and 1938 was in part caused by high monopoly prices, President Roosevelt asked Congress for funds for a full investigation by a special committee. These were granted and much interesting material was brought to light, particularly with reference to the patent laws and the monopoly conditions existing under them. After 1938 the anti-monopoly division of the Attorney General's office became increasingly active in opposing monopoly practices.

The activities of no type of American industry have been more subject to criticism in recent years than those of the public utilities, and this criticism began long before the depression. Inflated financial structures which bore little actual relation to the money invested or to the value of the property, and a complicated structure of holding companies imposed one upon the other, so confused the investing and consuming public as to make it difficult for them to determine the financial position of the corporations or the fairness of rates. State utility commissions, except in one or two states, were utterly incapable of controlling the situation, partly because the business had outgrown state boundaries. In 1936, as we have noted (p. 611 n.), the twelve largest utility holding companies controlled almost half the power produced in the nation, their lines crossing state boundaries in all directions. In brief, the business of producing and distributing electric power had reached a stage by the early 'thirties similar to that of the railroads a half century earlier. The conditions and abuses of the railroads in their early days were being duplicated and were leading again to the same sort of demand for federal control.

Federal regulation had begun in a tentative manner with the Federal Water Power Act of 1920, which set up a Federal Power Commission to exercise administrative control over all power sites erected on public lands of the United States and on navigable rivers. The Commission had the power to license for fifty years concerns desiring to erect such plants, and to require uniform accounting systems; and it was given power over security issues and over rates for power sold across state boundaries.[7] Perhaps the most important aspect of the utility problem which confronted the nation was whether the authority of this Commission should be extended to cover all companies operating in more than one state and all concerns transporting power across state lines. There was also the question as to whether the federal government itself should enter the field of power production. It was the latter question, as it turned out, which was taken up first.

The problem of government operation could hardly be dodged because the federal government had authorized during the First World War the building of two plants at Muscle Shoals on the Tennessee River to produce nitrates for the manufacture of explosives. To provide electric energy for these plants the Wilson Dam was also authorized; it was completed in 1925, making the total government investment about $145,000,000. Whether the government should operate these plants or turn them over at a nominal cost to private companies was the question before the nation. Congress twice passed bills authorizing enlargement of the plants and government operation; the first was pocket-vetoed by Coolidge, the second was vetoed by Hoover. Roosevelt was known to be more liberal toward government ownership and operation than Hoover, and the power question was a minor factor in the campaign of 1932. Before his inauguration he visited Muscle Shoals and announced that he would support a bill for government operation.

One of the most far-reaching and significant acts of the Roosevelt administration, and one that affected agriculture, industry, and other economic interests as well as public utilities, was the Muscle Shoals-Tennessee Valley Development Act (May, 1933). This created a board of three mem-

---

[7] As in the case of railroads, this power had been denied by the courts to state commissions.

bers, known as the Tennessee Valley Authority, to maintain and operate properties owned by the government at Muscle Shoals, Alabama, in the interest of national defense and the development of agriculture and industry in the Tennessee Valley, to improve navigation on the Tennessee, and to control the flood waters of that river and the Mississippi. The TVA was given wide authority to acquire real estate, build dams and power houses, install hydroelectric plants, develop a program of flood control, prevent soil erosion, and aid reforestation, besides manufacturing nitrogen products for fertilizers and explosives. The whole project is an important experiment in the development of a geographic region which is also essentially an economic unit. Although the Act affected many interests, the chief opposition in the courts came from the public utilities. Despite numerous legal attacks, the Act has been upheld by the Supreme Court. So certain was the administration of the success of the TVA experiment that in 1937 Roosevelt in a special message to Congress advocated that six similar regional planning agencies be set up which would cover most of the nation.

The great problem of more effective federal control and greater protection to the investing and consuming public was finally attacked in the Public Utility Holding Company Act (August, 1935), one of the most bitterly fought pieces of New Deal legislation. Among other things it granted to the Federal Power Commission authority to regulate rates and business practices of utilities doing an interstate business, prohibited holding companies beyond the second degree, and required federal sanction through the Securities and Exchange Commission for the issuance of securities, the acquisition of properties, and the handling of other kinds of business. After three years holding companies had to limit their operations to single integrated systems and to business directly connected with the supply of power service to consumers. At the time of its passage, the Act was loosely discussed as one which inflicted the "death penalty" upon holding companies. Whatever it did, it apparently has not yet injured the electric utility business for it was one of the first to push out of the depression and in 1937 enjoyed the greatest gross revenues of its history. Opposition by utility companies and the difficulties of reorganization have slowed up enforcement, but by 1942 the provisions of the Act were well on the way to attainment.

TRANSPORTATION

No branch of American industrial life felt the depression more than transportation. Much aid had already been extended through the RFC, but Congress in June, 1933, took a further step by passing the Railroad Emergency Act which set up a Federal Railroad Coordinator whose orders, unless revoked by the Interstate Commerce Commission to whom appeal could be taken, would have the force and effect of the Commission's. With the aid of coordinating committees of railroad representatives he was to devise means to avoid waste, to promote financial organization, to reduce fixed charges to the extent required by the public interest, and to improve the credit of the railroads. To accomplish these purposes, the anti-trust laws, if necessary, might be set aside. The Act repealed the famous but unsuccessful recapture clause of the Transportation Act of 1920 (Esch-Cummins Act),[8] but, on the other hand, it sought to remedy one great weakness of the earlier legislation by placing railroad holding corporations under the supervision of the Interstate Commerce Act. Although Coordinator Joseph B. Eastman and his aids made surveys of the railroad situation and recommendations for improvement—some of which were followed by the railroads—the most permanent effect of the Emergency Act of 1933, as far as railroads were concerned, appears to have been the modifications of the Act of 1920. The office of Federal Railroad Coordinator, created as an emergency measure, was discontinued in 1936. More important than the emergency legislation of 1933 was the Wheeler-Lea Transportation Act of 1940, which enlarged the powers of the ICC to include supervision over water carriers operating in coastwise, inland, and intercoastal trade. The Act also relieved the Commission of the necessity of proposing railroad consolidation, but no consolidation could be effected without the Commission's approval.[9]

It was not in railroads, however, that the Roosevelt administration made its greatest contribution to the problem of American transportation. One of the recommendations of Coordinator Eastman and his staff was for a federal act governing motor vehicles engaged in interstate commerce. By the Motor Carrier Act (October, 1935) motor vehicles engaged in interstate commerce were put under the regulation of the Interstate Commerce Commission and their activities coordinated with those of other carriers. A study of this Act reveals regulations suggestive of the earlier legislation regulating railroads. The Commission was empowered to establish just and reasonable rates and prescribe uniform systems of accounting, and the carriers were forbidden to grant rebates or to discriminate as to rates, localities, and persons. In brief, a real beginning was made in extending federal control to motor carriers engaged in interstate commerce.

Although the development of commercial aviation was temporarily halted by the depression, the industry did not collapse. On the contrary, it advanced rapidly during the 1930's. The government's problem was not one of saving aviation, but rather one of improving federal control. Charges of fraud and favoritism in awarding mail contracts led President Roosevelt in 1934 to

[8] Above, p. 616.
[9] Above, p. 617.

cancel all these contracts, and for a brief period the army carried the mail. By the Air Mail Act of 1934 the transportation of mail was returned under new contracts to private carriers, with government supervision divided among the Interstate Commerce Commission, the Secretary of Commerce, and the Postmaster General. Since this type of supervision was too clumsy, Congress in 1938 consolidated control under a Civil Aeronautical Authority, with a semi-independent Air Safety Board to investigate accidents and study safety measures. The work of these two bodies helped to inspire greater efficiency and safety in civil aviation and was popular with private air companies. It was believed to be non-political. Consequently, there was much criticism when the President in 1940, under the powers given him to reorganize the government service, placed these supervisory boards within the Department of Commerce. Here the responsibilities are divided between the Civil Aeronautics Administration and the Civil Aeronautics Board.

By 1936 a number of factors contributed to direct the nation's attention again to the question of the merchant marine. A succession of maritime disasters called for more thoroughgoing regulation and supervision, acute labor troubles pointed to the need of better working conditions, and the general decline of the merchant marine called for new measures if it was to be saved.[10] This situation was made particularly clear by a report from the Maritime Commission in 1937, which showed that of the 9,000,000 gross tonnage built during the previous decade only 5 per cent had been registered in the United States. Although this country still ranked second in tonnage volume, it ranked fourth in speed and last in age of vessels. At least one-quarter of the tonnage was obsolete and seven-eighths would be in that condition by 1942. To deal with this problem a Ship Subsidy Act was passed in 1936. It ended the construction loans under the old Merchant Marine Act of 1920, dissolved the former United States Shipping Board Merchant Fleet Corporation, and established a new agency known as the United States Maritime Commission. It directed the Commission to survey the American merchant marine to determine what additions and replacements were necessary, to investigate employment and wage conditions, and to consider applications for construction subsidies, at the same time laying down conditions under which they might be granted. The old system of subsidization through mail contracts was to be replaced by direct subsidies. These subsidies were chiefly of two kinds. First, ships might be built on government contract and sold to the shipper (on long-term easy payments) at cost minus the difference between the cost of building here and abroad. Second, operating subsidies might be granted to vessels engaged on essential trade routes,

[10] Above, p. 530.

these subsidies to be sufficient to offset the difference in cost between operating American and foreign ships. The Commission was also given power to determine wages, minimum crews, and working conditions, and a Maritime Labor Board was established to mediate labor disputes.

LABOR AND THE NEW DEAL

The detrimental effect of the depression on labor with respect to unemployment and decline in income has already been noted (p. 645). Income decreased more rapidly than the cost of living. There was conclusive evidence of an increase in industrial accidents reflecting a let-up in safety and accident-prevention activities; there was a general increase in sweatshop conditions and in the overworking of women and children. Until the tide was turned by the codes of the NIRA there was a lengthening of hours and a weakening of the position of union labor. On the other hand, the long-drawn-out depression, as we shall see, stimulated interest in new forms of legislation.

As far as labor was concerned, the crux of the New Deal was contained in Section 7 (a) of the NIRA. Briefly, it provided that employees should have the "right to organize and bargain collectively through representatives of their own choosing, and shall be free from interference, restraint, or coercion of employers of labor, or their agents, in the designation of such representatives or in self-organization." No employee as a condition of employment might be required to join a company union or to refrain from joining a labor organization of his own choosing, and employers had to comply with the code regulations of their industry respecting labor. Indeed, this seemed like a new "charter of liberty" to labor and under the circumstances it is hardly surprising that union membership increased rapidly.

In addition to advantages under Section 7 (a) of the NIRA, labor was expected to benefit under the codes established for the various industries. The first of the codes, somewhat typical of their general character, was that for the cotton textile industry; it forbade the employment of children under sixteen, prohibited the speeding up of work, and established minimum wages of $13 a week in the North and $12 a week in the South. Contrary to the intention of the administration, the minimum wages in the codes tended to become the maximum and as prices of commodities began to swing upward the benefit to labor was doubtful. The banning of child labor, however, was an unquestioned blessing.

The high hopes raised in the minds of labor by the NIRA were never realized. Opposition by many employers, widespread evasion of the codes, and the government's failure through the various labor boards vigorously to enforce the Act greatly weakened its operation long before the Supreme Court declared it unconstitutional in 1935. As the fact dawned upon labor that the NIRA was no short cut to the millennium and that in the end its enforcement was primarily their responsibility, the number of strikes increased rapidly. The number of employees directly involved in strikes, which had sunk to 158,114 in 1930, increased to 812,137 in 1933 and to considerably more in 1934. The serious strike situation in 1934 finally reached its climax in September with the nation-wide strike of the United Textile Workers.

These labor difficulties brought federal efforts to mediate or conciliate. Machinery for this, in fact, had been set up under the NIRA through national and local compliance boards, but the NIRA was barely in operation before their boards were swamped with complaints and proved inadequate. To enforce the labor provisions of the Act, therefore, Congress in 1933 established a National Labor Board, but even the NLB, with its nineteen regional boards, was ineffective. In the face of a rapidly spreading epidemic of strikes, Congress established under Joint Resolution No. 44 (June, 1934) a non-partisan National Labor Relations Board, which, it was hoped, might be more successful. In the meantime, threatened or actual strikes led the President to appoint boards of arbitration and adjustment to handle labor troubles among the longshoremen, the automobile workers, the steel workers, and the textile workers.

The Supreme Court decision which ended the NIRA (p. 662) did not involve the labor provisions and Congress attempted to perpetuate them in the National Labor Relations Act (July, 1935). The new Act sought to promote equality of bargaining power between employers and employees and to diminish the causes of labor disputes. Specifically, it forbade employers (1) to interfere with, restrain, or coerce employees in the exercise of their right to collective bargaining, (2) to refuse to bargain collectively, and (3) to dominate or interfere with the formation or administration of a labor organization or to interfere with membership in a labor organization by discrimination with regard to hire or tenure. To enforce the Act, a permanent National Labor Relations Board was established. Furthermore, Congress legislated regarding labor conditions in specific industries in the Bituminous Coal Conservation Act (later declared unconstitutional, p. 663) and in the Ship Subsidy Act (p. 667).

If adequately enforced, the National Labor Relations Act was bound to be extremely significant. It not only encouraged labor organization, but it made collective bargaining compulsory on the employer, and by its wording seemed to doom the company union. Enforcement, of course, was handicapped until the Supreme Court passed judgment, but the Act was eventu-

ally affirmed when the Court in a single day (April 12, 1937) upheld its
constitutionality in five decisions. These cases in general involved the question as to whether certain industries, including steel and men's clothing,
were sufficiently concerned with interstate commerce to be covered by the
Act. With the exception of the Fansteel decision in 1939, which virtually
banned sit-down strikes, the Court during succeeding months not only approved the constitutionality of the Act by implication, but time and again
upheld the procedure and decisions of the National Labor Relations Board.
During the first five years of its existence twenty orders of the NLRB,
contested by employers, finally reached the Supreme Court. In 18 of these
the Court upheld the Board in whole or in part. This protection given
the Board was extended in 1940 to protection against the lower courts,
when the Supreme Court in a unanimous decision held that "the findings of
the board, as to fact, if supported by evidence, shall be . . . conclusive." A
great triumph was achieved for both the Board and the unions on January 6, 1941, when in the H. J. Heinz Company case the Court supported
the Board's decision that a company must sign a written agreement with
a union after both sides had arrived at an oral understanding.

Important as was the National Labor Relations Act and its approval by
the Supreme Court, the growth of organized labor depended on other
factors as well. First of all was the need of regaining middle-class sympathy,
which had been lost in part during the 'twenties. The depression helped
in this because many were convinced that labor had suffered severely and
needed greater protection. Help came also from the activities of the Senate
Committee on Education and Labor, headed by Robert La Follette, which
received special instructions to investigate "violations of the rights of free
speech and assembly and undue interference with the right of labor to
organize and bargain collectively." As this committee spread on the record
the facts pertaining to the use of labor spies, strikebreakers, tear gas, and
deadly weapons by supposedly reputable employers and the abridgment
of civil liberties in company-controlled towns and regions, the public for
the first time realized the difficulties faced by labor in its efforts toward
organization.

More important than government aid was the ability of labor to help
itself. In the last analysis labor must do its own organizing. Spurred on
by the NIRA and the National Labor Relations Act, organized labor rose
to the occasion. Organizing machinery which had grown rusty was put in
commission, older leaders were sent out in the field, and younger men who
demonstrated ability were called on. By 1936 the A. F. of L. boasted a
membership of 4,000,000 and had added another million by 1942. In the
rapid drive for labor organization after 1933 it was found more practical

to organize every shop on the basis of industry rather than craft, and against its will the A. F. of L. granted many charters to these "federal unions." The new recruits included a large number of workers as yet unacquainted with the conservative traditions of A. F. of L. craft unionism. They gave a more militant tone to organized labor, a tone which was reflected in the annual convention of the A. F. of L. in 1934, when that organization voted over-whelmingly to promote industrial unionism in certain "mass industries," particularly steel, automobiles, rubber, radio, and aluminum. Failure of the executive committee of the A. F. of L. to pursue this mandate aggres-sively enough led certain of the larger unions under the leadership of John L. Lewis and the United Mine Workers of America to organize the Com-mittee for Industrial Organization.[11]

Although suspended from membership by the A. F. of L., the C.I.O. unions swung aggressively into action. The initial objective of the C.I.O. was the steel industry, but the movement for industrial organization spread so rapidly that, contrary to plans, the first battle was fought in the automobile industry. Following spectacular strikes early in 1937 in the General Motors and Chrysler Corporations the C.I.O. succeeded in effecting compromise settlements which recognized the C.I.O. automobile union as the bargaining agency for its own members. In actual practice this meant the recognition of organized labor in practically all of the major units in the hitherto un-organized automobile industry, except the Ford Motor Company. This con-cern finally gave in in 1941.

As the battle front shifted to the steel industry, the United States Steel Corporation, instead of opposing labor, reversed a lifelong policy to the surprise of all, and signed contracts with the C.I.O. Although other steel corporations immediately followed in granting recognition, a few of the more important "independents" did not, and a strike against these com-panies in the late spring of 1937 resulted in the first important reverse of the C.I.O. But, under the stress of war preparations, even the "independents" agreed later to recognition. In the meantime the C.I.O. spread rapidly. By 1942 it claimed over forty national unions and a membership of 5,000,000, approximately that of the A. F. of L. Despite efforts both within and without organized labor, the two factions were unable to reconcile their differences. In 1938 the Committee for Industrial Organization changed its name to the

[11] The unions composing the original committee which were expelled from the A. F. of L. in August, 1936, were as follows: United Mine Workers of America; Amalgamated Clothing Workers of America; International Ladies' Garment Workers Union; United Textile Workers of America; Oil Field, Gas Well and Refinery Workers of America; International Union of Mine, Mill and Smelter Workers; Federation of Flat Glass Workers of America; Amalgamated Asso-ciation of Iron, Steel and Tin Workers; International Union United Automobile Workers of America; United Rubber Workers of America. The I.L.G.W.U. later withdrew from the C.I.O. and eventually rejoined the A. F. of L.

Congress of Industrial Organizations, adopted a constitution, and took on a more permanent form. Its early leader, John L. Lewis, resigned the presidency in 1940 and was succeeded by Philip Murray.

The wave of strikes which accompanied efforts in 1937 to organize the automobile industry was watched with particular interest because for the first time in this country labor used the "sit-down" technique on a wide scale. This refusal by the worker to leave the plant during a strike on the theory that he had a vested interest in his job proved a powerful weapon because it forced the employer to commit the first violence in a strike. Employers, of course, denounced "sit-down" strikes as illegal trespassing on property rights and certain states passed legislation to ban them. The wide use of mass picketing during the labor conflicts of the 1930's sometimes resulted in violence and gave an opportunity for agitation for new laws to make labor more "responsible" in the courts by requiring incorporation. On the whole, labor was able to resist this kind of agitation.

RELIEF AND SECURITY

In addition to the New Deal legislation which bore particularly upon the problem of labor organization there was a series of acts and activities of the federal government that were aimed to improve the general standard of living of the wage earner. These, as we shall see, fall into two categories: emergency measures to provide immediate relief, and a more permanent long-term program. The Civilian Conservation Corps, already noted,[12] being omitted, emergency action for the relief of the millions of unemployed began with the Emergency Relief Act (May, 1933), which created the Federal Emergency Relief Administration and authorized the RFC to make available to it $500,000,000 for emergency relief to the states. Shortly thereafter, under the authorization of the NIRA, a Public Works Administration was established under the direction of the Secretary of the Interior, with an appropriation of $3,300,000,000 to promote construction in the public interest. To care for the unemployed outside of the construction industry, to broaden the work of the PWA, and particularly to carry the unemployed through the winter of 1933–1934 a Civil Works Administration was set up (it was discontinued in 1934). Congress in 1935 appropriated $4,880,000,000 for a second public works program, and in the hope of speeding reemployment the President by an Executive Order of May 6, 1935, established the Works Progress Administration to coordinate the program of relief. Additional appropriations were made in subsequent years so that by the middle of 1941 the PWA had spent over $4,000,000,000 and the WPA twice that amount. At the height of the program the government was providing jobs

[12] Above, p. 652.

for over 3,800,000 persons. Various relief agencies were consolidated in 1939 under the Federal Works Agency.[13]

Needless to say, the relief program was under bitter criticism and was continually charged with waste and inefficiency, with the expenditure of millions for political purposes, and with failure to accomplish its major objective—the elimination of unemployment. The best it could do was to reemploy about one-third of the jobless, and this often at wages which endangered the general level. In reply to criticism the administration insisted that the self-respect of millions had been saved by jobs rather than by the dole, that much necessary work had been done, and that the large amounts expended in this manner had helped materially to prime the pump of recovery. That much-needed work was accomplished through the various agencies listed in the preceding paragraph, it is impossible to deny. A mere catalogue of the work would make a book in itself. The WPA, for example, among many other accomplishments, completed by mid-September of 1936 some 22,785 miles of new roads, 3351 miles of new sewers, 1415 playgrounds, 1099 educational buildings (at the same time repairing 7176 others), 610 administration buildings, 425 parks, 7633 bridges, 45 landing fields, 1593 storage dams, and 1155 sewage treatment plants.

A real start was likewise made under the PWA on the problem of low-cost housing and slum clearance. To speed this program the Wagner-Steagall Housing Act of 1937 established a United States Housing Authority, with power to make loans and contributions for slum clearance and the building of low-rent houses. The Housing Authority was allowed to lend up to $800,000,000 for housing projects, with a limit of $4000 for a family dwelling in cities with a population up to 500,000 and a $5000 limit for cities above that population. The loans were to be made and the construction done in cooperation with local public housing agencies. By the middle of 1940 the USHA had made contracts for the construction of over 400 housing projects containing almost 150,000 homes. When it is remembered that one-third of the nation is poorly housed, the work of the PWA and later of the USHA seems but a tiny beginning. Nevertheless, it is a start in the right direction. Moreover, it has stimulated private interests to build new housing projects in slum areas.

The work of the WPA was essentially of an emergency nature, but the Great Depression and the New Deal also gave tremendous impetus to long-range reforms, such as old age pensions and unemployment insurance, which had made small progress during the boom years of the 'twenties. Up to the end of 1934, for example, only one state, Wisconsin, had passed

[13] In 1942 Congress ended further appropriations for the CCC, but efforts to discontinue appropriations for unemployment relief failed.

an Unemployment Insurance Act, but by the end of 1937 every state and the District of Columbia had some kind of unemployment insurance legislation. More rapid progress was made with old age pension schemes. By 1934 at least 29 states had some type of old age pension law, of which ten were passed in 1933 and two (Pennsylvania and Iowa) in 1934. It was the Social Security Act of 1935 as amended in 1939, however, that speeded the adoption of both unemployment insurance and old age pensions and made their application nation-wide. Primarily the Act provided for a system of old age pensions to aged needy persons over 65 years of age through federal grants on a fifty-fifty matching basis with the states, except that the federal government's share in no case would exceed $20 a month. To take care of the future the law provided for a contributory old age pension system to be paid for by an income tax on employees and a payroll tax on employers beginning with one per cent in 1937 and rising each three years until 1949, when the contribution from both would be 3 per cent. Under this scheme the monthly pension was expected to range between $10 and $85, depending on wages earned between January, 1937, and the retirable age. How widely extended would be the effect of this part of the Act can be seen by the fact that over 50,000,000 had registered by midsummer of 1940.[14]

In addition to old age pensions, the Social Security Act also sought to encourage the development of state systems of unemployment insurance that would meet certain minimum requirements. This is to be accomplished by a special federal tax on payrolls levied against employers. The employer is permitted to credit as an offset the amount which he contributes under an approved state unemployment insurance fund, but such credits are not to exceed 90 per cent of the federal tax for that year.[15] Other features of the Social Security Act carried appropriations—usually based proportionately on similar appropriations made by the states—to take care of needy dependent children; to promote the health of mothers and children in areas suffering severe economic distress; to provide medical, surgical, and corrective services for crippled children; to aid homeless and neglected children; to rebuild vocationally the physically disabled; to aid the needy blind; and finally, to promote adequate public health service. There were few who were satisfied with the provisions of the Act, but the country's general attitude in the following years was to improve the legislation rather than retreat from the position taken in 1935.

[14] Not all workers are included in the Social Security system. Among those excluded are hired agricultural laborers, domestic servants employed in homes, maritime workers in American waters, those working for federal, state, and local governments, and those employed by charitable, religious, and educational institutions.

[15] The unemployment insurance systems adopted by the states differed, but in general they provided for about half the weekly salary with a maximum of $15 for a maximum period of 16 weeks.

Even before the Social Security Act was passed the federal government had attempted in the Railway Pension Act of 1934 to take care of one group of employees by providing for retirement pensions based on contributions by the employer and employee. When this was declared unconstitutional in 1935 by a 5-4 decision on the ground that it violated the due process clause and that it was an unconstitutional use of the interstate commerce power, Congress made a second effort in that year. Before the new Act could reach the Supreme Court, however, the railroads and unions reached a voluntary agreement in March, 1937, which was to be incorporated in a third congressional Act and which the railroads promised not to challenge in the courts. It provides for the collection of a payroll tax beginning at 5 and increasing to 7 per cent and split half and half between worker and management. The scheme is administered by the Railroad Retirement Board and provides pensions with a maximum of $120 a month, the burden of the existing private pension schemes being taken over by the government.

Among other legislation designed to improve the status of labor was the National Employment Service Act of 1933 (Wagner-Peyser Act), which created a bureau, the United States Employment Service, in the Department of Labor for the purpose of establishing a national employment system to cooperate with the states in the promotion of employment. Specifically it was to coordinate the employment services of the states, and where such services do not exist, to establish them. The Act carried appropriations, three-fourths of which were to be distributed to the states on condition that they contribute an equal amount. Government employment agencies had been taken for granted for many years in Europe, but a major depression was necessary to bring them into existence in this country.

One piece of labor legislation that has far-reaching possibilities, if it can be enforced, is the Walsh-Healey Government Contracts Act of 1936. It provided that public contracts (except for certain specified articles) in excess of $10,000 made by any department or agency of the federal government must include stipulations requiring that the contractor be a manufacturer or regular dealer in the materials for which he is contracting, that he pay not less than the prevailing wages for persons employed in the industry, that he permit no one to work more than eight hours in one day or forty hours in any week, and that he employ no male under sixteen years of age and no female under eighteen. The work, furthermore, must be done under conditions that are not unduly hazardous.

The last important piece of New Deal legislation was concerned with labor and the standard of living. The Fair Labor Standards Act (Wages and Hours Act) attempted to put a cellar under wages and a ceiling on hours. Maximum working hours were set at 44 a week for the first year,

42 for the second, and 40 thereafter. Minimum wages were to start at 25 cents an hour for the first year and be increased to 40 cents over a period of seven years. The Act applied to all labor engaged in interstate commerce or the production of goods entering that commerce and was expected at the time to cover from 12,000,000 to 13,000,000 workers. Although the minimum wages under this Act bore little relation to a decent American standard of living, the provisions were generally accepted as a step in the right direction.

ECONOMIC SIGNIFICANCE OF THE NEW DEAL

The New Deal, which we have just scanned briefly, obviously included two types of legislation. Some of the Acts, as for example the NIRA, were of a temporary or emergency nature; others, such as the banking legislation and the Social Security Act, were more permanent. Certain of the Acts were designed primarily to hasten economic recovery; others were an effort to remedy abuses that had long cried for reform.

In the ardent heat of political and economic controversy, many criticisms were hurled at the New Deal legislation. To those economists schooled in the theories of classical *laissez faire,* there was little that could be said for it. Even its most ardent proponents found details in the various Acts to criticize. On the other hand, there were many who realized that whatever validity there might be in the *laissez-faire* theory, such a policy, if it ever existed, was not likely to be followed again. The economic catastrophe resulting from the First World War had brought throughout the world various types of government control of economic life. The New Deal, so called, was America's method of attacking the depression, and the general attitude apparently held that it was superior to the methods of many other nations and that it should at least be given a fair trial. If one thing was certain, it was that the era of "rugged individualism" was largely a thing of the past.

Perhaps the most frequent charge made against the New Deal was that it was socialism. That the legislation of the Roosevelt administration extended the supervision and control of our economic life by the federal government there can be no doubt. More than that, it involved, as in the case of the various government loan agencies, direct participation in the economic life of the nation. It did not, however, modify to any great extent the fundamental elements in the present economic system—the private ownership of the means of production and distribution, and the profit system. The proponents of the New Deal insisted that they were trying to save rather than destroy the existing economic system by eliminating some of its worst abuses. Whatever may have been the hope, one crying evil of the present system—the maldistribution of wealth—seemed hardly affected by the program. Judging from income tax returns in the late 'thirties, no appreciable change was effected.

Many also asserted that the New Deal marked a revolution in American history. Close study hardly bears out this point of view. The extension of federal control of business goes back at least to the Interstate Commerce Act of 1887 and the Sherman Anti-trust Act of 1890, and the history of humanitarian legislation in state and federal governments likewise extends back many years. There was, after all, little that was new in the New Deal; it was largely an extension and a continuation of an older method and an older philosophy.[16] The objective, as President Roosevelt himself described it, was to establish a "balance in our economic system—balance between agriculture and industry and balance between the wage earner, the employer and consumer." To this should be added a definite humanitarian motive. Said the President in 1937 in a special message urging the Wages and Hours Act, "The time has arrived for us to take further action to extend the frontiers of social progress. . . . One-third of our population, the overwhelming majority of which is in agriculture or industry, is ill-nourished, ill-clad and ill-housed. . . . A self-supporting and self-respecting democracy can plead no justification for the existence of child labor, no economic reason for chiseling workers' wages or stretching workers' hours." The *new* element in the New Deal was the acceleration of the decline of *laissez faire.*

SELECTED READINGS

Beard, C. A., and Smith, G. H. E., *The Old Deal and the New.*
Beard, Charles and Mary, *America in Midpassage,* Chaps. III–VI.
Hacker, Louis, *American Problems of Today,* Chaps. VII–X.
Lyon, L. S., *et al., The National Recovery Administration,* Chaps. I–X.
Pasvolsky, Leo, *Current Monetary Issues,* Chap. VI.
Shultz, W. J., and Caine, M. R., *Financial Development of the United States,* Chaps. XXVIII–XXIX.

[16] This point of view is developed more fully in H. U. Faulkner, "Antecedents of New Deal Liberalism," *Social Education,* III, 153–160 (March, 1939).

3I.

World Economic Relations

Export of American Capital

ONE of the most important effects of the First World War upon the United States was the rapidity with which she shifted from a debtor to a creditor nation. From the discovery of America until 1914, the flow of investment funds was from Europe here, and our economic development had to a considerable extent been financed from without.[1] Foreign investments in the United States in that year were estimated at between 4 and 5 billion dollars. At the same time the United States by that year had herself invested heavily abroad, to the extent of at least 2.5 billions,[2] leaving us still in debt to Europe by from 2.5 to 3 billions.[3] With the European war the situation speedily changed. In need of all their resources, Europeans who held American investments dumped them upon the market to the extent of $2,000,-000,000,[4] and heavy loans were contracted here both with private bankers and with the federal government. Private loans floated in the United States during the war period amounted to around $1,500,000,000, and our government made direct loans to European governments during the war or immediately after to the amount of over $10,500,000,000.[5]

These figures do not tell the whole story, or even the most important part. The war left Europe so exhausted economically that during the decade of the 'twenties the United States continued to be the great source of capital.

[1] Above, pp. 564 ff.

[2] One estimate of the American investments abroad at the close of 1913 is that of Fisk, *Inter-Ally Debts*, p. 307, quoted by R. W. Dunn, *American Foreign Investments*, p. 3.

COUNTRY	AMOUNT (in millions)
Canada	$ 750
Cuba	100
Mexico	1,050
Central America	50
South America	100
Europe	350
China and Japan	100
Philippine Islands	75
Puerto Rico	30

[3] R. W. Dunn, *American Foreign Investments*, p. 3.

[4] B. H. Williams, *Economic Foreign Policy of the United States* (1929), p. 18.

[5] R. W. Dunn, *American Foreign Investments*, pp. 16 ff.

Modern Industry—Automobile Body Assembly Line.

ern Industry—
anizing Tires
Steam-jacketed
Automatically
Controlled.

The Old and the New—A Southern Pacific Modern Streamliner Alongside of the Tiny "C. P. Huntington" in Operation in the 1860's.

A Transatlantic Clipper Plane.

A Parade of Coal Miners at Shenandoah, Pennsylvania, in the Coal Strike
of 1902.

William Green, President of the American Federation of Labor, and John
L. Lewis, Founder of the Congress of Industrial Organizations.

National Guardsmen Dispersing Strikers with Tear Gas at Greenville, South
Carolina, September, 1934.

A Line of Restaurant and Kitchen Workers in Front of City Hall, New York,
February, 1934, Where They Had Gone to Place Their Demands Before
Mayor La Guardia.

A California Oil Field.

New Deal—Excavating a Sewer Tunnel in Chicago, a Project Undertaken
with a WPA Allotment of $42,000,000.

Photo by Brown

New Deal—Jane Addams House, Chicago. A Slum Clearance Project Built Through the United States Housing Administration. It Covered 22 Acres of Land.

New Deal—Chemist: Building, University Tennessee, Erect with the Aid of WPA Loan and Grant of $355,698.

Photo by Brown Brothers

Photo by Brown Brothers

War Industry—An Assembly Line Working on Attack Bombers at the Douglas
Aircraft Plant.

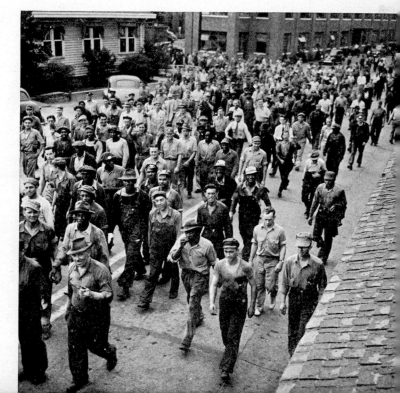

War Industry—Workers
Leaving a Newport News
Shipbuilding Plant in October, 1941.

Photo by Brown Brothers

War Industry—Building Engine Nacelles for Douglas A-20 Attack Bombers.

Squadron of Torpedo Planes in Echelon Formation.

American investments and loans abroad increased by $7,140,000,000 from 1922 to 1930. In 1914 this country was a net debtor by approximately $3,000,-000,000; in 1933 she was a net creditor by $20,645,000,000.[6] About half of this was in war loans made to foreign governments by our government. Wholesale lending on such a scale has inevitably thrown the United States pell-mell into the game of economic imperialism and brought with it immediate and difficult problems of a political and social as well as an economic nature. In the export of capital this country had gone far beyond the amount reached by any of the older European nations in 1914.

In a study of the debts owed to private American citizens the Department of Commerce in 1930 estimated that one-half of the money lent abroad was in the form of "portfolio investments"—that is, in ownership of foreign securities, public and private, by individuals or institutions in this country— and one-half in "direct investments" made by American corporations in agricultural, industrial, commercial, mining, public utility, and other enterprises abroad. The migration of billions of American dollars to other parts of the world did not come simply because the prosperity of the 'twenties created surplus wealth which high interest rates lured into foreign investment. It came in part because American economic interests were stretching far and wide to extend business. Most of the big American concerns, such as the Ford Motor Company, General Motors, General Electric, Standard Oil, International Telephone and Telegraph, and International Harvester, set up their own plants or bought control of foreign companies. Many economic factors led to this movement of capital into foreign industries, and of these the high tariffs which developed rapidly in the 1920's are probably the most important. When American manufacturers found it impossible to break through the tariff barriers, they simply set up branch factories abroad to serve foreign markets. Every traveler in Canada, for example, finds there numerous branches of American concerns which represent over two billion dollars of American direct investments.

The vast extension of foreign investments and our rapid shift from a debtor to a creditor nation have necessarily had a far-reaching effect upon our foreign and domestic policy. This changed situation the national government has in part recognized by efforts to promote and safeguard these investments. Such a policy was relatively easy with the weak nations of the Caribbean but difficult elsewhere. Although favorable to the expansion of foreign investments our government actually did little during the 'twenties to shape domestic policies to meet the new situation. Payment of interest and principal depended on world prosperity and the free move-

[6] Statement of George N. Peek, Special Adviser to the President on Foreign Trade, in a letter to the President dated May 23, 1934, made public at President Roosevelt's suggestion.

ment of international trade. The latter was greatly hindered by the American high tariff policy which was climaxed in the Hawley-Smoot Tariff of 1930. There could be no question regarding the need for American money in other parts of the world, but the loans so liberally granted often rested upon an insecure foundation. How insecure these investments were became clear enough after the crash of 1929.

The large stream of loans in the 1920's was reduced to a tiny trickle in the 1930's. Until the economic situation was artificially stimulated by the

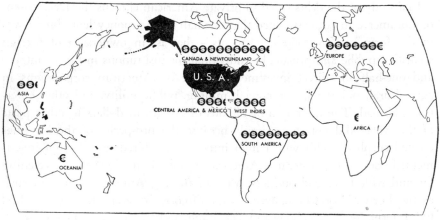

Each symbol represents 200 million dollars   PICTOGRAPH CORPORATION

AMERICAN DIRECT INVESTMENTS, 1940.
(From H. U. Faulkner and Tyler Kepner, *America, Its History and People*, Harper & Brothers.)

Second World War the income from direct investments in Latin America was relatively low. United States holdings in Latin-American dollar bonds (most of them government securities) amounted in 1940 to almost one billion dollars, but approximately two-thirds of these bonds were in partial or complete default. In continental Europe the situation was even worse. Total investments there amounted to $1,500,000,000 in 1940, almost all of which was in the Axis countries. For years exchange controls had prevented heavy remittances of income from these countries and the withdrawal of capital had been largely halted. The greater proportion of assets were frozen and when liquidation was permitted it was accompanied by heavy losses. In-direct (portfolio) investments there amounted to $530,000,000 at the end of 1940, but 59 per cent was in default. Moreover, the Debt Default Act of 1934 (Johnson Act), which prohibited loans to any government in default in its payments of obligations to the United States automatically ended the possibility of loans to most European governments. Foreign investments in 1940 as listed by the Department of Commerce are shown in the accompanying table.

UNITED STATES LONG-TERM INVESTMENTS IN FOREIGN COUNTRIES, BY TYPES OF INVESTMENT AND BY GEOGRAPHIC AREAS, DECEMBER 31, 1940 [7]

[In millions of dollars]

Area	Direct Investments	Portfolio Investments			Grand Total
		Foreign Dollar Bonds	Miscellaneous Foreign Securities	Total	
Canada and Newfoundland .	2,065	1,390	285	1,675	3,740
West Indies	755	74	5	79	834
Central America and Mexico .	650	26	...	26	676
South America	1,615	893	5	898	2,513
Europe	1,370	506	130	636	2,006
Asia	460	155	5	160	620
Oceania	135	95	3	98	233
Africa	105	2	17	19	124
International	25	...	...	...	25
Total	7,180	3,141[a]	450	3,591	10,771

[a] The estimated market value of these holdings was $1,791,000,000.

With the Second World War the situation with regard to foreign investments changed in important ways. As Germany invaded one small European nation after another, the American government froze the assets of these nations in the United States in order to protect the property of American nationals abroad. This, of course, was also done with German assets after our entry into the war. In the meantime, with private loans abroad declining because of unwillingness to take risks or prevented by the Debt Default Act and the Neutrality Acts, aid to the fighting democracies and to Latin-American nations devolved upon the government. For these reasons the RFC (through the Export Import Bank) and the United States Stabilization Fund have made virtually all of the foreign loans since the war began. Through these agencies loans and credits were extended in 1940 to twelve Latin-American countries, and $50,000,000 went to China; in July, 1941, a credit of $425,000,000 was extended to the United Kingdom. At least until the war ends, foreign financial transactions will be largely handled by governments.

[7] *Balance of International Payments in the United States in 1940*, p. 51. At the end of 1940 the Department of Commerce listed foreign long- and short-term investments in the United States at $9,695,000,000. *Ibid.*, p. 56.

Types of values used are as follows: Direct investments, book value; foreign dollar bonds, par value; miscellaneous securities, estimated value.

THE WAR-DEBT PROBLEM

Although the problem of the debts of the First World War seems academic today, it was closely interwoven with our international policy for two decades. When the United States entered that war, the credit of the Allied nations was exhausted and these loans were necessary to win the war. They were, however, supposedly made in good faith, with the expectation that they would be repaid. They had reached such staggering proportions that in 1922 the United States established a World War Foreign Debt Commission to take up with each nation the question of refunding the debt. The official attitude in this country was to make large reductions in the amounts owed, but to insist upon payment. Gradually over a period of seven years arrangements were made with fifteen European nations by which the total principal was fixed at $11,522,000,000 to be paid during a period of sixty-two years; the interest amounted to $10,621,000,000, and the grand total to $22,143,000,000. The annual payments were to vary from an average of $204,000,000 during the first decades to $414,000,000 during the last ten years. These arrangements involved a 23 per cent reduction of the British debt, a 46 per cent reduction of the Belgian debt, 52 per cent of the French, and 75 per cent of the Italian. While these reductions appear extremely liberal, it must be remembered that the debts were contracted during the high-price period of war time, that most of the money was used to purchase American commodities, and that the reductions merely tended to cancel wholly or in part the post-war deflation, on the basis of which the debts were to be paid.

Whether they were liberal or not, the agitation in Europe for complete cancellation continued. This was in part due to the fact that a large part of the reparations obtained from Germany came to the United States for the payment of Allied debts. The Treaty of Versailles originally fixed German reparations at $33,000,000,000, but it quickly became evident that Germany could not meet her payments. A committee headed by Charles G. Dawes adopted a plan in 1924 by which her annual payments were scaled down, and an effort was made to balance her budget and stabilize her currency. The failure of the Dawes Plan led to another attempt in 1929 by a committee under the chairmanship of Owen D. Young. The Young Plan radically reduced the German debt and provided that the size of certain yearly payments would be conditional upon a reduction of the Allied debts by the United States. This joining of reparation payments and Allied debts the United States would not officially recognize; but, practically speaking, such a connection existed, since four-fifths of the German payments eventually found their way to the United States. How close the connection was became evident in 1931 when the economic situation forced Germany to default and, to avoid a world economic collapse, President Hoover in June, 1931, after consultation with Allied governments, declared a moratorium for one year on all government debts and reparations payments. By June, 1933, only Finland made full payment of her interest; Britain, Italy, Latvia, Czechoslovakia, Rumania, and Lithuania paid a small part in silver as token, and Belgium, France, Hungary, Poland, and Estonia defaulted. After 1934 only Finland paid interest.

It was evident by 1932 that the whole war-debt problem would have to be reconsidered. The obvious possibilities were three: further postponement of payment, further reduction, or outright cancellation. There was considerable sentiment in this country for each of these plans, because many now felt with Secretary of the Treasury Mellon that "the entire foreign debt is not worth as much to the United States in dollars and cents as a prosperous Europe as a customer." Others believed that the money was not worth the harvest of hatred and suffering being reaped, and still others felt that we would never collect the money anyway and we might as well let it go on the best terms possible. At the other extreme was the sentiment, expressed by Coolidge, that the Allied nations had "hired it" (the money) and should pay it back. In any event the entire question provided a lesson which should prove valuable in the future.

Resentment over the European attitude regarding war debts along with other factors had led in 1934 to the Debt Default Act. It was also one of the many causes which led to a new program to maintain America's neutrality in future wars. A Senate investigation of the munitions industry greatly strengthened the belief that the United States had been drawn into the First World War because of the close economic relations which had bound her to one group of belligerent nations. Determined if possible to prevent the recurrence of certain influences tending to break down neutrality, Congress passed three Acts culminating in that of May, 1937. In addition to requiring all persons engaged in the manufacture of munitions to register with the Secretary of State and to export only under license, the Act provided for mandatory embargoes on loans, munitions, and implements of war to foreign belligerents or to factions in a civil strife of such proportions as to threaten the peace of the United States. It prohibited American citizens from traveling on belligerent vessels except under conditions prescribed by the President; it prohibited the transportation of munitions by American merchantmen, established the National Munitions Control Board with which all manufacturers and exporters of munitions must register, restricted the use of American ports as bases of supply in war time, allowed the President to exclude belligerent submarines and armed merchantmen from American ports, and prohibited the arming of American merchantmen. The Act of 1937 also gave the

President optional power for two years to embargo other commodities than loans and munitions, and when such embargo was proclaimed all trade in these commodities must be in accordance with the "cash and carry" principle. In other words, America's ownership in such commodities must end before they left our shores and they must be transported by foreign ships.

The Neutrality Acts represented the climax of a sentiment toward isolationism which had been growing since the First World War. Whether they could keep America out of an impending European war was, of course, problematical. That they meant the reversal of national policy, the sacrifice of the policy of "freedom of the seas," which this country had upheld for 150 years, was clear. That the type of isolationism represented by these Acts was a futile hope in a modern world was quickly proved. The Second World War began officially on September 1, 1939, when Germany invaded Poland; two days later Great Britain and France declared war on Germany. Although until Pearl Harbor (December 7, 1941) most Americans hoped that this country might avoid war, the great majority were firmly committed to the justice of the allied cause and the belief that help should be extended to the nations who were fighting for democratic principles. Shortly after the war broke upon Europe President Roosevelt called Congress into session and requested that the Neutrality Act be revised to allow the belligerents to purchase arms and munitions here. This was granted, but the purchase still had to be made on a "cash and carry" basis, and other provisions of the earlier Acts were maintained. A second step in breaking down the Neutrality Acts was taken in January, 1941, when the President called for "all-out aid" to the embattled democracies and asked for power to sell, exchange, loan, or lend any war equipment to any nation whose defense he might think vital to the defense of the United States. Bitterly opposed by those who believed that this was a definite step toward war, the legislation requested was finally granted after two months' debate. So also was the President's request for large grants to implement the Lease-Lend Act. This Act virtually nullified both the "cash and carry" principle and the Debt Default Act of 1934. That the administration was determined to reassert the old American principle of "freedom of the seas" which had been given up in the Neutrality Acts was evident in August, 1941, when at the famous Atlantic conference between President Roosevelt and Prime Minister Churchill the principle of freedom of the seas was made part of the Atlantic Charter.

THE PROBLEM OF INTERNATIONAL TRADE

Viewed superficially, the position of the United States in the realm of international trade seemed bright indeed in the decade following the First World War. Her volume of exports was maintained at a high level and she had substantial favorable trade balances each year. On the theory that this was a desirable condition tariffs were raised during the decade and every effort was made by the Department of Commerce and other government agencies to expand the export trade. In reality, however, the situation was by no means healthy. In an extended period of an unequal balance of trade, creditor balances can be paid only in gold or in goods. Gold was largely disappearing from the debtor nations and the free flow of goods was obstructed by high tariffs. In such a situation the balances due the creditor lead generally to foreign loans or to investments abroad. This was what was happening in the 1920's when American trade was to no small extent supported by such loans. This could not go on indefinitely, for the continued export of capital by the creditor nation merely accentuated an already unhealthy situation. Conditions were in the making which led to the complete débâcle of international trade at the end of the decade.

Many statesmen and economists were by no means blind to the dangers lurking in the area of international commerce. The League of Nations, for example, sponsored numerous conferences in an effort to reduce trade restrictions which, particularly during the First World War, had taken the form of embargoes, quotas, and other impediments. Impelled by the complaints of moving picture producers and automobile manufacturers who were suffering from quotas or prohibitions, the United States government finally became sufficiently interested to take part in the Conference on Import and Export Prohibitions and Restrictions held in Geneva in 1927. At the conference certain nations took the position that the problem of specific restrictions could not be separated from a consideration of the general tariff structure. The United States as a high-tariff nation disagreed. In the end, however, an agreement was reached which ignored tariffs but called for the abolition of import and export prohibitions and restrictions aside from those specifically excepted by the signing nations.[8] The United States was one of six nations to sign this agreement, but in 1933 she gave notice of withdrawal and in various trade agreements in the 1930's repeatedly resorted to the quota restriction.

The League of Nations was also interested in directly attacking the growing system of high tariffs. At the International Economic Conference of 1927 the United States joined in signing the conference report which said that "the time has come to put an end to the increase in tariffs and move in the opposite direction." The Hoover administration did not follow this policy, but the Democratic platform of 1932 advocated not only lower tariffs but also "an international economic conference to restore international trade and facilitate exchange." Such a conference was arranged by

[8] The United States, for example, maintained her prohibition on the export of helium gas.

the League of Nations to meet at London in 1933. Here the American delegation headed by Secretary of State Hull came out strongly for a modification of all unnecessary trade barriers. Certain of the European nations led by France insisted that a policy of tariff reductions must be accompanied by monetary stabilization. Mr. Roosevelt, who in preliminary conferences had agreed to this, now reversed himself and refused to participate in plans for currency stabilization. At that time he was convinced that the shortest road to recovery was through rising prices produced by currency inflation.[9]

This sudden reversal of policy brought the London Economic Conference to an untimely end. Nevertheless, the Roosevelt administration on its own part strove vigorously to improve international relations and revive foreign commerce. Its policy, in brief, was one of tariff reductions through reciprocal trade agreements with separate nations. This was facilitated by the Trade Agreements Act of June, 1934, authorizing the President for a period of three years (renewed for another three years in 1937 and again in 1940) to negotiate trade agreements without the advice and consent of the Senate and giving him power to raise and lower tariff rates by not more than 50 per cent. Enthusiastically pushed by Secretary of State Hull, who was firmly convinced that these reciprocal treaties would promote not only economic recovery but world peace, twenty-seven such treaties were signed up to May, 1943, and negotiations for others were pending. Although most of the treaties were with nations with whom our trade was not large, taken as a whole they included countries representing about one-third of our foreign trade. Because of the volume of trade between the two countries, probably the most important of these treaties was that with Canada. The first trade agreement with Canada, for example, made reductions on 180 commodities imported from this country and granted the lowest rate for any non-British country on 767 items; the United States on her part made large concessions particularly on agricultural products, lumber, and other commodities.

The idea of reciprocal tariffs was not new in American history. The great controversy with Canada over such a tariff during the Taft administration and its eventual failure was still remembered. The difficulty of helping certain economic groups without injuring others soon became clear. With few exceptions, imports under reduced tariffs were bound to come into competition with American industrial and agricultural products. If American industrial exports were to be increased they must go to the more backward nations and these nations ordinarily had only agricultural products and raw materials to give in exchange. As these same nations were

---

[9] Above, pp. 656 ff.

often not interested in importing agricultural products, any hope that the American farmer might be greatly benefited was bound to fade. It was a process of give and take in the hope that the long-term effect would be beneficial.

There was, of course, criticism of the reciprocal treaties during the campaign of 1936. Answering this criticism, the administration pointed to the

UNITED STATES
FOREIGN TRADE, 1940

NORTHERN
NORTH
AMERICA

18%
17%

41% EUROPE

39%

15%

ASIA &
OCEANIA
18%

9%
15%
8%
11%

5%
4%

AFRICA

SOUTHERN
NORTH AM.
CENTRAL
AM.

SOUTH
AMERICA

PICTOGRAPH CORPORATION

(From H. U. Faulkner and Tyler Kepner, *America, Its History and People,* Harper & Brothers.)

improvement in foreign trade, and to the greater fairness which it believed had been achieved by temporarily putting the tariff schedules in the hands of State Department experts rather than leaving them at the mercy of congressional lobbies. Finally, the administration contended that the treaties were influential in reversing the world-wide tendency that in the previous fifteen years had pushed tariff walls higher and higher. In this respect it should be noted that trade-agreement terms with any given nation applied also to the twenty-seven nations with which the United States has "most-favored-nation" agreements.[10] In other words, concessions to one nation automatically carried similar concessions on like products to all twenty-seven nations. Many, including Secretary Hull, believed that the trade-agreement treaties would also be an important influence in promoting peace in a world strained to a breaking point, but in this they were disappointed. Nevertheless, the trade agreements pointed to a condition of easier trade

[10] This does not apply to the Cuban trade agreement of 1934.

relations which most economists believed would have to be an essential part of the post-war world.

In the spring of 1943 the Administration asked Congress for a third renewal of the Trade Agreements Act. Republican victory in the congressional elections of 1942, however, had strengthened high-tariff sentiment as well as the power of the anti-Roosevelt bloc and efforts were made to modify the Act. In the end Congress renewed the Act, but for two years rather than three.

In addition to the trade agreements the Roosevelt administration attempted to improve international relations as well as the domestic economic situation by resuming diplomatic relations with Russia after sixteen years of non-recognition. At the same time a special commercial agreement was drawn up with her. The policy of promoting commerce through reciprocal tariffs was pushed with particular vigor in Latin America where it became an integral part of the "good-neighbor policy."

PREPARATION FOR WAR

It would take a volume adequately to describe the political and economic background of the Second World War as it developed from the Treaty of Versailles in 1919 to Pearl Harbor in December, 1941. As far as the conflict of arms is concerned, we now see a steady progression that began with the Japanese invasion of Manchuria in 1931 and moved steadily onward through the Italian conquest of Ethiopia in 1935, the fascist victory in Spain in 1938, and Hitler's occupation of Czechoslovakia in 1939 to the outbreak of the European war in September of that year. Although the United States made certain efforts during the fateful 1930's to ward off the coming catastrophe, she followed in general her traditional policy of avoiding European entanglements. This reached its climax in the Neutrality Acts of 1935–1937 in which our government reversed its policy of "freedom of the seas" and prepared to maintain neutrality in a future European war by avoiding any action which might involve us in the struggle.

This policy of neutrality was doomed from the start. Japan's invasion of China in 1937 and her announcement that she was "devoting her energy to the establishment of a New Order based on genuine justice throughout East Asia" was a direct challenge to the "open-door policy" and led inevitably to Pearl Harbor and war. Mr. Roosevelt's Chicago speech in October of that year, in which he denounced the aggressor nations who were promoting "international anarchy" and suggested a "quarantine" against international outlaws, was a direct indication that our government was no longer neutral with regard to aggressive fascism; in this the President expressed the attitude of the great majority of the nation. With Japan attempting to conquer China, the need of speeding American defense was obvious and it became even clearer with the outbreak of the war in Europe. After war began, the United States called conferences with the Latin-American nations to promote pan-American solidarity against the Axis powers, established a joint board of defense with Canada, effected an agreement with Great Britain for the lease of air and naval bases extending from Newfoundland to British Guiana, and in 1941 occupied Greenland and Iceland. At the same time military and naval appropriations were greatly increased and a Selective Service Act was passed in 1940 making all men from 21 to 45 liable for military service. In 1942 the draft age was lowered from 21 to 18.

MOBILIZATION OF RESOURCES

In the meantime, Congress in 1940 voted a total of $17,692,000,000 for the increase in the Army and Navy and other aspects of defense and in 1941 over $20,000,000,000. The latter appropriations were accompanied by the heaviest tax bill in our history up to that time, a bill which it was hoped would raise the total federal tax income to $13,000,000,000. Income taxes were increased steeply and exemptions were cut down to bring in 2,265,-000 additional taxpayers. In January, 1942, the President recommended to Congress $9,000,000,000 in additional taxes which would boost the revenue for 1943 to $25,000,000,000. After months of hearings the bill was finally passed in October. It imposed new levies designed to yield between $7,000,-000,000 and $8,000,000,000 and probably bring the total tax levy to the $25,-000,000,000 figure asked by the President. This was done again by increasing income taxes, by a 5 per cent "victory tax" on incomes over $624 a year (with deductions allowed or a proportion of the tax recovered after the war), by increasing surtax and excess profits rates on corporate taxes, and by stepping up the rates of the excise taxes.

By June, 1942, the staggering cost of the Second World War was becoming clear. The fiscal year ending on June 30 showed a national debt of $76,586,000,000 and a deficit of approximately $19,245,000,000. War appropriations cleared by Congress between June, 1940, and June, 1942, amounted to over $205,000,000,000, and other billions were voted in the subsequent months. By the end of 1942 the nation was spending $6,000,-000,000 a month, three times its expenditure in the First World War at its peak. Treasury reports predicted that expenditures for the fiscal year 1943 would amount to over $73,000,000,000, with a national debt on June 30, 1943, of around $130,000,000,000.

With such staggering appropriations it was clear that a "pay as you go" policy was out of the question. In June, 1942, the war was costing $1.15 per day per capita; receipts from taxation were 37 cents. As in earlier wars the government obtained its immediate income from taxation and loans. Greatly increased taxes on personal and corporation incomes and a wide extension of luxury taxes provided the chief current income for the payment of war costs. In addition, the government sold war stamps in denominations of ten cents to one dollar (to be later exchanged for war bonds) and several types of war bonds in denominations from $25 to $10,000, bearing interest at rates from 2.5 per cent to 2.9 per cent. Despite much advertising, the sale of stamps and bonds averaged only about $1,000,000,000 a month during 1942. When the Treasury launched the Victory Loan drive in December, however, subscriptions topped the $9,000,000,000 goal by over $3,000,-000,000. A Second War Loan drive in April, 1943, with an objective of $13,000,000,000 brought in more than $16,500,000,000.

It was one thing to vote money and call men into the armed service; it was quite another, and a far more difficult problem, to provide the needed equipment for the Army and Navy—warships, airplanes, munitions, tanks, and an innumerable variety of raw materials and manufactured goods. The "battle of production" was as important as the "battle of the armies," particularly in an age of highly mechanized warfare. Unlike Germany, America was keyed to peace-time manufacturing rather than to preparation for war. It was a long and difficult process to build new factories, convert and retool older plants for defense needs, control the use and production of raw materials, and meet the problems of labor and capital.

Efforts to coordinate this great task followed a procedure much like that in the First World War.[11] In May, 1940, the President established a Council of National Defense composed of the Secretaries of War, Navy, Interior, Agriculture, Commerce, and Labor. The Council was given an Advisory Commission of experts to obtain raw materials, supervise production, handle labor problems, manage farm products, supervise transportation, control prices, and deal with consumer problems. After seven months' trial it was evident that progress under this set-up was unsatisfactory. The difficulty was lack of coordination. To develop more speed and efficiency the President on January 7, 1941, established an Office of Production Management with William S. Knudsen, president of General Motors Corporation, as director, and Sidney Hillman, president of the Amalgamated Clothing Workers (C.I.O.) as associate director. Under OPM were grouped most of the activities of the Advisory Commission and the whole program of production was speeded.

[11] Above, pp. 594 ff.

But progress under the OPM was still too slow for the President and the nation. In September he created a new defense organization known as the Supply, Priorities, and Allocations Board (SPAB). Its chairman was Vice President Wallace and its executive director was Donald Nelson. Other members were Secretaries Stimson and Knox, OPM Directors Knudsen and Hillman, Lend-Lease Supervisor Harry Hopkins, and Price Administrator Leon Henderson. Except for the President, this board had the final direction of defense production. Progress under the OPM was still unsatisfactory, particularly after war began. There was obviously a divided responsibility which was slowing up the shift from a peace-time to a war-time economy. Late in January, 1942, the President abolished the OPM and in its place set up the War Production Board. At its head he placed Donald Nelson, and upon him put the final responsibility for the production and distribution of raw materials and finished products and their allocation among military and civilian needs. In addition to the chairman, the WPB included Vice President Wallace, Secretary of War Stimson, Secretary of the Navy Knox, Federal Loan Administrator Jesse Jones, and Price Administrator Leon Henderson. William Knudsen was assigned to the new Board as Munitions Director and Sidney Hillman was Labor Director for some months. These were the commanding generals in the battle of production in 1942.

After two years of organization and reorganization of various executive boards to promote the war effort, one might suppose that a solution had been reached. This was not the case. The old disputes among executives engaged in various phases of war production and the conflict between military and civil authorities over critical materials persisted. The fight against inflation seemed to be breaking down with a resulting increase in labor difficulties. The distribution of food was also breaking down and it was not being solved by rationing. In an effort to promote a better integration of the war effort the President determined in May, 1943, on one more reorganization at the top. This was to be an Office of War Mobilization, headed by James F. Byrnes, formerly Director of Economic Stabilization (below, p. 702), to unify the activities of federal agencies and develop unified programs. On it were the Secretaries of the Army and Navy; Donald Nelson, Chairman of the WPB; Harry Hopkins, Chairman of the Munitions Assignment Board, and Fred M. Vinson, who succeeded Byrnes as Director of Stabilization. For a long time many people had believed that the nation needed a strong war cabinet and many professed to see such a body in the OWM.

THE PRODUCTION FRONT

It was clear from the beginning that the Second World War was to be a mechanized war to a far greater extent than the conflict in 1914–1918. Fortunately the allied powers had the advantage in their control of the greater portion of the raw materials and factory facilities to turn these raw materials into tanks, airplanes, and guns. The problem was whether American factories could be retooled quickly enough to war mass production to turn the tide of battle. In its early stages the process was bound to be slow, for the technical difficulties of conversion were great. After our entrance into the war the whole program was speeded up tremendously. Less than six months after Pearl Harbor this phase of the war problem appeared to have been conquered. The United States, said Donald Nelson toward the end of May, 1942, "is actually doing things today which were unthinkable a year ago. It is executing programs which sounded utterly fantastic no more than six months ago." Production in virtually all phases, he said, was exceeding expectations. So rapidly was the conversion to war industries being effected that it was predicted that by the end of the year over 50 per cent of production would be centered in military supplies and over 17,000,000 wage earners would be engaged in war industries.

Mr. Nelson's predictions were more than fulfilled by the end of the year. The President's goal of 8,000,000 tons of shipping had been exceeded, with prospects bright for double that tonnage in 1943. Besides this there had been undisclosed additions to the Navy. Production in 1942 included 49,000 airplanes, 32,000 tanks and self-propelled artillery, and enormous amounts of guns and other materials. In his regular report early in December covering lease-lend materials the President announced that the amount spent for such materials in the preceding three months reached $2,367,000,000. To the British in Egypt had gone more than 1000 planes, hundreds of tanks, and 20,000 trucks. With Great Britain we had shipped to Russia during the year over the northern route alone more than 3000 planes, 4000 tanks, and 30,000 trucks. It was announced at the end of March, 1943, two years after the lease-lend program had begun, that total aid had reached $10,300,000,000. At that time the United Kingdom received 38 per cent and Russia 31 per cent.

By mid-summer of 1942 it was evident that the chief problem was no longer production, but rather obtaining certain raw materials. Bottlenecks in raw materials shifted as time went on. The first great shortage was in aluminum, and in the summer of 1941 the people were asked to contribute all the aluminum utensils that could be spared. Peace-time production in 1939 was 350,000,000 pounds. The shortage brought the govern-

ment into action with a government-owned but privately operated 640,-
000,000-pound expansion program which was doubled after Pearl Harbor.
The first expansion program was in operation by late summer, 1942, and
the aluminum shortage had vanished. This was not the case with other
metals, including iron. The United States has 50 per cent of the iron
resources of the world and surpasses any nation in productive capacity.
Moreover, the production of steel ingots reached an all-time high in June,
1942. The shortage was explained in part by failure to obtain scrap metal,
and this in turn was ascribed to the low ceiling on scrap prices. The main
difficulty, of course, was the fact that the fantastic war requirements had
finally outdistanced even the great productive capacity of America. Fortunately the situation improved as time went on.

As far as war needs were concerned, the two greatest shortages that developed in 1942 were ships and rubber. The shortage of ships was caused
primarily by the unexpectedly successful German submarine campaign in
the Atlantic which by November 1, 1942, had destroyed over 500 allied cargo
vessels. Fortunately the government objective of 8,000,000 tons in 1942 and
16,000,000 in 1943 was being achieved. By mid-1942 we were launching
two ships a day. At that time, however, ships were being destroyed more
rapidly than they were built, and the problem of delivering troops and
supplies to all parts of the world had become so acute that victory itself
depended on its solution. By mid-1943 the picture was brighter. Production
of ships had doubled and the battle against submarine warfare had become so effective that danger from lack of shipping had been overcome.

Far different from the aggressive efficiency with which the government
handled the aluminum problem was its muddling slowness in meeting the
rubber shortage. Japan's conquest of the East Indies completely closed the
source of virtually all the natural rubber used in this country, which
averaged 800,000 tons a year. It also cut off the United Nations' supply.
That a shortage would quickly develop was clear to everyone, and stocks
were frozen for war and essential civilian needs. Nevertheless, it was six
months after Pearl Harbor before government agencies actually organized
a synthetic rubber program. The processes of making synthetic rubber
had been largely discovered in America and were well known to rubber
chemists. The solution depended on deciding what type of synthetic rubber was to be produced, providing some $600,000,000 to build factories, and
obtaining steel and other materials to construct them. Confusion, divided
responsibility, and politics all slowed up the program. Politics entered when
the farm bloc discovered that synthetic rubber could be produced from
grain alcohol as well as from oil. In the end, however, the program finally
got under way. If all went well it was expected that by the middle of

1943 plants capable of producing 800,000 tons of synthetic rubber annually from an oil base would be in construction. Plants with a 200,000-ton capacity to make rubber from grain alcohol were also planned. In the meantime, the nation had to conserve its rubber to the utmost, eking out its needs from the reserve stock, reclaimed rubber, and the few thousand tons of the synthetic product being manufactured. Aggressive action came only after a special committee appointed by the President and composed of President James B. Conant of Harvard, President Karl T. Compton of the Massachusetts Institute of Technology, and Bernard M. Baruch had surveyed the situation, and the President had appointed William M. Jeffers as National Rubber Conservation Director.

The first manufacturing units for synthetic rubber were in actual production early in 1943. In the meantime, however, the need for aviation gas had increased to such an extent that it became necessary to reduce by 45 per cent the synthetic rubber program for 1943. Nevertheless, Director Jeffers confidently predicted a 250,000-ton output in 1943, and over 800,000 by 1944. By that time synthetic rubber would be available for civilian needs.

Shortage in foodstuffs occurred first in the two imported commodities, sugar and coffee. Americans normally consume 7,900,000 tons of sugar, most of which comes from Cuba, the Philippines, and Hawaii. With the declaration of war the Philippine supply was cut off, that from Hawaii seriously reduced, and that from Cuba curtailed by lack of shipping and submarine activity. At the same time, demand was increased by lend-lease shipments to England and Russia and by increased use of sugar in manufacturing alcohol for explosives. As a result Americans got their first taste of rationing early in May, 1942, when they registered for stamp books required henceforth for the purchase of sugar. As the months went by, shortages developed in other foodstuffs, but the only one of sufficient importance to cause rationing in 1942 was in coffee, most of which is imported from Brazil. As in the case of sugar, the immediate causes were exports to the allies and interference with shipping. Coffee rationing began late in November.

Production of most agricultural commodities had increased steadily in this country during the years 1939 to 1942 when certain crops had reached a record high. Although there was little fear of an acute shortage of foodstuffs at the opening of the war, the President in the interest of careful supervision appointed in June, 1942, a nine-man War Production Food Requirements Committee, headed by Secretary of Agriculture Claude Wickard. That careful conservation and supervision were needed was clear before the end of the year, when local shortages appeared in meat, canned goods, and other foodstuffs. In some cases they were caused by inefficient methods of distribution, in others by an actual shortage. Undoubtedly the increased demands of the Army and the needs of our allies were mainly responsible. By the end of the year our Army and lease-lend were absorbing 25 per cent of the supplies, particularly canned, bottled, frozen, and dried vegetables, fruits, juices, and soups. As these commodities began to disappear from grocers' shelves the nation was not surprised when Food Administrator Wickard on December 27 ordered Price Administrator Henderson to ration these commodities. Consumers registered in February for Ration Book No. 2 and on March 1, 1943, rationing of various kinds of canned and package goods went into operation under a "point system." Four weeks later rationing under the same system was extended to include meat, butter, lard, and other commodities. Rationing by that time covered 95 per cent of the food supply and insured a fairer distribution, but it by no means solved the problem of shortages. To promote efficiency Roosevelt named Chester C. Davis as Food Administrator and put in his hands the supervision of food production and distribution previously in charge of Wickard. Resigning in June, he was succeeded by Marvin Jones.

If the experience of the First World War meant anything, the problem of transportation was bound to be as difficult as that of production. The future was extremely unpredictable. Since 1917 America had more and more come to depend upon motor trucks and busses to supplement railroad transportation, and the cutting off of raw rubber supplies meant an eventual curtailment of motor transportation. As far as the railroads were concerned, the government was anxious to avoid, if possible, the responsibility of operation. Instead, in December, 1941, the President set up the Office of Defense Transportation to coordinate the domestic transportation policies and activities of the federal agencies and those of the private transportation groups. Joseph A. Eastman, chairman of the Interstate Commerce Commission, was appointed director. Working in close cooperation with the Office of Defense Transportation, the railroads met the challenge with increased efficiency and success. With one-third fewer locomotives and one-fourth less freight cars than in 1918, the greatest traffic year of the First World War, the railroads in 1942 moved 55 per cent more freight and 25 per cent more passengers. The freight load in 1942 was about one-third larger than in 1941 and more than double the annual average for the ten-year period ending with 1940. Passenger travel exceeded the previous peak year of 1920 by 13 per cent, and, as a whole, the job was done better. The miracle in freight movements was accomplished by an increase in the average load of freight cars and the length of the average haul. Average carload of freight was ten tons heavier than in the First World War and the average freight run almost 100 miles longer. This excellent performance of 1942 was even bettered in 1943.

The rôle to be played by the motor vehicle during the war depended upon the ability to distribute gas and provide rubber. The gas problem affected primarily the seventeen eastern seacoast states and Washington and Oregon. The nation, at least during the first year of the war, was well supplied with gasoline, but submarine interference with tanker shipments along the eastern coast had so curtailed the supply that gasoline rationing was established on the Atlantic seacoast and the two northwestern states in May, 1942, and made more stringent in July. It was extended to the entire nation on December 1. This rationing program attempted to provide gasoline for defense transportation and needed civilian business but to cut non-essential consumption to the bone. Solution of the gas shortage depended upon the ability of the railroads to speed up tank car deliveries, the building of new pipe lines, and the elimination of the submarine danger. Progress was made in all three ways. The railroads exerted heroic efforts to increase tank car movements. Congress in July authorized the building of a pipe line from the Mississippi to the east coast and the WPB released steel to build a pipe line from Texas to the Middle West. The Navy announced at the year's end that submarine losses in the Atlantic had been cut in half.

Closely allied to the gas problem was that of fuel oil. Like gasoline, fuel oil was produced during the first year of the war in sufficient quantities to meet the needs; the difficulty was transportation. The building of new pipe lines soon enough might have saved the East from fuel oil rationing and chilly houses during the winter of 1942–1943. Even if this had been done, a shortage of both gasoline and fuel oil was probably inevitable. By the time the transportation of these commodities was speeded, the greater demands of the armed forces following the invasion of Africa absorbed the increased shipments.

LABOR AND THE WAR

Two primary problems with respect to labor faced the federal government in its war efforts. The first was to obtain an adequate supply of trained personnel for war industries, and the second was to develop a sound and successful policy of handling labor disputes. The first problem did not become acute up to the middle of 1942. A far-sighted training program of "refresher courses" for adults and vocational training for youth during 1940–1941 added many workers for war industries and these were supplemented by thousands of women. Moreover, war industries after 1939 were able to absorb large numbers of unemployed. Provisions were also made in operating the Selective Service Act to retain essential men in war industries. There were, of course, cases of a shortage of labor in certain towns booming with war industries while unemployment was extensive in regions where civilian production had been curtailed.

At the beginning of 1940 about 500,000 persons were employed in war industries; by the end of 1942 at least 15,000,000 were so engaged, with the possibility of 20,000,000 by the end of 1943. This rapid increase in war workers accentuated earlier problems and produced new ones—training of apprentices, competition among war industries for skilled mechanics and pirating of labor by competing industries, the drafting of skilled mechanics for the armed forces, scarcity of labor in one section and an abundance in another. These and other problems led to the creation by the President on April 26, 1942, of a War Manpower Commission headed by Paul V. McNutt. The chairman was authorized "to establish basic national policies to assure the most effective mobilization and maximum utilization of the nation's manpower in the prosecution of the war." Although his power was undefined and rested largely on a basis of voluntary compliance, he was expected to supervise training, job recruiting, and placement, to formulate legislative programs, and to give "directives."

Following these directions Chairman McNutt issued a list of occupations essential to war industry, speeded up the whole program of vocational training, and with the aid of the Farm Placement Service of the United States Employment Service mobilized 3,000,000 workers for the fall harvests. As the shortage of labor became acute in the western lumber and non-ferrous mineral industries, a voluntary "employment stabilization plan" was worked out with labor representatives which practically froze workers in these industries in their jobs. Other local agreements of a similar nature were negotiated. So critical had the labor situation become by the end of the year that the President on December 5 enlarged the powers of the WMC to give it virtual control over the Selective Service system, authority to compel the hiring of labor through the United States Employment Service, and exclusive charge of all training for war industries. Under the executive order "no employer shall retain in his employ any worker whose services are more urgently needed in any establishment, plant facility, occupation or area designated as more essential." At the same time voluntary enlistment in the Army was restricted. In brief, the WMC was given the power to determine who should be drafted and the power to allocate labor.

During 1941 approximately 2,360,000 workers were involved in 4288 strikes.[12] This situation obviously could not continue in war time. With

[12] *Labor Information Bulletin*, May, 1942, p. 7.

the outbreak of hostilities many strikes then in progress were terminated and threatened strikes canceled. Leaders of both the American Federation of Labor and the Congress of Industrial Organizations voluntarily pledged these groups to maintain uninterrupted production of war supplies. At a conference of organized labor and employees called by the President in December a no-strike policy was officially formulated. To supervise the whole machinery of conciliation and mediation the President in January, 1942, appointed a twelve-member board, headed by William H. Davis and composed equally of representatives of the public, employers, and labor. If it was found impossible to settle a labor dispute with the existing machinery, the dispute could be certified by the Secretary of Labor to the War Labor Board for jurisdiction and determination through mediation or arbitration.

On the whole, the attitude and cooperation of labor were all that could be desired, at least until the coal strikes of May–June, 1943. Except for a few minor wildcat strikes, labor kept its promise of a non-strike policy. This policy was both wise and patriotic, but it put labor in a position in which the employer could take advantage. In the end, however, most disputes were handled by the War Labor Board and its subdivisions. In its effort to cooperate and maintain uninterrupted production, organized labor urged management to join with it in worker-management committees to find means of speeding production. This suggestion was backed by the War Production Board and hundreds of these committees were set up, to the great benefit of production.

Notwithstanding labor's generally cooperative spirit, there developed during the late spring of 1942 an aggressive anti-labor drive aimed at legislation to modify the Fair Labor Standards Act and to outlaw strikes in defense industries. Labor argued that the time-and-a-half basis for wage payments required by the Fair Labor Standards Act after 40 hours was not unreasonable in view of the rising cost of living and insisted that it was not trying to profit from the war. In any event, the administration opposed further labor legislation and the movement subsided for the time being. A few months later a new wave of criticism developed over the large amount of absenteeism in some of the war plants. Labor admitted that it was too large, but pointed out that much of it was caused by sickness resulting from inadequate housing in many war production centers, by the fact that hundreds of thousands of women normally concerned with household duties were now working in war plants and found it impossible to handle two jobs, and that breakdowns in routing raw materials or failures in management planning often held up production and encouraged workers to stay away. In any event, the situation improved during 1943.

This generally satisfactory labor condition ended in the late spring of 1943. The difficulty arose over a conflict between John L. Lewis and his 500,000 soft coal miners who demanded increases,[13] and the federal government's efforts to prevent inflation by holding wages to the "Little Steel formula." When workers in Little Steel had demanded higher wages, the War Labor Board granted an approximate 15 per cent increase (June, 1942) on the grounds that the cost of living had increased that much since January, 1941. On January 8, 1943, the President virtually ordered the WLB to hold wage increases to that amount. Although most miners had received the 15 per cent increase, if not more, mine leaders asserted that the cost of living had risen far beyond that amount and demanded a flat $2 a day increase. When negotiations with the mine owners broke down, the union leaders refused to take their case to the WLB on the grounds that it was powerless to rectify the situation, and called a strike on May 1. President Roosevelt replied by ordering Secretary of the Interior Ickes, Coordinator of Hard Fuels, to take possession of all coal mines in which stoppages had taken place, and in a radio broadcast urged the miners not to strike against the government but to resume work immediately. Shortly before the President went on the air, mine leaders called a 15-day truce and ordered the men to return to work.

Ignoring the WLB, the union leaders continued negotiations with the operators. When the WLB refused to meet the $2 a day demand and no progress was made in negotiations with the operators, a new strike began on June 1. The President ordered the men back to work and Lewis acceded, setting a new date line of June 30 for further negotiations. Mine leaders now shifted their demands from a $2 a day raise to a portal-to-portal payment, that is, payment for the time spent going from the door of the mine to their place of work and returning. On June 18 the WLB turned down all demands of the miners and in the succeeding days the miners walked out a third time. A third time Lewis ordered them back, this time until October 1, with the stipulation that the government continue to operate the mines.

Although many felt that the miners had real grievances, the nation as a whole was aroused over interruption in the production of a vital war necessity. Taking advantage of this resentment, anti-labor leaders in Congress pushed through the War Labor Disputes Act. Operative until six months after the war, the Act virtually bans strikes in government-operated plants by providing fines and imprisonment for anyone encouraging such strikes. It requires a 30-day cooling-off period and a secret strike ballot for war

[13] The United Mine Workers had been suspended from the A. F. of L. in 1936, had withdrawn from the C.I.O. in 1942, and during the coal dispute requested in May, 1943, readmission into the A. F. of L.

industries not operated by the government; gives the President authority to seize plants, mines, and other facilities affected by labor disputes; forbids a change in wages and working conditions in a seized plant without authority of the WLB; gives the WLB power to subpoena parties in a labor dispute; and forbids labor organizations, banks, and corporations organized under federal laws to make political contributions in any election involving officials of the federal government. Opposed by the administration and various government boards concerned with war production in the belief that it would injure rather than improve the generally satisfactory labor relations, the President vetoed the bill. It was immediately passed over his veto on June 25.

PRICE CONTROL

The greatest failure of the federal government during the First World War was its inability to control the price situation. Prices soared 100 per cent, greatly increasing the cost of the war and seriously injuring those whose income failed to keep pace with the cost of living.[14] Profiting from this earlier experience, the President in 1940 set up an agency headed by Leon Henderson to work toward the stabilization of prices. In 1941 this agency became the Office of Price Administration, established under the emergency powers of the President. Although its own powers were vague, it had, however, by the end of 1941 established price ceilings on over thirty commodities, chiefly raw materials, and maintained them with fair success. It accomplished this by persuasion, warnings, requests, and agreements.

By this time it was evident that the fight against inflation could not be won unless Congress granted wider and more definite powers. By February, 1942, wholesale prices had risen 28 per cent and retail prices 14 per cent over pre-war levels. As analyzed by the OPA, the trend toward higher prices was due to shortages of raw materials or facilities for production, heavy buying by government agencies, hoarding, increased costs, and profiteering. Congress was not oblivious to the need for price legislation, but passage of a bill was delayed because the farm bloc desired to exempt farm products from price ceilings and the anti-labor bloc wanted to include provisions for a ceiling on wages. These demands were opposed by both the administration and the OPA. In the end the bill was passed without the wage ceiling and with a compromise on agricultural products. The Emergency Price Control Act of January, 1942, gave the government wide power to establish maximum levels beyond which prices may not go, and full power to enforce them and to impose penalties for violations. The

---

[14] Above, p. 600.

Act provided that permission must be obtained from the Secretary of Agriculture for price ceilings on certain agricultural products and that these ceilings must be not less than 110 per cent of parity.

Even with power to establish price ceilings the battle was far from won. All kinds of aggressive action by the OPA would be needed, and it was evident before many months had passed that Congress was unwilling to grant adequate funds to enforce the Act. Moreover, many economic forces were at work to push prices up. The simultaneous increase of consumers' incomes and the decrease in consumers' goods provided a perfect background for inflation. The OPA estimated that income payments for 1942 would amount to approximately 117 billion dollars, of which 31 billions would be returned to the government either in taxes or in individual savings in the form of bonds and stamps, leaving a balance of 86 billions available for spending on civilian goods and services. At the same time it estimated that the goods and services which could be produced during 1942 would total approximately 69 billions. This would leave about 17 billions of purchasing power which would constitute a serious threat to the price structure. These estimates were not far from correct and they help to make clear the danger of inflation.

Publicity in the drive against inflation was aided by the President in a message to Congress on April 27, 1942, when he suggested seven methods of holding down the cost of living. They included heavy taxation to keep personal and corporate profits at a reasonable rate; the fixing of ceilings on prices paid by consumers, retailers, wholesalers, and manufacturers, and on rents in defense areas; the stabilizing of wages and salaries, and of prices received for farm products; the extension of war bond purchases; the rationing of essential commodities of which there is a scarcity; the contraction of credit and installment buying, and the payment of outstanding debts. On the following day the OPA announced regulations establishing price ceilings on most of the foods and other goods and services to take effect in the wholesale trade on May 11 and in retail trade on May 18. At the same time rents in 323 defense areas with an estimated population of 86,000,000 were frozen at the March, 1942, level, or at an earlier level if the rise had been too great. Later in the year these areas were widely extended. By other means efforts were made to curtail installment buying and credit expansion.

Whether these measures would be adequate or new ones, such as enforced savings, would be necessary was hard to predict. At one time or another the OPA felt it necessary to raise the ceilings for processors, distributors, or sellers of some commodity to keep them from bankruptcy, and many were quick to point to the danger of a general spiraling if a ceiling slipped upward on a single commodity. Furthermore, there was no ceiling on wages until the Little Steel formula, noted above, was worked out in June, 1942, and given official sanction in April, 1943. Since the situation continued to be unsatisfactory, the President in his Labor Day message of 1942 asked Congress for full power to regulate farm prices, and threatened that if Congress did not grant such power by October 1, he would accept responsibility for action. A bill in line with the President's wishes (including also power to stabilize wages and salaries) was passed on October 2. On the following day the President issued an order directing (1) the National Labor Board to limit wages and salaries, (2) the Office of Price Administration to fix ceilings on retail and wholesale prices and on rents not yet curbed, and (3) the Department of Agriculture and the OPA to cooperate to hold down farm prices. To supervise all this control he created an Office of Economic Stabilization and as its head appointed Associate Justice Byrnes, who resigned from the Supreme Court to accept the position. In the meantime Leon Henderson, who for more than two years had led the fight against inflation, resigned in December as Director of the OPA and was succeeded by Senator Prentiss M. Brown of Michigan, who had failed of reelection in November. It was clear from the start that the battle against inflation would be long and hard. It was also clear that the future happiness and security of millions would rest on the outcome.

A GLANCE BACKWARD

This book ends in the midst of the Second World War, a catastrophe so vast that the mind of mankind can hardly comprehend its significance. At such a time of crisis and reorientation it is easy enough to forget the inspiring drama of American history as it has unfolded before us. We have seen in this volume how the precarious settlements on the Atlantic coast grew into a mighty and wealthy nation. We have seen one generation of frontiersmen after another push their way farther and farther west until they conquered a continent and left for their children an unsurpassed heritage. We have seen a primitive agricultural people broaden its interests under the stimulus of limitless raw materials and become a nation whose economic life has widened into almost every activity. And we have seen an economically dependent people achieve first political, then economic, independence until finally it assumed a strong economic and political rôle and became a nation which proved the decisive factor in the First World War. It has been a history of the opening and exploitation of a region enormously rich in raw materials and overflowing with possibilities. Our people have met the task with confidence, buoyancy, and optimism. A continent has been conquered, but the methods have been crude and wasteful.

Much of value has been needlessly squandered and lost forever. Irreparable inroads have been made in our most valuable raw materials.

As we have grown rapidly and chaotically into a mighty manufacturing nation, the population has increased and concentrated in cities, economic groups have become more differentiated, and class feeling has grown stronger. We are now experiencing many of the economic and social problems of the older industrial nations of Europe, problems which have become far too complicated to be solved automatically under a policy of *laissez faire*. The Great Depression of 1929 opened a new era characterized by a rapid movement toward a more closely integrated economic and social life, a society in which economic planning was succeeding *laissez faire*. What the depression did to American economic life in the 1930's, the Second World War seemed destined to do for American international relations in the 1940's. Many indications pointed to a breakdown of isolation and *laissez faire* in international relations and in their place a closer integration with the political and economic life of the world.

SELECTED READINGS

Williams, B. H., *Economic Foreign Policy of the United States,* Chaps. I–VI.

Moulton, H. G., and Pasvolsky, Leo, *War Debts and World Prosperity,* Part V.

Dietrich, Ethel, *World Trade,* Chaps. II–VIII.

Sayre, F. B., *The Way Forward: The American Trade Agreement Program,* Chaps. IV, VIII, XIV.

Haines, C. G., and Hoffman, R. J. S., *The Origins and Background of the Second World War,* Chaps. V, VIII, XII, XV.

Bibliography

1. PHYSIOGRAPHIC FACTORS AND NATURAL RESOURCES

The interest of thinkers on the influence of geography upon history has been traced through the ages by H. E. Barnes, *The New History and the Social Studies* (1925), Chap. II. Perhaps the most famous contribution was made by H. T. Buckle, *History of Civilization in England* (1884), in his epoch-making introduction. The subject has been brilliantly followed by H. B. George, *The Relations of Geography and History* (1901). An economist's point of view may be found in Achille Loria, *Economic Foundations of Society* (1898). The best work on American history has been done by F. J. Turner in his famous studies; by Ellen C. Semple, *American History and Its Geographic Conditions* (1903), and *Influence of Geographic Environment* (1911); and by A. B. Hulbert, *Soil and Its Influence on the History of the United States* (1930).

The attempt of a geologist to interpret American history was made by A. P. Brigham, *Geographic Influences in American History* (1903). Two short but enlightening sketches are D. R. Fox's introduction to *Harper's Atlas of American History* (1920) and Chap. I of A. M. Schlesinger, *New Viewpoints in American History* (1922). The relations between geography and history have been emphasized by N. S. Shaler, *Nature and Man in America* (1899), and *The United States of America* (2 vols., 1897).

A preliminary discussion of products and resources is to be found in Livingston Farrand, *Basis of American History* (1904), Vol. II of the American Nation Series, and in Ellsworth Huntington, *The Red Man's Continent* (1919) in the Chronicles of America Series. Further figures and facts are obtainable in C. R. Van Hise, *Conservation of Natural Resources in the United States* (1910), revised in 1930 under the editorship of Loomis Havemeyer; in E. D. Durand, *American Industry and Commerce* (1930); in C. G. Gilbert and J. E. Pogue, *America's Power Resources* (1921); in R. S. Kellogg, *The Timber Supply of the United States* (1909); in J. R. Smith, *Men and Resources: A Study of North America and Its Place in World Geography* (1937); and in John Ise, *United States Forest Policy* (1920) and *United States Oil Policy* (1927). On soils C. E. Kellogg, *The Soils That Support Us* (1941) is an excellent introduction. In 1938 the Department of Agriculture devoted its entire yearbook to this subject under the title *Soils and Men*.

Numerous excellent textbooks on economic geography are available, including J. R. Smith and O. M. Phillips, *North America* (1940); H. H. McCarty, *The Geographic Basis of American Economic Life* (1940); E. Huntington and S. W. Cushing, *Principles of Human Geography* (2nd ed., 1922); and E. Huntington and F. E. Williams, *Business Geography* (1926). On the effect of climate on man, see E. Huntington, *Civilization and Climate* (1924). C. C. Colby, *Source Book for the Economic Geography of North America* (3rd ed., 1927) is helpful. The student who desires a basic knowledge of geology is referred to *Textbook of Geology, Part I, Physical Geology,* by C. R. Langwell, Adolph Knopf, and R. F. Flint (2nd ed., 1939), and Part II, *Historical Geology,* by Charles Schuchert and C. O. Dunbar (3rd ed., 1933).

A stimulating book is R. H. Whitbeck and O. J. Thomas, *The Geographic Factor: Its Rôle in Life and Civilization* (1932). Revealing observations of the effect of physical environment on social, political, and economic life are frequently found in Ernest Gruening (ed.), *These United States* (2 vols., 1923–1924). Interesting on frontier disease is R. C. Buley, "Pioneer Health and Medical Practices in the Old Northwest to 1840," *Mississippi Valley Historical Review,* Vol. XX, No. 4, pp. 497–520 (March, 1934). One of the ablest of the recent studies of climatic influence is Louis C. Hunter, "Seasonal Aspects of the Economic Life of the Ohio Valley Before the Age of Big Business," in *Smith College Studies in History,* Vol. XIX, Nos. 1–2 (Oct., 1933–Jan., 1934).

2. ECONOMIC BACKGROUND OF COLONIZATION

For Europe on the eve of expansion, see E. P. Cheyney, *European Background of American History* (1904), and his *The Dawn of a New Era* (1936). For general accounts of the late Middle Ages, see Carl Stephenson, *Mediæval History* (1935); J. W. Thompson, *Economic and Social History of Europe in the Late Middle Ages, 1300–1530* (1931); E. Lipson, *The Economic History of England* (3 vols., 1915–1931); and the early chapters of Curtis Nettels, *The Roots of American Civilization* (1938).

The story of the Commercial Revolution is summarized in W. C. Abbott, *Expansion of Europe* (2 vols., 1918), and in L. B. Packard, *The Commercial Revolution* (1927). Readable accounts of discovery and exploration are given in G. K. Jayne, *Vasco da Gama and His Successors* (1910); J. P. O. Martins, *The Golden Age of Prince Henry the Navigator* (1914); Edgar Prestage, *The Portuguese Pioneers* (1933); Joseph Jacobs, *Story of Geographical Discovery* (1904); J. N. L. Baker, *History of Geographical Discovery and Exploration* (1932); and J. Bartlett Brebner, *The Explorers of North America, 1492–1806* (1933). Albert H. Lybyer, "Influence of the Ottoman Turks upon the Routes of Oriental Trade," *Annual Report of the American Historical Association* (1914), Vol. I, pp. 125–133, clears up certain misconceptions. New light has also been thrown on Venice and the shifting trade routes by F. C. Lane, "Venetian Shipping During the Commercial Revolution," *American Historical Review,* Vol. XXXVIII, No. 2 (January, 1933), and in his *Venetian Ships and Shipbuilders of the Renaissance* (1934). The best life of Columbus is probably S. E. Morison, *Admiral of the Ocean Sea* (1942). Leading sources are in Cecil Jane (ed.), *Select Documents Illustrating the Four Voyages of Columbus* (1930-1933), with an essay on Columbus. The present situation in scholarship regarding Columbus is reviewed in C. E. Nowell, "The Columbus Question," *American Historical Review,* Vol. XLIV, No. 4, pp. 802-822 (July, 1939). Also important is Henry Vignaud, *Toscanelli and Columbus* (1902).

Richard Hakluyt, *Principall Navigations, Voyages, Traffiques, and Discoveries of the English Nation* (16 vols., 1885-1890) is indispensable for the background of English exploration and settlement. The early chapters of Louis M. Hacker, *The Triumph of American Capitalism* (1940), survey brilliantly the economic background of colonization. On the influence of the Protestant Revolt, see R. H. Tawney, *Religion and the Rise of Capitalism* (1926).

3. THE COLONIZATION OF AMERICA

The bibliography on the English colonies is extensive, ranging from single-volume introductions—like those of C. L. Andrews, *The Colonial Period* (1912), in the Home University Library; L. G. Tyler, *England in America* (1904), in the American Nation Series; E. B. Greene, *The Foundations of American Nationality* (1922); H. E. Bolton and T. M. Marshall, *The Colonization of North America, 1492-1783* (1921); M. W. Jernegan, *The American Colonies, 1492-1750* (1929); Carl Becker, *Beginnings of the American People* (1915); C. M. Andrews, *The Fathers of New England* (1919), Chronicles of America Series, Chap. IV; and S. G. Fisher, *The Quaker Colonies* (1919), Chronicles of America Series, Chaps. IV and IX—to more detailed works occupying several volumes. Among the latter are the scholarly volumes based upon the most recent investigations of H. L. Osgood, *The American Colonies in the Seventeenth Century* (3 vols., 1904-1907), *The American Colonies in the Eighteenth Century* (4 vols., 1924-1925); Charles M. Andrews, *The Colonial Period in American History* (1934–   ); and Edward Channing, *History of the United States,* Vols. I–III (1905-1912). The great cooperative work of Justin Winsor, *Narrative and Critical History of America* (8 vols., 1888-1889), is invaluable. The most noteworthy study by an Englishman is that of J. A. Doyle, *English Colonies in America* (5 vols., 1882-1907); consult also his contribution to *The Cambridge Modern History.* Interestingly written and historically sound are the two volumes by J. T. Adams, *The Founding of New England* (1921) and *Revolutionary New England* (1923). A successful effort to emphasize the social history and picture the life of the common man has been made by T. J. Wertenbaker, *The First Americans* (1927), and J. T. Adams, *Provincial America* (1927). Vols. II and III in A History of American Life. Two recent textbooks are O. P. Chitwood, *A*

History of Colonial America (1931) and Curtis Nettels, *The Roots of American Civilization* (1938), the latter emphasizing the economic phase. For the important simultaneous history of the West Indies, see F. W. Pitman, *The Development of the British West Indies, 1700–1763* (1917).

The more purely economic aspect is touched on in William B. Weeden, *Economic and Social History of New England* (2 vols., 1891), and Philip A. Bruce, *Economic History of Virginia in the Seventeenth Century* (2 vols., 1895). On land tenure, see B. W. Bond, Jr., "Quit Rent System in the American Colonies," in the *American Historical Review,* October, 1912, and V. F. Barnes, "Land Tenure in English Colonial Charters in the Seventeenth Century," *Essays in Colonial History* (1931), pp. 4–40. Usable and accessible collections of source material are E. L. Bogart and C. M. Thompson, *Readings in the Economic History of the United States* (1916); A. B. Hart, *American History Told by Contemporaries* (4 vols., 1901); William MacDonald, *Select Charters Illustrative of American History* (1904); and J. F. Jameson (ed.), *Original Narratives of Early American History* (13 vols., 1906–1912). A practical and almost indispensable aid to further study is the *Guide to the Study and Reading of American History* (rev. ed., 1912), by Edward Channing, A. B. Hart, and F. J. Turner.

A good introduction to the Spanish colonial system is the fifth chapter of H. H. Bancroft, *History of Central America,* Vol. I (1882); a more detailed account is W. Roscher, *The Spanish Colonial System* (1904). Excellent summaries of Spain in America are Bernard Moses, *The Establishment of Spanish Rule in America* (1898); E. G. Bourne, *Spain in America* (1904), in the American Nation Series; William R. Shepherd, *Latin America* (1914), especially good on the transplanting of Spanish culture; and William S. Robertson, *History of the Latin American Nations* (1922). Spanish civilization in America is competently described by H. I. Priestley, *The Coming of the White Man* (1929), Vol. I of A History of American Life. H. E. Bolton, *The Spanish Borderlands* (1921), should also be read. The spectacular features of the early years of Spain in America are covered in the classic volumes of W. H. Prescott, *The Conquest of Mexico* (1843) and *The Conquest of Peru* (1847). Further light on the economic aspects of New Spain may be gleaned from C. H. Haring, *Trade and Navigation Between Spain and the Indies in the Time of the Hapsburgs* (1918), and L. B. Simpson, *The Encomienda in New Spain* (1929). A source of never-failing interest is covered in C. H. Haring, *The Buccaneers in the West Indies* (1910) and P. A. Means, *The Spanish Main* (1935). A competent textbook is M. W. Williams, *The People and Politics of Latin America* (1930).

On France in America, consult R. G. Thwaites, *France in America* (1904), in the American Nation Series; W. B. Munro, *Crusaders of New France* (1918), in the Chronicles of America Series (Chaps. VIII–XI are best on New France); H. I. Priestley, *The Coming of the White Man;* the histories of Francis Parkman, especially *Pioneers of France in the New World* (1865), *The Old Régime in Canada* (1874), *Montcalm and Wolfe* (2 vols., 1884), and *A Half Century of Conflict* (2 vols., 1892). An important contribution is A. L. Burt, *The Old*

Province of Quebec (1933). French explorations are emphasized in Justin Winsor, *Cartier and Frontenac* (1894), and *The Mississippi Valley* (1895). Carl Wittke, *History of Canada* (rev. ed., 1941), is an excellent recent text.

On the Dutch in New York, see J. R. Brodhead, *History of New York* (2 vols., 1871); John Fiske, *Dutch and Quaker Colonies* (2 vols., 1899); T. A. Janvier, *The Dutch Founding of New York* (1903); J. H. Innes, *New Amsterdam and Its People* (1902); A. C. Flick (ed.), *History of the State of New York* (1933); and M. W. Goodwin, *Dutch and English on the Hudson* (1919), Chronicles of America.

4. COLONIAL AGRICULTURE AND LABOR

The best bibliographies of American agriculture are those by Louis Bernard Schmidt, *Topical Studies and References on the Economic History of American Agriculture* (rev. ed., 1923), and E. E. Edwards, *A Bibliography of the History of Agriculture in the United States,* Dept. of Agriculture, Misc. Pub. No. 84 (1930). On Indian agriculture the following are useful: P. A. Bruce, *Economic History of Virginia in the Seventeenth Century,* Vol. I (1895); L. Farrand, *Basis of American History* (1904), in the American Nation Series; John Fiske, *Discovery of America* (2 vols., 1891), Chap. I; J. W. Powell, "The North American Indians," in N. S. Shaler, *The United States of America,* Vol. I (1897); and G. K. Holmes, "Aboriginal Agriculture: The North American Indian," in Bailey's *Cyclopedia of American Agriculture,* Vol. IV (1909).

Adequate and scholarly are the treatments by Lyman Carrier, *The Beginnings of American Agriculture* (1923); P. W. Bidwell and J. I. Falconer, *History of Agriculture in the Northern United States Before 1860* (1925); and L. C. Gray, *History of Agriculture in the Southern United States to 1860* (2 vols., 1933). The ablest summary of our agricultural history is the article by E. E. Edwards, "American Agriculture—The First 300 Years," *Yearbook of Agriculture, 1940,* pp. 171–276. A general and popular survey is that of A. H. Sanford, *Story of Agriculture in the United States* (1915), and a more condensed but clearly stated account is that by T. N. Carver, "Historical Sketch of American Agriculture," in Vol. IV of Bailey's *Cyclopedia of American Agriculture.* Old but still usable for their details are A. S. Bolles, *Industrial History of the United States* (1878), which devotes some space to agriculture, and the contribution of C. L. Flint, "Agriculture in the United States, 1607–1860," in *Eighty Years' Progress* (1861). Virginian agriculture is exhaustively handled by Bruce, *Economic History of Virginia,* and suggestively treated by T. J. Wertenbaker, *The Planters of Colonial Virginia* (1922), and E. Q. Hawk, *Economic History of the South* (1934); glimpses of northern agriculture are given in Weeden, *Economic and Social History of New England.* Short but illuminating chapters by experts are to be found in Vol. V of *The South in the Building of the Nation.* Among the special studies are those of M. Jacobstein, *The Tobacco Industry in the United States,* Columbia University Studies in History, Economics and Public Law, Vol. XXVI,

No. 3 (1907), and L. G. Connor, "A Brief History of the Sheep Industry," in the *Annual Report of the American Historical Association* (1918). The most valuable and interesting contemporary account is the anonymously published *American Husbandry* (2 vols., 1775). That a few colonial farmers were intensely interested in colonial farming is evident in C. R. Woodward, *Ploughs and Politicks, Charles Read of New Jersey and His Notes on Agriculture* (1941). Other source material may be found in E. L. Bogart and C. M. Thompson, *Readings in the Economic History of the United States* (1916), and in L. B. Schmidt and E. D. Ross, *Readings in the Economic History of American Agriculture* (1925). T. J. Wertenbaker, *The First Americans* (1927), and J. T. Adams, *Provincial America* (1927), give pictures of an essentially agrarian society as exemplified in colonial America. An outstanding contribution to agricultural history is A. O. Craven, *Soil Exhaustion as a Factor in the Agricultural History of Virginia and Maryland, 1606–1860* (1926). A perusal of R. H. Gabriel, *Toilers of Land and Sea* (1926), Vol. III in the Pageant of America, an attempt to deal with American history through the medium of pictures, will be found rewarding.

The results of much earlier investigation have been brought together by U. B. Phillips in *American Negro Slavery* (1921) and in *Life and Labor in the Old South* (1929). More detailed studies in special fields are those of J. R. Brackett, *The Negro in Maryland* (1889); J. C. Ballagh, *Slavery in Virginia* (1902); and E. R. Turner, *The Negro in Pennsylvania, Slavery—Servitude—Freedom, 1639–1861* (1910). Source material appears in Elizabeth Donnan, *Documents Illustrative of the Slave Trade to America* (3 vols., 1930–1932). On the conditions of white servitude are the investigations of E. I. McCormac, *White Servitude in Maryland* (1904), Johns Hopkins Studies; J. C. Ballagh, *White Servitude in Virginia* (1895), *ibid.;* J. S. Bassett, *Servitude and Slavery in the Colony of North Carolina* (1896), *ibid.;* C. A. Herrick, *White Servitude in Pennsylvania* (1926); and K. F. Geiser, *Redemptioners and Indented Servants in Pennsylvania* (Supplement to the *Yale Review,* 1901). See also A. E. Smith, "The Transportation of Convicts to the American Colonies in the Seventeenth Century," *American Historical Review,* Vol. XXXIX, No. 2 (Jan., 1934). One of the best treatments of the indentured servant is in Edward Eggleston, *The Transit of Civilization,* pp. 293–307. A more recent study is Marcus W. Jernegan, *Laboring and Dependent Classes in Colonial America, 1607–1783* (Chicago, 1931). T. J. Wertenbaker, *Patrician and Plebeian in Virginia* (1910) and *Planters of Colonial Virginia* (1922) throw considerable light on class structure in that colony. An excellent summary of plantation labor appears in L. C. Gray, *History of Agriculture in the Southern States to 1860* (2 vols., 1933), Chap. XVI.

5. COLONIAL COMMERCE AND INDUSTRY

A brief survey of colonial industry is given in Clive Day, *History of Commerce of the United States* (1925) and in excellent chapters in Curtis Nettels, *The*

Roots of American Civilization (1938). L. M. Hacker, *The Triumph of American Capitalism* (1940) presents an intelligent interpretation.

The standard work and the one most satisfactory for student consultation is the cooperative work of Emory R. Johnson, T. W. Van Metre, G. G. Huebner, and D. S. Hanchitt, *History of Domestic and Foreign Commerce of the United States* (2 vols., 1915), based on monographs by other collaborators and published in the Contributions to American Economic History by the Department of Economics and Sociology of the Carnegie Institution of Washington. A useful bibliography will be found on pages 112 to 117 of Vol. I. Important in their special field are M. S. Moriss, *Colonial Trade of Maryland, 1689–1715*, Johns Hopkins University Studies, Series XXXII, No. 3 (1914); C. P. Gould, *Money and Transportation in Maryland, 1720–1765* (1915); and C. C. Crittenden, *The Commerce of North America, 1763–1789* (1936). Enlightening is J. S. Bassett, "The Relation Between the Virginia Planter and the London Merchant," *Annual Report of the American Historical Association* (1901), Vol. I, pp. 553–575.

English colonial policy can be best studied in the works of G. L. Beer, *Origins of British Colonial Policy, 1578–1660* (1908); *British Colonial Policy, 1754–1765* (1907), and *The Old Colonial System* (1913); these are among the most notable contributions made by an American scholar in economic history. A handy introduction to these volumes is the same author's *Commercial Policy of England Toward the American Colonies,* Columbia University Studies in Economics, History and Public Law, Vol. XI, No. II (1893). See also H. E. Egerton, *British Colonial Policy* (2d ed., 1909), and for a brief but most enlightening survey, C. M. Andrews, *The Colonial Period* (1912), in the Home University Library. Two valuable articles by C. M. Andrews are "Colonial Commerce," *American Historical Review,* Vol. XX (Oct., 1914) and "Anglo-French Commercial Rivalry, 1700–1750," *ibid.,* Vol. XXI (July, 1915).

On mercantilism, consult Gustav Schmoller, *The Mercantile System and Its Historical Significance* (1896). Edward Channing, in his *History of the United State* (Vol. II, 1908), devotes Chap. XVII to Colonial Industry and Commerce. The somewhat desultory but valuable *Economic and Social History of New England* by William B. Weeden (2 vols., 1890) contains much information.

On colonial finance, see D. R. Dewey, *Financial History of the United States* (rev. ed., 1928). On the medium of exchange in Virginia, see P. A. Bruce, *Economic History of Virginia in the Seventeenth Century* (2 vols., 1907), Vol. II, Chap. XIX.

Treatments of the slave trade are to be found in W. W. Claridge, *History of the Gold Coast* (1915); U. B. Phillips, *American Negro Slavery* (1921); and W. E. B. DuBois, *The Suppression of the American Slave Trade* (1896). On piracy, see the *Encyclopedia Britannica* (11th ed.); G. F. Dow and J. H. Edmonds, *The Pirates of the New England Coast, 1630–1730* (1923), and G. F. Dow, *Slave Ships and Slavery* (1927). On privateering, see Edgar S. Maclay, *History of American Privateers* (new ed., 1924), and J. F. Jameson (ed.), *Privateering and Piracy in the Colonial Period* (1924), a source book.

The best single volume on the subject is that by V. S. Clark, *History of Manu-factures in the United States, 1607–1860* (1916), published by the Carnegie In-stitution in a valuable series on American economic history. It contains an ex-tensive bibliography. Two books, now out of date but containing a mass of interesting detail not easily accessible elsewhere, are J. L. Bishop, *A History of American Manufactures from 1608–1860* (3 vols., 1866), and A. S. Bolles, *In-dustrial History of the United States* (1887). A briefer and later review is C. D. Wright, *The Industrial Evolution of the United States* (1897), which rests heavily upon Bishop. Brief accounts are contained in Malcolm Keir, *Manufactur-ing* (1928) under specific industries. Consult also E. L. Lord, *Industrial Experi-ments in the British Colonies of North America* (1898) in Johns Hopkins Studies in Historical and Political Science, Vol. XVII, and R. M. Tryon, *Household Manufactures in the United States, 1640–1860* (1917).

Two standard studies on particular sections are W. B. Weeden, *Economic and Social History of New England* (2 vols., 1890), and P. A. Bruce, *Economic History of Virginia in the Seventeenth Century* (2 vols., 1895). Other material on the South is contained in E. Q. Hawk, *Economic History of the South* (1934), and Kathleen Bruce, *Virginia Iron Manufacture in the Slave Era* (1931).

A good chapter on the fur trade is in the high school text by J. R. H. Moore, *Industrial History of the American People* (1913). See also Katherine Coman, *Economic Beginnings of the Far West* (1912). Invaluable is the scholarly H. A. Innis, *The Fur Trade in Canada* (1930). Very suggestive is his "Interrelations Between the Fur Trade of Canada and the United States," *Mississippi Valley Historical Review*, Vol. XX, No. 3 (Dec., 1930). A. T. Volwiler, *George Crogham and the Westward Movement, 1741–1782* (1926), and V. W. Crane, *The Southern Frontier, 1670–1732* (1928) deal with special regions, and the well-known study by C. A. Alvord, *The Mississippi Valley in British Politics* (2 vols., 1917), shows the influence of the fur trade upon imperial policy. The best studies on whaling and the fisheries are those of R. McFarland, *A History of the New England Fisheries* (1911), and W. S. Tower, *A History of American Whale Fishing* (1920), University of Pennsylvania Studies, No. 23. See also C. B. Hawes, *Whaling* (1924), and E. O. Hohman, *The American Whalemen* (1928). Other special studies include M. T. Copeland, *The Cotton Manufacturing In-dustry of the United States* (1912); B. E. Hazard, *The Organization of the Boot and Shoe Industry in Massachusetts Before 1873* (1921); A. H. Cole, *The American Wool Manufacture* (2 vols., 1926), and A. C. Bining, *British Regula-tion of the Colonial Iron Industry* (1933). An interesting article is that by Curtis Nettels, "The Menace of Colonial Manufacturing," *New England Quarterly*, Vol. IV, pp. 230–269. On the influence of slave labor upon industry, read M. W. Jernegan, "Slavery and the Beginnings of Industrialism in the American Colonies," *American Historical Review*, Vol. XXV (Jan., 1920).

A comparison of European industrial life during the same period is extremely valuable. Material with special reference to England may be found in George Unwin, *Industrial Organization in the Sixteenth and Seventeenth Centuries* (1904).

For accessible source material, see G. S. Callender, *Selected Readings in the Economic History of the United States* (1909), and E. L. Bogart and C. M. Thompson, *Readings in the Economic History of the United States* (1916). Source material in the form of pictures can be found in Malcolm Keir, *The Epic of Industry* (1926), Vol. V of the Pageant of America.

6. FRONTIER EXPANSION BEFORE THE REVOLUTION

Most of the studies of the significance of the westward movement in American history rest upon the pioneer work of Professor F. J. Turner, scattered in various articles published in magazines and the publications of historical societies. The most complete collection of references on the westward movement is that of F. J. Turner and F. Merk, *List of References on the History of the West* (rev. ed., 1922). Consult also E. E. Edwards, "References on the Significance of the Frontier in American History," U. S. Dept. of Agriculture, Biographical Contributions No. 25 (1935). A few of Professor Turner's essays have been collected in *The Frontier in American History* (1921) and *Significance of Sections in American History* (1933). Attempts to integrate a part of the story have been made by F. L. Paxson, *History of the American Frontier, 1763–1893* (1924), a Pulitzer Prize book, and by Dan E. Clark, *The West in American History* (1937). Upon Turner's contributions the author has drawn heavily for the three chapters in the present book on the westward movement. Concerning Turner and the Turnerian interpretation, read the brilliant essay by M. E. Curti, "The Section and the Frontier in American History," *Methods in the Social Sciences* (1931), pp. 353–367, and the able introductory essay by Fulmer Mood in *The Early Writings of Frederick Jackson Turner* (1938). In recent years Turner's emphasis on the frontier has been under some fire, particularly by L. M. Hacker, who has made pointed criticisms in his pamphlet, "The Farmer Is Doomed" (1933), and in the *Nation*, Vol. 137, pp. 109–110 (July 26, 1933). It has also been criticized in D. R. Fox (ed.), *Sources of Culture in the Middle West* (1934) and his *Ideas in Motion* (1935). See particularly G. W. Pierson, "The Frontier and Frontiersmen of Turner's Essays," *Pennsylvania Magazine*, Vol. LXIV, pp. 449–478 (Oct., 1940), and Murray Kane, "Some Considerations on the Frontier Concept of Frederick Jackson Turner," *Mississippi Valley Historical Review*, Vol. XXVII (Dec., 1940).

Most valuable on the geographic background of the pioneer advance, especially as regards routes of travel, is E. C. Semple, *American History and Its Geographic Conditions* (1903). Consult also Livingston Farrand, *Basis of American History* (1904).

The conflict between France and England is recounted by Parkman in a style so brilliant that history and literature may be said to join hands. The story of the frontier advance and Indian conflicts is interestingly told in Theodore Roosevelt, *The Winning of the West* (4 vols., 1889–1896), but with little attempt at interpretation. Detailed but dry are the narratives of Justin Winsor, *Mississippi Basin*

(1895) and *Westward Movement* (1897). C. W. Alvord, *The Mississippi Valley in British Politics* (2 vols., 1917), is a brilliant piece of research and essential to any understanding to colonial history. Since Turner and Alvord's work, the most significant contribution to frontier history is that of Walter P. Webb, *The Great Plains* (1931). This book touches only lightly on the colonial period, but on the plains frontier of the ninetenth century it deals illuminatingly with such important influences as water, fences, firearms, and windmills.

The expansion in Virginia is treated by H. L. Osgood, *The American Colonies in the Sevententh Century* (3 vols., 1904-1907); P. A. Bruce, *Economic History of Virginia* (1896); and John Fiske, *Old Virginia* (1897). On New England consult L. K. Mathews, *Expansion of New England* (1909); H. L. Osgood, *op. cit.;* C. F. Adams, A. C. Goodell, Jr., M. Chamberlain, and E. Channing, "Genesis of the New England Town," in *Massachusetts Historical Society Proceedings,* 2nd Series, Vol. VII, and the second essay in Turner's *Frontier in American History* entitled "The First Official Frontier of the Massachusetts Bay." The most exhaustive work yet done on the New England township system is the excellent monograph by R. H. Akagi, *The Town Proprietors of the New England Colonies* (1924).

The best introduction to the advance into the Piedmont is Turner's essay on "The Old West," Chap. III in his *Frontier in American History.* There are several excellent chapters in H. E. Bolton and T. M. Marshall, *The Colonization of North America* (1920), and much information in Roosevelt. More detailed on certain sections are Archibald Henderson, *The Conquest of the Old Southwest* (1920); C. L. Skinner, *Pioneers of the Old Southwest* (1919), in the Chronicles of America Series; H. E. Bolton, *The Spanish Borderlands* (1921), in the same series; and F. W. Halsey, *The Old American Frontier* (2 vols., 1901). See also F. J. Turner, "State Making in the Revolutionary Era," in *American Historical Review,* Vol. I. Recent important additions to the westward movement of the period include K. P. Bailey, *The Ohio Company of Virginia and the Westward Movement, 1748-1792* (1939); S. J. and E. H. Buck, *The Planting of Civilization in Western Pennsylvania* (1939); W. S. Lister, *The Transylvania Company* (1935); T. P. Abernethy, *Western Lands and the American Revolution* (1937), and the biographies by John Bakeless, *Daniel Boone* (1939), C. S. Driver, *John Sevier* (1932), and L. K. Koontz, *Robert Dinwiddie* (1941).

The part which certain nationalities played in this advance may be studied in G. D. Bernheim, *German Settlements in North and South Carolina* (1872); S. H. Cobb, *The Story of the Palatines* (1897); A. B. Faust, *The German Element in the United States* (1909); Oscar Kuhns, *The German and Swiss Settlements of Colonial Pennsylvania* (1901); H. J. Ford, *The Scotch-Irish in America* (1915); and C. A. Hanna, *The Scotch-Irish* (1902). Briefer but still useful are some of the state histories in the American Commonwealth Series. Americans of Irish descent have done much in recent years to "debunk" what they consider to be the "Scotch-Irish myth" and to emphasize the great contributions of the immigrants from southern Ireland. This material can be found in the publications of the American Irish Historical Society, and in M. J. O'Brien, *A Hidden Phase of American History* (1919).

Maps showing the settlements at various periods may be found at the end of Vol. II of Channing's *History of the United States* and in *Harper's Atlas of American History* (1920). Farrand and Semple contain maps showing portages and routes of travel. For pictorial material, examine Clark Wissler, C. L. Skinner, and W. Wood, *Adventurers in the Wilderness* (1925), and R. H. Gabriel, *The Lure of the Frontier* (1929), both in the Pageant of America. Excellent readings are I. F. Woestmeyer and J. M. Gambrill, *The Westward Movement* (1939).

7. ECONOMIC CAUSES OF THE REVOLUTION

The leading books on mercantilism and British colonial policy—those of Beer, Johnson, Harper, Egerton, and others—have already been cited in the bibliography for Chapter V. To these should be added W. S. McClellan, *Smuggling in the American Colonies* (1912), and A. M. Schlesinger, *The Colonial Merchants and the American Revolution* (1918). Among the special studies are C. H. Van Tyne, *The Causes of the War of Independence* (1922), an excellent recapitulation of the political and intellectual causes; H. E. Egerton, *Causes and Character of the American Revolution* (1923), a conservative and scholarly restatement by an Englishman; and C. M. Andrews, *The Colonial Background of the Revolution* (1924). Students in search of a bibliography of the best specialized work on the causes of the Revolution will find it in the footnotes and bibliographies of the able chapters (XXII–XXIV) in Curtis Nettels, *The Roots of American Civilization* (1938). See also J. T. Adams, *Revolutionary New England* (1923); C. A. Barker, *The Background of the Revolution in Maryland* (1940); Carl Becker, *The Eve of the Revolution* (1918), Chronicles of America; and A. M. Schlesinger, *New Viewpoints in American History* (1922), Chap. VII. For the South before the Revolution, see E. Q. Hawk, *Economic History of the South* (1934).

An interesting study of the background of the war, with good chapters on Boston of that time, is that by the Englishman, Henry Belcher, *The First American Civil War* (2 vols., 1911). Other cities are treated in V. D. Harrington, *New York Merchants on the Eve of the Revolution* (1935), and L. Sellers, *Charleston Business on the Eve of the Revolution* (1934). On the western phase, read C. W. Alvord, *The Mississippi Valley in British Politics* (2 vols., 1917). In Louis M. Hacker, "The First American Revolution," *Columbia University Quarterly*, Vol. XXVII, No. 3 (1935), the theses of Channing, Andrews, and Van Tyne are questioned and the point is brilliantly developed that the Revolution resulted from the constricted opportunities of colonial merchant capitalism. This thesis is largely reprinted in his *Triumph of American Capitalism* (1940), Chaps. XI, XII. The intellectual background of the colonial period can best be studied in V. L. Parrington, *The Colonial Mind, 1620–1800* (1927), Vol. I of *Main Currents of American Thought.*

Excellent sources will be found in the *Readings* both of G. S. Callender and of Bogart and Thompson; in S. E. Morison, *The American Revolution, 1764–1788, Sources and Documents* (1923), and in Willard Thorp, Merle Curti, and Carlos Baker, *American Issues* (2 vols., 1941).

8. ECONOMIC ASPECTS OF THE REVOLUTION

An excellent résumé of the financial aspect of the war is given in D. R. Dewey, *Financial History of the United States* (10th ed., 1928), and W. J. Shultz and and M. R. Caine, *Financial Development of the United States* (1937). More detailed studies are those of W. G. Sumner, *Finance and Financiers of the American Revolution* (2 vols., 1891); C. J. Bullock, *Finances of the United States, 1775–1789,* University of Wisconsin Bulletins (1895); R. V. Harlow, "Aspects of Revolutionary Finance, 1775–1783," *American Historical Review,* Vol. XXXV, pp. 46–68 (Oct., 1929); W. B. Norton, "Paper Money in Massachusetts During the Revolution," *New England Quarterly,* Vol. VII (March, 1934); E. P. Oberholtzer, *Life of Robert Morris* (1903), and Charles E. Russell, *Haym Salomon and the Revolution* (1930), a popular biography.

Material on the economic background can be found in V. S. Clark, *History of Manufactures in the United States, 1607–1860* (1916), Chap. X; W. B. Weeden, *Economic and Social History of New England, 1620–1789* (2 vols., 1890), Vol. II, Chaps. XX, XXI; E. R. Johnson *et al., History of Domestic and Foreign Commerce of the United States* (2 vols., 1915), Vol. I, Chaps. VII, VIII; S. E. Morison, *Maritime History of Massachusetts, 1783–1860* (1921); Allan Nevins, *The American States During and After the Revolution 1775–1789* (1924), especially Chaps. X and XI; Thomas C. Cochran, *New York in the Confederation* (1932); H. J. Eckenrode, *The Revolution in Virginia* (1916); R. A. East, *Business Enterprise in the American Revolutionary Era* (1938), and R. F. Upton, *Revolutionary New Hampshire* (1936). Most illuminating on the social aspects is J. F. Jameson, *The American Revolution Considered as a Social Movement* (1926). See also Michael Kraus, *Inter-Colonial Aspects of American Culture on the Eve of the Revolution with Special Reference to the Northern Towns* (1928). Of interest is O. W. Stephenson, "The Supply of Gunpowder in 1776," *American Historical Review,* Vol. XX, pp. 271–281 (Jan., 1925); E. C. Burnett, "Observations of London Merchants on American Trade," *ibid.,* Vol. XVIII, pp. 773–780 (July, 1913), contains valuable source material.

On the westward movement, read E. L. Sparks, *The Expansion of the American People* (1900); Justin Winsor, *The Westward Movement, 1763–1798* (1897); Theodore Roosevelt, *The Winning of the West,* 4 vols. (1889–1896); Archibald Henderson, *The Conquest of the Old Southwest* (1920); W. S. Lester, *The*

Transylvania Colony (1934), more objective than Henderson; and E. C. Semple, *American History and Its Geographic Conditions* (1903), Chaps. IV and V. A more extended bibliography is contained in F. J. Turner and F. Merk, *List of References on the History of the West* (rev. ed., 1922).

The part played by the loyalists is set forth in C. H. Van Tyne, *Loyalists in the American Revolution* (1902), and *The American Revolution 1776–1783* (1905), in the American Nation Series. Also see A. C. Flick, *Loyalism in New York* (1901); I. S. Harrell, *Loyalism in Virginia* (1926); C. H. Ambler, *Sectionalism in Virginia* (1910), and Chap. VII of H. E. Egerton, *The Causes and Character of the American Revolution* (1923). On political theories, read C. E. Merriam, *A History of American Political Theories* (1903), a lucid and condensed presentation. Material on this period is incorporated in the *Readings* of Callender, of Bogart and Thompson, and of Flügel and Faulkner; and also in S. E. Morison, *The American Revolution, 1764–1788, Sources and Documents* (1923).

The most authoritative study of the economic phases of the movement for the Constitution is that by C. A. Beard, *An Economic Interpretation of the Constitution of the United States* (1913). His conclusions must be reckoned with by any student of this period. Attention to social and economic conditions, as well as to the political story, is given in A. C. McLaughlin, *The Confederation and the Constitution* (1905), American Nation Series; in Max Farrand, *The Fathers of the Constitution* (1921), Chronicles of America Series; and in J. B. McMaster, *History of the People of the United States,* Vol. I, Chap. I. See also the old and popularly written but still valuable volume by John Fiske, *The Critical Period* (1888). Brilliant interpretative chapters are those in Charles and Mary Beard, *The Rise of American Civilization* (1927), Vol. I, Chaps. V and VI; Curtis Nettels, *The Roots of American Civilization,* Chap. XXIV; and Louis Hacker, *The Triumph of American Capitalism,* Chaps. XIII–XIV.

9. FINANCE AND TARIFF

Hamilton's reports may be found in *American State Papers, Finance,* Vol. I. The most satisfactory books for the general student are those of D. R. Dewey, *Financial History of the United States* (10th ed., 1928), containing a detailed bibliography; and W. J. Shultz and M. R. Caine, *Financial Development of the United States* (1937). On currency, see A. B. Hepburn, *History of Coinage and Currency in the United States* (rev. ed., 1915); J. L. Laughlin, *History of Bimetallism in the United States* (4th ed., 1897); and David K. Watson, *History of American Coinage* (1899). Interesting sidelights on the financial operations of the first Congress are to be found in E. S. Maclay (ed.), *Journal of William Maclay* (1890); this journal was republished in 1927 with an introduction by Charles A. Beard. See also R. I. Warshow, *The Story of Wall Street* (1929).

On the national bank controversy there is an extended literature. In addition to the valuable accounts in many of the general histories, more detailed studies are to be found in Ralph C. H. Catterall, *The Second Bank of the United States* (1903); Charles A. Conant, *History of Modern Banks of Issue* (1896; rev., 1915); William G. Sumner, *History of Banking in the United States* (1896); William MacDonald, *Jacksonian Democracy* (1906), in The American Nation Series; and John S. Bassett, *Life of Andrew Jackson,* Vol. II (1911; rev., 1916, 1 vol.). Also see David Kinley, *History, Organization and Influence of the Independent Treasury of the United States* (1893).

For the tariff, consult Percy W. L. Ashley, *Modern Tariff History* (3rd ed., 1920); Edward Stanwood, *American Tariff Controversies in the Nineteenth Century* (1903); and F. W. Taussig, *Tariff History of the United States* (7th ed., 1923).

On the economic collapse of 1837, consult R. C. McGrane, *The Panic of 1837* (1924), his "Some Aspects of American State Debts in the Forties," *American Historical Review,* Vol. XXXVIII, No. 4, pp. 673–686 (July, 1933), and his *Foreign Bondholders and American State Debts* (1935). On the general history of business cycles during these years, read Walter B. Smith, *Fluctuations in American Business, 1790–1860* (1935).

The conflict of economic theories during these years can be best studied in the writings of publicists, economists, and statesmen; but some short-cuts to this can be found in E. L. Bradsher, *Mathew Carey* (1912); H. D. H. Kaplan, *Henry Charles Carey* (1931); R. G. Stone, *Hezekiah Niles as an Economist* (1933); and Dumas Malone, *Public Life of Thomas Cooper, 1783–1839* (1926). There is no full-length objective life of Hamilton. The best is still the earlier one by W. G. Sumner, *Alexander Hamilton* (1890). For the other great secretary of these years, see Henry Adams, *Life of Albert Gallatin* (1880); J. A. Stevens, *Albert Gallatin* (1917); and Cheng Tseng Mai, *Fiscal Policies of Albert Gallatin* (1930).

For a general economic interpretation of the period, read C. A. Beard, *The Economic Origins of the Jeffersonian Democracy* (1915), and Charles and Mary Beard, *The Rise of American Civilization* (1927).

10. WESTWARD EXPANSION FROM THE REVOLUTION TO THE CIVIL WAR

The most complete bibliography of the westward movement during this period is that by F. J. Turner and F. Merk, *List of References on the History of the West* (rev. ed., 1922). Consult also L. B. Schmidt, *Topical Studies and References on the Economic History of American Agriculture* (rev. ed., 1923). Interesting source material is incorporated in Bogart and Thompson, in Flügel and Faulkner, in Callender, in A. B. Hart, *American History Told by Contemporaries,* Vol. III, and in I. F. Woestemeyer and J. M. Gambrill, *The Westward Movement* (1939). Among the most valuable of the contemporary accounts are Harriet Martineau, *Society in America* (1837); J. W. Monette, *History of the Discovery and Settlement of the Valley of the Mississippi* (1846), by an early inhabitant of the valley; Timothy Flint, *Recollections of the Last Ten Years* (1826), and *History and Geography of the Mississippi Valley* (1832); J. M. Peck, *Guide for Emigrants to the West* (1837); R. G. Thwaites (ed.), *Journals of Lewis and Clark* (1904–1905), and *Early Western Travels* (32 vols., 1904–1907).

For an interpretation of the movement the essays of F. J. Turner are the best, especially those collected in *The Frontier in American History* (1921). In F. J. Turner, *Rise of the New West* (1906), American Nation Series, the westward movement is interwoven with the political history. See also his "The Significance of the Section in American History," *Wisconsin Magazine of History,* Vol. VII, No. 3 (March, 1925), pp. 255–280, and his *The United States: 1830–1850* (1934).

Excellent chapters appear in Edward Channing, *A History of the United States* (1921), Vol. V, Chap. II; and J. B. McMaster, *History of the People of the United States* (6 vols., 1883–1896), Vol. II, pp. 144 ff.; Vol. III, pp. 100–142, 459–496; Vol. IV, pp. 381–428; Vol. V, pp. 160 ff. The work of McMaster, in the opinion of Channing, is "the best bit of writing" on the subject "that has been done." Valuable also are Theodore Roosevelt, *Winning of the West* (4 vols., 1889–1896). The story of this period has now been skillfully integrated in F. L. Paxson, *History of the American Frontier, 1763–1893* (1924) and in Dan E. Clark, *The West in American History* (1937).

The movement into the Northwest is developed in F. W. Halsey, *Old New York Frontier* (1901), L. K. Mathews, *Expansion of New England* (1909), and Beverley W. Bond, Jr., *The Civilization of the Old Northwest* (1934); and that into the Southwest in U. B. Phillips, "Origin and Growth of the Southern Black Belts," *American Historical Review,* Vol. IX, p. 798, and C. L. Skinner, *Pioneers of the Old Southwest* (1919), Chronicles of America Series. For western New York, see Paul D. Evans' chapter in A. C. Flick (ed.), *History of the State of New York* (1934), Vol. VI.

Most important for the region beyond the Mississippi is W. P. Webb, *The Great Plains* (1931), an original and significant approach. Consult also K. Coman, *Economic Beginnings of the Far West* (2 vols., 1912); C. Goodwin, *The Trans-Mississippi West* (1922); M. R. Werner, *Brigham Young* (1925); L. H. Greer, *Utah and the Nation* (1929); J. H. Evans, *Charles Coulson Rich, Pioneer Builder of the West* (1936), a biography of a Mormon leader; and Rena Stanley, *A Biography of Perley P. Pratt* (1937), another important Mormon. For the advance into Southern California read R. G. Cleland, *Pathfinders* (1929), and for early California, his *History of California, The American Period* (1922), and Owen C. Coy, *The Great Trek* (1931).

On the diplomatic background of the Mississippi Valley, see F. J. Turner, "Policy of France Toward the Mississippi Valley," *American Historical Review,* Vol. X, pp. 249–279 (Jan., 1905), and A. P. Whitaker, "New Light on the Treaty of San Lorenzo," *Mississippi Valley Historical Review*, Vol. XV, pp. 435–454 (March, 1929).

The land policy of the United States may be studied in P. J. Treat, *The National Land System, 1785–1820* (1910), in B. H. Hibbard, *A History of the Public Land Policies* (1924), and in Thomas Donaldson, *The Public Domain, Its History with Statistics* (1884). A. M. Sakolski, *The Great American Land Bubble* (1932), is a popular treatment of an important topic. Exhaustive research on land speculation is revealed in P. W. Gates, *The Illinois Central Railroad and Its Colonization Work* (1934), and his article, "Land Policy and Tenancy in the Prairie States," *Journal of Economic History*, Vol. I, pp. 60–82 (May, 1941).

The safety-valve theory is questioned in F. A. Shannon, "The Homestead Act and the Labor Surplus," *American Historical Review*, Vol. XLI, pp. 637–651 (July, 1936); and in Carter Goodrich and Sol Davison, "The Wage Earner and the Westward Movement," *Political Science Quarterly*, Vol. L, pp. 161–185 (June, 1935), and Vol. LI, pp. 61–116 (March, 1936); also in Goodrich and Davison, "The Frontier Safety Valve: A Rejoinder," *ibid.*, Vol. LIII, pp. 268–271, and Murray Kane, "Some Considerations on the Safety Valve Doctrine," *Mississippi Valley Historical Review*, Vol. XXIII, pp. 69–188 (Sept., 1936). The theory is defended in Joseph Schafer, "Concerning the Frontier as a Safety Valve," *Political Science Quarterly*, Vol. LII, 407–420 (Sept., 1937) and "Was the West a Safety Valve for Labor?" *Mississippi Valley Historical Review*, Vol. XXIV, pp. 299–314 (Dec., 1937). A criticism of the Turner thesis beyond the safety-valve theory is undertaken in Murray Kane, "Some Considerations of the Frontier Concept of Frederick Jackson Turner," *ibid.*, Vol. XXVII, pp. 379–400 (Dec., 1940).

For geography and routes of travel, see E. C. Semple, *American History and Its Geographic Conditions* (1903). On routes to the interior, read A. B. Hulbert, *Paths of Inland Commerce* (1920), Chronicles of America Series; and for pictorial source material, see R. H. Gabriel, *The Lure of the Frontier* (1929), Vol. II in the Pageant of America.

11. THE AGRICULTURAL ERA

Bibliographies include E. E. Edwards, "Guide for Courses in the History of American Agriculture," Dept. of Agriculture, Bibliographical Contribution 35 (1939); E. E. Edwards, "Bibliography of the History of American Agriculture," Dept. of Agriculture, Bibliographical Contribution 32; and L. B. Schmidt, *Topical Studies and References on the Economic History of American Agriculture* (rev. ed., 1937). The best condensed account is E. E. Edwards, "American Agriculture—the First 300 Years," *1940 Yearbook of Agriculture*, with excellent bibliography.

The standard treatise on agriculture in the North during this period is P. W.

Bidwell and J. I. Falconer, *History of Agriculture in the Northern United States, 1620–1860* (Carnegie Institution, 1925), equipped with an exhaustive bibliography. There are many articles of exceptional value in Vol. IV of Bailey's *Cyclopedia of American Agriculture*. A short and popular account is that by A. H. Sanford, *The Story of Agriculture in the United States* (1916). Among the best of the early accounts are those of C. L. Flint, "Agriculture in the United States," in *Eighty Years' Progress* (1869); also in the *Annual Report, U. S. Department of Agriculture* (1872), and in the *First Annual Report of the Massachusetts Board of Agriculture* (1854). See also the Introduction to the volume on Agriculture in the *Eighth Census of the United States* (1860), and W. N. Brewer, "Report on the Cereal Production of the United States" in the *Tenth Census* (1880), volume on Agriculture, Part II. For source material, consult L. B. Schmidt and E. D. Ross, *Readings in the Economic History of American Agriculture* (1925); T. N. Carver, *Selected Readings in Rural Economics* (1911); Bogart and Thompson, *Readings in the Economic History of the United States* (1916), and Flügel and Faulkner, *Readings in the Economic and Social History of the United States* (1929).

On New England farming of this period, read P. W. Bidwell, "Rural Economy in New England at the Beginning of the Nineteenth Century," in *Transactions of the Connecticut Academy of Arts and Sciences,* Vol. XX (1916), and "The Agricultural Revolution in New England," in the *American Historical Review,* Vol. XXVI, No. 4 (1921). Also consult Elizabeth Ramsay, *History of Tobacco Production in the Connecticut Valley* (1930), Vol. XV, Nos. 3–4, Smith College Studies in History.

On southern agriculture the most exhaustive study is that by Lewis C. Gray, *History of Agriculture in the Southern United States to 1860* (Carnegie Institution, 2 vols., 1933). Valuable also are M. B. Cairnes, *The Slave Power* (1863); M. B. Hammond, *The Cotton Industry* (1897); A. B. Hart, *Slavery and Abolition,* in the American Nation Series; F. L. Olmsted, *Journeys and Explorations in the Cotton Kingdom* (1861); James A. B. Scherer, *Cotton as a World Power* (1916), a study in the economic interpretation of history; M. Jacobstein, *The Tobacco Industry in the United States,* Columbia University Studies, Vol. XXVI, No. 3 (1907); and for an interesting general picture, U. B. Phillips, *Life and Labor in the Old South* (1929). Excellent chapters will be found in McMaster, Vol. VII, Chap. LXXVI; in Rhodes, Vol. I, Chap. IV; and in E. Q. Hawk, *Economic History of the South,* Chaps. VIII and IX. Important are A. O. Craven, *Soil Exhaustion as a Factor in the Agricultural History of Virginia and Maryland, 1660–1860* (1925); his "The Agricultural Reformers of the Ante-Bellum South," *American Historical Review,* Vol. XXXIII, pp. 302–314 (Jan., 1928), and his *Edmund Ruffin, Southerner; a Study in Secession* (1932). A first-class biography in the field of agricultural history has appeared in W. T. Hutchinson, *Cyrus Hall McCormick* (2 vols., 1930–1935). The story of the reaper has also been told by an admiring grandson in Cyrus McCormick, *The Century of the Reaper* (1931). An exceedingly valuable study on the effects of labor-saving machinery is Leo Rogin, *The Introduction of Farm Machinery in Its Relation to the Productivity of Labor in Agriculture of the United States* (U. of Cal. Pub. in Economics, 1931).

On the public domain, see I. Donaldson, *The Public Domain* (1884); L. H. Haney, *A Congressional History of Railways in the United States,* Vol. I, to 1850 (1908); Vol. II, *1850–1887* (1918), Bulletin of the University of Wisconsin (1910); R. T. Hill, *The Public Domain and Democracy,* Columbia University Studies, Vol. XXXVIII (1910); the Annual Reports of the Commissioner of the General Land Office from 1860 to 1900; P. J. Treat, *The National Land System, 1785–1820* (1910); R. G. Wellington, *The Political and Sectional Influence of the Public Lands, 1828–1842* (1914); George M. Stephenson, *The Political History of the Public Lands from 1840–1862* (1917); and B. H. Hibbard, *A History of the Public Land Policies* (1924). *The Centennial History of Illinois,* Clarence W. Alvord, editor-in-chief, contains much valuable material. See especially S. J. Buck, *Illinois in 1818* (1917), and T. C. Pease, *The Frontier State, 1818–1848* (1922). A. M. Sakolski, *The Great American Land Bubble* (1932), deals with speculation on the public domain. Also see Homer Hoyt, *One Hundred Years of Land Values in Chicago, 1830–1930* (1933).

Among the literature on this period are: Robert Dudley (pseud.), *In My Youth* (1914), the fictitious autobiography of a Quaker settler of Indiana in the middle of the nineteenth century; and Hamlin Garland, *A Son of the Middle Border* (1922), an autobiographical narrative of middle-western family life in the period after the Civil War, continued in *A Daughter of the Middle Border* (1921). Herbert Quick, *Vandemark's Folly,* deals primarily with Iowa in the 'fifties, but gives a picture of the life of western New York and Wisconsin settlements. A sequel, *The Hawkeye* (1923), pictures Iowa later in the century.

Many European travelers commented on agriculture; see especially Morris Birkbeck, *Notes on a Journey in America* (1818); and James Flint, *Letters from America* (1822), reprinted in R. G. Thwaites, (ed.), *Early Western Travels,* Vol. IX.

12. THE AMERICAN MERCHANT MARINE AND THE DEVELOPMENT OF FOREIGN COMMERCE

The standard history of American commerce is the cooperative work of E. R. Johnson, T. W. VanMetre, G. G. Huebner, and D. S. Hanchett, *History of Domestic and Foreign Commerce of the United States* (published by the Carnegie Institution in 2 vols., 1915, reprinted in 1 vol. in 1922). At the conclusion of Vol. II there is the most complete bibliography available on the subject. On the European background of the War of 1812, E. F. Hecksher, *The Continental System* (1922), is the best.

Possibly the best short account of the American merchant marine is that by J. R. Soley, one-time Assistant Secretary of the Navy, in Vol. I of N. S. Shaler (ed.), *The United States of America* (1897). Good chapters are also included in A. S. Bolles, *Industrial History of the United States* (1878). The ground is covered in more detail in W. J. Abbot, *American Merchant Ships and Sailors* (1902), and *The Story of Our Merchant Marine* (1919); W. Bates, *American Marine* (1893), and *American Navigation* (1902); C. E. Cartwright, *The Tale of Our Merchant Marine* (1924); A. H. Clark, *The Clipper Ship Era, 1843–1849* (1911); F. R. Dulles, *The Old China Trade* (1930); and K. S. Latourette, *Voyages of American Ships to China, 1784–1844* (1927). Delightfully written are R. D. Paine, *The Old Merchant Marine* (1919), Chronicles of America Series; and S. E. Morison, *Maritime History of Massachusetts, 1783–1860* (1921), the latter containing valuable bibliographies. The best work on a single port is that by R. G. Albion, *The Rise of New York Port* (1939). John Robinson and George F. Dow, *Sailing Ships of New England,* Marine Research Society *Publications* (Second Series, 1924, and Third Series, by Dow alone, 1928), gives beautiful reproductions of pictures of sailing ships in the famous Peabody Collection at the Essex Institute in Salem. A little-known phase of this subject can be studied in L. D. Baldwin, "Shipbuilding on the Western Waters, 1793–1817," *Mississippi Valley Historical Review,* Vol. XX, pp. 29–44 (June, 1933), and in A. B. Hulbert, "Western Shipbuilding," *American Historical Review,* Vol. XXI, pp. 720–733 (July, 1916).

On the whale fisheries, see W. S. Tower, *History of the American Whale Fishery* (1907); T. Jenkins, *A History of the Whale Fisheries* (1921); C. B Hawes, *Whaling* (1924); G. F. Dow, *Whale Ships and Whaling* (1925), Marine Research Society; E. O. Hohman, *The American Whalemen* (1928); R. McFarland, *A History of New England Fisheries* (1907); and F. R. Hart, "The New England Whale Fisheries," Colonial Society of Massachusetts *Publications,* Vol. XXVI, *Transactions 1924–26,* pp. 65–79, with interesting pictures of whaling captains. Much information on the early merchant marine is available in the numerous books bearing the imprint of the Essex Institute of Salem, Massachusetts. On privateering, see Bibliography for Chap. V; also E. S. Maclay, *A History of American Privateers* (1924), scholarly and well written; George Coggeshall, *History of the American Privateers and Letters-of-Marque During Our War with England in the years 1812, 13, and 14* (1856); and Nathaniel Hawthorne (ed.), *The Yarn of a Yankee Privateer* (1926).

On early subsidization, consult Royal Meeker, *History of Ship Subsidies* (1905), and M. M. McKee, *Ship Subsidy Question in United States Politics* (1922), in Smith College Studies VIII, No. 1. R. H. Dana, *Two Years Before the Mast,* a classic of the sea, gives an interesting picture of the early California trade and of conditions on shipboard, and life on a whaler is dramatically pictured in Melville's *Moby Dick.* Joseph Hergesheimer, *Java Head* (1919), a story of social life in Salem in the 'forties, pictures the decline of Salem in the Oriental trade.

The basic causes of the War of 1812 are discussed in J. W. Pratt, *The Expansionists of 1812* (1925); his failure to emphasize the agricultural causes sufficiently is rectified in G. R. Taylor, "Agrarian Discontent in the Mississippi Preceding the War of 1812," *Journal of Political Economy,* Vol. XXXIX, No. 4, pp. 471–505 (Aug., 1931). A history of the changing interpretations of the causes of the War of 1812 is given in W. H. Goodman, "The Origin of the War of 1812," *Mississippi Valley Historical Review,* Vol. XXVIII, No. 2, pp. 171–186 (Sept., 1941). On the embargo, consult W. W. Jennings, *The American Embargo, 1807–1809* (1921), and L. M. Sears, *Jefferson and the Embargo* (1927).

13. THE RISE OF THE FACTORY SYSTEM

The best study of manufacturing during this period is that by V. S. Clark, *History of Manufacturers in the United States, 1607–1860* (new ed., 1929), published by the Carnegie Institution of Washington, and containing the most complete bibliography available. Of the older books, the most valuable is that by J. L. Bishop, *History of American Manufacturers from 1608–1860* (3 vols., 1866), containing detailed accounts of specific industries in the early stage. Much information, not easily obtained elsewhere, is crammed into A. S. Bolles, *Industrial History of the United States* (1878). See also *Eighty Years' Progress* (1869), articles under the various manufacturing industries. Considerable information on this period is given in Malcolm Keir, *Manufacturing* (1928), a scholarly and suggestive book. On the English background the following are excellent: J. H. Clapham, *An Economic History of Modern Europe;* C. R. Fay, *Great Britain from Adam Smith to the Present Day* (1928); and Arthur Redford, *The Economic History of England, 1760–1860* (1931).

The census reports of the government will be found useful, as will also such special reports as those of Alexander Hamilton, *Report on Manufactures,* in F. W. Taussig, *State Papers and Speeches on the Tariff;* and of Louis McLane, *Report on Manufactures* (2 vols., 1833), House Doc. No. 308, 22nd Congress, 1st Sess. Much that is interesting and instructive is obtainable from the accounts of foreign travelers, extracts from which are contained in G. S. Callender, *Selections from the Economic History of the United States 1765–1860* (1909), in Bogart and Thompson, *Readings in the Economic History of the United States* (1916), and in Flügel and Faulkner, *Readings in the Economic and Social History of the United States* (1929).

On the tariff, consult F. W. Taussig, *Tariff History of the United States* (8th ed., 1931); P. Ashley, *Modern Tariff History* (3rd ed., 1920); and E. Stanwood, *American Tariff Controversies in the Nineteenth Century* (1903).

On cotton, see James A. B. Scherer, *Cotton as a World Power* (1916); James L. Watkins, *Production and Price of Cotton for One Hundred Years,* U. S. Department of Agriculture, Division of Statistics, Miscellaneous Series, Bulletin No. 9 (1895); Broadus Mitchell, *The Rise of Cotton Mills in the South* (1921), Johns Hopkins University Studies in Historical and Political Science, 39th

Series, and his *William Gregg, Factory Master of the Old South* (1928); M. T. Copeland, *The Cotton Manufacturing Industry in the United States* (1912); and Caroline F. Ware, *The Early New England Cotton Manufacture* (1931). Few adequate histories of specific industries have yet been written, but among those available are A. H. Cole, *The American Wool Manufacture* (2 vols., 1926); C. B. Kuhlmann, *Development of the Flour-Milling Industry in the United States* (1929); L. H. Weeks, *A History of Paper Manufacturing in the United States, 1690–1916* (1916); F. J. Allen, *The Shoe Industry* (1916); Howard and Ralph Wolf, *Rubber: A story of Glory and Greed* (1936); and Rudolph A. Clemon, *The American Livestock and Meat Industry* (1923). Consult also Kathleen Bruce, *Virginia Iron Manufacture in the Slave Era* (1931); and Blanche E. Hazard, "Organization of the Boot and Shoe Industry in Massachusetts Before 1875," in the *Quarterly Journal of Economics,* Vol. XXVII (Feb., 1913). On inventions, see the popular W. Kaempffert, *History of American Inventions* (2 vols., 1924).

The rise of the factory system may be studied in excellent histories of three New England factory towns: Vera Shlakman, *Economic History of a Factory Town: A Study of Chicopee, Massachusetts,* Smith College Studies in History, Vol. XX, Nos. 1–4 (1935); C. M. Green, *Holyoke, Massachusetts* (1939), and M. T. Parker, *Lowell, a Study in Industrial Development* (1940).

14. INTERNAL TRANSPORTATION AND COMMUNICATION
TO 1860

Perhaps the most valuable study of American transportation is the four-volume work by Seymour Dunbar, *History of Travel in America* (1915), somewhat diffuse but interestingly written and illustrated with many rare prints. An indispensable companion volume is that issued by the Carnegie Institution under the editorship of B. H. Meyer of the Interstate Commerce Commission and written by C. E. MacGill *et al., History of Transportation in the United States Before 1860* (1917), with a good bibliography. Shorter accounts may be found in E. R. Johnson and T. W. VanMetre, *Principles of Railway Transportation* (1922); S. L. Miller, *Railway Transportation* (1924); C. E. Carter, *When Railroads Were New* (1909); Slason Thompson, *A Short History of American Railways* (1925), and Agnes C. Laut, *The Romance of the Rails* (2 vols., 1929), a popular sketch. Very helpful is Malcolm Keir, *The March of Commerce* (1927), Vol. IV in the Pageant of America, and R. E. Riegel, *America Moves West* (1930). Excellent chapters are those in J. B. McMaster, *History of the People of the United States,* Vol. IV, Chap. XXXIII, and Vol. V, Chap. XLIV. See also A. B. Hulbert, *Paths of Inland Commerce* (1920), in the Chronicles of America. F. A. Cleveland and F. W. Powell, *Railroad Promotion and Capitalization in the United States* (1909) throws light on the early years.

For older accounts, see the chapters on travel and transportation in *Eighty Years' Progress* (1869); H. S. Tanner, *A Description of the Canals and Railroads of the United States* (1840); A. S. Bolles, *Industrial History of the United States* (1878); H. V. Poor, *Manual of Railroads* (1881), Introduction; and the *Census of 1880,* Vol. IV on Transportation. See also the *Readings* of Bogart and Thompson, of Callender, and of Flügel and Faulkner. Mark Twain, *Life on the Mississippi* (1883), and Mark Twain and C. D. Warner, *The Gilded Age* (1873), are history as well as humor. Interesting accounts of traveling conditions by coach, canal, and railway are to be found in the travels of Dickens, Martineau, the Trollopes, and other European commentators.

The literature on special phases is rapidly growing. T. B. Searight, *The Old Pike* (1894), and A. B. Hulbert, *The Old National Pike* (1901) and *Historic Highways* (15 vols., 1902–1905), are valuable for turnpikes. Helpful are the two popular books on river steamboating: F. E. Dayton, *Steamboat Days* (1925), and G. L. Eskew, *The Pageant of the Packets* (1929); and the articles by A. B. Hulbert, "Western Ship-Building," *American Historical Review,* Vol. XXI, pp. 720–733 (July, 1916), and L. D. Baldwin, "Shipbuilding on the Western Waters," *Mississippi Valley Historical Review,* Vol. XX, pp. 29–44 (June, 1933).

On canals, consult the *Preliminary Report of the Inland Waterways Commission, 60th Cong., 1st Sess., Senate Doc. No. 325* (1908), and read A. F. Harlow, *Old Towpaths* (1926). See also A. B. Hulbert, *Historic Highways,* Vols. XIII and XIV; E. L. Bogart, "Early Canal Traffic and Railroad Competition in Ohio," *Journal of Political Economy,* Vol. XXI; W. F. Dunaway, *History of the James River and Kanawha Company,* Columbia University Studies in History, Economics and Public Law, Vol. CIV, No. 2 (1922); C. L. Jones, *Economic History of the Anthracite Tidewater Canals,* University of Pennsylvania Series in Politics, Economics and Public Law, No. 22 (1908); G. W. Ward, *The Early Development of the Chesapeake and Ohio Canal Project* (1889); E. L. Bogart, *Internal Improvements and State Debts in Ohio* (1924); E. J. Benton, *The Wabash Trade Route in the Development of the Old Northwest* (1903); J. W. Putnam, *The Illinois and Michigan Canal* (1918); and N. E. Whitford, *History of the Canal System of the State of New York* (2 vols., 1906).

On· sections, consult U. B. Phillips, *History of Transportation in the Eastern Cotton Belt to 1860* (1908); W. F. Gebhard, *Transportation and Industrial Development in the Middle West,* Columbia University Studies, Vol. XXXIV, No. 1 (1900); Charles H. Ambler, *A History of Transportation in the Ohio Valley* (1932); George P. Baker, *The Formation of the New England Railroad Systems* (1937); Thelma M. Kistler, *The Rise of Railroads in the Connecticut River Valley,* Smith College Studies in History, Vol. XXIII, Nos. 1–4 (1938); R. E. Riegel, "Trans-Mississippi Railroads During the Fifties," *Mississippi Valley Historical Review,* Vol. X, pp. 153–173 (1923), and his *History of Western Railroads* (1926). For government aid, see H. L. Haney, *Congressional History of Railroads in the United States to 1850* (1908).

The history of several of the early railroads has been written; such books include Edward Hungerford, *The Story of the Baltimore and Ohio Railroad, 1827–1927* (2 vols., 1928), and *A Century of Progress, History of the Delaware and Hudson Company, 1823–1923* (1925); F. W. Stevens, *The Beginnings of the New York Central Railroad;* S. M. Derrick, *Centennial History of South Carolina Railroad* (1930); F. B. C. Bradlee, *The Boston and Maine Railroad* (1921); H. W. Schotter, *The Growth and Development of the Pennsylvania Railroad* (1927), and Paul W. Gates, *The Illinois Central Railroad and Its Colonization Work* (1934). A. F. Harlow, *Old Waybills* (1934), is an interesting popular history of the express companies. On the Santa Fé Trail, read Katherine Coman, *Economic Beginnings of the Far West* (2 vols., 1912); R. L. Duffus, *The Santa Fé Trail* (1930); Josiah Gregg, "Commerce of the Prairies," in R. G. Thwaites (ed.), *Early Western Travels* (1905), Vol. XX; and M. G. Fulton (ed.), *Diary and Letters of Josiah Gregg: Southwestern Enterprises, 1840–1847* (1941). A little-known phase is treated in L. B. Lesley, *Uncle Sam's Camels* (1929).

J. A. Miller, *Fares, Please!* (1941) is a spirited popular account of street railroads from horse cars to streamliners. A. D. Turnbull, *John Stevens: An American Record* (1928) is the biography of an early railroad experimenter.

Transportation maps may be found in MacGill, in McMaster, in Bogart, in *Harper's Atlas of American History,* and in C. O. Paullin, *Atlas of the Historical Geography of the United States* (1932).

15. POPULATION AND LABOR

A convenient statistical summary is the census monograph, *A Century of Population Growth* (1909). This should be supplemented by W. S. Thompson and P. K. Whelpton, *Population Trends in the United States* (1933). In Edward Channing, *A History of the United States,* Vol. V, Chap. II, there is an excellent study of the westward movement of population. A suggestive treatment of the development of the metropolitan economy in America is given in the last chapter of N. S. B. Gras, *An Introduction to Economic History* (1922).

On immigration, consult the *Preliminary Report of the Eighth Census* (1862), reproduced in part in Bogart and Thompson. The most voluminous and valuable collection of material is the *Report of the Immigration Commission* (42 vols., 1911), summarized in two volumes of abstracts. Edith Abbott, *Historical Aspects of the Immigration Problem* (1926) contains excellent contemporary material. Two important recent books are M. L. Hansen, *The Atlantic Migration, 1607–1860* (1940), emphasizing the European background, and C. F. Wittke, *We Who Built America* (1939), discussing the contribution of many of the non-English groups. Other studies should be noted: R. Mayo-Smith, *Emigration and Immigration* (1907); J. R. Commons, *Races and Immigrants in America* (1907); H. P. Fairchild, *Immigration* (1925), and G. M. Stephenson, *History of American Immigration, 1820–1924* (1926).

The most detailed account of the history of free labor during this period is given in John R. Commons (ed.), *History of Labor in the United States* (2 vols., 1918). Important source material upon which the first volume of this work is based appears in J. R. Commons *et al., Documentary History of American Industrial Society,* Vols. III–VIII. Shorter accounts based largely on the work of Commons and his associates are in Mary Beard, *A Short History of the American Labor Movement* (1920); Herbert Harris, *American Labor* (1939), and M. S. Clark and S. F. Simon, *The Labor Movement in America* (1938). From the left-wing point of view the following are helpful: James O'Neal, *The Workers in American History* (4th ed., 1921); Anthony Bimba, *The History of the American Working Class* (1927), and A. M. Simons, *Social Forces in American History.* Edith Abbott, *Women in Industry* (1910) contains good chapters on conditions surrounding the early mill operatives, as does Vera Shlakman, *Economic History of a Factory Town: A Study of Chicopee, Massachusetts,* Smith College Studies in History, XX, Nos. 1–4 (1935). Norman Ware, *The Industrial Worker, 1840–1860* (1924) is invaluable for the period after 1840. An early but still useful book is R. T. Ely, *The Labor Movement in America* (1886). The Bureau of Labor Statistics has a valuable study, *History of Wages in the United States from the Colonial Times to 1928* (1929).

Perhaps the best summary of communistic experiments is to be found in Morris Hillquit, *History of Socialism in the United States.* More detailed studies are those of J. H. Noyes, *History of American Socialism* (1870); Charles Nordhoff, *The Communistic Societies of the United States from Personal Visit and Observation* (1875), and W. A. Hinds, *American Communities and Cooperative Commonwealths* (rev. ed., 1908). A picture of Brook Farm is given in O. B. Frothingham, *George Ripley* (1882). Commons *et. al., Documentary History of American Industrial Society* has material on cooperatives, communal societies, and land reform. See also H. S. Zahler, *Eastern Workingmen and National Land Policy, 1829–1892* (1941), and R. M. Robbins, "Horace Greeley, Land Reform and Unemployment," *Agricultural History,* Vol. VII, pp. 18–41. Some idea of the intellectual ferment and reform drive during these years may be found in E. M. Schuster, *Native American Anarchism,* Smith College Studies in History, Vol. XVII, Nos. 1–4 (1932).

16. ECONOMIC CAUSES OF THE CIVIL WAR

Source material, extracts from contemporary sources, etc., have been collected by G. S. Callender, *Selections from the Economic History of the United States, 1765–1860* (1900); by E. L. Bogart and C. M. Thompson, *Readings in the Economic History of the United States* (1916); by F. Flügel and H. U. Faulkner, *Readings in the Economic and Social History of the United States* (1929), and by Ulrich B. Phillips, editor of the first two volumes of the *Documentary History of American Industrial Society* (1910), the whole work prepared under the direction of J. R. Commons and associates. The introduction to the first two volumes on slavery by Professor Phillips is, in the opinion of Channing, "the best brief survey of the system that has been written." Other sources are scattered through Hunt's *Merchants' Magazine and Commercial Review* (New York, 1839–1870), Niles' *Weekly Register* (Baltimore, 1811–1849), and *De Bow's Review* (intermittently in various places 1846–1880).

Short studies of slavery are included in the standard histories—e.g., J. F. Rhodes, *History of the United States,* Vol. I, Chap. IV, and Vol. III, Chap. I; J. B. McMaster, *History of the People of the United States,* Vol. VII, Chap. LXXVI; and Edward Channing, *History of the United States,* Vol. V, Chap: V. Thumbnail sketches of various phases of southern economic history are included in Vol. V of *The South in the Building of the Nation,* and Alfred H. Stone's article, "The Negro in the South," Vol. X. An interesting and well-balanced résumé with an excellent bibliography appears in A. B. Hart, *Slavery and Abolition,* in the American Nation Series. Recent histories of the American Negro are those of Ulrich B. Phillips, *American Negro Slavery* (1918), an expansion of many earlier studies; Benjamin Brawley, *A Short History of the American Negro* (1919), and *A Social History of the American Negro* (1921). Invaluable are Frederic Bancroft, *Slave Trading in the Old South* (1931); C. S. Sydnor, *Slavery in Mississippi* (1933); R. B. Flanders, *Plantation Slavery in Georgia* (1933); and C. S. Davis, *The Cotton Kingdom in Alabama* (1939). Still invaluable is W. E. B. Du Bois, *Suppression of the African Slave Trade* (1896).

Perhaps the finest study of southern civilization in the days before the war is that by Ulrich B. Phillips, *Life and Labor in the Old South* (1929). New light on the part played by the small and middle-class white farmer is given in F. L. and H. C. Owsley, "The Economic Basis of Society in the Late Ante-Bellum South," *Journal of Southern History,* Vol. VI, No. 1 (Feb., 1940), and in Blanche H. Clark, *The Tennessee Yeoman, 1840–1860* (1942). One phase of the slave system has been illustrated in J. S. Bassett, *The Southern Plantation Overseer as Revealed in His Letters* (1925), a study based on letters written to President James K. Polk by his plantation overseers. In Francis P. Gaines, *The Southern Plantation, a Study in the Development and Accuracy of a Tradition* (1924), a truer prospective regarding the plantation is attained. R. B. Russel, *Economic Aspects of Southern Sectionalism, 1840–1861* (1923), University of Illinois Studies in the Social Sciences, Vol. XI, Nos. 1–2, clarifies the background of the Civil War, as does J. G. Van Deusen, *Economic Basis of Disunion in South Carolina,* Columbia University Studies (1928). Important in understanding southern history is A. O. Craven, *Soil Exhaustion as a Factor in the Agricultural History of Virginia and Maryland, 1606–1860* (1925). The problem of soil, climate, and resources is also stressed in F. J. Turner, *The Significance of Sections in American History* (1932); in R. B. Vance, *Human Geography of the South: a Study in Human Resources and Human Adequacy* (1932), and in C. W. Ramsdell, "The Natural Limits of Slavery Expansion," *Mississippi Valley*

Historical Review, Vol. XVI, pp. 151–171 (Sept., 1929). On the social background, see G. S. Johnson, *A Social History of the Sea Islands* (1925), and especially A. C. Cole, *The Irrepressible Conflict* (1930).

The contemporary material on slavery is large. Very valuable are the works of J. E. Cairnes, *The Slave Power* (2nd ed., enlarged, London and Cambridge, 1863), an impersonal study by a famous English economist; Hinton R. Helper, *The Impending Crisis of the South* (1857), the best-known denunciation of the system by a Southerner; and J. S. Buckingham, *The Slave States of America* (1842), by an English traveler. Typical defenses of slavery are those of Professor C. F. McCay of Columbia, South Carolina, in *Eighty Years' Progress* (1869), and *The Pro-Slavery Argument* (1852) by several writers. See also Daniel R. Goodloe, *An Inquiry into the Causes Which Retard the Southern States* (1848), and T. R. Kettell, *Southern Wealth and Northern Profits* (1861). See also G. H. Barnes, *Antislavery Impulse, 1830–1844* (1933), and D. L. Dumond, *The Secession Movement, 1860–1861* (1931).

A mine of information on life and conditions in the pre-war South is J. D. B. DeBow (ed.), *The Industrial Resources of the Southern and Western States* (3 vols., 1852–1853); and the various works of Frederick L. Olmsted, the "best-known writer on conditions in the south prior to the outbreak of the Civil War," including *Journey in the Seaboard Slave States* (1859), *A Journey Through Texas* (1857), *A Journey Through the Back Country* (1860), and *The Cotton Kingdom* (1861). Interesting also are the observations of the famous actress, Frances Kemble, *Journal of a Residence on a Georgia Plantation in 1838–1839* (1863); of Edward Ingle, *Southern Sidelights* (1896), and of J. B. Angel, *Reminiscences of James Burrill Angell* (1912), who in Chapter II tells of a horseback journey and winter spent in the South in 1850 and 1851. Mrs. Harriet Beecher Stowe's *Uncle Tom's Cabin* (first published in 1852) should be read for its tremendous historical significance as an influence upon the generation which fought the Civil War, and also her *Key to Uncle Tom's Cabin* (1853).

The best study of cotton is that by M. B. Hammond, *The Cotton Industry,* Publications of the American Economic Association, New Series, No. 1 (1897). A more recent book, previously cited, is James A. B. Scherer, *Cotton as a World Power* (1916). See also A. H. Stone, "The Cotton Factorage System of the Southern States," *American Historical Review,* Vol. XX, pp. 557–565 (April, 1915). For the "cotton triangle" trade as it centered in New York, read R. G. Albion, *The Rise of New York Port,* Chap. VI. The whole background has been excellently summed up in W. E. Dodd, *The Cotton Kingdom* (1919), in the Chronicles of America. Results of the latest research are summarized in L. M. Hacker, *The Triumph of American Capitalism* (1940).

17. THE CIVIL WAR

The digested material on the economic history during the Civil War is still quite meager. The most satisfactory study of the South is that by John C. Schwab,

The Confederate States of America (1901), a financial and industrial history of the South during the conflict, devoting special attention to the financial phase and containing a good bibliography. What Schwab has done for the South E. D. Fite has done for the North in his *Social and Industrial Conditions in the North During the Civil War* (1910), but with more emphasis upon the social and industrial and less upon the financial. Popular accounts of the non-military aspects of the Civil War are given in Nathaniel Stephenson, *The Day of the Confederacy* (1919), and *Abraham Lincoln and the Union* (1918), both in the Chronicles of America. Important also are the later chapters in A. C. Cole, *The Irrepressible Conflict* (1934), and J. G. Randall, *The Civil War and Recon-struction* (1937), Chaps. XXVII, XXVIII. Further summaries of conditions in the South appear in J. F. Rhodes, *History of the United States* (1905), Vol. V, Chaps. XXVII and XXVIII, and in his *History of the Civil War, 1861–1865* (1917), Chaps. XI and XII. In Vol. V of *The South in the Building of the Nation,* there are a number of contributions on the economic background, notably those of J. C. Reed, "Economic Conditions in the South During the Civil War," "The Finances of the Southern Confederacy," and "The Labor Force and Labor Conditions." James A. B. Scherer, *Cotton as a World Power, a Study in the Economic Inter-pretation of History* (1916), contains interesting material on the rôle of cotton in the struggle. For a general history of the Civil War in most of its phases, per-haps the best is Edward Channing, *History of the United States,* Vol. VI. The most recent study of the Davis administration is E. C. Eckenrode, *Jefferson Davis, President of the South* (1930).

On special phases the following are valuable and detailed discussions: F. A. Shannon, *The Organization and Administration of the Union Army, 1861–1865* (2 vols., 1928); Albert B. Moore, *Conscription and Conflict in the Con-federacy* (1924); E. Lonn, *Desertion During the Civil War* (1928); M. C. Vaughan, *Women's Work in the Civil War* (1928); C. J. Stille, *A History of the United States Sanitary Commission* (1866), and F. L. Owsley, *States' Rights in the Confederacy* (1925). Useful reminiscences of war time include C. A. Dana, *Recollections of the Civil War* (1898); Mary B. Chestnut, *Diary from Dixie* (1905), and W. H. Russell, *My Diary North and South* (1863). B. S. Wise, *The End of an Era* (1899), a biography of H. A. Wise, Governor of Virginia from 1856 to 1860, also has value. In C. H. Wesley, *The Collapse of the Confederacy,* the defeat of the South is attributed to the internal breakdown of morale.

The financial history of the period is of special interest. That of the North is summarized in Davis R. Dewey, *Financial History of the United States* (10th ed., 1928); and in more detail in A. S. Bolles, *Financial History of the United States,* Vol. III, 1861–1885 (1886); also in W. C. Mitchell, *History of the Green-backs* (1903); in Don C. Barrett, *The Greenbacks and the Resumption of Specie Payments, 1862–1879* (1931), and in A. M. Davis, *The Origin of the National Banking System* (1910). On the finances of the Confederacy, see the book by John C. Schwab previously mentioned, and the following articles: "Finances of the Confederacy," *Political Science Quarterly,* Vol. VII, pp. 38–56 (1892); "The

Confederate Foreign Loan," *Yale Review,* Vol. I, pp. 175–186 (1893); "The Financier of the Confederate States," *Yale Review,* Vol. II, pp. 288–301 (1894), in part a review of Henry D. Capers, *The Life and Times of C. G. Memminger* (1894); and J. L. Sellers, "An Interpretation of Civil War Finance," *American Historical Review,* Vol. XXX, pp. 282–297 (Jan., 1925), and his "Economic Incidence of the Civil War in the South," *Mississippi Valley Historical Review,* Vol. XIV, pp. 179–191 (Sept., 1927). See also his Chap. XIX in *Cambridge Modern History,* Vol. VII. For prices during the war, consult the Report by Mr. Aldrich for the Committee on Finances and Prices, Wages, and Transportation, *Senate Reports,* 52nd Cong., 2nd Sess., 1892–1893, Special Session, March 4, 1893, Vol. III, four parts. See also E. P. Oberholtzer, *Jay Cooke* (2 vols., 1907), and Henrietta Larson, *Jay Cooke, Private Banker* (1936). The story of the most important single industry developed during these years is told in scholarly fashion in Paul H. Giddens, *The Birth of the Oil Industry* (1938).

The influence of railroads on the course of the Civil War may be traced in E. A. Pratt, *The Rise of Rail Power* (1916), Chaps. II, III, and IV. On an important topic read L. B. Schmidt, "The Influence of Wheat and Cotton on Anglo-American Relations During the Civil War," *Iowa Journal of History and Politics* (July, 1918), Vol. XVI, pp. 400–439, and Frank L. Owsley, *King Cotton Diplomacy* (1931), Chap. XIX. On the efforts to break the blockade, see Francis B. C. Bradlee, *Blockade Running During the Civil War and the Effect of Land and Water Transportation on the Confederacy* (1925); James R. Soley, *The Blockade and the Cruisers* (1890); and William M. Robinson, *Confederate Privateers* (1928). The European attitude is developed in D. Jordan and E. S. Pratt, *Europe and the American Civil War* (1931), and E. D. Adams, *Great Britain and the American Civil War* (2 vols., 1925), Vol. II, Chap. XVIII.

18. THE LAST FRONTIER

The history and significance of the westward movement since the Civil War have never been adequately summarized, although much has been done since F. J. Turner in 1893 pointed out the "Significance of the Frontier in American History," in the American Historical Association *Annual Report.* Other essays by Professor Turner, especially those in *The Frontier in American History* (1921), touch on this recent phase. The most complete bibliography of the period is in F. J. Turner and F. Merk, *List of References on the History of the West* (rev. ed., 1922). The earliest phases of the trans-Mississippi West are developed in Katherine Coman, *Economic Beginnings of the Far West* (2 vols., 1912), and the more recent in F. L. Paxson, *The Last American Frontier* (1910), and in Dan E. Clark, *The West in American History* (1937). See also F. L. Paxson, *History of the American Frontier* (1924); W. J. Ghent, *The Early Far West: A Narrative Outline, 1540–1850* (1931); and R. E. Riegel, *America Moves West* (1930).

On the miners' frontier, S. E. White, *The Forty-Niners* (1920), Chronicles of America, and R. G. Cleland, *California: The American Period* (1939), tell the early history of California; and Owen C. Coy, *The Grand Trek* (1931), the story of the 'forty-niners. The early days in Nevada are recounted in C. H. Shinn, *Story of the Mine* (1896), and E. Lord, *Comstock Mining* (U. S. Geological Survey, IV, 1883); Mark Twain's *Roughing It* gives an intimate picture of a stagecoach journey to the Far West and of the boom period in the Nevada silver mines. On mining, consult W. J. Trimble, *The Mining Advance into the Inland Empire, University of Wisconsin Bulletin,* No. 638 (1914), and T. A. Rickard, *A History of American Mining* (1932).

On ranching and the cow country, E. S. Osgood, *The Day of the Cattleman* (1929), E. E. Dale, *The Range Cattle Industry* (1930), and W. P. Webb, *The Great Plains* (1931) are invaluable and significant studies. Osgood is particularly valuable on the business and financial aspects of ranching, and Webb on the importance of firearms, barbed wire, and water as the background of plains settlement. Also important are Louis Pelzer, *The Cattleman's Frontier* (1936); P. A. Rollins, *The Cowboy* (1936); W. C. Barnes, *The Story of the Range* (1926); E. D. Branch, *The Cowboy and His Interpreters* (1926); R. A. Clemens, *The American Livestock and Meat Industry* (1923); and J. G. McCoy, *Historic Sketches of the Cattle Trade of the West and Southwest* (new ed., 1932), the latter by one of the pioneer cattle men. Intimate pictures of cowboy life are to be found in the books of Will James, but perhaps the most complete picture of ranching is that by Emerson Hough, *The Story of the Cowboy* (2 vols., 1897). See also F. L. Paxson, "The Cow Country," *American Historical Review,* Vol. XXII, pp. 65–84, and the following articles in the *Mississippi Valley Historical Review:* E. E. Dale, "The Ranchman's Last Frontier" (June, 1923); Louis Pelzer, "A Cattlemen's Commonwealth on the Western Range" (June, 1926); R. S. Fletcher, "End of the Open Range in Eastern Montana" (Sept., 1929); and Harold Briggs, "The Development and Decline of Open Range Ranching in the Northwest" (March, 1934). See also C. M. Lowe, "History of the Cattle Industry in the Southwest," *Southwestern Historical Quarterly,* Vol. XX (July, 1916). A popular summary is Emerson Hough, *The Passing of the Frontier* (1918) in the Chronicles of America. The life of Henry Miller, a cattle baron of California, is interestingly told in E. F. Treadwell, *The Cattle King* (1931).

On the public land policy, consult McLoughlin and Hart, *Cyclopedia of American Government* (1914), articles on Public Land, Land Grants, Homestead Act, etc., also G. M. Stephenson, *The Political History of the Public Lands from 1840 to 1862* (1917), and B. H. Hibbard, *A History of the Public Land Policies* (1924). T. Donaldson, *Public Domain* (1881), although inaccurate, is the only available detailed account up to that time. See also the *Public Land Report* (1880) and the *Report With Appendix* (1905). The most significant recent book is R. M. Robbins, *Our Landed Heritage; The Public Domain, 1776–1936* (1942). Important special studies are F. A. Shannon, "The Homestead Act and the Labor Surplus," *American Historical Review,* Vol. XLI, pp. 637–651

(July, 1936), and P. W. Gates, "The Homestead Law in an Incongruous Land System," *ibid.*, pp. 652–681. See also G. T. Du Bois and G. S. Mathews, *Galusha A. Grow, Father of the Homestead Act* (1917).

The Indian Wars are recounted in N. A. Miles, *Serving the Republic* (1911) and F. L. Paxson, *The Last American Frontier*. On the Indian, see F. E. Leupp, *The Indian and His Problem* (1910), and G. E. E. Lindquist, *The Red Man in the United States* (1923).

Material on the contribution of the railroads to the opening of the West may be found in H. K. White, *Union Pacific Railway* (1898); J. P. Davis, *Union Pacific Railway* (1894); E. V. Smalley, *The Northern Pacific Railway* (1883); *Memoirs of Henry Villard* (2 vols., 1904); E. P. Oberholtzer, *Jay Cooke* (2 vols., 1907); J. G. Pyle, *Life of James J. Hill* (2 vols., 1917); F. L. Paxson, "The Pacific Railroads and the Disappearance of the Frontier," *American Historical Association Annual Report* (1907), Vol. I, pp. 105–118; R. C. Overton, *Burlington West; a Colonization History of the Burlington Railroad* (1941); and particularly J. B. Hedges, "The Colonization Work of the Northern Pacific," *Mississippi Valley Historical Review* (Dec., 1926). See also his *Henry Villard and the Railways of the Northwest* (1930). The contribution to settlement by a railroad in the Middle West is developed in P. W. Gates, *The Illinois Central Railroad and Its Colonization Work* (1934).

19. THE AGRARIAN REVOLUTION

See the Bibliography for the preceding chapter for a partial bibliography on the ranchers' frontier, the last farmers' frontier, and other aspects of agricultural history. Full bibliographies on agriculture are available in L. B. Schmidt, *Topical Studies and References on the Economic History of American Agriculture* (rev. ed., 1937); in E. E. Edwards, *Guide for Courses in the History of American Agriculture*, Biographical Contribution 35, Dept. of Agriculture (1939), and in the same author's *Bibliography of the History of American Agriculture*, Bibliographical Contribution 32, Dept. of Agriculture (1939). The files of *Agricultural History* (1918–), published by the Agricultural History Society, will be found invaluable by any student of agricultural history. The *Annual Reports* of the United States Department of Agriculture are a mine of information. Particularly important are the historical articles in the *1940 Yearbook*. These have been gathered together as *Yearbook* Separate No. 1783 and printed under the title "An Historical Survey of American Agriculture." For the earlier years, consult the Introduction to the volume on Agriculture in the *Eighth Census*, the special reports on *The Cereals*, on *Flour Milling*, on *Meat Production;* and in the *Tenth Census*, Vol. III, the report on *Tobacco*. In Vol. V, pp. xvi–xxvii of the same census, there is a brief review of the *Agricultural Progress of Fifty Years, 1850–1900*. See also volumes on *Agriculture* in the recent census volumes.

Some historical material will be found in Bailey's *Cyclopedia of American*

Agriculture, Vol. IV. A short, popular, and well-written account is that of A. H. Sanford, *The Story of Agriculture in the United States* (1916). The best brief summary is E. E. Edwards, "American Agriculture—the First 300 Years," pp. 171–276 of the *1940 Yearbook of Agriculture,* also issued as *Yearbook* Separate No. 1730. J. F. Boyle, *Agricultural Economics* (1921), and Wilson Gee, *The Social Economics of Agriculture* (1932) will be found valuable; N. S. B. Gras, *History of Agriculture* (1925) is suggestive. *The Agricultural Problem in the United States* (1920) by the National Industrial Conference Board, Inc., is an interesting survey. For source material and readings, see T. N. Carver, *Selected Readings in Rural Economics* (1916), and L. B. Schmidt and E. D. Ross, *Readings in the Economic History of American Agriculture* (1925). Consult also the selections in Bogart and Thompson and in Flügel and Faulkner.

On farm machinery, see H. N. Casson, *The Romance of the Reaper* (1908); H. W. Quintance, *The Influence of Farm Machinery on Production and Labor* (1904), Publications of the American Economic Association, 3rd Series, Vol. V, No. 4; and Leo Rogin, *The Introduction of Farm Machinery in Its Relation to the Productivity of Labor in the Agriculture of the United States* (1931). On the reaper, see W. T. Hutchinson, *Cyrus Hall McCormick* (2 vols., 1930–1935) and Cyrus McCormick, *The Century of the Reaper* (1931). Helpful is O. E. Baker, *A Graphic Summary of Farm Machinery Facilities, Roads and Expenditures,* U. S. Dept. of Agriculture Misc. Pub. 264 (1937).

The history of government aid in the problems of agriculture may be found in the following: A. P. Chew, *The Response of Government to Agriculture* (1937); W. L. Wanlass, *The United States Department of Agriculture; a Study in Administration* (1920); A. C. True, *A History of Agricultural Extension Work in the United States, 1785–1923,* U. S. Dept. of Agriculture Misc. Pub. 15 (1928), his *A History of Agricultural Education in the United States, 1785–1925,* U. S. Dept. of Agriculture Misc. Pub. 36 (1929), and his "Agricultural Experiment Stations in the United States," *Yearbook of Agriculture, 1939,* pp. 513–548. On the problems of credit, consult A. C. Wiprud, *The Federal Farm Loan System in Operation* (1921); Clara Elliot, *The Farmers' Campaign for Credit* (1927), and E. S. Sparks, *History and Theory of Agricultural Credit in the United States* (1932).

On irrigation, see George Thomas, *The Development of Institutions Under Irrigation* (1920); R. P. Teale, *The Economics of Land Reclamation in the United States* (1927); J. W. James, *Reclaiming the Arid West* (1917), and P. B. Sears, *Deserts on the March* (1935).

The history of certain specific aspects of agriculture may be found in R. A. Cleman, *The American Livestock and Meat Industry* (1923); A. H. Cole, "The American Rice-Growing Industry," *Quarterly Journal of Economics,* Vol. XLI, pp. 595–643 (Aug., 1927); L. G. Connor, "A Brief History of the Sheep Industry in the United States," *American Historical Association Annual Report* (1918), pp. 89–197; C. B. Kuhlman, *The Development of the Flour-Milling Industry in the United States* (1929); C. W. Larson *et al.,* "The Dairy Industry,"

Yearbook of Agriculture, 1922, pp. 281–394; C. E. Leighty *et al.,* "The Corn Crop," *ibid.,* pp. 161–226; and T. R. Pirtle, *History of the Dairy Industry* (1926).

Two phases of southern agriculture are presented in M. B. Hammond, *The Cotton Industry* (1897), in the Publications of the American Economic Association, and by M. Jacobstein, *The Tobacco Industry* (1907), Columbia University Studies, Vol. XXVI, No. 3. For southern tenancy, consult R. P. Brooks, *The Agrarian Revolution in Georgia, 1865–1912* (1914), and for a general picture of the whole country, E. A. Goldenweiser and L. E. Truesdale, *Farm Tenancy in the United States,* Census Monograph No. 4, 1920 Census (1924).

20. DEVELOPMENT OF THE INDUSTRIAL REVOLUTION

The bases for the study of manufacturing since the Civil War are the census reports, especially Vol. VII of the *Twelfth Census of the United States* and the *Abstract of the Thirteenth Census.* Companion volumes of equal value are the *Reports on Manufactures* for 1905 and 1914. Essential for industrial developments, but unwieldy to handle is the *Report of the Industrial Commission* (19 vols., 1902), which took testimony for two years on general industrial conditions. Extracts from this report are included in the *Readings* by Bogart and Thompson and by Flügel and Faulkner. A valuable piece of work, beautifully done, is *A Graphic Analysis of the Census of Manufacturing, 1849–1919,* by the National Industrial Conference Board, Inc. (1923). The only comprehensive secondary account is V. S. Clark, *History of Manufactures in the United States,* Vol. II, 1860–1893; Vol. III, 1893–1928 (1929). An older book which covers part of this period is C. M. Depew (ed.), *One Hundred Years of American Commerce* (2 vols., 1895). More recent descriptive accounts are Malcolm Keir, *Manufacturing* (1928), and E. L. Bogart and C. E. Landon, *Modern Industry* (1927). B. J. Kendrick, *The Age of Big Business* (1921) is a popular introduction. N. S. B. Gras, *Industrial Evolution* (1930) is a valuable study of special industries.

Longer accounts of special industries may be traced in encyclopedias, especially the *Encyclopaedia of the Social Sciences,* and in the following books: T. M. Young, *The American Cotton Industry* (1903); P. H. Nystrom, *Textiles* (1916); M. T. Copeland, *The Cotton Manufacturing Industry in the United States* (1912); B. F. Lement, *The Cotton Textile Industry of the Southern Appalachian Piedmont* (1933); J. H. Burgy, *The New England Cotton Textile Industry. A Study in Industrial Geography* (1932); A. H. Cole, *The American Wool Manufacture* (2 vols., 1926); S. N. D. North, *A Century of American Wool Manufacture, 1790–1890* (1895); W. C. Wyckoff, *American Silk Manufacture* (1880); "Flour Milling" in the semi-centennial issue of the *Northwestern Miller* (1923); C. B. Kuhlmann, *The Development of the Flour Milling Industry in the United States* (1929); F. J. Allen, *The Shoe Industry* (1916); B. E. Hazard, *The Organization of the Boot and Shoe Industry in Massachusetts Before 1875* (1921); M. D. Swank, *History of the Manufacture of Iron in All*

Ages (2nd ed., 1892); H. N. Casson, *The Romance of Steel* (1907); J. R. Smith, *Story of Iron and Steel* (1913); J. V. Woodworth, *American Tool Making and Interchangeable Manufacturing* (1905), and A. O. Backert (ed.), *The A B C of Iron and Steel* (4th ed., 1921). Indispensable for the iron industry is B. J. Hendrick, *Andrew Carnegie* (2 vols., 1932). R. C. Epstein, *The Automobile Industry* (1928) emphasizes the commercial and financial aspects of the industry, and E. D. Kennedy, *The Automobile Industry* (1941) is more inclusive. The lumber industry is treated from two aspects in J. E. Defebaugh, *History of the Lumber Industry of America* (4 vols., 1906–1909), and in John Ise, *United States Forest Policy* (1920). The latter's *United States Oil Policy* (1927) is the best on that subject. For other industries, see the following: L. T. Sutherland, *Fifty Years of Portland Cement* (1923); William Haynes and E. L. Gordy (eds.), *Chemical Industries' Contribution to the Nation, 1635–1935* (1935); Howard and Ralph Wolf, *Rubber: A Story of Glory and Greed* (1936), an excellent history; R. A. Clemen, *The American Livestock and Meat Industry* (1923); J. H. Collins, *The Story of Canned Foods* (1924); A. P. Van Gelder and Hugo Schlalter, *History of the Explosives Industry in America* (1927); B. B. Hampton, *History of the Movies* (1931), and C. E. Puffer, *Air Transportation* (1941).

A popular history of many inventions is given in W. Kaempffert, *History of American Inventions* (2 vols., 1924).

21. CONSOLIDATION OF BUSINESS

Some of the most important source material on industrial and financial concentration is to be found in the various investigations made by the state and federal legislatures. Of these the most valuable are: *Preliminary Report of the Industrial Commission on Trusts and Industrial Combinations,* Vol. I of the Commission's Report (1900); *Final Report of the Industrial Commission,* Vol. XIX of the Commission's Report (1902); *Report of the Special Committee on Railroads Appointed Under a Resolution of the Assembly of February 28, 1879, to Investigate Alleged Abuses in the Management of Railroads Chartered by the State of New York,* Assembly Doc. No. 38, 1880 (Hepburn Committee), especially informative on rebates; *Report of the Committee Pursuant to House Resolutions 429 and 504 to Investigate the Concentration of the Control of Money and Credit* (1913) (Pujo Committee). See also the *Thirteenth Census Abstract,* Chap. X, and the *Abstract of the Census of Manufactures,* 1914, Chaps. VI and VII. The Commission of Corporations and, since 1914, the Federal Trade Commission have made many valuable reports on specific industries. Excerpts from their reports on the tobacco industry, the steel industry, the International Harvester Company, the meat-packing industry, and the concentration of electrical power are given in F. Flügel and H. U. Faulkner, *Readings in the Economic and Social History of the United States,* Chap. XIV.

General studies of the trust movement include J. W. Jenks and W. E. Clark, *The Trust Problem* (4th ed., 1917), a standard and scholarly work; Eliot Jones, *The Trust Problem in the United States* (1921); C. R. Van Hise, *Concentration and Control* (rev. ed., 1914); B. J. Hendrick, *The Age of Big Business* (1919), in the Chronicles of America, interestingly written; R. T. Ely, *Monopolies and Trusts* (1900); John Moody, *The Truth About the Trusts* (1904), with valuable statistical information by an expert; and John Moody, *The Masters of Capital* (1919), in the Chronicles of America. Essential to any understanding of business concentration is J. C. Bonbright and G. C. Means, *The Holding Company* (1932). A valuable survey is by H. R. Seager and C. A. Gulick, Jr., *Trust and Corporation Problems* (1929), primarily historical. On the Federal Trade Commission, G. C. Henderson, *The Federal Trade Commission* (1924), is exhaustive up to that date. It should be supplemented by T. C. Blaisdell, Jr., *The Federal Trade Commission* (1932). Recent important discussions of the general problem are given in M. W. Watkins, *Industrial Combinations and Public Policy* (1927); D. M. Keezer and Stacy May, *The Public Control of Business* (1930); J. D. Clark, *The Federal Trust Policy* (1931), and A. R. Burns, *The Decline of Competition* (1936). In a class by itself as the most important description of contemporary concentration is H. W. Laidler, *Concentration in American Industry* (1931). On the Webb Export Act, read L. T. Fournier, "The Purposes and Results of the Webb-Pomerene Act," *American Economic Review*, Vol. XXII, No. 1 (March, 1932). Sources are collected in W. Z. Ripley, *Trusts, Pools, and Corporations* (rev. ed., 1916).

The heaviest guns in the early anti-trust agitation were fired by Henry Demarest Lloyd in his unsparing denunciation of monopoly, *Wealth Against Commonwealth* (1894). See also C. Lloyd, *Life of Henry Demarest Lloyd* (2 vols., 1912), for a survey of the growth of anti-trust feeling. In later years Woodrow Wilson lifted his voice in favor of competition and small business in his *New Freedom* (1913), a collection of campaign speeches.

In C. C. Regier, *The Era of the Muckrakers* (1932), and in Louis Filler, *Crusaders for American Liberalism* (1939) can be found a résumé of the literature of protest; two of the most famous of the "muckrakers" contribute a wealth of interesting material in Charles Edward Russell, *Bare Hands and Stone Walls* (1933), and Lincoln Steffens, *Autobiography of Lincoln Steffens* (2 vols., 1931). A general discussion of the social unrest leading to reform legislation is that by H. U. Faulkner, *The Quest for Social Justice* (1931), Vol. XI in the History of American Life Series.

Special industries may be studied in Ida M. Tarbell, *History of the Standard Oil Company* (2 vols., 1904), a pioneer work based on first-hand research; in G. H. Montague, *Rise and Progress of the Standard Oil Company* (1903), a defense of the oil monopoly; in H. R. Mussey, *Combination in the Mining Industry* (1905); in Abraham Berglund, *The United States Steel Corporation* (1907), Columbia University Studies in History, Economics and Public Law, Vol. XVIII, No. 3; in H. L. Wilgus, *A Study of the United States Steel Cor-*

poration (1901); in Arundel Cotter, *The United States Steel—A Corporation with a Soul* (1921); in the *Report of the Commissioner of Corporations on the Steel Industry* (3 parts, 1911); in Eliot Jones, *The Anthracite Coal Combination*, Harvard Economic Studies, Vol. II (1914); and in Scott Nearing, *Anthracite: An Instance of Natural Resource Monopoly* (1915). See also *Report to the President on the Anthracite Coal Strike of May–October, 1902*, by the Anthracite Coal Strike Commission (1903), especially Appendix J; and *Report of the United States Coal Commission Transmitted Pursuant to the Act Approved Sept. 22, 1922* (1925).

On the legal aspect, consult W. H. Taft, *The Anti-Trust Act and the Supreme Court* (1914). For a summary of monopoly advantages and disadvantages, see L. H. Haney, *Business Organization and Combination* (rev. ed., 1913).

Most of the biographies of the industrial giants of the period are "official," and consequently undiscriminatingly laudatory. These include J. W. Jenkins, *J. W. Duke, Master Builder* (1927); I. M. Tarbell, *The Life of Elbert H. Gary* (1925); B. J. Hendrick, *Life of Andrew Carnegie* (2 vols., 1932); George Harvey, *Henry Clay Frick, the Man* (1928); and Carl Hovey, *The Life of J. Pierpont Morgan* (1912). Critical but based on sound research are the much more satisfactory Lewis Corey, *The House of Morgan* (1930); J. T. Flynn, *God's Gold* (1931); Harvey O'Connor, *Mellon's Millions* (1933); and Matthew Josephson, *Robber Barons: The Great American Capitalists, 1861–1901* (1934). Allan Nevins, *John D. Rockefeller: The Heroic Age of American Business* (2 vols., 1940) is a detailed and objective study. Useful also is Gustave Myers, *History of Great American Fortunes* (3 vols., 1910).

22. THE LABOR MOVEMENT TO 1914

For recent statistics, consult the *Statistical Abstracts* and the biennial *Census of Manufactures*. Excellent histories of the labor movement in America are Mary Beard, *A Short History of the American Labor Movement* (1920), a brief summary; G. C. Groat, *Organized Labor in America* (1919); F. T. Carlton, *History and Problems of Organized Labor* (rev. ed., 1920); and *Organized Labor in American History* (1920); G. S. Watkins, *An Introduction to the Study of Labor Problems* (1922); Selig Perlman, *A History of Trade Unionism in the United States* (1922); R. T. Ely, *The Labor Movement in America* (1905), good on the early period; N. J. Ware, *The Labor Movement in the United States* (1929), the most recent study of the period from 1860 to 1895; Leo Wolman, *Growth of American Trade Unions 1880–1923* (1924), and his *Ebb and Flow in Trade Unionism* (1936); M. S. Clark and S. F. Simon, *The Labor Movement in America* (1938), and Herbert Harris, *American Labor* (1939). The most detailed account is that by J. R. Commons *et al.*, *History of Labour in the United States* (2 vols., 1918). This has recently been continued in *History of Labor in the United States, 1896–1932* (2 vols., 1933–1935), of which the first volume, by D. D. Lescohier and Elizabeth Brandeis, covers labor conditions and employer policies; and the second, by Selig Perlman and Philip Taft, covers labor movements. A recent excellent general textbook is C. R. Daugherty, *Labor Problems in American Industry* (1933). L. L. Lorwin, *The American Federation of Labor* (1933) is the first adequate effort to deal with that organization. For the Negro, see C. H. Wesley, *Negro Labor in the United States* (1927). A tremendous collection of source materials gathered and edited by J. R. Commons and associates, but dealing chiefly with the period before 1860, is the *Documentary History of American Industrial Society* (10 vols., 1910–1911). Paul H. Douglas, Curtice N. Hitchock, and Willard E. Atkins, *The Worker in Modern Economic Society,* University of Chicago Press (1923), is an excellent collection of readings designed to supplement a textbook. For the official attitude of the American Federation of Labor, see D. J. Saposs, *Readings in Trade Unionism* (1925). Carroll D. Wright, "Historical Sketch of the Knights of Labor," *Quarterly Journal of Economics,* pp. 127–168 (Jan., 1887), is an excellent contemporary account of that movement. A more recent account is Powderly's autobiography, *The Path I Trod,* edited by H. J. Carman, Henry David, and P. N. Guthrie (1940). The best of the histories and interpretations by labor leaders are those of T. V. Powderly, *Thirty Years of Labor, 1859–1889* (1890), by the Grand Master of the Knights of Labor and particularly interesting on that organization; G. E. McNeill (ed.), *The Labor Movement, the Problem of Today* (1887), by one of the earliest state labor officials; John Mitchell, *Organized Labor* (1903), by the one-time president of the United Mine Workers of America; and Helen Marot, *American Labor Unions* (1914). No study of American labor would be complete without reading Samuel Gompers, *Seventy Years of Life and Labor: An Autobiography* (2 vols., 1925). An interesting episode is described in D. L. McMurry, *Coxey's Army* (1929).

There are numerous studies by experts, many of whom have received their inspiration from the researches and training of J. R. Commons. Among the best are J. R. Commons, *Trade Unionism and Labor Problems,* First Series (1905) and Second Series (1921), collections of readings; J. R. Commons, *Labor and Administration* (1913); T. S. Adams and H. L. Sumner, *Labor Problems* (1905); J. R. Commons and J. B. Andrews, *Principles of Labor Legislation* (4th ed., 1936); W. Jett Lauck and Edgar Sydenstricker, *Conditions of Labor in American Industries* (1917); D. D. Lescohier, *The Labor Market* (1919); and Hayes Robins, *The Labor Movement and the Farmer* (1922). W. B. Catlin, *The Labor Problem in the United States and Great Britain* (1926) is a scholarly interpretation. Important also are F. Frankfurter and N. Greene, *The Labor Injunction* (1930); Edward Berman, *Labor and the Sherman Act* (1930), and N. J. Ware, *The Boycott in American Trade Unions,* Johns Hopkins Studies, Series 34, No. 1 (1916). A standard volume on wages is P. H. Douglas, *The Theory of Wages* (1934). See also U. S. Bureau of Labor Statistics, *History of Wages in the United States from Colonial Times to 1928* (1929), and Paul F. Brissenden, *Earnings of Factory Workers, 1899 to 1927: An Analysis of Payroll Statistics,* Dept. of Commerce, Bureau of Census, Census Monograph X (1929).

On the labor of women and children, there is now a large amount of material. Pioneer government work was done in the *Report on Condition of Woman and Child Wage-Earners in the United States* (19 vols., 1910–1912), published by the United States Department of Labor, 61st Cong., 2nd Sess., Senate Documents, Vols. 86–104, and subsequent reports by the Women's Bureau and Children's Bureau of the Department of Labor. A recent study is that by Adelaide M. Anderson, *Women in the Factory* (1922). On the horrible conditions of child labor in the early mills, see Helen L. Sumner's work in J. R. Commons *et al., History of Labour in the United States* (1918), Vol. I, pp. 169 ff. An earlier work by John Spargo, *The Bitter Cry of the Children* (1906), is still valuable.

On the more radical developments, the books of P. F. Brissenden, *The I.W.W., a Study of American Syndicalism,* Columbia University Studies, Vol. LXXXIII (1919), and J. G. Brooks, *American Syndicalism: The I.W.W.* (1913), the latter emphasizing the philosophy of the movement and its international aspect, will be found valuable. The Brissenden book has now been supplemented and continued by J. S. Gambs, *The Decline of the I.W.W.* (1932). Carleton H. Parker, *The Casual Laborer and Other Essays* (1920), and John Spargo, *Syndicalism, Industrial Unionism and Socialism* (1913), are illuminating. A notion of European labor movements may be gained from Paul U. Kellogg and Arthur H. Gleason, *British Labor and the War: Reconstructors for a New World* (1919); and Louis Levine, *Syndicalism in France,* Columbia University Studies in History, Economics and Public Law, Vol. XLVI, No. 3 (1914). For recent radical developments, see George Soule, *The New Unionism in the Clothing Industry* (1920); D. J. Saposs, *Left Wing Unionism* (1920); Anthony Bimba, *The History of the American Working Class* (1927), and Nathan Fine, *Labor and Farmer Parties in the United States 1828–1928* (1928). J. A. Fitch, *The Causes of Industrial Unrest* (1924) is a sane study of the psychological background. An absorbing story of some of the more famous episodes of American class warfare is told in Louis Adamic, *Dynamite, the Story of Class Violence in America* (rev. ed., 1934).

The immigration problem may be studied in J. R. Commons, *Races and Immigrants in America* (1907), a succulent survey; J. W. Jenks and W. J. Lauck, *The Immigration Problem* (1917), a scholarly presentation; I. A. Hourwich, *Immigration and Labor* (1922); Philip Davis and Bertha Schwartz (comps. and eds.), *Immigration and Americanization* (1920), a book of selected readings; John P. Gavit, *Americans by Choice* (1922); F. J. Warne, *The Tide of Immigration* (1916); Grace Abbott, *The Immigrant and the Community* (1917); J. Drachsler, *Democracy and Assimilation* (1920); National Industrial Conference Board, Inc., *Immigration Problems in the United States* (1923); and two collections of source materials by Edith Abbott, *Historical Aspects of the Immigration Problem* (1926), and *Immigration, Select Documents and Case Records* (1924). For statistics, see the Report of the Immigration Commission, containing *Statistical Review of Immigration, 1820–1910,* and *Distribution of Immigrants, 1850–1900,* 61st Cong., 3rd Sess., Senate Document No. 756, Vol. XX (1911). Two excellent summaries are G. M. Stephenson, *History of American Immigration, 1820–1924* (1926), and R. L. Garis, *Immigration Restriction* (1927).

Three significant reports on specific strikes are the *Report to the President on the Anthracite Coal Strike of May–October, 1902,* by the Anthracite Coal Commission (1903); *Report of Strike of Textile Workers in Lawrence, Massachusetts* (1912), 62nd Cong., 2nd Sess., No. 870; *Report of the Steel Strike of 1919* by the Commission of Inquiry of the Interchurch World Movement.

Few full-length studies of specific unions have as yet been made. Among those that should be mentioned are Arthur Elliott, *Coal Miners' Struggle for Industrial Status* (1926); Herman Schluter, *The Brewing Industry and the Brewery Workers' Movement in America* (1910); E. C. Robbins, *Railway Conductors* (Columbia University Studies No. 148, 1914); Louis Levine, *The Women's Garment Workers: A History of the International Ladies' Garment Workers' Union* (1924), and particularly well done, Joel Seidman, *The Needle Trades* (1942).

The position of Negroes in the labor movement may be studied in C. H. Wesley, *Negro Labor in the United States* (1927); in his "Organized Labor and the Negro," *Journal of Negro Education* (July, 1939), and in H. R. Clayton and G. F. Mitchell, *Black Workers and the New Unions* (1939).

23. DEVELOPMENT OF TRANSPORTATION AND COMMUNICATION, 1860–1914

In addition to the various railroad magazines, Hunt's *Merchant's Magazine,* 1835–1870, and the *Commercial and Financial Chronicle* since 1870 will be found useful; also the yearly reports of the Interstate Commerce Commission. Seymour Dunbar, *History of Travel in America* (4 vols., 1915), well illustrated and interestingly written, is not so full on the period since 1860. Short résumés are E. R. Johnson and T. W. Van Metre, *Principles of Railway Transportation* (1922); C. F. Adams, Jr., *Railroads: Their Origin and Problems* (1878; rev. ed., 1893); A. T. Hadley, *Railroad Transportation* (1886); F. L. McVey, *Railway Transportation* (1921); I. L. Sharpman, *The American Railroad Problem* (1921); Eliot Jones, *Principles of Railway Transportation* (1924), and Slason Thompson, *History of American Railways* (1925). Exceedingly valuable are the standard studies by W. Z. Ripley, *Railroads, Rates and Regulations* (1912), and *Railroads; Finance and Organizations* (1915). For the reconstruction period in the South, see Carl Russell Fish, *The Restoration of the Southern Railroads* (1919), in University of Wisconsin Studies in the Social Sciences and History, No. 2. Popular presentations include M. D. Stevens, *Steel Rails* (1933); Labert St. Clair, *Transportation* (1933); J. W. Starr, *One Hundred Years of American Railroading* (1929), and R. S. Henry, *This Fascinating Railroad Business* (1942).

On special phases, consult L. H. Haney, *A Congressional History of Railroads in the United States, 1850–1887* (1910); S. J. Buck, *The Granger Movement* (1913), and the *Agrarian Crusade* (1920), in Chronicles of America; F. Cleveland and F. W. Powell, *Railroad Promotion and Capitalization* (1909); W. F. Gephart, *Transportation and Industrial Development in the Middle West,*

Columbia University Studies (1909); M. B. Hammond, *Railway Rate Theories of the Interstate Commerce Commission* (1911); E. R. Johnson and G. G. Huebner, *Railway Traffic and Rates* (1911); Leonor F. Loree, *Railroad Freight Transportation* (1922); Rogers MacVeagh, *The Transportation Act, 1920* (1922); Frank H. Dixon, *Railroads and Government; Their Relations in the United States, 1910–1921* (1922); W. J. Cunningham, *American Railroads: Government Control and Reconstruction* (1922), and I. L. Sharfman, *The Interstate Commerce Commission* (5 vols., 1931). Two excellent discussions of general problems are D. P. Locklin, *Economics of Transportation* (rev. ed., 1938), and Stuart Daggett, *Principles of Inland Transportation* (rev. ed., 1934).

The history of certain of the specific railroads has been written—e.g., H. S. Mott, *Story of the Erie* (1900); C. F. Adams, *Chapters of Erie* (1886); F. C. Hicks, *High Finance in the Sixties* (1929), chapters on the early history of the Erie; J. P. Davis, *The Union Pacific* (1894); Grenville Dodge, "How We Built the Union Pacific," *Senate Doc. 447,* 61st Cong., and Sess.; Nelson Trottman, *History of the Union Pacific* (1923); E. V. Smalley, *History of the Northern Pacific* (1883); Stuart Daggett, *Chapters in the History of the Southern Pacific* (1922); Edward Hungerford, *The Story of the Baltimore and Ohio Railroad 1827–1928* (2 vols., 1928); Milton Reizenstein, *The Economic History of the Baltimore and Ohio Railroad, 1827–1853* (1897); F. W. Stevens, *The Beginnings of the New York Central Railroad* (1926); S. M. Derrick, *Centennial History of the South Carolina Railroad* (1930); F. B. C. Bradlee, *The Boston and Maine Railroad* (1921); H. W. Shotter, *The Growth and Development of the Pennsylvania Railroad Company* (1927), and *A Century of Progress, History of the Delaware and Hudson Company* (1925). R. E. Riegel, *Story of Western Railroads* (1926), is a condensed account of the trans-Mississippi railroads, and J. I. Bogan, *The Anthracite Railroads* (1927), provides a similar treatment for the railroads serving northeastern Pennsylvania. Biographies which throw much light on early railroad building are H. G. Pearson, *An American Railroad Builder* (1911), relating the career of J. M. Forbes; E. P. Oberholtzer, *Jay Cooke, Financier of the Civil War* (2 vols., 1907); H. M. Larson, *Jay Cooke, Private Banker* (1936); J. G. Pyle, *Life of J. J. Hill* (2 vols., 1917); George Kennan, *E. H. Harriman* (2 vols., 1922); J. B. Hedges, *Henry Villard and the Railways of the Northwest* (1930); and the *Memoirs of Henry Villard* (2 vols., 1904). John Moody, *The Railway Builders* (1919), Chronicles of America, is chiefly biographical. A. D. Turnbull, *John Stevens: An American Record* (1928) deals with an important railroad pioneer.

Two legislative reports giving insight into early abuses are those of the "Hepburn Committee," New York State Assembly Document No. 38 (1880), and of the "Cullom Committee," Senate Reports, 49th Cong., 1st Sess., Serial Number 2356 (2 vols.). See also the *Report of the Industrial Commission on Transportation* (1902).

On waterways, consult the bibliography for Chap. XIV. H. J. Moulton, *Waterways vs. Railways* (1912) and *American Transportation Problems,* Chaps.

XXI–XXII, defends the economic advantages of railroads as against internal waterways. A. F. Harlow, *Old Towpaths* (1926), writes interestingly of the decline of canal transportation; Mildred H. Hartsough, *From Canoe to Steel Barge on the Upper Mississippi* (1934), traces transportation changes on the Mississippi; and N. E. Whitford, *History of the Barge Canal of New York State* (1922), tells of the revival of one early system. The history and problems of the Panama Canal are adequately handled in D. C. Minor, *The Fight for the Panama Route* (1940), and N. J. Pendleford, *The Panama Canal in Peace and War* (1942).

The two outstanding books on the history of the automobile are R. C. Epstein, *The Automobile Industry* (1928), which emphasizes the financial aspect, and E. D. Kennedy, *The Automobile Industry* (1941), which covers many phases.

Perhaps the best study on the recent history of highways is the joint report by the U. S. Bureau of Public Roads, U. S. Dept. of Agriculture and the Conn. State Highways Dept., *Report of a Survey of Transportation of the State Highway System of Connecticut* (1926). Mark Sullivan, *Our Times*, Vol. II, has a popular but excellent account of the early development of automobiles and airplanes in the United States. A popular history of the express business has been done by A. F. Harlow, *Old Waybills* (1934).

Street railways may be studied in Chap. VI of Stuart Daggett, *Principles of Inland Transportation* (rev. ed., 1934); in D. F. Wilcox, *Analysis of the Electric Railway Problem* (1921), and in E. S. Mason, *The Street Railways in Massachusetts* (1932). A popular but valuable account is J. A. Miller, *Fares, Please* (1941).

On aviation, C. E. Puffer, *Air Transportation* (1941) is outstanding. Also adequate on its phase is J. H. Frederick, *Commercial Air Transportation* (1942). Popular accounts of the early years are Eric Hodgins and F. A. Magoun, *Sky High* (1935), and H. L. Smith, *Airways* (1941).

An early history of the telephone is H. N. Casson, *History of the Telephone* (1910). T. A. Watson, *The Birth and Babyhood of the Telephone* (1926) is an account of the early years written by Bell's assistant. M. R. Danilian, *A. T. & T.* (1939) is exhaustive and critical. A. W. Page, *The Bell Telephone System* (1941) is a description of the operation and problems by a vice president of the A. T. & T. Horace Coon, *American Tel & Tel* (1939) is an interesting appraisal.

For the history and organization of the postal system, see D. C. Roper, *The United States Post Office* (1907), by a one-time First Assistant Postmaster-General, and A. F. Harlow, *Old Post Bags* (1928). See also K. M. Moon and J. Phillips, *John A. Moon, Father of the Parcel Post* (1941).

24. DOMESTIC AND FOREIGN COMMERCE

The chief sources for this subject are the various publications of the Department of Commerce. The best study of distribution costs is the work of the Twentieth Century Fund, Inc., *Does Distribution Cost Too Much?* (1939).

Two helpful textbooks on marketing are L. D. H. Weld, *The Marketing of Farm Products* (1919) and C. S. Duncan, *Marketing, Its Problems and Methods* (1921). On specific problems dealt with in this chapter, see E. R. A. Seligman, *The Economics of Installment Buying* (1927); W. S. Hayward and Percival White, *Chain Stores, Their Management and Operation* (1925); Frank Presbrey, *The History and Development of Advertising* (1929); F. E. Melder, *State and Local Barriers to Interstate Commerce in the United States* (1937); G. R. Taylor, E. L. Bertis, and F. V. Waugh, *Barriers to Internal Trade in Farm Products,* Department of Agriculture (1939), and D. H. Jacobson, *Our Interests as Consumers* (1941).

To the bibliography given under Chap. 12 should be added J. H. Frederick, *Development of American Commerce* (1932), a brief but serviceable textbook; Julius Klein, *Frontiers of Trade* (1929), a product of the optimistic 'twenties; W. S. Culbertson, *Commercial Policy in War Time and After* (1919), and *International Economic Policies* (1925); and Ethel Dietrich, *World Trade* (1939).

Besides the general books on the American merchant marine listed under Chap. XII, see R. Meeker, *History of Ship Subsidies* (1905); J. E. Sangstad, *Shipping and Shipbuilding Subsidies,* Trade Promotion Series No. 129, Bureau of Domestic and Foreign Commerce (1932); L. W. Maxwell, *Discriminatory Duties and the American Merchant Marine* (1926), and P. M. Zeis, *American Shipping Policy* (1938).

On the tariff, consult P. Ashley, Modern Tariff History (3rd ed., 1920); Edward Stanwood, *American Tariff Controversies in the Nineteenth Century* (1903); F. W. Taussig, *Some Aspects of the Tariff Question* (1915), and *Tariff History of the United States* (7th ed., 1923). Also C. W. Wright, *Wool Growing and the Tariff; a Study in the Economic History of the United States* (1910), Harvard Economic Studies, Vol. V. On the Fordney-McCumber tariff, see F. W. Taussig, "The Tariff Act of 1922," and A. H. Cole, "The Textile Schedules in the Tariff of 1922," both articles in the *Quarterly Journal of Economics,* Vol. XXXVII, No. 1 (Nov., 1922); and W. S. Culbertson, "The Making of Tariffs," in *Yale Review* (Jan., 1923). On the Hawley-Smoot bill, see F. W. Taussig, "The Tariff Act of 1930," *Quarterly Journal of Economics,* Vol. XLV, pp. 1–21 (Nov., 1930). An excellent symposium covering the many aspects of the subject is "Tariff Problems of the United States," *Annals of the American Academy of Political and Social Science,* Vol. CXLI (Jan., 1929). Also see Ethel Dietrich, *World Trade* (1939).

25. FINANCIAL HISTORY SINCE 1860

The *Annual Report on the Finances* by the Secretary of the Treasury forms an essential part of the material for detailed study of our finances. Special reports of value are that of the Special Commissioner of the Revenue, 1869, giving the results of David A. Wells' investigation of the money cost of the Civil War; and the *Monetary Commission Report,* 1898. Excerpts from both of these are given in Bogart and Thompson.

The most satisfactory textbooks in financial history are the standard work by D. R. Dewey, *Financial History of the United States* (12 ed., 1934), and the volume by W. J. Shultz and M. R. Caine, *Financial Development of the United States* (1937). Other volumes valuable for various phases of the subject are A. B. Hepburn, *History of Coinage and Currency in the United States* (rev. ed., 1915); A. D. Noyes, *Forty Years of American Finance* (1909), and the continuation, *The War Period in American Finance, 1908–1925* (1926).

On the struggle for the gold standard, see W. C. Mitchell, *A History of the Greenbacks* (1903), which contains useful tables; J. Laurence Laughlin, *History of Bimetallism in the United States* (4th ed., 1897), and Don C. Barrett, *The Greenbacks and Resumption of Specie Payments, 1862–1879* (1931). On a special phase, see Neil Crothers, *Fractional Money* (1930).

Of the general textbooks on money and banking the following are excellent: C. F. Dunbar, *Theory and History of Banking* (5th ed., 1916); J. T. Holdsworth, *Money and Banking* (3rd ed., 1921); H. P. Willis and G. R. Edwards, *Banking and Business* (rev. ed., 1925), and F. A. Bradford, *Money and Banking* (1935).

On the Federal Reserve system, consult W. Kemmerer, *The A B C of the Federal Reserve System* (1916); H. Parker Willis, *The Federal Reserve System* (1923); H. P. Willis and W. H. Steiner, *Federal Reserve Banking Practice* (1926); P. M. Warburg, *The Federal Reserve System* (2 vols., 1930), a rather complete history and criticism; S. E. Harris, *Twenty Years of the Federal Reserve Policy* (2 vols., 1933), exhaustive on this phase; J. L. Laughlin, *The Federal Reserve Act, Its Origins and Problems* (1933), best on the history of the Act; W. O. Weyforth, *The Federal Reserve Board* (1933); C. O. Hardy, *Credit Policies of the Federal Reserve System* (1932); C. S. Tibbetts, *State Banks and the Federal Reserve System* (1929), and S. E. Harris, *Twenty Years of Federal Reserve Policy, Including an Extended Discussion of the Monetary Crises, 1927–1933* (1933). Special topics on banking are adequately developed in A. M. Davis, *The Origins of the National Banking System* (National Monetary Commission Report, 1910); G. C. Barnett, *State Banks and Trust Companies Since the Passage of the National Banking Act* (1911); L. C. Helderman, *National and State Banks, a Study of Their Origins* (1931), and J. C. Smith, *The Development of Trust Companies in the United States* (1927).

On commercial crises and business depressions much has recently been written: O. M. W. Sprague, *History of Crises Under the National Banking System,* Senate Document No. 538, 61st Cong., 2nd Sess.; Otto C. Lightner, *History of Business Depressions* (1922); Alvin H. Hansen, *Cycles of Prosperity and Depression, 1902–1908* (1921), University of Wisconsin Studies in the Social Sciences and History, No. 5; W. C. Schluter, *Economic Cycles and Crises* (1933); Hudson B. Hastings, *Costs and Profits: Their Relation to Business Cycles* (1923), Pollak Foundation for Economic Research, No. 3; J. A. Shumpeter, *Business Cycles* (2 vols., 1939); W. C. Mitchell, *Business Cycles* (1913), Memoirs of the University of California, Vol. III; Warren M. Persons, *Forecasting Business*

Cycles (1931); Thorstein B. Veblen, *Theory of Business Enterprise* (1904); National Bureau of Economic Research, Inc., *Business Cycles and Unemployment* (1923), pp. xxvii-xl, and 1–405 in Conference on Unemployment (Washington, 1921); Report of Joint Commission of Agricultural Inquiry, *The Agricultural Crisis and Its Causes* (1921), House of Rep., 67th Cong., 1st Sess., Report No. 408. An outline of general conditions is given in W. L. Thorp, *Business Annals* (1926). Also valuable is A. F. Burns, *Production Trends in the United States Since 1870* (1934).

Much of interest is contained in the autobiographies of two men who were in the thick of the currency controversies of the period: Hugh McCulloch, *Men and Measures of Half a Century* (1889), by a Secretary of the Treasury who served under Lincoln, Johnson, and Arthur; and John S. Sherman, *Recollections of Forty Years* (1895), by Hayes' Secretary of the Treasury. Allen Nevins, *Grover Cleveland, A Study in Courage* (1932) is the best study of Cleveland. A racy account of the leading banker of the period is J. K. Winkler, *The First Billion, The Stillmans and the National City Bank* (1933). On the leading financier of these years, Carl Honey, *The Life of J. Pierpont Morgan* (1912) is conventional, and Lewis Corey, *The House of Morgan,* is critical.

26. ECONOMIC IMPERIALISM

The following are excellent résumés of American diplomatic history: J. H. Latané, *History of American Foreign Policy* (rev. ed., 1934); L. M. Sears, *A History of American Foreign Relations* (1927); S. F. Bemis, *A Diplomatic History of the United States* (1936); T. A. Bailey, *A Diplomatic History of the American People* (1940), and B. H. Williams, *American Diplomacy* (1936), the latter emphasizing the economic aspects.

On the general subject of imperialism and its economic phases, see B. H. Williams, *Economic Foreign Policy of the United States* (1929); Achille Viallate, *Economic Imperialism and International Relations During the Last Fifty Years* (1923); L. H. Jenks, *Migration of British Capital to 1875* (1927); P. T. Moon, *Imperialism and World Politics* (1926); and Herbert Feis, *Europe the World's Banker 1870–1914* (1930). Other studies of various economic phases appear in the following: F. M. Halsey, *Investments in Latin America and the British West Indies,* Department of Commerce Special Agent Series, No. 169 (1918); Francis W. Hirst and George Paish, *The Credit of Nations and the Trade Balance of the United States* (1910), National Monetary Commission Publications, No. 2, Senate Doc. No. 579. Of particular reference to American imperialism is Scott Nearing and Joseph Freeman, *Dollar Diplomacy* (1925), which should be supplemented by R. W. Dunn, *American Foreign Investments* (1929); Max Winkler, *Investments of United States Capital in Latin America* (World Peace Foundation, 1929), and his *Foreign Bonds, an Autopsy* (1933); and C. F. Remer, *Foreign Investments in China* (1933).

Valuable material can be found in biographical studies of those who played a leading part in the drama of expanding imperialism: C. S. Olcott, *William McKinley* (2 vols., 1916); H. F. Pringle, *Theodore Roosevelt* (1931); *Theodore Roosevelt, an Autobiography* (1913); H. F. Pringle, *The Life and Times of William Howard Taft* (2 vols., 1939); R. S. Baker, *Life and Letters of Woodrow Wilson* (7 vols., 1927–1937); H. C. Hill, *Roosevelt and the Caribbean* (1927); Tyler Dennett, *John Hay* (1933), and J. C. Jessup, *Elihu Root* (2 vols., 1938). Strong arguments against imperialism are presented in G. F. Hoar, *Autobiography of Seventy Years* (1913). The reminiscences of a bitter anti-imperialist Senator, interesting and containing information not easily available, are given in R. F. Pettigrew, *The Course of Empire* (1920).

The material on Latin America has become voluminous. Good general books include D. G. Munro, *The United States and the Caribbean Area* (1934), a brief survey; C. L. Jones, *The Caribbean Interests of the United States* (1916), and *Caribbean Backgrounds and Prospects* (1931); G. H. Stuart, *Latin America and the United States* (3rd ed., 1938), an excellent study. A result of the latest scholarly research on the backgrounds of the Spanish-American War is J. W. Pratt, *Expansionists of 1898* (1936). Walter Millis, *The Martial Spirit: A Study of Our War with Spain* (1931) is the best one-volume account.

On Cuba, Leland H. Jenks, *Our Cuban Colony: A Study in Sugar* (1928) is the best single volume as far as it carries the story. Carleton Beals, *The Crime of Cuba* (1933), highly colored, carries the story to the eve of the 1933 revolution. Harry F. Guggenheim, *The United States and Cuba* (1934) is a defense of the American domination by the ambassador of the United States during a part of the Machado régime. The most valuable in recent years is Foreign Policy Association, *Problems of the New Cuba* (1935). D. A. Lockmiller, *Magoon in Cuba: A History of the Second Intervention, 1906–1909* (1938) defends the Magoon administration. On Puerto Rico, B. W. and J. W. Diffie, *Porto Rico: A Broken Pledge* (1931) is extremely critical of American occupation. Victor A. Clark, *Porto Rico and Its Problems* (1930) is a scientific and intelligent survey. Also valuable is A. D. Gayer, P. T. Homan, and E. K. James, *The Sugar Economy of Puerto Rico* (1938). On the Virgin Islands, see L. K. Zabriskie, *The Virgin Islands of the United States of America* (1918), and C. C. Tansil, *The Purchase of the Danish West Indies* (1932).

American penetration in specific areas is covered in the following books. On Santo Domingo and Haiti the best single volume is M. M. Knight, *The Americans in Santo Domingo* (1928). See also U. S. Senate Select Committee, *Inquiry into Occupation and Administration of Haiti and Santo Domingo* (67th Cong., 1922); Carl Kelsey, "American Intervention in Haiti and Santo Domingo," *Annals of the American Academies of Political and Social Science,* Vol. C, pp. 109–202; "American Occupation of Haiti," *Foreign Policy Reports,* Vol. V, Nos. 19–20 (1919); and A. C. Millspaugh, *Haiti Under American Control, 1915–1930* (World Peace Foundation, 1931). On Central America, see Carleton Beals, *Banana Gold* (1932); C. D. Kepner and J. H. Soothill, *The Banana*

Empire (1935), and C. D. Kepner, *Social Aspects of the Banana Industry* (1936).

The story of Panama from various angles is discussed in the following: Philippe Bunau-Varilla, *Panama, Its Creation, Destruction and Resurrection* (1913), by the arch-conspirator of the affair; J. B. Bishop, *The Panama Gateway* (1913); E. R. Johnson, *The Panama Canal and Commerce* (1916); M. W. Williams, *Anglo-American Isthmian Diplomacy, 1815–1915* (1916); J. F. Rippy, *The Capitalists and Colombia* (1931); and D. C. Miner, *The Fight for the Panama Route* (1940). W. L. McCain, *The United States and the Republic of Panama* tells a full story of our relations with that country. On Colombia, J. F. Rippy, *The Capitalists and Colombia* (1931) is excellent.

To understand the relations between the United States and Mexico it is necessary to comprehend the Mexican scene. Two books showing a real understanding of Mexican civilization and tradition are Carleton Beals, *Mexican Maze* (1931), and Ernest Gruening, *Mexico and Its Heritage* (1928). American relations with Mexico are adequately handled in C. W. Hackett, *Mexican Revolution and the United States, 1910–1926* (World Peace Foundation, 1926), and J. F. Rippy, *The United States and Mexico* (rev. ed., 1931).

Among the best books on the Philippines are D. C. Worcester, *The Philippines Past and Present* (2 vols., 1914); C. B. Elliott, *The Philippines* (2 vols., 1917); F. B. Harrison, *The Corner-stone of Philippine Independence* (1922), by an anti-imperialistic governor-general; J. S. Reyes, *Legislative History of America's Economic Policy Toward the Philippines* (1923); and J. R. Hayden, *The Philippines: A Study in National Development* (1942).

On the Far East, Tyler Dennett, *Americans in Eastern Asia* (1922) covers the history to 1901; it should be supplemented with M. J. Bau, *The Open Door Doctrine and Relations to China* (1923), and Tyler Dennett, *John Hay* (1933). P. J. Treat, *Japan and the United States, 1853–1921* (2nd ed., 1928) is an authoritative study. See also the excellent volume by A. W. Griswold, *The Far Eastern Policy of the United States* (1938). Aspects of dollar diplomacy are covered in H. K. Norton, *China and the Powers* (1927); J. W. Overlach, *Foreign Financial Control in China* (1919), and C. F. Remer, *Foreign Investments in China* (1933). H. D. Croly, *Willard Straight* (1924) is a biography of the agent of the Morgan bankers in China.

27. AMERICA AND THE FIRST WORLD WAR

An effort to present a picture of American life during the decade and a half preceding the First World War with emphasis on the decline of *laissez faire* is H. U. Faulkner, *The Quest for Social Justice* (1931). The rise and decline of progressivism are developed in John Chamberlain, *Farewell to Reform* (1932). C. C. Regier, *The Era of the Muckrakers* (1932) is the best on this episode. See also Louis Filler, *Crusaders for American Liberalism* (1939), for a more complete picture of the reform movement as it functioned in the literature of exposure.

A standard volume on conservation is that of L. Havemeyer (ed.), *Conservation of Natural Resources in the United States* (1930). Other studies are C. G. Gilbert and J. E. Pogue, *America's Power Resources* (1921); Benton MacKaye, *Employment and Natural Resources* (1919), Publications of the Department of Labor; F. L. Lane, *Conservation Through Engineering* (1920), Bulletin 705, Department of the Interior, United States Geological Survey. A wealth of material is to be found in the *Proceedings of the Conference of Governors* (1909); in the *Annals of the American Academy of Political and Social Science,* Vol. XXXIII, No. 3 (1909); in the *Proceedings of the Second Pan-American Congress,* Dec. 27–Jan. 8, 1916, Section III; and in John Ise, *The United States Forest Policy* (1920).

Excellent studies of income have been made by the Staff of the National Bureau of Economic Research, Inc., *Income in the United States, Its Amount and Distribution, 1909–1919,* Vol. I, *Summary* (1921); Vol. II, Detailed Report (1922); also their *Distribution of Income by States in 1919,* Publication No. 3 (1922). See also W. I. King, *The Wealth and Income of the People of the United States* (1917); David Friday, *War, Profits and Prices* (1920); Federal Trade Commission, *National Wealth and Income* (1926); and the publications of the Treasury Department on income statistics. Important government investigations are the *Aldrich Report on Prices, Wages, and Transportation,* Senate Document 1394, 52nd Cong., 2nd Sess., March, 1893; *Investigation Relative to Wages and Prices of Commodities,* 61st Cong., 3rd Sess., Senate Document 847 (1911), and the *Report of the Massachusetts Commission on the Cost of Living* (1910). The Department of Labor studies the cost of living and reports regularly in the *Monthly Labor Review.* One of their most indispensable studies is *History of Wages in the United States from Colonial Days to 1928* (1929). Other important studies on wages and standard of living include Robert Hunter, *Poverty* (1904); John Ryan, *A Living Wage* (1906); R. C. Chapin, *The Standard of Living Among Workingmen's Families in New York City* (1909); F. H. Streightoff, *The Standard of Living Among the Industrial People of America* (1911); Whitney Coombs, *The Wages of Unskilled Labor in the Manufacturing Industries in the United States, 1890–1920* (1926), and Paul H. Douglas, *Real Wages in the United States, 1890–1926* (1930). Some of Douglas' conclusions have been challenged by A. H. Hansen in *American Economic Review,* Vol. XX, pp. 747–752 (Dec., 1930), and in other numbers. Consult also Leo Wolman, "Consumption and the Standard of Living," *Recent Economic Changes* (1929), Vol. I, pp. 13–78, and Morris A. Copeland, "The National Income and Its Distribution," *ibid.,* Vol. II; pp. 757–839.

Detailed studies of the war are to be found in the series, "Problems of War and Reconstruction," edited by F. G. Wickwire, and including G. O. Smith, *The Strategy of Minerals* (1919); W. F. Willoughby; *Government Organization in War Time and After* (1919), and E. L. Bogart, *War Costs and Their Financing* (1921). On the American section of the Carnegie series on the *Economic and Social History of the World War* the following volumes are important: W.

G. Leland and N. D. Mereness, *Introduction to the American Official Sources for the Economic and Social History of the World War* (1926); W. D. Hines, *War History of American Railroads* (1928), and J. M. Clark, *The Cost of the World War to the American People* (1931). On the cost of the war, in addition to the work of Bogart cited above, see J. H. Hollander, *War Borrowing* (1919); E. L. Bogart, *Direct and Indirect Cost of the Great World War* (1919); E. R. A. Seligman, "The Cost of the War and How It Was Met," *American Economic Review,* Vol. IX (Dec., 1919), and especially E. B. Rosa, "Expenditures and Revenues of the Federal Government," in the *Annals of the American Academy of Political and Social Science,* Vol. XCV, No. 184 (May, 1921).

For a brief summary of finance, consult A. D. Noyes, *War Period in American Finance: 1908–1925* (1926). America's participation in the war is told rather fully in B. Crowell and R. F. Wilson, *How America Went to War* (6 vols., 1921). On labor, read Samuel Gompers, *Seventy Years of Life and Labor* (2 vols., 1925), and U. S. Dept. of Labor, Wages and Hours Division, *War Time Policies on Wages, Hours and Other Labor Standards in the United States, 1917–1918* (1942). On transportation, see F. H. Dixon, *Railroads and Government, Their Relations in the United States* (1922). G. B. Clarkson, *Industrial America and the World War* (1923) is an excellent summary. Two recent important studies on special phases are C. O. Hardy, *War Time Control of Prices* (1940), and W. C. Mullendore, *History of the United States Food Administration, 1917–1919* (1941), with an introduction by Herbert Hoover written in 1920. Extremely valuable is B. M. Baruch, *American Industry in the War* (1941), a reprint of his Report of the War Industries Board and of the Commodity Section submitted to the President on March 3, 1921, and his memorandum for total mobilization submitted in 1931 to the War Policies Commission.

For the life of the people during war time read Preston Slosson, *The Great Crusade and After: 1914–1928* (1930), Vol. XII in the History of American Life Series; and Mark Sullivan, *Our Times,* Vol. V (1933). A discussion of the economic background of America's entrance into the war is given in C. Hartley Grattan, *Why We Fought* (1929). A good history of the Wilson administration is F. L. Paxson, *Pre-War Years, 1913–1917* (1936) and *America at War, 1917–1918* (1939).

28. THE GREAT ILLUSION

Probably the two most important books on American economic life during the decade of the 'twenties are *Recent Economic Changes* (2 vols., 1927), the report of the Committee on Recent Economic Changes of the President's Conference on the Unemployment, and *Recent Social Trends* (2 vols., 1933), the report of the President's Research Committee on Social Trends. A good survey of the legislative history during the same period is J. C. Malin, *The United States After the World War* (1930). Likewise consult Nathan Fine, *Labor and Farmer Parties in the United States, 1828–1928* (1928). P. W. Slosson, *The Great Crusade and After, 1914–1928* (1930) is a clever integration of post-war social history. A unique and valuable piece of research is R. S. and H. M. Lynd, *Middletown* (1929). See also E. L. Bogart and C. E. Landon, *Modern Industry* (1927); R. G. Tugwell, *Industry's Coming of Age* (1927), and E. D. Durand, *American Industry and Commerce* (1930). Useful surveys of manufacturing are the last three chapters in Vol. III of Victor Clark, *History of Manufactures in the United States* (3 vols., 1929). One of the most valuable studies of recent American marketing methods is E. R. A. Seligman, *The Economics of Installment Selling* (2 vols., 1927).

The literature and sources for the decade of the 'twenties are, in fact, almost exhaustless, and among them, of course, are many which critically appraise that period. These include J. T. Adams, *Our Business Civilization* (1929); Ralph Borsodi, *This Ugly Civilization* (1929); H. S. Raushenbush and H. W. Laidler, *Power Control* (1928); Stuart Chase and F. J. Schlink, *Your Money's Worth* (1927); Stuart Chase, *The Tragedy of Waste* (1925), and his *Prosperity, Fact or Myth* (1930). See also Norman Thomas, *The Way Out* (1931). A brilliant survey by a Frenchman is that of André Siegfried, *America Comes of Age* (1927). A purely economic survey of recent conditions is that of the National Industrial Conference Board, *A Picture of World Economic Conditions at the Beginning of 1930* (4 vols., 1930).

Important books on business consolidation include H. R. Seager and C. A. Gulick, Jr., *Trust and Corporation Problems* (1929); D. M. Keezer and Stacy May, *Public Control of Business* (1930); Frank A. Fetter, *The Masquerade of Monopoly* (1931); and J. L. Bonbright and G. C. Means, *The Holding Company* (1932). More valuable on actual consolidation during the 'twenties is H. W. Laidler, *Concentration in American Industry* (1931). See also A. A. Berle, Jr., and G. C. Means, *The Modern Corporation and Private Property* (1932), and W. Z. Ripley, *Main Street and Wall Street* (1927). These books should, of course, be supplemented in particular by the reports of the Federal Trade Commission on the Radio Industry, on the Control of Power Companies, etc. Useful also is the National Industrial Conference Board, *Public Regulation of Competitive Practices* (1925), and "The Anti-Trust Laws of the United States," *Annals of the American Academy,* Vol. CXLVII (1930).

An excellent start in the study of recent transportation is afforded by the chapters in *Recent Economic Changes* and *Recent Social Trends*. These should be followed by H. G. Moulton and associates, *The American Transportation Problem* (1933). Important studies of railroads include W. J. Cunningham, *American Railroads: Government Control and Reconstruction Problems* (1922); F. H. Dixon, *Railroads and Government: Their Relations in the United States* (1922); D. P. Locklin, *Railroad Regulation Since 1920* (1928); H. D. Wolfe, *The Railroad Labor Board* (1927); Rogers McVeagh, *The Transportation Act, 1920* (1923); and W. M. W. Splawn, *Government Ownership and Operation of Railroads* (1928). Perhaps the best study in its field is H. G. Moulton, C. G.

Morgan, and A. L. Lee, *The St. Lawrence Navigation and Power Project* (1929); this is critical. Enthusiastically favorable is Tom Ireland, *The Great Lakes-St. Lawrence Deep Waterway to the Sea* (1934). On the merchant marine, see National Industrial Conference Board, Inc., *The American Merchant Marine Problem* (1929), and American Bureau of Shipping, *The American Merchant Marine* (1933). On automobiles, read R. C. Epstein, *The Automobile Industry* (1928); H. L. Barber, *The Story of the Automobile* (1927), and for the most recent and comprehensive treatment, E. D. Kennedy, *The Automobile Industry* (1941). One of the most rewarding studies of roads is the U. S. Bureau of Public Roads report of a *Survey of Transportation of the State Highway System of Connecticut* (1926). P. T. David, *The Economics of Air Mail Transportation* (1934) adequately covers this phase. More recent and more comprehensive are J. H. Frederick, *Commercial Air Transportation* (1942), and C. E. Puffer, *Air Transportation* (1941). On transportation also see the bibliography for Chapter XXIII.

Besides the article by E. G. Nourse in *Recent Economic Changes,* and the *Yearbook of the Department of Agriculture* for the years after the war, probably J. D. Black, *Agricultural Reform in the United States* (1929), is the most useful in the field of agriculture. An excellent summary with bibliography is C. C. Davis, "The Development of Agricultural Policy Since the End of the World War," *Yearbook of Agriculture, 1940,* pp. 297-326. Valuable also is the symposium, "The Agricultural Situation in the United States" in the *Annals of the American Academy of Political and Social Science,* Vol. CXVII (1925). Other useful books of interpretation and otherwise which should be mentioned include Isaac Lippincott, *What the Farmer Needs* (1928); Wilson Gee, *Place of Agriculture in Our Life* (1930), and *American Farm Policy* (1934); E. R. A. Seligman, *The Economics of Farm Relief* (1929); and the National Industrial Conference Board, *The Agricultural Problem in the United States* (1926).

Two recent general discussions of the labor problem, both adequate, are Dale Yoder, *Labor Economics and Labor Problems* (1933), and C. A. Daugherty, *Labor Problems in American Industry* (1933). An invaluable study of organized labor is L. L. Lorwin, *The American Federation of Labor* (1933). Standard discussions of labor history covering this decade are in Vols. III and IV of J. R. Commons *et al., History of Labour in the United States.* Vol. III, by D. D. Leschohier and Elizabeth Brandeis, deals with working conditions and labor legislation; Vol. IV, by Selig Perlman and Philip Taft, with the general history of labor. Specialized studies particularly pertinent to the 'twenties include G. James *et al., Profit Sharing and Stock Ownership for Employees* (1926); R. F. Foerster and E. H. Dietel, *Employee Stock Ownership in the United States* (1926); R. W. Dunn, *The Americanization of Labor* (1927); H. W. Laidler and Norman Thomas (eds.), *New Tactics in Social Conflict* (1926); *Report on the Steel Strike of 1919 by the Commission of Inquiry, the Interchurch World Movement* (1920); W. J. Lauck, *Political and Industrial Democracy, 1776-1926* (1926), and Abraham Epstein, *The Problem of Old Age Pensions in Industry*

(1926). Exhaustive studies of wages have been made by the National Industrial Conference Board, and by P. H. Douglas, *Real Wages in the United States, 1890–1926* (1930). Valuable for the study of current labor history is the *American Labor Yearbook,* published annually; *The American Federationist,* the official organ of the A. F. of L., and the *Monthly Labor Review,* published by the United States government. For further labor material, see the bibliography for Chaps. 15 and 22.

29. ECONOMIC COLLAPSE

For a general background for the economic conditions and trends in the years preceding the New Deal the student is again referred to *Recent Economic Changes* and *Recent Social Trends.* In addition, much information may be obtained from F. C. Mills, *Economic Tendencies in the United States* (1932); National Industrial Conference Board, *The Banking Situation in the United States* (1933); H. W. Laidler, *Concentration in American Industry* (1931); and A. A. Berle, Jr., and G. C. Means, *The Modern Corporation and Private Property* (1932). For social history, see P. W. Slosson, *The Great Crusade and After, 1914–1928* (1930); R. S. and H. M. Lynd, *Middletown* (1929), and Mark Sullivan, *Our Times* (6 vols., 1926–1935). A skillful interwearing of economic, social, and political history is D. L. Dumond, *From Roosevelt to Roosevelt* (1937). Efforts at interpretation include Lewis Corey, *The Decline of American Capitalism* (1934); George Soule, *A Planned Society* (1932), and *The Coming American Revolution* (1934); Francis Neilson, *Control from the Top* (1933); and Lewis Mumford, *Technics and Civilization* (1934).

Among the more important pre-depression studies of business cycles are those of A. H. Hansen, *Cycles of Prosperity and Depression in the United States, Great Britain and Germany,* a study of monthly data, 1902–1908, University of Wisconsin Studies in the Social Sciences and History, No. 5 (1921); L. D. Edie (ed.), *The Stabilization of Business,* containing chapters by W. C. Mitchell, Irving Fisher, F. H. Dixon *et al.,* with an introduction by Herbert Hoover; W. C. Mitchell, *Business Cycles* (1913), and *Business Cycles and Unemployment,* Report and Recommendations of a Committee of the President's Conference on Unemployment (1921), including an investigation made under the auspices of the National Bureau of Economic Research. Perhaps the ablest of the recent studies are J. M. Clark, *Strategic Factors in Business Cycles* (1934), and W. C. Schluter, *Economic Cycles and Crises* (1933); J. A. Shumpeter, *Business Cycles* (2 vols., 1933), and W. M. Persons, *Forecasting Business Cycles* (1931). An excellent summary of the main theories is W. C. Mitchell's article, "Business Cycles," *Encyclopaedia of the Social Sciences,* Vol. III, pp. 92–106.

A more complete bibliography on the background of the depression will be found under the preceding chapter.

30. THE NEW DEAL

Perhaps the most satisfactory summary accompanied by keen analysis is Louis M. Hacker, *American Problems of Today* (1938). Another excellent summary is C. A. Beard and J. H. E. Smith, *The Old Deal and the New Deal* (1940). More spirited is Charles and Mary Beard, *America in Midpassage* (1939). A sympathetic analysis may be found in B. L. Landis, *The American Revolution* (1933), and S. C. Wallace, *The New Deal in Action* (1934).

The New Deal theoreticians have their say in R. G. Tugwell, *Industrial Discipline and Governmental Acts* (1933); H. L. Ickes, *The New Democracy* (1934); D. R. Richberg, *The Rainbow* (1936); and A. A. Berle, Jr., and others, *America's Recovery Program* (1934). Those with more conservative economic views criticize the program in such books as William McDonald, *The Menace of Recovery* (1934); D. V. Brown and others, *The Economics of the Recovery Program* (1933); L. P. Ayres, *The Economics of Recovery* (1933); and the Columbia University Commission, *Economic Reconstruction* (1934); more radical criticism may be found in Norman Thomas, *The Choice Before Us* (1934) and *Human Exploitation in the United States* (1934), and in John Strachey, *The Coming Struggle for Power* (1934). For a British appraisal, see Editors of the Economist, *The New Deal* (1937). An important appraisal from an ex-New Dealer is Raymond Moley, *After Seven Years* (1939). Any study of sources must include F. D. Roosevelt, *The Public Papers and Addresses of Franklin D. Roosevelt* (5 vols., 1938), edited and collected by Samuel I. Rosenman.

On agriculture, see H. A. Wallace, *America Must Choose* (1934), by the Secretary of Agriculture; Wilson Gee, *American Farm Policy* (1934), a sympathetic description; E. G. Nourse, J. S. Davis, and J. D. Black, *Three Years of the Agricultural Adjustment Administration* (1937), an objective and exhaustive study. Popular presentations of the agricultural problem are Stuart Chase, *Rich Land, Poor Land* (1936), and Ayres Brinser, *Our Use of the Land* (1939). The *Agricultural Yearbooks* for these years, particularly that for 1940, are important.

Excellent on money and banking are Leo Pasvolsky, *Current Monetary Issues* (1933); National Industrial Conference Board, Inc., *The New Monetary System of the United States* (1934); J. I. Bogen and M. Nadler, *The Banking Crises* (1933). On this phase and others the articles in the economic journals should not be neglected. These should include Bernard Flexner, "The Fight on the Securities Act," *Atlantic Monthly,* Vol. CLIII, No. 2, pp. 232–250 (Feb., 1934); F. A. Southard, Jr., "American Industry Abroad Since 1929," *Journal of Political Economy,* Vol. XLI, No. 4, pp. 530–547 (Aug., 1933); R. B. Westerfield, "The Banking Act of 1933," *ibid.,* pp. 721–749 (Dec., 1933); H. H. Preston and V. W. Bennett, "Agricultural Credit Legislation of 1933," *ibid.,* Vol. XLII, No. 1, pp. 6–33 (Feb., 1934); J. H. Taggart and L. D. Jennings, "The Insurance of Bank Deposits," *ibid.,* pp. 508–516 (Aug., 1934); S. D. Zagoroff, "The External Depreciation of the Dollar and Its Effect upon the Price Level in the United

States," *ibid.,* pp. 641–653 (Oct., 1934); R. L. Dewey, "Merchant Marine Act of 1936," *American Economic Review,* Vol. XXVII, No. 2, pp. 239–252 (June, 1937), and his "Transportation Act of 1940," *ibid.,* Vol. XXXI, pp. 15–26.

On the NRA perhaps the most objective is L. S. Lyon *et al., The National Recovery Administration* (1935). Also important is *The Recovery Problem in the United States,* prepared by the Brookings Institution. A vivid description of the career of the NRA by its first administrator is H. S. Johnson, *The Blue Eagle from Egg to Earth* (1935). His successor, Donald Richberg, has also written of it in *The Rainbow* (1936).

For labor, the following are excellent: C. R. Daugherty, *Labor Under the NRA* (1934); Emanuel Stein *et al., Labor and the New Deal* (1934); and G. E. Sokolsky, *Labor's Fight for Power* (1934). The conflict between the A. F. of L. and the C.I.O. is told in Edward Levinson, *Labor on the March* (1938), and J. R. Walsh, *C.I.O., Industrial Unionism in Action* (1937), both sympathetic with the C.I.O. A background is given in R. R. R. Brooks, *When Labor Organizes* (1938). The same author writes of the work of the National Labor Relations Board in *Unions of Their Own Choosing* (1938). For the background of the social security legislation, see E. M. Burns, *Toward Social Security* (1936); P. H. Douglas, *Social Security in the United States* (1937), and Maxwell Stewart, *Social Security* (1937).

31. WORLD ECONOMIC RELATIONS

The most accessible current material on foreign investment is to be found in the annual pamphlets published by the Department of Commerce on the *Balance of International Payments in the United States.* See also the following books: R. W. Dunn, *American Foreign Investments* (1929); Max Winkler, *Investments of United States Capital in Latin America* (World Peace Foundation, 1929), and *Foreign Bonds, an Autopsy* (1933); C. F. Remer, *Foreign Investments in China* (1933), and J. W. Overlach, *Foreign Financial Control in China* (1919). For other specific nations, consult the volumes listed in the bibliography for Chap. 26. An excellent appraisal of the problem is J. T. Madden, Marcus Nadler, and H. C. Sauvain, *America's Experience as a Creditor Nation* (1937).

On the war debt problem, H. G. Moulton and Leo Pasvolsky, *War Debts and World Prosperity* (1932) is exhaustive. On the problem of international trade, see B. H. Williams, *Economic Foreign Policy of the United States* (1929), and *American Diplomacy* (1936); Ethel Dietrich, *World Trade* (1939), and *Far Eastern Trade of the United States* (1940). On the tariff during the Roosevelt administration, see F. B. Sayre, *The Way Forward: The American Trade Agreement Program* (1939); J. D. Larkin, *Trade Agreements; a Study in Democratic Methods* (1940), and Grace Beckholt, *The Reciprocal Trade Agreement Program* (1941). Material on the "good-neighbor policy" may be found in H. C. Herring, *Good Neighbors* (1941); H. B. Hinton, *Cordell Hull* (1942); Carlton Beals,

Pan-America (1940); G. H. Graham, *Latin America and the United States* (3rd ed., 1938); Mordecai Ezekiel, *Economic Relations Between the Americas* (Carnegie Endowment for International Peace, 1941); J. F. Rippy, *Latin America in World Politics* (1938), and H. J. Trueblood, *Progress of American Cooperation* (Foreign Policy Reports, Vol. XV, No. 23, 1940).

For America's economic participation in the Second World War, the student is still largely dependent on contemporary newspapers and magazines, among the most useful of which are the New York *Times, Events, Newsweek,* and *Time.* Excellent background summaries of the Second World War are Dwight W. Lee, *Ten Years: the World on the Way to War, 1930–1940* (1942), and C. G. Haines and R. J. S. Hoffman, *Origins and Background of the Second World War* (1943).

Index